The Barbarian Empires of the Steppes

Kenneth W. Harl, Ph.D.

THE
GREAT
COURSES·

PUBLISHED BY:

THE GREAT COURSES
Corporate Headquarters
4840 Westfields Boulevard, Suite 500
Chantilly, Virginia 20151-2299
Phone: 1-800-832-2412
Fax: 703-378-3819
www.thegreatcourses.com

Kenneth W. Harl, Ph.D.
Professor of Classical and Byzantine History
Tulane University

Professor Kenneth W. Harl is Professor of Classical and Byzantine History at Tulane University, where he has taught since 1978. He earned his B.A. from Trinity College and his M.A. and Ph.D. from Yale University.

Professor Harl teaches courses in Greek, Roman, Byzantine, and Crusader history from freshman to graduate levels. A recognized scholar of coins and classical Anatolia, he also takes students to Turkey on excursions and as assistants on excavations of Hellenistic and Roman sites.

Professor Harl has published numerous articles and is the author of *Civic Coins and Civic Politics in the Roman East, A.D. 180–275* and *Coinage in the Roman Economy, 300 B.C. to A.D. 700*. His current work includes publishing the coin discoveries from the excavation of Gordion, Turkey, and a new book on Rome and its Iranian foes. Professor Harl also serves on the editorial board of the *American Journal of Archaeology* and is a fellow and trustee of the American Numismatic Society.

Professor Harl has twice received Tulane's coveted Sheldon Hackney Award for Excellence in Teaching (voted on by both faculty and students) and has received the Student Body Award for Excellence in Teaching on multiple occasions. He was also the recipient of Baylor University's nationwide Robert Foster Cherry Award for Great Teaching. In 2007, he was the Lewis P. Jones Visiting Professor in History at Wofford College.

Professor Harl's other Great Courses include *Alexander the Great and the Macedonian Empire*, *The Fall of the Pagans and the Origins of Medieval Christianity*, *The Era of the Crusades*, *Origins of Great Ancient Civilizations*, *The World of Byzantium*, *Great Ancient Civilizations of Asia Minor*, *Rome and the Barbarians*, *The Peloponnesian War*, and *The Vikings*. ■

Table of Contents

Table of Contents

SUPPLEMENTAL MATERIAL

The Barbarian Empires of the Steppes

Scope:

Our study begins with a description of the sack of Baghdad by the Mongols under Hulagu, grandson of Genghis Khan, in 1258. The Mongols ended the Abbasid Caliphate—a major shock to the Islamic world. To this day, Muslims regard this event as a catastrophe and a turning point in their history. The incident sums up popular images and stereotypes about the fierce steppe nomads. The course will examine the relationship of the barbarians of the Eurasian steppes with the sedentary civilizations of Europe, the Middle East, India, and China.

Lecture 2 starts with the peopling of the steppes in the Bronze Age, the domestication of the horse and camel, the invention of wheeled vehicles, and the spread of Indo-European speakers (Iranian and Tocharians) over the steppes—and then into Europe, Iran, and India. This was the first major movement on the steppes, and it went from west to east.

Then, we begin to explore the steppe nomads and their interaction with the urban civilizations and each other from about 600 B.C. to 600 A.D. We start with the eastern steppes, discussing Han China and the nomads. Wars and migrations led to the first travels across the steppes from east to west, thus influencing the central and western steppes. The last players in these migrations were the Huns and Hephthalites, the foes of Rome and Sassanid Iran, respectively. These nomads helped to bring a close to antiquity.

Lectures 14 to 25 deal with the steppes in the early Middle Ages, from about 600 to 1200 A.D., that is, before the Mongols. Again, we start in the east, with Tang China and the Turks who emerged on the eastern steppes and spread dramatically across Eurasia, displacing and assimilating Tocharian and Iranian speakers. The Turks apparently devised the stirrup and the composite bow to become dreaded horse archers. We will also deal with the Turkish nomads and Constantinople; these khaganates anticipated the later Golden Horde and played a decisive role with Byzantium and the caliphate.

In Lectures 19 to 25, we concentrate on the relationship between the Turkish-speaking nomads, or Turkmen, and Islam. Once the Turks embraced Islam and entered the Middle East, they assumed the dominant military role ever after and carved out new Islamic worlds in Anatolia and India. In time, Turkish dialects won out over other languages in the cities of Transoxiana. The Battle of Talas in 751 was pivotal, bringing together the Turkmen, Tang China, and the Abbasid caliphate. The Turks, who henceforth dominated the steppes (even under the Mongols), for the first time saw Islam rather than China as the most powerful civilization—a major change.

Lectures 26 to 35 explore the impact of the Mongols. We start with the Chin Dynasty in northern China (the typical Manchurian-Chinese frontier state) and Sung China, scrupulously posing as the heir to Confucian traditions and the Han Empire. This division was exploited by Genghis Khan, who rapidly expanded across the whole of the steppes, and his heirs, notably, his grandsons Khubilai Khan and Batu, who subjected the urban civilizations of Christian Russia, Muslim Iran and Transoxiana, and Sung China. This Pax Mongolica had a major cultural and technological impact. Ironically, it led to the spread of gunpowder that produced the first cannons and handheld firearms, which, when perfected by Christian Europe, put the steppe nomads out of business.

The Russians, starting with Ivan the Terrible, expanded across the steppes and ended the power of nomadic armies. But in the Islamic world, the Ilkhans converted to Islam, and the heirs of Genghis Khan, notably the conquerors Tamerlane and Baybur, ruled two of the great Muslim empires of the early modern age.

We close our course with the end of steppe power after 1500, notably with Ming China, Safavid Iran, and czarist Russia. Yet today, the steppes have again emerged as strategic, especially as the Soviet Union has fragmented and with prospects of separatist movements in Xinjang. ∎

Steppes and Peoples
Lecture 1

Mongols, originating from the Eurasian steppe, have been portrayed as civilization's worst nightmare; in many ways, the Mongols epitomized the typical barbarian. On the other hand, the Mongols were an exceptionally successful people. Genghis Khan and his three grandsons conquered a world empire; in fact, the 13th century is known as the Mongol century. In terms of military organization, logistics, vision of empire, and knowledge of the world, the Mongols surpassed all other previous nomadic peoples on the steppes. This course, *The Barbarian Empires of the Steppes*, is their story.

The Sack of Baghdad

- On February 13, 1258, a Mongol army under **Hulagu**, who was a grandson of **Genghis Khan** and ruler of the western domains of the Mongol Empire, sacked the city of Baghdad. Muslim chroniclers later reported that for 40 days, blood ran in the streets; 800,000 people may have been killed.

- The sack of the city was seen as a disaster by the Islamic world. It also confirmed every stereotype that civilized, literate societies had about peoples of the Eurasian steppe. Hulagu was no friend of Islam; he was married to two wives who were Nestorian Christians, and he himself was an animist and worshiper of Mongol spirits.

- Since the 9th century, Baghdad had been the intellectual center of the Islamic world. The destruction of Baghdad meant the destruction of the cultural and economic nexus of the entire Islamic world.

- The **caliph** of Baghdad was rewarded by being rolled up in a carpet and trampled to death by Mongolian cavalry. This was the traditional Mongol execution; they feared that if their swords or weapons shed the blood of a ruler, this could have bad repercussions in the animist world.

- Two years later, the Mongol army had retreated into central Asia. Baghdad never recovered, however, and has still not regained its role in the Islamic world. New centers of power emerged in the Islamic world as a result of this Mongol sack—first, Cairo and, later, Constantinople, Tehran, and Delhi.

Nomadic Life on the Steppe

- The Mongols were the last of a long tradition of empires of the steppes, going back to the 3rd century B.C. with the **Xiongnu** in China. Mongols maintained a traditional steppe way of life and warfare that had characterized nomads ever since these people domesticated the horse between 4800 and 4200 B.C.

- Life on the Eurasian steppe was severe, even under the best of conditions. The people of the steppes had to cope with an incredibly harsh climate and were in constant search of pasture land for their animals—goats, cattle, sheep, and above all, horses. Horses were essential for mobility, warfare, and herding. They originally were a form of food, providing both meat and dairy products.

- The people of the steppes were very much centered around their herds, and their social organization reflected this. They lived in kinship groups in homes called **yurts**, which were tents made of felt and wood.

- The Greek historian **Herodotus**, in the 5th century B.C., wrote of great caravans of **Scythians**, or Iranian-speaking nomads, on the steppes of what is today southern Russia. They had a diet consisting of meat, milk, yogurt, and *kumis*, or fermented mare's milk.

Trade with Settled Peoples

- Through trade, the nomadic peoples of the steppes were in constant contact with those who lived by agriculture. Thus, the nomads had access to grains, beer and wine, vegetables, all sorts of finished products, salt, and even iron.

The way of life on the Eurasian steppe has remained remarkably consistent for 6,000 years.

- In turn, the nomads traded dairy products, hides, furs, felts, and animals. For example, nomads traded horses to the Chinese because China itself could not produce the type of horses that could carry cavalry.

- In their life on the Eurasian steppe, the nomads evolved certain attitudes. Steppe peoples were suspicious of urban populations— even wary of entering any building with a roof. They believed that to live in a city was to become enslaved to the ways of the Chinese, the Romans, or later, the Muslims of Iran and the Middle East.

- Whatever attitudes and prejudices the people of the steppes had, the settled people returned the favor. Roman, Greek, and Chinese sources, from the earliest times, spoke with fear of these people. In return, the nomads themselves expressed contempt and fear of others.

- This interplay between the settled and the nomadic peoples created a frontier zone along the Chinese border, along the borders of the Middle East, and along the borders of Eastern Europe, in which steppe peoples and civilized peoples came to intermix. A particular type of frontier society grew up on those borders—a society that played an important role both for the steppes and the civilized zones.

Invention of the Saddle and Composite Bow
- The climate of the Eurasian steppe nourished a population hearty in hunting and war. One can argue that some of the greatest armies ever created were the nomadic warriors of the steppes. In earliest times, they rode light chariots, but from about 900 or 1000 B.C., in the period we call the Iron Age, the Scythians invented a type of wooden saddle that enabled warriors to ride and fight at the same time.

- What's more, they perfected a form of cavalry warfare that would dominate the battlefields of Eurasia and many civilized zones into the 14th century—a type of warfare that would only become obsolete with the advent of handheld firearms.

- People of the steppes also evolved a composite bow made up of wood, bone, and sinew. By holding the bow in one hand and pulling it, a warrior could launch an arrow with an enormous amount of power, even while on horseback. Based on experiments with modern bows, effective ranges suggest that the cavalry could shoot at least 100 yards. In combat, the enemy would be much closer.

Cavalry Warfare
- Adept at cavalry warfare, the nomads would ride up to a foe in groups, launching disciplined attacks. They would shoot a volley of arrows into the opponent's forces and encourage a chase. The enemy would lose cohesion, and then the horsemen would plow into the disorganized enemy and drive them off the battlefield.

- This strategy, based on stealth, rapidity, and brilliantly controlled fire, gave the nomads a distinct tactical advantage.

- The nomads were not particularly well armored; the real value was in the use of the bow. And, eventually, the bowmen were combined with heavy cavalry, armed as lancers, who would push in after the cavalry had broken up the enemy's organization. In the end, however, victory depended on the horse archers.

Influence of Geography
- The type of warfare that evolved on the steppes was also a function of geography. Geographic conditions dictated a great deal of how steppe nomads lived, how they moved, how they fought, how they traded, and even why they emigrated over the centuries into the settled zones.

- The Eurasian steppe consists of a 6,000-mile-long corridor stretching across Eurasia. When **Kublai Khan**, the grandson of Genghis Khan, died in 1294, the Mongol Empire stretched from the lower Danube, in the Carpathian Mountains—essentially the grasslands of Hungary today—in a corridor about 400 to 500 miles wide, across the whole of Siberia, ending at the forest of Manchuria.

- To the north were the vast **taiga** and **tundra** of Siberia. To the south were the arid deserts that split the central Asian steppes, and to the west were the great forests of Russia and Central Europe.

- The steppe zone has an incredibly harsh climate. Temperatures on the open steppes are extreme and restricted movement for both humans and animals, particularly in the winter.

- As a corridor, the steppes served as a kind of highway for people to move across inner and central Asia. This would have major consequences in the exchange of religions, cultural patterns, and profit-making along the Silk Road. The nomads played a vital role in the cultural exchange that enriched the great civilizations of China, India, the Middle East, and the Mediterranean world in Europe.

Mongol Dynasties

- The central Eurasian steppe areas and associated regions were divided between two separate Mongol dynasties. One was the dynasty of Hulagu, the so-called **ilkhans**, who ruled Iran, the Karakum Desert, the Kyzyl Kum, part of the steppes around the Aral Sea, and **Transoxania**.

- Most of the central steppes and the region around the **Tarim Basin**, with the caravan cities, were ruled by the family of **Chagatai**, one of the sons of Genghis Khan.

- The Mongolian homeland, the great eastern steppes that stretched from the **Xinjiang** to Manchuria, was the ancestral land of the Mongols—where Kublai Khan reigned.

Sources and Organization of Our Course

- This course uses a number of sources from the Western, Muslim, and Chinese worlds. An important point to remember is that very seldom do the steppe people speak to us directly; thus, we will have to supplement our information with archaeology and archaeobiology, such as DNA studies.

- Organization of this course falls into three broad chronological spans.
  - The first third of the course will deal with the nomadic steppe peoples from antiquity to 550 A.D. It will begin with the domestication of the horse by the earliest steppe peoples, known as Indo-Europeans, in the Pontic-Caspian steppes. We will carry that story through the interaction of steppe peoples with the civilizations of early China, the Near East, the Greeks, and imperial Rome.

  - The second third of the course will deal with the early Middle Ages. That period was dominated by the spread of Turkish speakers across the steppe zones; today, Turkish is still the language of the steppes.

- o The third component will deal with the Mongol impact, which began in the 12th century with the career of Genghis Khan. The 13th century is known as the Mongol century; we are still dealing with its ramifications today.

- With this course, you will begin to understand more about the nomadic peoples of the Eurasian steppe beyond the stereotypical image of the barbarian hordes sacking Baghdad. You will come to recognize the central role that these nomadic peoples have played in civilization and the influence and impact they still exercise today.

Important Terms

caliph: Ruler of the Muslim community. In 661, Muawiya established the first line of hereditary caliphs.

ilkhan: Meaning "loyal khan," the title granted by Kublai Khan to his brother Hulagu in 1260. It was carried by his descendants, the Ilkhanids (1265–1353), who ruled over Iran, Iraq, and Transoxania.

Scythians: The general name applied by classical Greeks to the Iranian-speaking nomads on the Eurasian steppe.

taiga: Forest zones of Siberia.

Tarim Basin: An area that encompasses the valleys of the tributaries of the Tarim River between the Tien Shan and the Tibetan highlands. The central zone comprises the Taklamakan Desert, and the eastern end is dominated by the salt depression of the Lop Nur. Today known as Xinjiang or eastern Turkestan, the region was home to caravan cities on the Silk Road.

Transoxania: Lands between the Oxus and Jaxartes rivers; in antiquity, known as Bactria and Sogdiana.

tundra: Arctic zones of Siberia.

Xinjiang: Eastern Turkestan.

Xiongnu: Altaic-speaking nomads who forged the first nomadic confederacy on the eastern Eurasian steppe. In 56–53 B.C., the Xiongnu divided into the southern and northern Xiongnu.

yurt: The residence and social bonds of the kinship group of a *ger*.

Names to Know

Chagatai (b. 1183; r. 1227–1242): Mongol khan; the second son of Genghis Khan and Börte and founder of the Chagatai khanate. In 1227, he was assigned the *ulus* in central Asia, originally comprising the Central Eurasian steppes, Tarim Basin, and Transoxania. He was notorious for his violent temper, but he ruled justly and was praised for his adherence to Mongol traditions. He resented his brother Ögödei, but he supported Töregene as regent in 1241–1242.

Genghis Khan (b. 1162 or 1167; r. 1206–1227): Born Temujin, he was the son of Yesugei (died c. 1171). He was the greatest conqueror of the steppes and founder of the Mongol Empire. In 1180–1204, he defeated his rival, Jamukha, and united the Mongol tribes. In 1206, the *kurultai* acclaimed Genghis Khan "Universal Lord." In 1209–1210, he compelled the Emperor Xiangzong (1206–1211) of Xi Xia to submit. In 1211–1216, he wrested northern China from the Jin (Jurchen) Empire. In lightning campaigns, he overthrew the empire of Khwarezm in 1218–1223 and, thus, opened the lands of eastern Islam to Mongol conquest. He died while planning his final campaign against the Jin Empire. His generalship and organizational genius place him among the great captains of warfare. By his principal wife, Börte, he had four sons: Jochi, Chagatai, Ögödei, and Tolui.

Herodotus (c. 490–425 B.C.): Known as the father of history. A native of Halicarnassus, he traveled through the Persian Empire and the lands around the Black Sea. He wrote his *History* to explain the wars between the Greeks and Persians. He gives a detailed account of the nomadic Scythians on the Pontic-Caspian steppes in the fourth book of the *History*.

Hulagu (b. 1218; r. 1256–1265): Mongol ilkhan; the son of Tolui and founder of the ilkhanate. In 1256–1260, he waged a war of conquest of the Islamic world, destroying Alamut, the seat of the Assassins, and sacking Baghdad in 1258. He halted his campaign against Mamluk Egypt and withdrew to support his brother Kublai Khan in his civil war against Arigh Böke. Kublai Khan bestowed on Hulagu the rank of *ilkhan*, "loyal khan"—the title held by his successors.

Kublai Khan (b. 1215; r. 1260–1294): Mongol khan; the second son of Tolui. Kublai Khan distinguished himself in campaigns against the Jin Empire in 1234–1235 and against Song China in 1257–1259. He was proclaimed khan by the Mongol army in 1260 and defeated his rival brother, Arigh Böke, in the civil war of 1260–1264. In 1268–1279, he completed the conquest of Song China. In 1274 and 1281, he launched two costly, abortive expeditions against Japan. In 1271, he assumed the Chinese temple name Shizu, the first of a new Yuan Dynasty (1271–1368). He founded a new capital, Dadu (Beijing), which Marco Polo called Kanbalu (Xanadu). Kublai Khan ruled through imperial servants of various nationalities rather than the Confucian bureaucratic classes. A convert to Buddhism, he assured the eventual triumph of Buddhism among the Mongol tribes.

Suggested Reading

Fyre, *The Heritage of Persia.*

Golden, *Central Asia in World History.*

Herodotus (Marcincola and de Selincourt, trans.), *The Histories.*

Hildinger, *Warriors of the Steppe.*

Saunders, *The History of the Mongol Conquests.*

Sinor, ed., *The Cambridge History of Early Inner Asia.*

Questions to Consider

1. Why did the Mongols epitomize the stereotypical ruthless barbarians of the Eurasian steppes? In what ways were the Mongol conquest and empire exceptional?

2. What are the determining geographic and climatic conditions across the Eurasian steppes that have shaped the course of human history? Where were the main points of contact between nomadic peoples and the sedentary literate civilizations based on cities and agriculture? What have been the usual interactions between the two?

3. How did terrain and climate produce a common way of life on the Eurasian steppes? What economic and social strategies did nomadic peoples evolve? How did these conditions lead to a distinct way of war?

4. What advantages did nomadic peoples possess down to the 15th century that allowed them to excel in warfare and trade? Why did they play such a decisive role in economic, religious, and cultural developments?

5. What are the main literary and documentary sources for our study? What prejudices and concerns do these authors of urban civilizations share in describing nomadic peoples? How have archaeology, anthropology, and biological and environmental studies transformed our understanding of these peoples?

Steppes and Peoples

Lecture 1—Transcript

On February 13, 1258, Hulagu, a grandson of Genghis Khan, led his Mongol army into the city of Baghdad, which is today in lower Iraq. This city, at the time, was the capital of the Abbasid Empire, the Abbasid Caliphate, and it was greatest city of Islam. The Mongol army carried out a sack that reputedly lasted for 40 days. The level of destruction was quite unimaginable at the time. The Abbasid Caliph, a rather gentle man who was the religious and political successor to Muhammad, had surrendered the city on terms back on the 10th of February. But because the city had resisted initially the Mongol Khan, Hulagu felt all bets were off and he turned loose his soldiers to conduct one of the great massacres of any Islamic city.

It was not only the colossal destruction of human life—and Muslim chronicles speak in great detail about the destruction—but it was also the cultural destruction that went on. Mongol soldiers ran through the city, deliberately destroying mosques, madrasas, plundering the libraries; thousands of manuscripts were thrown into the Tigris; and there are reports that the Tigris ran black with ink because of so much of the destroyed literature, and then the Tigris ran red with blood as the populations were marched out onto the Great Plains and they were executed, many of them by beheading, and great mounds of skulls were raised up to celebrate this Mongol victory. Furthermore, the city was largely burned; and with that went so many of the monuments, the palaces, the mosques that had been really the model for Islamic architecture since the eighth century A.D. The only population to be spared was a small group of Christians known as Nestorian Christians, and that is because, reputedly, one of the wives of the Mongol Khan was a Christian herself.

It is hard to calculate the losses, cultural and human, at Baghdad. Reports run as many as 800,000 people were in the city; clearly this city was one of the great urban populations of the world at the time. Someone put those numbers as high as one million; it was swollen with many refugees from the countryside at the start of the siege. In addition, the losses—the intellectual, the religious, the art losses—are enormous. Baghdad had been an intellectual center for centuries. It is where the Quran was edited in its final version;

where the great debates had taken place among Islamic theologians. Was the Quran the uncreated word of God spoken directly through Muhammad in Arabic, or was it to be taken allegorically? It is where Persian and Arabic scholars had drawn on the knowledge of Greek antiquity, of Hindu India, and of Persian Iran and gained great achievements in mathematics—they created algebra—in medicine, in geography, and in history. All of this legacy went up in flames in that destruction on that fateful day and the 40 days that followed.

The image is riveting, and it still endures in the Islamic world as one of the great catastrophes. In fact, many a Muslim might say that the Mongols represented a great catastrophe; their worst nightmare of barbarian. They typified the clash of barbarian peoples of the Steppes and the civilized people of civilizations such as Europe, the Islamic world, India, and China. But is this image true; is this the only image? Are the Mongols just ruthless conquerors, and so were the previous people of the steppes? Was their role to be either defeated or better yet civilized and incorporated and assimilated?

What we are going to look at is not only this image but perhaps other images that are equally telling of the relationship between nomadic peoples and the sedentary civilizations. In this course, I propose to look at all of these images: why they spring to us; why they have come down through the historical record; and why the people of the steppes have come to play such an important role, ever since the first people known as P.I.E. (Proto-Indo-European speakers) first domesticated the horse and made possible movement of peoples over the grasslands of Eurasia; a people who were hardy, capable of living on that climate and wresting a living from demanding conditions of following the seasons and their herds, ever-searching for pastures and water and constantly exchanging whatever goods they had for food and luxuries from the urban literate civilizations.

This course is a daunting challenge; and it has been put together, researched, and offered in response to customers of The Great Courses as well as my own students. These questions are arising largely because of a fascination, not only in the steppes but two of the great conquerors; two of the men that epitomize that image of the sack of Baghdad: One of them is the granddad of Hulagu who sacked Baghdad, and that is Genghis Khan, a household word;

and the other is Attila the Hun. Both of these conquerors are seen as the worst nightmare of civilized populations. They are great conquerors. We conjure up the images of the horse archers; the great cavalry armies that swept over the steppes. The image has been enduring; it fascinates; it repels; it has attracted many, many people to question: How did these conquerors come about and where do they fit in the larger scope of history?

I can say on a very unscientific method—polling my students over a number of years—that among the two conquerors, Genghis Khan, whose real name was Temujin (he gets the name Genghis Khan, "Universal Lord," in 1206, a great name) scores two to one over Attila the Hun (who has perhaps a better name, "Scourge of God") among students and various acquaintances of mine in terms of barbarian recognition; that is, Genghis Khan is seen as a greater and more ferocious conqueror than Attila the Hun. In my opinion, my favorite is Tamerlane, who is a really distant third. He has the title "Prince of Destruction"; I think that is perhaps one of the best titles of all time.

But seriously, these images of these great conquerors pose a daunting challenge, because what do they represent to us? How did they come about? What was their importance? Putting together this set of lectures for The Great Courses, I hope to answer some of those questions: Why were they successful and why did they build great empires? What were the secrets of that success; and at the same time why did these empires come to pass? Why did an empire, especially of Attila, fragment so quickly, whereas the Mongol Empire had a much greater and longer legacy for us today?

In addition, Attila and Genghis Khan have spawned all sorts of popular images and interests; and that can be measured in various ways, besides that very unscientific poll I take each year with my students. One is the image, for instance, of Attila the Hun in popular novels, in paintings, and in tales, in legends. Today, Hungarians and Turks claim Attila as one of their own; and this is very, very odd since Hungarians and Turks have fought each other for 400 years. Hungarians can proudly point—and it is on display, ironically, in Vienna at the Kunsthistorisches Museum—to the sword of Attila. This is some kind of legendary sword in Middle Ages that the kings of Hungary claimed had come from Attila; sure it is a legend, but the legend rings true of the importance of the image of Attila to later Hungarians even though they are not at all directly related to him. Other Turks are the same way: Many Turks have the name Attila; and ironically, the Turkish invasion of Cyprus in 1975, which toppled that military government and led to the partition of Cyprus today, was code named Operation Attila. Attila has also inspired some of my favorite Grade B movies. My favorite one is actually called *Sign of the Pagan*, released in 1954; and Jack Palance is the quintessential Attila on the big screen.

Genghis Khan has inspired almost as many images as Attila the Hun; and again, these images have fed into our understanding and researching of this course. He has not fared as well on the big screen, at least until recently. There is a film called *Mongol*, released in 2007, which is based on the *Secret History of the Mongols*, Tamujin growing up; and the Japanese actor there, Tadanobu Asano, plays a very, very credible Genghis, and the film really creates the world of the steppes in the 13th century quite successfully. There are also lots of statues especially put up in the current Mongolian Republic. In every public square, you get statues of Genghis Khan. Sometimes Genghis Khan is featured as almost an Abraham Lincoln type figure; rather amusing, but after all he did legislate Yassa, the customs of the Mongols. At other occasions he is seen as a conqueror. He is put on top of triumphal arches, which is a really weird mix of iconography; and sometimes the mounted Genghis Khan statue looks like it is leaping into the middle of thin air. There are also statues to Genghis Khan in the cities of Inner Mongolia, now part of the Republic of China. They do not seem to be quite as widespread; in some cases not as flattering either. But all of these images bring to bear very much that central question I asked: Why do these images endure?

There was also a third image—a third set of questions besides the two conquerors that fed into the creation of this course—and that was the image of the Silk Road. Customers of The Great Courses, students, and acquaintances of mine all have some sense of the Silk Road, the great caravans that twisted their way across dangerous steppes and through great mountain passes, across the Pamirs into Ferghana, the remote fabled cities of Samarkand and Bukhara. These are very glamorous, romantic images, and they have endured for a very long time in novels, in bad movies, in paintings, even the earliest archeologists who went there to excavate the cities of the Tarim Basin. In some ways, the images ring true. There is a certain glamour, even though it is pretty time consuming and not very comfortable to ride camels on caravans; but the images are significant in this regard: They balance that image of the bloodthirsty conquerors—that sack of Baghdad I had mentioned earlier—and they drive home the fact that the interaction between nomadic peoples of the steppes and the great civilizations of Europe, the Middle East, India, and China was more than just warfare but also involved cultural exchange, it involved trade, because on those routes would travel not only merchants but monks and mystics. Those routes would be very, very important for the spread of all sorts of religions across Eurasia, notably Christianity, and above all Buddhism and Islam. The impact of those religions and the distribution of those religions across Eurasia are a result of the great empires of these nomadic peoples and the Silk Road.

I want to return briefly to the starting point: the Mongols, sacking Baghdad in 1258. Yes, in some ways they are the epitome of the nomadic warrior; they are the epitome of the conditions of the steppes that can create such a great army as well as such great atrocities, and even the very genius of Genghis Khan and his grandsons. But on the other hand, we shall see that they are also something of exceptions. The image brings out two important issues I want to look at in this course; and that involves the steppe way of life, which we will repeatedly talk about, and how that conditioned the nomadic peoples and how that led to all of the developments we talk about, and the steppe way of war.

What were those conditions on the steppes, on the Eurasian Steppes? They go back at least to the fourth millennium B.C. At about that time, shortly after 4000 B.C., maybe around 3800 B.C., a group of peoples often called the P.I.E. (Proto-Indo-European speakers, and this is really a linguistic designation; we will get into that in the next lectures) perfected the nomadic way of life; and this way of life has remained consistent, remarkably, over the next 6,000 years or so. They are the ones who domesticate the horse; they learn how to ride horses to help move their animals to better pastures and to better sources of water; and they set the pattern of seasonal migrations as well as long-term migrations of whole peoples looking for new homelands that will people the steppes and then come to play a very, very important role in the history of all the civilizations of Eurasia, especially when we begin to get written records and we can trace the movement of these people.

In addition, they invent oxcarts, and felt tents that can convey family and friends across the steppes; those kinds of mobile homes are today essentially called *gers*, it is a Turkish-Mongolian word (there are undoubtedly earlier words). Each of these *gers* represents a yurt, the Turkish word for a family, a group, a kinship group; and a group of *gers* might be a yurt or a kinship (one might be). From the yurt, you build extended families and clans, and eventually political orders. Incidentally, the word *yurt* today in modern Turkish is used for people who share living quarters in a dormitory, which is a rather good extension of the word.

This pattern of moving across the steppes is already noted by the Greek historian Herodotus writing in the fifth century B.C.; it characterizes the movements of steppe nomads today. Furthermore, these animals were the source of milk, yogurt, and this fermented drink called *kumis*, fermented mare's milk, the favorite staple of Mongol armies. It sustained life, but at the same time the nomads needed to trade. They needed to trade for vegetables, for grains, for alcoholic beverages, and all the various luxuries that were available for the literate civilizations; and so from the start, the nomadic way of life was not only harsh but it was not independent. In variably, nomadic peoples have to come to terms with peoples who engage in agriculture, who build cities, who invent writing; and invariably there is always a tension between the nomads and the settled peoples. The steppes can get crowded very quickly; and traditionally nomads have moved into the civilized zones, not only for trade, but as immigrants, as raiders, and sometimes as invaders and conquerors. This is a pattern that is a result of the nomads being driven literally in a harsh life of survival, and it has major consequences in the development of great empires, as well as the redefinition and the change of nomadic life.

Seldom do the nomads themselves talk to us about this way of life. We do have some rare documents; and one of the rarest and one of the most important is the *Secret History of the Mongols*, which gives us a wealth of information about nomadic life centering on the remarkable career of Genghis Khan. Many of the details in that history can be applied to what archeology and what various incidental references in chronicles and geographies tell us about the nomadic peoples.

The way of life is remarkably consistent across time and space. The Indo-European speakers devise it; it is picked up by other speakers, particularly Turkish and Mongolian speakers; and that is because that pattern of life is dictated by the terrain, the extremes of temperature, the necessity of herding those animals, and following the relentless pattern of seasonal migrations. In addition, that way of life results in the development of a very distinct way of warfare; and this warfare gives the nomadic people, starting in what we call the early Iron Age—which is usually regarded as dating between 900 and 600 B.C.—of mounted horse archers; that is, cavalrymen who can ride in a saddle high on the horse and have what is called a composite bow. Initially, when this was perfected by a group of nomads called the Scythians, it is debated whether there were any stirrups or not. One suggestion is there may have been very, very primitive leather loops to steady the rider. By the early sixth century A.D., the Turks have introduced metal stirrups, and that gives stability to the warrior that allows them to do the kind of riding and battle tactics that would come to epitomize steppe warfare really for the next 1,000 years. With those saddles and stirrups, nomadic cavalry could perform all sorts of maneuvers, which the cavalry of the sedentary civilizations could not. There are several reasons for this: For one, the relentless pattern of nomadic life meant that every adult male had to know how to ride; every free adult male was, in effect, a warrior. They are trained at birth to ride these horses; and so when you speak of 1,000, or 10,000, or 20,000 warriors of Turks, that is essentially everyone from the age of 16 and 60 who can mount those horses and go into battle.

In addition, they are carrying a weapon that is perfected between the ninth century B.C. and the seventh century A.D.: the so-called composite bow; and this is sometimes known as a recurve bow. It looks like half a figure eight; it is a very, very powerful small bow. It is extremely difficult to make: You have to glue different types of horn and wood; it takes months for the thing to dry; then you have to string it and equip it with proper arrows. But once you perfect this bow-making, that weapon gives you a firepower that really is not exceeded until the invention of handheld firearms; and that meant horse archers, especially when they have stirrups, could ride close up to the opponents and shoot arrows into the opponents, maybe as close as 20 yards, 10 yards, and then turn on a dime and flee. Invariably, the armies of sedentary civilizations would get so angry they would pursue; they would lose formation; they would lose cohesion; and then those nomads could turn about and attack their opponents who were disorganized and drive them off the battlefield. If the opponent was more wary and would not engage in direct battle, the horse archers could then engage in strategic skirmishing, attacking of columns, of cutting off supplies, and eventually wearing down opponents until they essentially gave up. Both tactically and strategically, it is extremely difficult to bring these warriors to battle, and especially to decisive battle; and the nomadic horse archers maintain that military supremacy for the next 1,000 years and it comes to characterize warfare on the steppes. In the end, the best way to defeat steppe nomads is to mount your own steppe nomads, and many emperors realize this: the emperors of China, of India, the Abbasid Caliphs.

In addition to these two important aspects in the course—that is, the way of life and the way of war—we have to look at these developments and the use of nomadic institutions to build great empires, both on the steppes and in the surrounding areas, and we have to put them in space and time. As I mentioned, this is a daunting course. First, we are going to cover an awful lot of real estate; perhaps 2.5 million miles of Eurasian steppes and associated zones. These would include, for instance, the grasslands of central Europe, in Hungary and in Romania today; the grasslands leading up to the Caucasus and also on the other side of the Caucasus in Azerbaijan; the Kara Kum, the Kyzyl Kum, those deserts in Central Asia; the region of Transoxiana, where the great caravan cities are; the Tarim Basin, which we will be talking about, where there are more caravan cities; and also the borderlands of China. If you take all of those areas where nomads had historically moved about, where they have interacted with sedentary civilizations, you are looking at 6,000 miles in length; a corridor on the steppes could run anywhere from 250 miles to 500 miles; and this vast zone is essentially a highway. A highway compliments to the nomadic way of life: the domestication of the horse, learning to move on those steppes, and backed up by the military power and the way of warfare. We will keep that image of highway in mind because it explains a great deal of what will happen.

All you need to know at the moment geographically—because we will talk about geography in more detail as we move to the different parts of the steppes—there are essentially three zones: There is a western set of steppes, and these steppes stretch from the lower Danube essentially to the Ural north of the Caspian Sea, and they extend down to the Caucasus Mountains. I will be calling them the Pontic-Caspian Steppes or the South Russian Steppes. Then, continuously—there really is not any break—you have the Central Steppes; and they will stretch from the shores of the Caspian, east around the Aral Sea (or what used to be the Aral Sea; the place has really been drained in recent years by Soviet development projects), to the river Jaxartes, and eastward to the Altai Mountains; and that is a region we call the Central Steppes, and that is a distinct zone in itself. Then, from the Altai Mountains east, north of China—and it is bordered on the south by the Tarim Basin and the Gobi Desert—are the Eastern Steppes, these Mongolian grasslands, and they essentially stretch to Manchuria. Manchuria is divided off by the Khingan Mountains, and Manchuria is really a much more lush landscape with forests and valleys; and that defines the Eastern Zone. That is the great highway upon which this historical drama will be played.

It should also be noted that this highway has some important exit ramps. Those include exit ramps into Central Europe, especially the Danube; the great rivers of Russia provide contact of the nomadic peoples with the Black and the Caspian Seas; and then there are great passes over the Caucasus that allow nomadic peoples to go into what we would today call the Middle East. These are the Darial Pass, sometimes called The Gates of Alexander the Great, and the Derbent Pass. The nomads living on the Central Steppes, they have their own exit ramps, particularly across the Jaxartes; and that leads into a region we call Transoxiana today. Transoxiana is home to great caravan cities—Bukhara, Samarkand—and it is defined on the south by the Oxus River. Then finally, there are lots of exit ramps between the Eastern Steppes and the Chinese Empire, much to the dismay of many Chinese emperors.

Finally, I want to close with a sense of time. This drama occurs over a vast amount of time: 6,000 years starting in the fourth millennium B.C., and closes really with the end of the Mongol legacy in the 16th century. To order this information, we have to impose some sort of control; and what I have chosen is to divide time into three parts just as the steppes. You can put this down to a Classical education and learning to read Caesar at a very young age: All Gaul is divided into three parts; ergo everything is divided into three parts for any kind of Classicist. But it will prove very, very useful to think of these three periods. The first period comes after we invent the steppe nomads in that very, very early time before writing; and that period we will call antiquity. That is about the first third of the course; it goes to Lecture 13. That deals with the interaction of different nomadic peoples with early civilizations—with China, with Rome, with Persia—and that ends in the 6th century A.D. when there is a new period, and I will call that the early Middle Ages. That period will stretch from Lecture 14–25, and the great players in that period are the Turks; the Turkish people who spread across the steppes. They bring their languages: There are now 145 million Turkish speakers in the world today, most of them concentrated in the Republic of Turkey, Azerbaijan, which is in Iran, and Turkmenistan; and those languages were brought there in the 11th and 12th centuries. That is a result of the success of steppe nomads who brought those languages from the Mongolian heartland. The Turks are rather peculiar this way: They lose their homeland, but they win new homelands on the Central and Western Steppes and also in the heart of the Middle East. That period comes to an end in the 13th century. We open with the final period, the 13th and 14th centuries, and I like to call this the Mongol era. That is where we will look at the greatest conqueror of all, Genghis Khan, his grandsons, and the Mongol impact on the wider world; the interaction of the nomadic peoples on a hitherto great scale, a much greater scale than ever documented either in the literary records or the archeology.

With this perspective of the three periods and the three zones, I hope that we can come to an understanding with the peoples of the steppes. One other point in passing as we look at time and space, as we go through this course: Kick the map around of Eurasia. We are accustomed to looking north; turn the map around to look south. We are going to look from the nomadic viewpoint; we are going to look at the world as the nomads saw it; and in that case, the nomads are at the roof of the world, and the civilizations go from China to Rome in antiquity. That vision is going to be premised on most of what follows.

The Rise of the Steppe Nomads
Lecture 2

The earliest nomads of the Eurasian steppe were those peoples dwelling in the Pontic-Caspian steppes. Because no writing survives from then, we depend on archaeology and linguistics to understand who these people were. In this lecture, we'll examine the origins and development of the Indo-European language family. We'll also look at what the archaeology of the area tells us about the landscape, the domestication of the horse, and the shift to nomadism that gave rise to the steppe nomads' patterns of life and their distinctive way of waging war.

Proto-Indo-European

- The study of Indo-European linguistics has been an occupation of Western scholars since the 18th century. Previously, the Indo-European family of languages was known as the family of **Aryan** languages (*arya* means "noble" in **Sanskrit**). William Jones, a philologist working at the Asiatic Institute in Calcutta, discovered that Sanskrit, Greek, and Latin were related languages, whose common roots were Indo-European.

- An important point in studying languages is that people speaking a particular language can be from a variety of ethnic and racial backgrounds. Nomads, in particular, learn a variety of languages to communicate with trading partners and neighboring areas. In some circumstances, the nomads actually assimilate a larger settled population.

- Scholars who have studied the grammar and phonology of Indo-European determined that at some point, about 5000 B.C., there was a **Proto-Indo-European (PIE)** language. No one actually spoke Proto-Indo-European; it was essentially created by scholars. However, it gives us an idea of what the parent language is for some 75 percent of the world's population.

Indo-European

- The oldest written texts in an Indo-European language were in the Hittite or **Anatolian** language family; those were represented in **cuneiform** tablets dating between 1650 and 1190 B.C.

- The Anatolian language family probably broke away first. It is speculated that sometime between 4000 and 3500 B.C., the ancestors of these people moved out of the Pontic-Caspian steppes into Asia Minor—what is now Turkey—and brought the **Anatolian languages** there.

- Another group of languages that broke off after the Anatolian is known as the **Tocharian** language family. People who spoke this language inhabited the Tarim Basin.

Centum and Satem

- Indo-European gave rise to a more familiar branch of families, the **centum** branch, which includes Germanic, Celtic, Italic, Greek, and possibly Armenian. The **satem** branch includes Baltic and Slavic languages and Iranian and Indic languages.

- The difference between centum and satem represents changes in the treatment of certain sounds. For example, the kw sound in Indo-European became a hard k in the western languages (*centum* is the Latin word for "100"). In the east, that sound weakened to an s (*satem* means "100" in Sanskrit).

- These languages became differentiated by about 2000 B.C. The other significant point that comes out of the study of the Indo-European language family is not only the relationship of the languages but also the origins and homeland of the original speakers of Proto-Indo-European.

- If we study the common cognates in Indo-European languages, they demonstrate that before the daughter languages broke away, they had a common vocabulary for such words as *horse*, *chariot*, *wheel*, and various steppe animals. As the groups of people broke off and settled in other areas, distinct versions of the original words evolved.

Domestication of the Horse

- Archaeology tells us that around 6500 to 5000 B.C., humans moved onto the Pontic-Caspian steppes and shifted from hunting and gathering food to raising stock. They adopted nomadic patterns of life and domesticated various animals—most importantly, the horse.

- Around 6500 B.C., the vast majority of horses to be domesticated were found on those steppes. Very few horses survived in the rest of Eurasia; the species had died out in North America.

- The domestication of the horse, between about 4800 and 4000 B.C., was vital. Initially, it is speculated, the horse was domesticated for winter food. It was also a source of mare's milk.

In 6500 B.C., estimates are that 50 percent of all horses were in the steppe zone; it makes sense, therefore, that the early Indo-Europeans domesticated this animal.

- By 4200 B.C., the steppe nomads began to ride horses bareback to help them herd animals. Herding on horseback meant that many more animals could be handled and expanded the range of the nomads.

Invention of the Wheel
- Another crucial invention was the wheel. People from the Russian steppes, identified as the Yamnaya, had learned to harness carts to oxen. The wheel meant people had mobility; they could move all their possessions in vast wagon trains in search of better pastures or to exploit seasonal advantages of water, move away from drought conditions, and find new homes.

- After the technology of carts and wheeled vehicles was perfected, spoked wheels were invented, which led to the light chariot. The light chariot became the weapon extraordinaire of the middle and late Bronze Age, from roughly 2000 to 1200 B.C. These chariots acted as platforms in battle, which gave the nomads a military edge.

Migrations East and West
- By 2500 to 2000 B.C., Indo-European speakers started to migrate both west and east. Migrations west took them into the forest zones of Western and Central Europe, which gave birth to the Germanic and Celtic languages. They also migrated into the Mediterranean world, which gave birth to the Greek language and to the Romance languages.

- Those who stayed in the original steppe zones moved into the forests of Russia and became the ancestors of the Baltic and Slavic peoples. But there was also a great eastern expansion; the majority of Indo-European speakers who spread east spoke a version of the Indo-Iranian languages.

- These people migrated out of their original homeland on the western steppes of the great arm of Eurasia to steppes north of the Aral Sea and then drifted down into Transoxania into regions acquired by the Greeks: Bactria and Margiana. There, they settled and brought their distinct technology of chariots, use of domesticated horses, and language.

- The complex in Transoxania was the original homeland for the ancestors of Iranian speakers and for the speakers of Indic languages that gave rise to Sanskrit and, eventually, to the languages of modern India: Hindi and Urdu.

Iranian and Indic Speakers

- The early Iranian and Indic speakers who had moved into the area of Transoxania and northern Iran were in close association for a long time. Scholars have noted similarities in their two languages and parallels in cultural patterns, such as a sense of caste, or *varna*. They also worshiped many of the same gods.

- They broke off in two directions, one to the west and one to the east, and in so doing evolved into the later Indian and Iranian peoples.

- Among their common features was the horse sacrifice and the use of *soma*, an alcoholic beverage given as an offering to the gods. A branch of these people, generally known as the **Mitanni**, a military elite, moved into northern Iraq. The Mitanni spoke a language very close to Vedic and Avestan Iranian.

New Techniques of Warfare

- Migrations during the middle and late Bronze Age brought Indo-European speakers into the central steppes, into Iran, and even into the Middle East. The next major migration of nomadic peoples arose as a result of another pair of breakthroughs: the use of saddles to ride horses in battle and the development of the composite bow.

- These breakthroughs led to the second migration of Indo-Europeans, Iranian speakers, from the central Asian steppes into the Tarim Basin, where the Tocharians had eventually settled. This led to settlements farther east, to the fringes of the Chinese Empire. Scythians, or Iranian speakers from the southern Russian steppes, invaded the historic civilizations.

- A group of people known as the Cimmerians apparently crossed over the Caucasus Mountains, invaded provinces of the Assyrian Empire, and smashed into the Phrygian kingdom of King **Midas**.

- There are records of attacks extending from 1716 to 654 B.C. The Cimmerians disrupted the entire political order of the Near East, which tipped the balance to the emperors of the Assyrians, who united the Near East in the early Iron Age.

A Common Steppe Way of Life
- In Transoxania, in the central Asian steppes, were a group of people known as the Sacae (or Scyths). A component of people who probably originated from Iran in the Middle East had moved into the Tarim Basin and intermixed with the earlier Tocharian people.

- These people, who probably emigrated during the early Bronze Age, now intermixed with a new group of nomads, settled in the caravan cities, adopted civilized ways of life, and melded with the populations of the western zones.

- The Iranian speakers, or Scythians, spread their way of nomadic life across the whole of the Eurasian steppe. By 500 B.C., from the lower Danube to the edges of the Manchurian forest, a common steppe nomadic way of life now prevailed.

Persians and Indo-Aryans
- Most successful were the Medes and Persians, who came out of Transoxania and settled in Iran. The Persians would go on to build the most successful of the ancient empires, the **Achaemenid** Empire, which was based on cavalry armies.

- Other members of the Indo-Iranian steppe people, the Aryans or Indo-Aryans, moved into India. They overthrew the Indus Valley civilization and moved into the upper Indus area, then into the Ganges basin area. They became the people who eventually blended with the local populations to create classic Indian civilization.

- In the next lecture, we will move our focus east to the steppes of Mongolia. We will examine how the Iranian and Tocharian nomads came into contact with China, and the repercussions of their interaction for the great civilizations bordering them.

Achaemenid: The royal family of the great kings of Persia (559–329 B.C.).

Anatolian languages: The first language family to diverge from Proto-Indo-European (4000–3800 B.C.). Speakers of these languages who migrated into Asia Minor circa 2500–2300 B.C. were ancestors of those speaking Hittite, Luwian, and Palaic.

Aryan: From Sanskrit *arya*, meaning "noble": (1) designation of related languages that has been replaced by Indo-European languages; (2) speakers of Sanskrit who entered India circa 1500–1000 B.C.

centum languages: Western language families that evolved out of Proto-Indo-European in 3000–2500 B.C. These language families shared common changes in sound and morphology. They include the language families of Celtic, Italic, Germanic, and Balkan Indo-European languages (the putative mother language for later Greek, Macedonian, Phrygian, Illyro-Thracian languages, and possibly Armenian).

cuneiform: The first writing system, devised by the Sumerians circa 3500–3100 B.C. The wedge-shaped writing was inscribed by a stylus on wet clay.

Mitanni: Indo-Aryan speakers who migrated from Transoxania into northern Mesopotamia in the 16th century B.C., where they established a kingdom over Hurrian- and Amorite-speaking populations. Their language is closely related to Sanskrit and Avestan Iranian.

Proto-Indo-European (PIE): The reconstructed mother language of the Indo-European languages, circa 6000–5000 B.C.

Sanskrit: The sacred literary language of Hinduism.

satem languages: The eastern branch of language families that evolved out of Proto-Indo-European circa 3000–2500 B.C. The language families share sound changes and morphology. These include the Balto-Slavic and Indo-Iranian language families.

Tocharian: The name given to two, possibly three, related Indo-European languages spoken in the Tarim Basin and used to translate Buddhist texts between the 6th and 9th centuries. The ancestors of the Tocharians migrated from the original Indo-European homeland on the Pontic-Caspian steppes to the Altai Mountains and then the Tarim Basin in circa 3700–3500 B.C.

varna: From the Sanskrit for "outward appearance," any one of the original four castes of Indo-Aryan society described in the Rigveda: Brahmins (priests), Kshatriyas (warriors), Vaishyas (merchants), and Shudras (laborers). Only the first three castes were considered twice born; the Shudras represented the subjected populations.

Name to Know

Midas (c. 725–696 B.C.): King of Phrygia. Constructed a great royal tumulus near his capital, Gordion. He was remembered by Greeks for his patronage of the oracle of Delphi. He committed suicide after the Cimmerians, Iranian-speaking nomadic invaders, destroyed his kingdom.

Suggested Reading

Anthony, *The Horse, the Wheel, and Language*.

Kelenkna, *The Horse in Human History*.

Mallory, *In Search of the Indo-Europeans*.

Mallory and Mair, *The Tarim Mummies*.

Okladnikov, "Inner Asia at the Dawn of History."

Piggott, *The Earliest Wheeled Vehicles from the Atlantic Coast to the Caspian Sea*.

1. How have philologists reconstructed the ancestral mother language (PIE)? What led to the divergence of this language into so many daughter languages? How has the field of comparative linguistics also contributed to our knowledge about the origins and early culture of the Proto-Indo-European peoples?

2. How has archaeology clarified the world of Proto-Indo-European speakers? Why was the horse domesticated? Why did the peoples of the Yamnaya culture (c. 3600–2300 B.C.) shift to a nomadic way of life?

3. How did the act of migration by the early Anatolian-speaking and Tocharian-speaking peoples transform their language and cultural identity? What was the nature of such migrations in the Bronze Age?

4. What accounted for the success of Indo-Iranian speakers in the middle Bronze Age (2000–1500 B.C.) and Iranian-speaking nomadic peoples in the early Iron Age (c. 1000–500 B.C.)? What were the long-term consequences of their success?

5. Why did chariots in the Bronze Age and cavalry in the early Iron Age prove so decisive in battle?

The Rise of the Steppe Nomads
Lecture 2—Transcript

In this lecture, I plan to deal with the earliest Steppe nomads we know of, and these are peoples dwelling on what we call the Pontic-Caspian steppes, sometimes referred to as the South Russian steppes. This is a zone I talked about in the opening lecture as essentially the western arm of that great corridor that stretches across Asia, or Eurasia to be more accurate. The earliest people dwelling there are known from archaeology. We have no writing and we depend on archaeology and linguistics to understand what actually happened on these steppes, why the horse was domesticated, and who these people were. This will require us to look at the origins and development of the Indo-European language family. In older textbooks, it was generally known as the Aryan languages, which was a perfectly good term from Sanskrit; *arya* means "noble" in Sanskrit. It was used to apply to a great language family in the 18th century by William Jones, the philologist working at Calcutta at the Asiatic Institute when he discovered that Sanskrit, Greek, and Latin were related languages. Of course, the poor word got ruined by the Nazis and Fascists, and we come up with the cumbersome Indo-European as an explanation for this language family. So we will look at the evolution of these languages. The second important point is the archeology: what it tells about the landscape and above all the domestication of the horse, and the shift to the pattern of pastoral life characteristic of the nomads that gave rise to that distinct pattern of life and that distinct way of war. With that in mind, let us move to the question of language first.

The study of Indo-European linguistics has been an occupation of western scholars since the 18th century. I have to put in a couple of caveats: When you study language families, these should not be mistaken for race. Peoples will change language quite frequently; the speakers of one language, sometimes a minority, will actually assimilate a majority of other people to their language. This has happened many times. Anthropologists have done considerable study on this with modern language families, and there is a theory known as distributive theory or distributive survival theory. That explains that nomadic peoples are particularly skillful, because of their climate, because of their struggle in life, in learning languages and adapting to different language systems. That meant nomads, for instance, who spoke Iranian languages in the period of antiquity, or Turkic languages in the early Middle Ages, or Mongolian languages in the later Middle Ages came to learn a variety of other languages; they adopted what are known as loan words, words for items that they did not have in their native language; and they also spread their language as a koiné, as a means of communication, across the steppes. You will find on various occasions that the nomads will actually assimilate a larger settled population. This is a theme that will repeat itself throughout this course. We will see that particularly with Turkish speakers; we believe the same was true of early Indo-European speakers in the prehistoric age where we do not have written records and we depend on archaeology. It is important to stress from the start that language is not necessarily race in any sense of the word. People speaking a particular language could be from a variety of ethnic and even racial backgrounds.

The second important thing that we want to talk about in the Indo-European language family is that these relationships have been established by scholars who have studied very carefully the grammar, the phonology—that is, the sound systems of Indo-European languages—and they have come to the conclusion that at some point, about 5000 B.C., there was a Proto-Indo-European language; P.I.E. is how it is usually abbreviated in scholarly texts. This language is reconstructed. There are a lot of jokes in graduate school about it when you study it. For instance, no one ever really spoke Proto-Indo-European, it was essentially created by scholars; but there is belief that we have some idea of what the parent language was, the mother language of these numerous language families that will spread across much of Asia and Europe, and today some 75 percent of the world's population speak as their first language or their main language of communication Indo-European language. That would include many of the languages of Western Europe, but also languages of India, Iran, and really some quite diverse languages that would not jump to mind immediately.

These changes can be studied and it is predictable how the daughter languages break away; how they evolve into independent languages mutually unintelligible to the mother language; and then later daughter languages that break away from that mother language P.I.E., Proto-Indo-European. Based on the best analysis of the languages and the text available to us—and again, we are looking at written text that come a lot later than 5000 B.C.—the oldest written text of an Indo-European language are the languages of the Hittite or the Anatolian language family. Those are represented in cuneiform tablets from the city of Hattusa in Asia Minor; roughly most of these texts date between 1650 and 1190 B.C. What it proves is that the Anatolian language family broke away probably first. There are features in its grammar that are very, very archaic that seem to retain older features that were dropped by the later daughter languages. It is speculated that sometime between 4000 and 3500 B.C., the ancestors of these people moved out of the Caspian-Pontic Steppes into Asia Minor, what is now Turkey, and brought the Anatolian languages there. Another daughter that broke off is the group of languages known as the Tocharian language family. That was a bit later than the Anatolian. They did not go west and south, they went east. They apparently peopled the Tarim Basin. That is the basin that has been subject to intensive archaeological study, particularly by Victor Mair and his team working with Chinese scholars who have uncovered these remarkable mummies that show people who have a DNA, ancestry, and physical look to the people of Western Europe, and the language that we later know there. The mummies date from anywhere from about 1000 B.C. to the first century A.D.; and the languages apparently spoken there were Indo-European languages going back to this early daughter language from Proto-Indo-European. They are represented by Buddhist texts written from approximately the seventh through the ninth century A.D. Again, they represent three different distinct versions of that language. These are two early breaks, and probably breaks from that Pontic-Caspian Steppe region.

The other breaks in Indo-European languages are later. This gives rise to a more familiar branch of families. The so-called Centum branch, the branch that broke off largely in Western Europe; Germanic, Celtic, Italic, Greek, possibly Armenian are all languages that come out of that branch. Then there is the so-called Satem branch. That would be the branch more easterly: The Baltic and Slavic languages represent a family; the Iranian and the Indic languages (that is, the languages based off Sanskrit in much of India) are part of that family. That again represents changes in the treatment of certain sounds, above all the "kw" sound in Indo-European became a hard "k" in the western languages, hence *Centrum*, the word "100" in Latin. In the east, that sound weakened to an "s," a sibilant sound, such as "sh" or "s," "suh," hence *Satem* branch of languages, "100" in Sanskrit. Therefore, there are other changes that fall with that pattern. These languages become differentiated by about 2000 B.C.

The other significant point that comes out of the study of the Indo-European language family is not only the relationship of the languages but the origins and homeland of the original speakers of Proto-Indo-European. This is controversial, and it is attempting to match linguistic study—very learned study based on ancient text by scholars who just essentially do language—with archaeological evidence. As I mentioned, there is no writing to help us out, and there is no way, even if you had sufficient skeletal remains, to do a very, very careful DNA analysis on these people; there is no way of pinning this to particular racial groups either. This could get you into very, very dangerous grounds if you start trying to match up bones and material culture with language. But if you study the Indo-European languages and you look at the common cognates—*cognate* is a word that comes from the Latin word meaning "cousins" or "related"—the cognates in all these daughter languages show that the basic vocabulary for horses, for chariots, for wheels, a variety of different types of animals that would be associated with the steppe zone rather than a forest zone or a settled agricultural zone indicates that these daughter languages, before they broke away, had a common vocabulary for these words, which then evolved into distinct versions of those original words as these groups broke off and settled in different areas. That locates the region to the Caspian-Pontic Steppes.

Archaeology tells us several important points that are undeniable facts: Around 6500–5000 B.C., humans moved onto those steppes and they shifted from hunting and fishing and gathering food to stock raising and seasonal patterns of nomadic life by domesticating various animals, above all the horse. The horse is that common word, along with the wheeled vehicles, that ties those Indo-European languages together. Around 6500 B.C., the vast majority of horses to be domesticated are to be found on those steppes. There are very few horses surviving in the rest of Eurasia—in the rest of the Old World, in fact—and the species had died out in North America. One estimate is 25 percent—other estimates are 50 percent—of all horses or equines in the year 6500 B.C. were in that steppe zone; and therefore it makes sense that the early Indo-Europeans saw this animal and found out how they could domesticate it and then eventually ride it. Initially, the thought is it was domesticated for winter food. You could slaughter horses in the winter; they can graze under the snow; they can get in under those grass roots. You have to remember the grasses are fantastic carpet over this steppe area; the roots go very deep, they renew themselves, and even in the winter if those horses can pull up the snow and get down there and feed on that grass they will survive. It also is a source of mare's milk; and I talked about how that fermented mare's milk was a very, very important commodity for all of these people starting from the Scythians in the 6th century B.C. to the Mongolians, the Mongols of the Mongol Empire, in the 13th century A.D. By 4200 B.C., they began to learn to ride the horses bareback to help them herd animals. One experiment is if you are walking on foot with a dog, you can herd maybe 200 sheep at best, probably half that number; but if you are on a horse with a couple of dogs, you can herd 500 or more. That is, it expands the number of animals and the range that you can herd. So the domestication of the horse between about 4800 B.C. and 4000 B.C. was vital; and the speakers of the early Indo-European languages all shared those common words for horse and the related items of the horse.

Another important invention is the wheel. There is a lot of controversy as to when wheeled vehicles were readily available. The earliest uncontested depictions generally come from the Near East; but already this is a very, very well-known technology. From the Standard of Ur in 2600 B.C., we have depictions of clumsy carts that are being dragged into battle by onagers or donkeys; some kind of wild ass, not even by horses. These vehicles, however, are clearly late in the tradition. What we do find in archaeology is people who are identified on the steppes as the Yamnaya Culture—and that comes from a major site on the Russian steppes—had learned to harness carts, to get the harnessing equipment on the wheeled carts, harness them to oxen, and create the so-called *gers* or a kind of cart that will move your dwellings across the steppes. These are generally framed buildings of felt and hides that you can set up as tents; but you could also actually live on these things when they are mounted on the *ger*, and the *gers* are essentially a physical manifestation of the social group known as yurt in Turkish. So you gain mobility: You can move all of your possessions in these vast wagon trains drawn by oxen across the steppes; you could herd your animals with horses. We have descriptions of these from Herodotus writing in the fifth century B.C. about the Scythians dragging huge numbers of carts and people across the steppes in search of better pastures or to exploit seasonal advantages of water, getting away from drought, finding new homes, whatever it is.

By perfecting the technology of carts and wheeled vehicles, at some point it is surmised—and the evidence is really still not there, but the best surmise is—that people on the steppes invented spoked wheels and fashioned these wheels to what we call the light chariot, which became the weapon extraordinaire of the middle and late Bronze Age from roughly 2000 B.C. to 1200 B.C. The vast majority of depictions of light chariots come from the Middle East again, they come from historic periods, they come from New Kingdom Egypt, from the Hittite Empire; yet there is enough evidence coming out of burials from the Altai Mountain zone—that is out in the eastern steppes where you get the Altaic languages as a language family, which are the language families of Turkish and the Mongolian languages— of what seem to be these early vehicles; there is evidence also from burials as far west as Poland. Sometime before 2000 B.C.—some scholars would like to push this back to 3000 B.C.; we really do not have the evidence—they perfect the making of the light chariot. These chariots acted as platforms in battle. Men could ride in; they could attack infantry armies from the flanks; they could ride across the front of an infantry army; they could use a version of the composite bow I described, which is later used by mounted horsemen to disorganize the enemy; and that gave the nomads a new military edge, as well as mobility for their families, as well as better stock raising. That was the third vital innovation on the steppes.

Perhaps by 2000 B.C., 2500 B.C., and by virtue of that—the carts, the stock-raising, the riding of horses to herd animals, and the light chariots—the Indo-European speakers started to migrate both west and east. The migrations west will take the ancestors of the speakers of many European languages into the forest zones of Western and Central Europe. It will take them into the Mediterranean world and give birth to the Greek language, to the various romance languages; in Western Europe, to Germanic and Celtic languages. Those that stay in the original steppe zones and move into the forests of Russia become the ancestors of the Baltic and Slavic peoples.

But there was also a great eastern expansion, and the majority of Indo-European speakers who spread east spoke versions of what are classified as the Iranian language family, or more properly the Indo-Iranian languages. These people migrated out of that original homeland on the western steppes of the great arm of Eurasia to steppe lands north of the Aral Sea, and then drifted down into Transoxiana into regions called by the Greeks Bactria and Margiana. In there, they settled and brought their distinct technology of chariots, the use of domesticated horses, and their language. That complex in Transoxiana was the original homeland for the ancestors of what became the Iranian speakers and the speakers of Indic languages that gave rise to Sanskrit and eventually to the languages of modern India today: Hindu, Urdu, and what we know. That migration represented a very important migration of steppe nomadic peoples from the original core area east. Other Iranian speakers went farther east, across the Central Asian steppes as far as the upper course of the Yellow River, the Huang He, in the Ordos area, which is this great loop in the Yellow River, a desert area that fades into the Gobi, and they settled in that region. Therefore, the peopling of the steppes was largely a phenomenon brought about by Indo-European speakers moving out of that heartland, brought about first by the introduction of chariots in the middle and late Bronze Age and later by the perfection of riding horses with saddles, which led to another distribution farther east. In contrast to the historic periods where we have good written records, the movement of nomadic peoples across Eurasia in the earliest period is west to east; and that is an important point I wish to stress because that is going to have major repercussions in the upcoming lectures.

The early Iranian and Indic speakers who had moved into that area of Transoxiana and Northern Iran were in close association for a long time. Scholars who study the Rig Vedas, which are the earliest texts of India in Sanskrit, and the Avesta, particularly the earlier passages of the Avesta that is a very antique language of Iranian, scholars have noted close association of these two languages; similarities in cultural patterns whereby the early Iranians and early Indian peoples, the ancestors of these people, had a sense of caste. They also worshipped a lot of the same gods. As a result, they broke off in two directions, one to the west and one to the east, and in so doing they evolved into the later Indian and Iranian peoples. Among the common features we know about is the use of horse sacrifices; the use of Soma, which is an alcoholic beverage, in order to get inspired contact with the ancestral spirits. A branch of these people—generally known as the Mitanni, a military elite, and known in the text as the *maryannu* or the young charioteers—moved actually into the Middle East, into Northern Iraq, and they are known from Hittite texts. They were known as great horsemen, and they brought the horse and light chariot into Northern Mesopotamia sometime around 1600 B.C. Those texts were quite a revelation; it shows that the Indo-European speakers of the Mitanni spoke a language very close to Vedic and Avesta Iranian. Those migrations represent an important migration of the middle and late Bronze Age that brought Indo-European speakers into the central steppes, into Iran, and even into the Middle East.

The next major migration of nomadic peoples really came as a result of another breakthrough: learning to ride horses in battle on saddles; the development of the composite bow, which I had talked about in the very first lecture. Sometime after 1000 B.C., Nomadic peoples on the steppes—almost certainly Iranian speakers known as Scythians in Classical sources and described in detail by Herodotus—perfected a type of saddle. It did not yet have stirrups—some scholars surmise perhaps it had primitive leather stirrups—but they create a saddle that could sit on these superior horses they had been breeding (I guess something like 13–14 hands high would be the distance in modern terms), and these horses had a saddle with a wood frame, leather cushions, eventually a tree or a back on it that allows the man to sit up with a composite bow; and that superior saddle, that bow, allowed for the development of horse archers.

Once this technique of warfare was known, it led to that second migration of Indo-Europeans, Iranian speakers, from the Central Asian steppes into the Tarim Basin, where the Tocharians had eventually settled. It led to settlements farther east to the fringes of the Chinese Empire. Scythians or Iranian speakers from the Southern Russian steppes, from the western arm, invaded into the historic civilizations. The first disastrous records we have of this are a group of people known as the Cimmerians who apparently crossed over the Caucasus Mountains, invaded provinces of the Assyrian Empire, smashed into the Phrygian Kingdom of King Midas (King Midas of the golden touch) at Gordian; there are records of attacks extending from 1716–654 B.C. As a result, these Cimmerians disrupted literally the political order of the Near East, which tipped the balance to the emperors of the Assyrians, who united the Near East in the early Iron Age.

In Transoxiana, in the Central Asian steppes, we encounter in the Classical sources a group of people known as the Sacae. They settled in the region of Ferghana, which I will be talking about. They enter into the western zones of the Tarim Basin. Iranian-speaking peoples moved into the Tarim Basin; and the mummies have proved that a component of people who probably originated from Iran in the Middle East had moved into the Tarim Basin and intermixed with the earlier Tocharian people, whose mummies show people with reddish hair, light eyes; whose textiles resemble very much the Tartans of Scotland and Ireland; and suggest that these people who probably immigrated during the early Bronze Age now intermixed with a new group of nomads who came in, settled in the caravan cities, adopted eventually the civilized ways of life, and fused into the populations of these western zones that later the Chinese encounter.

What is also important is that the Iranian speakers, or the Scythians if you want to use the Greek term, spread this common way of nomadic life across the whole of the Eurasian steppes. By 500 B.C., from the lower Danube to literally the borders of the Manchurian forest, we suspect that a common steppe nomadic way of life now prevailed. That included all the carts, the diet we have talked about, the way of life. Some of these Iranian speakers have now entered into the settled zones. The most successful are the Medes and Persians who came out of Transoxiana, settled in Iran; and the Persians would go on to build the most successful of the ancient near empires, the Achaemenid Empire, which, significantly, was based on cavalry armies. Other members of that Indo-Iranian steppe people moved into India; the so-called Aryans or Indo-Aryans. They overthrew or assisted in ending—I think they really overthrew—the Indus Valley civilization known in archaeology, called by the Sumerians Malua; there are faint memories of this in the Rig Vedas. They moved into the Land of the Five Rivers, of the upper Indus, and then into the Ganges and became the people who will eventually fuse with the local populations to create classic Indian civilization.

These movements in what we call the early Iron Age, from about 1000–500 B.C., had major, major consequences for the development of civilization in the Near East and India; and as we will see in an upcoming lecture, in China as well. It tied together the whole of the steppes with this cultural koine, with this common way of life, which would come to dominate the steppes through all of antiquity and only change in the sixth century A.D. with the arrival of the Turks.

Our goal is to see the implications of these changes on the steppes in the coming lectures. It is people from the steppes who are responsible for important exchanges of technology and cultural ideas that will help stimulate early Chinese civilization, or at least enrich it to be more accurate; much of Chinese civilization will be sui generis, but there will be an important component there. Their very pressure on the empires of the Near East and the empires of the Mediterranean will lead to major confrontations and changes in the great Persian Empire, in the empire of Alexander the Great, and ultimately in the successor states of the Roman Empire and the Parthian states that follow those empires. The plan now is to move our focus from the original homeland of the Indo-Europeans on the Pontic-Caspian Steppes east to those steppes of what are now Mongolia to look at how these Iranian and Tocharian nomads come into contact with China, their interaction, and what those repercussions will be like across the central and western steppes and for the great civilizations bordering them.

Early Nomads and China
Lecture 3

Interaction between the early steppe nomads and the Chinese had significant repercussions, which led to the movement of people from east to west. DNA has increasingly confirmed that nomadic peoples on the western and northwestern frontiers of early China were probably Indo-European speakers—using Tocharian, or Iranian-based languages. In this lecture, we begin with China because the excellent Chinese records allow us to take a close look at the first significant conqueror of the steppes: Modu Chanyu. He was the leader of the Xiongnu and, in many ways, was the prototype for many of the later conquerors, such as Attila the Hun, Genghis Khan, and Tamerlane.

Early Chinese Civilization

- Chinese civilization, which was based on the cultivation of millet in the Huang He valley and the cultivation of rice in the Yangtze, was in constant contact with nomadic peoples.

- Chinese civilization stretches back into the Neolithic, with the domestication of animals and plants. While China developed a distinct urban, literate civilization, it was clearly subject to outside influences in its formative period. What the archaeology proves is that this civilization owed a great debt to nomadic peoples.

- In tombs from the **Shang Dynasty** (around 1600 B.C.), jade and other objects from the Tarim Basin have been found. Another important indication of contact is evidence of chariots, horses, and wheels, especially spoked wheels. Chinese warfare was very much based on chariot warfare, yet the technology, even some of the vocabulary, clearly was not originally Chinese.

- Knowledge of horses, the wheel, and light chariots was due to trade or some other kind of contact with Indo-European speakers, probably Iranian or Tocharian nomads.

Origin of Chinese Writing

- Although the point is controversial, copper and bronze technology may have been transmitted by the nomadic peoples from the Near East to China.

- We see, in the early period of Chinese civilization, primitive forms of writing, **oracle bones** used in divination, particularly from the Shang period. There are also bronze tablets from the **Zhou Dynasty** that followed. Some scholars claim that these early forms of Chinese writing, using ideograms, could be read in as many as six different languages.

- An important question is whether or not the Chinese invented writing completely on their own. We do not have evidence of that; we do not see early developments from pictures to writing. The idea of writing might have come from the nomads, and then the Chinese put together their own writing system.

- What is key is that early Chinese civilization was the product of a number of different peoples. There may have been contact between the early Chinese and the nomadic peoples known as the **Yuezhi**. The Yuezhi were the ancestors of the Kushan, the Wusun, and the Xiongnu (hence, "Huns").

The Xiongnu

- The first emperor of China, **Shihuangdi**, unified China in the **Qin Dynasty**, from 246 to 206 B.C. He ordered the burning of books; one speculation is that he was essentially centralizing the cultural and aesthetic traditions of his empire and eliminating other languages besides Chinese.

- Early Chinese rulers, especially the emperors of the Zhou Dynasty, became quite alarmed by the threat of various nomadic peoples, who had learned the art of horseback riding with a saddle and fought with the composite bow.

- In the 3rd century B.C., the Xiongnu were the barbarians of most concern to the early Chinese emperors. In our best estimation, the Xiongnu spoke an **Altaic** language.

- The Altaic language family consists of two important branches: Turkish and Mongolian languages. Those two languages and their offspring languages are much closer to each other than any of the Indo-European languages. They diverged much later.

Warring States
- In the early Iron Age, China consisted of a series of competing states that vied for power in the heartland of China, between the Huang He and the Yangtze. This central area was where the cities and the agricultural wealth were concentrated. It was the core of the classic **Han Dynasty**; everything else was extension.

- As these states battled for supremacy, they were far more concerned about their Chinese neighbors. Nonetheless, the northern states could not neglect their frontiers, and already as early as the 6th century B.C., some of these states were building walls along their northern frontier to protect themselves from the horse-riding nomads.

Shihuangdi
- An important change occurred in 246 B.C. One of the contenders, Shihuangdi, united the various states of China into the first empire. By doing so, he took control of China and its urban civilization.

- Shihuangdi was a brutal emperor. He carried out the burning of books; he ruthlessly reordered Chinese civilization along legalist principles. Legalism was one of the philosophical systems that emerged in the period of **Warring States**, along with Confucianism and the more mystical Daoism. He mercilessly mobilized labor. Above all, he had imperial ambitions.

- In contrast to many later Confucian emperors, Shihuangdi put military success at a high value. Now, Chinese expansion went

Shihuangdi is well known to many people because in 1974, his mausoleum was found with thousands of the famous ceramic warriors.

in different directions—to the northeast, toward Manchuria and Korea, and to the south, to control what we now know as Vietnam.

Tribal Organization

- Foremost of concern was the northern frontier, where tribes had been organized under a ruler, known as a *chanyu*, named **Touman**. Touman organized various clans consisting of Altaic speakers—the true Xiongnu—and other associated tribes.

- Turkish and Mongolian tribal structures consisted of the inner tribes of the original confederation, usually speaking the same or closely related languages, and the outer tribes, allies affiliated with the Xiongnu. This sort of organization was first perceived under Touman and his son and successor, **Modu Chanyu**.

- Shihuangdi commissioned his general **Meng Tian** to deal with the nomads. Meng Tian pursued the nomads north, leading a massive army up the valley of the Huang He. He tried to drive them into the arid zones across the Gobi.

- Meng Tian's notion of victory was to take real estate on the frontier zones, mark it out, and define the northern frontier as China and everything on the other side as barbarian land. In that sense, the expedition was a success; Meng Tian, in fact, may have ordered walls to be linked together, a precursor to the Great Wall.

A Military Disadvantage

- Facing an enemy on horseback, Shihuangdi and the next set of emperors, during the Han Dynasty, learned that Chinese horses were just not strong enough to be ridden. The soil in China does not have enough selenium to allow horses to develop the kind of strong bones necessary to carry a mounted warrior. The Chinese had to resort to chariots of two or four horses.

- These chariots were inadequate for fighting nomads on grasslands in arid conditions. From the start, the Chinese found themselves at a military disadvantage. Their heavy infantry, their crossbows, and their chariots were not going to bring a Xiongnu army down in battle.

Modu Chanyu

- In 209 B.C., shortly after the death of Shihuangdi, Modu Chanyu came to power. He had an extraordinary reputation in successfully waging warfare, and he proved to be able, not only as a commander but also as an organizer. Modu Chanyu organized the Xiongnu into an illustrious confederation of inner and outer tribes. He was served by two subordinates: the righteous king of the right and the righteous king of the left.

- Modu Chanyu also appreciated the advantages of Chinese civilization. The Xiongnu used Chinese bureaucrats to facilitate trade. They developed a peculiar kind of writing that was clearly in imitation of the Chinese. Some of their political institutions, such as the notion of the mandate of heaven, were influenced by China.

- There was an enormous amount of cultural exchange going in both directions, and the advantages gained by the interaction with the Chinese allowed the Xiongnu to organize themselves more successfully.

Gaozu and the Han Dynasty

- In 206 B.C., **Gaozu**, who originally started off his career as a jailer under the Qin Dynasty, turned rebel and eventually seized the throne and instituted the Han Dynasty.

- The Han Dynasty was the quintessential Confucian state. The first emperor of the Han created the Confucian order as we understand it. The Confucian order will dominate much of our discussion of the eastern sects.

- Gaozu also chose to confront the Xiongnu as a threat. He sent armies north to battle and encountered the same difficulties as his predecessor, Shihuangdi.

- There was an embarrassing defeat in 200 B.C. on the plateau near Mount Baideng, in today's Shanxi province. The imperial army was badly beaten by the usual nomadic tactics.

The Five Baits

- In response, Gaozu shifted from confrontation to courting and accommodation. He developed the tribute system, or what the Chinese called the five baits. This plan was to court the leader of the Xiongnu by the assurance of marriage to a Chinese princess and by promises of silk, rice, and all the commodities that the Xiongnu needed to sustain life.

- If the Chinese could control and regulate trade, they could change raiding to trading and thereby secure their frontier. The five baits became a principle of diplomacy that would reappear in relationships between Chinese dynasties and the nomadic peoples.

Deteriorating Relationships

- For the Xiongnu, this was a splendid arrangement. There was no risk of combat, the Han regularly showed up with gifts, and Modu

Chanyu married a Chinese bride. Everything raised his esteem in the eyes of the righteous king of the right, the righteous king of the left, and all his subordinate rulers. This became a pattern of many nomadic conquerors: not to defeat China but to exploit China.

- In turn, the Xiongnu provided vital products to the Chinese— above all, an enormous number of horses—and they secured the trade of the beginning of what is known as the Silk Road.

- However, later Chinese emperors began to chafe under this exchange. For one, it challenged the fiction of the Middle Kingdom. The question was: If the son of heaven truly was the only ruler, why did he have to deal with the Xiongnu ruler as an equal?

- Eventually, the traditions of the Confucian state and the notion of the Middle Kingdom conflicted with the existing relations with the nomads. The arrangement rankled the Mandarin elite so much that the Han emperor Wudi, when he came to the throne about 140 B.C., decided to substitute war for diplomacy. As a result, he embarked on a crusade that was to have major consequences both to the Han Empire and the Xiongnu.

Important Terms

Altaic languages: A family of languages with common agglutinative grammar and syntax, vowel harmony, and vocabulary. The major branches are Turkic, Mongolian, and Tungusic; Korean and Japanese may also be branches of this language family.

chanyu: Meaning "son of endless sky," this was the title of the ruler of the Xiongnu reported by Han and Song Chinese sources. In the early 5th century, the title was abandoned, and steppe nomadic rulers henceforth styled themselves as khan.

Han Dynasty: Rulers of imperial China as the Former or Western Han (206 B.C.–9 A.D.) and then as the restored Later or Eastern Han (25–220). The usurper Wang Mang, who overthrew the Former Han Dynasty, failed to establish his own Xin Dynasty (9–25).

oracle bones: Inscribed divination bones of the Shang Dynasty (1600–1046); they are the first examples of Chinese writing.

Qin Dynasty: The dynasty (221–206 B.C.) founded by Shihuangdi (257–210 B.C.), when he unified China in 221 B.C.

Shang Dynasty: The first historical dynasty of China (c. 1600–1046 B.C.), centered in the lower and middle Huang He (Yellow River).

Warring States: Kingdoms in the period of political disunity in China following the collapse of effective rule by the Zhou Dynasty (481–221 B.C.).

Yuezhi: The Chinese name for Tocharian-speaking nomads who dwelled on the central Asian steppes north of the Tarim Basin. In 155 B.C., the Xiongnu drove the Yuezhi west into Ferghana, where Zhang Qian visited them in 128 B.C. These Tocharian speakers, called Da Yuezhi ("Great Yuezhi") were the ancestors of the Kushans.

Zhou Dynasty: The second imperial dynasty of China (1045–256 B.C.), ruling in the early Iron Age. After 481 B.C., Zhou emperors lost control over their vassals, and China lapsed into the period of Warring States.

Names to Know

Gaozu (b. 247 B.C.; r. 206–195 B.C.): First Han emperor of China. Overthrew the Qin Dynasty. Born Liu Bang and of humble origin, he preferred negotiation to war with Modu Chanyu after he suffered an embarrassing defeat at Mount Baideng in 200 B.C. Gaozu instituted the tribute system whereby nomadic tribes could be turned into allies dependent on Chinese silk and goods.

Meng Tian (d. 210 B.C.): The leading general of the Qin emperor Shihuangdi. In 221 B.C., he led a major expedition against the Xiongnu and established the empire's northern frontier. He directed the construction of the continuous Great Wall of China.

Modu Chanyu (b. c. 234 B.C.; r. 209–174 B.C.): Succeeded his father, Touman, as *chanyu* of the Xiongnu. He gave the tribal confederation administrative organization and effective leadership in raiding China, and he defeated the army of Han emperor Gaozu at the Battle of Mount Baideng in 200 B.C. Thereafter, he received gifts and silk from the Han court in return for an alliance and sale of horses to the Han armies.

Shihuangdi (b. 259 B.C.; r. 246–210 B.C.): Founded the Qin Dynasty and united the warring states of China. He took strong measures against the Xiongnu and ordered the construction of the Great Wall.

Touman (c. 220–209 B.C.): First known *chanyu* of the Xiongnu; organized the first nomadic confederation on the eastern Eurasian steppe. He warred with the Qin emperor Shihuangdi and with the rival Yuezhi (Tocharians) for control of the Gansu corridor.

Suggested Reading

Barfield, *The Perilous Frontier.*

Chang, *Shang Civilization.*

Hucker, *China's Imperial Past.*

Kinoshita and Portal, eds., *The First Emperor.*

Waldron, *The Great Wall of China.*

Ying-shi Yu, "The Hsiung-nu."

———. *Trade and Expansion in Han China.*

Questions to Consider

1. How significant were the contributions of steppe nomads to the formation of early Chinese civilization? Why are these contributions, surmised from archaeology, so controversial and politically charged?

2. How successful was the Qin Shi Huang in confronting the threat posed by the Xiongnu? What were the strategic, tactical, and logistical challenges faced by Qin armies operating on the steppes?

3. What accounted for the success of Modu Chanyu in creating a confederacy of steppe nomads? How did Chinese institutions and ideas influence Xiongu organization and material culture?

4. What were the advantages of the tribute system to Han emperors and the Xiongnu? Who had the superior position in this exchange?

Early Nomads and China
Lecture 3—Transcript

In this lecture, I wish to deal with early nomadic peoples and early China. The interaction is extremely important; and you might ask why we start with China? Part of it is because we have extremely good records; and we have earlier records of the interaction of steppe peoples with settled peoples—we will be talking about them later—but the Chinese records are particularly good. The second important point is, as I mentioned at the close of the last lecture, that we will start looking at the migrations of peoples from east to west. The earliest populations moved from the western steppe zone out—these are the Iranian speakers—and DNA has increasingly confirmed that the nomadic peoples that would have dwelled on the western and northwestern frontiers of early China were in origin probably Indo-European speakers, Tocharian languages, which came to be very important in the Tarim Basin, or Iranian-based languages. We start with China for those two reasons. The interaction between the steppe nomads and the Chinese led to very important changes, very important repercussions; and it will then result in movements of people east to west, really until the end of the course.

Another reason why I choose to deal with China is not only are the records very good, the records allow us to look at the first significant conqueror of the steppes, who will be featured later in this lecture. His name is Modu Chanyu (that is a Chinese rendition of his name); he is the leader of the Xiongnu, and he in many ways is the prototype for many of the conquerors better known to you as Attila the Hun, Genghis Khan, Tamerlane. Starting with early China and the nomads is really a good point to tie together key themes of the entire course as well as this new movement now that goes from east to west.

I mentioned that DNA and archaeology have indicated that nomadic peoples dwelling on the western and the northwestern frontiers of China—this would be in the region of Guangzhou, the corridor that links China to the Tarim Basin to the Ordos triangle, and you have to think of the Yellow River as this vast river that bisects northern China, and it loops up, it starts in the Tibetan Highlands, it loops around, and in that loop is a very arid zone, very attractive to nomadic peoples, not very attractive to agriculturists; Chinese emperors are always concerned about controlling it because it is part of the river valley of the Yellow and therefore essential for protecting their capitals An Yang, Lu Yang, and later capitals of the Tang period—so the archaeology and DNA indicates Chinese urban civilization, which was based on the cultivation of millet in the Yellow River Valley and the cultivation of rice in the Yangtze (or as it is now generally rendered the Yangzi) that these urban centers, these early settlement regions, were in constant contact, a very important contact, with nomadic peoples.

I should make a note that in the course of talking about China, I will tend to use the new system, the Pinyin system. I was actually trained on an older system of Chinese transliteration—that is, the so-called the Wade Giles system—and sometimes I kind of mix the two systems in my pronunciation, so please forgive me if that happens. Yangzi is the common way it is rendered now; Yangtze is the more traditional way that I know and many English speakers still use.

What the archaeology shows us is that Chinese civilization was subject to outside influences in its formative period. This does not mean that the Chinese were not original. This does mean that the Chinese themselves apparently learned the cultivation of rice very early, mastered the cultivation of millet, developed important settlements; and also the architecture that comes to characterize early China: this rammed-down earth construction where you put wooden frames, you ram down the earth, you use them as platforms to build palace structures; we see that as early as the Xia Dynasty, roughly around 2000 B.C. It was later used in the construction of the Great Wall and other types of features. Chinese civilization stretches way back into the Neolithic with the domestication of animals and plants. It develops a distinct urban, literate civilization.

On the other hand, what the archaeology proves is that this civilization, however, owed some very important gifts from the nomadic peoples. This has come from tombs particularly. One of the major items that has been found in tombs of the early period, particularly of the so-called Shang dynasty—traditionally the Shang are dated as starting in 1766 B.C., many scholars would date that now a little later, around 1600 B.C.; but in the Shang and in the earlier period generally known as the Xia (it is sometimes rendered as "Hs-," Xia is now the common way of rendering it)—in these dynasties, jade and other objects have been imported from the Tarim Basin, which is a considerable distance away. You have to go across that corridor, through the so-called Jade Gate, the great pass that links China to the outside world; clearly there was some kind of trade connection bringing the goods in.

Another important point is the appearance of chariots, horses, and wheels, especially spoked wheels. These are particularly characteristic of the Shang Period. Chinese warfare is very much based on chariot warfare; yet the technology, even some suspect some of the words, are clearly not originally Chinese. The knowledge of horses, the wheel, the light chariots was due to trade or some kind of contact with nomads, and these would have been Indo-European speakers, probably Iranian or Tocharian. There are arguments that copper and bronze technology may have been transmitted by the nomadic peoples from the Near East to China.

Even more controversial is the notion of the writing. We have in this early period of Chinese civilization early writing: oracle bones used in divination, particularly from the Shang period; there are also later bronze tablets from the so-called Zhou Dynasty that follows. They are ideograms. Some scholars claim that these early forms of Chinese writing could be read in as many as six different languages, again a very controversial point. Did the Chinese invent writing completely on their own? We do not have evidence of that. We do not have early developments from pictures to writing; the system as we have it is full-blown. That might be a result of the fact that we do not have the earlier examples the way we have in Sumar, where we can see how you go from pictograms (essentially pictures) to full writing. Or, the idea of writing might have been another one of those gifts, compliments of the nomads, brought to China and the Chinese had an idea of writing and then put together their own writing system.

This is a very controversial and sensitive point; there really is not enough evidence to decide one way or the other. What is key, though, is that Chinese civilization was the product of a number of different peoples (early Chinese civilization); and that nomadic peoples later known as the Yuezhi or the ancestors of the Kushans, the Wusun, and above all the Xiongnu or Xiangnu—who may really have been pronounced "Xiongnu" according to one argument, hence "Huns"—that these people had some sort of contact. We also know that there were periodic burnings of books. The first emperor (as opposed to a king in China) we know about, Qin Shi Huangdi, who unifies China in the so-called Qin Empire from 246–206 B.C., ordered burning of the books and one speculation is that he was essentially centralizing the cultural and aesthetic traditions of his empire on Chinese and other languages were to be removed.

The notion of an unbroken succession of Chinese dynasties stretching back to the very origins of the heavenly kings is really a historical conceit created in the Han period and later; that is, the first great imperial dynasty of the third century B.C. The notion that Chinese history has always been an unbroken succession of rulers and that disunity when it comes is an aberration, it is not the norm, it is being done by non-Chinese bozos, barbarians, whatever the stereotype, that this is a conceit that is imposed on the earlier period. The archaeology suggests that it was much more complicated than what we have in the written tradition later on, starting in the Han and later.

The other important point is that these early Chinese rulers, especially the later Shang and the emperors of the so-called Zhou Dynasty (again, it could be rendered as "Ch" or "Czh" depending on which transliteration system you are using) became quite alarmed that they had to deal with various nomadic peoples. These nomadic peoples somewhere around 1000 B.C. had clearly learned the art of horseback riding, with the mounted saddle and the composite bow. The nomadic peoples dwelling on the northern and western frontiers of the Chinese world are not very well known to us. We do not have any written texts; well, we have a few texts later of the Xiongnu and they are very controversial, but we really do not know what languages they are speaking. The best guess is on the western side they were Tocharian speakers, and they would be the Yuezhi, the later Kushans, a people who will migrate eventually into India; or the Wusun, some have tried to identify them with Iranian speakers including Alans; and then to the north we encounter a bewildering array of names, the Chang, the Ti peoples, these are names that start appearing in the eighth and seventh centuries B.C.; and finally, in the third century B.C., we hear largely of the Xiongnu. The Xiongnu become the barbarians par excellence that concern the early Chinese emperors.

The Xiongnu, our best estimation, is they spoke an Altaic language. I spoke of the Indo-European language families; and the Indo-European language families had broken up in very, very early times, distributed themselves across Eurasia and Western Europe, and really broke up into a large array of different languages, mutually unintelligible. The Altaic language family consists of several branches. The two most important branches in this course will be the Turkish languages and the Mongolian languages. Those two languages and their daughter, offspring, languages are much, much closer to each other than any of the Indo-European languages, and they diverge much later. The suggestion is that in the early Iron Age—from 900 to, say, 300 B.C.—the speakers of what eventually became Turkish and Mongolian languages were dwelling on the Mongolian steppes bordering the Manchurian forest zone, and these are the people who come into contact with the Chinese. They learn the pastoral nomadic way of life from the Iranian nomads immediately to the west. That is again a very important point I wish to stress: It was undoubtedly intermixture, intermarriage, a swapping of ideas. These nomadic peoples do not see themselves as Indo-European speakers versus Altaic speakers; they think in terms of tribe and clans. Tribe and clan can expand and incorporate newcomers; the people can be assimilated.

The Chinese found all of these people alarming; and in the early Iron Age, China was a series of competing states. Whoever the early Zhou rulers were who succeeded to the Shang, they broke up into what are known as the Warring States: the states of Yan, Zhao, Wei, Qin. All of these vied for power in the heartland of China, which is essentially between the Yellow River and the Yangtze, or Yangzi if you wish to call it that; the region where the heartland of the cities, the agricultural wealth, is located. That is the heartland of the classic Han Chinese; everything else is extension. As these states battled for supremacy, they were far more concerned about their Chinese neighbors; nonetheless, the northern states could not neglect their frontiers, and already, as early as the sixth century B.C., some of these states were building walls along their northern frontier to protect themselves from these horse-riding nomads.

An important change comes in the middle of the third century B.C. In 246 B.C., one of the contenders, the king of the state of Qin, Qin Shi Huangdi—

well known to many people because in 1974 his mausoleum was found and we got thousands of the famous ceramic army; we actually have some examples of them here in minature, which represents the army of the first real emperor of China as opposed to a king, a man who could rule the whole Chinese heartland and had wider ambitions in the frontier zones— he had interned with him this essentially personal army, which is actually a very good look at the type of armies that the Xiongnu encountered in their wars, especially in the second century B.C., which we will talk about in an upcoming lecture. Anyway, Qin Shi Huangdi unites the various states of China into the first empire. He has essentially control of China and the urban civilization. He was a hard master. He carries out the burning of the books, as I said; he ruthlessly reorders Chinese civilization following what is often known as legalist principles. Legalism was one of the philosophical systems that emerged in the period of Warring States along with Confucianism and the more spiritual mystical Daoism. He ruthlessly mobilized labor. Above all, he had imperial ambitions. In contrast to many later Confucian emperors, Qin Shi Huangdi put military success at a high level.

Chinese expansion was in different directions. To the northeast, towards Manchuria, Korea; to the south to control, of course, the regions we now know as Vietnam; but foremost in concern was that northern frontier, and above all the *chanyu* of the Xiongnu. The *chanyu* is apparently some kind of royal title, and the first one we hear of is a man named Touman. Touman apparently organized the various clans. They probably included people of different language backgrounds; not only Altaic speakers, true Xiongnu, but other associated tribes. You have to get used to a policy that occurs in both Turkish and Mongolian tribal structures; later, it is put very simply: Any tribal coalition on the steppes consists of two components. There are the inner tribes; those are the real tribes of the original confederation, usually speaking the same language or very closely-related languages. Then there are the outer tribes; these are tributary and ally tribes affiliated to the Xiongnu. It is always very nice in steppe nomad society: You really know whether you are in or out. If you are in the inner tribe, you are in on the really good goodies; you are going to get the first of the pick of the loot (in the case of China that means silks and other goodies). When you are in the outer tribes, you are in a vassal relationship; some of them can be promoted, some can be demoted. But this sort of organization is first perceived under Touman and then, when he dies, under his son, Modu Chanyu, the successor.

Both of these two kings are known from Chinese sources. The rendering of their names is from the Chinese characters; but what we can say is that they posed enough of a threat that the Qin emperor commissioned his general, Meng Tian, one of the very able generals of early China, to deal with the nomads. We see in this first expedition a typical pattern that emerges; that is, what does an organized state, an organized bureaucratic state (the first Chinese emperor), expect victory to be? The general, Meng Tian, is ordered to pursue the nomads north, and he does. He leads an enormous army up the valley of the Huang Ho; he tries to drive them out of the Ordos triangle; then into the arid zones across the Gobi; and he counts success in the following way: Have we captured the Xiongnu leader? Have we captured any kind of settlements? What areas can we mark off with a wall, and bring in colonists, set up settlements, tax them, and declare a victory? His notion of victory is taking real estate on the frontier zones, marking it out, and defining the northern frontier as China and everything on the other side as barbarian land. In that sense, the expedition is a success; and Meng Tian, some of whose thoughts have survived to us, is apparently the general who ordered linking some of these walls together that became the basis of the Great Wall.

You have to actually deprogram yourself from thinking of what the Great Wall of China was like when it was built by Qin Shi Huangdi and his general Meng Tian. The Great Wall is not what you see today. What you see today is a monument built in the Ming period of masonry architecture, which is essentially an emotional overreaction to the fact that the Mongols had ruled China. There is an old adage, I remember when I was boy starting to decide what field of history I would major in, and it went something like this: Rome fell because China built the Great Wall. The Great Wall in third century B.C. was hardly anything like what we think the Great Wall is today. It was rammed earth; that is, there was an earth platform built. That is earth that is pounded down within a wooden frame. On top of it, there would be rough constructions; there would be wooden palisades. The wall was not really continuous; it will stretch 2,500 miles, but there were sections of it where you used the natural boundaries of mountains. You constructed it from wood and earth. The labor was from great *corvees*; that is, massing together peasants to build this thing. It is an immense testimony to the organization of early China, but it is nothing like a Maginot Line. It was intended to mark the boundary and operate as a frontier system to monitor and to regulate the movement of the Xiongnu across the Chinese frontier because in the very costly expedition of trying to run these nomads down, the Chinese very, very quickly learned they do not have the horses to do it.

One of the rude awakenings that Qin Shi Huangdi and the next set of emperors, the Han emperors, learn is Chinese horses are just not strong enough to be ridden. The soil in China does not have enough selenium that allows the horses to develop the kind of strong bones necessary to carry a mounted warrior, so Chinese chariots of two or four horses is the best you can do. These are inadequate for fighting nomads on grasslands in arid conditions; the Mongolian grasslands, the Gobi Desert, the Ordos triangle, or even that corridor of the Guangzhou that links China to the Tarim Basin. From the start, the Chinese for the first time find themselves at a military disadvantage. Their heavy infantry, their crossbows, their chariots just are not going to bring a Xiongnu army to battle, not very easily. What you do is you mark out a system of frontier fortifications that allow you to monitor and regulate, perhaps regulate trade. This policy will be inherited next by the Han emperors.

When Qin Shi Huangdi, who was so successful in organizing the first Chinese empire, dies, he does not leave a set of very, very successful successors. The dynasty is quickly replaced in 206 B.C. At the same time, in 209 B.C., shortly after the death of Qin Shi Huangdi—he dies in 210 B.C.—Modu Chanyu, the son of Touman, comes to power in his own right. He had been in association with his father; he had racked up an incredible reputation in raids and warfare; and he proved to be able not only as a commander, but also as an organizer. Modu Chanyu organizes the Xiongnu into a great confederation of inner and outer tribes. He is served by two subordinates: the righteous king of the right; the righteous king of the left. You have to understand that when you are dealing with the Xiongnu or later Turkish or Mongolian peoples, they see the world from the roof of the world; they are looking out on the map. They are not looking the way we do, projection north; they are at the north looking to the rim of the world. They are in the center of the known world. The right to them is the west; the left to them is the east. He had two subordinate kings with lesser kings; all of these people tied to the Xiongnu, and in turn reward it with plunder and booty. That meant he could tie the tribes together.

He also appreciated the advantages of Chinese civilization. The Xiongnu used Chinese bureaucrats. They want trade goods. They develop a peculiar set of writing, which is still controversial as how to read it; but it is clearly in imitation of the Chinese. Some of their political institutions, such as the notion of the mandate of heaven, too seem to be a borrowing from China, where the Xiongnu is apparently the embodiment of heaven itself. There is an enormous amount of cultural exchange going in both directions, and those advantages allow the Xiongnu to organize themselves much more successfully.

There is always a weakness in these confederations, and that is in the nature of succession. Succession within nomadic states is generally lateral succession; that is, when a ruler dies, very often his brother succeeds rather than his sons. This will cause repeated civil wars: a later one among the Xiongnu that the Chinese exploit; you will see the same when Attila the Hun dies in 453. You will see the same in the great Mongol civil war, which puts Kublai Khan on the throne. There is always that danger of the confederation breaking up over the succession. But Modu Chanyu has the ingredients of success: organization, the welding of the great tribes, and raiding China.

The raids on China were never intended to overthrow the Chinese Empire. They put pressure on the Qin Dynasty. It was a contributory factor to the fall of the Qin; but in 206 B.C., a new man, Gaozu, who originally started off his career as a jailer under the Qin and turned rebel and eventually seized the throne, instituted in a civil war what we call the Han Dynasty. The Han Dynasty is the quintessential Confucian state. The first emperor of the Han creates the Confucian order as we understand it; and that Confucian order will be articulated, improved upon, and will dominate much of our narrative of the eastern sects.

Gaozu, who was also successor to the policies of Qin Shi Huangdi, initially chose to confront the Xiongnu as a threat; he tried to lay a trap for them. He also sent armies, again, north to battle and encountered the same difficulty very, very quickly that the armies could easily be trapped and bushwhacked. There was an embarrassing defeat in 200 B.C. on the plateau near Mount Baideng, today Datong in Shanxi province. The imperial army was badly cut up by the use of the usual nomadic tactics; and so Gaozu shifts from confrontation to courting and accommodation. He develops what the Chinese eventually call the tribute system, or better translated as the "five baits"; and this was to court the leader of the Xiongnu by the promise of a marriage to a Chinese princess, by promises of silk, of rice, all the commodities that the Xiongnu needed to sustain life. What Gaozu realized was—and the same thing was true of Modu Chanyu—is that most true nomads are poor nomads; and if the Chinese can control and regulate the trade, they could change raiding to trading and therefore secure their frontier. This tribute policy, this "Five Baits" as it is sometimes called in Chinese, becomes a principle of diplomacy that will reappear in relationships between Chinese dynasties and the nomadic peoples, particularly from those kings who realized that confrontation was very, very difficult to win. Gaozu, himself a usurper, realized he could not afford defeats at the hands of the Xiongnu; and he very sensibly followed this policy, which secured his northern frontier.

On the other hand, for the Xiongnu this was a great arrangement. There was no risk of combat, getting defeated; the Han regularly showed up with gifts; Modu Chanyu got a Chinese bride; everything raised his esteem in the rise of the righteous king of the right, the righteous king of the left, of all of his subordinate rulers, and he became the source of all the goods that went to the various inner and outer tribes. This becomes a pattern of many nomadic conquerors: not to destroy China, not to defeat China, but to exploit China. In turn, the Xiongnu provided vital products to the Chinese, above all horses; they secured the trade of the beginning of what is known as the Silk Road; they brought in an enormous number of horses.

The Chinese never really got reconciled to this. I think the Xiongnu were more than happy to follow this tribute system, but later Chinese emperors began to chafe under this exchange. For one, it challenged the fiction of the middle kingdom; that the son of heaven truly was the only ruler that mattered. He had to deal with the Xiongnu ruler as some kind of, if not equal, near equal; and the price always went up. The Xiongnu were not stupid, they would count the silk; and so you go from 6,000 pieces of silk to 30,000 pieces of silk. There are even reports of precious metal being exchanged; and the emperors were sending even more lofty bribes to these rulers. Eventually, the traditions of the Confucian state, the notion of the middle kingdom, rankled the Mandarin elite so much that the great Han emperor Wudi, when he came to the throne about 140 B.C., decided to substitute war for diplomacy, and as a result embarked on a war that was to have major consequence both for the Han Empire and the Xiongnu.

The Han Emperors and Xiongnu at War
Lecture 4

In this lecture, we examine the relationship between the Han Empire of China and the confederacy of the Xiongnu. Wudi, one of the most important of the Han emperors, wanted to control the vital area between the steppes and the Tibetan plateau that linked the Tarim Basin with western China. Although the Han envoy Zhang Qian was captured, his reports provided important information about inner Asia and the movements of tribes from east to west. Wudi was partly successful; his victories committed Chinese emperors to the control of a narrow corridor, the Jade Gate, which would be important to the Silk Road. By 9 A.D., however, the Han Empire had fragmented.

Emperor Wudi

- The Han emperors found the five baits system of tribute humiliating. The Han minister **Chao Cuo**, who died around 154 B.C., wrote a memorandum to Emperor **Wen** advising how to battle the Xiongnu instead of courting them. In addition to recommending heavy infantry backed by men with crossbows, he recommended using barbarians as mercenaries and allies.

- By the time the emperor **Wudi** came to the throne, probably in 141 B.C., he already had a blueprint for how to deal with the northern barbarians.

- Wudi was perhaps the most important emperor of the entire Han Dynasty. Some would see him as the architect of not only the Confucian state but also the letters and aesthetics that we have come to associate with classical China. During his reign, education and mastery of the classics were emphasized. He also saw himself as ruling according to the principles of a well-ordered Confucian state.

- Wudi intended to expand the frontiers of the Confucian state. Not only did he want to destroy the Xiongnu, he also wanted to control the vital area known as **Gansu**, the Hexi Corridor—a thin corridor of land between the steppes and the Tibetan plateau that linked the Tarim Basin with western China.

- After gaining control of that corridor, the plan was that Wudi would move Chinese armies into the Tarim Basin itself and secure the various caravan cities. They were extremely wealthy cities to tax. The region would also give him access to Ferghana, where the best cavalry horses were found.

The Chinese put great trust in the coordination of arms, that is, cavalry with infantry, archers with standard shock phalanx infantry, and above all, in crossbows.

Zhang Qian

- To seek out barbarian allies, Wudi chose an envoy named **Zhang Qian**. He was dispatched to the **western regions** to seek out allies among barbarian tribes that had been pushed westward by the Xiongnu. The Wusun were a nomadic tribe, possibly Iranian speakers, sometimes identified with the later Alani. Another group of Tocharian speakers, known as the Yuezhi, had also been driven from their homeland by the Xiongnu.

- The idea was to court these tribes into alliance. They had large cavalry armies and could help take on the army of the Xiongnu.

- Unfortunately, Zhang Qian was captured by the Xiongnu and married off to a Xiongnu wife. He lived in captivity for the next 10 years, had a son, and eventually escaped sometime around 128 B.C.

- He wrote up a report when he returned. Zhang Qian's account proved vital, providing important information about inner Asia, the movements of tribes from east to west, and details about the perceptions of the barbarians by the Han Chinese. Furthermore, he cast light on the Bactrian kingdom and the **Parthian** Empire.

Costly Campaigns

- In 127 B.C., Wudi began a series of campaigns against the Xiongnu that proved very costly. One particularly capable general was **Wei Qing**. He not only headed up the campaigns against the Xiongnu but also was involved in bringing many of the western districts under control.

- Wudi mounted a huge army—perhaps up to 100,000 men—and invaded the homeland of the Xiongnu in a series of columns commanded by different generals, with Wei Qing taking the lead.

- There was a systematic effort to hit the Xiongnu settlements. Repeatedly, Wudi's forces would drive the Xiongnu back into the depths of Mongolia, try to pin them down, round up livestock, and drive off the captives.

- The Han losses were devastating. The Chinese had to cross the Gobi Desert, water was a problem, and they never had enough horses. Each campaign resulted in enormous numbers of deaths; the wars were ruinous and costly. The campaigns cannot be overlooked as having a long-term impact on the Han Dynasty, an impact that eventually led to its breakup and demise.

- On the other hand, the Han won several significant battles and broke, at least temporarily, the power of the Xiongnu. By 114 B.C., Wudi had essentially destroyed the effective field army of the Xiongnu; they were no longer a threat on the northern frontier.

Into the Tarim Basin

- Wudi then mounted a series of expeditions into the Tarim Basin. This proved a momentous turn of events not only for the Han emperors but for all of China. It henceforth committed Chinese emperors to the control of the narrow corridor called the **Jade Gate**, an important pass on the Silk Road.

- Chinese Turkestan, which is today the Uighur Autonomous Region of Xinjiang, was a region with cities and trade routes; it could be incorporated and taxed. The caravan trade was highly lucrative.

- The cities submitted to the Chinese, garrisons were built, and tribute was imposed. The envoy Zhang Qian was once again sent out to negotiate with the Wusun trade connections and form alliances to secure the northern frontier and mutual interests between the cities of Chinese Turkestan and the Chinese.

- China now acquired an important western extension; control of this western extension would persist throughout Chinese history, into today.

War of the Heavenly Horses

- In securing this area, the Han emperors also realized that they were in close contact with Ferghana, the source of the supply of so-called heavenly horses, or cavalry horses.

- Two expeditions were mounted. The war is often known as the War of the Heavenly Horses. By the time the second expedition was over, most of the army had been lost. Only a couple of thousand horses ever made it back to China.

- Nonetheless, Chinese power had moved into a valuable region: a corridor that linked the central steppes with Iran and the Middle East. However, these victories over the Xiongnu and the Tarim Basin, along with the War of the Heavenly Horses, bankrupted the empire.

- Over the next 25 years, the Han emperors had increasing problems meeting their military obligations and faced repeated shortfalls in revenues, debasement of the currency, and increasing opposition within their empire. The nomads themselves did not topple the Han state; the collapse was a result of internal conditions.

Xiongnu Civil War

- In 58 B.C., the Han emperors were able to exploit a civil war within the Xiongnu and essentially disrupt the Xiongnu confederation into two groups. This was a significant change.

- The southern Xiongnu, dwelling immediately along the northern frontier of the Chinese Empire, along the Great Wall, were brought into alliance. The northern Xiongnu, in the Mongolian homeland and farther west into the central steppes, were targeted as the enemy.

- The idea was to use the southern Xiongnu to destroy the northern Xiongnu. The Chinese came to distinguish the inner barbarians from the outer barbarians.

- The inner barbarians dwelled in the Chinese frontier zones and intermixed with the Chinese population to form a kind of martial provincial Chinese society, part Chinese and part nomadic. They were important for the defense of future Chinese empires.

Emperor Guangwu

- The Han Dynasty eventually came to an end in 9 A.D. **Wang Mang**, a usurper, seized power, ended the Han Dynasty, and issued sweeping reforms. He renewed some of the wars against the northern Xiongnu. However, he alienated forces within China and, in 23 A.D., was overthrown by another member of the Han family, Liu Xiu, who took the dynastic name of **Guangwu**.

- In 25 A.D., Guangwu had secured power over the Han state and initiated the Later Han Dynasty, which ruled China until 220 A.D. Guangwu and his successors renewed imperial expansion into Korea and Vietnam and recommenced the war against the Xiongnu.

- The Tarim Basin and its important caravan route had fallen out of Chinese control during Wang Mang's reign. The later Han emperors sent their best generals into the region to drive off the Xiongnu and eventually broke the power of the northern Xiongnu. That confederation finally dissolved somewhere around 50 A.D.

Thereafter, we really have very little evidence that the northern Xiongnu posed a serious threat.

- By 91 A.D., the Tarim Basin was in the power of the Han emperor. In addition, he set in motion a number of important administrative reforms that led to colonization of these regions.

Contact with the West
- In 97 A.D., the Chinese emperor sent out another envoy, **Gan Ying**. He was sent west to collect information rather than to seek out grand alliances.

- The route Gan Ying took gives us good idea of the routes used for the Silk Road. When Gan Ying arrived at the Persian Gulf, he received reports of a mighty empire to the west, Da Qin. This was the Roman Empire, and we have, for the first time, a Chinese report of the Western world.

The Three Kingdoms
- Han power disintegrated very rapidly in the 2nd century A.D. The empire did not so much fall as fragment into three warring states, often known as the **Three Kingdoms**.

- The northern kingdom, which was along the Great Wall, depended on nomadic cavalry power. The northern area had close contacts with the steppe peoples.

- The southern kingdoms had the bulk of the silk, rice, cities, and the Confucian tradition. These kingdoms were the true heir to the Confucian Han tradition.

- This dichotomy would persist until a new set of emperors from the frontier northern kingdom reunited China under the great **Sui** and **Tang** dynasties.

Gansu Corridor: The narrow zone between the Eurasian steppe and the Tibetan highlands that connects China with the Tarim Basin.

Jade Gate: The name for the strategic Yumen Pass on the Silk Road that connected the Tarim Basin to China.

Parthians: An Iranian-speaking tribe melded into a kingdom, and then a Near East empire of the Arsacid kings (246 B.C.–227 A.D.).

Sui Dynasty: The dynasty (581–618) that reunited China and founded the third great imperial order; immediately succeeded by the Tang Dynasty.

Tang Dynasty: Founded by Emperor Gaozu, the Tang Dynasty (618–907) represented the greatest imperial family of classical China.

Three Kingdoms: The period of political division (220–280) in China after the fall of the eastern Han Dynasty.

western regions: Also called Xiyu, the designation by the Han and Tang emperors of their provinces in the Tarim Basin.

Chao Cuo (c. 200–154 B.C.): Han minister and legalist writer; composed a memorandum to Emperor Wen (180–157 B.C.) in which he presented the strategy for battling the Xiongnu. The emperor Wudi (141–87 B.C.) based his strategy on the recommendations of Chao Cuo.

Gan Ying (fl. 1st c. A.D.): Han envoy; sent by Ban Chao on a mission to contact imperial Rome in 97. He visited Sogdiana, Bactria, Gandhara, and Parthi, and likely reached the shores of the Persian Gulf. He wrote the only Chinese account about the Roman world and gained important new information on the lands of the Near East and Transoxania.

Guangwu (b. 5 B.C.; r. 25–57 A.D.): Han emperor; restored the Han Dynasty and moved the capital to Luoyang. He pursued a defensive policy against the nomadic tribes, but he reimposed Chinese rule over what is now Korea and Vietnam.

Wang Mang (b. 45 B.C.; r. 9–23 A.D.): Usurper who overthrew the Former Han Dynasty and issued sweeping reforms. He failed to maintain the northern frontier against the Xiongnu.

Wei Qing (d. 106 B.C.): Han general of imperial descent; the strategic genius behind the victories over the Xiongnu. He and his nephew Huo Qubing captured the Mobei, the tent capital of Ichise Chanyu. Thereafter, he retired from active service and served as strategic advisor to Emperor Wudi.

Wen (b. 541; r. 581–604): Sui emperor; reunited China under the Sui Dynasty (581–618). He promoted Buddhism, secured the northern frontiers by reconstructing the Great Wall, and initiated the Grand Canal.

Wudi (b. 157 B.C., r. 141–87 B.C.): Han emperor; presided over the territorial expansion of China. In 133 B.C., Wudi initiated war against Gunchen, *chanyu* of the Xiongnu. By campaigning across the Gobi in 127–119 B.C., his general broke the power of the Xiongnu. In 121–115 B.C., Wudi's armies imposed Han suzerainty over the western regions (Tarim Basin). His wars, however, proved costly and nearly bankrupted the imperial treasury.

Zhang Qian (200–114 B.C.): Official of the Han court. Sent by emperor Wudi as envoy to the Yuezhi (Tocharians) to form an alliance against the Xiongnu in 137–125 B.C. Zhang Qian failed in this mission; twice he was captured by the Xiongnu. His account of the western regions is an invaluable source on the customs of the Xiongnu and the reigns of the *chanyus* Gunchen (161–126 B.C.) and Ichise (126–114 B.C.). His account was incorporated into the *Shiji* ("Historical Records") by the historian Sima Qian in the 1st century.

Suggested Reading

Barfield, *The Perilous Frontier*.

Hill, *Through the Jade Gate to Rome*.

Hirth, *China and the Roman Orient*.

Waldron, *The Great Wall of China*.

Ying-shi Yu, "The Hsiung-nu."

————, *Trade and Expansion in Han China*.

Questions to Consider

1. Why did the emperor Wudi favor war over diplomacy in dealing with the Xiongnu? How effective were Han armies? Why did they fail to bring the Xiongnu to decisive battle?

2. How important were the caravan routes and cities of the Tarim Basin to both Xiongnu and Han emperors? What accounted for Han success in controlling the western regions (Xiyu)?

3. What were virtues of the tribute system devised by the Han emperors? Who benefited most from these exchanges? Why did the Xiongnu need access to Chinese markets and tribute? How meaningful was the Xiongnu acknowledgment of the mandate of the Han emperor in practice?

4. How did the Han conceit of ruling the Middle Kingdom influence their dealings with the Xiongnu? What do the accounts of Xuan Zhang in 129–119 B.C. and Ban Chao in 97 A.D. reveal about Chinese attitudes to the nomadic peoples?

5. What were the consequences of the Sino-Xiongnu War (133–154 B.C. and 73–88 A.D.) for China the Eurasian steppes?

The Han Emperors and Xiongnu at War
Lecture 4—Transcript

In this lecture, I want to follow up the issues I raised in the past lecture, and that is the relationship between the Han Empire of China and the confederacy of the Xiongnu. This is the great nomadic confederacy that probably stretched from the forests of Manchuria across eastern and probably much of the Central Asian steppes. With the death of Modu Chanyu, who was the real creator of this confederation—and that occurred somewhere after 180 B.C.—successive Han emperors found the tribute system really humiliating and onerous. It would turn out that paying tribute was far less expensive than waging war. Nonetheless, the terms of the arrangement, particularly the sending of Chinese brides as well as high silk items to the barbarians, was seen as somehow undermining the pretenses and really the whole conceit of the emperor being the son of heaven. There were discussions among the ministers of the Han court, particularly a fellow named Chao Cuo, who died around 154 B.C., and he wrote a memorandum to the Emperor Wen recommending how to battle the Xiongnu. Chao Cuo based his analysis on previous encounters. He recommended the use of heavy infantry, but the heavy infantry had to be backed up with men carrying crossbows to give them fire. He recommended very tight military formations supported by heavy cavalry, and above all the use of barbarians as mercenaries and allies. That is, the Chinese themselves could not provide the horses for the cavalry, so you hire foes, you hire allies from among the nomadic peoples, and hope that you can have these horses operate in tandem with classic Chinese forces and somehow bring the Xiongnu to battle. The decisive battle would crush their military ability and therefore end the threat.

They put great trust in the coordination of arms; that is, cavalry with infantry, archers with standard shock phalanx infantry, and above all in crossbows. Crossbows go back at least to the sixth century B.C., probably earlier, and the weapon allows an infantryman a greater distance and a greater penetrating power so he can knock those nomads right off their horses and protect the infantry from the favorite nomadic tactic of riding up, shooting arrows, and drawing the Chinese into an ill-advised attack. In addition, on the strategic level there were recommendations to repair the great fortifications; to use colonists, military colonists, along the frontier zone; and so by the time a new emperor, an emperor by the name of Wudi, comes to the throne, probably in 141 B.C., he already has in front of him a blueprint of how to deal with the northern barbarians.

Wudi is an extremely important emperor; he is perhaps the most important emperor of the entire Han Dynasty. Some would see him as the architect of not only the Confucian state, but also the letters and aesthetics that we come to associate with classic China. It is in his reign that education, mastery of the Classics, the beginning of the formation of the Confucian canon come into being. He also saw himself as ruling according to Confucian principles, moderating the tough military logic, the so-called legalist way of approaching an empire that went back to Qin Shi Huangdi and some of the early Han emperors, with the principles of a well-ordered Confucian state. In many ways, Wudi creates classic China, or he at least sets it in motion.

But it is also sometimes forgotten that this Confucian vision had an imperial dimension to it; and Wudi intended to expand the frontiers of that Confucian state. He targeted various areas, but above all he wanted to smash that barbarian coalition. He found the terms of the tribute system, the so-called "Five Baits," as humiliating; and he had at his disposal a very good plan of how to attack the enemy. Furthermore, he had several clear aims in mind. Not only did he want to destroy the Xiongnu, he also wanted to control the vital area known as Gansu, the Hexi Corridor, and that is that very thin corridor of land between the steppes and the Tibetan plateau that links the Tarim Basin with Western China. That area is right on the border of the steppes, the Xiongnu patrol it, they tax it, they protect the caravans, and Wudi wanted to gain control of that corridor and then move Chinese armies into the Tarim Basin itself and secure the various caravan cities; we will be talking about those cities when we deal with the Silk Road; they are already very, very wealthy cities to tax. Also, it would give him access to the region of Ferghana, just beyond the Tarim Basin, where the Chinese know that certain horses—they are usually called the "heavenly horses that sweat blood," and we have many later depictions from the Tang period; one right here on the table is a very clear example of it—and these are horses that are reputed to be the best cavalry horses around, and the sweating of the blood is the result of some kind of parasite that lives on the horse and causes the sweating.

Wudi had clear aims in mind. He wanted to secure regions that would give him revenues; he planned to send in military garrisons in the Tarim Basin; he would refortify that northern frontier; and he would break the power of the Xiongnu confederacy. One of the most intriguing figures in this new policy was the envoy that the emperor came up with to seek out those barbarian allies. Remember, it was recommended that you hire foes of the Xiongnu or allies to the Han to help fight the war. In 138 B.C., the man who was chosen to head up a mission to meet these barbarians was a member of court who was known as Zhang Qian. He was dispatched to the western regions to seek out allies among barbarian tribes that had been pushed westward by the Xiongnu; and these were the so-called Wusun. They were a nomadic tribe, possibly Iranian speakers, sometimes identified with the later Alans. They dwelled immediately to the north of the Tarim Basin; and farther away on the western side of the Tarim Basin on the central steppes were apparently another group, Tocharian speakers, known as the Yuezhi, who had also been driven from their homeland by the Xiongnu. The idea was to court these tribes into alliance. They had large cavalry armies, and they could help take on the army of the Xiongnu.

Zhang Qian was an interesting fellow. He was provided with a guide, actually a Xiongnu guide who spoke Chinese; he had been brought up as a slave at the court and he was a bilingual. He and his companion Ganfu set out to find these barbarian allies. The routes were fairly obvious; actually there is only one way to go: You have to go through the so-called Jade Gate and then go across the Tarim Basin. Of course, these routes are patrolled by the Xiongnu; and in no time, as soon as they left Chinese territory, they ran into a band of Xiongnu who arrested these rather interesting-looking fellows. They brought them before the Xiongnu, his name is Gunchen in Chinese; and Gunchen was really impressed by this guide. First, he was from the High Court. He knew how to read and write; that is always useful. He had all sorts of information about Wudi's court and also Chinese bureaucrats, Mandarins, merchants; they were all valued, and the Xiongnu always liked having Chinese brides because these women brought all sorts of goodies and they provided the silk and prestige. What happened is this poor Chinese envoy was married off to a Xiongnu wife and essentially lived with her for the next 10 years, had a son; and eventually, somewhere around 128 B.C., he escaped. He made his way west and contacted the two tribes he was supposed to find nearly 10 years earlier. He eventually found them. He later wrote up a report when he got back 13 years later and gives us some rather interesting details, which are going to be very important for understanding how these tribes were pushed from the eastern steppes to the central steppes.

On the other hand, once he got essentially a negative response, particularly from the Yuezhi—they had fought the Xiongnu; they were not about to take them on again—he really had no success. On his way back, he essentially followed the same route and he was captured again and had to spend yet more time; he was returned to his Xiongnu wife who, from his later account, apparently he despised. Xiongnu women were ugly; they did not know how to prepare rice properly; they were promiscuous; they were noted for divorcing their husbands and marrying other men; they did not understand a proper marriage. All this comes out later once he makes his way back to the Han court around 125 B.C. nearly 13 years later.

Nonetheless, his account proved very vital. It provided important information about inner Asia; the movements of some of these tribes from east to west; and above all is a flood of information about the perceptions of the barbarians by the Han Chinese. Furthermore, he casts very important light on the Bactrian kingdom; the Greco-Bactrian kingdom, the successor kingdom of Alexander the Great. There is information on the Parthian Empire we will be talking about; the ancestors of the Kushans, who are so important for the empire in India. All of this information is written up in a memorandum, in a report, and it has survived in later accounts.

One thing about these reports written by envoys and generals in the Chinese tradition: There is a single author who sits down and writes it. Later commentators will write commentary; will write editions and supplements; and eventually this gets merged, and so what was originally an individual work to a large extent becomes a collective achievement as more and more is added. These works were not read by the emperor himself, but by his various scribes and officials who read them for information in order to advise the emperor on strategy. They are different from contemporary Classical works that talk about the nomadic peoples—we will be turning to authors like Herodotus, Ammianus Marcellinus, Tacitus, well-known figures from Greek and Roman history—and the work is the work of that man, whereas in the case of Zhang Qian, the work as it comes down to us has lots of commentary, additions, and supplements. That is a caution for you should you delve into that work and sometimes you get a bit confused: There are later editions that have been put in there and run together.

Meantime, while the diplomatic front did not go anywhere, the emperor was impatient; and in 133 B.C., he decides to open his war against the Xiongnu. That means mounting a huge expedition across the Gobi Desert to bring the Xiongnu to battle. Instead of mounting the expedition immediately and knowing what the previous failures were like, the emperor tries a ruse. This sounds like something right out of the manual of Sun Tzu; that is, a border town is selected—I believe the name is Mayi; it is in Shanxi province today—and the border town was well known to the Xiongnu due to trade connections; it is where there was an exchange of different types of horses, silks, and food; and what was done is the town was simply left as an open invitation to attack. The Xiongnu at the time, Gunchen—who actually happened to be the host of Zhang Qian—decided to take the bait; he crossed the Gobi Desert; he was going to attack the town; and then his caution got the better of him and he realized this was too easy, this is too open and he sent in a small force. The Han forces revealed themselves too quickly and he knew immediately this was a trap, and the Xiongnu army quickly eluded the Han forces because they were essentially a mounted army.

At that point, Wudi had no choice but to go the traditional route and invade the Xiongnu homeland. He could not count on any kind of barbarian allies in the attack; and so in 127 B.C., he opened up a series of campaigns over the next 10 or 11 years that proved very, very costly. He had some very capable generals. The one that comes down to us is a man by the name of Wei Qing. He headed up not only the campaigns against the Xiongnu, but later was involved in bringing many of the western districts under control; he had a part in that operation as well. What was done is large armies—scholars debate the size, we are told 100,000 men; we are told great armies of colonists—were moved in along the frontier; large numbers of chariots. The numbers are so great that one might doubt that the Han logistical system could support such an army. Nonetheless, the army is very large. The idea is to hit the homeland of the Xiongnu in a series of columns commanded by different generals—Wei Qing taking the main lead, another fellow named

Huo Qubing led another major column—and the idea was by converging columns to trap one or all of the major armies of the Xiongnu and destroy them in decisive battle.

At the same time, settlements were targeted. There are known to be Xiongnu settlements because of trade connections; livestock and captors were to be seized. They understood that it was just not a matter of defeating a particular Xiongnu force, but also destroying the means of that confederacy to continue. Capturing livestock, horses, cattle would deny food to the Xiongnu during the winter. The captives would include many members of families, women, children, which would demoralize the Xiongnu warriors who had not fallen in battle or who had not been captured. There was a systematic effort to hit the settlements. These were relatively small tent encampments. They were very similar to the early Mongol settlements. Karakorum, the so-called capital of Genghis Khan, which was not really a city until the reign of his son, was a huge tent city that would spring up where trade could take place. Repeatedly, they would drive the Xiongnu back into the depths of Mongolia, try to pin them, round up livestock, and drive off the captives. The losses were enormous. The Chinese had to cross the Gobi Desert; water was a problem; horses were always a problem, they never had enough horses. Each campaign resulted in enormous number of deaths, new recruitment drives, and money. The wars were very ruinous and costly, and they cannot be overlooked as having a long-term impact on the Han Dynasty, which eventually led to its breakup and demise at the end of the first century B.C. As successful as Wudi was, he committed his successors to a very, very expensive war.

On the other hand, several significant battles were won; and these battles broke, at least temporarily, the power of the Xiongnu. That was important because these battles by 114 B.C. had essentially destroyed the effective field army of the Xiongnu, and that meant they were no longer a threat on the northern frontier. For Wudi, this is what he wanted. He had plenty of captives; he knew it would take a generation for the Xiongnu to recover. That allowed him to pull those generals, pull those forces, out of the north and send them west. What happened is a series of expeditions were now mounted into the Tarim Basin.

This proved a momentous turn of events for not only the Han emperors, but for China. It henceforth committed Chinese emperors to the control of that narrow corridor, the so-called Jade Gate, which will be very important when we discuss the Silk Road, and also into the region of Chinese Turkistan, today known as Xinjiang or Shinjang as it used to be known. It is today the Uyghur Autonomous Turkistan Republic of China; it is populated by both a population of Chinese and Turkish speakers. This region was a region that had cities, it had trade routes; it could be incorporated and taxed. It was not originally part of China; but the Han emperors, from 121 B.C. when they send their initial expeditions in while they are still fighting the Xiongnu, are under the impression that they can actually control and tax this region.

The result is success as they understand it: They were able to move in and capture a number of those cities. This did not mean a capture and colonization as we understand it. Instead, what happened was the cities submitted; there were some Chinese garrisons; tribute was imposed. Actually, our envoy Zhang Qian was once again sent out there to negotiate with especially the Wusun trade connections and alliances to secure the northern frontier and mutual interests between them and the Chinese; but the upshot was that China now acquired this important western extension, and the control of this western extension will persist through Chinese history really down to today. It had to be denied the nomads; it was just too important. The caravan trade was much too lucrative.

In securing this area, the Han emperors also realized that they were now coming into very close contact with the source of the horses: Ferghana. Ferghana is where the supply of heavenly horses comes from; and the result of breaking the power of the Xiongnu temporarily and acquiring the Tarim Basin was one of the more peculiar wars in Chinese history. The brother of the emperor's favorite concubine, Li Guangli, was commissioned to move an army in 102 B.C. from the Jade Gate—the army is reputedly 180,000–200,000 men—west across the Tarim Basin to cross the Pamir mountain range and descend into the upper valley of the Jaxartes and bring under control the source of those horses. Two expeditions are mounted; the war is often known as the War of the Heavenly Horses. By the time it is all over with the second expedition, most of the army had been lost; I think only a couple of thousand horses ever made it back to China. Nonetheless, a Chinese power has moved into the region that is really today modern Tajikistan, really into Transoxiana, into that very, very important region; that corridor that links the central steppes with Iran and the Middle East.

These victories—the victories over the Xiongnu, the Tarim Basin, the kind of victory on the War of Heavenly Horses—bankrupted the empire. Over the next 25 years, the Han emperors had increasing problems meeting their military obligations and faced repeated shortfalls in revenues, debasement of the currency, and increasing opposition within their empire. The nomads themselves did not topple the Han state, it was internal conditions that finally knocked them over; but the wars against the Xiongnu contributed decisively to the bankrupting of the monarchy and a lot of the internal problems that emerged in the first century B.C.

Actually, in 58 B.C., the Han emperors were able to exploit a civil war between two brothers of the Xiongnu and essentially disrupt the Xiongnu confederation into two groups; and this was a very significant change. The Xiongnu dwelling immediately along the northern frontier of the Chinese Empire—that is, along the Great Wall—were known as the Southern Xiongnu. They were brought into alliance. One could think of them as something like the Germanic Federates of the Roman Empire; they were tribal regiments that were under the control or alliance of the emperor of China. They received certain gifts, but the relationship was clearly subordinate. The Northern Xiongnu in the Mongolian homeland, and also farther west into the central steppes, were targeted as the enemy; the idea was to use the Southern Xiongnu to destroy the Northern Xiongnu. This becomes a common policy that persists through Chinese history; that is, they come to distinguish the inner barbarians from the outer barbarians. That distinction is very important. The inner barbarians are dwelling in the Chinese frontier zones and they intermix with the Chinese population and form a kind of martial provincial Chinese society, part Chinese and part nomadic. They will be important for the defense of future Chinese empires. The Northern Xiongnu, or the outer barbarians, are usually targeted as the enemies.

The Han Dynasty, because of its difficulties, eventually comes to an end in 9 A.D. He was related to the imperial court, but he was not a direct member of the imperial family; a man by the name of Wang Mang, a usurper, probably one of the most clever reformers in Chinese history (he invents gold coinage as far as we can tell). He seizes power in 9 A.D., and ends the Han Dynasty and issues sweeping reforms. He renews some of the wars against the Northern Xiongnu; that is not a good idea. He alienates forces within China; and in 23 A.D., he is overthrown by another member of the Han family, a collateral branch of the old imperial family, a man named Li Xiu, who takes the temple name, the dynastic name, of Guangwu. In 25 A.D., he has secured power over the Han state and initiates a new Han Dynasty, sometimes known as the Later Han Dynasty as opposed to the earlier former Han Dynasty; and this dynasty will rule China down to 220 A.D.

Guangwu and his successors renew imperial expansion in various directions: into Korea; into Vietnam; and above all they want to renew the war against the Xiongnu and make sure they can seize control of the Guangzhou corridor and the Tarim Basin, that very, very important caravan route. The area had fallen out of Chinese control during Wang Mang's usurpation in 9–23 A.D., and as a result these later Han emperors send their best generals into those zones to drive off the Xiongnu, and they do eventually break the power of those Northern Xiongnu. That confederation finally dissolves somewhere around 50 A.D. Thereafter, we really have very little evidence that they posed a serious threat.

The Chinese also moved into the Tarim Basin and they campaigned against local tribes, against various caravan cities; they brought in different submissions by the cities; and by 91 A.D., the general Ban Chao—who was from a very, very distinguished family at the Han court known for diplomats and generals in the last three generations—is sent into what the Han call the Western Zones, and he secures the various cities by diplomacy and force. In 91 A.D., the Tarim Basin is now in the power of the Han emperor. In addition, he sets in motion a number of important administrative reforms that lead to colonization of these regions, and he also takes a very important decision in 97 A.D.: He sends out another envoy. This envoy is known as Gan Ying. He was sent west; and he was more sent west to collect information rather than to really search out for grand alliances. At this point, the Chinese position in Central Asia is pretty secure. We have some idea of the route he takes; and what it does is give us a pretty good idea of the routes that are being used for the so-called Silk Road. We know, for instance, that he visits the Kushan emperors, or the domains of the Kushan emperors. He also gets to the land of Parthia, and we will be talking about the Parthians; they are a nomadic, Iranian-speaking people who dominate the Iranian plateau. He calls them the Anxi, meaning "the Arsacids," after the dynastic name. Above all, he does not get there. He probably gets down to the Persian Gulf—that is probably as far as he gets—perhaps to the trade city of Charax, and there he gets reports of a great empire to the west, the Da Qin. This is the Roman Empire; and we have for the first time a Chinese report of the Western world, this great Roman Empire. Again, he retraces his steps back to his commander. Gan Ying eventually writes up his report; it is incorporated; it becomes part of the memorandum of the Han court.

The Han success under these later emperors did come with a price. It followed soon after with increasing instability; the cost of war helped bring about usurpations; and Han power disintegrates very, very rapidly in the second century A.D. The Han Empire does not so much fall as fragment into three warring states, very often known as the Three Kingdoms. What comes out of that division is something very significant: The Northern Kingdom, Wei, which is along the Great Wall; that is a kingdom that rests on nomadic cavalry power. This will be a feature in the division of China ever after. The Southern kingdoms, particularly the Wu kingdom and the Shu kingdoms in the Yangzi or Yangzi Valley, those states have the bulk of the silk, the rice, the cities, and the Confucian tradition. The pattern of Chinese history in division henceforth will be a division of that Northern Zone, which has close contacts with the steppe peoples upon which military power rests, and then the South, which is the true heir to the Confucian Han traditions. This dichotomy will persist until a new set of emperors from the Northern Zone, from that frontier martial zone, will reunite China under the great Sui and Tang emperors.

Scythians, Greeks, and Persians
Lecture 5

In this lecture, we'll turn to the western and central steppes and the Scythians, an Iranian-speaking nomadic people. The patterns of trade and movement of peoples that evolved with the Scythians would repeat themselves in later periods. In many ways, the Scythians wrote the script for how to dominate the western Eurasian steppe. They accomplished this by exploiting trade and by accommodation with the civilized states. As we will see, however, there was always the danger that the system would be undone by newcomers pressed east because of the wars between Chinese emperors and other nomadic peoples on the eastern steppes.

Western and Central Steppes

- The western and central steppes fell into two main zones. The western zone, the original homeland of the Indo-European speakers, extended from the Volga and Ural rivers in the east to the middle and lower Danube in the west. Importantly, in the western steppes, the rivers run north to south—a fact that accounts for a different history and trade patterns between the nomads and the settled peoples.

- The rivers of Russia flowing into the Black Sea linked the steppe peoples with the populations of the Black Sea, Mediterranean world, and Baltic Sea. The Darial Pass, known as the Gates of Alexander the Great, and the Derbent Pass offered access to the Middle East.

- The central steppe region extended from the Caspian Sea in an arch eastward to the upper banks of the Jaxartes River. Here again, interaction between steppe and settled peoples was much more accessible than on the eastern steppes.

- The river offered grasslands on both sides, and the nomads migrated south into the region we call Transoxania. Transoxania was the focal point of interaction between nomads and settled peoples. It was known in antiquity as the **upper satrapies** of the Persian Empire.

Reports of Herodotus

- These regions were occupied by the Scythians, who dwelled there from the early Iron Age (900–800 B.C.) to around 300 B.C. They are largely known to us through archaeology, but we also have excellent literary sources—most notably, the Greek historian Herodotus.

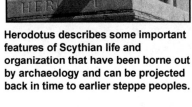

- In 450 B.C., Herodotus visited the city of Olbia, a Greek colony on the shores of the Black Sea. There, he had direct contact with Scythians.

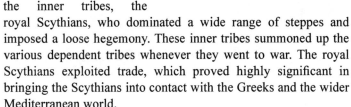

Herodotus describes some important features of Scythian life and organization that have been borne out by archaeology and can be projected back in time to earlier steppe peoples.

- Herodotus describes the inner tribes, the royal Scythians, who dominated a wide range of steppes and imposed a loose hegemony. These inner tribes summoned up the various dependent tribes whenever they went to war. The royal Scythians exploited trade, which proved highly significant in bringing the Scythians into contact with the Greeks and the wider Mediterranean world.

- Grain was in great demand in the Greek world. It was grown by the dependent tribes of the Scythians, usually dwelling along the shores of the Black Sea or in the river valleys, and it was extracted as tribute by the inner tribes and exported. The profits, of course, went primarily to the inner tribes, the royal Scythians.

The Scythians

- In addition to grain, the Scythians offered other principal products to the Greek world: flax, timber, amber, and slaves. The Scythians pioneered a unique relationship between the Mediterranean world and the northern worlds of the Baltic, Central Europe, and the Russian forest zones.

- They were the intermediaries who dominated the river systems of Russia. They controlled the transit of goods from the Baltic to the Black Sea or along the Volga to the Caspian Sea. This would be a pattern of trade taken over by later Turkic confederations, notably the **Khazars** and, finally, by the Mongol **Golden Horde** itself.

- The Scythians were admired for their military ability, especially as cavalry riders and archers. They were hired as mercenaries by the armies of Greek tyrants who seized power in Greek city-states. They were later hired into the armies of the Hellenistic kings, the successors to **Alexander the Great**. In Athens, a bodyguard of Scythians was retained as the police force.

- Furthermore, Scythian jewelry and other objects were highly prized. The exchange between Greeks and Scythians was very productive and persisted through the classical age.

King Cyrus of Persia

- The Scythians also came into contact with the peoples of the Near East: in Asia Minor, the Fertile Crescent in Iran, and the upper satrapies known as Transoxania.

- In 550 B.C., **Cyrus the Great** of Persia deposed his overlords and united most of the Near East, creating the Persian Empire. The Persian Empire, or Achaemenid Empire, was built by Iranian speakers, themselves descendants of nomads who had moved into this area in the middle to late Bronze Age.

- They brought with them the traditions of horses and cavalry. King Cyrus, whose ancestors were nomads, based his armies on mounted horse archers, not infantry.

- The Achaemenid Empire was a great bureaucratic state. The empire had possessions from Europe to the Indus. The Persian kings, as a result of their successes, inherited a long northern frontier, a frontier shared with the Scythian world.

King Darius I

- The great king of Persia had to establish a way of dealing with the nomadic peoples. That meant patrolling the borders of the Caucasus and the two great passes that provided entrance into the Near East. Areas that had fallen under the control of the Persian kings were Transoxania, the Jaxartes River, and the western frontier along the Black Sea regions and the lower Danube.

- Around 512 B.C., King **Darius I**, the third of the great kings of Persia, marched an army across a bridge of ships at the Dardanelles, crossed Thrace, and invaded the Pontic-Caspian steppes, attacking the Scythian homeland.

- The expedition proved a fiasco. In many ways, Darius was frustrated by the typical steppe tactics. The Scythians refused to come to battle.

- An anecdote in Herodotus captures the essence of the campaign. The Scythians had sent a message to the Persians: a bird, a mouse, a frog, and five arrows. The immediate reaction of Darius was that this was an indication of surrender, on earth and water.

- One of his ministers, however, said the message meant that unless the Persians can fly like birds, burrow into the ground like mice, or leap across water like frogs, they would be full of Scythian arrows—and that is essentially what happened.

- The Scythians pursued a scorched-earth policy, and eventually, Darius had to call off the expedition. Darius's experience would be repeated by many armies in the future. Fighting steppe nomads was extremely difficult. Few armies, either in classical or medieval times, ever devised the proper tactics and strategy to deal with the steppe nomad armies.

Alexander the Great

- The next ruler to come into contact with the Scythians was Alexander the Great. From 334 to 327 B.C., Alexander, king of Macedon, overran the Persian Empire. He was, without a doubt, one of the mightiest conquerors of all times.

- His success meant that he inherited the frontiers of the Persian Empire and the problem of the nomads. He confronted them on the Danube and, by some clever tactics, beat back a group of them, punished them, and secured the frontier. However, he did not make the mistake of waging a war of conquest against them, as Darius had done.

- Later, Alexander ran into those same Scythians on the Jaxartes River. Already, the cities of this region were engaged in the beginnings of a caravan trade across the Tarim Basin to China. Furthermore, these upper satrapies, or Transoxania, were home to powerful Iranian nobles who had to be brought under control.

- Alexander initially tried to set up a border, establishing military cities, such as Alexandria Eschate. He quickly realized that the best way to deal with nomads was to regulate the migration of tribes and the flow of trade—and then to tax it.

- By the time he withdrew from this region to invade India and, eventually, march home, Alexander had established a number of colonies in Bactria on the Oxus River. These colonies evolved into Greek-style cities under the Greco-Bactrian kingdom. With Alexander's death in 323 B.C., his empire was partitioned.

Greco-Bactrian Kingdom

- The region known as Bactria, today encompassing parts of Afghanistan and Turkmenistan, eventually broke away under its own rulers. In 250 B.C., **Diodotus** rebelled and set up his own independent Greek kingdom.

- This kingdom was known in Chinese sources, thanks to the reports of the Han envoy to the Xiongnu, Zhang Qian, who reached the Greco-Bactrian Kingdom somewhere around 128 B.C.

- Zhang Qian was very impressed by this area, which he called Daxia. His account also mentioned other important groups of people. Foremost were the Yuezhi, or Kushans. They probably called themselves Tocharians. Both the Sacae, who were Iranian speakers, and the Kushans were courted by the Chinese as allies.

- Around 140 B.C., the Sacae destroyed the Greco-Bactrian kingdom and subsequently invaded India. But the Tocharians, ancestors of the Kushans, settled in the prosperous area of Bactria. They took over the Greek cities and brought an end to Alexander's political legacy there, although the Hellenistic civilization persisted.

The Sarmatians

- The collapse of the world of the Persian Empire taken over by Alexander and his successors was caused by movements resulting from the wars between the Xiongnu and Han Chinese.

- The wars had pushed the Tocharian and Iranian speakers westward from their homes on the frontiers of the Chinese Empire. This was a pattern that would repeat itself. The nomadic tribes eventually entered into Transoxania in the Middle East.

- The Scythians, farther west, disappeared sometime in the 3rd century B.C. They gave way to a new people known as the Sarmatians. These were Iranian nomads whom the Romans would encounter. The Sarmatian migration, east to west, is surmised to be yet another spinoff of the Xiongnu–Han conflict.

- The ancestors of the Sarmatians had started out in the regions around the Aral Sea in the central steppes. They migrated westward and, sometime shortly after 300 B.C., took over the Scythian confederation and dominated the western Eurasian steppe.

Important Terms

Golden Horde: The western part of the Mongol Empire (1240–1502), established by Khan Batu.

Khazars: Members of the Ashina clan and western Turkish khaganate, who established their own khaganate (c. 670–967) over the Pontic-Caspian steppes. The Khazar court converted to Judaism in the late 8th century. Circa 965–967, the Khazar capital was sacked by Prince Svyatoslav of Kiev and the Pechenegs.

Names to Know

Alexander III, the Great (b. 356 B.C., r. 336–323 B.C.): King of Macedon; son of Philip II (359–336 B.C.) and the Epirote princess Olympias (375–316 B.C.); arguably the greatest commander in history. In 334–329 B.C., he conquered the Achaemenid Empire and defeated King Darius III of Persia (336–329 B.C.). He subdued Bactria and Sogdiana (Transoxania) in 329–327 B.C. and the Indus Valley in 327–325 B.C. Alexander defeated the nomadic Sacae, secured the Upper Satrapies (Bactria and Sogdiana), and established a frontier on the upper Jaxartes. His Greco-Macedonian military colonies in the Upper Satrapies were the basis for the Greco-Bactrian kingdom (c. 250–125 B.C.).

Cyrus the Great (b. c. 590 B.C., r. 559–530 B.C.): Achaemenid king; founded the Persian Empire, conquering Lydia in 546 B.C. and Babylonia in 539 B.C. He was hailed in classical sources as the greatest conqueror before Alexander the Great. He was killed in a frontier war against the Massagetai, a Scythian tribe, north of the Jaxartes River.

Darius I (b. c. 550 B.C.; r. 521–486 B.C.): Achaemenid king of Persia; succeeded to the throne during the Great Revolt of 522–521 B.C. He organized the satrapies of the Persian Empire and built the capital of Persepolis. In 515 or 512 B.C., he waged unsuccessful war against the Scythians on the Pontic-Caspian steppes.

Diodotus I (250–230 B.C.): Greco-Bactrian king who declared his independence from his Seleucid overlord Antiochus II (261–246 B.C.).

Suggested Reading

Cribb and Herrmann, eds., *After Alexander.*

Herodotus (de Selincourt, trans.), *The Histories.*

Frye, *The Heritage of Central Asia.*

Fuller, *The Generalship of Alexander the Great.*

Holt, *Alexander the Great and Bactria.*

Melyukova, "The Scythians and Samartians."

Reder and Treiser, *Scythian Gold.*

Sulimirski and Taylor, "The Scythians."

Tarn, *The Greeks in Bactria and India.*

Questions to Consider

1. What accounted for the success of the Scythians? How was trade conducted, and how did it enrich and transform Scythian society?

2. In what ways was Scythian contact with Greeks and Persians comparable to the later exchanges between the Xiongnu and Han China? In what significant ways did it differ?

3. Why did the Persian kings Cyrus and Darius I fare so poorly in fighting the Scythians? What accounted for the success of Alexander the Great? What were Alexander's strategic aims in the Upper Satrapies (Transoxiana)? Did his frontier policy promise long-term success?

4. What was the relationship between the Greco-Bactrian kings and their subjects with the Scythian nomads in the 3rd and 2nd centuries B.C.? How did this contact contribute to increasing trade across the Tarim Basin that linked the Hellenistic world and Han China?

Scythians, Greeks, and Persians
Lecture 5—Transcript

In this lecture, I plan to look at the Scythians, an Iranian-speaking nomadic people, and I am going to change the focus away from the eastern steppes to the western and central steppes.

In the last two lectures, we dealt with the interaction between the Xiongnu and the Han Chinese Empire, and that took place on that eastern third of the great Eurasian steppes, which essentially extends from the Manchurian forest westward to the Altai Mountains in the southwest and further west to around Lake Balkhash today. That entire area was in play in the trade relationships and war between the Xiongnu and Han China.

The repercussions of the interaction between the Chinese and the Xiongnu will actually form part of the closing of this lecture, but we will get to that a bit later on. What I want to do is focus on those western and central steppes. They fall essentially into two zones: The Western Zone was the original homeland of the Indo-European speakers, or the Proto-Indo-European speakers; and that extends from essentially in the east around the Volga River, the Ural River, which empty into the Caspian Sea westward across the great rivers of Russia, and it terminates on the middle and lower Danube. The grasslands of Hungary and Romania are bisected by this reverse "L" mountain range, known as the Carpathians. Another important feature I wish to stress on those western steppes is the rivers run north to south. That is very important. It accounts for a very different history and trade patterns between the nomads and the settled peoples in contrast to what we talked about with the Xiongnu in China. The Xiongnu were largely defended by the Gobi Desert; Chinese armies could never really get to them, it was extremely difficult. On the other hand, the pattern of Russian rivers—the Volga flowing into the Caspian, the Don, the Dnieper, the Dniester, the Bug; all of these great rivers of Russia flowing into the Black Sea—linked the steppe peoples with the populations of the Black Sea, the Mediterranean world, and also with the people of the Baltic Sea area; and that is an important distinction.

In addition, those steppes swept south through the so-called Kuban up to the foothills of the Caucasus. The two great passes—the Darial Pass, known as the Gates of Alexander the Great, and the Derbent Pass—offered access to the Middle East. The middle steppe region essentially starts from around the Caspian Sea where the Ural River flows into the Caspian Sea in the Ural Mountains, and it swings in an arc eastward to the upper banks of the Jaxartes River—better known today as the Syr Darya by its Turkish name—and it encompasses a very, very rich and important steppe zone area. Here again, the access between steppe and settled is much easier than it would be on the eastern steppes because the Jaxartes is really a political boundary. The river offers grasslands on both sides; and instinctively the nomads arriving in that area would migrate south into the region we call Transoxiana. That is a region that terminates at the Oxus River, known by a Turkish name today, Amu Darya; and that area Transoxiana is a cockpit of the interaction between nomads and settled peoples. It is a very diverse landscape, and we will be talking about that later in the lecture. It would be known in antiquity as the Upper Satrapies of the Persian Empire.

These entire regions I have just described were occupied by the Scythians. This is a term that is applied to the people dwelling there from the early Iron Age, from about say 900–800 B.C. to about 300 B.C. They are largely known to us by archaeology; but, as in the case of the Xiongnu, we have excellent literary sources, above all the Greek historian Herodotus, often known as the "Father of History," or to the less charitable scholars in the 19th century as the "Father of Lies." Actually, I have always objected to that term; I am a strong proponent for Herodotus, even though by inclination I prefer Thucydides as an ancient historian. But Herodotus is a man who observed very carefully the peoples that he encountered on his many travels and he also gathered an enormous amount of information on the Scythians when he visited the city of Olbia, which is a Greek colony on the shores of the Black Sea. Olbia was one of those Greek towns on the shores of the Black Sea—today the Crimea, which the Greeks would have called the Tauric Chersonesos—and he would have been there about 450 B.C. or thereabouts. Herodotus had direct contact with Scythians. He saw them in the markets. He would have talked to people who had direct dealings with the Scythians, particularly Greek merchants.

He tells us some very important features about Scythian life and organization, and this has been borne out by archaeology. In fact, the matching up of Book Four of Herodotus, which deals with the Scythians and archaeology, is remarkably good; and what Herodotus tells us about Scythian habits and customs also can be projected backward in time to the early Proto-Indo-European peoples who had occupied those very same steppes and had domesticated the horse, invented the light chariot, and finally the riding of horses and the composite bow itself. For one, Herodotus tells us of royal Scythians, as opposed to the dependent tribes. I mentioned in passing in a previous lecture that the organization of these tribal confederations very much consisted of an inner group of tribes and an outer group of tribes that are dependents. In this case, Herodotus is describing essentially the same operation that the Chinese would have observed. I am sure that nomads as early as the Yamnaya period—that is, the Yamnaya culture, which is the archaeological culture of the Proto-Indo-Europeans—would have probably had a very, very similar structure. That meant the inner tribes, or the royal Scythians as Herodotus would call them, dominated the wide range of steppes and imposed a loose hegemony. It was their rulers who summoned up the various dependent tribes whenever they went to war. It was also the royal Scythians who were prospering and exploiting the profits of trade; and that trade proved very, very significant in bringing the Scythians into contact with the Greeks and the wider Mediterranean world.

We know some of this information on trade from Herodotus; he gives us reports of some of the items that are swapped. For one, grain was in big demand in the Greek world; there was never enough grain to feed the hungry populations, particularly the city of Athens. Grain was grown by the dependent tribes of the Scythians, usually dwelling along the shores of the Black Sea or in the river valleys, and it was extracted as tribute and exported. The profits went, of course, primarily to the princes and royal families of the great inner tribes or the royal tribes, or the Royal Scythians as Herodotus would call them. We also document it very much from archaeology, particularly from an unusual set of graves. These graves have been excavated by Soviet archaeologists, then by the Russian and Ukrainian archaeologists. They are collectively known as kurgans; and these kurgans reveal an enormous wealth of goods, particularly gold. The Scythians prefer gold to silver. We have beautiful ornamental bridles and bits; no stirrups yet, no metal stirrups. We suspect there may have been leather stirrups. These have been found in great pits, essentially shaft graves, dug into the ground and then a huge tumulus of earth put over it. It could be as high as 120 feet.

In addition, the graves are very instructive in confirming not only Herodotus but other Greek stories. At least a third of the graves are those of apparently women of high rank. It is often believed that this tradition of burying women in the graves reflects warrior princesses, women who intermixed with male society, and it gave rise to the legends of the Amazons, well known from Greek mythology and legend. Many scholars would make this connection that Amazons are essentially a version of the Scythian princesses and warrior princesses that are buried in these kurgans.

In turn, the Scythians offered very important products to the Greek world. Not only was it agricultural goods, grain, but they also offered the flax, the timber, amber, slaves, much of this exacted from the peoples of the forests. In some ways, the Scythians pioneer a relationship between the Mediterranean world and the northern worlds of the Baltic and Central Europe, the Russian forest zones, in which they are the intermediaries who dominate the river systems of Russia; they control the transit of goods from the Baltic to the Black Sea, or in some cases along the Volga to the Caspian Sea; and this will be a pattern that will be taken over by later Turkic confederations, notably the Khazars, and finally by the Mongol Golden Horde itself. In this regard, the Scythians very much pioneered the basis of tribal confederations on the Pontic-Caspian Steppes that will endure really down to the 16th century when the Russians conquer the area.

Due to this trade, Herodotus and Greeks in general came into contact with the Scythians. Herodotus tells us some very important points about them. He is intrigued by their various burial customs. He gives us detailed explanations of the burials. Above all, he gives us a very, very vivid—one would even say a grim—description of horse sacrifices and the gutting of horses and the stuffing of them, mounting them on poles, and then the killing of the appropriate number of riders (Herodotus says it is usually 50); and then these grooms are likewise gutted and stuffed and mounted on poles and suspended over the grave of a great ruler or figure. In the early 19th century when Herodotus was being read with great interest, a lot of these reports would be doubted. Nonetheless, there are now finds, archaeological finds going back even to the Bronze Age but certainly from the Scythian period, which suggest that this was standard fare; that there was a whole cult of worshipping horses. Horse sacrifice is a tradition that would be carried on in Vedic India and even into historic India. There are references to it in the Greek world, not perhaps sacrificing the grooms with it. But it seems to go back to this early Indo-European practice of the first nomads on the Pontic-Caspian steppes, and it was retained by the Scythians well into the Classical age, probably as late as the fourth and third centuries B.C.

In addition, Scythians were very much appreciated for their military ability, especially as cavalry and archers. We know they are hired into the armies of Greek tyrants, men who seize power in Greek city-states. They are later hired into the armies of the Hellenistic kings; those are the successors of Alexander the Great. In Athens, a bodyguard of Scythians was retained as the police force known as Toxotai, meaning "the archers." These are men depicted in Greek art with that distinct recurved bow; that is, the half figure eight bow. They are shown with felt caps, leather trousers; they also have a peculiar bow case rather than a true quiver. These objects have been confirmed in archaeology from tombs, from depictions on Greek vases, and relief sculpture from the pediments of Greek temples.

Furthermore, Scythian jewelry and objects were prized. It is as if the nomadic peoples had a particular genius in working jewelry. They put many of their creative activities into jewelry and woodwork, leather work, rather than monumental architecture. This is seen in the type of jewelry that comes out of the tombs and jewelry styles, usually generally called animal-style jewelry, which influences the jewelry of the Greek world and eventually the entire Classical world. It is seen in the great rhytons or the drinking cups in which some kind of animal head acts as the base of this vast container for drinking wine. To the Greeks, the Scythians drank their wine unmixed whereas the Greeks would cut it with water, and those Greeks who pick up this bad Scythian habit are known to go mad. One of them is my favorite king of Sparta, King Cleomenes, who really went off his rocker right before the Persian invasion in 490 B.C. It is because he was hanging around Scythian ambassadors too long and picked up this bad habit.

In any case, the exchange is very fruitful and it persists through the whole of the Classical age. Given the nature of the Greek political system, the Greeks and the Scythians had a very, very successful symbiosis. They never posed a threat. The Greeks were there on the shore in certain colonies; they were there by permission and very useful.

The Scythians, however, came into contact also with the peoples of the Near East; and by that I would mean the regions of Asia Minor, today the so-called Fertile Crescent, and Iran, and also those upper satrapies known as Transoxiana. There had been contact between the nomadic peoples and the Middle East going back well into the Bronze Age. However, in the sixth century B.C., King Cyrus of Persia, he came to the throne in 559 B.C. but in 550 B.C., he overthrew his Medean overlords—those were an Iranian people that would today be around Hamadan, the ancient city of Ecbatana; and Cyrus ruled from Persia or Persis, today that would be Fars province in Southwestern Turkey—he overthrew his masters and eventually united most of the Near East. His son Cambyses conquered Egypt; that was about the only thing that had escaped Cyrus. He was remembered as a great conqueror.

Two significant points about this Persian Empire: This Persian Empire, which we often refer to as the Achaemenid Empire, was an empire built by Persians, Iranian speakers, who themselves were descended of nomads who had moved into this area in the middle to late Bronze Age. They were part of an archaeological complex archaeologists affectionately abbreviate the BMAC, the Bactriam-Argiana Archaeological Complex, which is essentially the region of Transoxiana where ancestors of the Persians migrated from the Pontic-Caspian steppes and they later broke off and moved into Iran, whereas cousins and kindred moved into India. We will talk about that subsequently. They brought with them the traditions of horses and cavalry.

King Cyrus, whose ancestors were nomads, nonetheless had very much absorbed and built upon the culture of the ancient Near East. His empire was based on cavalry armies; and very much a cavalry army that owed its origins to steppe traditions, the steppe way of war, mounted horse archers, javelin men fighting from a distance, not closing and shock action, tends not to use infantry other than in a supporting role. But other than that, the Achaemenid Empire was a great bureaucratic state. It was the successor to the Near Eastern empire stretching back to the first conquerors: Sargon of Akkad, Hammurabi of Babylon, the great Neo Assyrian emperors of the Iron Age. The Persian Empire was the summation of that tradition. It stretched in time from the lower Danube—it actually had possessions in Europe—to the Indus.

The Persian kings, as a result of their successes, inherited a long northern frontier. That frontier marched along the southern borders of essentially the Scythian world. In fact, the entire of the Scythian world shared a border running from the Danube in that great arc across those steppes to the Jaxartes. There are different Scythian tribes that are named in the sources, such as the Daha, the Massagetae, later the Soki; all of these tribes were apparently parts of that wider Scythian confederation or peoples, nation, family of nations. The Persian kings therefore had to deal with the threat somewhat along the lines of the Chinese emperors; but in many ways, the Persian kings—the Great King of Persia, as he like to be called in the Greek sources—had to pioneer dealing with these nomadic peoples in a way that later states that would come to dominate the Near East would; and the one that will come to mind later in this course in the medieval period will be the Abbasid Caliphate. That meant patrolling the borders of the Caucasus and the two great passes that gained entrance into the Near East. Another was Transoxiana, the Jaxartes River, and also the western frontier, along the Black Sea regions and the lower Danube; all areas that had fallen under the control of the Persian kings.

In 512 B.C.—some scholars would date it a bit earlier to 515 B.C.; you will find both dates cited—King Darius I, the third of the great Persian kings, decided to march an army across a bridge of ships at the Dardanelles (the Greeks would have called it the Hellespont), across Thrace (roughly Bulgaria today), cross the lower Danube, and invade the Russian steppes, the Pontic-Caspian steppes, to bring the Scythians to bear. In contrast to his Chinese contemporaries, Darius led the army himself, whereas Chinese emperors always sent out able generals and did not get involved in these things. The expedition proved a fiasco. In many ways, Darius was frustrated by the typical steppe tactics. The Scythians refused to come to battle. There is an anecdote in Herodotus that captures the whole essence of the campaign: The Scythians sent a message, which was a bird, a frog, I believe it was perhaps a fish, and five arrows; no, it is not a fish, a bird, a frog, a mouse, and five arrows. The immediate reaction of Darius: "This is a submission; earth and water. It was one of his ministers who said, "No, the message means unless the Persians can fly like birds, burrow into the ground like mice, or can leap across water the way frogs do, they are going to be full of Scythian arrows"; and that is essentially what happened. The Scythians pursued a scorched earth policy; and eventually Darius had to call off the expedition, return that army to Europe with great cost, and had achieved very little. Darius's experience would be repeated by many armies in the future, and fighting steppe nomads would turn out to be a very, very difficult task. Few armies, either in the Classical age or the medieval age, ever really devised the proper tactics and even strategy to deal with the steppe armies.

The next person who came into touch with these Scythians and had to essentially deal with the frontiers of the Persian Empire was Alexander the Great. From 334–327 B.C., Alexander, King of Macedon, overran the Persian Empire. He is without a doubt one of the greatest conquerors of all times. In my opinion, he is number one; but I am prejudiced. Nonetheless, his very success meant that he inherited the frontiers of the Persian Empire and how to deal with these nomads. He confronted them on the Danube, and by some very clever tactical devices—by stealth and by close coordination of infantry and cavalry—he beat back a group of nomads along the Danube, punished them, and secured that frontier. But he did not make the mistake of waging a war of conquest against them as Darius had done.

Later, as he has conquered the entire Persian Empire, he runs into those same Scythians on the Jaxartes River—today that would be the Syr Dayra—and there he confronted a far more daunting task. This was a much larger river; it involves regulating the interchange between Scythian nomads and the settled people of Transoxiana. These were the ancient regions of Sogdiana and Bactria, home to very important caravan cities; the most famous under the Greek name of Maracanda is close but not identical to the later Samarkand. Already the cities of this region were engaged in the beginning of a caravan trade across the Tarim Basin to China. Furthermore, these satrapies, these Upper Satrapies—Transoxiana as we would call it—were home to very important Iranian nobles and barons who had to be brought under control; they were very powerful; and they represented a potential threat to Alexander and later his successors, the Seleucid kings of Syria; that is, the family of the general Seleucus who succeeded Alexander's Asian Empire. Alexander initially tried to set up a border. He established military cities,

Alexandria's—Alexandria Eschate is one of the most famous—and he made the mistake of cutting off that contact between the Scythians, often known as Dahae or Sacae, these are tribes of the Scythians, and the various caravan cities. This just was not going to work. Alexander defeated them—defeated them in a very, very famous tactical battle—but he came very quickly to realize that the whole way of dealing with nomads was not setting up a kind of Maginot Line, but regulating the flow, the migration of tribes, the tempo of trade, and taxing it.

Alexander, by the time he withdrew from this region to invade India and eventually march home, had established a number of Greek Macedonian colonies in Bactria on the Oxus River, which could be supported by agriculture—the reports are over 20,000 were settled—and for the next 125 years after his death, these cities evolved into Greek-style cities. We often call the region Greco-Bactrian or the Greco-Bactrian Kingdom. North of Bactria in Sogdiana, along the upper Jaxartes and well the whole Jaxartes really, those areas were only loosely affiliated to the Greco-Bactrian kingdom.

With Alexander's death in 323 B.C., his empire was partitioned. Eventually, the Asian domains fell to the general Seleucus. He fell heir to Alexander's policy of dealing with Scythian nomads; however, that region known as Bactria, which would today be parts of Afghanistan and Turkmenistan, broke away under its own rulers. A fellow by the name of Diodotus, somewhere around 250 B.C., rebelled and set up his own independent Greek kingdom. This kingdom is actually known in Chinese sources, particularly our erstwhile envoy to the Xiongnu, Zhang Qian, who actually reached the Greco-Bactrian kingdom somewhere around 128 or 127 B.C. after a long stay with a Xiongnu wife, and he reported on the existence of this kingdom. He was very impressed by it; it is called Daxia in his account. But he also reports of two other important people: Foremost are people we met in the last lecture, the Yuehzhi or Yue-Chi, that peculiar Chinese rendition of a name that eventually gives rise to the famous Kushans—they probably really called themselves Tocharians, which is the name of the language on the Buddhist texts and essentially a version of the name used by the Greek sources; they seem to be the same people—and then the Sacae, who are also known to the Chinese. Both the Sacae, Iranian-speakers, and the Kushans, the ancestors of the Kushans—let us call them Tocharians—were courted by the Chinese as allies. They were not particularly interested in getting involved, and both of them were in their locales; that is, north of Sogdiana in the case of the Sacae, and in the case of the Kushans just to the northeast of that region. They had been displaced here by the fighting between the Xiongnu and the Chinese. They took it upon themselves somewhere around the middle of the second century B.C. to migrate into the settled zone of Transoxiana. We're not exactly sure why; they were probably driven by local conditions. The Sacae moved first, and they swept in in 140 B.C. and did a pretty destructive job on the Greco-Bactrian kingdom; they pretty much smashed it. The Kushans came maybe 15 or 20 years later, and they moved into Bactria. The Sacae kept on moving into the Helman Valley; they crossed the Bolan Pass and entered India. But the Tocharians, the ancestors of the Kushan emperors, they settled in the very prosperous area of Bactria. They took over the Greek cities and brought an end to Alexander's political legacy there, although the Hellenistic or the Greek style of civilization persisted.

The collapse of that frontier—of the Iranian world; that Hellenistic Iranian world; the world of the Persian Empire taken over by Alexander and his successors—was related, caused, by the very movements that were a result of the Xiongnu-Han wars that had pushed these tribes, Tocharian speakers and Iranian speakers, westward from their eastern homes on the western and northwestern frontiers of the Chinese empire. This is a pattern that will repeat itself; and these tribes have moved, they find new locales, and they eventually enter into Transoxiana in the Middle East. You will see this again with the migration of the Turks.

The Scythians themselves, farther west, the bulk of the Scythians, disappear somewhere in the third century B.C., and they give way to a new people known as the Sarmatians. These are the Iranian nomads whom the Romans will encounter; and the Sarmatian migration, which seems to have, again, originated from an east-to-west direction, are thought—or, perhaps better, surmised—to be yet another spinoff of that Xiongnu-Han conflict. The ancestors of the Sarmatians had started out in the regions around the Aral Sea; they were on the central steppes; they migrated westward, they crossed the Ural; and sometime shortly after 300 B.C., they took over the Scythian confederation and dominated now those western Eurasian steppes, essentially from the lower Danube to the Volga. The result is that the patterns we see evolving with the Scythians are patterns that are going to repeat themselves at later periods. The Scythians in many ways are the rulers who wrote the script of how to dominate those western Eurasian steppes. It is done by trade; it is done by coming into accommodation with the civilized states; but there is always the danger that the system can be unhinged by newcomers who have been pressed east because of the wars between Chinese emperors and other nomadic peoples out on the eastern steppes.

The Parthians

Lecture 6

In this lecture, we will study the Parthians, the Iranian-speaking nomadic peoples who were an offshoot of the Scythians. The Parthians were remarkably versatile and successful for 400 years. They ruled Iran and the wider Middle East from horseback. They were interlopers, but by a judicious combination of diplomacy with the Romans and the Kushans, by promoting the Silk Road through their domains, and by coming to terms with the existing populations, they created the first nomadic empire in the Near East ruled from the steppes. Their culture provided a model for the later and more successful nomads from the steppes, the Seljuk Turks.

Seleucid Kings
- Between 247 and 129 B.C., the Parthians carved out a large empire stretching from what is Iraq today into parts of Afghanistan and Turkmenistan. They wrested control of the Iranian heartland from the Seleucid kings.

- The Seleucid kings were a family of Macedonian generals who had fought with Alexander the Great. In 312 B.C., the founder, King **Seleucus**, took the title king of Babylon, and he and his successors ruled over the Asian sections of the empire of Alexander.

The Parthians
- In 247 B.C., the **Arsacid** kings of Parthia—governors in the Seleucid Empire—asserted their independence. It had been increasingly difficult for Seleucid kings to keep control over distant provinces. In one area along the northern frontier, there was a tribe of Iranian speakers known as the Parni who migrated into the northern districts of Iran. They exploited the Seleucid weakness to create their own principality.

- Two brothers, **Arsaces** and Tiridates, carved out a realm. From Arsaces, we get the name Arsacid. The son of the first Arsaces,

Arsaces II, who ruled between 211 and 191 B.C., united various groups in that region and took the name Parthian.

- Arsaces II was an astute and adroit king, who considered himself a vassal of the Seleucid king, **Antiochus III**. Antiochus marched off to India and eventually made his way back to the Mediterranean world.

- Unfortunately, Antiochus's activities came to the attention of Rome, and in 190 B.C., the Romans destroyed his army at the Battle of Magnesia. This was a great victory that demonstrated the superiority of the Roman legion over the Macedonian phalanx. Seleucid power began to fragment rapidly thereafter, which presented an opportunity for the Parthian rulers to assert their independence.

Mithradates I

- The turning point came during the reign of a king known as **Mithradates I**. Mithradates had several important achievements to his name.

- In 140 B.C., he decisively defeated and captured **Demetrius II**, the Seleucid king. That victory assured that the Parthian kings would gain control of Iran, particularly the ancient lands of Media and Persia.

- Increasingly, the Parthian kings came to assume many of the roles of the king of Persia. Mithradates defeated the Greek kings ruling in Bactria.

- Although the Seleucids tried to make a comeback in 129 B.C., the Parthian kings eventually came to rule the eastern half of the former Seleucid Empire. It was a stunning achievement by nomads.

- The reign of Mithradates also marked another important turning point. From now on, the Parthian kings ruled not only the nomadic peoples along the northern frontier of the Iranian world but also the heartland of Iran itself and the wealthy cities of Babylonia, including the city of Babylon.

Parthian Silver Coins

- The Parthian kings began to change the way they represented themselves, as we see on Parthian silver coins. These silver coins have come down to us in great numbers.

- The coins document how the Parthians, nomadic invaders, came to terms with the traditions of a bureaucratic state. It is significant, for instance, that the Chinese envoy Zhang Qian remarked how impressive Parthian silver coins are because they carry the portraits of kings.

- The coins acted as an important record and guide to Parthian political and cultural pretentions. Starting with Mithradates I, royal portraits were increasingly modeled after Seleucid kings.

- On the coins, the Parthian king discards the traditional nomadic felt cap and begins to wear the diadem—the pearl headdress used in ancient Persian royalty, which was adopted by Alexander the Great and many of the Hellenistic monarchs.

- It is also significant that the coins carry their inscriptions in Greek, which was recognized as an administrative and commercial language across much of the Near East.

- This tradition persisted on Parthian coinage to the end of the dynasty, 227 A.D., when they were defeated and overthrown by a native Persian dynasty, the **Sassanids**. The Sassanids restored the traditional Persian bureaucratic state and eliminated Parthian interlopers.

Lateral Succession

- The Parthians proved themselves adept conquerors and employed some of the techniques Modu Chanyu used in building his confederation of the Xiongnu.

- The Parthian king came to terms with numerous rulers within his empire, with the kings of Persia, with rulers in Mesopotamia, and with rulers on the eastern frontiers. The Parthian king invested these lesser kings with titles and ruled them much like a tribal confederation.

- In particular, in the eastern areas, where the Parthian kings faced serious threats from the Sacae and the Kushan emperors, they entrusted control to one of the leading families, known as the **Suren** family.

- This was a hereditary group of commanders who ruled as a combination of local princes and satraps, as well as marshal commanders of the Arsacid armies. A member of the Suren family defeated the Roman army at Carrhae in 53 B.C.

- The Parthians were always children of the steppes. One could argue that they ruled their Iranian Empire from horseback. That meant that they also practiced lateral succession. There was no strict succession from father to son.

- When an Arsacid king died, the next senior male relative was in the best position to take over. That always risks the danger of civil war, particularly if there were several possible candidates. This is what plagued the confederacy of the Xiongnu, which the later Han emperors exploited. It is a weakness we see in the Parthian state.

Four Eurasian Empires
- The Parthians, through their conquests, gained an important segment of the Silk Road, and they reaped great profits from it. While they themselves did not engage in trade, their subjects did.

- The Parthians, however, had a major strategic problem. If we look at the political world order in the year 1 A.D., there were four great Eurasian empires: the Han Empire of China, the Kushan Empire of central Asia and north India, the Roman Empire in the Mediterranean world, and the Parthian state. The other empires exerted constant pressure on the Parthian state.

The Roman Empire

- On their western frontier, the Parthians faced a ruthless and dangerous opponent: Rome. In 69 B.C., **Lucius Licinius Lucullus** won the Battle of Tigranocerta in one of the greatest Roman victories. That battle made Rome the arbiter of the Middle East. Henceforth, Roman power stretched to the Euphrates.

- The Romans, in 53 B.C., under **Marcus Licinius Crassus**, attempted to conquer the Parthian Empire. That ended in a disaster. The Suren, using a combination of heavy cavalry and horse archers, lured the legions of Crassus onto the battlefield of Carrhae and wiped out a Roman army of some 50,000.

- It was a major disgrace for the Romans, and it assured that the Parthians could keep the upper Euphrates as their frontier. It also taught the Romans to respect Parthian cavalry on the plains and grassland of the Middle East and Iran and the high tableland of Armenia.

- That victory presaged a new set of relationships between Rome and the Parthians. The Romans wanted revenge. However, the emperor **Augustus**, after settling the Roman revolution and consolidating and creating the Roman Empire, preferred to negotiate rather than to invade.

- By a diplomatic settlement in 20 B.C., Augustus regained the lost honor of Rome by recovering whatever captives were left from Carrhae, as well as the legionary standards.

- The diplomatic arrangement by Augustus suited both empires. The Parthians had not the means to conquer Rome. The Romans, on the other hand, really did not have the means to conquer the Parthians, although Rome in many ways was the superior military power.

War of Armenian Succession

- The diplomatic arrangements of Augustus were maintained for almost 75 years, when in 54 A.D., a war erupted with the ruling king of Parthia, **Vologeses I**, who tried to put his brother on the throne of Armenia. This led to a war of the Armenian succession, and it, too, ended in a diplomatic settlement.

- The king of Armenia would be a Parthian prince crowned by Rome. Both states could rest satisfied that Armenia was protected. It was the borderland and the route between the two empires, as well as the entrance ramp for the barbarians coming off that steppe highway over the Caucasus.

- It was in the joint interest of the Romans and Parthians to maintain a peace settlement. There were successive wars against the Romans, but the campaigns waged by Rome against the Parthians ultimately contributed to the undermining of the Arsacid state.

The Sassanid Empire

- The Romans picked up important real estate in the Middle East and emerged from these wars as the dominant power. The weakening of the Parthian state in the end would come to plague the Romans, however.

- In 227 A.D., the Parthians were overthrown by a rebellion headed by none other than their vassal king of Persia, who defeated and killed the last Parthian king and proclaimed a new neo-Persian Empire, the Sassanid Empire.

- The Sassanid Empire was a bureaucratic state that was Zoroastrian in faith and committed to the reconquest of all the domains of the older Persian Empire, including the eastern half of the Roman world. The Romans were far better off dealing with the Parthians than they ever were with the Sassanid shahs.

Arsacid: The royal family of the kings of Parthia (246 B.C.–227 A.D.).

Sassanid: The dynasty of Zoroastrian shahs of the neo-Persian Empire (227–651).

Suren: The hereditary commander of the Drangiana and Arachosia (today, western Afghanistan and Pakistan). The Suren had the right to crown the Arsacid king of Parthia.

Names to Know

Antiochus III, the Great (b. c. 241 B.C.; r. 223–187 B.C.): Seleucid king. Restored the power of his empire. In 309–203 B.C., he conducted an eastern expedition and received the homage of the Parthian prince Arsaces II and the Greco-Bactrian king Euthydemus. At the Battle of Panium in 200 B.C., he defeated the Ptolemaic army, conquering Phoenicia, Coele-Syria, and Judaea. He was decisively defeated by the Roman consul Lucius Cornelius Scipio Asiaticus at Magnesia in 190 B.C. Thereafter, the Seleucid Empire fragmented.

Arsaces I (246–211 B.C.): Prince of the Iranian-speaking tribe Parni and founder of the Arsacid Dynasty in northeastern Iran. His descendants ruled as the kings of Parthia.

Arsaces II (211–191 B.C.): King of Parthia and a vassal of the Seleucid kings. In 190 B.C., he asserted his independence after the Romans decisively defeated the Seleucid king Antiochus III (223–187 B.C.) at the Battle of Magnesia.

Augustus (Gaius Julius Caesar Octavianus) (b. 63 B.C., r. 27 B.C.– 14 A.D.): Roman emperor; the nephew and adopted son of Julius Caesar (101–44 B.C.). Augustus ended nearly 60 years of civil war and, in 27 B.C., founded the principate.

Crassus, Marcus Licinius (115–53 B.C.): Roman senator and consul in 70 and 55 B.C.; a leading commander of the republic and a member of the First Triumvirate. He was defeated and slain by the Parthians at the Battle of Carrhae in 53 B.C.

Demetrius II Nicator (b. c. 160 B.C.; r. 147–141 B.C., 129–125 B.C.): Seleucid king and son of Demetrius I Soter (161–150 B.C.). This dashing monarch was defeated and captured by the Parthian king Mithradates I in 141 B.C. Demetrius lived in gilded captivity at the Arsacid court and married the sister of Phraates II. In 129 B.C., King Phraates II, at war with Demetrius's brother Antiochus VII, released Demetrius to raise a rebellion in Syria. Demetrius regained his throne but failed to restore Seleucid power.

Lucullus, Lucius Licinius (118–56 B.C.): Consul in 74 B.C.; assumed the command as proconsul against Mithradates VI, king of Pontus, in 73–66 B.C. In 69 B.C., his victory at Tigranocerta over King Tigranes II of Armenia and Mithradates VI made Rome the premier power in the Near East.

Mithradates I (171–138 B.C.): King of Parthia, defeated and captured the Seleucid king Demetrius II in 140 B.C. and then the Greco-Bactrian king Eucratides. He conquered Media, Persia, Mesopotamia, Margiana, and Aria.

Seleucus I Nicator (b. 358 B.C.; r. 312–281 B.C.): Macedonian noble and general. A minor figure in the initial succession wars after the death of Alexander the Great in 323–321 B.C. In 320 B.C., he obtained the satrapy of Babylonia, and between 312 and 281 B.C., he fell heir to the Asia domains of Alexander's empire.

Vologeses I (51–78): Arsacid king of Parthia. Supported his brother Tiridates to the throne of Armenia in a war against Rome. In 66, he concluded a peace with the emperor Nero, whereby Tiridates retained the Armenian throne but recognized the hegemony of Rome.

Suggested Reading

Curtis and Stewart, eds., *The Age of the Parthians*.

Debevoise, *A Political History of Parthia*.

Frye, *The Heritage of Persia*.

Isaac, *The Limits of Empire*.

Millar, *The Roman Near East, 31 B.C.–A.D. 337*.

Shavegan, *Arsacids and Sasanians*.

Tacitus (Grant, trans.), *Annals of Imperial Rome*.

Yarshater, ed., *The Cambridge History of Iran*.

Questions to Consider

1. What factors led to the emergence of the Parthians as heirs to the eastern lands of the Seleucid Empire? What were the decisive points in the Parthian conquests?

2. In what did the Arsacid kings remain nomadic warriors, ruling their empire from horseback? What institutions of their subject peoples did the Arsacid kings adapt?

3. How did the Arascid kings promote commerce and culture? What contributions did they make to the development of the Silk Road? In what ways were they phihellene kings? In what ways did they pose as the heirs to the Achaemenid kings of Persia? Why are coins such an important sources about Parthian political ideology?

4. How should the Parthian achievement be evaluated? In what ways did the Parthians anticipate the Sejuk Turks?

The Parthians
Lecture 6—Transcript

In this lecture and the next lecture, we are going to deal with three new steppe nomadic peoples: the Parthians, the Sacae, and Tocharian speakers who eventually came to be known as the Kushans. I think it would be useful before we plunge into this lecture that will be dealing particularly with the Parthians that we look for a moment where we have been and where we are going.

The Parthians are an Iranian-speaking nomadic people. They, in effect, are an offshoot of the Scythians, of whom we have spoken. The Sacae are also Iranian speakers. The Kushans, or the ancestors of the Kushans, are Tocharian speakers. All three of these people in the third and second centuries B.C. came to play an extremely important role in both Northern India and the Middle East. It is useful to remember that their activities are more or less contemporary with the Xiongnu; and, in fact, at least two of these people, the Sacae and the Kushans, were set in motion by fighting with the Xiongnu as well as the struggle between the Xiongnu and the Han emperors. That gives you some kind of chronological context: We are now dealing with that central steppe area, approximately at the same time that the Chinese have their first serious dealings with nomadic peoples; and we will see certain similarities in the relationships between the nomadic peoples of the central steppes and the civilized societies that we saw with China and the Xiongnu.

With that in mind, let us turn to the Parthians. The Parthians, between 247 and 129 B.C., carved out a large empire stretching from what is today Iraq into parts of Afghanistan and Turkmenistan. They essentially gained control of the Iranian heartland, and they wrested control of this region from the Seleucid kings. The Seleucid kings, as you may recall, were a family of Macedonian generals who had fought with Alexander the Great; the founder was King Seleucus, who in 312 B.C. took the title of King of Babylon. He and his successors ruled over the Asian sections of the empire of Alexander, which had stretched from the Aegean to the Indus; and that empire had tended to fragment steadily over time. What had happened to the Seleucid state is that by the middle of the third century B.C., in 247 B.C. when we get our first record of the Arsacid rulers—that is the Arsacid kings of Parthia—

that the satraps (and the satraps refer to the governors) or governors in the Seleucid empire, had more or less asserted their independence; and it was increasingly difficult for Seleucid kings in Babylon and the great capital of Antioch to keep control over these distant provinces.

In one area along the northern frontier, the traditional frontier that divides the nomadic people from the Iranian heartland—and that would be an eastern extension of the Elburz Mountains that extends beyond the Caspian; this region that is later known as Khurasan in Islamic times—there was a tribe of Iranian speakers known as the Parni who migrated into the northern districts of Iran; and they exploited the Seleucid weakness to essentially create their own principality. There are two brothers according to the Greek sources, a fellow named Arsaces and his younger brother Tiridates. It is from Arsaces, the elder of the two, that we take the name "Arsacid," which means "descendants of Arsaces"; it is a typical way of referring to dynasties. They carved out a principality; they came to terms with the Seleucid king and essentially were recognized as rulers who functions as satraps or governors; and the son of the first Arsaces, Arsaces II, who ruled after his father between 211 and 191 B.C., actually began to synthesize the various elements, unite the various groups in that region, and took the name Parthian.

Parthia originally referred to a district. At the time Alexander the Great had moved through there about 125 years earlier, it had been a geographic designation. But this king, Arsaces II, turns it into an ethnic designation. It comes to mean the various Parthian retainers of the Arsacid king who give their loyalty to the king and remain fundamentally nomads in their political organization, in their way of war, and a good deal of their customs. What the Parthian kings do is conquer an Iranian empire and attempt to rule it from horseback. In this regard, they will act in a way as prototypes for the later Turkish dynasts known as sultans and emirs who will do very much the same in the medieval period; that is, conquer the great cities of the Islamic world and attempt to rule them based on nomadic military power and coming to some kind of accommodation with the existing institutions.

Arsaces II was a very astute and adroit king. He submitted to the Seleucid king Antiochus III. Antiochus III, who took the name "Great"—he appropriated for himself, and no one knew better than Antiochus—saw himself as the embodiment of Alexander the Great. He conducted a great anabasis, an eastern march, to bring all the eastern satrapies under control. Of course, the Parthians submitted. Arsaces recognized himself as a vassal of the great Seleucid king. Antiochus marched off to India, got more elephants, and eventually made his way back to the Mediterranean world. Unfortunately, Antiochus's activities came to the attention of Rome; and in 190 B.C. the Romans destroyed his army at the Battle of Magnesia in one of the great victories that demonstrated the superiority of the legion over the Macedonian phalanx. Seleucid power began to fragment very rapidly thereafter. That gave an opportunity for the Parthian rulers to assert their independence. Starting from 190 B.C. down to essentially 63 B.C., successive Parthian kings gathered up the eastern heritage of the Seleucid kings.

The turning point comes in the reign of a king known as Mithridates I. The name "Mithridates" is significant: The name is taken after the Indo-Iranian god Mitra or Mithras, who becomes a popular god in the Roman Empire. He is known in the Rig Vedas; he is known among the earliest of the Iranian gods; and it is suggestive that the Parthians had always retained that ancient polytheistic Iranian rites. They were not Zoroastrian monotheists; we will get into that later on in the talk. Mithridates I has several important achievements to his name. In 140 B.C., he decisively defeated and captured King Demetrius II, the Seleucid king; put Demetrius under house arrest. Demetrius then went on to a very colorful career. He tried to escape several times; he was married to a princess of the Parthian royal family. He was an absolutely irrepressible figure, and eventually was released in 129 B.C. by the Parthian king in order to plague his family back in Syria and in Mesopotamia. But that victory in 140 B.C. assured that the Parthian kings would gain control of Iran, particularly the ancient lands of Media and Persia. Increasingly, the Parthian kings came to assume many of the roles of the Great King of Persia and had to come to terms with that bureaucratic ancient monarchy of the Achaemenid kings. Mithridates also defeated the Greco-Bactrian rulers. These were the Greek kings ruling in Bactria; that would today be Northern Afghanistan. Their capital was the city Bactra, today Balkh on the upper Oxus River, studded with important caravan cities; and the Bactrian kings also exercised control over Ferghana—that is, ancient Sogdiana—and were involved in the trade across the Tarim Basin to China.

Certain districts were wrested from the control of these kings; notably Margiana, which is the modern city of Merv, and Areia, Herat, two critical caravan cities on the emerging Silk Road. The Seleucids tried to make a comeback in 129 B.C. It is decisively defeated by the Parthian king, Phraates II, who defeats that Seleucid comeback under Antiochus VII; he actually kills the Seleucid king. At that point, the Seleucids are pretty much out of it and the Parthian kings come to rule the eastern half of the former Seleucid Empire. It is a stunning achievement by nomads. In part, this is because on the terrain of Iran and Central Asia, the classic nomadic cavalry tactics are very, very much useful against Macedonian-style armies depending heavily on the traditional infantry phalanx and heavy cavalry. In all instances, the Parthians usually wear down their opponent by skirmishing and strategic withdrawal, and then in the decisive battle they usually are able to encircle and defeat an already exhausted Seleucid army. This accounts for their successive victories fighting against the Seleucid kings.

The reign of Mithridates I also marks another important turning point: From now on, these Parthian kings are ruling, not just the crucial nomadic peoples along the northern frontier of the Iranian world, but they were now ruling the heartland of Iran itself, as well as the wealthy cities of Babylonia; that is, today lower Iraq. That includes the city of Babylon. It also includes an important new city that was established by the Parthian kings, and that is Ctesiphon, on the Upper Tigris. It is in the vicinity of Baghdad today, and it becomes essentially the Parthian capital where the court resides. There also is nearby a Seleucid city, Seleucia ad Tigrim, which is essentially on the east bank and slightly south of Ctesiphon on the Tigris, and those two twin cities become essentially the court and capital of this Parthian Empire and fuel a great deal of the economic development.

At the same time, the Parthian kings begin to change the way they project themselves. One of our best pieces of evidence is Parthian coins. It has often been remarked that we would know very little about the Parthians had it not been for the survival of large numbers of silver coins. These silver coins have come down to us in great numbers, and by studying the coins it documents how the Parthians, a nomadic invader, came to terms with the traditions of a bureaucratic state. It is significant, for instance, that the Chinese envoy, our friend Zhang Qian, the erstwhile envoy to the Xiongnu, when he finally made it west somewhere around 128–127 B.C., he actually discovered a kingdom he calls [Anxi], which apparently is a Chinese rendering of Arsacid; that is, using the dynastic name to designate the Parthian kingdom. He remarks, for a man who comes from a world in which only copper coins are used, he remarks how impressive Parthian silver coins are because they carry the portraits of kings and Chinese coins only carry calligraphy, designating the date and the emperor when the coin was put out; those are cast bronze coins. The coins therefore act as a very important record and guide to Parthian political and cultural pretentions.

Starting with Mithridates I, royal portraits are modeled increasingly first after Seleucid kings. The Parthian king discards the traditional nomadic felt cap and begins to wear the diadem; that is, the pearl headdress used in ancient Persian royalty and was adopted by Alexander the Great and many of the Hellenistic monarchs. By the way, those pearls come from the Red Sea, and it is an important royal monopoly that emerges in the Parthian and the later Sassanid periods. The reverse of the coins shows an archer dressed in traditional nomadic dress with felt cap, the usual leather breeches, and, of course, that ubiquitous recurve bow; that is, the half figure eight bow. He is usually seated in a position to remind the viewer that this is the source of royal power. That type remains the same throughout Parthian coinage on these silver coins, which are known as drachma.

It is also significant that the coins carry their inscriptions, or as numismatists like to call them legends, in Greek. That might be curious for a moment; why Greek? They are ruling an Iranian state; Aramaic is a commercial language; as far as we can tell, the Parthians spoke an east Iranian dialect; and the reason they used Greek is because it is recognized as an administrative and commercial language across much of the Near East. Several languages in the history of the Near East have played this role. The first was Akkadian, written in cuneiform; the second was Aramaic; and the third was Greek, written in alphabetic system. For all international correspondence between kings or merchant princes, or even kings to their governors, the written language used was known by the scribe; and the Parthian king would speak in his native language, his native Iranian language, the scribe would however write the letter in Greek. The letter would then be sent to the other end, and the scribe at that end, who also knew Greek, would then translate the Greek into the appropriate language; it could be Iranian, it could be Tocharian, or in some cases if he was corresponding with the Roman emperor it would be Latin. Greek and Aramaic played that function across the Near East. They were privileged written languages, and most nomadic conquerors very quickly came to terms with this fact and employed these languages rather than their native language in communication. The Sacae and the Kushans did very much the same, as we will see in an upcoming lecture. The adoption of Greek is in effect saying, "We are serious monarchs."

The king Mithridates II, who had a very, very long reign and a very important reign—he ruled in the second and early first century B.C.; died somewhere in 88 or 87 B.C.—he begins to sport the full regalia of the Great King of Persia, and his coins project an imperial rank; that "We are now not just nomadic conquerors, but also the heirs to the Achaemenid Empire." This tradition persists on Parthian coinage really down to the end of the dynasty, usually dated in 227 A.D. when they are defeated and overthrown by a native Persian dynasty, the so-called Sassanids, who will then restore the traditional Persian bureaucratic state and essentially get rid of these Parthian interlopers who are a bunch of nomads off the steppes whom the Persians never particularly cared for, and anyway, to the Persians they are not even good Zoroastrians; so there are a lot of things wrong with the Parthian rulers to the traditional Persians.

In addition, besides taking on these royal pretentions from the Achaemenid period, the Parthians proved themselves adaptable conquerors and in some ways employed some of the techniques that we saw with Modu Chanyu in putting together his confederation of the Xiongnu. The great king of the Parthians, the Arsacid king of the Parthians, came to terms with numerous rulers within his empire: at the city of Charax on the Persian Gulf; with the kings of Persia, Fars province today, who eventually would overthrow them; with rulers in Mesopotamia; and also with rulers on the eastern frontiers. There, the Parthian king invested these sub-kings with titles and essentially ruled them as an extension of the old notion of a tribal confederation.

In particular, in the eastern areas where the Parthian kings faced serious threats from the Sacae and the Kushan emperors—and we will talk about them in the next lecture—there, in regions that historically were known in the

Classical age as Drangiana, which is today essentially Sīstān, and Arachosia, which is now Baluchistan, part of Pakistan, in that important border area the Parthian kings entrusted control to one of the leading families, and this was the Suren family. This was a hereditary group of commanders who essentially ruled as a combination of local prince and satrap, as well as martial commander of the Arsacid armies. We know none of the names of these men—they are only called the Suren—but they held this hereditary position through the Parthian age. It would be one of these men, a Suren, who would defeat the Roman army at Carrhae in 53 B.C. Some scholars believe that the Suren gave rise to one of the famous heroes of medieval Persian literature, and that is the hero Rustam who is well known in Persian miniatures and combat scenes and is a figure who is known in Persian epic. It is believed that this figure, the Suren, gave rise to that epic figure well known in the *Shahnameh*, the *Epic of the Kings*, in medieval Persia. It also points to the loose structure of the Parthian state.

Another feature of that loose structure was the Parthians were always children of the steppes; and one could argue that they ruled their Iranian Empire from horseback to a large extent. That meant they also practiced lateral succession. I mentioned that fact with the Xiongnu in the lectures on their relationships with the Chinese Empire, and that is there was not a strict hereditary succession from father to son; far from it. There was some kind of rough and ready approval by the leading families—and there were apparently seven of them, including the Suren family—that come to some kind of consensus, an agreement without voting, that when an Arsacid king dies who is the next senior relative, male relative, in best position to take over? It could be a brother; it could be a cousin; sometimes it is an uncle. That always risks the danger of civil war, particularly if there are several possible candidates. This is what plagued the confederacy of the Xiongnu, which the later Han emperors exploited. It is a weakness that you see in the Parthian state; in a moment, we will talk about how the Roman emperors also exploited it. Again, it is a weakness that we will see even in the Mongol Empire, especially after the death of Genghis Khan in 127 A.D.; the Mongol Empire is a rocked by a series of succession crises arising from that lateral succession principle.

Even so, it is astonishing at how successfully the Parthians ruled their empire. Part of it was their general policy of toleration of various cults and divinities. The coins depict various gods from the Greek Pantheon; those were the coins issued in the great cities, notably Seleucia ad Tigrim, which issued particularly large silver coins known as tetradrachm. Relief shows that the Greek god Heracles, the ancient Persian divinities such as Mithra, were all approved of. There was no effort to favor one religious tradition over another; and again, that is a very traditional pragmatic policy of the steppes. We will see that with the Kushan emperors when they come to rule an empire in India; these are people who are Tocharian speakers who come off the steppes. We will see it in some of the early Turkish khanates, and above all in the Mongol khanate. This is just a pragmatic policy pursued by all steppe conquerors.

In addition, they will exploit very much the Silk Road. The Parthians by their conquests had gained an important segment of the Silk Road stretching from the modern city of Merv across the northern cities of Iran, notably Hamadan, ancient Ecbatana, Tiberias; also into the Roman Empire where the goods would have been shipped ultimately to the Roman port of Antioch on the Mediterranean; and then on the eastern end Merv, caravans would go into Central Asia across the Tarim Basin to China. That important trade route was now under the control of the Parthian kings and they reaped great profits from it. We will be discussing in detail how this Silk Road—or *Seidenstrasse* as it was first called in 1877—becomes such an important, pivotal role in the economic life of the ancient and medieval world and also the main avenue of cultural and religious exchange; and the Parthians played an important role there. They themselves did not engage in trade—it was largely their Sogdian- and Aramaic-speaking merchants, their subjects, who did it—but they made it possible.

The Parthians, however, had a major strategic problem. From the start, this state—and if you looked at the political world order in, say, the year 100 A.D., there are four great Eurasian empires: one is the Han Empire of China, one is the Kushan Empire of Central Asia and North India coming up, the other is the Roman Empire in the Mediterranean world, and the fourth is the Parthian state—is really sandwiched in between what is the great Kushan Empire and the Roman Empire to the west. Those empires were exerting constant pressure on the Parthian state. The early migrations of the Sacae and the Tocharian speakers out of Central Asia into their future homes—it will take both people eventually into India—but those migrations started in 140 B.C. when the Sacae pushed southwest from their homeland along the Jaxartes River; that is, into Transoxiana. They disrupted the Greco-Bactrian Kingdom, and they eventually made their way through Afghanistan into Western India. In fact, today the Jats claim descent from the Sacae; those are one of the warrior castes of India favored by the British as a martial race. The Kushans, or the ancestors of the Kushans—those would be known as Yuezhi in Chinese sources, the Tócharoi in Greek sources, or Tocharian—pushed into the regions of Bactria (that is, the former Greek kingdom), and eventually would cross the Hindu Kush into Northern India. Both the Tocharians and the Sacae defeated Parthian armies. At least two separate Parthian kings lost their lives battling these "invaders." The one, Phraates II, who fell probably in 128 B.C., fell fighting because he had hired a bunch of nomadic allies, they failed to turn up at the decisive battle, and then since they had not been paid they were trashing the eastern frontier and so the king rushed in and, of course, he fell fighting these ancestors of the Kushans. So they felt pressure on their eastern frontier.

On their western frontier, they faced a far more dangerous opponent, and that was Rome. In 69 B.C., my favorite Roman commander—a man whom I study in my travels in Eastern Asia Minor—Lucius Licinius Lucullus won the Battle of Tigranocerta in one of the great Roman victories. That battle made Rome the arbiter of the Middle East. Henceforth, Roman power stretched to the Euphrates. The Romans in 53 B.C., under Lucius Licinius Crassus, attempted to conquer the Parthian Empire. That ended in a disaster, a *clades* in Latin, in which the Suren, using a combination of heavy cavalry and horse archers, lured the legions of Crassus onto the battlefield, really an open plain, northeast of the modern city of Haran, today Carrhae, and essentially wiped out a Roman army of some 50,000, capturing the Roman legions. It was a major disgrace for the Romans, and it assured that the Parthians could keep the Upper Euphrates as their frontier vis-a-vis Rome. It also taught the Romans to respect Parthian cavalry on the plains and grassland of the Middle East and Iran, and also, above all, the high tableland of Armenia.

That victory at Carrhae announced a new set of relationships between Rome and the Parthians. The Romans wanted revenge. Rome could never accept a defeat like this. The Emperor Augustus, who after settling the so-called Roman revolution and consolidating and creating the Roman Empire, in 20 B.C. preferred to negotiate rather than to invade. By a diplomatic settlement in 20 B.C., he regained the lost honor of Rome by recovering whatever captives were left from Carrhae as well as the legionary standards. At the same time, he received hostages from the then-reigning king, King Phraates IV. Phraates IV sent a number of his sons, four of them, to be raised at Rome. He received in return a Greek courtesan known as Musa, Thea Urania Musa, the only lady to appear on Parthian coins, and from her he had his favorite son Phraates V who succeeded. The diplomatic arrangement by Augustus suited both empires. The Parthians had not had the means to conquer Rome. The Romans on the other hand really did not have the means to conquer the Parthians, although Rome in many ways was the superior power. The diplomatic arrangements of Augustus were maintained for almost 75 years when in 54 A.D. a war erupted between the ruling king of Parthia, Vologeses I, who tried to put his brother Tiridates on the throne of Armenia. This led to a war of the Armenian succession, as it is often called, and it too ended in a diplomatic settlement. The king of Armenia would be a Parthian prince crowned by Rome. Both states could rest satisfied that Armenia was protected. It was the borderland and the route between the two empires as well as the entrance ramp for all those barbarians coming off that steppe highway over the Caucasus; and that was in the joint interest of the Romans and Parthians to maintain a peace settlement.

There were successive wars against the Romans; against Trajan, Marcus Aurelius, Septimius Severus. These wars always favored the Romans, who had the military edge. The campaigns waged by Rome against the Parthians ultimately contributed to the undermining of the Arsacid state. In the meantime, the Romans picked up important real estate in the Middle East, and emerged from these wars as the dominant power. The weakening of the Parthian state in the end would come to plague the Romans, because in 227 A.D. the Parthians were overthrown by a rebellion headed up by none other than their vassal king of Persia, a man named Ardashir. He defeated and slew the last Parthian king Artabanus V and proclaimed a new Neo-Persian Empire or Sassanid Empire, a bureaucratic state that was Zoroastrian in faith and committed to the reconquest of all of the domains of the older Persian Empire, including the eastern half of the Roman world; and the Romans were far better off dealing with Parthians than they ever were with the Sassanid shahs.

In summing up the Parthian achievement, there are two significant points I would like to stress: First, they were remarkably versatile and successful for 400 years. They ruled Iran and the wider Middle East from horseback. They are very, very difficult to fit in the current national histories. They were not Zoroastrians; they really were not Iranians; they were interlopers. But by a judicious combination of diplomacy vis-a-vis the Romans and the Kushans, by promoting the Silk Road through their domains, and coming to terms with the existing populations, they had ruled the first nomadic empire in the Near East from the steppes, and in so doing, unwittingly provided a model for the later and more successful nomads from the steppes, the Seljuq Turks.

Kushans, Sacae, and the Silk Road
Lecture 7

In this lecture, we'll look at two nomadic peoples: the Sacae and the Kushans. While the Parthian kings were conquering Iran and Mesopotamia, these peoples were moving to the east of them in Transoxiana and, ultimately, in India, and these migrations were extremely important. The Tocharians were driven west and smashed into the Sacae, who were dwelling in the valley of the Jaxartes in Ferghana. About 140 B.C., the Sacae then moved into Transoxiana and ultimately ended up in India. About a decade later the Tocharian speakers essentially followed the route of the Sacae and also arrived in India. These migrations led to the rise of important kingdoms in India and the great Kushan emperors.

The Sacae

- The **Sacae** were an Iranian-speaking people. Classical sources usually identify them with the Scythians. We have depictions of them as early as the reign of King Darius on the Behistun Rock. They undoubtedly had been dwelling on the central steppes since the early Iron Age, from about 900 to 600 B.C.

- Some of the Sacae had moved east and southeast. They settled in the southwestern corner of the Tarim Basin, particularly around the city of Khotan. The Sacae established a symbiosis with the cities of **Sogdiana** and **Bactria**, the two districts of Transoxiana in the ancient period.
  - The Sogdians, also an Iranian-speaking people, lived in towns and were engaged in farming. They inhabited an important city called Maracanda.

  - Bactria was at the south end of Transoxiana, in the upper valley of the Oxus River. It was densely populated, with cities and agriculture.

- These two areas were collectively called the **Upper Satrapies**. They came under the control of Alexander the Great in 329/328 B.C., and Alexander quickly learned that the only way to secure Transoxiana was to win the elites of the cities, the merchant princes. He also found that he could regulate the movement of the nomads but not stop it.
    - Alexander initially tried to set up fortifications on the Jaxartes. That would've prevented the Sacae from crossing over and engaging in trade with the cities and the agriculturalists of Transoxiana.

    - When those cities rebelled against Alexander, they called in their nomadic allies. This would be a common pattern in Transoxiana. Both Iranian-style cities and Greek cities needed contact with the steppes, particularly to obtain horses and camels.

- Somewhere around 145/140 B.C., this symbiosis fell apart. The Sacae were forced to leave their homes and migrate into Transoxiana. They probably came from several routes and disrupted the Bactrian kingdom along the way. They ended up on the borders of what is today southeastern Iran, the region of Sistan.

- These migrations were catastrophic for the Greek cities, which existed not only in Bactria but also in northern India, all tracing their origins back to colonies of Alexander the Great. Many of these cities fell to the Sacae. The Sacae are probably responsible for extinguishing the political legacy of Alexander the Great, but they embraced the Hellenistic culture.

- We have limited information about the Sacae, sometimes called Indo-Sacae or Indo-Scythians. We have a number of coins that bear a strange mixture of both Greek and Indian elements in their iconography. One of the most important kings we know from the coins is **Azes**, who ruled from perhaps from 57 B.C. to around 30 B.C.

Tocharian Speakers

- The **Kushans**, Tocharian speakers, are first discussed in Chinese sources and eventually moved west. They were noticed by Greek sources and discussed in Buddhist sources, particularly their greatest emperor **Kanishka**, who ruled in the early 2nd century A.D. and was remembered as a convert to Buddhism.

- The nomadic peoples known as the Yuezhi were a people on the western borders of China, just above the Gansu corridor. They had been in early contact with China and had absorbed a great deal of Chinese civilization. They were perhaps behind the earliest trade from the Tarim Basin around Khotan to the early Shang emperors, then later, the Zhou Dynasty. They were still an important force in the time of the Han.

- These Tocharian speakers were quite formidable. Our diplomat from the emperor Wudi, Zhang Qian, finally contacted the Yuezhi in 128 B.C. and reported that they were a great power. A number of defeats had steadily driven these Tocharian speakers west, out of the orbit of China and essentially into Transoxiana. Once they showed up in Transoxiana, they pushed the Sacae south and southeast into India and into Transoxiana in eastern Iran.

- These Tocharians quickly took over the Greek cities of Bactria and began issuing coins. They embraced Hellenic culture and followed some of the same routes as the Sacae. They clearly were a confederation of five tribes, participating in some kind of partnership, with a rotating leader among the tribal rulers.

- One of these early rulers issued coins in the Greek style. The coins show a man clearly from the steppes, with evidence of the ritual deforming of the head as a child to result in a high forehead.

Sources on the Kushans

- Until recently, we were in the dark about how these nomads turned themselves into the Kushan emperors. But an unusual set of sources has come to our assistance. The key source is an important inscription found in 1993 near the site of **Rabatak**, a town in Afghanistan today.

o This monumental inscription was set up by the Kushan emperor Kanishka I. It provides us with a list of four important Kushan emperors: **Kujula Kadphises**, who ruled in the early 1st century A.D.; his son, **Vima Taktu**; another king known as **Vima Kadphises**; and finally, Kanishka himself. From other sources, we know that Kanishka's son was **Huvishka**.

o These emperors collectively stretched throughout most of the 1st and 2nd centuries A.D. They are contemporary with the Roman emperors from Tiberius to Marcus Aurelius.

o The inscription also tells us that Kanishka switched from the official language of Greek to an Aryan language, which could have been Bactrian, an Iranian language, or a vernacular of Sanskrit. This was the first conscious effort in the early 2nd century A.D. to create a Kushan Empire without dependence on Greek.

o Further, the inscription tells us that Kanishka set up images of his ancestors to worship and that the various ancient Iranian gods were invoked, particularly the goddess Nana.

• In addition to the inscription, we have a gallery of portraits of these emperors on stunning coins, particularly gold coins, which began to be issued in the reign of Vima Kadphises. The reverses of the coins show various gods and inscriptions. The coins dovetail with the inscription beautifully.

o The emperors are often depicted with halos and carrying ceremonial maces. Sometimes, they are shown in portrait; other times, as standing figures at sacrifice. The inscriptions are in both Greek and the Kharosthi script, which was used to write a vernacular of Sanskrit. Their titles are clearly those of great power and divinity.

o Interestingly, this greatness is proclaimed by rulers who are wearing traditional steppe nomadic costumes. They have clearly been exposed to Chinese civilization and are projecting themselves essentially as the nomadic version of the Son of Heaven.

o The coins also show an array of gods. One of the most frequently seen is Oesho, an old Iranian god. He's shown with the attributes of the Greek god Heracles, but he closely resembles Shiva. The Bactrian goddess Nana appears virtually as Tyche, the Greek goddess of good fortune. Some coins show seated figures who may be the Buddha.

- The coins and inscription together now allow us to get some sense of the boundaries that these five emperors ruled over.
  o Starting with the first emperor, Kujula Kadphises, the Kushans came over the Hindu Kush and began to conquer the Indus Valley. That was not finished until probably the end of the 1st century A.D.

  o By the time of Kanishka's reign in the early 2nd century A.D., the Kushan Empire extended from the Jaxartes and beyond to the cities of the Tarim Basin, across Transoxiana, Afghanistan, the Indus Valley, and most of the Ganges. This emperor ruled over a vast territory, including the cities on the middle Ganges where many of the important Buddhist sites were located.

The Kushan Emperors
- It is now clear that Kanishka, who was fondly remembered in Buddhist texts, built a state which was ultimately on par with the early **Mauryan Empire**, the empire of Ashoka. The Kushan Empire was an Indian empire plus parts of the central Asian steppes and Transoxiana. In some ways, it also anticipated the great empire of the **Mughal**.

- The Kushan emperors were also behind the development of the Silk Road, which became the first great international trade system. They

The relief work on the gates at Sanchi, carved in the period of the Kushan emperors, shows the Buddha depicted in human form for the first time.

controlled the middle portion of those routes that linked the Middle East and Rome with China. In so doing, they encouraged the development of cities and enabled the dissemination of Buddhism across the Silk Road, where it would become the second great cultural influence on the steppes after China.

- In addition, the Kushan emperors embraced the Greek arts, and under their auspices, the art of Gandhara developed. This is a composite of Indian and Greek traditions that produced the first great images of the Buddha, seen on the great gates of the stupa at Sanchi.

- Under the Kushans, Buddhism transformed itself into a universal religion and, in the process, won East Asia. Ironically, at the same time, the Kushans began to lose their homeland in India. The Kushan Empire fell to the Gupta emperors in the 4th century, who mounted a recovery of Hinduism.

Bactria: Today, northern Afghanistan. This is a fertile region of the upper Oxus River. Its principal city, Bactra, was the nexus of routes of the Silk Road between central Asia and India.

Kushans: Tocharian speakers who forged an empire embracing the central Asian steppes, Transoxania, and northern India (30–230). They promoted Buddhism and trade along the Silk Road.

Mauryan Empire: The first empire of India (322–185 B.C.), established by Chandra Gupta (320–298 B.C.). The emperor Ashoka (268–232 B.C.) converted to Buddhism.

Mughal Empire: The last Muslim empire (1526–1857) in India; established by Babur (1526–1530), a descendant of both Genghis Khan and Tamerlane.

Rabatak: The site in Afghanistan where a Kushan royal inscription in the Bactrian language was discovered in 1993. The Kushan emperor Kanishka I (127–147) gives his genealogy and names the tutelary gods of the empire.

Sacae: An eastern branch of the Scythians dwelling on the central Asian steppes. In 145–135 B.C., they migrated across Sogdiana and Bactria into the Helmand Valley, then via the Bolan Pass into India in the early 1st century B.C., where they were known as the Indo-Scythians.

Sogdiana: Lands of northern Transoxania and the Fergana Valley; the Sogdians spoke an eastern Iranian language that was long the commercial language of the Silk Road.

Upper Satrapies: The Greek designation of the satrapies of Bactria and Sogdiana (Transoxania) in the Achaemenid Empire of Persia (550–329 B.C.).

Azes I (c. 58–38 B.C.): Indo-Scythian king, conquered the Indus valley, and was remembered by Buddhists, who took his year of accession as the first year for reckoning by the Vikrama era.

Huvishka (147–180): Kushan emperor, succeeded Kanishka I. He consolidated Kushan rule in India and patronized Buddhism and the leading Hindu cults. His coinage reveals that he venerated all the gods of his empire.

Kanishka (127–140): Fourth Kushan emperor; revered as convert to Buddhism, although he was more likely a patron who promoted favorable conditions for the spread of Buddhism into central Asia and Han China. He is credited, anachronistically, by a later Buddhist tradition with summoning a Fourth Buddhist Council in 78.

Kujula Kadphises (30–80): Kushan emperor; crossed the Hindu Kush and conquered Taxila and Punjab. He forged a confederation of the Tocharian tribes in Bactria into a bureaucratic state. He is hailed in the Rabatak inscription as the founder of the Kushan royal family.

Vima Kadphises (105–127): Kushan emperor; received envoys from the Roman emperor Trajan. He extended Kushan domains in India and introduced gold coinage.

Vima Taktu (80–105): Kushan emperor; the son and successor of Kujula Kadphises. He is known from the Rabatak inscription and minted an extensive coinage but without the royal name.

Suggested Reading

Frye, *The Heritage of Central Asia from Antiquity to the Turkish Expansion.*

Gupta and Kulashreshtha, *Kuṣāna Coins and History.*

Hill, *Through the Jade Gate to Rome.*

Mallory and Mair, *The Tarim Mummies.*

Narain, "Indo-Europeans in Inner Asia."

Tarn, *The Greeks in India and Bactria.*

Questions to Consider

1. Why did the rise of the Xiongnu on the eastern Eurasian steppes in the 2nd century B.C. generate the first major migrations from east to west? What were the natures of these migrations? How did migrations change or create new identities?

2. Why did the Sacae migrate into India around 145 to 125 B.C.? What impact did they have on the cities of the Sind and Gandhara?

3. How did the Tocharian-speaking tribes known to the Chinese as the Yuezhi turns themselves into the imperial Kushans between the late 1st century B.C. and the early 1st century A.D.?

4. Why did the Kushan emperors pursue such generous policies to their diverse subjects? What accounted for the cultural diversity and changes in the Kushan Empire? How was Buddhism transformed from an Indian into a world religion?

Kushans, Sacae, and the Silk Road
Lecture 7—Transcript

In this lecture, I plan to look at two new nomadic peoples: The first are the Sacae; and the second are best known under the name Kushans, and they have a number of other names in Classical and Chinese sources.

We are going to have to recall that while the Parthian kings, the Arsacid kings of Parthia, were conquering Iran and Mesopotamia, there were movements to the east of them in Transoxiana and ultimately in India and they were conducted by these two contemporary nomadic peoples. The migrations of the Sacae and the Tocharians prove to be extremely important. For one, it is the first of what I like to call a domino effect; that is, the Tocharian speakers who were known in Chinese sources as the Yuezhi or the Yuzechi, they use both terms, were driven west having been defeated in the mid-second century B.C. They smashed into the Sacae, who were dwelling more or less in the valley of the Jaxartes, in Ferghana; and the Sacae then moved about 140 B.C. into Transoxiana and ultimately ended up in India. Then about a decade later, these Tocharian speakers essentially followed the route of the Sacae and they too will ultimately end up in India. This is a pattern that will repeat itself. Later we will see that with the Huns, the Hephthalites, various Turkish tribes, the Kara Khitans; it is the changes of the political dynamics between the Chinese Empire and nomads on the eastern steppes that will invariably have repercussions sending peoples west.

The other important point about these migrations: It led to the rise of important kingdoms in India, particularly the second migration, the great Kushan emperors; and that will have profound consequences for Buddhism and also the emergence of the Silk Road, two subjects we will be talking about later in this course. First, let us take a look at the Sacae. They entered into our urban literate civilization sooner than the Tocharian speakers. The Sacae are an Iranian-speaking people. Classical sources usually identify them with the Scythians. We have depictions of them as early as the reign of King Darius, the great Persian emperor who set up the Behistun Rock where the Sacae are shown being brought into submission. They undoubtedly had been dwelling on the Central Steppes since the early Iron Age; let us say from about 900–600 B.C. Some of these Sacae had moved east and southeast. We know that some entered the Tarim Basin. They settled in the regions of the southwestern corner of the Tarim Basin, particularly around the city of Khotan; and much later documents prove there was an east Iranian language being spoken there as well as Tocharian. The DNA testing of Tarim Basin mummies have shown there was probably an Iranian component in the population; we discussed that evidence earlier where the very early mummies seem to point to Indo-European speakers coming from the west. Furthermore, these Sacae, being nomads, were very, very adept at horseback riding and may well have been involved in the early domestication of the Bactrian camel—that is, the two-humped camel—that becomes so important in the trade of the Silk Road; again a subject coming up in a future lecture.

The Sacae established a symbiosis with the cities of Sogdia and Bactria. Those are the two districts of Transoxiana in the ancient period; and they are essentially the north and the south sections of Transoxiana. The Sogdians— they were also an Iranian-speaking people—lived in towns, particularly oasis towns. They were engaged in farming. They inhabited an important city called Maracanda, which is the predecessor but not identical to later Samarkand. Bactria was at the south end of Transoxiana. It was the upper valley of the Oxus River. It was heavily, densely populated with cities and agriculture. These two areas were collectively called the Upper Satrapies. They came under the control of Alexander the Great in 329–328 B.C., and Alexander quickly had to learn—as the previous Persian kings learned and as later Arab emirs who were trying to run this area in the eighth and ninth centuries learned—that the only way to secure Transoxiana is to win the elites of the cities, merchant princes; and also, you cannot set up a frontier barrier. You can regulate the movement of the nomads; you cannot stop it. Alexander initially tried to set up fortifications on the Jaxartes. That would have prevented the Sacae from crossing over and engaging in the typical trade with the cities and the agriculturalists of Transoxiana; it just destroyed the pattern. When those cities rebelled against Alex, they called in their nomadic allies. Again, this is a common pattern in Transoxiana. Starting in the antiquity and really running down through the Mongol period and beyond, the caravan cities of Transoxiana were in close association with the nomads on the Central Steppes; and the relationship between Alexander and these Sacae underscore it.

I discussed earlier that Alexander's empire broke up, that a general of his called Seleucus took over the eastern domains; and then in 250 B.C., a governor of this Seleucid Empire—that is, the descendants of the General Seleucus—usurped power in the Upper Satrapies. He is known as Diodotus; he was a Greek. He styled himself as a king at Bactra. That is the city of Balkh today; it is the capital of Bactria. Bactria is the country; Bactra is the capital city on the Oxus. He ruled as a Hellenistic king in the fashion of the great kings such as the Ptolemies, known through Cleopatra of Antony and Cleopatra fame, and the Seleucids in the west, and lesser dynasts. We know about these Greek kings largely through their coins and just snippets of information from the Greek historians. However, what is clear, especially from archeology, is there were a number of Greek-style cities in Bactria; and then in Sogdiana—that is, the northern section of Transoxiana, places such as Maracanda—the Sogdian merchant princes held sway.

Whether they were Sogdian—that is, Iranian-style cities—or Greek cities, they needed contact with the steppes; they needed the interaction with those Sacae. The Sacae were selling them horses and camels. We have on Greco-Bactrian coins beautiful examples of the horses of Ferghana. Those are the horses that are known in Chinese sources as the heavenly horses that sweat blood. They later become the objective of a number of important Chinese diplomatic and military efforts. These horses are depicted on the coins of several Greco-Bactrian kings, and they are the steeds upon which the Dioskouri, Caster and Pollux, are riding. They are unmistakably the same horses; the horses that are also depicted in Tang art. This was probably a major lucrative trade between the Sacae and the Greco-Bactrian kings.

Somewhere around 145–140 B.C., this whole symbiosis fell apart. The Sacae were suddenly forced to quit their homes and they migrated into Transoxiana. They probably came from several routes. There is speculation one group came directly over the Hindu Kush through the Khyber Pass. Another group clearly swung around in a wide arc, crossing the Jaxartes, disrupting the Bactrian kingdom; probably sacking cities, destroying agricultural fields. They ended up on the borders of what is today southeastern Iran, the region of Sistan (actually, it takes its name from the Sacae), Baluchestan. They made their way up to Kandahar, crossed the Bolan Pass, and descended into the Indus Valley.

These migrations were a catastrophe for the Greek cities. There were Greek cities at this point not only in Bactria, but also in northern India; these all trace their origins back to colonies of Alexander the Great. Many of these cities fell to the Sacae. The Sacae are probably responsible for extinguishing the political legacy of Alexander the Great. On the other hand, they embraced the Hellenistic culture a great deal; and as we shall see, their successors, the people who followed them—that is, the Kushans—the people who put them in motion in the first place, these Tocharian speakers, they would take the same route. They would be very, very favorable to the Hellenic arts and letters and aesthetics.

We have limited information about these Sacae. Sometimes they are called Indo-Sacae or Indo-Scythians. We do have a number of coins, and the coins are a strange mixture of both Greek and Indian elements in their iconography. One of the most important kings we know from his coins is Azes. He ruled perhaps from 57 B.C. somewhere down to around 30 B.C.; and actually his accession date is still remembered today in many Buddhist communities because it is used as the date of reckoning. It is known as the Vikrama Era, or sometimes just the Sacae Era. Undoubtedly, the Sacae had a big impression on the Buddhist community in India.

Let us turn to the fellows who were pushing the Sacae into Transoxiana and India; and that takes us to one of the most remarkable of the early empires of the steppes, the Kushans. It is remarkable for several reasons because in order to reconstruct it, we have to use a bizarre range of sources. As we look at the Kushans, we are going to start on the confines of the Chinese Empire, in the extreme western ends of the Chinese Empire. These Tocharian speakers are first being discussed in Chinese sources, and eventually they are going to move west; they get noticed by the Greek sources, and they end up essentially being discussed in Buddhist sources, particularly their greatest emperor Kanishka, who ruled in the early second century A.D. and was remembered as a convert to Buddhism.

The best guess is—it is not a guess anymore; it is now pretty conclusively accepted in an earlier academic literature, and we will find out in a moment why it was not so certain—the nomadic peoples known as the Yuezhi or the Yuzechi (both forms are found) were a people on the western borders of

China; they were just above the Gansu corridor. They had been very early contact with China and had absorbed a great deal of Chinese civilizations. It is speculated that these people were perhaps behind the earliest trade, especially in jade, from the Tarim Basin around Khotan to the early Shang emperors, then later the Zhou Dynasty. They were still an important force in the time of the Han. As you will recall, the Han is really the first great Chinese empire. [...] The Han Empire is looked upon as the epitome of the first great early Chinese empire. These Tocharian speakers were very, very formidable. Our diplomat from the Emperor Wudi, Zhang Qian, made his way to these people, the Yuezhi. He finally contacted them in 128 B.C. after about 10 years with his Xiongnu wife, and he reports to us that these are a great power; they have 100,000–200,000 horse archers. That was why the emperor Wudi was interested in courting these guys: He wanted to use them as allies against the Xiongnu, and with good reason. When Zhang Qian contacted these Tocharian speakers, they were dwelling in Ferghana. They had gone very, very far west; and the reason for that is the Xiongnu had pushed them there. Modu Chanyu, the great organizer of the Xiongnu confederacy, had it in for these rivals. He is known to have defeated them; he turned the head of his defeated Yuezhi opponent into a goblet. There were a number of defeats that steadily drove these Tocharian speakers west out of the orbit of China and essentially into Transoxiana. Once these people showed up in Transoxiana, they then pushed the Sacae south and southeast into India and into Transoxiana in eastern Iran; your domino effect.

I mentioned that once these people got there—and we can now start calling them the Tócharoi, because they now come into the view of Greek sources or Tocharians, the term that links them to those later Buddhist texts in the Tarim Basin—these Tocharians very, very quickly took over the Greek cities of Bactria. They began issuing coins, they embraced a lot of the Hellenic culture, and they followed some of the same route as the Sacae. We have some information about them: They clearly were a confederation of some five tribes, and these tribes had some kind of partnership in which there was a rotating, essentially chairman of the board among the tribal rulers. They probably held a title equivalent to the later Turkish title, Yabgu. The Greeks translate that title apparently as "tyrant," *tyrannos*. It is a title that loosely means "prince"; it is not really a royal title. One of these early rulers issued coins in the Greek style; his name is Aureus in Greek. The coins are in

Greek, and it shows a man clearly from the steppes. He actually shows this ritual deforming of the head as a child to give you a high forehead from the portrait. This is later reported to be done by the Huns and various Turkish peoples, and confirms that these Tocharians are clearly steppe nomadic peoples who entered into Transoxiana (that is, Bactria).

Up until recently, we were really in the dark how these nomads turned themselves into the Kushan emperors. Here we got an unusual set of sources that have come to our assistance, because up until this time we depended on very, very limited sources. The key source in this is an important inscription that was found in 1993. It was found near the site of Rabatak. Rabatak is a town in Afghanistan today; it is on an old trade route to India. It is a monumental inscription—it weighs something like half a ton—and it is currently in the Kabul Museum. This inscription was set up by the Kushan emperor Kanishka I, the great emperor regarded as a convert to Buddhism. In it—the document is very, very important—it gives us a list of the Kushan emperors; Kanishka names his successors. In this list, there are four important emperor's names: The first is Kujula Kadphises, who ruled in the early first century A.D.; then the man who is his son, a man that we were not quite sure of before until we got this inscription, his name is Vima Taktu; then another king known as Vima Kadphises; and finally, Kanishka himself. From other sources, we know that Kanishka's son is Huvishka, who followed. All of a sudden we have a sequence of five emperors, and from what we can tell this is a succession from father to son. These emperors collectively stretched from most of the first and second centuries A.D. They are contemporary with the Roman emperors from Tiberius to Marcus Aurelius; they had very long reigns.

The inscription is informative in other ways. It tells us, for instance, that Kanishka switched from the official language of Greek to an Aryan language, by which he might mean Bactrian, an Iranian language; some have speculated maybe a vernacular of Sanskrit. But whatever it is, this was the first conscious effort in the early second century A.D. to create a more Kushan Empire without depending on Greek. Furthermore, the inscription tells us that Kanishka set up images to his ancestors to worship; that the various ancient Iranian gods were invoked, particularly the goddess Nana. This is a revelation, because if you depended just on the Buddhist text you would think that these emperors were strict Buddhists, and they are clearly not. The inscription proved a very, very important discovery. It was not translated until a couple years later. It is in the Kabul Museum and there are really a lot of fears about what might happen to it in the fighting going on there right now.

In addition to the inscription, and the inscription really becomes our baseline, we have a gallery of portraits of these emperors on stunning coins, particularly gold coins—they started issuing gold coins in the reign of Vima Kadphises—and the coins are marvelous because they now match up with the inscription. We know the sequence of these emperors, and what the coins give us are a portrait gallery of Kushan emperors; and you have to realize, we have very little other sources about these men. In addition, the reverses of the coins carry various gods and inscriptions.

The coins are very, very revealing and they dovetail with that inscription beautifully. For one, looking at how these emperors depict themselves: They are very often with halos. They are carrying ceremonial maces. Sometimes they are portraits; sometimes they are standing figures at sacrifice. The inscriptions are in both Greek and the so-called Kharosthi script, which is used to write a vernacular of Sanskrit; they are bilingual inscriptions. The titles are clearly titles of great power and divinity. In Greek, they are mega, *soter*, great, powerful, savior. Some of the titles look very much like the titles of the great Iranian kings, the Persian kings, King of Kings. Others clearly show indications of familiarity with the cults of Shiva, the great god of the Hindus. All of this is being proclaimed by rulers who are wearing traditional steppe nomadic costumes—that is, the leather breeches; they sometimes carry the felt caps of the steppes—and they clearly represent a group of nomadic conquerors who have been exposed to Chinese civilization; they are projecting themselves essentially as the nomadic version of the Son of Heaven, the Chinese emperor. They have picked up notions from the Hellenistic world; they have come into contact with early Iranian cults as well as cults of Hinduism.

On the reverse, we see the same group of images; and this is seen in the divinities that the emperors choose to venerate on their coins. It is a wide array of gods. None of these emperors—even Kanishka who is very, very well remembered in the Buddhist tradition—was a strict Buddhist and simply followed Dharma, The Way, and nothing else. There's a wonderful coin, particularly of the last of those five rulers, Huvishka. He ruled in the middle to late second century A.D.; the dates are not really that well known. He is shown mounted on an elephant in full regalia like a Hindu prince, and the iconography suggests he was making a royal progress, the *dig-vi-jaya* in later Hindu tradition, in which he moves among the four corners of the world, summoning his vassals in a great show of pageantry. In addition, there is quite an array of gods. One of the most frequent ones found on the coins is Oesho, an old Iranian god. He is clearly shown with the attributes of the Greek god Heracles, Hercules to the Romans, but also he is almost a dead ringer for Shiva. He is shown with four arms; he has the bull as his vehicle (that would be Nandi in the Hindu tradition). The Bactrian goddess, I mentioned Nana; she is worshipped in the inscription. She appears virtually as a Greek goddess, Tyche, the goddess of good fortune. There are some coins that suggest that there are seated figures who may be the Buddha. Clearly, there is an array of gods well known from Persian texts such as Mithra, gods such as Hermes and Heracles from the Greek tradition. It is a medley of divinities in the Kushan pantheon.

This, too, is a feature of the steppe nomads; I have mentioned it in passing, but it will be particularly relevant to the Mongol period. Nomadic conquerors were very, very pragmatic about the gods. Any holy man, any mystic, any individual who had contact with the other powers, it was worth listening to him or her. These could be sorceresses; these could be the equivalent of Greek Pythias; they were shamans on the steppes. That meant all of the gods were venerated; all of the gods were seen as a contact to the divine. Nomadic conquerors were unusually tolerant of the different faiths within their multinational empires, and so you do not get on the iconography of the coin nearly the same kind of strict iconography you will get from their successors; that is, the two states that partition this Kushan Empire in the fourth century: the resurgent Iranian Empire under the Sassanid shahs who are strict Zoroastrians and that is all you get on their iconography, or in India the great Gupta emperors who essentially are mounting a comeback for the Hindu cults.

The coins and the inscription together also now allow us to draw a map and really get some sense of the boundaries that these five emperors ruled over. Starting with the first emperor, Kujula Kadphises, the Kushans came over the Hindu Kush and began to conquer the Indus Valley; and that was not finished until probably the end of the first century A.D. By the time of Kanishka's reign in the early second century A.D., the Kushan Empire extended from the Jaxartes, even beyond on the steppes, on the cities of the Tarim Basin, across Transoxiana, Afghanistan, the Indus Valley, most of the Ganges; and this emperor ruled over a vast territory, including the areas that were the cradle of Buddhism: the very, very important cities on the middle Ganges where many of the important Buddhist sites were located, particularly Sarnath, where the Buddha himself had had his enlightenment. This has been quite a revelation. It has been gained by the distribution of coins—that is, where are they found—as well as the information from the inscription that names very, very specific Indian cities that are under the control of the Kushan emperor.

That gets us perhaps to the most important aspect about this empire; and that is whatever these Kushan emperors were like—and we really do not have the literary sources that make these men come to life; we have wonderful portraits of them, we can surmise how they projected themselves, we have this marvelous inscription that is an insight into their religious beliefs, but who they are as personalities and individuals such as Attila the Hun or later Genghis Khan, the information is not there—there are two important activities that these kings clearly carried out. It is also now clear that Kanishka, who was very fondly remembered in the Buddhist text, was even credited with summoning a Buddhist counsel to try to work out the issues of dogma, that these emperors built a state that is now recognized as on par with the early Mauryan Empire—the empire of Ashoka, which is regarded as the first empire of India—and then the successor state known as the Gupta. The Kushan Empire was an Indian empire plus parts of Central Asian steppes and Transoxiana. In some ways, it also anticipates the great empire of the Mughals, which will come much later in the course; the final summation of the Muslim imperial tradition in India. This is a revelation to us. Much of what we knew about the Kushans had been very, very speculative up until the 1990s. Reconstructing the success of this nomadic empire is really a triumph of archeology, numismatics, philology, all of those specialized fields and culling information from a wide variety of literary sources.

Two points are clear: The Kushan emperors, given their origin, promoted what becomes the Silk Road, especially that spur that leads into India. They are behind the development of the Silk Road that becomes the first great international trade system; we will be talking about that in a separate lecture. They control really the middle portion of those routes that link the Middle East and Rome with China. In so doing, they encourage the development of cities; and it is in those cities where Buddhist monks began to translate the scriptures from Sanskrit into the vernacular languages. It enabled the dissemination of Buddhism across the Silk Road, where it would become the second great cultural influence on the steppes (the first, of course, being China).

In addition to that, the Kushan emperors embraced all of those Greek arts. They ruled in the city of Taxila, which was a Greek-style city. They clearly had winter residences in Bactra; that is, former cities of the Greco-Bactrian kings. They sponsored a great deal of marvelous art: the art of Gandhara, very well known to art historians in northern India. It is a composite of Indian traditions and Greek traditions; it brings in Greek naturalism with the Indian traditions of sculpture and produces the first great images of the Buddha. This is occurring under the auspices of the Kushan emperors. How much they were involved in it we do not know; but clearly this work was going on in the very capitals, winter palaces, and cities of the Kushan state.

The Kushans clearly favored Buddhism. They may not have embraced it, but they were very great patrons. This has been borne out not only by the evidence of some of the coins, which may sometimes be interpreted as having Buddhist symbolism, but particularly at the great monastery complex at Sanchi. Sanchi is perhaps one of the earliest Buddhist sites in India. It is a great monastery going back to Ashoka's day. There is a stupa, and the stupa is much earlier; but in the first century A.D., in the period of the Kushan emperors, there are these great gates, *toranas*, which are built. On those gates is marvelous relief work of the incidents of the life of the Buddha; and for the first time, the Buddha is now depicted in human form. This is an influence from the Greek artistic traditions merging with the Indian, creating a new iconography for Buddhism of the greater vehicle; that is, the Buddhism destined to win the loyalties of so many peoples in Transoxiana and Central Asia. Significantly, there is an inscription from Sanchi that praises Kanishka for his donations. The connections are real; they are not imagined. The Kushan emperors really stood behind Buddhism as one of the great faiths of their empire, and that is why Kanishka was regarded so fondly by later Buddhist writers.

In that perhaps is the greatest tradition of the Kushan legacy: Buddhism. Under their auspices, Buddhism transformed itself into a universal religion, and in the process won East Asia. Ironically, at the same time they start losing their homeland, India; for the Kushan Empire in India fell to the Gupta emperors in the fourth century. The Gupta emperors not only ended Kushan rule, but they also mounted a recovery of Hinduism.

Rome and the Sarmatians
Lecture 8

In this lecture, we'll look at a group of people known as the Sarmatians. They were Iranian speakers, remote kinsmen to the Parthians and the Sacae; however, they operated on the steppes immediately to the west. They came to dominate the Pontic-Caspian steppes, which was the original homeland of the Indo-European speakers. These Sarmatians appear in classical sources starting in the beginning of the 2nd century B.C. Later, they controlled important trade from the Baltic to the Black Sea. Even more so than the Scythians, the Sarmatians were prized as mercenaries.

The Sarmatians in the Southwestern Steppes

- The **Sarmatians** originally dwelled in the lands to the east of the Ural Mountains, that is, the steppes north of the Caspian and Aral seas. They moved into the important corridor stretching from the northern shores of the Caspian to the Aral Sea and the upper Jaxartes, probably in response to local circumstances, such as the need for pastures, severe droughts, and clashes with neighboring tribes.

- The region occupied by the Sarmatians is what we today call the southwestern steppes. On its southern borders is the Black Sea. To the north stretch the great forest zones of Russia, leading to the Baltic. Not only was this area ideal for stock raising, but it also encompassed the great river systems of the Volga, the Don, the Dnieper, the Dniester, and the Bug.

- The Sarmatians came to control trade going from the Baltic to the Black Sea or the Caspian Sea. They exploited the transit of this trade by taxing and levying customs on it, by providing protection, and by offering markets themselves. All the products of the forest came through essentially Sarmatian domains and headed to the Greek ports on the Black Sea, particularly the cities of the Crimea.

- The Sarmatians were prized as soldiers, especially as mercenaries, even more so than the Scythians. We have a number of reports of Sarmatian mercenaries being hired in Hellenistic and even Roman armies. As a result of mercenary service, many Sarmatians intermarried with Greek or Greek-speaking populations and brought back a taste of goods from the Mediterranean world. This taste, of course, fueled additional trade.

- After 100 B.C., the Sarmatians began to move out of the Pontic-Caspian steppes. We know them from several different tribes that are offshoots of the Sarmatians and are recognized as independent groups in Greek and Roman sources. Among these are the **Jazyges**, the **Roxolani**, and the **Alani**.

- The first two groups traveled westward and southwestward, moving into the region known today known as the Dobruja, which is the delta of the Danube, a heavy marsh area that's attractive for nomads herding their animals during the winter. They also occupied eastern Hungary and the Hungarian plains. The Sarmatians were essentially looking for new grasslands and new areas to exploit. Undoubtedly, they subjected and assimilated preexisting populations.

Military Technology and Tactics

- The Roxolani and the Jazyges came into contact with central European cultures, including the Dacians, who dominated most of what is today eastern Romania and the Carpathian Mountains. They also came into contact with Celts and, eventually, Germanic peoples. As a result, there was a great deal of trade and intermarriage, and the Sarmatians gained an enormous of amount of metal technology. The Sarmatian aristocracy amassed great wealth, with which they acquired horses and arms.

- By the time of the emperor Trajan (98–117 A.D.), the Sarmatian tribes that bordered on the Danube provinces had long been in contact with Romans and the Germanic peoples of central Europe. Reliefs from this era show that the Sarmatians still depended on the mounted horse archer.

Roman reliefs, such as those on Trajan's Column, offer a number of depictions of Sarmatian cavalry.

- o Sarmatian forces were likely 90 percent cavalry, with a significant 10 percent heavy cavalry.

- o They wore heavy **lamellar armor**, that is, armor with overlapping sets of scales, and were called by the Greeks and Romans *cataphracti*. They also wore distinct conical helmets.

- Steppe cavalry armies were no longer just horse archers. They probably started with an attack by horse archers, but they also carried well-mounted *cataphracts*, that is, lancers who could enter a melee and destroy the enemy close up.

- In any Sarmatian cavalry force, out of 10,000 cavalry, enemies could expect to encounter some 1,000 to 2,000 heavily armed *cataphracti*. In fact, the Romans themselves, starting in the 2nd century A.D., mounted such cavalry and hired Sarmatians as Roman auxiliary units.

- The Sarmatians also had an effective system of regimental commands. The Romans tell us that Sarmatians went into battle in military units distinctly designated by such symbols as inflated leather dragons, or *dracones*. These dragons were ultimately of Chinese origin and were used by the Sarmatians to spur troops into battle.

- We have an unusually good tactical manual by a man named **Arrian** that deals with a group of Sarmatians who attacked into Roman Asia Minor, or Anatolia.
  - Arrian commanded a force of about 11,500 legionaries and assorted auxiliary units. He had with him some 5,000 cavalry. He records a detailed order of march and explains how the battle line was drawn up, with legionaries in the center, supported by wings of advanced auxiliary infantry with many archers. The back two lines were archers, infantry, and horse archers shooting over the infantry as a barrage.

  - The Roman cavalry was held in reserve, and the idea was to draw in the nomadic cavalry and punish it with the fire of the infantry archers. When the nomads closed, the Roman cavalry would charge out, encircle, and destroy them. Such tactics required remarkable discipline and perfect timing, but it was the only response that an army from an urban civilization could come up with to gain any kind of tactical advantage against the nomadic cavalry.

Sarmatians and Romans

- On the upper and lower Danube, the Sarmatian tribes essentially became Roman allies. The Romans understood that in order to patrol these frontiers, they had to control trade routes and access, and they had to regulate settlement and the use of pasture lands within the Roman world. They did not try to draw a Maginot Line but, instead, built a set of highways and fortified blocks to regulate the flow of barbarians over the frontier.
  - The tombstone of a Roman governor of the province of Moesia, **Tiberius Plautius Aelianus**, relates how he broke

up an attack by the Roxolani and took measures to secure the province thereafter.

- o He took hostages from the barbarians north of the Danube and selectively settled 100,000 of these people as colonists. Some Dacians and probably some Germanic peoples were also scattered through the provinces to relieve the pressure that would cause them to migrate.

- o This sensible policy was pursued for the next 200 years along the Roman frontiers.

- The Alans seem to have migrated out of the Pontic-Caspian steppe region into the Kuban and the grasslands just north of the Caucasus. They proved to be a common foe to both the Romans and the Parthians.

- o We have a number of reports of Alan attacks; a famous one in 72 A.D. was recorded by Josephus, in which perhaps 10,000 or 20,000 Alans crossed over into the Caucasus and raided across Mesopotamia.

- o The passes through the Caucasus became extremely important, and the Romans and Partians came to some kind of agreement over Armenia, in part to ensure that the routes leading over the Caucasus and into Armenia were monitored and regulated as early warning signals for attacks of Alans and other nomadic peoples.

- The Sarmatians, well-armed and with excellent trade routes, became addicted to Roman goods and never acquired the kind of great leader who could weld the various tribes into an effective confederation. The Sarmatian tribes never gained much of a political sense of how to organize themselves against the Romans.

- In part, this is explained by the fact that the Romans never dealt with barbarians in the same way that other peoples did. The Roman emperor was a military dictator who represented a republic, and he was still a magistrate. The idea of sending princesses to marry Sarmatian rulers, as the Chinese had sent to the Xiongnu, was impossible under Roman law. Thus, there was never the same kind of political exchange between Rome and the Sarmatians that would allow the Sarmatian tribes to learn the political institutions and organization that other nomadic tribes did by exposure to the Chinese or Persian empires. The tribes remained divided.

- In the 3rd century A.D., a people from Scandinavia, the Goths, left their home in Scandinavia. They traveled the trade routes onto the Pontic-Caspian steppes, and starting from about 235 to 250 A.D., began to raid and attack the Roman Empire. They subjected the Sarmatian peoples, turning them into clients and allies. They learned horse-riding techniques from the Sarmatians and set up a loose confederacy on the Pontic-Caspian steppes, but the Goths, too, never managed to establish an effective political organization. They were driven back in the 3rd century and remained in a loose Roman alliance down to the arrival of the Huns in 375.

- The Roman experience with Sarmatian tribes seems to have led the Romans to a sense of complacency and self-satisfaction. These tribes were relatively easy to divide and conquer and to manipulate into following traditional Roman policies; the Romans merely had to regulate their trade. When a serious threat came off the steppes in the 370s from the east, Rome didn't know how to handle a great steppe confederacy. That situation would contribute directly to the breakup of the western Roman Empire in the 5th century A.D.

Important Terms

Alani: Sarmatians who settled on the steppes north of the Caucasus in the 1st century B.C. In A.D. 375, many Alani submitted to the Huns, while others, along with Goths, migrated west. The Alani entered the Roman Empire as allies of the Vandals in 406–407.

cataphracti: Heavily armored shock cavalry wearing chain mail or lamellar armor. This heavy cavalry, first attested among the Sarmatians, was adopted by the Romans during the reign of Hadrian (117–138).

Jazyges: Sarmatians who settled as allies of Rome on the eastern Pannonian grasslands west of Dacia in the mid-1st century.

lamellar armor: Armor of overlapping plates sewed together and often worn as a second layer of protection over chain mail armor.

Roxolani: Sarmatians who settled on the grasslands between the Carpathian Mountains and the Black Sea in the 1st century.

Sarmatians: Iranian-speaking nomads who succeeded the Scythians on the Pontic-Caspian steppes between the 3rd century B.C. and the 3rd century A.D. The tribes included the Alani, Roxolani, and Jazyges.

Names to Know

Arrian (Lucius Flavius Arrianus) (86–160): Native of Nicomedia (Izmit); a Roman senator and historian who composed a history of Alexander the Great. He also wrote a treatise of his battle line against the Alani in 135, when he was governor of Galatia-Cappadocia.

Plautius Silvanus Aelianus, Tiberius (c. 15–85): Roman senator and consul (45 and 74) of patrician lineage. As legate of Moesia in 66–67, he repelled Sarmatian attacks against the Greek cities and secured the lower Danube against nomadic invaders.

Suggested Reading

Agusti, *Sources on the Alans*.

Bachrach, *A History of the Alans in the West*.

Burns, *A History of the Ostrogoths*.

Goldsworthy, *The Roman Army at War, 100 B.C.–A.D. 200*.

Lecture 8: Rome and the Sarmatians

Frye, *The Heritage of Central Asia.*

Melyukova, "The Scythians and Sarmatians."

Rice, "The Scytho-Sarmatian Tribes of South-Eastern Europe."

1. In what ways did the Sarmatians differ in their political organization and effectiveness from the Scythians or Xiongnu? What might have accounted for the failure of the emergence of a powerful confederation?

2. What were the routes and possible reasons for migrations of the Sarmatians westward? How did these migrations transform and create distinct tribal entities for the Alans, Roxolani, and Jazyges?

3. How did trade with Rome, Dacia, and the Germanic peoples transform Sarmartian society? What accounts for the less imposing kurgan and grave goods from the Sarmartian period? Does this archaeological record necessarily document an economic decline or, rather, a change in social practices and religious outlook?

4. How did the Roman imperial army respond to the threat of Sarmatian horse archers? How formidable were the *cataphracti*? Why was the order of battle adopted by Arrian against the Alans so effective? What frontier policies did Rome adopt vis-á-vis the Sarmatians?

Rome and the Sarmatians

Lecture 8—Transcript

In this lecture, I want to deal with a group of people known as the Sarmatians. They are Iranian speakers; remote kinsmen to the Parthians and the Sacae; however, they are operating on the steppes immediately to the west and they come to dominate the Pontic-Caspian steppes, which was the original homeland of the Indo-European speakers.

These Sarmatians appear in Classical sources starting end of the third, beginning of the second century B.C.; and so they are contemporaries with the Sacae, those Tocharians who eventually become the Kushan emperors, and the Parthians. But as I noted, they were originally dwelling in the lands to the east of the Ural Mountains; that is, the steppes north of the Caspian and Aral Seas. They seem to have connections with tribes that had some kind of contact with the Chinese Empire. When we discuss several of the tribes that are known from Classical sources, notably the Alans, it will be evident that there is some kind of connection with China. We are not sure whether these tribes in remote times were members of the Xiongnu confederacy, whether they had ancestors that once bordered on the western and northwestern frontiers of China, but there has been a lot of learned scholarship to try to connect the two. More significantly and immediately, they move into this homeland, probably due to local circumstances: The need for pastures, severe droughts, clashes and blood feuds with neighboring tribes brought the Sarmatians to occupy this very important corridor stretching from essentially the northern shores of the Caspian over to the Aral Sea and the Upper Jaxartes. That area is an important corridor that will link the western steppes to the central steppes and eastern steppes; and the Sarmatians are on that nexus of routes in, say, 300 B.C.

From there, they decide to migrate west. Exactly why, we are not sure; we have no real written records on this. Some have tried to connect them with the Sauromatae; those are a tribe that is known to be vassals in the fifth century B.C. to the Scythians, they are mentioned in Herodotus. But whatever happens, somewhere around 300 B.C. the Sarmatians begin to move west and eventually cross the Volga and enter into that Pontic-Caspian steppe zone; that region that stretches from the Dniester River to the Volga.

Today, we actually call that the southwestern steppes. On the southern borders of it is the Black Sea; to the north stretch the great forest zones of Russia, which then lead to the Baltic. As I noted, the Sarmatians move into not only an ideal area for their stock raising, but also the great river systems of the Volga, the Don, the Dneiper, the Dniester, the Bug; all of these great river systems that flow from north to south across the steppes and link the Caspian and Black Sea by trade routes to the Baltic.

The Sarmatians, just as their predecessors the Scythians, come to control that important trade that goes from the Baltic to the Black Sea, or to the Caspian Sea if it is coming down the Volga River; and they, too, exploit the transit of this trade by taxing and levying customs on it, by providing protection, by offering a market themselves, setting up market towns and settlements. Therefore, all the products of the forest—the great amber prized in Classical sources; the goods from the Arctic—would have to come through essentially Sarmatian domains and would head to the Greek ports on the Black Sea, particularly the cities of the Crimea, which the Greeks called the Tauric Chersonesus. Those Greek cities will flourish through the Roman Empire really into the early Byzantine age.

Another important aspect about the Sarmatians is they are prized as soldiers, especially as mercenaries, even more so than the Scythians; and we have a number of reports of Sarmatian mercenaries being hired in Hellenistic and even Roman armies. In the great clash between Mithridates VI of Pontus, who ruled in Eastern Asia Minor, and the proconsul Lucius Licinius Lucullus, both sides recruited Sarmatian *cataphracti*—these are heavily armored cavalrymen, quite distinct from the horse archers; we will get into in a moment why the Sarmatians are able to do this—and so the Sarmatians become a military force. As a result of mercenary service, many Sarmatians go into Greek towns; they serve in the wider Hellenistic world; they intermarry with Greek or Greek-speaking populations; and they bring back a taste of goods from the Mediterranean world. This taste, of course, fuels the trade.

Another item that is big and something that the Scythians undoubtedly engaged in—we have a lot of evidence from the Roman period—is in the slave trade. Slaves are excess population, sold on the ports of the Greek cities; and this will become a tradition henceforth on these steppes of selling slaves, labor, and in the Muslim world soldiers off the Pontic-Caspian steppes into the wider Middle East and Mediterranean world. That is another important feature of the trade developed by these Sarmatians.

The Sarmatians after 100 B.C. begin to move out of that Caspian-Pontic steppe region, or the Pontic-Caspian steppes as I have been calling them. We know them from several different tribes. These are offshoots of the Sarmatians and they are recognized as independent groups in Greek and Roman sources. One of them is the Iazgyes or Iazgyes—that Latin "I" is pronounced as a "J"; that initial "I" is really a consonant in Latin—and the other is the Roxolani. A third group is the Alans; we will discuss them in a moment. The first two groups, they move westward and southwestward. This is a natural route to follow; we will see that a number of steppe nomadic peoples in the Middle Ages will follow those routes. They leave the south Russian steppes; they move into the region today known as the Dobruja, which is the delta of the Danube, a heavy marsh area that is very, very attractive for nomads to herd their animals during the winter; also the regions today that are Eastern Hungary, especially the traditional region of Wallachia, very good grasslands there. Another zone they move into is the Hungarian plains, or as the Romans would call it the Pannonian plains. The Sarmatians are essentially attracted to find new grasslands, new areas to exploit; and they are undoubtedly subjecting and assimilating the preexisting populations there.

These two new tribes, the Roxolani and the Iazgyes come into contact with Central European cultures. These include the Dacians. The Dacians dominate most of what are today Romania and the Carpathian Mountains. They are a Thraco-Illyrian speaking people; they are Indo-European speakers. Their language goes back to P.I.E., Proto-Indo-European; it broke off very early. Linguistically today they would be remotely related to Albanians, actually. They also come into contact with Celts and eventually Germanic peoples. As a result of this contact, there is a great deal of trade, intermarriage, and exchange; and the Sarmatians gain an enormous of metal technology. The Sarmatian aristocracy amasses great wealth. They do not seem to put it into great tombs, kurgans, as the Scythians did. What they seem to do is spend that wealth in other ways, foremost in acquiring good horses and arms. It is clear from depictions—and here the Romans help us a great deal; the Romans being such a visual people like to put up reliefs of all sorts of individuals, especially conquered individuals—and we have a number of depictions of Sarmatian cavalry, and it is clear they are getting horses off the steppes, probably breeds related to the heavenly horses that sweat blood, the so-called Ferghana horses.

Another aspect about these reliefs is they show that the Sarmatians are unusually well armed. We can get a sense of the military potential of the Sarmatians because of these later Roman reliefs and Roman sources. By the time of the Emperor Trajan, from 98–117 A.D., the whole of the Rhine Danube and the Dacian areas have long been Roman provinces, and the Romans have set up secure frontiers along the Rhine and Danube. The Sarmatian tribes that border on the Upper, Lower, and Middle Danube provinces have been in long contact with Romans and the Germanic peoples of Central Europe. Because of their trade connections, they gain a great deal of wealth, and this undoubtedly is put into better armament. The reliefs show that the Sarmatians still depend very much on the mounted horse archer; and there is every reason to believe, especially when we deal with Roman tactical manuals, that the Sarmatians are 90 percent light cavalry. But a significant 10 percent are heavy cavalry, and that means men who are armed in this heavy lamellar armor—that is, an overlapping set of scales—and they are called in Greek and Roman sources *cataphracti*. That terms becomes a generalized term in the Roman age and then into the Byzantine and early Medieval age for heavy cavalry lancers. The Parthians, too, apparently had such cavalry, but we have unusually few depictions of it from the Parthian army; we are really depending on depictions of Sarmatians as they have come down through the Romans.

Furthermore, they are armed with a very distinct conical helmet; a helmet that will go on to live very much—a version of this helmet; it is a more elaborate version—that gets to be the common helmet worn by Turkish tribes and later Mongol tribes in the Middle Ages. Steppe cavalry armies now are differentiated; they are not just horse archers. They surely now start with an attack by horse archers; but invariably these armies carry well-mounted cataphracts, lancers, men who can enter into a melee and destroy the enemy close up. This is a combination that the Romans are very, very well aware of in dealing with the Sarmatians on their northern frontier. In any kind of Sarmatian cavalry force—such as Alans operating out of the Caucasus, or Roxolani on the Danube—out of 10,000 cavalry, you could expect to encounter some 1,000–2,000 heavily-armed *cataphracti*; and the Romans themselves starting in the second century A.D. mount such cavalry and repeatedly hire Sarmatians as Roman auxiliary units. I think Marcus Aurelius actually hires some 7,000 of them; 6,500 of them are sent to Britain as auxiliary forces, and that gives rise to that rather strange movie that was released on King Arthur several years ago where they are turned into Sarmatians serving in Britain, which is something of a strange fantasy. But nonetheless, it is based in the fact that the Romans come to appreciate both the light cavalry and the heavy cavalry and are incorporating them into their own army.

As another point I would like to make—and again to stress some of the improvements in military technology that are probably available to all the steppe peoples at this point—besides the heavy cavalry, besides the horse archers, it is clear that they have an effective system of regimental commands. We suspect this in the army of the Xiongnu just by the titles of the kings, but the Romans tell us Sarmatians go into battle in military units. These battles are designated by distinct manners, among them the inflated leather dragons—*dracones* would be the Roman terms for it, the Latin—and these dragons are, again, ultimately of Chinese origin. There really are no dragons in Greek and Roman mythology; there are great serpents. Dragons in Chinese society, in Chinese tradition, of course, are creatures associated with the spirit of mountains; they are actually beneficial creatures. They are picked up by nomadic peoples as symbols and emblems for the different tribal regiments; they are brought into battle to spur on the troops; the Romans notice them and adopt them; and it is probably through the Sarmatians that the classic medieval dragon to be slain by the heavily armored medieval knight passes into the European consciousness. This is a steppe nomadic mediation of a Chinese notion that eventually gets into Western European traditions.

We have an unusually good tactical manual by a man named Arrian dealing with a group of Sarmatians who have attacked into Roman Asia Minor or Anatolia. His name is actually Lucius Flavius Arrianus Xenophon; he is a

Greek speaker from Asia Minor. He actually comes from, I believe, the city of Nicomedia, today Izmit, in Turkey. He served as a Roman senator, and he was a governor of the province of Galatia Cappadocia in Asia Minor. In 135 A.D., he had to deal with a group of the Sarmatian cavalry; and he wrote a tactical manual that is known as the tactical battle array against the Alans. Some have regarded it as a theoretical military manual, but it is not. What it is, it is a very, very detailed analysis of how he set up a battle line to counter an attack of nomadic cavalry that had passed through the Dariel Pass in the Caucasus and had entered into Asia Minor. That manual, which has come down to us from the Middle Ages, is one of our earliest accounts of how to deal with a threat like this. It probably, with proper changes, could be applied to the Chinese armies of the Han Dynasty, as well as to later medieval armies, to probably Sassanid armies dealing with later nomadic powers.

Arrian commanded a force of about 11,500 legionnaires and assorted auxiliary units. He had with him some 5,000 cavalry. This is unusual proportion for a Roman army. Roman armies usually have a proportion of 1:7 cavalry to infantry; this is literally 1:2; 1:2, 1:3 becomes the common proportion in dealing with steppe nomads. Arrian records a very detailed order of march. He explains how you draw up the battle line with the legionaries in the center occupying a gently sloping hill, the upper level of it. The legionaries are to be supported with wings that are advanced of auxiliary infantry with lots of archers. Even the legionary line is modified, where they are to stand in close ranks presenting an unbroken front of *pila*—that is the Roman throwing spear, but instead they are using it as a phalanx rather than casting it at the foe—and the back two lines, the 9th and 10th ranks, are archers, infantry and horse archers, shooting over the infantry as a barrage. The Roman cavalry is held in reserve behind, and the idea is to receive the attack of the nomadic cavalry, of horse archers, which is to break up the Roman infantry formations so that that heavy cavalry can ride in and get it; but to draw that cavalry close, to punish it with a firepower of infantry archers, and then when they come too close for that Roman cavalry to charge out, encircle, and destroy. That type of tactic requires remarkable discipline. It would require fighting for hours to get the Alans or any nomadic cavalry to commit themselves to such a close order battle, and then it requires perfect timing to launch your cavalry attacks to encircle it.

If you changed a few of the details and the names it was probably a similar type of formation that was used in 119 B.C. by the Han armies to encircle and destroy one of the forces of the Xiongnu. The only difference is that the Han general Wei Qing had crossbows and chariots. He had some cavalry provided by his steppe nomads; but it would be a similar type of arrangement: heavy infantry in the center, two advanced flanks of infantry with missile weapons, followed by cavalry attacks out in an enveloping attack. This is the only response that an army from a literate urban civilization can really come up with to gain any kind of tactical advantage fighting nomadic cavalry, and it is a rare number of states—from the Romans and the Han Chinese; really down to the advent of modern firearms, which is the 16th century—that are able to field such armies and to defeat nomadic cavalry in set battles. As we shall see, the nomadic cavalry have an immense tactical advantage on the battlefield, and bringing them to bay is very, very difficult. The manual of Arrian gives us one of our best glimpses into serious efforts to counter the nomadic way of war.

What about these three tribes themselves? Besides their importance in illuminating the military relationships between literate civilizations and nomadic peoples, what sort of role do they come to play in the Roman Empire, and what do the Romans learn by their interaction with these nomadic peoples? This is a subject that is still under consideration; there has been some very, very good work done in archeology showing how these Sarmatian tribes were transformed. On the Upper and Lower Danube—not the Middle Danube, because that is broken up by the Carpathians—the Sarmatian tribes were essentially turned into Roman allies. The Romans—just as Alexander the Great had to learn by experience and which the Chinese Han emperors understood certainly at the start of the Hun Dynasty—understood that in order to patrol these frontiers, it was again a matter of controlling trade routes, access; making sure that if the nomads come onto our side of the frontier that we regulate where they trade, how many can come in; and above all, should they want to seek lands, pastures, settlement within the Roman world, this would have to be regulated and supervised. The Romans did not try to build a Maginot Line any more than the Han emperors did, or we suspect the later Sassanid shahs did in Transoxiana (that is, the successors to the Parthians). What they did build was a *limes*, a set of highways and fortified blockhouses really and fortresses to regulate the flow of barbarians over the frontier.

We have a remarkable tombstone of the governor of the Roman province of Moesia, which approximately is sort of Bulgaria today; Northern Bulgaria along the Lower Danube. This governor Tiberius Plautius Aelianus in the time of Nero reports how he managed to break up an attack by the Roxolani, and then he took measures to secure the province thereafter. He took hostages from the barbarians north of the Danube, and he selectively settled 100,000 of these people as colonists; they would be known as *coloniae* in the Roman legal accounts. These were Roxolani; there were some Dacians, probably some Germanic peoples; and they were scattered through the provinces to relieve the pressure that would cause these people to migrate. This is a very, very sensible policy; it is a policy that is pursued for the next 200 years along the Roman frontiers; and it is a policy that we suspect is also very similar to the type of policies the Han emperors used. The Han emperors brought in Chinese settlements in the Ordos triangle on the upper reaches of the Yellow River. They came to terms with lesser tribes of the Xiongnu. Recall that when the Xiongnu confederation broke in two, the southern tribes were enrolled as sort of allies of the Han emperor; they had favorable treatment; the more distant ones were outer barbarians. The Romans essentially resort to similar types of practices along the Danube and stabilize their frontier quite successfully.

The other group of Sarmatians we know about are the Alans. They seem to have migrated out of the Pontic-Caspian steppe region into the Kuban and the grasslands just north of the Caucasus. There are people who claim descent from these Alans down to this day in what is now the Russian Republic. The Alans prove to be a common foe to both the Romans and the Parthians. Several times, they break through the so-called Dariel and Derbent passes. These are the great passes that allow the nomadic peoples to cross over the Caucasus or into the Elburz Mountains and enter either into the Middle East or into Iran. We have a number of reports of Alan attacks; a famous one in 72 A.D. is recorded by Josephus where reports that something like 10,000 or 20,000—and these are very vague terms—crossed over into the Caucasus and raided across Mesopotamia and Media, and sacked cities, and it was a horrible experience, and then the invaders withdrew. The Alans are, again, the people of whom Arrian writes when he draws up that tactical manual in 135. This is obviously a group of Alans who have crossed the Caucasus and have hooked a right turn rather than a left turn, so they run into Roman Asia Minor; and hence the tactical manual. In this case, those passes become extremely important and the Romans and Parthians come to some kind of agreement over Armenia, in part to make sure that the routes leading over the Caucasus into Armenia are monitored and regulated by Armenians and Georgian allies as early warning signals for Alans or other nomadic peoples—later they will be Turks—raiding into the settled zones.

What was the sum total of the experience of Rome with the Sarmatians? The Sarmatians never fuse into an effective confederacy. It is a question that is seldom posed, but I think is really central to trying to understand not only how Romans dealt with Sarmatians, but with later a more powerful nomadic threat, the Huns. The Sarmatians, well-armed with excellent trade routes, became addicted to Roman goods and never acquired the kind of great leader like a Modu Chanyu or later an Attila the Hun who could weld the various tribes of the Pontic-Caspian steppes into an effective confederation. This may be in part because for all of the trade goods and all of the advantages—including grape wine, which is reported a great deal—that the tribes obtain from the Romans, they never really gain much of a political sense of how to organize themselves against the Romans. The Xiongnu came into immediate contact with the Chinese emperor. That whole tribute system of the "Five Baits" resulted in Xiongnu kings getting Chinese brides who came with great retinues; with Xiongnu rulers and princes—like the Righteous King of the West, or the Right as he would be called, the Righteous King of the Left—receiving Chinese mandarins, technicians, and specialists who could actually create some kind of court, some kind of sense of a wider institutional monarchy, around which you could weld the inner and outer tribes into an effective confederation. That was never available due to the contact with the Romans; in part because the Romans never dealt with barbarians the same way many other peoples did, Chinese, Parthians, even Persian kings. The Roman emperor was a military dictator who represented a republic. He was still a magistrate. The idea of sending Roman princesses, even if the term is relevant, was impossible under Roman law. Romans do not marry peregrines, barbarians. There was never the same kind of political diplomatic exchange between Rome and the Sarmatians that allowed those Sarmatian tribes to learn the kind of political institutions and organization that other nomadic tribes did by exposure to the Chinese Empire, or to the Persian Empire in the case of the Middle East; and so the tribes remained divided.

In the third century A.D., a people from Scandinavia, the Goths, had left their home in Scandinavia. They traveled those trade routes onto the Pontic-Caspian steppes; and starting from about 235– 250 A.D., the Goths—and these are Germanic peoples from Sweden—began to raid and attack the Roman Empire. They subjected the Sarmatian peoples; they turned them into clients and allies. They learned the horse riding techniques from the Sarmatians, and set up a loose confederacy on the Pontic-Caspian steppes. But the Goths, too, never managed to get the kind of political organization that they were in a position to dictate and change the Roman world the way the Xiongnu were able to dictate terms to the Han emperor. The Goths were driven back in the third century. They were put under a Roman alliance structure, and they remain in a loose Roman alliance down to the arrival of the Huns in 375.

In my opinion, the Roman experience with nomadic tribes, Sarmatian tribes, led the Romans to be rather complacent and self-satisfied in dealing with them. These are relatively easy tribes to manipulate, to divide and conquer, to follow traditional Roman policies; just regulate the trade. When a really serious threat came off the steppes in the 370s from the east, a people who had had exposure to Chinese civilization, a people who probably are a spinoff of the Xiongnu and came to be controlled by one of the great conquerors of the steppes, Attila, Rome was really in no position to know how to handle a great steppe confederacy; and that will result in a very, very different situation that contributes directly to the breakup of the Western Roman Empire in the fifth century A.D.

Trade across the Tarim Basin
Lecture 9

I n this lecture and the next, we will turn our attention to the Silk Road. This term was coined in 1877 by a German explorer, and it conjures up images of the exotic, of luxury goods being shipped from China to Rome. It's both a popular image and one that embodies a great deal of truth. In this lecture, we'll look at the legendary Silk Road and all its trade connections—running from Samarkand across the Tarim Basin to the Jade Gate and extending into China, the steppes, northern India, and across the Middle East. We'll also look at the corresponding and complementary oceangoing routes, which appeared in the 1st century B.C. as part of this wider trade network.

Routes of the Silk Road

- Probably the most important points in the entire network of the **Silk Road** were in Han China, the great capitals of Luoyang and, later, Chang'an. These two imperial cities were the jumping-off points for trade that would move west. Silk was the main commodity that drew foreign merchants into these Han capitals.

- Leaving those cities meant leaving the protection of the Han emperors, as envoys sometimes learned to their dismay. Heading west, travelers reached the Gansu Corridor, a narrow strip of land connecting the upper areas of China to the Tarim Basin to the north of the steppes; to the south is the great Tibetan Plateau. There was the Yumen Pass, popularly known as the Jade Gate, through which all the trade had to pass.

- The northern route from this point skirted the Taklamakan Desert, an alkaline desert that was almost impossible to cross except in small nomadic groups. This route moved along the northern fringe of the desert among various oasis cities. The southern route also skirted the desert. The nexus of the two routes was the city of Kashgar.

- From Kashgar, travelers crossed over the formidable Pamir mountain range, which led into one of three river systems, all of which headed in different directions to the west.
  - The northern system descended into the river we know as the Jaxartes. This route led travelers into the region of Ferghana where the famous horses were found. From there, one could go on to the Aral Sea and, following the steppe routes across the Aral Sea, eventually reach the ports of the Black Sea.

  - The middle route descended into a river that is today called the Zeravshan. That route, too, led into Transoxiana and, ultimately, to the cities of central Asia, such as Bukhara, and across the cities of northern Iran to the ports of the Mediterranean.

  - The third route led into the Upper Oxus River, now known as the Amu Darya; in antiquity, the great city there was Bactra, the capital of Bactria. This was the center of that Greco-Bactrian kingdom and a major jumping-off point for routes going into India, crossing the Khyber Pass.

  - The city of Samarkand was the lynchpin of the middle and northern routes. From there, the way led down to Merv and Bukhara.

- At the same time, there was a complementary sea route that was pioneered largely by the peoples of the Mediterranean world. Around 116 to 114 B.C., a fellow named **Eudoxus of Cyzicus** is credited with understanding how to use the monsoon seasons to propel ships across the Indian Ocean.
  - By the opening of the 1st century B.C., there was regular communication by sea from Egypt, which was controlled by the Greek dynasty of the Ptolemies, down the Red Sea, across the Indian Ocean, to the ports on the western shores of India. This trade route did not displace the Silk Road. It was, in a way, a spur or an extension of the Silk Road.

- Once Rome secured the Mediterranean world (by 31 B.C.), the imperial court and the city of Rome developed an appetite for Chinese silks, Indian spices, and gems from Indian mines. Enormous levels of trade went down the Red Sea to what the Romans called Arabia Felix (Yemen), then made their way over to Indian ports, where they could obtain Chinese silks.

Moving Goods

- Moving goods from one point to another along these routes was an arduous task. Both wheeled vehicles and pack animals were used for overland travel. One of the great breakthroughs of the 2nd century B.C. was the extensive use of camels, which offered several advantages.

  - Camels could travel much farther and for longer periods than horses, mules, or donkeys. Further, using packs of camels allowed merchants to increase their carrying capacity by at least 50 percent. Camels can carry 300 pounds, whereas a good mule can carry perhaps 200 pounds.

  - Unlike wheeled vehicles, camels don't break down, and they're extremely efficient animals, conserving food and water in their systems. They became the prime beast of burden that made possible trade on the Silk Road.

- Some of the great caravans that traveled along the Silk Road had as many as 600 to 1,000 camels and hundreds of merchants, along with military detachments, usually nomads, hired to protect them. Such caravans were virtually miniature moving cities and could travel thousands of miles. With rest periods and stops to take on new goods, they might take six months to reach their final destinations.

- In addition, many lesser trade groups moved along the same routes. The cities in the Tarim Basin have produced 4th-century documents that discuss some of these lesser groups.

- There was constant movement of goods along these routes, and often, merchants dealing in one commodity carried along tag goods, that is, lesser items picked up along the way, such as interesting Buddhist manuscripts.

- Every major participant in the Silk Road trade had something of great prestige and value to trade. The Romans had grape wine, certain types of aromatics and spices, finished products, and purple dye. The Chinese had the silks. The Sogdians also had grape wine, along with linens.

The use of camels as pack animals started in the 6th century B.C. with Aramaic-speaking peoples in the Fertile Crescent and eventually reached China.

Family Networks

- From the earliest trade records we have from the Middle East, it seems that goods were moved through networks of families and something like family guilds. Certain types of families speaking specific languages did much of the carrying trade.

- Most of the people moving goods on the overland routes spoke Aramaic, a Semitic language widely used in the Fertile Crescent and later displaced by Arabic. It is the language that Jesus would've preached in.

  o Aramaic-speaking merchants from such cities as Bostra or Palmyra had kinsmen in all the key cities of the Silk Road trade.

  o When they set out from Palmyra, they knew they could stop in these cities, where they had friends and kinsmen who could provide credit, stand surety with the local authorities, provide translations, and relate information about markets and prices.

- At Merv, this network was taken over by Sogdians, who spoke an Eastern Iranian language related to Persian. They were located in Maracanda, the future Samarkand. Documents discovered in the early 20th century indicate that Sogdian merchants had the same kind of networks linking Chang'an and Loyang, the Han Chinese capitals, through Dunhuang, the cities of the Tarim Basin, and all the way back to Maracanda.
  - We have some remarkable documents of these Sogdian merchants. One of them is a report in which a merchant in the city of Dunhuang expresses concern about the reported sacking of the Chinese capital in 313. The merchant hasn't heard anything from his family concern in that city for three years.

  - Another one is a moving letter about a woman and her daughter left without enough money to pay for their passage back to Samarkand.

- These trade routes were made possible for two reasons. First, from the 2nd century B.C. to the 2nd century A.D., there were four great imperial orders that imposed peace over most of the routes: the Han Empire of China, the Kushan Empire that extended from the southern cities of the Tarim Basin across Transoxiana into northern India, the Parthian Empire, and the Roman Empire. In addition, there were powerful tribal confederacies that appreciated and benefited from the trade.

Silk Road Commodities

- The emperors of China profited immensely from the production and regulation of silk. We will see the development of the silk industry, especially in the Tang and Song period. This was in response to this overseas market. Some would argue the building of the great canal system to link the Yellow River to the Yangtze was in part to move silk up to the northern capitals and then to export.

- Also traded along the Silk Road were the spices and aromatics of India. These made their way to China, as well as to the Roman world. Roman glassware, grape wine, and aromatics crossed the

Silk Road, while the peoples of the steppes profited immensely from the sale of horses and leather goods and products.

- Finally, one commodity that's often forgotten in this exchange is people. The ease of travel made possible by the use of camels, security, and the trade networks set up by merchants, allowed different types of individuals who were not merchants to pass over the Silk Road.

  o The great courts constantly sent missions to one another. For example, we're told that the emperor Augustus in Rome received musicians and other emissaries from the raj of Taprobane (Sri Lanka) via the sea.

  o Craftsmen were another group who traveled over the Silk Road, attested by a papal envoy to Güyük, a great Mongol khan.

  o Above all, especially in later medieval periods, slaves were one of the most important commodities. In the Islamic period, young Turkish men between the ages of 13 and 16 were often captured, sold into slavery, converted to Islam, and drilled to be bodyguards or elite forces of Turkish rulers.

  o Perhaps the most important people traveling on the road for the wider cultural ramifications of the civilization of Eurasia were missionaries, monks, and merchants who had embraced new faiths, such as Christianity, Manichaeism, and Buddhism. The Silk Road brought these religions to the peoples of the steppes and, with them, writing and a wider view of their own world. In turn, this would lead to the organization of more effective states on the steppes and would draw the peoples of the steppes into increasingly closer relationships with the literate, urban civilizations.

Important Term

Silk Road: The network of caravan routes across central Asia that linked China with Europe and the Mediterranean world. The German explorer Ferdinand von Richthofen coined the term in 1877.

Name to Know

Eudoxus of Cyzicus (fl. c. 130–90 B.C.): Greek navigator for King Ptolemy VIII (126–116 B.C.); credited with the discovery of the use of the monsoon season to sail the Indian Ocean.

Suggested Reading

Bulliet, *The Camel and the Wheel.*

Golden, *Central Asia in World History.*

Hansen, *The Silk Road: A New History.*

Harl, *Coinage in the Roman Economy, 300 B.C.–700 A.D.*

Liu, *The Silk Road in World History.*

Ying-Shi Yu, *Trade and Expansion in Han China.*

Questions to Consider

1. What stimulated the demand for the different luxury goods that gave rise to the Silk Road? What were the prime routes, and why did Aramaic and Sogdian merchants and the nomadic tribes play such a vital role?

2. What were the major routes on the Silk Road? How was trade organized and conducted? Why was the domestication and spread of the camel so important for the expansion of trade?

3. What were the profits of trade, and how did they transform caravan cities in the Tarim Basin and the nomadic peoples?

4. What material culture, knowledge, and organizational skills were gained by steppe peoples that allowed the creation of later Turkish khaganates and the Mongol Empire?

Trade across the Tarim Basin
Lecture 9—Transcript

In this lecture and the next lecture, I want to slow down a bit in dealing with various nomadic peoples from antiquity. What I wish to concentrate on in this lecture is something known as the Silk Road. It was a term coined in 1877 by a German explorer, *Seidenstrasse* in German, and it conjures up images of the exotic, of long-distance goods being shipped from China to Rome, silks, grape wine, all of this. It is a popular image, an image that is very attractive in a number of ways; and yet at the same time, remarkably, there is a great deal of truth to this image. The term, as I said, was coined by a German traveler, a fellow by the name of Ferdinand von Richthofen; and he had traveled out to Central Asia, the cities of the Tarim Basin actually. In 1877, he began excavating sites in what are now essentially Chinese Turkestan (used to be known as Xinjiang), and his marvelous discoveries drew attention to this region, which you have to remember in 1877 was a pretty wild and wooly area; very little of it was known by Europeans. Incidentally, this traveler is the uncle of the famous Manfred von Richthofen, who is the "Red Baron" of the first World War, just sort of an interesting aside; a prominent family in Germany.

More important was a British adventurer, archaeologist; if anyone has a claim to the kind of Indiana Jones legacy, it is Sir Aurel Stein, who was a native of Budapest who eventually became a naturalized British subject. Stein carried out four expeditions, running from 1900–1930. He made off with an enormous haul of texts and Buddhist manuscripts, coming especially from the Mogao caves in the vicinity of the city of Dunhuang, which is a largely Chinese city near the Jade Gate, the Yumen Pass, and a jump off point on the Silk Road. The finds were fabulous: Stein's excavations revealed documents that were written in Chinese; in early Turkish languages, particularly Uighur Turkish (we will talk about Uighurs later on); in Tocharian, that very unusual Indo-European language that apparently broke away from the parent language centuries earlier; Sogdian, which is an Eastern Iranian language widely spoken in the cities of Transoxiana and was a commercial language. There are all sorts of Buddhist texts; Manichee texts; texts of early Christianity, the Eastern Christianity known as Nestorian. The finds were incredibly rich. Stein has been criticized for not carrying out the kind of scientific excavations that one would do today; but nonetheless, the collection in the British museum today owes its existence to the efforts of Stein.

These documents have given us a flood of light as to the question of international trade. In this lecture, I want to look at this legendary Silk Road and all of its trade connections; not just that connection that would run from Samarkand, more or less ancient Maracanda, across the Tarim Basin to the Jade Gate, but its extensions into China, its extensions into the steppes, there is a big spur that goes off into North India, and the extension across the Middle East that would take goods to the courts of the Mediterranean world, notably the city of Antioch in the Roman period, today Antiochia in Turkey, which is a great export city. We will also look at the corresponding and complementary oceangoing routes, which is something that also appears in the first century B.C. as part of that wider trade network.

The Silk Road has great romantic images to it, but it is also historically extremely important. What I would like to do first is sketch out a bit of the way there; that is, what were the routes used to move these goods? Then we will look at actually the goods themselves that were moved; and finally the merchants, the type of people who moved these goods; and then what were the ramifications of what some would call the first steps to a kind of international, or if you will global economy, which emerges between the second century B.C. and the second century A.D.?

Let us take our primary overland route, and let us start from the point that was really probably the most important point in the entire network: Han China. I had reasons to stress Han China in dealing with the nomadic peoples; and in terms of the Silk Road, the great capitals of the Han Empire—Luoyang, and then later Chang'an in the Yellow River; those two great imperial cities—are the jump off point for trade that would move west; and what they are carrying first and foremost is Chinese silk. The Chinese emperors come to regulate silk production—what we would call a *sericulture* is the fancy term for it—and silk was the main commodity that was drawing all these foreign merchants into those Han capitals. You would leave those cities; you would leave the protection of the Han emperors as you move farther west, as envoys learned to their dismay on several occasions; and you would get into what is known as the Gansu corridor. That is a narrow band of land connecting the upper areas of China to the Tarim Basin to the north of the steppes; to the south is the Great Tibetan Plateau. There is a pass, the Yumen Pass—popularly known as the Jade Gate—through which all the trade has to pass. The Han emperors made sure that the Great Wall extended out to this point and offered protection; and furthermore, when China was strong enough, the emperors stationed garrisons in that vicinity at the Yumen Gate on the other side in Dunhuang in order to tax trade and regulate the exports.

From that point, you moved in one of two directions. You could move along a northern route. This route was to skirt the Taklamakan Desert. The Taklamakan Desert is essentially an alkaline desert, which is almost impossible to cross except in small nomadic groups. You would move along the northern fringe of that desert among various oasis cities. These included the cities of Hami, Turfan, Yanqi, Korta, Kucha, Aksu (which means "white water" in Turkish); there was a southern route that followed Dunhuang, Niya, Khotan, and Yarkand. Whether you went on the northern route or the southern route, and it is sort of like a circle around this great desert depression, you would end up at the city of Kashgar; that is the nexus of these two routes. From Kashgar, you crossed over the Pamir Mountain range. That was a formidable barrier; it would lead you into one of three river systems. Each of these river systems would take you into different directions to the west.

The northern one would descend into the river we know in the west as the Jaxartes, or as it is known by its Turkish name, the Syr Darya; and that was a very, very important route because that would lead you down into the region of Ferghana where the horses are. From that route, you could follow on to the Aral Sea and follow the steppe routes across the Aral Sea, north of the Caspian, and you would pop out on the ports of the Black Sea. Essentially, that route would take you from Greek cities on the Black Sea all the way to the Jaxartes River, over the Pamir Mountain range, ultimately to China. The middle route descends into a river that the ancients knew as the Polytimetus; that would be the name that Alexander the Great would apply. Today that is the Zeravshan River. That route, too, would lead you into Transoxiana. It would take you ultimately to the cities of Central Asia such as Bukhara, eventually to Merv, Margiana in ancient times, and across the cities of

Northern Iran to the ports of the Mediterranean. The third route would lead down into the Upper Oxus River. That Oxus River is now known as the Amu Darya; and in antiquity, the great city there was Bactra, the capital of Bactria. This was the center of that Greco-Bactrian Kingdom; and Bactra becomes a major—it is today the modern city of Balkh—jump off point for routes going into India especially, crossing the Khyber Pass.

Foremost, the city of Samarkand was the lynchpin of those two northern routes: the middle and northern route. Many routes coming over that northern and middle route ended up in Samarkand—its predecessor was Maracanda—and from there it would go down to Merv, it would go to Bukhara, you could go to the steppes, you could go to Iran. All of these cities—Bukhara, Samarkand, Balkh, Kashgar—would have long histories on this trade route known as the Silk Road; and these cities were just as legendary as the cities of the Tarim Basin and the Jade Gate.

At the same time, there was a complementary sea route that was pioneered largely by the peoples of the Mediterranean world. We get varying accounts on this, but usually it is dated around 116–114 B.C. A fellow by the name of Eudoxus of Cyzicus is credited with understanding how to use the monsoon seasons to propel ships across the Indian Ocean, which the Romans called the Erythraean Sea. This is credited to Eudoxus. There is another fellow that is sometimes credited, Hippalus; and the usual thought is that Hippalus was the actual skipper of the ship and we got two contradictory ports, one coming out of Strabo and one coming out of this document known as the Periplus of the Erythraean Sea. Whoever is actually responsible, by the opening of the first century B.C. there was regular sea communication from Egypt, which was controlled by the Greek dynasty of the Ptolemies, down the Red Sea, across the Indian Ocean, to the ports on the western shores of India.

This trade route is complementary. It did not displace the Silk Road; far from it: It was in a way a spur or an extension of the Silk Road, for two reasons: Once Rome secured the Mediterranean world—and that was clear by 31 B.C., where the Mediterranean world was consolidated by the emperor Augustus—the Roman court, the city of Rome, its senators, the imperial court, the wealthy provincial cities of the Mediterranean world had an appetite for Chinese silks and Indian spices, and also gems coming from

Indian mines. That meant enormous amounts of trade went down the Red Sea to ports on the Red Sea, particularly the port of Berenice, which has been excavated, which is on the shores of the Red Sea in Roman Egypt. It would leave in mid-July, go down to what the Romans called Arabia Felix, today Yemen, and then make its way over to the Indian ports. We have a very good navigational manual written from the first century A.D. that describes this. We know the ports, the distances, the locations—and one of the most important ports was Muziris, which is more or less in the vicinity of Cochin, it was in the pepper areas; the Romans are very familiar with Sri Lanka—and above all, what they wanted in landing in the Indian ports were Chinese silks that were coming overland from Balkh, from Bactra, brought in by the Silk Road. In the ancient and medieval world, there is always this oceangoing extension of the Silk Road; but it never displaces, it is not in competition, it is really complementary. The displacement of the Silk Road by oceanic routes is really a phenomenon that occurs in the 16th and 17th centuries and changes the whole dynamics of steppe peoples and steppe empires; and that will come later in the course.

Besides these trade routes, we want to know a bit of: How do you get the goods from one place to the other? This is an arduous task. You have to travel overland. While there are various ways to do it—one is by wheeled vehicles, another is pack animals—but one of the great breakthroughs by the second century B.C. is the extensive use of camels. Camels were domesticated both in Arabia, and that would be the dromedary, the one-humped camel, and the Bactrian, the two-humped camel, in Central Asia, which is more resistant to the cold. Later on, Muslims from the 9th to 11th century would breed a kind of hybrid, which would wipe out the Bactrian camel in its homeland and bring in this one-humped hybrid, which is stronger and better adapted to the cold. Camels offered several advantages. First, they could go a lot farther and longer than horses, mules, and donkeys. Furthermore, by using packs of camels, you would increase carrying capacity by at least 50 percent. Camels are thought to carry 300 pounds, whereas a good mule maybe 200 pounds. They did not have to be shod. You did not have the problem of breakdown with wheeled vehicles if you went to pack animals. Above all, camels conserve food and water in their systems and they are extremely efficient animals. They live much longer than donkeys and other types of draft animals; and so the use of camels, which had spread starting in the sixth century B.C. with Aramaic-speaking peoples in the Fertile Crescent, across Central Asia, and eventually camels will reach China, they become the prime beast of burden, and that makes possible the trade on the Silk Road.

In addition, you have to keep in mind that caravans varied. They were not all extensive, long distance caravans. We do know of great caravans. They could comprise of 600 or 1,000 camels traveling with hundreds of merchants; with a military detachment, usually nomads who have been hired to protect it. Along it would travel all sorts of entertainment groups; there would be lesser merchants. This was virtually a mini moving city; and we have such reports of these types of caravans leaving Chinese cities, arriving in Samarkand, particularly from the medieval period. Kashgar was home to many of these great caravans because that is the lynchpin where everything is coming out of the Tarim Basin and is ready to move out. These caravans would travel 1,000 miles in order to get to the destination. They would not travel it all at once. Calculation is on an average speed a caravan could cover 1,000 miles in 40 days; very few caravans ever did that. Caravans would stop; they would have rest periods; they would take on new goods; they would trade. Caravans could take really half a year to get from the jump off point to the final destination.

In addition, there were lots of lesser trade groups moving along; that is, local and regional trade that followed along the same routes. The cities in the Tarim Basin have produced documents of the fourth century, a series of letters that were found by Stein's group excavating near Dunhuang that apparently talks about some of these lesser trade routes. There is constant movement of goods; both the long distance high prestige items, lesser regional and local trade moving along the same routes. Very often merchants were dealing in one commodity and they carried along what is called a tag good; that is, a lesser item that you pick up along the way, kind of a conversation piece: "What is it?" "We don't know, but we can sell it; we pick it up in Turfan, we're really dealing mainly in Chinese silks. These were some interesting Buddhist manuscripts; we can sell them at a profit once we get to Samarkand." There is a lot of this type of trading going on along the Silk Road; and so you have to envision this as a route that is in constant trade and commerce moving along there.

This is a way of transporting goods; these are the types of goods that are being moved, high prestige goods; and what is important to note is that every major participant has something of great prestige and value to swap. The Romans have grape wine; they have certain types of aromatics, spices, finished products, purple dye. The Chinese have the silks. The Sogdians actually are growing their own grape wine; they have carpets and linens. All sorts of prestige goods are being moved along by all of the participants in the Silk Road.

How do you move these goods? How do you get them from Point A to Point B, especially in a world that does not have modern banking instruments and certainly does not have all the advantages of high technology? The way goods were traditionally moved in all trade concerns, from the earliest trade records we have from the Middle East—those would be the Sumerian merchants of, say, 3500–3000 B.C.—really down to the Modern Age was through networks of families and almost family guilds. That meant certain types of families speaking very specific languages did much of the carrying trade.

Let us move to the western arm of the Silk Road, which I know the best and I have done quite a bit of study with in tandem with the Roman Empire. Most of the people moving goods on the overland routes spoke Aramaic. This was a Semitic language widely used in the Fertile Crescent in the Near East, later displaced by Arabic. It is the language that Jesus would have preached in. It is the second lingua franca of the Eastern Roman Empire; the first is Greek, which is a very privileged literary administrative language. Aramaic-speaking merchants from cities such as Bostra or Palmyra had kinsmen in all the key cities: at Charax, the port on the Persian Gulf; in Ecbatana or Hamadan; in Merv, Margiana, which is today in Afghanistan. Along there, you had family, consortiums, and friends; when you set out from Palmyra you knew that you could stop in these key sites, these cities, and there you would have friends, probably kinsmen, who could provide credit, who could stand surety with the local authorities, tell you what you need, what you need to do, provide translations, tell you what the market prices were, tell you where to sell, how to sell, and how to buy. They could also extend credit as well as redeem all sorts of letters of credit that you were carrying from home.

Once you got to Merv, it was taken over by Sogdians. Sogdians were people who spoke in Eastern Iranian language; it is related to Persian. They are located in Maracanda, the future Samarkand; it is spoken in Kashgar. It is widely known all through the Tarim Basin, all the way to the Chinese capitals. The documents discovered by Sir Aurel Stein indicate that Sogdian merchants had the same kind of networks linking essentially Chang'an and Loyang, the Han Chinese capitals, through Dunhuang, the cities of the Tarim Basin, all the way back home to essentially Samarkand (ancient Samarkand; really its ancient name, Maracanda). They took care of the same moving of goods.

For the sea networks, it would be Greek. It would be the language of this time. We get some remarkable documents of these Sogdian merchants that were found by Stein. One of them is a report where one merchant is very, very concerned. He is in the city of Dunhuang and he has heard that the Chinese capital has been sacked in 313—that is verified by the Chinese annals—and he is not sure if the profits would come in; he has not heard anything from the family concern in that city for three years. Another one is a very moving letter about a woman and her daughter, who are left penniless, and she is complaining that her husband has abandoned her, and she is stuck there and she cannot get enough money to pay her passage back to Samarkand. These letters cast a glimpse at some of the kinds of conditions that went on on the Silk Road; and you have to keep remembering there is a constant movement of people across that route with different conditions, different situations.

These trade routes were made possible for two reasons. First, from the second century B.C. to the second century A.D., based on the lectures we have given so far, we have four great imperial orders that have imposed peace over most of this route: That is the Han Empire of China; the great Kushan Empire that extends from the southern cities of the Tarim Basin across Transoxiana into Northern India; the Parthian Empire; and the Roman Empire. In addition, there are powerful tribal confederacies such as the Xiongnu and other nomadic peoples who appreciate and benefit from the profits of trade; hire themselves out as guards, guides, suppliers of all sorts of commodities to sustain the caravan route; and everyone profits from it.

The emperors of China profited immensely. The whole production and regulation of silk: We will see the development of the silk industry, especially in the Tang and Song periods, is in response to this overseas market. Some would argue the building of the great canal system to link the Yellow River to the Yangzi or the Yangtze River was in part to move silk up to the northern capitals and then to export. There are also other reasons—that is, you need to feed the northern capitals with rice—but there are a number of reasons for that going on. It influences Chinese foreign policy from the reign of Wudi on; that is, the Chinese effort to control the great corridors leading all the way to Kashgar.

Another important commodity traded along the Silk Road was the great spices and aromatics from India. These would make their way to China as well as to the Roman world, and they were part of that network. Roman goods, Roman glassware, remarkably shipped overseas as well as over land; grape wine, aromatics; all of this stuff crossed the Silk Road. For this trade network to remain in place, some kind of sense of value had to be exported from one end to the other end. The peoples of the steppes profited immensely in the sale of horses to the Chinese and to the various empires; to the sale of all sorts of leather goods and products; so all of the participants had a reason to maintain and extend this Silk Road, which was so important in the economic development not only of the civilized, literate, urban civilizations, but also of the nomadic pastoral populations across the Eurasian steppes. So the second century B.C. to the second century A.D. is really a period of remarkable prosperity and intellectual and cultural exchange.

Finally, one commodity that is often forgotten in this exchange is people; and it is important to stress that the ease of travel along the Silk Road made possible by these conditions—the improved travel conditions with camels; the security; the whole set of trade networks set up by merchants—allowed for different types of individuals who are not merchants necessarily to pass over the Silk Road, but also all sorts of people were part of that trade network. What do we mean by that?

The great courts constantly sent missions between each other. Think of, for instance, reports of the emperor Augustus in Rome. It is told to us that on the sea routes he received musicians; various types of people from the Raj of Taprobane, which is today Sri Lanka, including an extraordinary man who had no arms but could play a lyre with his toes. At the Tang court—

this is a bit later, from the eighth century A.D.—Xuanzong, one of the great emperors of the seventh century, and his favorite mistress, a rather notorious lady, and favorite consort Yang Guifei, they enjoyed all sorts of acrobatics and dancers. They made a concerted effort to attract dancers and entertainers from Central Asia, which generally shocked many members of the Confucian court; eventually they have to be banned. Craftsmen were another group of men who traveled over the Silk Road; and this is a tradition that lasts through the entire period. We have extremely good reports from the Mongol period, particularly from the Papal envoy to the court of the great khan Güyük; his name is Giovanni Carpini, we will be talking about him later. He traveled to the great Mongol court at Karakorum, which is today in Mongolia. He notes the numerous craftsmen, merchants from all over the world, who had come to do business at the Mongol court because of the conditions on the Silk Road. It was ideal: You had markets; you had demand; you had security; you had some order; you had the predictability that would allow profits to proceed and therefore trade could go forth.

Above all, we will find in later medieval periods, slaves were one of the most important commodities; and in the Islamic period, remarkably the most important slaves would be men destined to be soldiers in Islamic armies. These would usually be Turks, young men between the ages of 13 and 16 who would be captured, who would be sold into slavery, converted to Islam, and drilled to be the bodyguard or the elite forces of Turkish rulers. They are often known by a variety of names, one of the most common names is Mamluk; and that is a peculiar tradition of medieval Islam. All of these commodities passed along the Silk Road in great numbers.

But perhaps the most important people travelling on the road for the wider cultural ramifications of the civilization of Eurasia were missionaries, monks, and merchants who had embraced new faiths, such as Christianity, Manichaeism, and above all Buddhism; because the Silk Road brought to the peoples of the steppes these religions and with them writing and a wider view of their own world, of its geography, of its political ramifications, new views of the religious reality. The impact of these religions on the peoples of the steppes would be profound: It would lead to the organization of more effective states on the steppes, and it would draw the peoples of the steppes evermore into closer relationships with the literate, urban civilizations.

Buddhism, Manichaeism, and Christianity
Lecture 10

In the last lecture, we discussed the various commodities exchanged along the Silk Road, but this lecture will concentrate on the exchange of ideas and, above all, religions. Perhaps the most important items that were transmitted along the Silk Road to nomadic peoples were various religions, especially Buddhism, but there were others, including Nestorian Christianity, Manichaeism, Zoroastrianism, and, even later on, Judaism. These religions were appealing for a number of reasons, not only to the caravan cities but also to the nomadic peoples who participated in the process of moving goods along the Silk Road. They presented a new world vision and brought missionaries, monks, and even merchant princes who introduced the art of writing to the nomadic peoples.

The Success of Buddhism

- Buddhism was clearly the most successful of the religions between the 4th and 8th centuries A.D., and it was appealing to people along the Silk Road for a number of reasons. Among these was the fact that the teachings of the Buddha had been reinterpreted for a wider appeal.

- In addition, Buddhism represented a reaction to the caste structure, to the sacrifices administered by the **Brahmins**.
  - **Siddhartha Gautama** himself was a mentor of the **Kshatriya** caste, that is, the warrior caste that produced the princes and kings of northern India; they were the highest of the twice-born caste. The Brahmins were supposed to be second, but already in the time of the Buddha, the Brahmins were beginning to assert themselves as the top caste, and that is what is recognized today in Hindu India. Below them was a merchant class, followed by the **Shudras**, and finally, those with no caste.

  - Caste, or *varna*, was a way of defining one's position in society, as well as an individual's relationship in the cycle of life. Buddhism represented a rejection of this. All people who

The decorations in the Ajanta rock monasteries in India may have been donated by wealthy merchants in thanks for their prosperity and the karma they achieved just by conducting their trade.

embraced the enlightenment and the teachings of the Buddha were able to achieve *moksha*, liberation from the eternal cycle of life, and a type of nirvana, an extinction of one's individual soul into the greater soul of the universe.

- From the start, there were debates about the meaning of the Buddha's message. How broad ranging was it? What was the role of monks who would achieve enlightenment? What was the relationship between the monastic community and the laity that supported it?

- Several Buddhist councils were held, the first one around 400 B.C. The third one, in 247 B.C., was particularly important. This council was held under the auspices of the Mauryan emperor Ashoka, who had come to embrace Buddhism. The councils led to a division within the Buddhist community into, essentially, the Theravada and the **Mahayana** schools of Buddhism. These divisions were based on questions about the original teachings and whether the teachings should be translated into the vernacular.

- Another important point that came out of these debates was that anyone who embraced the teachings of the Buddha, even at the lowest levels, could achieve some level of enlightenment. In the Mahayana (Greater Vehicle) tradition, all individuals had the potential to achieve some understanding and potentially become buddhas themselves. This vision was extremely appealing to merchants and rulers who were not Indian; hence, it was this vision that was exported along the Silk Road.

- There were two forces at work disseminating Buddhism along the Silk Road: the profits of trade and the translation of Buddhist texts by monks who traveled the routes.
  o Many members of the **Vaishya** caste, the merchants in Hindu India, came to embrace Buddhism because it was their *dharma* to conduct trade and prosper. Thus, merchants often acted as unofficial missionaries in the caravan cities and among the nomadic tribes with which they came into contact.

  o In addition, the monks who began to travel along the Silk Road, particularly under the Kushan emperors and later, translated Buddhist texts into languages that were readily used along the routes. In this way, Buddhist texts were disseminated across Transoxiana and central Asia in a variety of languages that were readily understood by the literate classes who were engaged in trade.

- The monks themselves settled in monasteries, large complexes in which the ascetics were supported by the donations of believers. For instance, the early rock monasteries in India at Ajanta were beautifully decorated with murals that were probably donations made by wealthy merchants.

- It was from this context along the Silk Road that Buddhist missionaries arrived in China and began to translate various texts into Chinese. This was already taking place in the 2nd century A.D. and probably earlier. These translations were from, perhaps, Sanskrit originals or Sogdian and Tocharian originals. By the 3rd century A.D., there were a number of Buddhist texts, **sutras**, available from a variety of Buddhist schools.

- The most remarkable figure coming out of this Buddhist world created on the Silk Road was a Chinese pilgrim named Xuanzang (602–664). He traveled along the Silk Road in search of manuscripts and went on a long pilgrimage, first to central Asia, then into northern India. He brought back to China many Sanskrit texts and was commissioned to do more accurate translations that became extremely important in the dissemination of Buddhism under the Tang and, later, the Song empires. Xuanzang is representative of the process of turning what was almost a spinoff of Hinduism into a universal faith in East Asia.

Dualistic Manichaeism

- The religion known as **Manichaeism** represents the teachings of Mani, perhaps one of the most enigmatic and remarkable figures to burst upon the Silk Road and the Middle East. He was apparently born into some kind of Christian Jewish community about 216 A.D. in what is today lower Iraq. He was crucified in 276 A.D. on orders of the shah for teaching essentially heretical messages that were at odds with Zoroastrian traditions.

- Mani taught various schemes of cosmic redemption involving the battle between light and darkness. The Mani Codex, discovered in Cologne, which contains the life of Mani and his early teachings, shows us a well-worked-out religion that had certain similarities to Buddhism. It also had a system of levels of reality that was not too dissimilar from the Buddhist notions of successions of reincarnation through *dharma* and improved **karma**, leading to *moksha*.

- Again, Manichaeism was universalist in appeal, and merchants found it extremely attractive because it justified their position. We know of a an 8th-century Turkish monarch, **Khagan Bögü**, who officially converted to Manichaeism and brought his whole tribe, the **Uighurs**, over. The Uighurs remained Manichees well into the 9th and 10th centuries and brought the religion into the Tarim Basin, where they migrated after their khaganate collapsed in 840.

- Manichaeism was another faith that brought new values and ideas to the nomadic peoples. The Manichee missionaries were apparently behind devising a script for writing Uighur Turkish. They also were regarded as people who had skills and expertise, such as in organizing taxes and assessments for would-be nomadic rulers.

Christianity on the Steppes

- A third religion that made its way onto the steppes via the Silk Road was Christianity, perhaps next successful after Buddhism and Manichaeism. This is not the Christianity we associate with the Roman Empire. In fact, these are the losers in the Roman Empire in a way. This version is often called **Nestorian Christianity**.

- The Nestorian Christians were followers of Nestorius, who had been patriarch of Constantinople from 429 to 431. He held that Mary gave birth only to the man Christ, and the Christ logos entered after his birth; thus, Mary is not the Mother of God. That position was struck down at the Third Ecumenical Council in 431. Rather than give up their faith, the Nestorians moved across the frontier into the Persian domains of the Fertile Crescent and adapted their Christianity to local conditions.

- The Nestorians adopted Aramaic as their liturgical language, abandoning Greek. They culturally assumed the mores and traditions of the people of the Middle East, including multiple marriages. They quickly turned themselves into a Middle Eastern version of Christians who could travel along the Silk Road, following the same routes as the merchants and winning converts.

They had a particularly powerful network of bishops in the cities of central Asia, particularly Samarkand.

- The Nestorian monks and ascetics were apparently seen as local versions of **shamans**. The ability of these Christian monks to carry out healing cures is what probably endeared them to a number of Turkish tribes. We have some interesting reports from the 6th century A.D. of Turkish tribes that had embraced Nestorian Christianity because, reputedly, the Turks had been protected from a plague by the sign of the cross.

The Coming of Islam
- In the 12th and 13th centuries, Islam increasingly moved in and displaced these religions. Particularly, there would be something of a duel between the Buddhists and the Muslims for the religious loyalties of the steppe peoples. As a result of the Silk Road, on the eve of the Islamic conquest, these religions had made an immense impact on the nomadic peoples and the caravan cities.

- All of these religions were represented with major shrines, and all had important recommendations. First, they were carried by scholars, monks, ascetics, and healing miracle men who could be associated with shamans and traditional healers in nomadic society. They also were responsible for bringing writing and organizational skills that would allow the nomadic peoples, particularly the Turkish peoples, to organize more effective confederacies and kingdoms than the Xiongnu or other peoples on the steppes. Finally, they put the nomadic peoples in close contact with urban centers.

- Up until 751, all of these religions were practiced and embraced by different individuals, tribes, and monarchs. In 751, the armies of the Abbasid caliph won over the armies of the Tang emperor of China at the Battle of Talas. Although that battle has been exaggerated and misunderstood, it was the first sign of a new religion on the Silk Road, a religion that was now associated with victory: Islam.

Brahmin: In Hinduism, the first or priestly caste.

dharma: In Hinduism, the moral law that dictates the cycle of reincarnation.

karma: In Hinduism and Buddhism, the individual merit acquired by an individual through meritorious deeds.

Kshatriya: In Hinduism, the caste of warriors.

Manichaeism: The dualist, monotheistic faith proclaimed by the prophet Mani in Sassanid Mesopotamia. The faith was popular among Sogdian merchants of the Silk Road; the khagan of the Uighurs converted to Manichaeism in 763.

Mahayana Buddhism: The "Greater Wheel" was the school of Buddhism that emerged in India in the 1st century B.C., stressing the divine status of the Buddha. The schools of Mahayana Buddhism today are in East Asia (Tibet, Mongolia, China, Korea, and Japan).

moksha: The liberation of an enlightened Hindu who is freed from the cycle of rebirths, according to *dharma*.

Nestorian Christianity: The Christian church that followed the teachings of Patriarch Nestorius of Constantinople (429–431), who taught that Mary gave birth only to the man Jesus rather than man and God. The Nestorians, condemned at the Third Ecumenical Council (431), spread their faith across the Silk Road, converting Turkish and Mongol tribes.

shaman: A mystic prized for insights gained by contact with the spiritual world through trances often induced by hallucinogens, notably hashish.

Shudra: In Hinduism, the caste of laborers or peasants.

sutra: A Buddhist sacred text of aphorisms.

Uighurs: Turkish-speaking nomads who founded the third Turkish confederation on the eastern Eurasian steppe (744–840). They converted to Manichaeism in 763.

Vaishya: In Hinduism, the caste of merchants.

Bögü Khan (759–780): Uighur khagan; promoted trade and settlements within the Uighur khanate. In 762, he converted to Manichaeism.

Gautama, Siddhartha (563–483 B.C.): The Buddha, a prince of the Kshatriya Shakya clan, was the sage who founded Buddhism. Around 534 B.C., he assumed an ascetic life to achieve understanding of human suffering. In the deer park at Sarnath, he achieved enlightenment and went on to teach the noble truths of the Middle Way, the fundamental tenets of Buddhism.

Xuanzang (596–664): Buddhist monk and Chinese pilgrim; wrote an account of his travels in the western regions and India in 629–645. He visited the court of Harsha Vardhana (606–647) at Kannauj on the Ganges. He revealed the international network of Buddhist monasteries in central Asia and India on the eve of the Islamic conquests.

Suggested Reading

Elvergskog, *Buddhism and Islam on the Silk Road.*

Fowden, *From Empire to Commonwealth.*

Golden, *Central Asia in World History.*

Foltz, *Religion of the Silk Road.*

Lieu, *Manichaeism in the Roman Empire and Medieval China.*

1. What were the respective appeals of Buddhism, Manichaeism, and Christianity to the caravan cities of Transoxiana and the Tarim Basin and to the Eurasian nomads?

2. Why was Buddhism such an attractive religion to merchants? How did commerce and travel along the Silk Road profit from the creation of a Buddhist network of monasteries?

3. How did the Chinese pilgrims Faxien and Xuanzang reflect the world of Buddhism during the heyday of the Silk Road? Why did they pen such perceptive accounts of their travels? Why are their accounts such important sources?

4. Why was the translation of scriptures of the new faiths into Tocharian, Sogdian, and Turkic so important? Why were merchants so important in promoting religious beliefs?

5. What accounted for the success of Buddhism over the other new religions on the Silk Road? Why did Buddhism succeed in China whereas the other faiths remained those of foreign minorities?

Buddhism, Manichaeism, and Christianity
Lecture 10—Transcript

In this lecture, I want to continue discussing the importance of the Silk Road. We have discussed the various commodities exchanged along the Silk Road; but this lecture is going to concentrate on the exchange of ideas and, above all, religions.

Perhaps the most important item that was transmitted along the Silk Road to nomadic peoples was various religions; especially Buddhism, but there are others: Nestorian Christianity, Manichaeism, Zoroastrianism, even Judaism later on is exchanged along the Silk Road. There are a number of reasons why these religions were appealing, not only to the caravan cities but to the nomadic peoples who were very much caught up in the whole process of moving goods across the Silk Road. These reasons were connected with, in part, what those religions represented, especially to the nomadic peoples. They presented a new world vision. It generally involved the adaptation of writing, a concept that was largely unknown to many of the nomadic peoples. We will see that it will be missionaries, monks, even merchant princes of these religions who would engage in debate; who bring the art of writing to the nomadic peoples and give us the opportunity to hear the voices of some of these people later on in the early Middle Ages, particularly of Turkish speakers.

First and foremost among the religions was Buddhism. It was clearly the most successful of the religions between the fourth and eighth centuries A.D. There were a number of reasons why Buddhism would have been appealing to people along the Silk Road. For one, the vision of the Buddha— Siddhartha Gautama, who lived in the sixth and early fifth centuries B.C.— these teachings had been reinterpreted for a wider appeal. There is very little that is clear about the life of the Buddha. Siddhartha Gautama was supposedly a prince. He was born on the border between what is now Nepal and Northern India. There are a number of stories of why he was moved to seek his enlightenment, which came at age 35, and eventually preach in the deer park at Sarnath to his followers. Basically, what troubled the Buddha was the question of suffering; and he devised a very simple system known as the Four Noble Truths on how to handle that suffering was universal within the human experience. That involved detaching oneself from the material world and all sorts of connections and pursuing what he would call a Middle Way; not the extreme asceticism practiced by some of the Jains and even some of the Hindu fakirs, and not a full indulgence protection from the ugliness of life, which had characterized Siddhartha's early life according to the legendary histories.

In addition, Buddhism also represented a reaction to the caste structure; to the sacrifices administered by the Brahmins. Siddhartha Gautama himself was of the Kshatriya caste; that is, the warrior caste who produced the princes and kings of Northern India who go back to the early Rig Vedas as the highest of the twice born caste. The Brahmins were supposed to be second; but in the time of the Buddha, already the Brahmins were beginning to assert themselves as the top caste, and that is what is recognized today in Hindu India. Then below them was a merchant class, and then the so-called Suddhras, and finally those with no caste. Caste, or *varna*, was a way of defining one's position in society, as well as his relationship or her relationship in the cycle of life. Buddhism represented a rejection of this. All people who embrace the enlightenment and the teachings of the Buddha were able to achieve *moksha*, liberation, breaking from the eternal cycle of life, and then achieving a type of nirvana, an extinction of one's individual soul into the greater soul of the universe. These teachings, as they have come down to us—and you have to remember that the original Sanskrit texts do not survive—the lives of the Buddha that have been reported, these hagiographical texts, are much later in time; and most of what we know about the early Buddhist texts are actually in translations, not in the Sanskrit that might have been used in the sixth and fifth centuries B.C. (although the suspicion is Siddhartha probably spoke in Prakrit; that is the vernacular at the time).

From the start, there were divisions as to what was the meaning of the Buddha's message. How broad-ranging was it? What was the role of monks who would achieve enlightenment? What was the relationship between the monastic community, the *sangra*, and the laity supported that monastic community; that is those who were concentrating on enlightenment to break from the cycle of life and who would live in what we would call proto-monasteries (*vihara* is eventually what they would become to be called)?

There were several Buddhist councils held; the first one around 400 BC and two others following. The third one was particularly important in 247 B.C. These councils—the third one was actually held under the auspices of the Mauryan emperor Ashoka, who had come to embrace Buddhism, and he was the emperor of the first great Indian Empire—led to a division within the Buddhist community.

The terms keep changing as to what the various groups are, but today they would essentially be represented by the Theravada school of Buddhism, extremely common, for instance, in Thailand and Sri Lanka; and the Mahayana vehicle (they were often called vehicles), the Greater Vehicle of Buddhism. These divisions really came down to a question of: What were the original teachings? Should they be translated into the vernacular? The Mahayana Buddhist tradition, the Greater Vehicle tradition, essentially stressed the message over the language; that is, translation was acceptable because content was all important, not necessarily adhering to original Sanskrit words if that indeed was the language that was used. Another important point that comes out of that is that anyone who embraces the teachings of the Buddha, even at the lowest levels, could achieve some level of enlightenment. That was his dharma, the law of social and religious inevitability, if you will; the cycle of one's life; a notion that is shared by Hindus, Buddhists, and Jains; the law of dharma that dictates the way you are to live, the way you are to achieve enlightenment. Enlightenment was achieved at different levels; and the notion in the Greater Vehicle was that all individuals could achieve some kind of understanding and potentially become Buddhas themselves. There was a whole history of Buddhists—Bodhisattvas, if you will—enlightened ones who preceded the historical Buddha and will follow afterwards.

This vision, this Greater Vehicle vision, this Mahayana vision, is the vision that really gets exported along the Silk Road. The reasons for it is it was extremely appealing to merchants, particularly members of the merchant caste in Hindu India, who were only at the third level in the strict caste system that had pervaded across India at least since the early Iron Age when the Indo-Arians had settled on the Gangic Indus plains. It was also very appealing to rulers who were not Indian in origin, such as the Kushan emperors who came to rule Northern India in the first and second centuries

A.D. I mentioned in a previous lecture that the Kushan emperor Kanishka I, usually dated between 127 and 147 A.D., was revered as a convert. He is credited with holding a fourth Buddhist council in order to reconcile the differences. But even if he did not convert, he clearly promoted Buddhism and Buddhist monks who were operating along the Silk Road.

There are various reasons for this. There are two forces at work disseminating Buddhism along the Silk Road. First, the profits of trade: The Vaishya caste in India, the merchant caste in Hindu India; many of them came to embrace Buddhism because it was their dharma to conduct trade and to prosper; and prosperity was actually a manifestation of their dharma and gave them what is called karma, which is good value that will lead to a better life in the next reincarnation. Those notions were strongly engrained in Greater Vehicle teachings of Buddhism, and merchants very often acted as unofficial missionaries along the routes in the caravan cities among the nomadic tribes with whom they came into contact because very often they hired the tribesmen as guards; your other option was to fight them off as brigands. Furthermore, merchants made enormous amounts of money; they built palatial homes; often held debates; collected texts. In addition, the monks who began to travel along the Silk Road, particularly under the Kushan emperors and later, translated the Buddhist texts into languages that were readily used along the Silk Road; above all, the vernaculars that had come out of Sanskrit, such as Prakrit and later Pali. They would also translate into Tocharian, the language of the Tarim Basin and probably the language of the Kushan emperors themselves. Eventually, text would be translated into Turkic languages and dialects; into other Iranian dialects, notably Sogdian; and so the Buddhist texts were then disseminated across Transoxiana and Central Asia in a variety of languages that were readily understood by the literate classes who were engaged in trade. This made the message particularly appealing. The monks themselves settled in these monasteries—*vihara* is the technical term of a function like a Christian monastery—and these were large complexes in which the ascetics were supported by the pious donations of believers. We have some remarkable examples of the type of pious donations that could be given. These include, for instance, our earliest rock-cut monasteries in India at Ajanta, which are beautifully decorated with murals, probably donations by wealthy merchants in thanks for their prosperity and the karma they achieved by just conducting their daily lives. Others were found in the so-called Mogao caves in the vicinity of Dunhuang. These were excavated by Sir Aurel Stein; and again they show spectacular fresco paintings of donors, of wealthy merchants, Sogdians, Tocharians, Chinese, all engaged in this activity in which Buddhism was part and parcel of their lives.

It was from this context along the Silk Road that Buddhist missionaries arrived in China and began to translate various texts into Chinese to make them available to a Chinese audience; and this is already happening in the second century A.D. and probably earlier. We have a number of names; we do not know much about them. These translations were out of perhaps Sanskrit originals, or Sogdian and Tocharian originals, but what is clear is that by the third century A.D., there are a number of Buddhist texts, sutras, now available, and these come from the different Buddhist schools—not just the Greater Vehicle, but the Lesser Vehicle schools—that were already penetrating into China; and as we will talk about in the later Chinese dynasties, the foreign dynasties, just as the Kushans, tended to favor Buddhist texts.

The most remarkable figure coming out of this Buddhist world created on the Silk Road is a Chinese pilgrim by the name of Xuanzang, born in 602 and dying in 664. He traveled along the Silk Road in search of manuscripts and he went on a long pilgrimage, first to Central Asia. He actually studied at the monastery beneath the great Buddhists at Bamiyan, those two marvelous rock-cut figures that were blown up by the Taliban as retaliation against their political opponents in Afghanistan and the crazy fighting going on there right now. He then entered into Northern India and he ended up at Sarnoff, the very place where the Buddha had taught. He brought back to China all sorts of Sanskrit text, and essentially was commissioned to do more accurate translations that became extremely important in the dissemination of Buddhism under the Tang and later the Song empires. He is representative of the whole process of turning what was Indian, almost a spinoff from Hinduism, into a universal faith of East Asia that would have powerful appeal on the Silk Road and powerful appeal upon all of these peoples of the Central and Eastern nomadic steppes. Buddhism, which still prevails on the eastern steppes, was the religion of choice in Central Asia, on the

Central Asian steppes, in the Tarim Basin deep into the Middle Ages; and only gradually was it displaced by Islam.

If Buddhism was the most successful, there were a number of other religions that were exchanged across the Silk Road. Again, they are not as spectacular and we do not have the same examples that we have from our Chinese pilgrims; but these included, for instance, Zoroastrianism. That was the official religion of the Sassanid shahs. We will be talking about the Sassanid shahs, who will come to power in the third century A.D. and represent a resurgence of the ancient Persian traditions. They will rule as agents of Ahura Mazda, the god of good who is in internal struggle against the evil forces. This is sometimes characterized as a dualistic religion. Really, Zoroastrianism as we have it today is a monotheistic creed that is very Iranian in its ethnicity but universal in its appeal; and the Zoroastrianism we are talking about is a religion that really is reformed in the third century A.D. associated with the reformer Kartir, now known through some important inscriptions, and particularly the first two shahs of the Sassanid Dynasty, Ardashir and Shapur I.

Besides Zoroastrianism, another faith that was originally on the Persian provincial zone is Manichaeism. These are the teachings of Mani, perhaps one of the most enigmatic and remarkable figures to burst upon the Silk Road and the Middle East. Mani apparently was born into some kind of Christian Jewish community about 216 A.D. in what is today Mesopotamia, lower Iraq, which the ancients called Mesopotamia. He was crucified in 276 A.D. on orders of the Shah for teaching essentially heretical messages that were at odds with Zoroastrian traditions, especially the Zoroastrian traditions as represented in the Avesta; and that is the collection of the Gathas, the early sayings of Zoroaster, which are now the canonical text of Zoroastrians. Mani taught schemes of cosmic redemption, as many scholars of religion would call it; and these schemes involved also a dualism and the dark fight between Light and Darkness. They were very, very ill-understood because most of our information on Manichaeism came from their opponents, particularly Christian critics. But the discovery of the Mani-Codex in Cologne , which contains the life of Mani and his early teachings, show us a very, very well-worked out religion that has certain similarities to Buddhism—a division between the Elect; the enlightened one pursuing an ascetic life; the laity who are supporting them—it also has a system of levels of reality that is not too dissimilar from the Buddhist notions of successions of reincarnation through dharma, improved karma that leads you to *moksha*, to spiritual liberation; and it is speculated by some that Mani was influenced by both Buddhist and Hindu traditions. Again, it was Universalist in appeal; and merchants particularly found it extremely attractive because it justified their position.

We know of a Turkish monarch: He is Kaghan Bögü—and that is "B-O-G-U," and the "g's" in Turkish language, or the "gh," are actually a silent sound; it is known as *yumushak* in modern Turkish, it acts as a glide—but Bögü, the khan of the Uighur Turks in the eighth century, converted officially to Manichaeism and brought his whole tribe over. These Uighurs as a group embraced Manichaeism because it was a higher religion. It had a powerful vision of lightness and darkness; cosmic redemption; a powerful monarch was the agent of the forces of good. The Uighurs remained Manichees well into the 9th and 10th centuries and actually brought it into the Tarim Basin where they migrated after their khanate collapsed in 840. This was another faith that brought new values, new ideas to the nomadic peoples. The Manichee missionaries are apparently behind devising a script for writing Uighur Turkish. They also were regarded as people who knew how to do things, particularly Manichee and merchants. Merchants would be prized for their expertise, their skills. They could organize taxes and assessments for would-be nomadic rulers. So Manichaeism and Buddhism also played that very important cultural role in enriching the lives of nomadic peoples.

Furthermore, Buddhist monks—Manichaean elect as they were called—were viewed as versions of the traditions shamans; the shamans of nomadic tribes, Turkish and Mongolian tribes, who were often in communication with the other world through hallucinogens, were envisioned as mounting the world tree on a horse, having insights into the spiritual world. These traditions are probably very, very early. They may well have been believed by Indo-European nomads, we do not know; but they are clearly believed by Turkish- and Mongolian-speaking nomadic peoples persisting well into the Mongol Empire and beyond, and even today among some of the tribes, they are still shamanists. Buddhists ascetics, Manichaean elect were put in that category. They were essentially shamans who could perform miracles and healing; they had expertise and knowledge; and therefore many of the nomadic peoples who embraced either Buddhism or Manichaeism still retained a good deal of their shamanist beliefs and were able to accommodate the two religious systems very readily.

A third religion that made its way onto the steppes compliments of the Silk Road that gained many, many adherents—there were some devotees of Zoroastrianism, but as I noted that remained a very nationalist Iranian religion, it did not gain too many adherents; it was essentially Buddhism and Manichaeism that won the numbers—probably third most successful was Christianity. This is not the Christianity we associate with the Roman Empire; in fact, we are dealing with the losers in the Roman Empire in a way. It is often called Nestorian Christianity; it is something of a misnomer. They, today, would call themselves the Church of the East. The Nestorian Christians were followers of Nestorius, who had been patriarch of Constantinople from 429–431; and his position on the nature of the birth— that Mary gave birth only to the person Jesus, the historical figure Jesus, and the Christ logos entered after his birth, and so Mary is not really Mother of God—that position was struck down at the Third Ecumenical Council in 431. There was a reconciliation of some of the Nestorians back into the mainline imperial church of the Roman Empire, the church that eventually gives birth to Catholic Western Christianity and Orthodox Eastern Christianity. If the Protestants are a reform group off the Catholic Church of the Reformation, essentially most of the Christian communities today come out of what is called the Council of Chalcedon in 451; the Nestorians represent a group that had broken earlier.

They left the Roman Empire. Rather than give up their faith, they moved across the frontier into the Persian domains of the Fertile Crescent; and they very quickly adapted their Christianity to local conditions. They adopted Aramaic as their liturgical language. They abandoned Greek; very important. They culturally assumed the morays and traditions of the people of the Middle East including multiple marriages; it was perfectly acceptable. The Nestorian Christians quickly turned themselves into a Middle Eastern and almost East Asian version of Christians who could travel along the Silk Road following the same routes by merchants and winning converts. They had a particularly powerful network of bishops in the cities of Central Asia; Samarkand, in particular, the great jump off point on the Silk Road—which is today remembered as the capital of Tamerlane; and most of the buildings you would see, the spectacular buildings, are Timurid buildings of the 14th century—when the Arabs first arrived there in the 8th century, Samarkand housed not only Buddhists and Manichaean shrines, but also very significant Christian churches. This is true of Nestorian communities across Transoxiana. There are some in the Tarim Basin; but they scored success among a number of the Turkish and Mongolian tribes of the central and eastern steppes. It is a little curious why they did so, but one of the explanations is that they spoke a well-known commercial language, Aramaic; and again, they had the advantage of knowing writing, and this was useful to nomadic peoples if they wanted to record anything. But again, their monks and ascetics were apparently seen as local versions of shamans; and the ability of a Nestorian ascetic or monk, a Christian monk, to carry out healing cures, particularly healing miracles, is what probably endeared them to a number of Turkish tribes.

We have some interesting reports from the 6th century A.D. of Turkish tribes that had embraced this Nestorian Christianity because reputedly it had been protected; the sign of the cross was seen as a protective device. In 588, a number of Turks were captured by the Sassanid shah, or actually the Sassanid shah's general—it is an important battle in the fighting between Turks and Persians over Central Asia—and Bahrām Chobin, the commander, took all of these Persians and he was surprised to find that many of them had tattooed on their foreheads little crosses. He was told by a number of the captives that the mothers of these men had done this when they were children because the sign of the cross was seen as very, very valuable in warding off a plague that had been apparently ripping through the tribe. The Nestorian monk was there telling them to believe in Jesus, to accept the new faith, and that would be a guardian to them; and apparently it worked, and the result was these fellows were tattooed with crosses. How strong they were Christians; what did their Christianity mean is another matter? But nonetheless, they would regard themselves as Christians, and again they would reconcile these Christian beliefs, superficial perhaps, with their shamanistic beliefs; and there are reports of conversions of Turkish tribes as late as the early 11th century. In the 12th and 13th centuries, this situation will change as Islam increasingly moves in and will displace these religions; and particularly there will be something of a dual between the Buddhists and the Muslims for the religious loyalties of the steppe peoples.

As a result of the Silk Road, on the eve of the Islamic conquest, these religions had made an immense impact upon the nomadic peoples and the caravan cities of the Silk Road. All of these religions were represented with major shrines, with Buddhist temples, Christian churches; there were even some significant Jewish communities on the Silk Road. We will later discover that a Turkish people, the Khazars, perhaps in 730 or thereabouts, sometimes it is dated to 860, that even a Turkish people—or at least the upper classes—will embrace Judaism. All of these religions had important recommendations. First, they were carried by scholars, monks, ascetics, and healing miracle men who could be associated with shamans and traditional healers in nomadic society. They also were responsible for bringing writing and all sorts of organizational skills that would allow the nomadic peoples, particularly the Turkish peoples, to organize far more effective confederacies and kingdoms than the Xiongnu or other peoples on the steppes. This is distinct from Parthians and others who would move into the settled areas and adopt the political institutions of the existing bureaucratic states. Finally, they put the nomadic peoples in close contact with the urban centers and create this dynamic that connects the great caravan cities to the nomadic peoples ever more strongly; the economic interchange, the interchange of material goods and ideas, which is a constant theme running through the Middle Ages and will culminate in the great cultural exchange and economic development under the Mongol Empire.

Up to, in my opinion, 751, all of these religions were practiced; they were all embraced and chosen by different individuals, tribes, and monarchs. But in 751, there will be a significant victory by the Muslims, by the armies of the Abbasid caliph, won over the armies of the emperor of China, the Tang emperor of China; this is the Battle of Talas. While that battle was exaggerated in many, many ways and misunderstood, that battle was the first sign of a new religion on the Silk Road; a religion that was now associated with victory. We will be talking about that religion, and that will be the religion of Islam.

Rome and the Huns

Lecture 11

This lecture begins a series that deals with the end of antiquity and the role of the steppe nomadic peoples in the transition from the ancient world to the Middle Ages. We will look at several nomadic peoples, first and foremost, the Huns. We'll devote two lectures to the Huns, both because we have a good bit of information on them, particularly on Attila, and because they play a pivotal role in the collapse of the Roman world and the advent of the Middle Ages, at least in Europe and the Mediterranean world. In later lectures, we'll look at other groups, including the Hephthalites and the Turks.

Goths versus Huns

- Around 376 A.D., the Goths fought a major battle against the **Huns**. They were overwhelmingly defeated, and their king, **Ermanaric**, committed suicide out of the grief. The defeat was quite a shock, not only to the Goths but also to the Romans. For some 150 years, the Goths and their Sarmatian subjects had been in alliance with the Roman Empire.

- The last Roman coins to celebrate a victory over a specific barbarian people were coins issued by Constantine celebrating his victory over the Sarmatians and, by extension, we suspect, the Goths. But this confederation came crashing to an end.

- The Germanic poets and, later, the Norse poets in the Viking age remembered this Gothic-Hun conflict in a very distorted way. The Goths themselves, who petitioned to be admitted to the Roman Empire to escape the Huns, appeared on the Lower Danube in the next year, and the emperor Valens reputedly brought 150,000 or 200,000 Goths from the barbarian side to the Roman side of the frontier. This made sense from Valens's point of view because he needed soldiers for his war against the Persians.

- Information we have from **Ammianus Marcellinus**, a Roman officer involved in diplomatic and administrative military affairs, paints a rather frightening picture of the Huns from the Roman viewpoint. The Goths were regarded as particularly savage among the Germanic peoples, but the Huns were barbaric on a whole new level. Over time, even the name "Hun" became associated with extreme ferocity.

The image of the Huns as ferocious warriors was transmitted from the Roman period throughout European history, down to the present day.

  o Ammianus tells us that they lived on fermented mare's milk. They didn't cook their food but sliced off chunks of meat from animals, put it under their saddles, and hoped the friction of riding would heat it up. They decorated their horses with severed heads and turned the heads of their opponents into drinking goblets.

  o At the same time, the Huns were ferocious and invaluable warriors; one Hun was equal to five Goths, and every Roman knew that one Goth could outfight any other German barbarian.

Origins of the Huns

- There has been great speculation about the origin of the Huns. It's clear that when Attila ruled the Huns, from approximately 434 to 453 A.D., it was a confederation of many different peoples—Germanic, Iranian, and apparently Proto-Turkish speakers. A good argument can be made by studying graves on the Russian steppes that seem to date to this period that the inner tribes of the Huns were probably Turkic speakers. They had East Asian features,

Lecture 11: Rome and the Huns

although they obviously intermarried with all sorts of people, and the population was very mixed.

- There is also a suggestion that somehow, they were scions of the Xiongnu. There's a belief that "Xiongnu" in ancient Chinese may have been pronounced closer to "Hunna." The Xiongnu, as you recall, were a great confederacy that Han emperors had fought for close to 300 years before finally breaking their power.
  o There had been a civil war in 58–54 B.C., in which the Xiongnu had broken up into northern and southern groups. The southern group dwelled in the regions that today would be called Inner Mongolia. They became allies of the Han emperor. The northern group was considered outer barbarians and was targeted by the Han emperors.

  o Eventually, Han armies and their southern Xiongnu allies pushed the northern Xiongnu further west. Ultimately, the northern confederation was broken up by the campaigns of the Han general **Ban Chao** from 75 to 102 A.D.

- It's thought that the northern Xiongnu on the central and east-central steppes of Eurasia probably broke up into different tribes, and the Huns who appeared in Europe about 370 A.D. were a spinoff from that confederacy. They probably took the name Xiongnu, Hunna, or Hun because it was considered ferocious.

- It is significant that somehow the ancestors of the Huns had come into close contact with Chinese civilization. Their tribute system in particular suggests a collective tribal memory of the five baits system of the Chinese.

- No written text of the Hun language survives, but the suspicion is that it was some kind of Turkic or Proto-Turkic language—not Indo-European. If so, they are the first Turkish speakers to appear in Europe. The arrival of the Turkish speakers across the steppes marked the turning point from the ancient world to the Middle Ages for at least the peoples of the Eurasian steppes.

Hun Expansion

- After the Huns achieved their victory over the Goths, they took possession of the Pontic-Caspian steppes. From that position, they invariably expanded, first, to the south, toward the Caucasus Mountains. There, they met up with the Alans, who guided them toward raiding into the Middle East.

  o There are reports of Hun invasions across the Caucasus and into the Sassanid Empire in the late 4th and early 5th centuries. The Huns ransacked Armenia, Mesopotamia, and northern Syria.

  o After taking plunder, these Huns withdrew, refusing to face the full Sassanid army and leaving the Sassanid shahs with the need to defend against a new threat from the northwest. This resulted in cooperation between the eastern Roman court and the Sassanid shahs to try to garrison and control the passes over the Caucasus.

- The Huns also moved west, following routes that the Sarmatians followed. They were naturally drawn to the grasslands of the Danube, today, the regions of the Hungarian plain in Transylvania and the Wallachian Plains of eastern Romania. All of these are traditional grasslands that would attract nomadic peoples from the steppes of southern Russia into Central Europe.

Eastern and Western Views of the Huns

- The appearance of the Huns in Central Europe, as opposed to the eastern steppes, posed an interesting problem for the Roman imperial government. These movements began probably around 395.

  o By the time the Huns arrived in Central Europe, the Roman Empire was divided in two. There was a western Roman emperor ruling from the city of Milan; the first one was the emperor Honorius, who came to the throne in 315 A.D. at the age of 11. His elder brother took over the eastern half of the Roman world, centered in the city of Constantinople.

  o The two courts were often at loggerheads over the first half of the 4th century. The western court was under the control of, essentially, a military strong man, who commanded various armies largely made up of barbarian mercenaries. In the eastern court, the emperors were just as ineffectual but ruled through a civil bureaucratic class that maintained control of the government.

- This division of the two courts was very much to the advantage of the Huns. The eastern court saw the Huns initially as an annoyance and, eventually, a major threat, whereas the western court saw the Huns as rather useful allies. The warlords of the western empire hired Huns as mounted soldiers to keep the German barbarians in line along the Rhine and Danube. The late Roman Empire of the west was essentially a game of the Roman master of the soldiers (*magister militum*) maintaining control using Hun mercenaries.

- This was an ideal situation for the Huns to exploit. We hear of a pair of brothers, **Rugila** and **Octar**, who ruled the Huns resident in Central Europe in the early 5th century. Rugila, in particular, was closely allied with the western court, especially with the general **Aetius**. From Rugila and Octar, Aetius had on command 60,000 Hun and Hun-allied soldiers. Aetius turned a blind eye to Hun raids into eastern Roman territory.

- The eastern Roman emperors at Constantinople had a very different view of these Huns. They were much closer to the locus of Hun power—the Pontic-Caspian steppes—and the Hun raids became increasingly difficult to contain.
  - Initially, the imperial government had been concerned about Goths. As we said, they entered the Roman Empire in 395 and sacked Rome in 410, an event that is often taken as a symbol of the breakup of Roman power. The Goths who had been pushed into the Roman Empire eventually migrated to carve out an independent kingdom with Roman blessings in southern Gaul. That would be the first of a series of Germanic barbarians being accommodated within the Roman Empire.

- When those Goths moved into the Roman Empire and east, that meant the Huns now bordered on the lower and middle Danube, that is, the frontier of the eastern Roman Empire, and were dangerously close to Constantinople. They raided repeatedly into the eastern Roman Empire for captives and gold.

- One response was to build the great walls of Constantinople. These included a trench, 25 feet deep and 50 to 60 feet across; a 25-foot-high outer wall with towers and fortified gates; and a 40-foot-high inner wall. These walls sealed off Constantinople from direct attack, although the government was forced to accept the fact that the Huns could still ravage their European provinces; at least the capital was preserved, and the Huns could not cross over into Asia Minor. It was the construction of the walls that turned Constantinople, the capital of the eastern empire, into the queen of cities and the bastion of the future Byzantine Empire.

- Another response to the Hun threat was to try to pursue a tradition of divide and conquer, that is, to play different Hun rulers off one another.
  - That approach worked only until a figure arrived on the scene to unite the various tribes, and that was Attila. Until his appearance, eastern diplomatic policies were rather sound and, in some ways, corresponded to the Huns' activities and traditions.

  - The Romans really had no experience in dealing with a great nomadic confederacy, but that would change dramatically with the emergence of Attila. He would organize a confederacy that bore no resemblance to any nomadic threat the Romans had ever faced and one that would threaten the very existence of the Roman world.

Huns: Altaic-speaking nomads who conquered the Pontic-Caspian steppes circa 375 and, under Attila, forged a barbarian empire from the Rhine to the Volga that challenged the Roman Empire. The Huns were probably descendants of subject or allied tribes of the northern Xiongnu.

magister militum: "Master of the soldiers," the supreme commander of field armies in the Roman Empire. From the reign of Constantine I (306–337), commanders of the cavalry and infantry commanded regional field armies. After 395, their supreme commander was designated *magister militum*, one for the western and one for the eastern Roman Empire.

Aetius (d. 454): A *magister militum* (425–454) from a military family in Moesia. By his influence with King Rugila and, later, Attila, Aetius secured Hun *foederati* so that he dominated policy at the court of the western emperor Valentinian III. His policy of alliance with the Huns was ruined by the invasions of Attila in 451–452. In 454, Aetius was executed on grounds of treason.

Ammianus Marcellinus (c. 325–391): A historian of imperial Rome, a native of Antioch, and a staff officer. He wrote a history of the Roman world from the reign of Trajan (98–117) to Valens (364–378). His work provides invaluable information on the Goths, Alani, and Huns, as well as Roman relations with the Sassanid Empire.

Ban Chao (30–102): Han general who completed the subjection and organization of the western regions in 75–91 and ended the power of the northern Xiongnu.

Ermanaric (d. 376): King of the Goths; committed suicide upon the defeat of his people by the Huns. He was remembered in the Norse legend of the Volsungs as the tyrant Jörmunrek.

Octar (c. 420–430): Ruled over the western Huns on the Pannonian grasslands; he was the father of Attila (434–453) and Bleda (434–445).

Rugila (c. 420–434): King of the Huns; ruled over the eastern tribes of the Huns between the lower Danube and the lower Volga. His brother Octar (c. 420–430) ruled over the western Huns on the Pannonian grasslands. He was succeeded by his nephews Attila and Bleda.

Uldin (r. c. 395–412): King of the Huns. Directed attacks of the Huns into the Balkans to extort subsidies and trading privileges from the eastern Roman emperor Arcadius. He commanded Hun contingents sent on request of the western Roman emperor Honorius in 406.

Suggested Reading

Ammianus Marcellinus (Hamilton, trans.), *The Later Roman Empire (A.D. 354–378).*

Gordon, *The Age of Attila.*

Meaenchen-Helfen (Knight, ed.), *The World of the Huns.*

Sinor, "The Hun Period."

Thompson, *The Huns.*

Questions to Consider

1. Why did the defeat of the Goths by the Huns in 376 excite such fear and attention in the Roman world? How accurate is the description of the Huns by Ammianus Marcellinus?

2. What was the composition of the Hun confederation in 376? What factors might have led their ancestors to migrate from the eastern Eurasian steppes? How did their conquests and migrations into Central Europe transform the Huns?

3. Why did the rival Roman imperial courts at Constantinople and Ravenna pursue different policies toward the Huns? How did the Hun kings Uldin

and Rugila exploit the rivalry and the Roman Empire? In what ways did they anticipate Attila, the Hun Scourge of God?

4. What accounts for the image of the Huns as the quintessential nomadic barbarians in Western literature thereafter? Why did the Romans and Germans agree that the Huns represented new, outlandishly ferocious barbarians? How did their view compare to those voiced by Chinese writers of the Han Empire about the Xiongnu?

Rome and the Huns
Lecture 11—Transcript

In this lecture, I want to open up a set of lectures that deal with the end of antiquity and how the steppe nomadic peoples played a role in the transition from what we call the ancient world or antiquity to the Middle Ages. That will involve us looking at several different nomadic peoples, first and foremost the Huns; and I devote two lectures on the Huns for several reasons: One is because the amount of information that we have on them, particularly on Attila who will really deserve his own lecture; and in addition, the Huns play a very, very important role—a pivotal role—in the collapse of the Roman world and the advent of the Middle Ages, at least in Europe and the Mediterranean world. We will also look later on at other groups, notably the Hephthalites who are often known as the White Huns, and we will bring on the first Turks. But for the next two lectures—for this lecture and the next one—we will be dealing largely with the Huns.

The Huns, as I said, are particularly well-documented; and that is because they come to the attention of Roman authors, above all a man by the name of Ammianus Marcellinus. He was a Roman born in either Antioch, or today the city of Beirut; Berytus would be the Roman name. He spoke Latin as his first language. He was a Roman officer; not a line officer, but someone more involved in diplomatic and administrative military affairs. He travelled widely across the Roman Empire. He came into contact with all sorts of people, and he gives us a very, very detailed description of the Huns when they entered the Pontic-Caspian steppes somewhere between 370 and 375 A.D. His information is very good. He got the information from Goths— from East Germanic peoples who fought the Huns and also lost—but the information matches up very well with a lot of the social institutions and customs of the Xiongnu described by Han sources, particularly Zhang Qian, that envoy who spent so many years wandering among the Xiongnu and eventually returned home to write an account of their customs. In a moment, we will also see that there may be some connection between the Xiongnu and the Huns.

Ammianus was astonished. The Goths had fought a major battle against the Huns, usually dated about 376 A.D. They were overwhelmingly defeated, and their king, a man by the name of Ermanaric as he is recorded in Jordanes writing in the sixth century A.D., committed suicide out of grief. This was quite a shock, not only to the Goths, but also to the Romans. For some 150 years now, the Goths and their Sarmatian subjects had been in alliance with the Roman Empire. In fact, they had submitted during the reign of Constantine. The emperor Constantine had waged some kind of campaign on the steppes, he had crossed the Lower Danube; and actually the Sarmatians and Goths had submitted to Rome and agreed to send federates (that is allies; *foederati* in Latin means "allied forces"). The last Roman coins to celebrate a victory over a specific barbarian people were coins issued by Constantine celebrating his victory over the Sarmatians, and by extension we suspect the Goths as well because the two were in cooperation. In any case, this confederation came crashing down. Ermanaric lived on as a quintessential tyrant king in both Germanic and Norse literature. He becomes a pivotal figure in the story of the Völsungs where he orders the death of Svanhild, the daughter of Gudrun. In Norse mythology, she is torn apart by horses. The evil gothic king is attacked by her half brothers, Sorli and Hamther. It is great stuff, and it remotely remembers, "Yeah, there are Huns in the background that are somehow behind all of this." The Germanic poets and later the Norse poets in the Viking Age still remember this Gothic-Hun conflict in a very distorted way.

The Goths themselves, who fled into the Roman Empire and petitioned to be admitted to the Roman Empire to escape the Huns, appeared on the Lower Danube in the next year, in 377, and the emperor Valens reputedly brought 150,000 or 200,000 Goths from the barbarian side to the Roman side of the frontier. This made sense from Valens's point of view because he needed soldiers; he was fighting a war against the Persians. The Goths and their Sarmatian allies had long been furnishing soldiers to the Roman army anyway, and so it was a matter of resettling these barbarians on Roman territory. This would prove a fateful move that would have really dire consequences for the political and military integrity of the Roman Empire; but in 377, no one was looking that far ahead. It is from these Gothic refugees who arrived in the Roman Empire from whom Ammianus Marcellinus obtained his information.

The information paints a rather frightening picture from the Roman viewpoint. The Huns clearly were very, very different from the Goths. The Goths were regarded as particularly savage among the Germanic peoples, but the Huns were something else. The Romans had never quite seen people like this. The closest dealings they had had with nomadic opponents were Sarmatians, Iranian-speakers; separate tribes such as the Roxolani, the Alans, with whom the Romans had dealt individually and, as I had stressed, had never really come together in a confederation. The Huns clearly were perceived as different. The description of them is they are particularly ugly. They wear fur and living clothing they never washed; the clothing just falls off of them. Various stock stories that would really match up very well with prejudices and stereotypes in Han Chinese record show they are ferocious warriors. They ride these ugly ponies. They are clearly horse archers. They are a whole other set of barbarians. This image is transmitted from the Roman period through the ages through European history right down to the present day.

There is a famous irony in this of those of you familiar with modern European history: In 1900, Kaiser Wilhelm told the German forces that were marching off to put down the Boxer Rebellion in Beijing to fight like Huns; that is, to bring back to the Asiatic menace the same ferocity that the Huns had once perpetrated on the Germanic tribes. This is a whole bunch of overblown, silly German nationalism of the early 20th century, but the name stuck; and ironically, the Germans are called Huns in the First World War. The British have a wonderful time depicting the Germans as new Huns, raping Belgium, and going across France; and they are as barbaric as Attila and his Huns. In the Second World War, FDR always referred to the Germans in his memos as "Huns," and this notion stuck. Ironically, it is not exactly what the Kaiser wanted; but that is true of a good deal of the Kaiser's career: It is not exactly what he wanted, but this is what he got. The name "Hun" became associated with a particular ferocity. It was almost a generic term, and was so applied in medieval chronicles, really starting from the end of the Roman Empire from the 5th century A.D. running into the 16th century A.D., where barbarian people after barbarian people, nomadic peoples that came across the southwestern steppes, were generally dubbed "Huns" by Europeans because they could not think of anything more ferocious and they have all got to be related one way. Ammianus tells us that they live on that fermented mare's milk; they ride on these horses. They do not really cook their food; they slice off chunks of meat from animals, put it under their saddles, and hope the friction of riding will heat it up for them. They decorate their horses with severed heads; they turn the heads of their opponents into drinking goblets. I mean, one after another of the stereotypes. They also indicate the Huns are afraid of roofs and houses; that they roam incessantly over the steppes. On the other hand, they are ferocious and invaluable warriors. One Hun is equal to five Goths, and every Roman knows that one Goth can outfight any other German barbarian—when you get lower down the totem pole you get to people like Vandals who do not even count—but the Huns are put up in this category.

There has been a great speculation as to the origin of these people. We really have very little information. We have no information on the Hun names; even the name Attila is apparently Germanic in origin. It is clear that when Attila ruled the Huns from approximately 434–453 A.D.—after he died of that hemorrhage from overindulging at a marriage festival—that it was a confederation of many different peoples, Germanic, Iranian, and apparently Proto-Turkish speakers. There is a good argument to be made by studying graves on the Russian steppes that seem to date to this period that the Huns, at least what would be called those inner tribes of a nomadic confederation, were probably Turkic speakers. They had East Asian features; they were not Europoid in appearance, although they obviously intermarried with all sorts of people along the way—Iranian speakers, later Germanic speakers—and the population was very mixed.

There is also a suggestion that somehow they are scions of the Xiongnu. This was an identification made in the 19th century; it has been hotly debated. But there is a very good argument made by Chinese scholars—I not being an expert in ancient Chinese have to follow the majority opinion on this—but there is a belief that Xiongnu in ancient Chinese may have been pronounced closer to "Hunna." The Xiongnu, as you recall, were a great confederacy that the Han emperors had fought for really close to 300 years before they finally broke the power of the Xiongnu. There had been a civil war in 58–54 B.C. where they broke up into a northern and southern group. The southern group dwelled in the regions today would be called Inner Mongolia; they became allies of the Han emperor. The northern group was outer barbarians and targeted by the Han emperors. Eventually, Han armies and their southern Xiongnu allies pushed those northern Xiongnu further and further west; and it was that migration that triggered the movement of the ancestors of the Kushans and the Sacae, some would even say the Parthians, and they moved ever steadily west. They end up north of the Chin Shan; and that northern confederation is broken up by the campaigns of Ban Chao, the great late Han general from 75–102 A.D. who conquers the Tarim Basin and organizes the so-called western districts, the later four garrisons of the Tang period. It is thought that some kind of confederacy of the Northern Xiongnu on the central and east-central steppes of Eurasia broke up into different tribes, and the Huns who appear in Europe about 370 A.D. were probably a spinoff from that confederacy. They probably took the name Xiongnu, or Hunna, or Hun because it was a ferocious name; just the same way Kaiser Wilhelm invoked the name when he was waving bye-bye to all those German soldiers who were going off to fight the Boxers (and by the way, they arrived too late to have any significant effect on the Siege of the Legations in Beijing, but that is again another story for European imperialism).

That is a significant fact: that somehow the ancestors of the Huns had come into close contact with Chinese civilization; and remember, a number of aspects of their dealings with the Chinese, particularly the tribute system, the so-called "Five Baits," where the Chinese would court nomadic allies who would otherwise be raiding their empire and buy bolts of silk, buy Chinese brides who would be sent, princesses of different rank, providing specialist technicians who could teach the Xiongnu in different types of activities that would be useful. There is some sort memory—tribal memory, collective memory—of the Huns, of that connection, which I think explains a great deal of Attila's own dealings with the Roman Empire, which we will discuss in the next lecture.

Again, I mentioned we have no language surviving, no written text of the Hun language; but the suspicion is that it was some kind of Turkic language or Proto-Turkic language; that it was not Indo-European. If, so they are the first Turkish speakers to appear in Europe; and the arrival of the Turkish speakers across the steppes—that movement from east to west, as we will discuss in coming lectures—really marks the turning point from the ancient world to the Middle Ages for at least the peoples of the Eurasian steppes.

The Huns achieved a great victory over the Goths and took possession of the Pontic-Caspian steppes, just as earlier the Sarmatians had and before them the Scythians; that is, the original heartland of those early Indo-European nomads now fell under the rule of the Huns. In that position, they invariably expanded in two different directions. One was to go immediately to the south, towards the Caucasus Mountains. They met up with the Alans, that Sarmatian people who had plagued the Romans and the Parthians; and the Alans now told the Huns, "By the way, there are these things known as the Dariel Pass and the Derbent Pass, and even farther on there are passes through the Elburz Mountains, and we can raid into the Middle East." There are reports of the late fourth century and early fifth century of Hun invasions across the Caucasus into the Sassanid Empire, and these were particularly destructive. The Huns ransacked Armenia, Mesopotamia, Northern Syria. Actually, Saint Jerome in Bethlehem at the time, working on his Latin translation of the Bible, the so-called Vulgate, makes report of these horrible invasions on the scale of the Mongols; and he uses the same language that later Christian monks and chroniclers would use of Mongol invasions.

Eventually, these Huns withdrew; they were there for raiding, taking plunder, and goodies. They refused to face the full Sassanid army, and it left the Sassanid shahs with a new threat of trying to defend their empire from the northwest from these Huns across the Caucasus; and that resulted in efforts of cooperation between the eastern Roman court and the Sassanid shahs to try to garrison and control those passes over the Caucasus, which becomes an important strategic position through the whole of the Middle Ages: control of those passes, and therefore the movement of nomadic peoples out of Southern Russia into either Asia Minor, the heartland of the later Byzantine Empire, or into the lands of the caliphate, what we would today call Iraq and Iran. For the Sassanids, this was an unexpected and new nomadic menace; one that they really did not want to deal with because, as we shall see in an upcoming lecture, they have a lot more problems on their northeastern frontier trying to control Transoxiana from yet new nomads.

Meanwhile, the Huns also moved west. They followed routes that the Sarmatians followed. They would naturally be drawn to the grasslands of the Danube; that would be the regions today of the Hungarian plain and Transylvania. It would also be to the regions of Wallachia, the Wallachian

Plains of Eastern Romania. All of these are traditional grasslands that nomadic peoples would move from the steppes of Southern Russia into Central Europe. Again, to some extent they were occupying areas that had once acknowledged Gothic suzerainty; these had once been home to the Sarmatians—and undoubtedly they intermixed and assimilated nomadic peoples already living there.

The appearance of the Huns in what we would call Central Europe, as opposed to the eastern steppes, posed an interesting problem for the Roman imperial government. These movements began probably around 395. We know of a Hun ruler named Uldin who ruled approximately from 395 and died sometime after 412 A.D. He is seen as an ally of the emperor of Constantinople, the eastern Roman emperor; and the Huns were seen, again, as useful allies providing federate soldiers. But by the time the Huns arrive in Central Europe, the Roman Empire has divided in two. There is a Western Roman Emperor ruling from the city of Milan. The first one was the emperor Honorius, who came to the throne in 315 A.D. at the age of 11, the younger, ineffectual, and rather obstinate son of the emperor Theodosius I and the last emperor to rule over a united empire, and then his elder brother at age 17 took over the eastern half of the Roman world—that was centered in the city of Constantinople—and the two courts were often at loggerheads over the first half of the fifth century A.D. That is because the western court fell under the control of generalissimos, *magister militum* was the official title. The first one was a man named Stilicho who was the generalissimo, the master of the soldiers of the western armies, from 395 until he was executed for treason in 410; and then, later on, the general Aetius, who in the middle of the fifth century A.D. would dominate the western court, which at that point had moved to Ravenna in 402. You have a western court under the control of essentially a military strongman, one would even say a warlord, who could command the various Roman armies, at this point largely comprising barbarian mercenaries; and then an eastern court, where the emperors were just as ineffectual but were ruled through a civil bureaucratic class that maintained control of the government. The generals were ultimately supported, were paid, and subordinate to the civil government, to the imperial court; and generals could be fired and executed rather than lured into suspicious arrangements and murder, which is what happened to both Stilicho and Aetius.

That division of the two courts was very much to the advantage of the Huns. The eastern court saw the Huns initially as an annoyance and eventually as a major threat, whereas the western court saw the Huns as really rather useful allies; in fact, so useful that Stilicho and later Aetius, the two essentially military warlords of the western empire, loved hiring Huns from the rulers of the Huns as a way of getting excellent mounted soldiers who could keep all the German barbarians in line along the Rhine and Danube and who were now settled within the western provinces of the Roman empire and provided the main military force. Ironically, the late Roman Empire of the west, in the last 75 years of the western Roman Empire in the fifth century—it collapses in 476, or officially ends; it already had collapsed—is essentially a game of the Roman master of the soldiers maintaining control by using Hun mercenaries, Hun allies, to keep his German allies and federates in line.

This was an ideal situation for the Huns to exploit. If it is true that the Huns had some kind of connection to the Xiongnu, they understood how to play the game; how to exploit a great imperial state in the way that the Sarmatians and the Scythians never did. The kings who follow Uldin, it is hard to know exactly who they are. We hear of a pair of brothers, a man named Rugila or Ruga—he has several names—and a brother Octar, who are known to be ruling the Huns, at least the Huns resident in Central Europe, in the early fifth century. Their power may have extended over the southwestern steppes. We know that they are in place in the 420s and 430s because the Romans are sending missions up to these fellows more or less in the vicinity of where Budapest is today. These two brothers apparently shared power and may well have divided power between them in a classic system of lateral succession, which we have seen with other nomadic peoples.

In any event, Ruga or Rugila in particular was closely allied with the western court, especially with that general Aetius. Aetius had made himself master of the western court in 425. When the first western Roman emperor Honorius mercifully died in 423 A.D., there was a brief civil war and Aetius actually backed the usurper, a fellow called Johannes; but the legitimate emperor put on the throne was Valentinian III, the son of Galla Placidia, one of the formidable Roman empresses of the Late Roman world, and Aetius pledged his loyalty to her. Aetius had on command from Rugila and Octar 60,000 Hun soldiers. That probably meant Huns and Hun allies; there were not all Huns.

But it was clearly the most formidable field army in the Western Roman Empire; and Aetius could bully his way into dominating the imperial court and essentially running the western provinces under the title of Patrician, which was a civil title that gave him control over the taxing and administering of Roman Gaul, as well as his title of master of the soldiers. He could call those Huns on cue to attack recalcitrant Germanic tribes; the most famous one was either in 436 or 437 where Rugila or Ruga leant Hun soldiers, who ruthlessly destroyed the Burgundian Germans at the city of Worms, and that massacre of the Burgundians lived on later Germanic legend that fed into the legend of the Niflungs or the Nibelungs, the Nibelungenlied in middle high German, or the Niflungs in Norse mythology. It was remembered as a great attack. Furthermore, Aetius made sure to keep on excellent terms; if the Huns raided Roman territory, not a problem. They were allowed to plunder the Balkans, and Aetius was pretty much indifferent to what the Huns did vis-à-vis the eastern court.

The eastern Roman emperors at Constantinople had a very different view of these Huns. They were much closer to the locus of Hun power, which was that Pontic-Caspian steppes. There has been a lot of learned discussion that when the Huns settled in what is today Hungary they lost their cavalry edge, because the Hungarian plain cannot sustain the large numbers of horses necessary to maintain steppe cavalry; and there have been several significant articles and monographs written along those lines. That is true, except that whoever was the charismatic leader who could dominate the Hun confederation could summon many, many Hun forces from the Pontic-Caspian steppes; and we believe that is eventually what Attila the Hun did. He may have resided on the Hungarian plain, but his authority ranged widely probably to the Volga if not to the Aral River where he had large numbers of steppe cavalry that he could summon with promises of plunder; and that gets at the crux of the problem.

For the eastern imperial government, they faced Huns whose raids increasingly became more and more difficult to contain. Initially, the imperial government had been concerned about Goths who would enter the Roman Empire in 395; eventually would migrate. They would sack Rome en route in 410, which is often taken as a symbolic act of the breakup of Roman power. But the Goths, who had been pushed into the Roman Empire, rebelled and eventually migrated through the Roman Empire to carve out an independent kingdom with Roman blessings in Southern Gaul; and that would be the first of a series of Germanic barbarians being accommodated within the Roman Empire. When those Goths moved into the Roman Empire and moved west, that meant the Huns now bordered on the Lower and Middle Danube—that is, the frontier of the eastern Roman Empire—and were dangerously close to Constantinople. They raided repeatedly into the eastern Roman Empire for captives, for gold, for payoffs because this is the way the Huns would reward their various supporters. That was quite in the tradition of the Xiongnu; they would raid the Chinese Empire for silk, the Huns are raiding the Roman Empire for gold.

One response was to build the great walls of Constantinople. These were ordered by the empress Aelia Pulcheria, the older sister of the emperor Theodosius II, and the walls were built along the four mile land side of Constantinople. Constantinople is essentially a triangle. On the north is the Golden Horn, the river flowing into the Bosporus; one the other side is the Sea of Marmora; and then it is facing the Bosphorus Straits. You cut off that land side with four miles of wall that turn the city into an invincible island. Those walls, which are being rather heavy-handedly restored but nonetheless restored by the current government in Istanbul, were awesome. There was a huge fosse or trench 25 feet deep, 50–60 feet across; an outer wall with towers, and that outer wall was 25 feet high with towers and fortified gates; there was an inner wall 40 feet high with 60 foot towers, some 95 of them have been counted. These walls literally sealed off Constantinople from direct attack, so any Hun attack over the Danube into the Balkans would hit those walls and essentially ricochet west; and that is, the government in Constantinople accepted the fact that the Huns would ravage their European provinces, but at least the capital would be preserved and the Huns could not cross over into Asia Minor. It was the construction of those walls of Constantinople that turned the new Rome—Constantinople, the capital of the eastern empire—into the queen of cities and the bastion of the future Byzantine Empire, which would defy barbarian after barbarian; nomadic tribe after nomadic tribe would fail before those walls. That was one way of dealing with the Hun threat.

The other was to try to pursue a tradition of divide and conquer—that is, to play the different Hun rulers off with each other; to pay them bribes of gold and the like—and that worked only so far until a figure managed to unite those tribes, and that was Attila. Up until the appearance of Attila, eastern diplomatic policies were rather sound and in some ways corresponded to what the Han did; and the Romans really had no experience of dealing with the great nomadic confederacy. But that would change dramatically with the emergence of Attila, the Scourge of God; and he would organize a great nomadic confederacy that bore no resemblance to any nomadic threat the Romans had ever faced, and a nomadic confederacy that could threaten the very existence of the Roman world.

Attila the Hun—Scourge of God
Lecture 12

In the last lecture, we introduced the Huns as the first Turkic-speaking nomads or Proto-Turkic–speaking nomads to enter the steppes of southern Russia and move into the grasslands of Central Europe. In this lecture, we will finish the history of the Huns, particularly Attila, the Scourge of God, who succeeded to sole rule over the Huns after apparently orchestrating the murder of his brother while hunting, an incident dated usually to around 444 or 445 A.D. The image of Attila as a pitiless conqueror has endured for centuries.

The Legend of Attila

- The image of **Attila** has inspired novels, films, and artwork over the centuries, and he has been admired by later rulers. For instance, the Arpad kings of Hungary, who were **Magyars**, identified themselves with Huns or Hungarians because the name Attila struck such fear in the hearts of Western Europeans. They even claimed to have the sword of Attila.

- The Ottoman Turks—having no direct connection to Attila—also identified with the steppe conqueror because they saw themselves as *ghazi* warriors, warriors of the steppes. Indeed, the names Attila and Genghis are still popular in Turkey today.

- In European traditions, especially among the Germanic peoples who were subjects of Attila, he lived on as a great lord. Roman sources who visited Attila's court (thought to be somewhere near Budapest) describe it as a great hall, like something out of *Beowulf*. In Norse legend, Attila was known as Atli and seen as somehow responsible for the destruction of the Burgundian family of Gunnar.

- All these images that have come down to us resulted because Attila is the first steppe conqueror of whom we have a real sense of identity. Attila had a profound effect on both the eastern and

Attila even appears in Romantic paintings of the 19th century, particularly some by French painters who conjured up images of the destruction of Gaul by hordes of Huns.

western Roman Empires and an important influence in dictating the course of European history.

Rise to Power

- Attila and his brother **Bleda** came to the throne jointly in 434, succeeding their uncle, Rugila, who had a longstanding alliance with the western Roman court. The brothers shared power and initially pursued traditional Hun policy, that is, attacking and looting in the east and allying with the west.

- The brothers lent their horse archers and Hun vassals to the armies of Aetius and the western Roman emperor. At the same time, they began systematic attacks into the Balkan provinces, a loose region called Illyricum that is today largely Bulgaria. These provinces came under increasing attack in the 440s, enabling Attila and Bleda to capture large numbers of Roman specialists, such as urban and military engineers.

- Starting in the 440s, the Huns not only raided but began capturing Roman cities. They were able to storm the heavily fortified masonry architecture walls of cities in the Balkans that had controlled the Roman road network. The Huns must have had good information about the goings on at the imperial court because they timed their attacks generally when the eastern arm was preoccupied elsewhere.

- Attila seems to have had knowledge of the overall geographic dimensions of the Roman world, which allowed him to frame rather sophisticated attack strategies. The Hun victories netted plunder, captives, and gold—the ingredients that sustained the Hun Empire.
  - o Attila probably never envisioned a methodical conquest of the Roman Empire. His subjects, including the German tribes, numbered perhaps 800,000 or 1 million, compared to the Romans' 55 or 65 million. This disparity was a determining factor in the strategies of Attila.

  - o His objective was to wrest control of certain crucial border areas to break down the barriers on the Danube and gain easy access into the Roman provinces; there, he could acquire plunder to reward all his vassal rulers and sustain his position. The goal was to ensure that the Roman frontier stretching along the Danube became a highway, allowing the movement of Huns.

  - o This is clearly the thrust of a treaty negotiated in 447 by the Roman envoy Anatolus, who was then the master of the eastern Roman army and a representative of the emperor **Theodosius**. This treaty promised very heavy tribute—2100 pounds of gold. It also essentially dismantled the Roman frontier along the Danube. And it ensured that Attila would be recognized as the leader of the Hun confederation, with some sense of equality to the western Roman emperor.

- In 444 or 445, Attila had a falling out with his older brother, Bleda, and dispatched him in a hunting "accident." From that point on, Attila was the unquestioned ruler of the various Hun tribes— essentially a barbarian counter-empire to the Roman world. He waged war ruthlessly in the eastern Roman Empire and destroyed the imperial frontier. The Roman cities in the European provinces existed only on the sufferance of Attila.

Western Invasion
- In 445 A.D., Attila was at the height of his power. He commanded a confederation and a number of nomadic warriors clearly on the order of the Xiongnu confederation under Modu Chanyu. Many scholars believe that at this point, he dramatically changed his policy and invaded the western empire, which hitherto had been his ally. To understand this change, we need to look at the politics of the western imperial court and some aspects of Roman law and nomadic customs.

- In 450 A.D., Attila received a ring and apparently what he took as a marriage proposal from the Empress **Honoria**, the elder half-sister of the then-reigning western emperor, **Valentinian III**. Valentinian was a weak and ineffectual emperor, dominated by his mother and his master of the soldiers, Aetius, who hated each other. Honoria likewise resented Valentinian. She felt that she had a better claim to the throne than her half-brother, which meant that anyone she married would have a better claim, as well.

- Finally, Valentinian and Aetius decided that the only way to neutralize her was to marry her to an elderly boring senator. But Honoria sent a ring to Attila, who interpreted it as a marriage offer and, thus, recognition that he was the greatest lord in the world. Attila replied that he would accept control of Gaul and Spain as his bride's dowry.

- This was unacceptable to the Roman emperor, who still operated under the laws of the republic. Valentinian's refusal of Attila's proposal was tantamount to an act of war. In early 451, Attila levied a huge barbarian army, probably 50,000 to 100,000 strong, with large numbers of mounted horsemen.

- These forces swept over the Rhine and began to sack the cities of Western Europe as thoroughly as they had sacked the cities of the Balkans. Many late Roman cities known today by their modern names—Strasbourg, Worms, Mainz, Cologne, and others—fell to the Hun armies. One of the few major cities not to fall was Paris because the local Saint Geneviève appeared and allegedly warded off the Hun hordes.

- Otherwise, the Huns did a thorough job of destroying eastern and central France, which ultimately destroyed the very military basis of the western Roman state. Aetius had no choice but to seek allies among the Visigoths and other Germans settled within the Roman Empire. He put together a coalition army of Romans and largely German federate allies to oppose this great Hun invasion.

The Battle of the Catalonian Plains

- Aetius raised a siege of Orleans, and Attila began to withdraw east, in the general direction of what today is the city of Châlons. In the summer of 451, the two met at the Battle of the Catalonian Plains, which was likely fought between Châlons and Troyes.

- The Hun army was enormous, drawn up in three forces. The best forces, Attila's nomadic cavalry, the Huns, were in the center, with various allied forces on the flanks, including Ostrogoths, Alans, Burgundians, and others. For his part, Aetius put his weakest forces in the center to receive the Hun attack. Then he stationed his more powerful forces, the Visigoths, on the right and Romans and Franks on the left.

- The battle opened with a charge of the Hun cavalry that drove deep into the Roman center and scattered it. It seemed as if the Roman army would be broken in half. The two Gothic forces, Attila's Ostrogoths and Aetius's Visigoths, clashed in a violent attack. The Romans and

Franks plowed into the exposed flank of Attila and eventually forced him to quit the battlefield. The fight ended in a draw.

Aftermath of the Battle

- Attila withdrew east, making a beeline back to his capital and vowing to return the next year, which he did. In 452, he invaded northern Italy with another huge barbarian army. He penetrated to the Po Valley, and it seemed as if the way to Rome was open. There were no imperial forces opposing him because the German federates had no interest in fighting for Italy.

- It was there that Pope **Leo I** met Attila and convinced him to withdraw, for reasons that are still obscure. Attila pulled back to his capital and celebrated in a great marriage festival. He had married a German girl, Ildico. He drank to excess, and in the night a blood vessel burst in his head, and he drowned in his own blood. The girl was killed on suspicion that she had murdered him. She would live on in Norse legend as Gudrun, the Germanic princess who avenged the death of her relatives at the hands of Attila.

- Attila's death resulted in the fragmentation of his empire. The subject tribes were raised in rebellion, complements of money paid by the new eastern Roman emperor, Marcian, a tough soldier-emperor who had actually supported the western government in its struggle against Attila. Attila's sons ruled some Hun tribes on the Pontic-Caspian steppes, but they were never again the force they had been.

- The real victors at Châlons and in the invasion of northern Italy were the Germanic tribes who were left to partition what was left of the Roman Empire into independent kingdoms. Meanwhile, the eastern court had learned its lesson well: Trust in the walls surrounding Constantinople and make sure that no future Attila ever emerged on the steppes. The emperor invented Byzantine diplomacy to prevent the revival of another steppe conqueror.

ghazi: The epitome of the heroic nomadic warrior, prized by Turks.

Magyars: Finno-Ugric nomads who migrated from the Siberian forests east of the Urals to the Pontic-Caspian steppes in the 9th century. In 896, they settled on the Pannonian grasslands; they are in fact ancestors of the Hungarians.

Attila (b. c. 410; r. 434–452): Regarded as the second greatest conqueror of the steppes. He and his brother Bleda succeeded their uncle Rugila as joint kings of the Huns. Circa 445, Bleda was murdered by Attila. In 442–443 and 447, Attila launched devastating raids into the Balkans, earning the sobriquet "Scourge of God." In 451, he invaded Gaul and suffered at Châlons a strategic defeat from a Roman-Gothic army under Aetius. In 452, he invaded northern Italy but withdrew due to the intercession of Pope Leo I. Attila died in 452 from overindulgence at his wedding celebrations. The Hun Empire collapsed within two years after his death.

Bleda (434–445): King of the Huns and elder son of Octar. He ruled jointly and clashed repeatedly with his brother Attila, who ordered Bleda's murder.

Honoria (417–454): Daughter of Galla Placidia and Constantius III; created Augusta in 425. Honoria, who despised her brother, the western emperor Valentinian III, precipitated the invasion of Attila in 451.

Leo I, the Great (b. c. 390; r. 440–461): The first pope of a noble Roman family. Leo upheld papal primacy against the patriarch of Constantinople. He defined the creed of the western church in his *Tome* (449), accepted at the Fourth Ecumenical Council in 451. He won a moral victory by convincing Attila to withdraw from Italy in 452.

Theodosius II (b. 401; r. 408–450): Flavius Theodosius, the son of Arcadius and Eudocia (daughter of the Frankish general Bauto); succeeded as a minor. The emperor was directed by his ministers and his older sister, Aelia

Pulcheria. Theodosius agreed to humiliating treaties dictated by Attila the Hun in 443 and 447.

Valentinian III (Flavius Placidius Valentinianus) (b. 419; r. 425–455): Son of Galla Placidia and Constantius III. As western Roman emperor, Valentinian lost the remaining provinces in Spain and North Africa. His mother, who directed affairs of state, clashed with the powerful *magister militum* Aetius. Valentinian III, murdered by a clique of senators, left no heirs; thus, the western Roman Empire disappeared within 20 years of his death.

Suggested Reading

Ferrill, *The Fall of the Roman Empire.*

Gordon, *The Age of Attila.*

Meaenchen-Helfen (Knight, ed.), *The World of the Huns.*

O'Flynn, *Generalissmos of the Western Roman Empire.*

Sinor, "The Hun Period."

Thompson, *The Huns.*

Questions to Consider

1. What accounts for the enduring popularity of Attila as one of the greatest barbarian conquerors? How do these perceptions match or differ from the sources on Attila?

2. What were the qualities that made Attila such a remarkable conqueror? How much did he depend on the prowess of the Huns as horse archers? How much did he depend on the weakness of the Roman Empire?

3. Why did the eastern and western Roman Empires pursue different policies with regard to Attila? Were Attila's aims consistent throughout his career? Why did his empire fragment so quickly upon his death?

4. What was the impact of Attila's invasions of Gaul and Italy in 451–452? Was the Battle of Châlons decisive?

5. How did Attila's career mark the beginning of the medieval world for both Europe and the south Russian steppes?

Attila the Hun—Scourge of God
Lecture 12—Transcript

In this lecture, I want to finish the history of the Huns, and particularly Attila, the Scourge of God, who succeeded to the sole rule over the Huns after apparently orchestrating the murder of his brother during a hunting accident, dated usually around 444 or 445 A.D.

In the last lecture, we introduced the Huns as the first Turkic-speaking nomads, or Proto-Turkic-speaking nomads, to enter the steppes of Southern Russia— that is, the Pontic-Caspian steppes—and then move into the grasslands of Central Europe. The exploits of Attila the Hun are really legendary. He is a figure that captured not only the imagination of contemporary authors—we have a number of accounts and even a description of him by a Roman envoy Priscus who actually visited Attila—but the image of Attila as the pitiless conqueror, the barbarian of the distant steppes of the east, this is endured for centuries and it has inspired all sorts of presentations, novels, films, and artwork over the centuries. Furthermore, Attila has been admired in many instances. For instance, the later kings of Hungary, known as the Arpad kings of Hungary, themselves nomads—their real name is Magyars, but we call them Hungarians because Western Europeans in the 9th and 10th century identified them with the Huns, and Hungarian is really a misnomer for these people—took upon themselves to become Huns or Hungarians since the name of Attila struck such fear in the hearts of Western Europeans. They even claimed to have the sword of Attila; that was a medieval legend that some shepherd had found a sword, had brought it to Attila, it was a promise of universal world dominations, sort of a nomadic version of *Excalibur and King Arthur*. It passed to, of course, Attila and then was lost for centuries, but magically found by the Hungarian kings. This sword is actually on review in the Künsthistorisches Museum in Vienna. It eventually gets into the hands of the Hapsburgs, who essentially marry every ruler in Central Europe you can come up with in the 16th and 17th centuries, so most everything ends up in Vienna one way or the other. In any case, it is indicative of how Attila was viewed.

The Ottoman Turks, themselves having no direct connection to Attila the Hun, admired the steppe conqueror because, as we will discuss later on in the course, the Ottoman sultans—or the Ottoman sultan caliphs to be more accurate—in Constantinople saw themselves as *ghazi* warriors, warriors of the steppes; that is a traditional term to designate Turkish warriors in the Muslim period. Therefore they identified with Attila the Hun and with Genghis Khan. They very much compare the two, and the names Attila and Genghis are still very popular names in Turkey today. In fact, in 1974, when the Turks intervened in Northern Cyprus, they codenamed the operation Operation Atilla or Attila. Usually in Turkish the name is spelled "Atilla," but it is the same name.

In European traditions, especially among the Germanic peoples who were subjects of Attila the Hun, Attila lived on as a great lord. We have descriptions from Roman sources, particularly Priscus and others who had arrived at Attila's court, thought to be somewhere near Budapest, the Roman city of Aquincum, and the description is that of a great hall that reads like something right out of *Beowulf* or Norse saga. Attila was known in Norse legend as Atli, a great king. The Norse did not really know much about Huns, whether they were cavalry people, nomads, or anything; but they had the image of Attila as a great king, an avaricious king, somehow responsible for the destruction of the Burgundian family of Gunnar, who is based on that historical Burgundian king wiped out in 436 or 437 by Huns operating as auxiliaries of the Roman master of the soldiers, Aetius. Atli lives on in Norse legend; he is associated with the Völsungs. He lures Gunnar and his family into a great hall; there is a great battle in which the Burgundians are killed; but the sister Gudrun avenges herself by killing Atli because she had been married to him after she had lost her true love, Sigurd. This story is retold in the *Nibelungenlied*, except Attila there, known as Etzel in German, is a sympathetic figure who is really quite astonished that his wife wants vengeance on her Burgundian kinsmen.

Whatever version of the story you take—the Icelandic or the Middle High German—Attila rings largely as a great figure. He appears in romantic paintings of the 19th century, particularly by French painters who were conjuring up images of the destruction of Gaul, of France, by the hordes of the Huns. He is also linked with the great famous meeting of Pope Leo I, of whom we will speak about later in this lecture; Leo I, who reputedly prevents Attila from attacking Rome. That dramatic scene was a painting:

There was a painting commissioned by Pope Julius II done by Raphael in which Julius II is Pope Leo I; it is a kind of nice coincidence there of the great Renaissance pope being linked with that great medieval pope.

In more modern times, there are the pop movies, great films, classical biblical spectacles as I like to call them, in which Attila is portrayed in a number of movies. He has even been reprised, the role has been reprised for some made-for-TV movies; but still in my mind, the quintessential Attila the Hun on the big screen is Jack Palance, starring in a little-known (and deservedly little-known) film known as *Sign of the Pagan* with Jeff Chandler playing the emperor Marcian and an incredible Rita Gam being the warrior daughter of Attila in the movie. There are several other renditions of Attila in the movie tradition, but really Jack Palance is the best. He also plays a very credible Ögedei, the third son of Genghis Khan, in a movie called *The Mongols*, which is loosely based on the Mongol invasion of Europe, which we will get to later in the course.

All of these images that have come down to us of Attila have resulted because he is the first steppe conqueror of whom we have a real sense of who he was; and this is because of the nature of the sources. We have some information on Modu Chanyu, but all of the other steppe conquerors that we have discussed so far, we only have snippets about them and general discussions of these rulers; the mores and the customs of their peoples. Attila, we actually have some information. He had a profound effect on both the Eastern and Western Roman Empires, and really an important effect in dictating the course of European history and also announcing what we think is a very, very important ethnic and linguistic transformation; and that is the gradual shifting of the peoples of the steppes from Iranian-speaking languages to Turkish-speaking languages, which marks the beginning of the Middle Ages on the steppes, in my opinion.

In any case, Attila and his brother Bleda came to the throne jointly in 434, succeeding their uncle, Rua or Rugila, who had a longstanding alliance with the western Roman court. The brothers shared power; they may have actually divided the tribes among themselves. We are not sure what the arrangement was, but initially they very much pursued traditional Hun policy, which is attack the east, loot the east, ally with the west; that is, the Western Roman

Empire). The brothers were more than willing to lend their horse archers and their Hun vassals to the armies of Aetius and the western Roman emperor. At the same time, they began systematic attacks into the Balkan provinces; and this region was loosely called Illyricum, which would embrace the former Yugoslavia, and Thrace, which is today largely Bulgaria. These provinces came under increasing attack in the 440s. The attacks were designed to extort loot, captives, all sorts of specialists who could manufacture things. It was also hoped that the eastern Roman court, ruled by the incredibly ineffective Theodosius II, who had a dreadfully long reign from 408–450, and his only claim to fame is he was a calligrapher; he did not even bother to read the law code that bears his name. The walls of Constantinople bear his name, the Theodosian Walls; they were really built by his older sister and the prefect Anthemius. He was an incredibly lazy emperor and creature of the court; but he was served by a very able sister and competent generals and ministers who were able to preserve the Eastern Roman Empire against the attacks of Attila.

These attacks increased in intensity, and it seems that Attila and his brother Bleda were able to capture large numbers of Roman specialists. We have stories of this told by that Roman author Priscus who visited Attila. He gives us marvelous stories how a Roman merchant was captured by the Huns and decided to go Hun; and there is a long conversation between the Roman envoy and this former Roman merchant and he tells of his virtues: "Look, I was married to a Hun wife. I can ride around and fight and pal around with the Huns. I gain wealth and honor whereas in Rome I'm despised," and it is very, very suggestive anecdote. You remember, our Chinese envoy Zhang Qian was also married to a barbarian wife, the Xiongnu, except he rebelled and wanted to go back to China; but in this case, this Roman merchant went native and joined the Hun elite. We are told of Roman specialists such as engineers who built bathhouses for the Huns. Clearly Attila and Bleda have Roman-trained engineers who are able to build engines of war, because starting in the 440s, the Huns not only raid, but they are capturing Roman cities. They are able to storm heavily fortified masonry architecture walls of Roman cities in the Balkans, cities such as Viminacium, Singidinum, Siscia; all of the great cities that check and control the Roman road network across the Balkans are now subject to direct Hun attack.

Furthermore, Attila and his brother have very, very good information about the goings on at the imperial court. They time their attacks generally when the eastern army is preoccupied elsewhere and the main military forces are in Africa fighting Vandals or tied up on the eastern frontier. This is another aspect about these great nomadic confederations put together by charismatic leaders: They create tent capitals; these great cities that attract craftsmen and specialists, all sorts of trade. Attila had more knowledge probably of the overall geographic dimensions of the Roman world—where to attack, when to attack—and his position, his knowledge near the Roman Empire allowed him to frame really rather sophisticated strategies. This bears comparison to Genghis Khan and his grandsons who had waged great campaigns and probably had the best geographic knowledge in the world during the 13th century; and this is a function of a nomadic society engaged in long-distance travel, knowledge of the wider steppes, as well as attracting all of these people to the great court of Attila who ruled essentially (the term is anachronistic) like a great khan, the way the Mongol khans would rule. Attila had a powerful vision of what he could do, where he could attack into the eastern Roman Empire, why he had these arrangements with the Western Roman Empire. The victories netted plunder, captives, above all gold. These were the ingredients that sustained the Hun Empire.

One could argue to some extent Attila never envisioned a methodical conquest of the Roman Empire any more than the Xiongnu did. For one, the numbers were against you in both cases. The Xiongnu in the second century B.C., Attila in the fifth century A.D.; the most that Attila could account among all of his subjects—including the German tribes of Central Europe who are now vassals, the grasslands of eastern Europe, the tribes on the Pontic-Caspian steppe—maybe a million subjects, 800,000. The adult men, however, were all warriors, and particularly those horse archers were ready to go. The Xiongnu probably had a similar number, maybe a million. The same was true of the eastern steppes under the Mongols. The great sedentary empires, the Roman Empire or the Han Empire, there you are looking at empires running somewhere between 55 and 65 million people; and this disparity is a determining factor in the strategies of Attila as well as later steppe conquerors, particularly the Mongols but even lesser conquerors of Northern China. His objective was to wrest control of certain crucial border areas to break down the barriers on the Danube to allow him easy access into the Roman provinces so he could plunder and gain gold and captives and reward all of his vassal rulers and sustain his position. That was important; that is, to make sure that that Roman frontier stretching along the Danube was no longer a frontier but now was a highway that would allow the movement of Hun forces on their road looking for goodies. This is clearly the thrust between a treaty that we have in detail signed in 447 negotiated by the Roman envoy Anatolius, who was then the master of the eastern Roman army and a representative of Theodosius. That was a treaty that not only promised very heavy tribute—the previous tribute paid to the Huns was more like a subsidy of 700 pounds of gold, he treaty triples it to 2,100 pounds, arrears are made up, there are other arrangements—but the real key is that the Roman frontier along the Danube is now essentially dismantled, and the Romans are not to approach the Danube from the south or from the west from a distance of something like five days, which is by Hun standards, traveling on horses, you are looking anywhere from 100–200 miles depending on what they would want to claim. One objective was to make sure that that frontier zone was now securely in Hun hands.

The other important point was to exploit tribute; to exploit a system that his ancestors would have been familiar with, with the Chinese emperors, the Han emperors; that is, at some point Attila would be recognized as the great leader of the confederation and from that would come some kind of imperial marriage, some kind of recognition, some sort of sense of equality, and in the case of the eastern Roman emperor, actually subordination to this great conqueror.

In 444 or 445, Attila had a falling out with his older brother. We are not sure what it was; the sources give some colorful anecdotes. Bleda is presented as a brother with an incredibly acid and even nasty wit. He took to using a dwarf—a Roman dwarf from Mauritania, I think—who had been captured in a raid as a way of criticizing Attila at court, embarrassing his brother. There was a horrible falling out. There is always this problem within these nomadic confederations when there are two brothers. Eventually, one brother is more charismatic, more successful than the other, and invariably it leads to either a civil war, a parting of the ways, or one brother doing in the other; and Attila did in Bleda in a hunting accident somewhere around 445.

From that point on, apparently Attila is the unquestioned ruler of the various Hun tribes in a great confederation that essentially is a barbarian counter-empire to the Roman world. He had no restraints at this point. He waged war ruthlessly in the Eastern Roman Empire. He extorted that treaty in 447, which essentially gave him access to the Balkan provinces of the Roman world. He destroyed that imperial frontier. Theodosius II and his government had to consent to annual payments of 2,100 pounds of gold. I have calculated what this might represent in real buying power to the Roman emperor; it probably was cheaper than trying to fight the Hun armies. Clearly, later Han emperors discovered the same: It was cheaper to buy the Xiongnu as allies than to wage a direct war, which is what Wudi did starting with his great campaigns in the 130s and 120s B.C. But it was humiliating. Attila loved calling Theodosius his slave in all of these exchanges. Furthermore, the Roman cities in the European provinces really existed on the sufferance of Attila. He had the hordes of horse archers, numerous other barbarian allies, an engineering corps that could capture cities, and should he be moved he could capture and sack any of these cities at will to demonstrate his power. Furthermore, the emperor behind those powerful walls—those powerful Theodosian walls—all of a sudden felt very vulnerable when those walls were badly damaged in an earthquake in 447, and the entire population of the city was put to work to repair those walls and have them up and running in early 448 because they feared a Hun attack. That is how successful Attila was vis-à-vis the eastern Roman government.

In 450 A.D., Attila was at the height of his power. He commanded a confederation and a number of nomadic warriors clearly on the order of the Xiongnu confederation under Modu Chanyu; and those two confederations are comparable in a number of ways. It is at this point that a peculiar circumstance—doubted by some scholars, but I suspect it is true; I really believe it is true, in fact—resulted in Attila dramatically changing his policy by invading the western empire, which hitherto had been his ally.

This gets us a bit into lurid Roman politics of the court of Ravenna, where the western emperors had resided since 402 A.D.; and also to some aspects of Roman law and the nomadic customs and expectations that Attila believed in. First, in 450 A.D., Attila received a ring and apparently what he took as a marriage proposal from the Empress Honoria. Honoria was the elder half-sister of the then-reigning western emperor Valentinian III, an incredibly weak and ineffectual emperor dominated by his mother and, of course, his master of the soldiers, Aetius. His mother and his warlord generalissimo both hated each other. Honoria likewise resented her brother. She felt that she had a better claim to the throne, and therefore anyone she married would have a better claim to the throne than her half-brother. She was caught in a number of plots and intrigues. There were a number of scandalous stories. She had been playing around with the chief chamberlain; that did not look good. Finally, Valentinian and Aetius decided the only way to neutralize her was to marry her to a very elderly and very boring senator. Apparently Honoria got it in her head to send this ring and message to Attila—and this would have been known since Atilla was in regular communication with the western court—and essentially said, "Save me." Furthermore, one speculates whether this rather bored late Roman empress, cloistered in the palace and hearing all these wild stories about Hun barbarians and the kind of savage men they were, had all sorts of exciting ideas of what this new husband would be like; certainly a far better option to her than the elderly senator that her half-brother had lined up for her. In any case, Attila got the message and the ring.

In my opinion, Attila thought, "It's come. The final marriage offer; the imperial family now recognizes me as the greatest lord in the world." Xiongnu rulers, *chanyu*, would expect a Chinese imperial bride, silks, a whole retinue of members coming from the Chinese court to indicate that you are now a great ally, and really in many ways on par with the son of heaven himself. This is what Attila expected that message was; and so he sent back saying, "Yes, and by the way I would like to take control of Gaul and Spain, which are the dowry of my wife to be." This was unacceptable to Roman emperors. They still operated under the laws of republic. First, the empress should not have married without her brother's permission; and second, by the way, she is a Roman citizen, he is not a citizen, and this was just politically impossible," and they had to refuse. When Attila gets the refusal, this is tantamount to an act of war.

All of a sudden, the western court is caught in a dilemma because Attila declares war. There is no negotiation on this; and in early 451, Attila levies the barbarian army to end all barbarian armies. He summons all of the Hun tribes across the steppes, his Germanic allies; Roman sources speak of as many as 700,000 people on the move, probably an exaggeration, some say the army is more like 50,000, 100,000. How much infantry there is we do not know. Many German tribes join along the way; they really had no choice but to join. It clearly included large numbers of mounted horsemen. These forces swept over the Rhine—there was no barrier—and began to sack the cities of Western Europe, of Gaul, as thoroughly as they had sacked the cities of the Balkans. Many late Roman cities known today by their modern names—Strasbourg, Worms, Mainz, Cologne, Trier, Metz, Reims, Tournai, Cambrai, Amiens, Beauvais—fell to the Hun armies. One of the few major cities not to fall was Paris, Latin Lutetia, and that was because the local Saint Geneviève appeared miraculously and had warned off the Hun hordes. Otherwise, the Huns did a job on Eastern and Central France, sweeping across, destroying cities, deporting populations, and doing a thorough job of destruction, which ultimately destroyed the very military basis of the western Roman state by that invasion.

Aetius had no choice but to seek allies among the Visigoths and other Germans settled within the Roman Empire, and those included Franks, a detachment of Alans and lesser tribes; and he put together a coalition army of Romans and largely German federate allies, primarily Visigoths, to oppose this great Hun invasion. His army moved and forced Attila to raise the siege of Orleans; and Attila began to withdraw east. He withdrew east in the general direction of what today is the city of Châlons, and we are not exactly sure where the battle is fought. It is called the Battle of the Catalonian Plains, and that could be anywhere on the plains between Châlons and today Troyes, probably closer to Châlons than Troyes. We know that the Hun and Roman flanks rested on the Marne River; so somewhere in that vicinity a great battle was fought on an afternoon in the summer of 451.

The Hun army was enormous, and Attila drew up his army in three forces. He placed his best forces, the Huns, in the center; his nomadic cavalry with the intention of breaking through the Roman army with typical tactics; and then he deployed his various allied forces on the flanks. These included Ostrogoths, Alans, various Germanic peoples like Burgundians; all sorts of other subject peoples. In the case of Aetius, he weakened his center; he put in his center his weakest forces to receive the Hun attack. Then he stationed his more powerful forces—that is, his Visigoths—who actually opposed their kinsmen, the Ostrogoths, on the other side of the Hun army; and then the Romans and Franks took up the other Roman flank. That was the left. The Visigoths were on the Roman right and the Franks and the Romans were on the Roman left with a weak center. The Ostrogoths were opposed to their kinsmen on the Hun side, and then the Romans and Franks faced various Hun allies.

The battle opened with a charge of the Hun cavalry that drove deep into the Roman center and scattered it; and it looked like the Roman army was going to be broken in half. The two Gothic forces clashed in a violent attack; Ostrogoths and Visigoths, essentially the same people, went at it. The Romans and the Franks plowed into the exposed flank of Attila and eventually forced Attila to quit the battlefield. It ended in a draw. Later sources said the battle was so fierce that the warriors continued to fight in the sky. Attila withdrew east, making a beeline back to his capital and vowing to return the next year; and he did. In 452, he invaded Northern Italy with another huge barbarian army. He penetrated to the Po Valley, and it looked like the way to Rome was open. There were no imperial forces opposing him because all those German federates would fight for Gaul; they had no interest in Italy, and Aetius was powerless. It is there that Pope Leo I met him and convinced Attila to withdraw for reasons that are still obscure, but it bolstered the reputation of the pope in Western Europe. Attila pulled back to his capital somewhere in the area of Budapest and celebrated a great marriage festival. He had married a new German girl, Ildico was her name. He drank to excess and in the night a blood vessel burst and he drowned in his own blood. The girl was killed thinking she had murdered him, and she would live on in Norse legend as the Gudrun or the Kriemhild of epic; that is, the Germanic princess who avenged the deaths of her relatives at the hands of Attila.

Attila's death saw the fragmentation of his empire. The subject tribes were raised in rebellion, compliments of money paid by the new eastern Roman emperor Marcian, a tough soldier-emperor who came to the throne in 450 and had actually supported the western government in a struggle against Attila. The empire quickly fragmented; and Attila's sons ruled some Hun tribes on the Pontic-Caspian steppes, but they were never again the force they ever were.

The career of Attila the Hun essentially shattered the power of the western empire. The real victors at Châlons and the invasion of Northern Italy were not Attila, but the Germanic tribes who were left to partition what was left of the Roman Empire into independent kingdoms. Meanwhile, the eastern court had learned its lesson well: Trust to the Theodosian Walls and make sure that no future Attila ever emerges on those steppes. The emperors soon to be known as Byzantine emperors invented Byzantine diplomacy to prevent the revival of another steppe conqueror like Attila the Hun.

Sassanid Shahs and the Hephthalites
Lecture 13

I n this lecture, we'll cover two new nomadic peoples known as the Hephthalites, or "White Huns," and the Gök Turks, actually ancestors of many of the Turkish peoples living today in the Middle East and central Asia. In the last two lectures, we dealt with the Huns, who in some ways represent the climax and conclusion to the nomadic steppe peoples of antiquity on the western steppes. In this lecture, we'll turn to the central steppes, the regions that essentially are around the Caspian and Aral seas and Transoxiana, and deal with events taking place there at the same time the Huns were assaulting the Roman Empire.

The Sassanid Empire

- The Sassanid Empire was the contemporary empire and rival to the late Roman world. We talked about the Sassanids briefly in our lecture on the Parthians because the shahs **Ardashir I** and his son **Shapur I** restored the great bureaucratic Persian Empire known as the Sassanid or Neo-Persian Empire that saw itself as the direct successor of the Achaemenid Empire of the 5th through the 4th centuries B.C. They had overthrown the Parthian rulers and founded an effective bureaucratic state.

- The Sassanid shahs saw themselves as the vice-regents of a new Zoroastrian state. **Zoroastrianism** was a monotheistic religion centered on a supreme god, **Ahura Mazda**, the god of lightness, good, and truth. The ancient fire altar became the symbol of Ahura Mazda, and fire altars were set up across the Sassanid Empire as symbols of his power. Animal sacrifice was ended, and a much more devotional worship took its place.

- The monarchy was closely tied to the veneration of Ahura Mazda. On some of the Sassanid coins, the fire altar appears flanked by two guardians, perhaps royal figures or military attendants but not magi or priests. In some instances, within the flames of the fire altar is apparently Ahura Mazda conceived in human form, and in one case, it may well even be the portrait of a king.

- There was a close association between the king and Ahura Mazda. Both the king and the god were locked in internal battle with the forces of evil, represented by the counter-god Ahriman. This struggle was also reflected in human affairs between the shah and his political rivals, such as the Roman emperor or, later, the kings of the Hephthalites and the **khagans** of the various Turkish tribes.

- The Sassanid state was much better organized than the Parthian and, with its tax collection, could support a far more professional army. The Sassanids could capture and rule cities in a way that the Parthians never could and posed a considerable danger to the Roman emperors.

Clashes with Rome
- In the 3rd century A.D., starting with the first shah, Ardashir I, down through the shah Narses, Roman and Sassanid armies clashed for control of Armenia and Mesopotamia. In the end, the Romans won this round of fighting but not before suffering some humiliating defeats, particularly in the reign of Shapur I. One Roman emperor, Gordian III, is shown on Shapur's victory reliefs as defeated and slain. The successor of Gordian III, Philip I, known often as Philip the Arab, is shown as a suppliant to Shapur.

- These events occurred in 243 to 244 A.D. In 260, Shapur defeated the emperor **Valerian**. He lured the emperor into a conference and captured him. Valerian, too, is shown on the reliefs in a subordinate position to the shah. These victories exalted the power of the Sassanid shah over Rome because the shah demanded the eastern half of the Roman Empire as part of his legacy. However, the Romans regrouped and counterattacked, and by 300 A.D., the shah signed a treaty relinquishing provinces to the Roman emperor.

- That situation lasted for about 60 years. Then, a new war erupted, which ended in the defeat of the Roman emperor Julian III in 363 by Shah **Shapur II**. The result was a series of treaties starting in 364 that gave the shah the better position in the Middle East, with formerly Roman fortresses in Mesopotamia and control over Armenia.

Pressures on the Sassanids

- The Persians discovered that the door prize for their victories over the Romans was dealing with the nomadic peoples coming over the Caucasus by way of the Dariel and Derbent passes. In particular, the Derbent Pass, which is close to the Caspian Sea, led directly into Azerbaijan, a large grassland that was instinctively attractive to nomadic peoples. The Huns broke in repeatedly, and the shah had to deal with them throughout the 4th and into the 5th centuries.

- At the same time, the shah faced new pressures on the northeast in Transoxiana, along the upper regions of the Jaxartes. Those pressures arose from two new groups, the first of which was the **Hephthalites**, or "White Huns." These were probably Tocharian speakers, along with some Iranian speakers and Turkish elements, who had been pushed into the Tarim Basin as a result of the collapse of the Han Empire in China.

  - The immediate reaction of the Sassanid shahs was to hire the Hephthalites as mercenaries in their attempts to further expand their empire. The Sassanids had taken over the core areas of the Parthian Empire, but that was not enough. They sought to acquire the regions that are today Afghanistan, Pakistan, and the central Soviet Republic.

  - The first two shahs, Ardashir and Shapur I, had imposed their authority over Transoxiana and the Kushan princes ruling in northern India, doubling the size of the Sassanid state. In the 3rd century A.D., these domains provided gold and silver and access to nomadic tribal allies, all of which had enabled the shahs to wage expensive wars against the Romans.

  - That convenient situation began to break down at the end of the 4th century, when the Hephthalites appeared on the banks of the Jaxartes. Initially, the shahs sought to settle them on the frontiers as allies and auxiliaries, but the Hephthalites realized the advantages of controlling the caravan routes of Transoxiana and quickly turned from allies to rivals.

○ The Hephthalites overran much of Transoxiana for most of the 5th and early 6th centuries and ruled under their own titles. As a result, the shahs found themselves losing valuable provinces to the east.

Current studies of coins and archaeology indicate that the Hephthalites, much like the Kushan emperors, were pragmatic conquerors.

• Shah **Peroz I**, who ruled in the mid-5th century, mounted several campaigns against the Hephthalites, and in one, he was captured and eventually forced to ransom himself and his son in a humiliating treaty. It's even reported that the then-ruling eastern Roman emperor Leo I offered to help pay part of the ransom because he found it far more convenient to deal with the Persian shah than Hephthalites running over the Middle East. Shah Peroz regained his throne but was killed in battle in 484.

• His son Kavadh came to the throne but was challenged by his uncle and chased out of Persia. He eventually cut a deal with the Hephthalites to form an army of horse archers to put himself back on the Persian throne and, in return, agreed to a treaty confirming essentially the Oxus River as the boundary between the Sassanid and Hephthalite empires.

• This was a severe blow. It was a major territorial loss and resulted in the emergence of an impressive Hephthalite state controlling Transoxiana, dominating at least the western cities of the Tarim

Basin, the central steppes, and parts of northern India. This Hephthalite state looked increasingly like the old Kushan Empire.

- The shahs were never reconciled to this loss and took a number of important measures to counter this eastern threat, including constant exchanges with Constantinople to cement good relations with the Byzantine emperor.
  - They also erected an impressive set of fortifications known as the Gorgon Walls that extend east of the Caspian Sea and cut off key passes that would give access to nomads coming from the steppes. These fortifications were probably manned by between 15,000 and 30,000 guards.

  - But the best way to defeat nomadic horse archers is to hire other nomadic horse archers, and that's what a new shah did. Shah **Khosrow I**, who came to the throne in 531, contacted possible allies, the **Gök Turks**, who could help him beat this new menace that controlled the valuable eastern lands.

The Gök Turks
- In 557, Khosrow entered into negotiations with a leader of the Turks, **Istami**. The Gök Turks ("Sky Turks") were the newest nomadic power on the eastern steppes and had rapidly expanded across the steppes. The shah wasn't aware of how large this confederation really was. He contacted these potential allies and made arrangements to conduct a joint war against the Hephthalites and share the spoils.

- That was a momentous decision. The shah agreed to take a Turkish princess, the daughter of Istami, into his harem. He also released great numbers of steppe cavalry to help the Turks wipe out the Hephthalites.

- As always the case with Turkish horse archers, they did their jobs well. The Hephthalites left, and their possessions in India essentially fell into the hands of Indian native rulers. Central Asia fell under the control of the Gök Turks. Now, the shah realized that he had a far more powerful foe than he had ever imagined in his former allies.

- Quite unwittingly, Khosrow I brought into the Middle East a new people, the Gök Turks, who had numerous advantages and political and military organizations that previous nomads had not. What the shah had done was to open a new chapter in the history of the steppes. The Turks were destined to propel the Eurasian steppes and all of its associated civilizations out of antiquity and into the early Middle Ages.

Important Terms

Ahura Mazda: The supreme god of creation in Zoroastrianism.

Gök Turks: The "Celestial Turks" who overthrew the Avar khanate in 551–552. Khan Bumin established the senior Gök Turk khaganate (551–744). His brother Istami (551–575) established the western Turkish khaganate (553–659) on the central and western Eurasian steppe. In 681, after ending Tang Chinese overlordship, the western khaganate was reconstituted as the Confederation of the Ten Arrows.

Hephthalites: The "White Huns" were Tocharian-speaking nomads, driven from the eastern Eurasian steppe by the northern Wei emperors of China and Avar khagans. They founded an empire (408–670) encompassing the western Tarim Basin, Transoxania, and northern India.

khagan: Meaning "khan of khans," a Turkish term denoting a great royal figure ruling over many subordinate khans.

Zoroastrianism: The monotheistic religion of the Iranians, based on the teachings of Zoroaster, born circa 628 B.C. The Sassanid shahs favored Zoroastrianism as reformed in the 3rd century.

Ardashir I (227–240): Shah of Persia; overthrew Parthian rule and founded the Sassanid Neo-Persian Empire. He initiated the first of a series of wars by the Sassanid shahs to conquer the eastern provinces of the Roman Empire.

Istami (553–575): *Yabgu* of the western Gök Turks; brother of Khagan Bumin, who commissioned Istami to pursue the Avars, who had fled west. Istami established western Turks on the central Eurasian steppe. In 557–561, in alliance with Shah Khosrow I, he occupied Transoxania and ended the Hephthalite Empire.

Khosrow I (531–579): Sassanid shah; waged two wars against Justinian, emperor of the eastern Roman (Byzantine) Empire, in 530–532 and 550–545. He sought prestige, plunder, or subsidies of gold under treaty from Justinian rather than conquest. In 557–561, he allied with Istami, *yabgu* khagan of the western Turks, to defeat the Hephthalites.

Peroz I (457–484): Sassanid shah; was deposed by his brother Hormizd II. He regained his throne with a Hephthalite army provided by King Khush-Nevaz. Peroz twice waged campaigns against his former ally Khush-Nevaz. In either 469 or 472, Peroz suffered a defeat and had to pay a ransom for his release. In 484, he was slain near Herat, enabling the Hephthalites to raid deep into Iran.

Shapur I (240–270): Sassanid shah; waged three major wars against the Roman Empire, in 242–244, 253, and 254–260. In the third war, he took the Roman emperor Valerian captive. His victories are celebrated on the rock reliefs at Naqsh-e Rostam. Shapur failed to conquer Roman territory, and in 262, he faced a counterinvasion by Odenathus, merchant prince of Palmyra and ally of Rome.

Shapur II (309–379): Sassanid shah; waged two wars against the Roman Empire, in 335–350 and 358–363. He repelled the Roman invasion of lower Mesopotamia led by the emperor Julian II. The retreat and death of Julian enabled Shapur II to conclude a favorable treaty from the new emperor, Jovian, who relinquished the strategic fortresses of upper Mesopotamia.

Valerian (b. c. 193; r. 253–260): Roman emperor; waged two Persian wars. He was captured by Shah Shapur I and died ignominiously in captivity. As a result of Valerian's defeat and capture, Shah Shapur ravaged Roman provinces in eastern Asia Minor and northern Syria in 260. He ordered the second empire-wide persecution of Christians in 258–260.

Suggested Reading

Canepa, *The Two Eyes of the Earth.*

Daryaee, *Sasanian Persia.*

Pourshariati, *Decline and Fall of the Sasanian Empire.*

Sinor, "Establishment and Dissolution of the Türk Empire."

Questions to Consider

1. How successful were the Sassanid shahs in creating a new bureaucratic monarchy in the Near East? How effective was the shah's power? What was the value of Zoroastrianism to the shah?

2. How did the Sassanid Empire differ from the Parthian Empire, whose Arsacid kings ruled from horseback? How did the Sassanids view the nomadic peoples of the steppes?

3. Why did the Sassanid shahs wage so many wars against imperial Rome? How did these wars compromise defense along the northern frontiers?

4. Who were the Hephthalites? Why were they considered Huns? In what ways did the Hephthalites re-create the Kushan Empire?

5. Why did the collapse of the Hephthalite Empire benefit the Gök Turks?

Sassanid Shahs and the Hephthalites
Lecture 13—Transcript

In this lecture, I plan to cover two new nomadic peoples known as the Hephthalites or "White Huns" and the Gök Turks, actually ancestors of many of the Turkish peoples today living in the Middle East and Central Asia. In the last two lectures, we dealt with the Huns, who probably were a Proto-Turkish-speaking nomadic people who in some ways represent the climax and conclusion to the nomadic steppe peoples of antiquity on those western steppes. What I want to do in this lecture is turn to the central steppes, the regions that essentially are around the Caspian and Aral Sea and Transoxiana. We discussed them earlier in conjunction with the Kushans, the Sacae, and the Parthians; I want to return to that central steppe region and deal with events going on there at the same time the Huns are assaulting the Roman Empire.

This means we first must look at the Sassanid Empire, which is the contemporary empire and rival to the late Roman world. We talked about the Sassanids very briefly in the conclusion on the Parthians, because the Sassanid shahs Ardashir I and his son Shapur I restored the great bureaucratic Persian Empire known as the Sassanid or Neo-Persian Empire that saw itself as the direct successor of that Achaemenid Empire of the fifth through the fourth centuries B.C. They had overthrown the Parthian rulers, the Arsacid kings who were seen as interlopers from the steppes; and they founded an effective bureaucratic state. There is still a considerable debate among scholars as to how centralized was this state; but clearly the Sassanid state was far more powerful, wealthy, and better organized than the Parthian kingdom ever was, or probably even the Saca rulers in India or the Kushan emperors. Furthermore, these new Persian emperors were extremely important because they wanted to restore that Persian Empire in its fullest extent. That would have some major consequences not only for Rome, but for the nomadic peoples dwelling on the Central Eurasian steppes.

First, let us give us some idea of what this monarchy is all about; what its aspirations are; and then we can look at how these Neo-Persian shahs—and the word *shah* is legitimately used; this is how they would style themselves in their public inscriptions, on their coins, and in their official documents—how these shahs came into conflict with Rome and the nomadic peoples.

First, they saw themselves as the vice-regents of a new Zoroastrian state. This Zoroastrianism was a monotheism. It emerged out of religious reforms, apparently in the third century A.D., taken in tandem by a great thinker known as Kartir, who is now known from inscriptions and religious monuments that were set up in Persia, as well as the shahs themselves. This Zoroastrian faith, which centered now on a supreme god Ahura Mazda, who represents the god of lightness and good and truth, can be traced back clearly on coins not only of the Sassanid kings but their predecessors, kings who were vassals of the Parthians going back at least to the second century B.C. The ancient fire altar became the eternal flame and symbol of Ahura Mazda; and fire altars were set up across the Sassanid Empire as symbols to the power of Ahura Mazda. Animal sacrifice, which had been characteristic of the Persians in earlier times—and we do think that those early Persian kings of the sixth century B.C. were probably polytheists; they were not strict Zoroastrians—animal sacrifice was ended; there was a much more devotional worship. The monarchy was closely tied to the veneration of Ahura Mazda. On some of the Sassanid coins, silver coins, the fire altar appears flanked by two guardians. Sometimes they look like royal figures, sometimes they look like military attendants; they do not look like magi or priests as far as I can tell on the numerous coins I have seen. In some instances, within the flames of the fire altar is apparently Ahura Mazda conceived in human form; and in one case, on a very rare coin of Vahram V, it may well even be the portrait of the king.

There is a close association between the king and Ahura Mazda. The king is not divine, but he is his vice-regent; and he is locked in eternal battle, both the king and Ahura Mazda, with the forces of evil; with the counter-god Ahriman, the evil one. This is a struggle that is also reflected in human affairs between the shah and his political rivals, such as the Roman emperor or later the kings of the Hephthalites and the *kaghans* of the various Turkish tribes. Persian coins make that very clear. Persian coins carry on the obverse the head of the shah in a magnificent special crown; around it are often concentric circles with symbols of power of earth and the heavens, and the crown pierces it. The symbolism of the coin is the shah is in the middle of the earth and he is designated by Ahura Mazda himself to rule justly over a world empire. These visions are repeated on coins and on Sassanid iconography. They are part of the reason for the success of the Sassanid state.

In addition, the Sassanid state is much better organized: in its tax collection; it can support a far more professional army than the Parthians. It is not just tribal levies and nomadic allies from the steppes; they have a siege train, they have logistics. They can capture and rule cities in a way that the Parthians never could, and so they pose a danger to Roman emperors that is considerable. Unlike the Parthians, whom the Romans could always have the better end of any battle or war with them, the Sassanids proved a far tougher opponent.

We need not get into the details of the wars between the Romans and the Sassanid shahs; that belongs more properly to a history of Roman and Sassanid foreign policy. On the other hand, there are a couple of important points to note. In the third century A.D., starting with the first Shah, Ardashir I, down through the shah Narses—who signs a very, very important treaty with the Romans either in 299 or 300 A.D.—Roman and Sassanid armies clash for control of Armenia and Mesopotamia. They wage repeated and destructive wars. In the end, the Romans win this round of fighting, but it is not until after suffering some very, very humiliating defeats, particularly in the reign of Shapur I. One Roman emperor, Gordian III, who waged a war against Shapur, was apparently lynched by his soldiers in a mutiny engineered by his praetorian prefect. He is shown on Shapur's victory reliefs as a defeated and slain emperor being trampled. The successor of Gordian III, Philip I, known often as Philip the Arab, in 244 is shown as a suppliant, supplicating Shapur on his relief, and signed a disgraceful treaty promising a subsidy of 10,000 gold pieces to the shah. These events occurred in 243–244. In 260 A.D., Shapur defeated the emperor Valerian; he lured him into a conference and captured the Roman emperor, who became a captive. He, too, is shown on the reliefs in a subordinate position to the Shah. These victories exalted the power of the Sassanid shah over Rome because the shah demanded the eastern half of the Roman Empire as part of his legacy. However, the Romans regrouped, counterattacked, and by 300 A.D. the shah is signing a treaty relinquishing provinces to the Roman emperor.

That situation obtained for about 60 years. Then a new war erupted, which ended in an inglorious defeat by the Roman emperor Julian III who was killed in 363 in an attempt to defeat the then-ruling shah Shapur II, an ancestor of the first Shapur, and he ruled from 309–379. The result was a series of treaties in 364 in which the shah now had the better position in the Middle East. In 364, the Romans surrender many of the fortresses of Mesopotamia; in a treaty either in 379 to 382, the Persians take control of the region of Armenia, which is very, very strategic. They think they have the advantage over the Romans, and then the Persians discover to their surprise that the door prize for these victorious wars over the Romans is dealing with the nomadic peoples coming over the Dariel and Derbent passes. The Dariel Pass is often identified as the Gates of Alexander the Great in medieval legend, where Alexander built a great gate to keep the barbarians out. These are the barbarians of Gog and Magog, who are these creatures manufacturing barbarians somewhere under the Pripet Marshes I would assume in Central Russia, releasing nomads to plague the civilized world. Great medieval legend; it persists in both medieval Western Europe, in the Islamic world. These gates are just encased with all sorts of legend. The reality was that the Sassanid shah now had the problem of defending those critical passes across the Caucasus Mountains that gave nomadic peoples direct access into the Middle East.

Furthermore, the Derbent Pass, which is in the Caucasus and close to the Caspian Sea, led directly into Azerbaijan. Azerbaijan is a very important grassland. In its climate and its conditions it is a part of Central Asia. It was instinctively attractive to nomadic peoples, and repeatedly nomads will come over the Caucuses to settle in that zone. Today, Azerbaijan is an independent republic; part of Azerbaijan is actually in Iran, and it is home to Turkish speakers, Turks who migrate there in the Middle Ages and find that, "Gee, this is not too different from Central Asia; we can maintain our animals here." Azerbaijan, as we shall see, will later become a cockpit of wars between different states. The most famous will be the two Mongol grandsons of Genghis Khan—that is, Hulagu, the Ilkhan of Iran, and his cousin Batu, the Khan of the Golden Horn—are going to fight for control of Azerbaijan because that is where you can sustain horse archers and cavalry. The shah was now saddled with defending these regions and keeping out invaders. I mentioned in the last lecture, across the Caucuses were Huns.

These are the same people who are attacking the Roman Empire; they break in repeatedly; and the shah has to deal with these Huns through the whole of the fourth and into the fifth century. This was a problem enough, now having a western frontier that was under pressure.

At the same time, the shah was now facing new pressures on the northeast in Transoxiana, along the upper regions of the Jaxartes, along the steppes of the Caspian and Aral Seas. These pressures arose not from the Huns that were plaguing the Roman Empire, but from other nomadic peoples who arrived about the same time the Huns were entering the Roman world. They consisted of two groups; and the first group to arrive was a group of people known as the Hephthalites. The Hephthalites are of obscure origin. They are called in Classical sources the "White Huns." The Byzantine historian Procopius, when he is not criticizing Justinian and telling all the lurid details about his infamous wife Theodora, gives a long passage explaining that the Hephthalites or White Huns were probably different from the Huns that the Romans knew: that they were more European in features; they had fair hair and fair eyes. The suspicion is—and this is, again, only an intelligent surmise—that they were probably Tocharian speakers, just as the Kushans had been; that they comprised of people who had migrated from the early Indo-European populations into the Tarim Basin. They were on the borders of the Chinese Empire. They also comprised of Iranian speakers. There may have also been Turkish elements because some of the Hephthalite rulers carry Turkish personal names; there are certain terms that come down through the literature that might suggest a Turkish connection. Undoubtedly, they were a confederation of inner and outer tribes comprising of several different linguistic and ethnic groups loosely called the Hephthalites and identified by Classical sources as the White Huns.

The significant point is they were pushed out of the border zones of the Chinese Empire due to the very complicated fighting we will be discussing in the upcoming lectures with the collapse of the Han Empire. With the collapse of the Han Empire, eventually nomadic tribes came to rule Northern China, styled themselves as Chinese dynasties; the most successful will be the so-called Northern Wei Dynasty. They ruled from 386–535 A.D. and they are probably responsible for pushing these Hephthalites west just as the Xiongnu had pushed the Kushans west. The Hephthalites show up in the late fourth century, about the same time the Huns show up on the Roman world; and the immediate reaction of the Sassanid shahs is, "We can hire these guys."

I had mentioned that the shahs of Persia had seen themselves as the heirs of the earlier kings of Persia, and when they defeated the Parthians and took over what is today Iraq, Iran, and parts of Afghanistan, the core areas of the Parthian Empire, that was not enough. Most of what is today Afghanistan, Pakistan, the so-called Central Soviet Republic such as Turkmenistan and Uzbekistan, all of those regions were also considered integral to the Persian Empire. These would be the regions of Transoxiana, between the Oxus and Jaxartes Rivers, where all those wealthy caravan cities are. Those cities were largely homes to Sogdian merchants. It also had Aramaic speakers. It was home to a diverse set of religions; we discussed them: They would be Manichees; they would be Zoroastrians; people worshiping the old Persian gods before the Zoroastrian reforms. Many coins show from this period that the goddess Anahita, an ancient Iranian goddess, had her own public great temples in these cities. There were also many, many Buddhist monasteries and sanctuaries. In fact, the most common religion in the cities of Transoxiana was probably Buddhism, at least in the cities. In the countryside, there were agriculturalists who believed in the ancient Iranian gods; may have inclined to some of the newer religions. Within Transoxiana, there were a number of small numbers of tribes and clans of nomadic people living in symbiosis with the agriculturalists and with the cities who were shamanists. It was a very diverse, very wealthy area. It represented the old Upper Satrapies in the Classical age. So the shahs immediately campaigned to move into this region.

As you recall, these regions had been part of the heartland of the Kushan Empire. The first two shahs, Ardashir and Shapur I, essentially subjected Transoxiana, imposed their own governors—Persian governors who ruled as princes; sometimes we call them Kushano-Sassanid rulers or princes—and then they also imposed their authority over Kushan princes ruling in Northern India. What happened is the Sassanid state doubled in size. It conquered essentially the core areas of the old Kushan state. In the third century A.D., these domains provided gold, silver, access to nomadic tribal allies, and all of that enabled the shahs to wage those expensive wars against the Romans.

That very convenient situation began to break down at the end of the fourth century in the 370s and 380s when the Hephthalites appeared on the banks of the Jaxartes. They had been pushed steadily west by pressure from tribes in alliance with the Northern Wei dynasts of China, from local conditions of drought, in searching of new pastures, and the immediate reaction of the shahs is to settle them on the frontiers as allies and auxiliaries. Very, very quickly these Hephthalites turned from allies into rivals. They saw immediately the advantages of controlling the caravan routes of Transoxiana, and they quickly expanded. You have to remember that the shahs are locked in mortal combat with the Roman emperors. They are going to get that northwestern frontier to defend against the Huns, and at the same time now they face these wayward allies, these Hephthalite allies, who very, very quickly overrun much of Transoxiana largely for most of the fifth and early sixth century and rule as their own under their own titles that are of Chinese origin, very similar to the Kushan emperors. As a result, the shahs find themselves losing these very, very valuable provinces to the east.

This was intolerable; you just could not accept this, and the shahs were going to fight for this area. The shah Peroz, who rules in the mid-fifth century, mounts several campaigns against the Hephthalites. In one campaign—and the date is a little uncertain when it took place; one date is 472—he ends up getting captured by the Hephthalites and eventually forced to ransom himself and his son in a humiliating treaty. It is even reported that the then-ruling Eastern Roman emperor Leo I offers to help pay part of the ransom because the Byzantine emperor finds it far more convenient to deal with the Persian shah than a bunch of Hephthalites running over the Middle East. He recovers his throne; he gets back; he engages the Hephthalites again; but he is killed in battle in 484. His son Kavadh comes to the throne; he is challenged by his uncle; he is chased out of Persia. He finds refuge among the Hephthalites and eventually cuts a deal with the Hephthalites to get an army of horse archers to put himself back on the Persian throne, and in return agrees to a treaty confirming essentially the Oxus River as the boundary between the Sassanid and Hephthalite Empires.

This is a severe blow. It is a major territorial loss, and it results in emergence of a very, very impressive Hephthalite state dominating Transoxiana; dominating at least the western cities of the Tarim Basin, the central steppes, and parts of Northern India. This Hephthalite state is increasingly looking like something of the old Kushan Empire; and that is based on the current studies of coins and archaeology, artifacts that indicate that the Hephthalites, very much like the Kushan emperors, were pragmatic, nomadic conquerors. For instance, they used as their official language an East Iranian dialect sometimes known as Bactrian, written in Greek letters just as the Kushans did. Based on the iconography of the coins—many of these coins are imitative of Sassanid coins—they seem to have tolerated all the cults. They were not interested in posing a strict Zoroastrian faith as the shahs were from Persia, which undoubtedly caused an awful lot of hard feelings in many of the cosmopolitan and religiously diverse cities of Transoxiana. They linked India to the wider trade network and invariably are seen and remembered as patrons of Buddhism. In fact, the Chinese sources—the contemporary Chinese sources—make a clear identification. They see the Hephthalites as nothing more than later versions of the Kushans and call them in Chinese the Da Yuezhi; that is, the Great Yuezhi. The Yuezhi was the Chinese name for the ancestors of the Kushans back in the second century B.C. The Hephthalites build up a very, very successful empire embracing the central steppes and extending down into Northern Empire; and this state, which is very similar to the Kushan state, will prefigure a number of medieval states created by later Turkish conquerors in the Middle Ages, really down to the period of the Mongol conquest.

As I said, the shahs were never reconciled to this loss; and they decided to challenge Hephthalite policy, and that meant despite the humiliating defeats and the agreement that the Oxus was now the border, the shahs took a number of important measures to counter this eastern threat. It is countering this eastern threat that actually benefited the Roman Empire, because in the fifth century A.D. and early sixth century A.D., the shahs were so much concerned with these barbarians in the northeast that they paid far less attention to the western frontier. One was constant exchanges with Constantinople to cement good relations with the Byzantine emperor, the eastern Roman emperor. In several instances, these exchanges stressed common interests between Constantinople and Ctesiphon; that is, the capital of the shah. The shah Khosrow II says that Rome and Persia are the two eyes of the world from god and that they should rule as twin emperors; that is, there comes to be something of an accommodation in the fifth and early sixth centuries A.D. between new Rome, Constantinople, and the new Persian Empire.

At the same time, the shahs take strong measures to counter the Hephthalite threat. There is an impressive set of fortifications known as the Gorgon Walls or barriers that extend east of the Caspian Sea and cut off key passes that would give access of nomads coming from the steppes around the eastern shores of the Caspian, the Aral Sea, or swinging in through routes that would lead them through Samarkand and Bukhara. This is an impressive set of fortifications. They are actually much longer than the Roman walls of Britain combined. They probably were manned by between 15,000 and 30,000 men, and they represent an effort by the later Sassanid shahs to monitor their vulnerable eastern border and link up their positions on the Caspian Sea with their positions on the Lower Oxus River. This is in part, we think, initially a barrier against the Hephthalites; it will later be used as a barrier against the Gök Turks. There are measures along the northeastern frontier; while we do not have literary sources about it, just vague references to it and Classical sources, nonetheless archaeology has revealed concerted efforts by the Sassanids to build these fortifications.

Finally, the best way to defeat nomadic horse archers is to hire other nomadic horse archers. This is what a new shah, Shah Khosrow I—who comes to the throne in 531, dies in 579; he is a contemporary of the great Byzantine or Eastern Roman emperor Justinian—he contacts possible allies that could help him beat this new menace that controls these valuable eastern lands; and the people he contacts are known as the Gök Turks. In 557, he enters into negotiations with a leader of the Turks. He apparently is Ishtemi; we will be talking about him in the next lecture. He is a subordinate ruler of the western Gök Turks. Gök Turks means "Sky Turks"; they are the newest nomadic power on the eastern steppes who have rapidly expanded across all of the steppes. The shah is not aware of how large this confederation really is. Nonetheless, he contacts these potential allies who are north of the Jaxartes River and makes a number of arrangements. The arrangement is essentially, "We will jointly go to war against the Hephthalites and share the spoils."

That is a momentous decision. When the shah made this decision, he probably was not quite aware of how powerful these Turks would be. There is a marriage alliance; the shah agrees to take a Turkish princess into his harem. It is a daughter of Ishtemi. Ishtemi is not really a *kaghan*; he probably holds a lesser title, *yabgu*, which means he is sort of a subordinate kaghan to his nephew who is ruling back in the homeland. He releases great numbers of steppe cavalry to help the Turks wipe out the Hephthalites. As always is the case with Turkish horse archers, they do their job really well. The Hephthalites exit. Their possessions in India essentially fall into the hands of Indian rulers, and Central Asia falls under the control of the Gök Turks; and now the shah realizes that he has a far more powerful foe than he had ever imagined in his former allies. Quite unwittingly, Khosrow I has brought into the Middle East a new people, the Gök Turks; people speaking an Altaic language who have originated on the eastern steppes. Their homeland is in the Orkhon Valley. They have rapidly expanded across the steppes. They have all sorts of advantages in political and military organization that previous nomads have not done. What the shah has unwittingly done is opened a new chapter in the history of the steppes: He has brought in the Turks, and the Turks are destined to propel the Eurasian steppes and all of the associated civilizations out of antiquity into the early Middle Ages.

The Turks—Transformation of the Steppes
Lecture 14

With this lecture, we move our course into the early Middle Ages, that is, the period from roughly the 6th century A.D. to the end of the 11th century A.D. This period is defined particularly by the emergence of the Turks. We will first shift our focus back to the eastern steppes—the grasslands of Mongolia—where we will see the origins of the Turks and look at the interaction between the early Turks and China after the Han Dynasty. Turning back to the western steppe zones, we will deal with the relationship between the Turks and Byzantium, and finally, we will explore the interaction of the Turks with the peoples of the Middle East in the central steppe zone.

Emergence of the Turks

- The Turks apparently emerged in the Orkhon Valley. Ironically, with their expansion into the central Asian steppes, the Turks lost their homeland in Mongolia.

- The Turkish languages are closely related and show far less divergence than Indo-European languages. They diverged from the parent Proto-Turkish language relatively late, perhaps in the 1st century B.C. or the 3rd century A.D. The constant reinforcing of traditional Turkish as different groups intermarried and assimilated across the steppes also contributed to the homogeneity of the Turkish languages.

- This is seen quite well in two modern Turkish languages: Uzbek, which has been heavily influenced by Persian languages, and the Turkish of the Turkish Republic. In the 5th century A.D., all the Turkish tribes spoke what we might call dialects that were probably mutually intelligible. They didn't diverge into independent languages until the 11th century.

- The **Avars** emerged in the 4th century B.C. Their rulers—khagans—put together the first significant confederacy of Turks on the steppes.

- By the opening of the early Middle Ages, the Turks had acquired superior saddles and stirrups, which allowed archers to guide their horses and use both hands for their weapons.
  - There were also certain improvements in the composite bow, and the Turks perfected the forging of iron and steel. Turkish speakers living in the Altai Mountains were known for producing fine armor, conical helmets, scimitars, and battleaxes.

  - Thus, at the start of the Middle Ages, the Turkish nomadic warriors were far better equipped and armed than any of the earlier nomadic peoples. Invariably the nomadic armies now had heavy cavalry—lancers—and large numbers of horse archers.

- The Avars were Turkish speakers who dominated the eastern steppes from about 330 A.D. down to 551 or 552. Their effective armies enabled them to negotiate terms with the dynasties then ruling in China, particularly the emperors of the **northern Wei Dynasty**. They also engaged in border wars with the Hephthalites, and as a result, they participated in trade to acquire silks and other goods.

- Sometime in 551 or 552, a vassal ruler of this confederacy, a man named **Bumin**, ruler of the Gök Turks, overthrew the Avars. This was essentially an internal rebellion. Bumin had a private quarrel with the last Avar khagan; he had been denied a royal marriage. Bumin's followers were particularly well armed because they were the people producing the weapons that armed the confederacy of the Avar khaganate.

- As a result, Bumin, who died soon after the rebellion, established the second great khaganate on the steppes. He seized the Orkhon Valley and was acclaimed khagan, probably by an assembly of **khans** and princes, who gave their approval for this man to lead the confederation.

Eastern and Western Gök Turks

- The Gök Turks did not confine their activities to just the eastern steppes. They were responsible for a rapid expansion of the Turks across the central and western steppes. In the course of the 6th century, Turkish speakers extended all the way into the Pontic-Caspian steppes, penetrating to the shores of the Black Sea and to the steppes around the Caspian and Aral seas. They came into contact with the Sassanid Empire and the Byzantine Empire, as well as with the various kingdoms in China.

- That expansion saw several important changes, including a linguistic transformation of the steppes. The Turks proved extremely adaptable in assimilating other steppe peoples, who up until this point mostly spoke Iranian languages. With Turkish becoming a common language, the various steppe peoples also became culturally united.

- Bumin gave his brother Istami the commission to go west and pursue the Avars, who eventually ended up in western Europe, trying to flee the Gök Turks and enter into alliance with Constantinople. After Bumin died, the Gök khaganate essentially divided into two: the eastern Gök khaganate, centered on the traditional homelands, and the western Gök khaganate, centered on the central lands and with aspirations to bring the western steppes under control.
  - This division was not just a matter of lateral succession but also a matter of size. The military abilities of the Gök Turks were so great that they were able to incorporate much of the steppes under a single confederacy. Thus, the political division was forced as a result of considerations related to time and communication.

  - Bumin was ruling in the Turkish heartland, in what is today central Mongolia—3,000 miles away from where his brother was operating on the shores of the Caspian or fighting the Sassanid shah in Transoxiana. This state could not be ruled from a single center.

- o This partition of great khaganates became a feature ever after and was seen in the Mongol Empire conquered by Genghis Khan.

- The eastern khaganate drew the attention of the Chinese emperors, particularly the Tang emperors. In 618, the Tang emperors unified China into a great military state and immediately targeted the northern lands as a region to bring under control. They waged major wars against the Gök Turks, culminating in a campaign in 629–630, in which the Chinese general **Li Jing** destroyed the army of the khagans. The eastern khaganate collapsed, and thousands of Turks were captured and sent back to China to serve in the Chinese army or were settled as colonists.

- In 657, Tang armies also inflicted a serious defeat on the western Turks in central Asia. From this point down into the 680s, the central and eastern steppes were ruled by the Chinese emperor. This was a major achievement; no other urban civilization of the entire Middle Ages or even of antiquity ever won such victories as the Tang emperor did.

- However, this situation could not last, and the Tang Empire went into a decline, particularly brought on by the **An Lushan Rebellion**, which broke out from 755 to 763. The weakening of the Tang Dynasty allowed the Turks to reestablish their independence. They shook off Tang control in a rebellion in 680–681. We have a remarkable set of inscriptions that were set up by these restored Turkish khagans in the Orkhon Valley—the earliest examples of Turkish.

  - o The **Orkhon inscriptions** are written in a runic script. They describe a *yabgu*—a subordinate

The Orkhon inscriptions represent our first direct evidence from the Gök Turks and are regarded as a World Heritage site today.

khagan—named **Tonyukuk**, who put the khagan **Bilge** on the throne.

- o In the inscription, Tonyukuk warns his khagan and his people not to become too assimilated to Chinese ways, not to build Daoist temples or Buddhist stupas, and above all, not to lose their military virtues.

- o The Orkhon inscriptions mark the height of the Gök Turk khaganate. Within 20 years of the inscriptions, the khaganate was overthrown by a subject tribe of the confederation who were also Turks.

The Uighurs

- Between 742 and 744, a new group of Turks, known as Uighurs, constructed the third khaganate, which in some ways represented an improvement over the previous two. Essentially the western zones, even much of the central steppes, were loosely affiliated with this khaganate.

- The Uighurs quickly came to embrace Manichaeism, developed their own script, and established settlements. They turned their tent encampments into what looked like insipient towns. The Uighurs established a close relationship with the caravan cities and the later Tang emperors. As a result, important cultural influences emanating from China and the caravan cities of the Silk Road entered into the eastern and central steppes. For this reason, the Uighurs were regarded as the most accomplished and civilized among all the Turks.
  - o This view is documented in their political dealings with the Chinese Empire. At least half of the Uighur khagans married Chinese princesses, who would have arrived from the Tang court, along with artisans, entertainers, and scribes. The Uighurs were receptive to all these cultural influences.

  - o They were also tolerant of all religions, even though they favored Manichaeism. They allowed the dissemination of Nestorian Christianity and Buddhism across the eastern steppes.

- The Uighur khaganate lasted for about a century before it was overthrown, again, by subject tribes. The capital was destroyed in 845. Many of the Uighurs migrated into the cities of the Tarim Basin and eventually merged with the sedentary populations, bringing their language and traditions.

- These three Turkish khaganates—the Avars, the Gök Turks, and the Uighurs—were the dress rehearsals for the great Mongol Empire of Genghis Khan. They forged more impressive political organizations and brought the Turks into intimate contact with settled civilizations, particularly the civilization of Islam. Indeed, the interaction between the Turks and Islam would change the life of the steppes and change the emerging Islamic world.

Important Terms

An Lushan Rebellion: A rebellion (755–762) raised by the Tang general An Lushan against the emperor Xuanzong (712–756). The revolt, even though it failed, wrought great destruction throughout China and compelled the emperor to withdraw garrisons from the Tarim Basin.

Avars: Peoples who founded the first confederation of Turkish-speaking tribes on the eastern Eurasian steppe (330–551). In 551–552, Bumin of the Gök Turks overthrew the Avars, who then migrated west to establish a new khaganate on the Pannonian plains (580–796).

khan: Turko-Mongolian royal title, meaning "king."

northern Wei Dynasty: Sinicized nomadic rulers (386–535) of northern China and the Gansu Corridor. They promoted Buddhism along the Silk Road. They were Turkish-speaking Tuoba, the royal clan of the Xianbei tribes.

Orkhon inscriptions: The earliest memorial inscriptions in Turkish (722); written in a distinct runic alphabet.

yabgu: The subordinate of a khan or khagan; among the Khazars, the leading commander of the army.

Bilge (b. c. 683; r. 717–734): The fourth Ashina khagan of the Gök Turks (or eastern Turks) since the end of the Tang overlordship in 681. The protégé of his *yabgu* and father-in-law Tonyukuk, Bilge restored the power of the Gök Turks on the eastern Eurasian steppe. His deeds are celebrated on the memorial inscriptions in the Old Turkic language in the Orkhon Valley (today Mongolia).

Bumin (546–553): Khagan of the Gök Turks and a member of the Ashina clan. He ruled as vassal king to the Avars over the Turks dwelling in the Altai Mountains. In 552–553, he overthrew his Avar overlord Anagui and established the Gök Turk khaganate on the eastern Eurasian steppe.

Li Jing (571–649): Tang general and chancellor; proved the ablest commander under emperors Gaozu and Taizong. In 629–630, he defeated and captured Khagan Illig, thereby ending the eastern Turkish khaganate.

Tonyukuk (646–726): A *yabgu* of the eastern Turkish khaganate and advisor to Bilge Khan (717–734). He restored the power of the khaganate after the end of the Tang overlordship in 681. In 716, he erected a memorial inscription of his deeds and his advice in the Old Turkic language at Bayn Tsokto in the Orkhon Valley (today Mongolia).

Suggested Reading

Barefield, *The Perilous Frontier*.

Golden, *Central Asia in World History*.

———, "The Peoples of the South Russian Steppes."

MacKerras, "The Uighurs."

Sinor, "The Establishment and Dissolution of the Türk Empire."

1. Why did the expansion of Turkish-speaking nomads across the Eurasian steppes prove so important? Where did the Turks find new homes? How does this wide distribution of Turkish speaking peoples still influence the world today?

2. What decisive advantages did Turkish horse archers enjoy over other foes?

3. What led to the rapid rise and fall of the Avar, Gök Turk, and Uighur khaganates? How did these khagans seek to make their power effective among so many diverse tribes within these confederations? In what ways did these efforts anticipate the Mongol Empire?

4. How did trade and the reception of new religions, such as Buddhism, Manichaeism, or Christianity, transform these early Turkish empires? Why did the civilization of China have such a profound impact?

The Turks—Transformation of the Steppes
Lecture 14—Transcript

With this lecture, we are going to start the second component of the course. The next 11 or 12 lectures are dealing essentially with the early Middle Ages. By that I mean the period from roughly the 6th century A.D. to really the end of the 11th century AD; that is, what is happening on the steppes and the associated literate, urban civilizations up to the eve of the Mongol conquests. This period is defined particularly by the emergence of the Turks.

We are going to shift our focus again back to the eastern steppes; that is, the grasslands of Mongolia today, the steppe lands essentially running from Lake Balkhash and the Altai Mountains east to the forests of Manchuria. It involves also the arid zones of the Gobi Desert, the regions of Inner Mongolia, because in that area we see the genesis of a new people who come to be called the Turks speaking a distinct set of languages. In addition, we wish to look at the interaction between these early Turks and essentially China after the Han Dynasty; that is, what happens to China after 220 A.D. when it fragments into the three kingdoms and eventually will reconstruct itself into the so-called Tang Empire. That reunification of China begins in 581.

Then we will look at the dynamics of the Turks and the Chinese and how the Turks have transformed the steppes linguistically, culturally, ethnically; and we can then move our focus back to the western and central steppe zones. In the case of the western steppe zones, we will deal with the relationship between these new Turkish peoples and Byzantium, or as we often call it, New Rome; that is, the Eastern Roman Empire, which redefines itself as a Greek-speaking Roman Christian empire in the seventh century. We finish with the relationship between New Rome and the Turks; and that will have some very, very major consequences because it will see the creation of Russia and the emergence of the Russian principalities, which in the end will conquer the steppes and essentially close down that highway starting in the 16th century.

Then finally, we can turn and look to the interaction of the Turks with the peoples of the Middle East. We go back to that vast central steppe zone stretching essentially from the northern shores of the Caspian all the way over to the Pamirs and the Tarim Basin. Not only will we look at the Turkish interaction with civilized life, the great caravan cities again, but also the interaction of the Turks with Islam. That interaction between the Turks and the Islamic world will fundamentally change the Turks as well as change the Islamic world; and that cultural, linguistic, and military interaction is really on par with the interaction between nomadic peoples and Chinese civilization on the eastern end of the steppes.

It is a tall order in the next coming lectures, but it is a fascinating story about the Turks and the role they come to play essentially between the 5th and 11th centuries A.D.

The emergence of the Turks is still a question that plagues linguists. We do not have nearly the information that we would like to have on, say, the development of Indo-European languages. What can be said about the Turks is that they emerged apparently in the Orkhon Valley. That would today be in the center of Mongolia; and one of the ironic aspects about Turkish expansion is that the Turks essentially lost their homeland. They have relocated themselves to new homelands on the Central Asian steppes, in the Tarim Basin, also on the western steppes; and they have spread their language across the Near East in what today would be Turkmenistan, parts of Iran—those would be the Azerbaijanis who speak a Turkish language— and above all Turkey. The concept of Turkey does not really emerge until the 14th century A.D.; and ironically the majority of Turkish speakers are essentially in Turkey, Iran, and Turkmenistan, regions very, very far from the Turkish homeland of the 5th century A.D., which is now the homeland of Mongolian speakers.

The Turkish languages are closely related and show far less divergence than Indo-European languages, and there are several reasons for that. One is they diverge from the parent Proto-Turkish language relatively late; some linguists would say in the first century B.C., others would say in the third century A.D. The languages are still very close. They break into essentially a western and eastern branch and then a northern Lir branch, which is almost extinct; there are only a few peoples who speak the versions of that Turkish in Russia today. But today, a modern Turkish speaker in the Republic of

Turkey in say Ankara would look at the Turkish of Azerbaijanis, of people of Turkmenistan, and say, "Well, it's Turkish, but not quite right"; and then when they got farther east to where today you have the Uighurs in Eastern Turkestan, you would have Uzbeks, they would say, "That Turkish is related, it's a little weird," but they could still make a great deal of sense not only of the words, but also of the syntax.

All the Turkish languages share certain grammatical features that are very important in designating them. One is they are a gluten of languages; that is they are languages that stick together, monosyllabic combinations. Everything is done by suffixes to indicate the function of words. This is peculiar not only to Turkish, but also to the Mongolian languages; and the Turkish and Mongolian languages are a larger branch known as Altaic languages. There are a couple of other families to it, but those are the two main families that survive today. Furthermore, they show very similar tendencies and traits in grammar; in the way the verbs are treated; in what is known as vowel harmony. That is, Turkish languages only have eight vowels; four in one class, four in another. A pure Turkish word should always have words only of that single class. There are no diphthongs; there are no two vowels coming together.

There are numerous other features that keep these languages close together. It is not only a function of time—that is, they diverge from each other much later than the Indo-European languages diverged from their mother—but it is also the nature of nomads; that is, there is a constant reinforcing of traditional Turkish as nomadic peoples cross the steppes, as different Turkish groups intermarry and assimilate, and there is a tendency to keep a certain homogeneous feature of the Turkish languages, which does not happen when people settle down and the languages become generalized among many non-Turkish speakers, there are lots of loan words that are borrowed. This is seen very well in two modern Turkish languages: One is Uzbek, which has been heavily influenced by Persian languages; another one is the Turkish of the Turkish Republic, what we would call Turkish. It has shown enormous amount of influences from Arabic and Iranian in grammar and language, loan words as we call them, as well as certain concepts. Nonetheless, in the 5th century A.D., all of these Turkish tribes spoke languages that were probably mutually intelligible and may better be called dialects; and they really do not diverge into independent languages until probably at the end of this period in the 11th century.

What I wish to do in this lecture is to look at three major Turkish confederations that emerged between the fifth and really the ninth centuries A.D. These confederations in some ways are similar to what we saw under the Xiongnu; that is, the confederation of really the end of the third, second centuries B.C. that poses a threat to China. In this lecture, I want to concentrate a lot on the Turks themselves. We will talk a little bit about China. The interaction between China and these Turkish nomads we shall reserve for an upcoming lecture. In any case, the first confederation we know about emerges in the fourth century A.D.., somewhere in the 330s. There are a group of rulers who go by the name of khan, *kaghan* to be more exact—and that gives rise to names such as khan, which would be a modern rendition of it in English or European languages; but that "g" is really a soft "g," a glide, in Turkish; *yamusak* is the technical term—the Avar khans, who put together the first significant confederacy of Turks on the steppes; they would be centered again on those eastern steppes, particularly on the Mongolian grasslands.

There are several features or several advantages that the Turks had acquired by the opening of the early Middle Ages. One of these is superior saddles; and with superior saddles, stirrups. We believe as early as 300 A.D. nomadic people had devised what is often called the leather loop stirrup. It is essentially a toehold attached to a rather high-backed saddle that would give you more support in riding; it would assist the archer in steering his horse and using both hands for his weapon. These leather straps gave way to metal stirrups; and metal stirrups are attested certainly from the fourth and fifth centuries A.D. on. They are very, very quickly adopted by the Chinese; and when we talk about the clash between the Chinese and Turkish armies in the Sui and Tang dynasties, the Chinese are armed just as well as their Turkish opponents with better leather saddles and that metal stirrup. There also were certain improvements in the composite bow. Above all, the Turks turn out to be extremely skilled metallurgists. They perfect the forging of iron and steel; in fact, the name *Turk*, which comes to become a general name for people speaking all of these related languages, is a term that was originally applied only to those speakers of Turkish living in the Altai Mountains who are really vassals of the Avar khans, and they got their claim to fame because they were excellent metalworkers. They could produce fine armor, the conical helmets, the various scimitars, and battle axes needed for close order fighting.

At the start of what we would call the Middle Ages, certainly by the 4th and 5th centuries A.D., the Turkish nomadic warriors are far better armed and equipped, have far better saddles and stirrups than any of the earlier nomadic peoples, the Xiongnu, the Tocharian speakers, the Saca, the groups that we have discussed earlier in antiquity; and therefore they are a far more formidable cavalry force. Invariably, these nomadic armies now have a component of what we would call heavy cavalry, lancers; men who could close and fight in close order. They have the body armor and the weapons, as well as large numbers of horse archers who would open the attack by harassing the enemy, wearing them down, luring them into a premature attack. All of the khanates that we are talking about—the Avars, the Gök Turks who follow them, and then the Uighur Turks—all of them field similar armies; similar types of armored warriors, horse archers, and they employed the same tactics and strategies. Remarkably, these tactics and strategies will dominate the battlefield, really into the 15th century. As I have mentioned before, it is only the advent of firearms that really undermines this entire system of fighting. You have to understand that these Turks are trained from birth to fight as warriors, to hunt. In fact, the famous kind of polo game played by Turks still survives across Central Asia and into Mongolia, Buzkashi, which is a rough and ready polo played with the carcass of a goat. It is a pretty brutal sport, and a sport that also trains you for the kind of expert horse riding that would require men to ride within 10 or 20 yards of the foe, shoot arrows into him, flee before the enemy can even react, then turn on a dime to counterattack should the enemy give you that opportunity.

The Avars, as we best as we can determine, were Turkish speakers; and from 330 A.D. or thereabouts down to a rebellion that was carried out by their subject Turks in the Altai Mountains—a man named Bumin, who in 551–552 overthrew the Avars—they dominated the eastern steppes based on these armies. They were able to negotiate terms with the dynasties then ruling in China—and we will return to these dynasties in China in the upcoming lecture—and these included particularly Chinese emperors of what are known as the Northern Wei Dynasty. What they really were were related Turks, called in Chinese sources the Tobau people (they have a variety of names) who have established themselves in Northern China, in the Yellow River valley, along the Great Wall—although the Great Wall is falling out of use because they really do not have the resources to maintain it—and they are nomadic warriors trying to rule Northern China in the guise of Chinese emperors. They also clash with the Hephthalites, probably Tocharian speaking people, who succeeded to the empire, the Kushans who attempted to dominate the Tarim Basin and the cities of Transoxiana; that is, those wealthy caravan cities that really net so many advantages to the nomadic peoples. The Avar khans repeatedly negotiated with the emperors of the Northern Wei; they exchanged embassies as well as lots of border wars with the Hephthalites; and as a result they got in on part of that trade, again to acquire the silks and the other goods, which allow the khans to rule a confederation of inner and outer tribes.

I mentioned that very abruptly somewhere in 551–552 a vassal ruler of this confederacy, a man named Bumin, who ruled a group of people who come to call themselves the Gök Turks—and the Gök Turks means the "Sky Turks," the "Celestial Turks"; Gök is still a Turkish word for "sky," it means the "blue sky," and it is associated with the blue color and is probably a Turkish version of the notion of the Son of Heaven in Chinese ideology—they overthrow the Avars very rapidly; it is essentially an internal rebellion. Bumin had a private quarrel with the last Avar khan; he had been denied a royal marriage; there really had been some kind of a dishonoring of him. His followers were particularly well-armed because they had been the people producing the weapons that armed the confederacy of the Avar Khanate. As a result, Bumin, who dies soon after the rebellion, establishes the second great khanate on the steppes. He seizes the traditional regions; the Orkhon Valley. He is acclaimed khan by probably an assembly that already resembles the Kurultai; that is, the assemblies of rulers, of khans, *kaghans*, and princes who give their approval to the man who will lead the confederation. This is a feature of not only various Turkish confederations, but also the Mongols. You have to be approved by this assembly. Do not mistake it for democracy; it is an assembly of the greater ones.

The significant point about the Gök Turks is they do not confine their activities to just the eastern steppes, the Tarim Basin; they are responsible for a very rapid expansion of the Turks across the central and western steppes. In the course of the sixth century, Turkish speakers now extend all the way into those Pontic-Caspian steppes, penetrating to the shores of the Black Sea, to the steppes around the Caspian and Aral Seas. They come into contact with the Sassanid Empire and the Byzantine Empire, as well as with the various kingdoms in China, not yet quite reunified until 581 under the Sui Dynasty. This Turkish confederacy borders on all three of these great literate, urban civilizations.

That expansion sees several important changes: It begins a linguistic transformation of the steppes. The Turks prove extremely adaptable in learning as well as assimilating other steppe peoples, who up until this time mostly spoke Iranian languages. Between the sixth century A.D., when literally Bumin gives his brother Ishtemi, his younger brother, the commission, "Look, you go west; you pursue the Avars"—who eventually end up in Western Europe, they actually end up ultimately in Hungary, trying to flee the Gök Turks and enter into alliance with Constantinople in part to escape their overlords, their would-be overlords, the Gök Turks—he tells his brother Ishtemi, "You run these guys down and bring the various other steppes under control," which he very successfully does. After Bumin dies, either in 552 or 553 shortly after he overthrew the Avars, this khanate essentially divides into two. There is the eastern Gök khanate centered on the traditional homelands, and there is a western Gök khanate that centers on the central lands and has aspirations to bring the western steppes under control. This is not just a matter of lateral succession, but also a matter of size; that the military abilities of the Gök Turks are so great, they are able to incorporate so much of the steppes under a single confederacy, that that forces a political division because of questions of time and communication. You have to remember that Bumin is ruling in the Turkish heartland in what is today Central Mongolia, close to the later capital of Genghis Khan; and that is 3,000 miles away from where his brother is operating on the shores of the Caspian or fighting the Sassanid shah in Transoxiana. You just cannot rule this state from a single center; and so this partition of great khanates becomes a feature ever after, and it is a major feature of the Mongol Empire conquered by Genghis Khan and especially his grandsons.

The second important point I mentioned, of course, is that you have a major linguistic and ethnic transformation going on; that is, Turkish language has now become the language of the steppes and with that comes a sort of cultural koine that unites the various steppe peoples henceforth. Also, this is a matter of power. The khanates, the Gök Turk khans, have military power on an order that no one has seen on the steppes really, at least the central and eastern steppes, since the time of Modu Chanyu and the Xiongnu.

This eastern khanate runs into trouble. It draws the attention of the Chinese emperors, particularly the Tang emperors. The Tang emperors in 618 unify China into a great military state, and they immediately target the northern lands as a region to bring under control; and we will be discussing the Tang emperors. They find the reintroduction of that tribute system; that is, providing Chinese brides, bolts of silk in exchange for some kind of submission as well as access to the horses of the steppes. That is unacceptable. The first Tang emperors rule virtually as generals and conquerors themselves, and I will argue to some extent they are products of the martial society of Northern China. As a result, the Tang emperors wage major wars against these Gök Turks. The fighting climaxes in a campaign in 629–630 when the Chinese general—and his well-known from his military manuals—a man by the name of Li Jing is commissioned to wage a major campaign against the eastern Turks, and it is a perfect strategic operation and envelopment. He nails the army of the khans, destroys them with the kind of tactics we have discussed before, and as a result the eastern khanate collapsed. Thousands of Turks are captured; they are sent back to China to serve into the Chinese army or settled as colonists.

In 657, Tang armies also inflict a serious defeat on the western Turks in Central Asia; and by 657, really down into the 680s, the central and eastern steppes are literally being ruled by the Chinese emperor. The Tang emperor, the second Tang emperor Taizong, could style himself not only as the emperor of China, but also effectively as the khan of the nomadic peoples, the people of the Felt Tents. This was a major achievement; no other urban civilization, organized army, of the entire Middle Ages or even of antiquity ever won such victories as the Tang emperor did.

However, this could not last; and the Tang Empire went into a decline, particularly brought on by the An Lushan Rebellion, which breaks out from 755–763, we will discuss that in the upcoming lecture. What happens is that the weakening of the Tang Dynasty allows the Turks to reestablish their independence. They shake off the control of the Tang in a rebellion in 680–681; and we have a remarkable set of inscriptions that were set up by these later restored Turkish khans in the Orkhon Valley, and these are the earliest examples of Turkish. They are written in a runic script, a script that looks a lot like Germanic runes but is unrelated to it; and in it, the man who is what is known as a *yagbu*—that is a subordinate khan, his name is Tonyukuk; he put the khan on the throne, the khan Bilge—he has a long inscription that is quite significant because it is the first time we have direct evidence from these nomadic peoples. He, Tonyukuk, warns his khan and his people not to become too assimilated by Chinese ways; not to build Daoist temples, not to build Buddhist stupas; to be careful in the material culture; and above all not to lose the military virtues. This is an issue that will be raised again in the Mongol Empire as well as Turkish tribes who enter into the Islamic world. The inscription, which is today—and the whole site, which is regarded as a World Heritage site—known to all Turkish speakers today; any Turk would know, "Yes, that is the first Turkish that we have"; and the modern Turkish languages are still fairly closely related to that early form of Turkish from the 720s. Those inscriptions really mark the height of the Gök Turk khanate.

Within 20 years of those inscriptions, the khanate collapsed. It was overthrown, again by subjects; that is, a subject tribe of the confederation who were also Turks. Between 742 and 744, a new group of Turks known as Uighurs—they are known to people who have been following the news in the relationship between the Uighurs and the Chinese and Chinese Turkestan or Xinjiang today, we used to call it Hsin-chiang; but they are not there yet, they are actually on the Mongolian steppes—construct the third khanate. In some ways, they represent a new improved khanate over the previous two. Their power does not extend as far west; essentially the western zones, even much of the central steppes are loosely affiliated with this khanate.

But the Uighurs are important for several reasons: One, they very quickly come to embrace Manichaeism. There is an official conversion to that faith brought by Sogdian merchants. The Uighurs develop their own script, ultimately based on the Brahmi script. They quickly also establish settlements. They turn their tent encampments into what look like insipient towns. The Uighurs establish a very, very close relationship with the caravan cities and with the later Tang emperors, and that results in important cultural influences emanating from China and from the caravan cities of the Silk Road entering into the eastern and central steppes. That is one of the most important roles they play; and as a result, the Uighurs, among all of the Turks, are regarded as the most accomplished and civilized. This is, for instance, documented in their political dealings with the Chinese Empire. We know of 13 different Uighur khans; 7 of them, essentially half, married Chinese princesses. These would have been women who arrived from the Tang court; some of them were from the imperial family, other from high members of the court. They would have arrived with great retinues; would have been received by the Uighurs. That was essentially equivalent to grand caravans, and with it came artisans, entertainers, and scribes; and the Uighurs were extremely receptive to all of these cultural influences and really enriched the society of the eastern steppes. They were tolerant of all the religions, even though they favored Manichaeism; and when we turn to the Mongol Empire, the Uighurs were regarded as the natural administrative staff for the Mongols. Genghis Khan immediately starts; as soon as his is on his world conquest, he is using Uighurs to run his empire. They also allow the dissemination of Nestorian Christianity and Buddhism across the eastern steppes. On the eve of the unification of the Mongol tribes by Genghis Khan, many of the tribes are already Buddhists, some are Nestorian Christians. There are still some Manichees; many of them have departed from their traditional animist religion.

The Uighur Kaghanate also lasts for about a century before it, too, is overthrown. Again, it is overthrown by subject tribes. The capital is destroyed in 845, it is abandoned; and the successors—these Kyrgyz Turks, who are the ancestors of today the Turks of Kyrgyzstan—they essentially overthrow Uighur power and then leave. Many of the Uighurs migrate into the cities of the Tarim Basin and eventually merge with the sedentary populations and bring their language and their traditions there.

I want to stop with a couple of conclusions about these three Turkish khanates: First, they were the dress rehearsals for the Mongolian Empire, the great Mongol Empire of Genghis Khan. Second, they forged more impressive political organizations and brought the Turks into contact with the settled civilizations very intimately, and above all with the civilization of Islam, which is soon to emerge. It is the great interaction between the Turks and Islam that will change the life of the steppes and also change the emerging Islamic world.

Turkmen Khagans and Tang Emperors
Lecture 15

In the last lecture, we talked about three early Turkish khaganates: the Avars, Gök Turks, and Uighurs. The last two of these khaganates were brought down by rebels who had been egged on and financed by Chinese emperors. That brings us back to the role that China played vis-à-vis the nomadic peoples of the eastern steppes. This lecture, then, provides an update on events in China since the fragmentation of the Han Dynasty in 220 A.D. Then, we look at the interaction between the Chinese and the Turkish-speaking peoples who settled in northern China. Finally, we consider the unification of China under the Sui and Tang emperors and their relationship with both the Gök Turks and the Uighurs.

The Northern Wei and Sui Dynasties

- As mentioned earlier, the empire of the Han (206 B.C.–220 A.D.) was roughly contemporary with the Roman Empire. The Han Empire initiated many of the policies and priorities on the Chinese political agenda that actually continue down to this day. Successive Chinese emperors were influenced by that notion that the Middle Kingdom had the right to rule the various areas along the northern frontier and into central Asia to control the vital Silk Road.

- In 220, the Han Empire fragmented into three competing kingdoms. They were briefly united by the Jin emperors but then collapsed into 12 or 15 competing principalities. In this political landscape of civil war, rebellions, and migrations, there are a couple of important facts to keep in mind.
  - First, the locus of Chinese civilization shifted from the Yellow River south into the Yangtze River basin. The southern regions of China offered a great deal more opportunity to exploit the landscape, support great cities, and become the repositories of Chinese civilization. Already in the period of the 3rd, 4th, and 5th centuries A.D., there was a migration of Chinese to the south.

- Another important feature in this period is that nomadic peoples begin to migrate inside of China. Specifically, in the 4th century, Turkish speakers moved into the northern regions of China. They were contemporary with the Avar khagans, but they carved out their own frontier kingdom in the Yellow River basin and began to rule as if they were Chinese emperors. These emperors took the Chinese dynastic name Wei.

© Worapip Kunteerapaseart/iStock/Thinkstock.

- The northern Wei rulers set the pattern for future nomadic conquerors of China, including the Mongols. The Wei learned that the Chinese could not be ruled by horseback. It was necessary to co-opt the Chinese administrative class and to tax the peasantry, rather than simply plundering it. Above all, these rulers were great sponsors of Buddhism, and it is because of these early emperors that Buddhism entered China and spread across the population.

The second northern Wei emperor commissioned five colossal statues at Yungang that show earlier incarnations of the Buddha.

- In 581, Emperor Wen began a series of campaigns to reunite China. By 589, he had battled his way to control the entire Middle Kingdom. The northern Wei were brought under his control. All the southern kingdoms were reunited, and once again, China was a single imperial state.

- The second emperor of the Sui Dynasty, **Yangdi**, got involved in wars against the Koreans and with steppe nomads. He left no powerful successor, and when he died (617/618), he was succeeded by Li, a duke, who established the Tang Dynasty.

The Tang Dynasty

- The Tang Dynasty was essentially a continuation of the Sui. Li, who took the throne name **Gaozu**, was from a powerful military family, and he and his son Taiyüan (**Taizong**) proved to be extraordinary emperors.

- The Tang Dynasty is looked upon as the apex of early Chinese civilization. In one sense, it was the empire in which China achieved its greatest territorial extent. However, it is significant that the Tang Empire was not purely a Chinese empire. It owed a great deal to the frontier society along the northern Chinese border. The Chinese people and the nomads there had been interacting at least since the 3rd century B.C.

- Gaozu and Taizong were not typical Confucians; they were known to be great equestrians and reveled in battle. They commanded armies, were involved in military reforms, and hand-picked excellent generals. In the early Tang period, the army was reorganized into seven divisions. These were powerful field armies, with 20,000 men and at least 4,000 cavalry assigned to each division.
  - The logistics of the Chinese army were clearly superb. Tang armies numbering between 50,000 and 150,000 are reported to have mobilized against distant objectives in Korea, against the steppe nomads, and in the south, along the borders of what today would be called Vietnam.

  - The general Li Jing and his colleagues were behind this military reorganization, and they perfected the strategy and tactics to bring the nomads to battle.

- In 628, after some humiliating defeats at the hands of the Gök Turks, the emperor Taizong decided to reckon with the Turkish khagan, **Illig**. A huge army was mobilized; one, commanded by Li Jing, penetrated into the Turkish homeland, and on May 2, 630, brought the Gök Turk army to bay. The khagan himself was captured, and the eastern Gök khaganate collapsed. Turkish tribes acknowledged the authority of Taizong.

- By the late 640s, the Tang armies had swept through the Tarim Basin and brought that entire area back under Tang control. In 657, a Tang army won an even more significant victory over the western Gök Turks and forced them to acknowledge the authority of the emperor of China. By 660, all the central and eastern nomadic zones were essentially ruled by the Chinese emperor. It was without a doubt the greatest imperial order on the globe at this point.

- The Tang Dynasty was extremely successful, and we have a wealth of information about how the emperors organized what they called the four garrisons.
  - The Tarim Basin was divided into four garrisons based on caravan cities and put under the command of four military governors, with an overall superintendent of the entire region. The garrisons had Chinese military colonists, as well as native populations and many nomadic peoples.

  - Surviving documents of the military garrisons show that the Chinese had a major impact in stimulating the development of cities in the Tarim Basin. For example, soldiers were paid in "cash coins," which monetized markets in the caravan cities. Chinese settlers and pilgrims came to the region, and the Chinese language became well known.

- The Tang established an impressive political order, but it was expensive to maintain. Already at the end of the 7th century, the imperial budget faced increasing military and frontier costs.
  - These resulted from the fielding of great armies and garrisons, notably in the western region, and from expeditions in Korea and to the south.

  - Further, the Tang emperors repaired and manned the Great Walls and began to link the various canal systems into what would eventually become the Grand Canal. The canal systems were necessary for moving forces and supplies between northern and southern China and for shipping silk out of the south.

○ Costs were also associated with maintaining the northern frontiers.

End of the Tang

- In 751, the Tang Dynasty suffered three significant defeats on the frontiers. The first was in Korea; the second was in the region that would be Yunnan today, another border area; and the third—the one that really hit home—was the defeat on the Talas River.
  - ○ At the Talas River, a Chinese army for the first time ran into an army of the Abbasid caliphs. Both sides fielded nomadic cavalry. The Chinese army had state-of-the-art crossbows and heavy infantry. But the Tang's nomadic allies, the Turks, deserted over to the Muslim side. The result was a decisive win for the Muslims.

  - ○ That accomplishment would make Islam the religion of victory in the eyes of the nomadic peoples, and it was a significant blow to the credibility of the Tang emperors.

- Those defeats, which fed into the fiscal demands and weaknesses and into the perceptions that the Tang emperors had lost the mandate of heaven, resulted in the explosion of the An Lushan Rebellion. This was led by a Uighur Turkish general who had fallen out of favor. In the end, the Tang emperors triumphed. They put the rebellion down, but it turned out to be a demographic and fiscal disaster.
  - ○ The Chinese armies were withdrawn from the western garrisons. The Tibetans controlled the Tarim Basin and Silk Road for the next 75 years. Although Tang armies reappeared in the 840s and 850s and reimposed some authority over the Tarim Basin, it was never the same.

  - ○ The Tang emperors made deals with warlords to regain the throne, and by 907, the Tang Dynasty fragmented, just as its predecessor, the Han Empire, had. As a result, China once again became home to competing warlords and new nomads settling in the Middle Kingdom.

○ Above all, the defeat on the battlefield of Talas marked a turning point in the history of the steppes and of China: For the first time, the power of Islam had projected itself over the steppes.

Names to Know

Gaozu (b. 566; r. 618–626): Tang emperor of China. One of the greatest soldier-emperors of Chinese history. Under the Sui emperors, Gaozu, or Li Yuan, ruled strategic borderlands in Shanxi. In 618, he seized power. He waged war against the Gök Turks of the eastern khaganate.

Illig Khagan (r. 620–630): Ruled over the eastern Turkish khaganate. His raids into northern China precipitated war with the Tang emperor Taizong. In 626–630, the Tang general Li Jing defeated and captured Illig, thereby ending the eastern Turkish khaganate and imposing Chinese overlordship in 630–681.

Taizong (b. 598; r. 626–649): Tang emperor of China. Defeated the Gök Turks in 629–630 and brought the eastern Eurasian steppe under Chinese rule. His generals Li Jing and Li Shiji subjected the Tarim Basin, defeated the Tibetans, and advanced Chinese influence to the Jaxartes River.

Yangdi (b. 569; r. 604–618): Sui emperor; reorganized the imperial army, recruiting Turkish cavalry. He initiated the conquest of what is now Vietnam, but expeditions against Korea proved costly failures. His assassination precipitated a brief civil war, whereby the general Li Yuan seized the throne as Gaozu, first emperor of the Tang Dynasty.

Suggested Reading

Barefield, *The Perilous Frontier*.

Graff, *Medieval Chinese Warfare, 300–900*.

Lewis, *China between Dynasties*.

Li, trans., *The Great Tang Dynasty Record of the Western Regions*.

Skaff, *Sui-Tan China and Its Turko-Mongol Neighbors*.

1. What role did the nomadic barbarians plays in the disunity in China in 330–581? Why did successful Turkish generals and princes embrace Chinese institutions and aesthetics whenever they carved out a kingdom in northern China? What impact did the nomads have on the society and mores of northern China?

2. What accounted for the success of the northern Wei as Sinified rules? Why did they fail to unite China? What accounted for the success of the Sui emperors? Why did they fail to deal with the Turkish khaganates?

3. What accounts for the extraordinary success of the Tang emperors Gaozu and Taizong against the nomadic Turks? How important was Li Jing as general and strategist in Tang success?

4. What was the impact on Tang civilization of the nomadic peoples and the cities of the Tarim Basin in the 7th and early 8th centuries?

5. How did setbacks in frontier policy lead to the An Lushan Rebellion? How were fiscal weakness, oppressive taxation, and rebellion ultimately linked to the costs of imperial defense? How did the later Tang emperors fail?

Turkmen Khagans and Tang Emperors
Lecture 15—Transcript

In this lecture, I wish to deal with the interaction between the Turks and the Chinese Empire. I mentioned it in passing in the previous lecture that Turks and Chinese have long been in contact with each other, and that Chinese civilization is one of the great forces that exert cultural influence and change on the Eurasian steppes. In this lecture, I want to examine that question much more thoroughly.

In the last lecture, we talked about the three great early Turkish khanates. The first of them were the Avar khans, who ruled from about 330–552. They were overthrown by an internal rebellion. The second two khanates, however—the Gök Turks, or as we sometimes call them the "Celestial Turks," which would be an English translation—and then their successors the Uighurs, both of those states were brought down not only by internal rebellion, but by rebels who had been egged on and generally financed by the Chinese emperors. That brings us back to China and the role that China plays vis-à-vis the nomadic peoples of the eastern steppes, and also the struggle between the Chinese and nomadic confederations to control the crucial eastern arm of the Silk Road; that is, the routes running from Northern China through the Jade Gate, the Yumen Pass, into the cities of the Tarim Basin, over the city of Kashgar that is today in Tajikistan, and then to the cities of Central Asia (Samarkand, Bukhara), cities well-known as the fabled caravan cities of the Silk Road.

This requires us to do a couple of things in this lecture: First, we want to update what has been happening in China ever since the Han Dynasty fragmented in 220 A.D. Then we want to look at the question of the interaction between the nomads who settled in China; not the confederacies I just talked about—the Avars, the Gök Turks, and the Uighurs—but Turkic-speaking peoples who actually settled in Northern China and passed themselves off as Chinese emperors. Then we want to look at the unification of China under the Sui and the Tang emperors, and their relationship with both the Gök Turks and also the Uighurs.

First, some update on what has happened to China since 220 A.D. I mentioned in a previous lecture that the empire of the Han, the great dynasty established in 206 B.C. and running to 220 A.D., was roughly contemporary with the Roman Empire, and that the Han Empire had evolved the initial policies; in fact, it could be attributed to the emperor Wudi, who initiated a war against the Xiongnu in 133 B.C. and in many ways sets a lot of the priorities on the Chinese political agenda, diplomatic front, really down to this day. One can argue that successive Chinese emperors really were influenced by that notion that the Middle Kingdom, China, had the right to rule these various areas along the northern frontier and deep into Central Asia to control the vital silk route. In 220 A.D., the Han Empire fragmented. It fragmented into three competing kingdoms, and this fragmentation into three kingdoms reproduced earlier patterns before the year 221 B.C. when the first empire was established, the so-called period of the Warring States usually dated from 481–221 B.C. There were three kingdoms contending in the south; briefly they were united by emperors known as the Jin emperors. They maintained a brief unity, and then it collapsed again into well over 12 or 15 competing principalities.

In this political landscape of civil war, rebellions, migrations, there are a couple of important facts to keep in mind. First, the locus of Chinese civilization shifts. It shifts from the Yellow River down into the Yangtze or Yangza River basin; that is to the south. It is in the south where many Chinese will migrate from their traditional homeland into regions that offered better opportunity, particularly for the cultivation of rice, the cultivation of silk (what we would call sericulture), as well as stock raising. The southern regions of China offered a great deal more opportunity to exploit the landscape, support great cities, and also to become the repositories of Chinese civilization. Already in the period of the third, fourth, and fifth centuries A.D., there was a migration of Chinese south. Some of this was encouraged by the southern kingdoms such as the kingdom of Wu, the kingdom of Qi, which were located in the south. These were local dynasties that ruled only part of Southern China. Nonetheless, they encouraged immigrants, and above all they maintained themselves; these courts maintained themselves as the true Confucian rulers, the Confucian rulers who followed the proper way. In many ways, they will anticipate the great Song Dynasty, which will come to power in 960 and will rest in Southern China and will really uphold the position that they are heirs to the Han Empire even though they do not control the Han heartland; that is, the traditional capitals of Luoyang and Chang'an, which are on the Yellow River in the lower and middle reaches of the Yellow River and had been the capitals of so many earlier Chinese civilizations.

Another important feature in this period is that nomadic peoples begin to migrate inside of China. This does not mean the borderlands just north of the Great Wall; this period witnesses actual movements of people who are Turkish speakers primarily. In Chinese, they are known as the Tuoba, the Tabgach; one name. They are apparently Turkish speakers; and in the fourth century they move into the northern regions of China. They are contemporary with the Avar khans; but they are not subjects of the Avar khans, quite the contrary. They carve out their own frontier kingdom in the Yellow River basin and in those frontier zones—the Orhdos triangle, the regions of Inner Mongolia—and they begin to rule increasingly as if they were Chinese emperors. The rulers take Chinese names. They style themselves as if they are more or less conforming to the Confucian norms; and the first ruler that we know, the founder of this dynasty, Daowu, he in a sense ruled not only as a nomadic khan, as you will, who had access to nomadic cavalry but also as a Chinese-style emperor. He and his successors sponsored Buddhism. They put access to the Silk Road as a top priority. They garrisoned the Jade Gate. They encouraged that type of trade; and furthermore they took the Chinese dynastic name Wei. It is an old dynastic name, and they are often known as the Northern Wei to distinguish themselves from that earlier Chinese kingdom. They set the pattern for future nomadic conquerors of China, including the Mongols, above all the Mongols, that when you enter into China, when you take parts of China proper, you cannot rule them by horseback. You have to co-op the Chinese administrative class, the men who come to be known as the Mandarins, who follow the Confucian classics. You have to have administrators. It is also better to tax the peasantry rather than to simply plunder it and turn Chinese cities into pastures. The Northern Wei play an important role there.

Above all, they are great sponsors of Buddhism; and it is because of these early emperors—especially the second one, Taiwu—that Buddhism enters China and really begins to spread across the Chinese population, not only in Northern China, but also in Southern China. Taiwu commissions a remarkable set of colossal statues at the city of Yungang, which is today really an international tourist treasure. They are five colossal statues that show earlier incarnations of the Buddha, and this is the emperor himself Taiwu and his ancestors essentially projecting themselves as earlier avatars or incarnations of the Buddha if you will.

The Northern Wei set the agenda and set the model of future nomadic conquerors and the relationship of nomads when they come into the Chinese world. Genghis Khan and above all his grandson Kublai Khan learn very important lessons, if they had followed the way of a script; and significantly they would too take a Chinese name, sponsor Buddhism, and follow a number of the same policies.

In 581, a fellow by the name of Emperor Wen began a series of campaigns to reunite China. By 589, he had battled his way to control the entire middle kingdom. The Northern Wei were brought under his control; all of the southern kingdoms were united; and once again China was a single unitary imperial state. The second emperor, Yang, of the Sui Dynasty blundered into waging a war against the Koreans; he got involved in wars with steppe nomads; he left no powerful successor. When he died in either late 617 or perhaps early 618 he was succeeded by a Li, a duke, who was related to the imperial family through his mom's side, and he established a new dynasty that we call the Tang Dynasty. The Tang Dynasty is essentially a continuation of the Sui. Gaozu is the throne name that this warlord took; throne names are the names that Chinese emperors are known by historically. He was from a powerful military family called the Li family, and he and his son Taiyüan, both of them, proved to be extraordinary emperors.

The Tang Dynasty is looked upon as the apex of early Chinese civilization; and in one sense, it is the empire in which China achieves its greatest territorial extent, far greater than the earlier Han Empire. However, it is significant that this Tang Empire was not purely a Chinese empire. It owed a great deal to the frontier society I discussed in earlier lectures along the Northern Chinese border of which the Northern Wei were just one manifestation in which Chinese and nomadic peoples had been interacting at least since the third century B.C. Gaozu and Taizong, the first two Tang emperors, were not typical Confucians. They were known to be great equestrians. They reveled in battle. Of course, the first emperor was a Li, or duke—that was his job on the frontier—but the early Tang emperors, quite uncharacteristically of later Tang rulers and especially of Chinese emperors from the Song Dynasty down really until the overthrow of the monarchy and the end of the Republican revolution, they were not commanders; they did not go out and wage war personally. That was done by generals. They were the son of heaven; they had more important duties to do back in the Chinese homeland. Yet the Tang emperors, quite the contrary, were emperors who were expert in fighting; they were known to command armies; they were personally involved in military reforms. They also had a hand in picking excellent generals.   The most important general is a man named Li Jing—I have mentioned him earlier—and he is behind the reform of the early Tang army under the first two emperors.

Chinese armies had been always impressive. They were essentially based on *corvee* labor; that is, all the adult males of the Chinese Empire owed their labor services to the emperor either on great building projects such as the Grand Canal or other such public projects or one year's military service and possibly a second year of garrison service. This had characterized Chinese armies since the Han period. The army was reorganized in the early Tang period, quite significantly into seven divisions. These were very, very powerful field armies with 20,000 men, at least 4,000 cavalry assigned to each division; that is, 20 percent of the force. This is cavalry armed in the up to date weapons that the Turks had pioneered; that is, metal stirrups, the lamellar armor, it included horse archers. Above all, the Chinese divisions were well equipped with archers, crossbow men, and field artillery. The logistics of the Chinese army, which is only imperfectly understood, were clearly superb. Tang armies numbering between 50,000 and 150,000 are reported as mobilized against distant objectives: in Korea, against the steppe nomads, and down in the south along the borders of what today would be called Vietnam into what is now Yunan Province, which was then a wild and wooly frontier zone. Li Jing and his colleagues were behind this military reorganization, and they also perfected the strategy and tactics to bring the nomads to battle.

In 628, after some humiliating defeats at the hands of the Gök Turks, the emperor Taizong decided to reckon with the Turkish khan; the khan at the time was a fellow by the name of Illig. A huge army was mobilized. Two great columns, one commanded by Li Jing, penetrated into the Turkish homeland and on May 2, 630 brought the Gök Turk army to bay, forced it into a battle using very much the tactics I discussed earlier that the Romans had devised against nomads; it is almost a textbook copy of it. Similar problems generally generate similar solutions, and Li Jing was clearly one of the great generals in all of Chinese history. The victory is decisive. The khan himself was captured; the Turkish army goes down in defeat. As I mentioned, many Turks were recruited into the imperial army. One aspect about the Tang and later armies, the Chinese emperors: These armies were above nationality. Once you were recruited into the army, into those divisions, you were essentially going to be assimilated as a Chinese soldier. The victory over the khan meant the eastern Gök khanate collapsed. The Turkish tribes acknowledged the authority of the Tang emperor, Taizong.

In 641, Tang armies reappeared in Korea. Shortly afterwards, by the late 640s, the Tang armies had swept through the Tarim Basin and had brought that entire area back under Tang control. In 657, a Tang army won an even more significant victory over the western Gök Turks and forced the western Turks to acknowledge the authority of the emperor of China. By 660, all of the central and eastern nomadic zones, all of those regions, essentially were ruled by the emperor of China almost in the capacity of a khan, while to his Chinese subjects he ruled as the Son of Heaven. It was without a doubt the greatest imperial order on the globe at this point. However, it rested very much on these Chinese emperors adopting an aggressive military policy, being directly involved—hands-on involved—with the campaigns along the frontiers; and it is easy to forget this fact if one studies Chinese history simply from its internal developments, from the great classics, from the writings of the Confucian historians. In the later tradition, there is great admiration particularly for Gaozu and Taizong, the first two Tang emperors; those are throne names that are taken by many lesser men in later dynasties. Nonetheless, you get the sense there is always this ambiguous feeling: They really were not fully Confucian emperors. They spent too much time paling around with their generals, going out and riding and carrying out hunting expeditions; and these are activities that later Chinese emperors tended to avoid, stressing far more knowledge of the classics, calligraphy, and creating a huge court to distance themselves between their subjects and their servants and the Son of Heaven.

The Tang Empire to some extent is not only Chinese, but it is also a product of the interaction of Chinese civilization with the nomadic peoples going back to the Xiongnu. It was extremely successful. Its success has been tested in several ways, and that is a result of finds, archaeology. This would be the regions that the Chinese had historically called the western regions. These regions had been under Han control, particularly after the great Han victories, essentially between 75 and 91 A.D., really extending into 102 A.D.; notably Ban Chou, the later Han general who brought those areas under control. We have some documents from the Han period. They have survived from garrison cities in the Tarim Basin. We have a wealth of documents surviving from the Tang period. These are on bamboo, leather and wooden tablets, parchment, scrolls; they are documents. What they give us is a wealth of information of how the Tang emperors organized what they called the Four Garrisons.

The Tarim Basin was divided into four garrisons, four separate military governors, with an overall superintendent of the entire region. They were based on the great caravan cities: Khotan, Kucha, Kashgar, and Yanqui, to pronounce it in its Chinese form. These four garrisons had Chinese military colonists. They also included native populations and many nomadic peoples, probably Turkish speakers on the basis of the names, who are now serving the emperor of China. The documents of the military garrisons show that the Chinese had a major impact in stimulating the development of cities in the Tarim Basin. For one, large amounts of stock raising—and horses were particularly needed—and the Tang developed those activities in the Tarim Basin. The soldiers had to be paid. Thousands of examples of what are known as Chinese cash coins: These are cast coins going back to the Han Period; the basic day to day currency is a cast bronze coin. The word *cash* is actually a loan word from the Portuguese through the Malay dialects from a later period. Nonetheless, they are paid in coins and the soldiers start spending this money in the caravan cities and monetize markets. It is clear in the eighth and ninth centuries that coins were in common use throughout the cities of the Tarim Basin, even when Tang rule over this region lapsed in the late eighth and early ninth centuries.

In addition, it brought many Chinese settlers, Chinese pilgrims. The Mogoa caves near Dunhuang indicate a significant influx of Chinese. Chinese now becomes a language well known in the Tarim Basin. It is really the basis for the development of the Chinese population now living there in what the Uighurs would prefer to call eastern Turkestan—I have called neutrally the Tarim Basin—it goes back to this Tang settlement; and it results in a very, very subtle interaction between the Tang court, the caravan cities, and the various tribes of the central and eastern Eurasian steppes.

This is an impressive political order. However, it was expensive to maintain. We do have some accounts of the rising costs, and the rising costs are staggering. Already at the end of the seventh century A.D., the imperial budget is increasingly facing military and frontier costs; and these came from several items on the budget. First was the fielding of great armies and garrisons, notably in the western region, in the western districts; the so-called Four Garrisons. It also resulted from expeditions. These were expeditions that were waged not only on the steppes, but in Korea and into the south. Furthermore, the Tang emperors carried out certain important activities that were very costly. One was the repair and the manning of the Great Walls. These had fallen in disarray after the fall or the fragmenting of the Han Dynasty, and it was repaired and extended under the Tang. It was expensive. It was particularly expensive to maintain and repair, to garrison. Generally, many men called up for military service under the conscript system would then be sent off to do garrison duty; so you could at least take two or three years out of your life serving the emperor with the obligatory military service.

The Tang emperors and the predecessors, emperor Win and Yang of the Sui Dynasty, also began to link the various canal systems that go back really to the Han and before into what eventually becomes known as the Grand Canal, which stretches some 1,400 miles and connects the Yellow River region with the Yangtze or the Yangzi. That canal systems was necessary for military movement, for moving forces and supplies between northern and southern China, but above all for supply of foodstuffs and silk; that is, Southern China increasingly was producing the rice and silk that sustained the monarchy. Silk was the commodity on the Silk Road. It was the prime currency for all major transactions; that is, pieces of silk, bolts of silk, were counted out in order to make major payments to contractors, to foreign princes, to nomadic warlords, whatever, and then the bronze coins and rice were used in everyday transactions. So the canal was necessary for the moving of the silk out of the Yangtze valley into the cities of Chang'an and Luoyong, the classic cities of Northern China, the ancient capitals, and then through the Jade Gate and west. In addition, the Yellow River valley system, which had been the homeland of Chinese civilization, certainly the core of Chinese civilization grew there, that homeland apparently was becoming drier and less fertile over the early centuries of the first century A.D. By the third, fourth, and fifth centuries, we hear of problems of flooding; the crops and conditions are not so good. That could account in part for the migration of Chinese into the southern lands. Part of the reason for building that canal was to feed the great capitals in the north, the historic centers. Henceforth, the Grand Canal is strategic not only for the control of China, but for feeding the northern capitals, for shipping the silk out to points west; and that was an immense expense on the Tang budget. The figures have been calculated; they rise considerably: an annual budget of some 2,000 cash; military expenditure starts to jump to figures of 15,000–20,000, many times the original expenditures by the end of the seventh century. This is a fiscal pressure that all Tang emperors are under.

The second important pressure on the monarchy is maintaining the northern frontiers. We have, fortunately, some figures from the early Tang period, and these come from the years 712–755; that is, on the eve of the An Lushan Rebellion, which is in part a rebellion against the fiscal demands. In 712, military expenditures were reckoned at 2 million strings of cash; that would be a hundred bronze coins strung together. By 742, it has risen to six times to 12 million. By 755, on the eve of the Rebellion, it is now 15 million strings of cash. Under these pressures—pressures to pay the army, the heavy building costs to maintain the capitals, the Grand Canal—all of this lost the emperor a great deal of sympathy. It contributed to a major rebellion from 755–763 that was headed up by a disaffected general, An Lushan, and one could argue that the dynasty was really done in by internal matters.

But that is only part of the story. Before the outbreak of that rebellion, four years earlier in 751, the Tang Dynasty suffered several significant defeats. Actually, in 751, they suffered three significant defeats on the frontiers, and these were by armies commanded by their generals. The first was in Korea. There is always a problem invading Korea, and any emperor with any sense would avoid Korea. The second one was in the distant regions today; that would be Yunnan, which was another border area. But the third one, the one that really hit home, was the defeat in 751 on the Talas River. We will be talking about this battle when we are dealing with the interaction between Islamic civilization and the Turks. In that battle, a Chinese army for the first time ran into an army of the Abbassid caliphs; that is, the caliph of the Islamic world. Both sides fielded nomadic cavalry; and the Chinese army was state of the art crossbows, heavy infantry supported by nomadic cavalry. But what happened in that battle is the nomadic allies, the Turks, deserted over to the Muslim side. The Chinese army was badly defeated even though it was essentially fighting withdrawal from the battlefield; and the result was a decisive win for the Muslims. That victory for the Muslims would make Islam the religion of victory in the eyes of the nomadic peoples, and it was a very, very important blow to the credibility of the Tang emperors. Those defeats, which fed into the fiscal demands and weaknesses, which fed into the perceptions that the Tang emperors had lost the Mandate of Heaven, resulted in the explosion of the An Lushan Rebellion, led by a Uighur Turkish general who had fallen out of favor and really was driven to rebellion because of scandals about him in the court.

In the end, the Tang emperors triumphed. They put the rebellion down, but it turned out to be a demographic and fiscal disaster. The Chinese armies were withdrawn from the western garrisons. The Tibetans controlled the Tarim Basin and Silk Road for the next 75 years. While Tang armies reappeared in the 840s and 850s and re-imposed some authority over the Tarim Basin, it was never the same. Above all, the Tang emperors had made deals with the warlords to regain their throne, and by 907 the Tang Dynasty, the Tang Empire, again fragmented just like its predecessor the Han Empire; and as a result, China once again becomes home to competing warlords and new nomads settling in the middle kingdom. But above all, the defeat on the battlefield of Talas marked a new turning point in the history of the steppes and of China, because for the first time the power of Islam had projected itself over the steppes. That will be the subject of the following lectures.

Avars, Bulgars, and Constantinople
Lecture 16

I n this lecture, we will shift our focus away from the eastern Eurasian steppes and the Chinese world, back across those steppes to the western arm. That would be the region stretching from essentially the lower and middle Danube River to the Ural River that empties into the Caspian Sea. We want to focus on the interaction of the Turkish peoples with the greatest Christian civilization of the early Middle Ages, that of the Byzantine Empire, centered on Constantinople, or New Rome. In the next three lectures, we'll look at the relationship between Byzantine civilization and the peoples of the steppes.

Lessons Learned by the Byzantines

- To understand the Byzantine perception of the northern nomads, recall that the emperors who ruled in Constantinople saw themselves as heirs to the Roman Empire going back to Augustus, and they were particularly conscious of the crisis that late Roman emperors had encountered from the Huns in the 5th century A.D.

- The emperors had drawn several important lessons from their dealings with Attila the Hun. One was to pursue a policy of divide and conquer to undermine any kind of insipient confederacy on the steppes. It has often been remarked that Byzantine diplomacy is perhaps the most contorted and clever of all diplomacies ever created. It was largely devised for dealing with steppe nomads.

- The other important lesson the Byzantines learned was to trust the walls of Constantinople. The walls were such an effective barrier that no nomadic conqueror, no matter how sophisticated his engines of war, could possibly breach them. The Roman masonry architecture defied any invader until the advent of artillery. Even provincial cities, such as Thessalonica, were well fortified and could defy nomadic invaders.

- The Byzantines, who had problems dealing with the Islamic world and their own internal religious issues, failed to have the same kind of impact on the peoples of the western Eurasian steppes that the Chinese and, as we shall see, the Muslim world had on steppe nomads. The nomadic peoples dwelling on the steppes from the Danube to the Caspian never embraced Orthodox Christianity.

Negotiations and Alliances with the Turks
- The first time the Byzantines encountered the Turks was during the reign of the emperor **Justinian I**, who ruled from 527 to 565 and attempted to reconquer the western provinces. Avar envoys arrived at the court at Constantinople, seeking to enter into an alliance with the Byzantine emperors. They were seen as an exotic people, quite beyond the imagination of those living in Constantinople.

- The Gök Turks claimed that these Avars were wayward vassals. This opened up a series of negotiations between the court in Constantinople and the rulers of the western Gök Turks. One of the big stumbling blocks in these negotiations was the question of the Avars, whom the Byzantines hope to use as possible allies.

- Another issue was the question of trade routes. The Byzantines sought access to an extension of the Silk Road from the southern shores of the Aral Sea across the steppes to ports on the Black Sea. This issue was raised repeatedly between the imperial government and the nomadic tribes of the steppes.

- Meanwhile, the Avars turned out to be not the best of allies. To escape the control of the Gök Turks, they moved west and settled on the Hungarian plain, the same area that Attila had controlled. Having escaped the power of the western Turkish khagans, they began to raid into the Byzantine Empire.
  - Like all nomadic rulers, the Avar khagan needed gold to pay off his various followers. In addition, the Avars found that the imperial frontiers along the Danube were particularly vulnerable, largely because the imperial government had commitments elsewhere.

- In the late 6th century, the Avars followed the river systems of the Balkans and ravaged many of the same cities once ravaged by the Huns.

- The imperial government responded in part with diplomacy and gifts. There's a famous story that the emperor **Maurice Tiberius** (r. 582–602) sent an elephant and a gold couch to the Avar khagan as novelties to try to convince him to ally with the Byzantines. The gift backfired, suggesting to the nomads that they could acquire more exotic gifts if they further pressured the Byzantines.

The Byzantines attempted to respond to Avar aggression with diplomacy and gifts, but the Avars realized that if they increased pressure on the Byzantines, they might receive even more exotic and valuable goods.

Conflicts with Persia and the Avars

- Maurice Tiberius is also credited with writing a strategic manual, the *Strategikon*, in which he described how to cope with nomadic cavalries. This document reveals that the Byzantines were now mounting cavalry with metal stirrups, had adopted some of the cavalry tactics of the steppes, and were hiring nomadic horse archers.

- The difficulty for the Byzantines in dealing with nomadic invaders was the fact that they were at war with Persia, the Sassanid shahs. These wars dragged out over the 6th and 7th centuries, erupting in 568 and continuing on and off down to 628. Indeed, Persian and Byzantine emperors were in almost constant warfare over Armenia, Syria, and the traditional battlefields of the Middle East for almost 90 years.

- In 590, the legitimate Sassanid emperor, **Khosrow II**, was overthrown by one of his generals, and civil war broke out in Persia. Maurice Tiberius lent Khosrow the Roman army, which put him back on the throne in 591. That bought the Byzantine Empire a brief respite from Persian wars, allowing Maurice to go after the Avars.

- Maurice blundered in trying to have his army winter on the steppes of eastern Russia, and his forces rebelled in 602. They murdered Maurice and put a man named Phocas on the throne, who turned out to be incompetent. The Persian shah took advantage of this situation by invading the Byzantine Empire and, between 602 and 626, came very close to overthrowing the empire in Asia.

- The Avars saw their chance. They entered into an alliance with the Sassanid shah and, in 626, besieged Constantinople on the European side. This alliance failed, largely because of the brilliant campaigns of the emperor **Heraclius**. While his capital was besieged, the emperor moved the imperial army by sea into Armenia and hooked up with the Gök Turks. Together, they waged a war against the Sassanid Empire that ended in total Byzantine victory by 628.

- As a result of this victory, Heraclius recovered all of his Asian provinces in Egypt, and the Turks occupied strategic passes of the Caucasus and Transoxiana. The Persian Empire was bankrupt and reduced to its Iranian core. The Persians became vulnerable to Arab attack and, in 639, came crashing down.

- In one sense, the Byzantine victory over the Persians was a poison legacy because the Byzantine Empire lost its most wealthy provinces in Syria, Egypt, and North Africa to Arab armies. However, the Byzantine state reconfigured itself as a regional power based on Asia Minor, the Balkans, and Italy. There, the Byzantines had to deal with nomadic peoples as a potential threat to their state.

End of the Avars

- Very soon after the initial Muslim conquest, Constantinople was able to stabilize its frontiers and come to an understanding with the caliphate, but the nomadic peoples were another matter.

  o For instance, the Avars—sometimes allies, sometimes raiders—dominated the steppes of eastern Europe; they repeatedly invaded the Balkans and disrupted imperial control there. Meanwhile, the Lombards, Germanic peoples, crossed the Alps and invaded Byzantine territory in Italy.

  o Slavic peoples moved in and settled the Balkans, resulting in an ethnic transformation from Latin- and Greek-speaking provinces into the Slavic principalities and kingdoms of the later Middle Ages.

- The Avars had suffered a significant check when they failed to take Constantinople in 626. The result was that Avar power receded. In the course of the 7th and 8th centuries, the Avars refocused their attacks on western Europe.

- Those attacks drew the Avars to the attention of the Franks, who reunited western Europe, especially under the emperor **Charlemagne** (r. 768–814). Charlemagne eventually captured the main settlement of the Avars and broke their power in 796. But the Avars had shown that a steppe nomadic conqueror could mobilize the power of the Slavic tribes, challenge Constantinople, and extort gifts as either tribute or plunder.

The Bulgars

- The successors to the Avar policy were a group of people called the Bulgars. They were apparently a Turkish tribe that had migrated west to escape the power of the western Turkish khagans. In 681, the Bulgars crossed the Danube into imperial territory and were initially admitted as imperial federates or allies. The relationship between the Bulgars and the Byzantine Empire was a major feature of the 9th and early 10th centuries.

- Up until the mid-860s, when the khagan **Boris I** converted to orthodox Christianity and began to build cities and rule as a Byzantine-style monarch, the rulers of the Bulgars were essentially nomadic khagans ruling in the Balkans and the eastern European steppes. With that power of Slavic infantry and nomadic cavalry, they repeatedly attacked the Byzantine Empire and inflicted embarrassing defeats on imperial armies.
  - The most famous one was in 811, when the khagan **Krum** destroyed the army of Emperor **Nicephorus I**, killed the emperor, and turned his skull into a drinking goblet.

  - These defeats forced the Byzantine state to acknowledge that most of the Balkans had passed under the authority of the Bulgar khagan.

- In 864, the situation improved for the Byzantines. In that year, Khagan Boris converted to Orthodox Christianity. As a result, Boris, now Tsar Boris, started to organize a Byzantine-style kingdom, collect taxes, establish cities, and initiate a major economic recovery in the Balkans. In the process, the Bulgars became Bulgarians; that is, the Turkic ruling class was assimilated into the wider Slavic population.

- The second son of Tsar Boris waged two major wars, from 894 to 897 and from 911 to 924, in an attempt to become the Byzantine emperor. His attempts failed and, in the end, so weakened the incipient Bulgarian kingdom that it was later incorporated back into the Byzantine Empire.

- Constantinople may have drawn some incorrect lessons from the conversion and assimilation of the Bulgars, believing that future nomadic people who threatened the security of Constantinople could likewise be turned into subjects of the emperor. That would have fateful consequences when the Byzantines dealt with new nomadic peoples on the steppes, particularly the Seljuk Turks.

Strategikon: Byzantine military manual, attributed to the emperor Maurice, with sound recommendations for countering nomadic cavalry.

Boris I (r. 858–899): Tsar of Bulgaria; converted to Orthodox Christianity in the 860s and, thus, assured the conversion of the southern Slavs. He presided over the conversion of the Bulgar khanate into a Christian Slavic kingdom.

Charlemagne (Charles the Great) (b. c. 747; r. 768–814): King of the Franks; forged the Carolingian Empire. He was crowned Roman emperor in 800, thereby founding the Holy Roman Empire. He built the first effective state in western Europe since the collapse of Roman power. In 791–796, he destroyed the Avar khaganate.

Heraclius (b. c. 576; r. 610–641): Byzantine emperor and exarch of Carthage; overthrew the usurper Phocas (r. 602–610). Heraclius rescued the eastern Roman Empire from near collapse and transformed it into the Byzantine state. He defeated Shah Khosrow II in 626–628 and recovered the eastern provinces. He nearly succeeded in reconciling the monophysites and Chalcedonians. Incapacitated by illness, the aging Heraclius failed to prevent the loss of Syria and Egypt to the Arab armies in 636–641.

Justinian I (b. 482; r. 527–565): Known as Justinian the Great; the greatest emperor since Constantine. He promoted the most talented at his court without regard to birth. He restored imperial rule in Italy and Africa, sought religious reconciliation, and sponsored arts and letters. His most enduring achievements are the Hagia Sophia and the *Corpus Juris Civilis.*

Khosrow II (591–628): Last great Sassanid shah. He gained his throne with the support of the Byzantine emperor Maurice. In 602–628, he waged a war of conquest of the eastern provinces of the Byzantine Empire. In alliance with the Avars, he besieged Constantinople in 626. In 622–628, the emperor Heraclius, along with Turkish nomadic allies, launched offensives in Armenia, Iran, and Mesopotamia that led to the defeat and overthrow of Khosrow II. Heraclius recovered his lost eastern provinces, so weakening the Sassanid state that it fell to Arab armies in 636–651.

Krum (r. c. 803–814): Khan of the Bulgars; defeated the Byzantine emperors Nicephorus I and Michael I. He negotiated the first treaty with Byzantium that delineated the Bulgar state.

Maurice (582–602): Byzantine emperor; waged campaigns against the Avars in the Balkans and ended the Persian war (572–590) by supporting Shah Khosrow II to the Sassanid throne. He is credited with writing the *Strategikon*, a manual of tactics against nomadic horse archers.

Nicephorus I (802–811): Byzantine emperor; served as treasurer of the empress Irene (797–802). He was an Arabian by birth and seized power as Irene lost popularity. He suffered humiliating defeats at the hands of the Abbasid caliph Harun al-Rashid. He was defeated and slain by Khan Krum of the Bulgars.

Suggested Reading

Curta and Kovaley, eds., *The Other Europe in the Middle Ages.*

Golden, "The Peoples of the South Russian Steppes."

Oblensky, *The Byzantine Commonwealth.*

Runciman, *A History of the First Bulgarian Empire.*

Szádeczky-Kardoss, "The Avars."

Whitby, *The Emperor Maurice and His Historian Theophylact Simocattta on Persian and Balkan Warfare.*

Whittlow, *The Making of Byzantium, 600–1025.*

1. How did the emperors of Constantinople view the nomadic peoples dwelling on the Pontic-Caspian steppes in the 5th through 9th centuries? What were the imperial interests? How well did emperors between Justinian and Michael III secure these aims?

2. Why did the Avars pose such a threat to Constantinople? What advantages did the Avars possess over Attila and the Huns? How did they change the course of Byzantine civilization?

3. What accounted for the success of the Bulgars between 680 and the 830s? What were the achievements of the Bulgar khans? How did they contribute to the revival of trade and towns in the 9th century?

4. Why did the conversion of Boris to Orthodox Christianity transform the Bulgars from a steppe empire into a lesser Orthodox kingdom?

5. What impact did the Avars and Bulgars have on Byzantine policy and civilization?

Avars, Bulgars, and Constantinople
Lecture 16—Transcript

In this lecture, I want to shift our focus away from the eastern Eurasian steppes and the Chinese world back across those steppes to the western arm. That would be the region stretching from essentially the Lower and Middle Danube Rivers to the Ural River that empties into the Caspian Sea. We want to focus on the interaction of the Turkish peoples with the greatest Christian civilization of the early Middle Ages, which happens to be Constantinople or New Rome. We frequently call it the Byzantine Empire. Usually that designates the Eastern Roman Empire that survived the imperial collapse of the fifth century, was shorn of its eastern and southern possessions by the Arabic expansion of the seventh century A.D., and came to rest on the peninsula of Asia Minor, the Balkans, and Southern Italy. Very often when we think of the Middle Ages, we think of Western Europe; but at the time of the Sui and the Tang dynasties, the great nomadic confederations of the Avars, the Gök Turks, and the Uighurs, it was Constantinople not Western Europe that represented the great urban civilization on the western end of the Eurasian steppes. In the next three lectures, this one and the succeeding two, we will look at the relationship between Byzantine civilization, the Byzantine emperors, and the peoples of the steppes.

As a way of understanding what the Byzantine perception was of these northern peoples, we should recall that the emperors who ruled in Constantinople saw themselves as Roman emperors, saw themselves as heirs to the empire going back to Augustus, and they were particularly conscious of the crisis that late Roman emperors had encountered from the Huns in the fifth century A.D. The emperors had drawn several important lessons due to the dealings with Attila the Hun. One was to pursue a policy of divide and conquer; that is, to undermine any kind of insipient confederacy on the steppes, and that would be any collection of inner and outer tribes that would be united under a Khan stretching from the Danube essentially to the Volga River, and make sure that the tribes fought among themselves. It has often been remarked that Byzantine diplomacy is perhaps the most contorted and clever of all diplomacies that anyone has ever created. It was largely devised for dealing with steppe nomads, not so much the people of the Balkans or the great Islamic powers.

There is an anecdote that captures the attitude of the steppe peoples themselves to the Byzantines, particularly Byzantine diplomats who were known as the *basilikoi*—that is, representatives of the emperor; the emperor is *Basileus* in Byzantine Greek—and one of them, a man named Valentinus, probably in 575 A.D., was sent to negotiate with Tardush, who was the leader of the western Gök Turks. His official title at the time was probably not khan but *yabgu*, a subordinate title. As the envoy approached—and Tardush had been in contact with the Byzantines before—he saw the Byzantine envoy in his presence and he immediately said, "Oh my gosh, it's a typical Roman who speaks 10 languages and the one lie." That is, the Byzantines are constantly to use diplomacy to maneuver these people around with the same type of artful, fast-talking diplomats and gifts that the Han and Tang emperors used.

The other important lesson that they drew was to trust to the walls of Constantinople. I discussed those walls in conjunction with Attila and the fact that the Great Walls acted as a barrier to nomadic peoples who would enter into the eastern empire by crossing the Danube and invading the European provinces, and that the walls were such a barrier that no nomadic conqueror, no matter how sophisticated his engines of war were, could possibly breach those walls. That was proved historically time and time again: Avars, Bulgars, Cumans, Pechenegs, even the Rus—that is, Vikings on ships who appear before Constantinople—failed to take the great city, and that is because the masonry Roman architecture could defy any invader really until the advent of artillery, which is quite in contrast to what Han and Tang emperors encountered; that is, as impressive as the fortifications of the Great Wall might seem to us today, those are Ming fortifications of the 14th century. In the Tang period, at the time that is contemporary with the early Byzantine state of which we are speaking, they were much less formidable walls. They were rammed-earth and wooden palisades, and when the nomads penetrated into China they got over the defenses—which meant all of the military forces along the Great Wall—they were in. The capital of Luoyang is sacked three times that we know of by so-called Xiongnu; that is, northern barbarians. The most famous is the 311 sack, which is noted in that letter that was found by Aurel Stein out in the Tarim Basin. That does not happen in Constantinople. Even provincial cities such as Thessalonica, the great city of Greece, was very, very well fortified and could defy nomadic invaders. That was an advantage that the Byzantine emperors had.

Finally, the Byzantines, who have their own problems dealing with the Islamic world, which they never really fully understood, and their own religious internal issues remarkably failed to have the same kind of impact on the steppe peoples of the western Eurasian steppes, on the Pontic-Caspian steppes, that the Chinese and, as we shall see, the Muslim world had on steppe nomads. It is a curious fact that the nomadic peoples dwelling on the steppes from the Danube to the Caspian really never embraced Orthodox Christianity; Orthodox Christianity made very, very few inroads. When the Mongol army of Batu appears on the western steppes for the great Mongol conquest, starting really in 1236–1237, the vast numbers of Turkic peoples there (Kipchak Turks, Cumans), they are still worshiping their ancient ancestral gods, heaven, Tengri as he would be known in Turkish, they followed their shamans. They had acquired some of the material culture of Byzantium, but a lot more of the Islamic world; and really these regions will convert to Islam in the 13th and 14th centuries with very little reference to Constantinople. We will be investigating why that is so in the coming lectures; that is, Orthodox Christianity never really scored a major triumph in culturally and religiously assimilating the Eurasian steppes. Their triumph would be the Russians, the Rus, the Scandinavian Slavic peoples of the forest, and that would have major consequences for the steppes; but we shall reserve that issue for later on.

Let us take a look at how Byzantine emperors were dealing with nomadic powers contemporary with those faced by the Tang emperors of China; and actually, the story will go a bit later into the so-called Song Dynasty. First, the Byzantines found that they were in a real quandary when these Turks showed up. The first time the Byzantines get a firsthand look at the Turks is in the reign of the Emperor Justinian—the great emperor who ruled from 527–565, who attempted to re-conquer the western provinces—when envoys come from the Avars. These are clearly members of the inner tribes of the Avars, of the Avar khan, who had been driven west by Bumin and the Turks when they had overthrown the Avar khanate in 552. The envoys arrived, and they are clearly dressed with these long braids, their appearance excited comment, their leather breeches, their bows. They were seen as a new and an exotic nomadic people quite beyond anything what the people in Constantinople had seen. The Avars wanted to enter into an alliance with the Byzantine emperors for good reason. The Gök Turks claimed that these Avars were wayward vassals and belonged to their authority, and this opened up a series of negotiations between the court in Constantinople with the rulers of the western Gök Turks. That would be Ishtemi, the brother of Bumin, who first ruled over the western tribes and then later Tardush; he is the fellow that makes the comment about the 10 tongues and the one lie of the Byzantine envoys.

One of the big stumbling blocks in these negotiations is the question of the Avars. The Byzantine court, the imperial court, hoped to use the Avars as possible allies. They accepted the Avars into alliance; whereas the Gök Turks wanted those Avars under their authority. Another issue that was raised between the Byzantine court and these Turks on the steppes were trade routes. We get some of the first detailed information from contemporary Byzantine sources, particularly a man named Menander the Protector who records a number of these missions, that the Byzantines starting in the reign of mad emperor Justin II, the nephew of Justinian, entered into negotiations in order to obtain access to what is clearly an extension of the Silk Road that is coming from the cities of Khorasan—that is, on the southern shores of the Aral Sea—that is receiving silk from Kashgar that is making its way across the steppes to the ports on the Black Sea. One of the most important ports was the city of Cherson, which was a Byzantine possession. It is in the Russian Crimea today and it is a Greek-speaking city. There is where a lot of the diplomatic activity took place. Immense profits were made because the Byzantines could obtain Chinese silks and other exotic goods. Since 555, the Byzantines had begun to set up their own silk manufacture; they had obtained the secret. Nonetheless, there was never enough silk in Constantinople to satisfy the demand for trade for the upper class, and there was always a desire for imports. This was another feature; that is, the Byzantines wanted access to those trade routes terminating on the Black Sea. They will deal with the Gök Turks, later with the Khazars, later with the Pechenegs, and the Cumans. This is a constant issue that is raised between the imperial government and the nomadic tribes of the steppes.

Meanwhile, the Avars turned out to be not the best of allies. To escape the control of the Gök Turks, they moved west following the routes that many nomadic peoples had taken, and they end up settling on the Hungarian plain. We only know of one Avar khan in Western Europe, and his name is Bayan. He ruled at the end of the sixth century and into the early seventh century A.D.; and usually the Byzantine sources simply referred to the Avar khan, they do not even designate him by name. The Avars settled on the Pannonian plain, the same area that Attila had controlled. They had escaped the power of the western Turkish khans who were ruling over the Pontic-Caspian steppes and points east, and there they began to raid into the Byzantine Empire. The reason for that was the Avar khan, just like all nomadic rulers, needed gold; he needed wealth to pay off his various followers. In addition, the Avars found that the imperial frontiers along the Danube were particularly vulnerable; that the imperial government had commitments elsewhere; that they had exhausted themselves by waging wars of reconquest in Italy and North Africa. In the late sixth century, the Avars followed the river systems of the Balkans, usually following the Middle Danube down to the Moravia River, the Margus River, and entered into the Balkans and ravaged many of the same cities once ravaged by the Huns.

The imperial government responded in part with diplomacy and gifts. There is a famous story that the emperor Maurice Tiberius actually sent an elephant and a gold couch to the Avar khan as novelties to try to convince him that an alliance would be better. It did not really work; it backfires. It is the usual problem that if you give too many good gifts to the nomads they might think, "Well, we could actually get more. If this is what they're willing to give us, perhaps a little pressure will gain us even more." The Chinese make the same comment in their diplomatic texts. Furthermore, Maurice Tiberius, who ruled from 582–602, is also credited with writing a strategic manual, the *Strategikon*, in which he comes up with the same military recommendations that Li Jing a generation later would do for the Tang emperor; that is, how to cope with nomadic cavalries. It is an extremely instructive document. It also reveals that the Byzantines are now mounting cavalry with metal stirrups, that they have adopted some of the cavalry tactics of the steppes, and that they are hiring nomadic horse archers just as Tang emperors did.

What is restricting the Byzantines in dealing with the nomadic invaders is the fact that they are at war with Persia, the Sassanid shahs. These wars drag out over the sixth and seventh centuries A.D. One erupts in 568 in negotiations when the emperor Justin goes mad and does not accept certain treaty obligations. By 572, the two empires are at war; this rages down to 590–591. Another war breaks out and rages from 602–628; and really in the last hundred years of the Persian and Byzantine emperors, almost 90 years of it are in constant warfare over Armenia, Syria, and the traditional battlefields of the Middle East. Maurice Tiberius is restricted in what he can do vis-à-vis the Avars.

In 590, he lucks out. There is a civil war in Persia. The legitimate emperor Kushrau II is overthrown by one of his generals. He goes to Constantinople and Maurice Tiberius lends him the Roman army, which puts Khusrau back on the throne in 591. That buys the Byzantine Empire a brief respite from Persian wars, and with it Maurice goes after the Avars. He blunders in trying to have his army winter on the steppes of Eastern Europe. They rebel in 602. They murder Maurice and put a man by the name of Phocas on the throne, who turns out to be incompetent. The Persian shah invades, first as an act of vengeance for his old patron Maurice Tiberius, and then he realizes the Byzantine Empire is such a shambles, why not conquer it. The Persian shah Khusrau II, between 602 and 626, comes very close to overthrowing the Byzantine Empire in Asia. The Avars now see their chance. They enter into an alliance with the Sassanid shah, and in 626 the Avars besiege Constantinople on the European side, and a Persian army is on the Asian side at the ancient city of Chalcedon, attempting to cross and capture New Rome. This alliance of nomads with the shah of Iran fails largely due to the brilliant campaigns of the emperor Heraclius, who while his capital is besieged by Avars and Persians, takes the imperial army, moves it by sea into Armenia, and hooks up with the Gök Turks. They together wage a war against the Sassanid Empire that ends in total Byzantine victory by 628.

The Byzantine victory over the Persians, a story well-known in Byzantine history, had resulted in the Byzantine and Persian Empires fighting themselves to exhaustion; but it was also a Turkish victory. The Turks, the western Turks at this point, who were essentially operating as independent khans and are the future ancestors probably of the Khazars who are in the next lecture, they had entered into alliance with Heraclius; they had provided cavalry. They had also put pressure on the Persians; and by the time the war is over in 628, it is not only the Byzantine Empire that has prospered—Heraclius recovers all of his Asian provinces in Egypt—the Turks now occupy the strategic passes of the Caucasus and Transoxiana. The Persian Empire has been reduced to its Iranian core; it is fiscally bankrupt and becomes very, very vulnerable to Arab attack; and in 639 A.D. will come crashing down.

The Byzantine victory over the Persians ends up being a sort of poison legacy because the Byzantine Empire loses its most wealthy provinces in Syria, Egypt, and North Africa to the Arab armies under the banner of Islam; and that becomes an issue that we deal with in later lectures about the caliphate. On the other hand, the Byzantine state does reconfigure itself as a regional power based on Asia Minor, the Balkans, and Italy. There, the Byzantines have to deal with nomadic peoples; in fact, the nomadic peoples emerge as a major threat, a potential threat to the Byzantine state. The Byzantine emperor can always come to terms with the caliph; and very quickly after the initial Muslim conquest, Constantinople is able to stabilize its frontiers and come to an understanding with the caliphate. But the nomadic peoples are another matter. The Avars, for instance, sometimes allies, sometimes raiders. They dominated the steppes of Eastern Europe, the Hungarian plain, the Wallachian plain; they repeatedly invaded the Balkans and disrupted the imperial control of the Balkans, one of their heartlands. They also had come to an agreement early on with a group of people known as the Lombards, Germanic peoples, dwelling in Hungary back in 567, to wipe out a common foe, the Gepidae. Then the Lombards, having common sense, crossed the Alps and invaded Italy, and those Germanic peoples shattered Byzantine control of Italy. The Avars personally directly were responsible for disrupting two of three imperial heartlands: Italy and the Balkans. They themselves did not settle. They sent the Lombards into Italy and the Avars, who were nomadic peoples, attacked the Balkans, disrupted imperial communications, sacked cities, destroyed the road networks, and Slavic peoples moved in and settled in the Balkans. That results in the great ethnic transformation of the Balkans from Latin- and Greek-speaking provinces into the Slavic principalities and kingdoms of the later Middle Ages. The Slavs technically were subjects of the Avar khan. They were agriculturalists; they were organized by clan and family. They were the ideal subjects for a nomadic conqueror because they lacked cohesion. They were easily taxed; they were easily directed. They provided the infantry to support the raids of the Avar attacks.

The Byzantine government had its own difficulties. Part of it was an internal dispute over the images; they were essentially waging a civil war among themselves between 726 and 843. The Avars had suffered a significant check when they failed to take the city of Constantinople in 626. The result was Avar power receded. In the course of the seventh and eighth centuries, the Avars refocused their attacks on Western Europe. Those attacks drew the Avars to the attention of the Franks, who reunited Western Europe into the first effective Western European state, especially under the emperor Charlemagne from 768–814. Charlemagne eventually broke the power of the Avars, capturing their main settlement, the so-called Six Rings—that is, the six fortresses of the Avars, we suspect in the vicinity of Budapest—and ended Avar power by 796.

The Avars, however, had left a powerful legacy. They had shown how a steppe nomadic conqueror could, if he wished, mobilize the power of the Slavic tribes, challenge Constantinople, and extort numbers of gifts either in tribute or in plunder. The finds that have come to light in Hungary bear testimony to the success of this policy. Marvelous items have been found in Hungarian tombs dated to the Avar period; all sorts of objects that originated from the Byzantine world that had arrived in trade, tribute, and plunder to the Avar khans in the course of the seventh and eighth centuries.

The successors to the Avar policy were a group of people called the Bulgars. They are in part the ancestors of the modern Bulgarians, but the Bulgars were a Turkic people. They were apparently a Turkish tribe that had migrated west to escape the power of the great khans of the western Turks, who eventually would reinvent themselves as the Khazar khans. In 681, these Bulgars crossed the Danube into imperial territory and were initially admitted as imperial federates or allies. The relationship between the Bulgars and the Byzantine Empire is a major feature of the 9th and early 10th centuries. Up until 864, when the khan Boris converted to Orthodox Christianity and began to build cities and rule as a Byzantine-style monarch, the rulers of the Bulgars were essentially nomadic khans ruling in the Balkans and the

Eastern European steppes. With that power of Slavic infantry and nomadic cavalry, they repeatedly attacked the Byzantine Empire when it was at its weakest. It was waging essentially a religious war, a civil war, over the use of images. Bulgar khans inflicted embarrassing defeats on imperial armies. The most famous one is in 811 when the khan Krum bushwhacked the army of the emperor Nicephorus I, destroyed the army, killed the emperor—the emperor was actually captured and executed—and turned the emperor's skull into a drinking goblet. This is a common feature of nomadic warriors; I have mentioned it in tandem with the Scythians who took heads and scalps. There are stories of the Xiongnu doing the same; even stories of the Scythians, King Cyrus of Persia, his head gets detached from his body by Queen Tomyris of the Massagetae and she uses it as some kind of symbol of victory. These defeats force the Byzantine state, especially the Byzantine emperor Leo V, to acknowledge that most of the Balkans had passed under the authority of the Bulgar khan, and that imperial power in the Balkans was restricted to the cities on the shore in Greece and to the peninsula of Asia Minor and the immediate hinterland of Constantinople. The Bulgar khan ruled as a virtual equal vis-à-vis the emperor of Constantinople.

It is only in 864 that the situation improves for the Byzantines. In that year, Khan Boris decided to convert to Christianity. He toyed with Catholic Christianity, but he eventually went with the Orthodox version of it, in part because two brothers, Saints Cyril and Methodius, had devised a Slavic alphabet—it is known as the Cyrillic alphabet—and they had begun to translate the Christian scriptures and Bible into a language known as Old Church Slavonic, and that would have been a Slavic dialect understood by many of the subjects of the Bulgar khan. Furthermore, Christianity offered organization, it offered hierarchy; and as a result, Khan Boris, who became Czar Boris upon the conversion, could start to bring about the organization of a Byzantine-style kingdom, collect taxes, establish cities, and really start a major economic recovery in the Balkans. In the process, the Bulgars became Bulgarians; that is, the Turkic ruling class was assimilated into the wider Slavic population and essentially became Orthodox Bulgarians henceforth speaking a Slavic language. The second son of Czar Boris got it into his head—because he studied at the University of Constantinople—that he could become emperor. He waged two major wars, one ranging from 894–897, another one breaking out in 911 and ending in 924, in an attempt to pressure Constantinople into giving him an imperial marriage. This failed. In the end, it so weakened the incipient Bulgarian kingdom that it was later incorporated back into the Byzantine Empire; that would be accomplished by the emperors John I and Basil II later in the 10th century. The nomadic component of that Bulgar khanate essentially passes.

The Byzantines, in their experience with the Bulgars and Avars, perhaps might have drawn some incorrect lessons. The Avars and Bulgars both were regional powers. They were not a great confederacy. They came into contact with Constantinople right off the steppes. Both of them were scions of the great western Turkish khanate or the Gök Turk khanate. They were impressed by Byzantine civilization. The Franks eliminated the Avars from concern. The Bulgars, however, had been converted and ultimately assimilated; and I think Constantinople might have drawn some incorrect lessons here. They might have believed that future nomadic peoples who offered threats to the security of Constantinople could likewise be converted to Orthodox Christianity; turned into potential subjects of the emperor of Constantinople. This will have fateful consequences when the Byzantines deal with new nomadic peoples on the steppes, particularly the Khazars, later Pechenegs and Cumans, and then Seluk Turks, Turks of Central Asia who will enter Asia Minor. The Byzantines always thought that somehow they could convert the Seluk Turks; that somehow Byzantine civilization and Orthodox Christianity would prevail. What the Byzantines did not take into account: The Bulgars were a small minority ruling a Slavic population, and these Turks had not come under the power of Islam. The Turks will embrace Islam, and in so doing will define themselves ethnically into a very, very distinct population and a people who can assimilate rather than who are going to be converted. The Byzantines were not aware of this process, and we will see how it takes place in one of the upcoming lectures about Islam and the Turks.

Khazar Khagans

Lecture 17

This lecture introduces a new group of nomadic people, the Khazars. The khagans of the Khazars ruled as members of the Ashina family. This family claimed descent from the original khagan Bumin who overthrew the Avars in 552 A.D. The Khazars are significant for several reasons, including the fact that the upper classes converted to Judaism sometime at the end of the 8th or beginning of the 9th century. Further, they played an important role in Byzantine foreign policy and in the Byzantine wars against the Arab caliphate. In this lecture, we'll explore who these people were, why they didn't convert to Orthodox Christianity, and why the Byzantines failed to win the Khazars over to the Byzantine commonwealth.

Rise of the Khazars

- The Khazars were Gök Turks. Undoubtedly, their ancestors were among those Turks who had concluded an alliance with the emperor Heraclius in 625–626 to make common cause against the Sassanid emperor. As a result, large numbers of Turkish cavalry were released for imperial service.

  o In 627–628, some 10,000 Turkish horsemen crossed over the Caucasus and invaded Iran, ravaging Azerbaijan, penetrating as far south as the modern city of Hamadan, and causing great distress to the Sassanid emperor. Other subjects of the khagan passed into Byzantine service.

  o Starting with Heraclius, the imperial army fielded regular units of Turkish horse archers as part of its strike force.

- This alliance proved beneficial to the western Turks. The Sassanid shah was overthrown and was followed by a succession of weak and short-lived rulers. The Turks gained control of Transoxiana and access to strategic passes in the Caucasus, allowing Turkish armies to enter Armenia and Iran. These territorial aims didn't trouble the Byzantine emperor because they basically corresponded with his own.

- In 634, Arab armies crossed the imperial frontiers of Syria. These areas had just passed back under imperial control after that exhausting war with Persia. The Arab armies cut up an imperial force. Initially, the emperor Heraclius, who was ill, simply dismissed this as another raid by Arab nomads. The Romans were far more concerned with Persia and the northern steppes, but as we'll see later, the early raids escalated into Islamic conquests. The emergence of Arabic power drew the western Turks and the Byzantines closer together.

- In the early 7th century, the western Turks had separated themselves from their eastern kinsmen. After a complicated series of civil wars, the western tribes reconfederated themselves into what's known as the Confederation of the Ten Arrows. In 670, one of the leading tribes of this confederation, the Khazars, emerged to dominate the steppes from the Aral Sea down to the borders of Persia.
  - The inner tribes of this confederation were those of the Khazars, including the immediate family of the khagan, who was revered as a celestial figure. Indeed, the khagan became such an important religious figure that he designated administrative and military affairs to a subordinate, a *bek* (modern Turkish: *bey*).

  - Starting from the 670s and 680s, this Turkish power began to emerge on the steppes between the Caspian Sea and the Volga region and expanded its sway westward over the tribes of the lower Dnieper. Eventually, their power was felt as far as the Hungarian and Wallachian grasslands in eastern Europe.

- The Khazars enjoyed an unusually close relationship with the Byzantine emperors. As the Khazars were reconfiguring themselves into the next great confederacy on the steppes in the 670s, Constantinople was in a battle for its life, dealing with Avars in the Balkans and the Arab caliphs of Damascus. From 626 to 843, the Byzantine Empire was also in a veritable civil war over the use of icons in religious worship. Under these circumstances, the Khazar khagans represented a godsend of an alliance.

- o The Byzantines departed from their Roman legal practices and carried out alliances, including marriage alliances, with the Khazars; this would have been unthinkable in earlier Roman periods. There were also constant diplomatic exchanges.

- o Apparently, the Byzantine court was impressed by the Khazar court. It represented a great power on the steppes and a valuable ally against the caliphate.

Conversion to Judaism

- From a practical military viewpoint, the Khazars proved to be invaluable allies. They were able to field large armies of cavalry and periodically could cross either the Dariel Pass or the Derbent Pass and invade the caliphate directly, taking pressure off the Byzantine emperor. In addition, the caliphs decided that the conquest of the Khazars was probably as significant as the conquest of the Byzantine Empire, and Arab armies repeatedly crossed the Caucasus in attempts to bring the Khazars to battle and defeat them.

- Here, the **Umayyad** caliphs ran into the same problems that the early Persian kings and the Sassanid kings encountered, that is, bringing steppe horse archers to battle. Already in the early 8th century, the Arab chroniclers stated that the Turks on horseback could outride and outshoot Arabs. In 737, the future caliph **Marwan** led an army across the Caucasus, defeated the Khazars, and forced a conversion to Islam.

- That defeat and forced conversion was immediately repudiated, and sometime at the end of the 8th or the beginning of the 9th century, the Khazar court embraced Judaism. For a long time, scholars accepted the date of 860 for this conversion, but the discovery in Scandinavia of coins issued by the Khazars suggests that the date is a generation or two earlier.

- How did the embrace of Judaism come about?
  - One of the great achievements of the Khazars was their promotion of trade along the northern extension of the Silk Road. In addition to the products of the Roman world, this trade also involved the products of the forest: amber, furs, and above all, slaves, usually Slavic peoples sold as labor into the Islamic world, as well as Turks captured in raids and sold as soldiers.

  - The Khazars exploited all these trade networks. The movement of goods within the early Islamic Empire was usually in the hands of minorities, and several groups emerged in prominence, foremost, the Jews.

  - Jewish bankers and trading houses extended from Muslim Spain across North Africa to Egypt and Syria. There were large communities in Cordova and Cairo, and it's almost certain that Jews were also prominent at the Khazar capital at Atil.

The Cairo Genizah documents, found in a medieval synagogue, give us a sense of the extent and range of Jewish merchandising and banking at the time of the Khazars.

- In the late 700s or early 800s, the Khazar khagan probably decided that Judaism was a worthy monotheistic religion. Given that it wasn't Orthodox Christianity and it wasn't Islam, it also marked the khaganate as a separate great state. Thus, the court converted to Judaism.

- With the conversion came enormous advantages. The Muslim geographer and historian Ibn Fadlan, who traveled to the Volga in 921–922, commented on the numbers of Jews, Christians, and Muslims trading in the city of Atil. The fact that there were so many people of different nationalities meant that special courts had to be set up to adjudicate questions of contract and commerce. Ibn Fadlan was also impressed by the extent of the slave trade, the powers of the khagan, and the wealth of the khaganate.

Downfall of the Khazars

- The Khazar khagans had constructed the most successful confederacy on the western steppes until the Golden Horde of the Mongols. It was light-years ahead of the Scythians and Sarmatians and would be far more sophisticated than the **Pechenegs** and **Cumans** who would follow them. The problem was that the khagans spent so much of their time on trade and commerce and the benefits of material culture that they failed to enforce their will over the subject tribes. This led to challenges within the confederacy.

- Two tribes in particular would come to play an important role in the demise of the Khazars. One was the Magyars, speakers of a **Finno-Ugric language** who had moved onto the western steppes and adopted a pastoral way of life.
  - They proved to be unruly vassals of the Khazar khagan and ended up migrating into eastern Europe. There, they got involved in the Byzantine–Bulgarian wars and were eventually sent ricocheting into Hungary, where they settled and became the Magyars of the Hungarians we know in 897.

  - En route to their final destination, they did quite a job of disrupting the khagan's control of his subject tribes.

- The other unruly group was the Pechenegs, who came to dominate the southern Russian steppes; that is, the areas around the Don and Dnieper rivers.
  - The Pechenegs entered into an alliance with a third group of people who were total interlopers. These were the Rus, Scandinavians from Sweden, who had been exploiting the trade route on the Volga since the 8th century. They were especially active in the slave trade and were operating as merchant princes by permission in the Khazar khaganate.

  - In the early 9th century, when the Pechenegs came to dominate the south Russian steppes and were at loggerheads with the Khazar khagans, the Rus switched the axis of their trade from the Volga to the Dnieper. They established cities at the future Russian towns of Novgorod and Kiev. They aligned their trade route on Constantinople and entered into alliance with the Pechenegs. This Pecheneg-Rus alliance undermined a good deal of the trade routes that had previously gone to Atil.

- Both the Pechenegs and the Rus came to see the Khazars as foes. And for various reasons, the emperor in Constantinople came to prefer the Pechenegs and Rus as allies over the Khazars.

- Sometime in 965 or 967, the Rus and the Pechenegs destroyed the Khazar capital, and the Khazar khaganate fragmented shortly thereafter. After the destruction of the khaganate, the Khazar Jews were probably absorbed into later Turkish confederations.

- But the Khazars had created a great steppe empire based on trade. They had proved immensely successful in defining themselves and provided a model for the next successful rulers of the western steppes: the family of Batu, the grandsons of Genghis Khan, the rulers of the Golden Horde.

Important Terms

Cumans: Western Turkish-speaking nomads and scions of the Kipchak Turks, who migrated from the central Asian steppes into the Pontic-Caspian steppes in the 11th century.

Finno-Ugric languages: A family of the Altaic languages, which includes Magyar (Hungarian), Estonian, Finnish, and the Samoyedic languages of Siberia.

Pechenegs: Turkish-speaking tribes whose confederation dominated the Pontic-Caspian steppes west of the Don River from circa 860 to 1091.

Umayyad caliphate: The first hereditary line of caliphs (661–750), established by Muawiya (661–680) and ruling from Damascus.

Name to Know

Marwan II (b. 688; r. 744–750): Umayyad caliph; moved the capital from Damascus to Harran. In 737, as governor in Armenia, he waged a campaign north of the Caucasus and compelled the Khazars to accept Islam. In 750, he was defeated by as-Saffah at the Battle of the Zab and, later, captured and executed.

Suggested Reading

Brook, *The Jews of Khazaria.*

Curta and Kovaley, eds., *The Other Europe in the Middle Ages.*

Dunlop, *The History of the Jewish Khazars.*

Oblensky, *The Byzantine Commonwealth.*

Golden, "The Peoples of the Russian Forest Belt."

———, "The Peoples of the South Russian Steppes."

———, et al., eds., *The World of the Khazars.*

Ostrer, *Legacy: A Genetic History of the Jewish People.*

Whittlow, *The Making of Byzantium, 600–1025.*

1. How did the Khazars so quickly establish their hegemony over the tribes of the Pontic-Caspian steppes in the 7th century? Why was the power of the Ashina khagan of the Khazars so respected?

2. Why did the Khazars prove to be such valuable allies to the Byzantine emperors? How did the Byzantines view this alliance?

3. What accounted for Khazar success in checking the expansion of the Umayyad caliphate? Why did the Khazar court embrace Judaism in the later 8th century?

4. How did the development of far-flung trade routes strengthen the power of the Khazar khaganate? How did trade transform Khazar society? In what significant ways was Khazar success comparable to that of the contemporary Uighur khagans?

5. Why did the Pechenegs and the Rus princes of Kiev undermine and eventually overthrow the Khazar khaganate?

Khazar Khagans
Lecture 17—Transcript

In this lecture, I want to introduce a new nomadic people known as the Khazars, sometimes pronounced "Kazars." The khans of the Khazars ruled as members of the Ashina family. This is a family that claimed descent from the original khan Bumin, who overthrew the Avars back in 552 A.D., and a number of different khans on the western and central Eurasian steppes in the early medieval period claim some kind of connection. That gave them a sort of legitimacy; it was often associated with the favor of the sky god Tengri, who is essentially cast as the benevolent protective god similar to the Mandate of Heaven in Chinese ideology.

The Khazars are significant for several reasons. One of them is the controversy that they have stirred up, at least the upper classes—the khan, his family, and his *bek*, or leading commander, warlord, a Khazar version of the later Turkish word *bey*—converted to Judaism sometime at the end of the eighth or beginning of the ninth century. Furthermore, they play a very important role in Byzantine foreign policy and come to play a decisive role in the Byzantine wars against the Arab Caliphate. Who are these people? Why do they occupy this peculiarly important role in Byzantine history? Again, we will be examining that question I raised in the previous lecture: Why did they not convert to Orthodox Christianity? Why did they go over to Judaism, and why did the Byzantines, for all of their dealings with these people in the seventh, eighth, and ninth centuries fail to win the Khazars over to what many historians call the Byzantine commonwealth; that is, the conversion of various peoples of Eastern Europe to Orthodox Christianity, which then becomes the basis of Eastern Europe today?

The Khazars were western Turks, Gök Turks; and undoubtedly their ancestors were among those Turks who had concluded an alliance with the emperor Heraclius back in 625–626 to make common cause against the Sassanid emperor. The ruler at that time was a man named Tong Yabgu, Yabgu Kahn would be his official title, which means the "subordinate khan"; he recognized as his superior the khans ruling out in the east near the borders of China. Their agreement was to take on the armies of Sassanid Persia, then ruled by Khusrau II, the emperor, the Persian shah with ambitions of conquering Constantinople. As a result, large numbers of Turkish cavalry were released for imperial service. We know in 627–628, some 10,000 Turkish horsemen crossed over the Caucasus and invaded Iran, ravaging the regions of Azerbaijan, penetrating as far south as the modern city of Hamadan, and causing great distress to the Sassanid emperor. Other subjects of the khan passed into Byzantine service, and starting with the emperor Heraclius—who again ruled from 610–641 during these wars with the Persians—the imperial army comes to field regular units of Turkish horse archers as part of the strike force, the field army used in major operations.

As I mentioned in a previous lecture in passing, this alliance proved very beneficial to the western Turks. By the time that the shah surrendered— actually, Khusrau II was overthrown—there were a succession of very weak and short-lived shahs that followed him. The Turks actually walked off with the lion's share of the territorial gains. They gained control of Transoxiana; so when the Muslim armies, the Arabic armies under the banner of Islam, overthrow the Persian Empire and penetrate to the Oxus River, all of Transoxiana is under the protection of the Turkish khan, the khan of the western Turks, and that will have significant consequences for the interaction of the Islamic world under the Arab Caliphs and the Turkish nomads. The other great benefit they gained was access to those strategic passes in the Caucasus, and this actually was quite acceptable to Constantinople. Those passes allowed Turkish armies to enter Armenia and enter Iran. Armenia was a land of Christian kingdoms; but they were seen by the Byzantine emperor as heretics, as monophysites, and often making common cause with the Persian shah or later with the Arab caliph. So it did not trouble the Byzantine emperor that these passes were in the hands of Turkish allies. Throughout the seventh, eighth, and ninth centuries, the territorial ambitions of these western Turks more or less corresponded with the territorial aims of the Byzantine emperors. Both of them had common cause to fear the Sassanid shahs.

In 634, Arab armies crossed the imperial frontiers of Syria. These areas had just passed back under imperial control after that exhausting war with Persia some four years earlier. The Arab armies cut up an imperial force. Initially, the emperor Heraclius was extremely ill and incapacitated; he could not lead the imperial armies. Simply dismiss this as another typical raid by Arab nomads. Actually, for centuries the Romans had regarded the frontier with the Arabians as a minor frontier. One Roman emperor, Trajan Decius, reputedly argued that, "You want to check Arab raiders along the desert frontier? Simply increase the lion population; that'll do the job for you." The Romans were far more concerned with Persia, far more concerned with the northern steppes. These raids escalated into the Islamic conquests. What the Byzantines did not know and what the Persians did not know is that the Arab army starting in 636 under the banner of Islam would carry out some of the most spectacular military conquests in human history. They would overthrow the Sassanid Empire; they would overrun Syria, Egypt, North Africa. All of the wealthy southern and eastern provinces of the Roman emperor of Constantinople would now be incorporated with Arabia and Iran into a new world empire called the Caliphate.

We will discuss the implications of those invasions and successes in a future lecture. What is significant for us to know at the moment is that the emergence, the dramatic emergence, of Arabic power under first the Rashidun caliphs, the first four rightful caliphs down to 661, and then the Umayyad caliphs who ruled as dynastic monarchs essentially in the city of Damascus from 661 down to 750, that the emergence of this powerful Muslim Arabic state drew the western Turks and the Byzantines close together.

The western Turks had also reconfigured themselves in the early seventh century. It is a bit obscure what happened, but several important developments resulted in the khans of the western Turks going their own separate ways from their eastern kinsmen. In 657, a Tang army operating out of the Tarim Basin inflicted decisive defeat on the western Turks north of the Jaxartes River; and from 657–681, the western khan—actually the subordinate khan; he would have probably been called *yabgu* khan—acknowledged the authority of the Tang emperor; and that led to a fragmenting of the western khanate. There is a complicated succession of civil wars, re-confederations of the tribes. Eventually they are re-confederated into something known as the On Ok, the Ten Arrows; and in 670, one of the leading tribes out of this confederation, the Khazars, emerge as the dominant tribe occupying the steppes, essentially around the Aral Sea and down to the borders of Persia.

The Khazars were 1 of the 10 inner tribes of this confederacy; their khan was recognized as supreme. He made claims of being a descendent of the Ashina clan; that is, the family of the original khans who overthrew the Avars. They were able to make their claim stick for several reasons: One is the eastern khanate was long under Chinese domination, it reasserted itself, it went a separate path. The central steppes, where there were a number of Turkish tribes, became locked into a struggle with the Arab caliphate over the cities of Transoxiana. The steppes stretching essentially from the Aral Sea into Southeastern Europe, those steppes were essentially free of outside influence and the Khazars could exercise their power over a wide range of different tribes and eventually brought them into a typical confederation of inner and outer tribes; the inner tribes being the tribes of the Khazars, the immediate family of the khan, who was revered as a celestial figure, almost as a nomadic version of the emperor of China, and a ritual figure. In addition, the khan became such an important religious figure that he designated administrative and military affairs to a subordinate. That subordinate we encounter is a man who is usually designated as a *bek*, or *bey* as you would say in modern Turkish. Starting from the 670s and 680s, a new Turkish power began to emerge on the steppes between the Caspian Sea and the Volga region, and they expanded their sway westward over sundry tribes of the lower Dnieper, Don River. Eventually, their power was felt as far as the Hungarian and Wallachian grasslands in Eastern Europe.

The Khazars enjoyed an unusually close relationship with the Byzantine emperors. As the Khazars were reconfiguring themselves into the next great confederacy on the steppes in the 670s, Constantinople was in the battle for her life. Not only did they have to deal with Avars in the Balkans, Slavs settling in their Balkan provinces, but they were under constant attack by the Arab caliphs of Damascus. Twice, the city of Constantinople was besieged in 674–677, again in 717–718; both times the Arab armies were beaten back. Shortly after that second siege, the emperor Leo III initiated a debate over why is the empire suffering defeats? He concluded it was because people were worshiping icons as if they were idols; those are icons in Orthodox worship. He wanted the icons removed. For the next several generations, from 626 when his edict was published removing the icons down to the restoration of icons in 843, the Byzantine Empire is in a veritable civil war over the use of icons in religious worship.

Under these circumstances, with an empire under constant assault by a greater caliphate, with an empire whose control over the Italian peninsula and the Balkans has been shattered compliments of the Avars, the Khazar khans represent a godsend of an alliance. These alliances went back to the reign of Heraclius, and they were repeatedly cemented through the seventh, eighth, and ninth centuries. The Byzantines actually departed from their Roman legal practices and carried out alliances with the Khazars that would have been unthinkable in the earlier Roman periods. We know of marriage alliances; this is very, very unusual. The emperor Heraclius considered marrying one of his daughters to a Khazar khan; he is called in the sources Ziebel. We are not exactly sure who he is; it is hard to match this source in literary sources with known Turkish names. Nonetheless, it was seriously considered. That type of marriage was impossible at the time of Attila the Hun.

We know of several other marriage alliances. One of the most colorful ones is of the emperor Justinian II. He was autocratic even by Byzantine standards. He had two reigns, one from 685–695; he was overthrown in 695 because of his autocratic and erratic policies, and in keeping with Byzantine policy he was disfigured, he had his nose slit. He is known in the sources as Justinian Rhinotmetos, the slit nose. What the emperor did is he had a gold nose made up that he attached to hide his disfigurement, and he was sent in exile to Cherson—that is, the port on the Crimea—which is the main port by which the Byzantine court communicates with the Khazars, who have their court at the city of Atil at the mouth of the Volga on the Caspian Sea. Justinian II manages to escape. He makes his way to the Khazar court. The khan is really impressed by Justinian. First, they are fellow autocrats; they can get along that way. They have a lot of items they can share like how to impress your subjects. The second thing they had in common is the disfigurement. The khan probably thought the slit nose was actually neat—there are all kinds of ritual deformity of heads on the steppes, cutting, tattooing, body art—so he gave his sister in marriage to Justinian and gave him an army to recover his throne. Justinian recovered his throne, proved just as autocratic as before, was overthrown, and this time he was not disfigured, he was beheaded, and ended his career. We know of a later marriage between the emperor Constantine V and a Khazar princess known as Chichek; that is how you would render the Greek word, it means "flower." She is, of course, renamed with a Greek name, Irene, and the son of that union, Leo IV, became emperor of Constantinople.

There are constant diplomatic exchanges. Apparently the Byzantine court is very, very impressed by the Khazar court. It represented a great power, a great confederacy on the steppes and it was an alliance against the caliphate. It is still a debated issue how this came about, but in the eighth and ninth centuries several Byzantine emperors were selected by a beauty pageant. It sounds a little silly to us; but the idea was that the emperor was so great he should be served by the most beautiful woman in the world. He was the vice regent of Christ, and these beauty contests were held. They were clearly rigged; generally the dowager emperor's mom—or in the case of one of them, stepmom in the case of the emperor Theophilus—had the answers all prepared; there was a question and answer session. This type of pageantry, this type of selection, was apparently characteristic of the Khazar court. We have comments about that, particularly by Arab sources. It seems to be a practice that was adopted by the Byzantines, in part in imitation of the Khazar court. It makes sense: The Khazar khan came to be a ruler virtually in the guise of a Chinese emperor. He was the Son of Heaven; he was the celestial khan, the Gök khan, the Sky khan. He was so busy with religious rites and matters that he had no time for mundane things like fighting Arabs or dealing with other types of trade missions and the like; and therefore, this Khazar practice apparently was adopted by Constantinople and is a very, very telling incident of the relationship between the two courts.

From a practical military viewpoint, the Khazars proved to be invaluable allies. They were able to field large armies of cavalry and periodically could cross either the Dariel Pass or the Derbent Pass and invade the caliphate directly, taking pressure off the Byzantine emperor. In addition, the caliphs decided that the conquest of the Khazars was probably as significant as the conquest of Rome—that is, the Byzantine Empire—and Arab armies repeatedly crossed the Caucasus in attempt to bring the Khazars to battle and defeat them. Here, the Umayyad caliphs ran into the same problems that the early Persian kings and the Sassanid kings encountered: bringing horse archers, steppe horse archers, to battle. In these early encounters, both against the Khazars and then against their Turkish kinsmen in Transoxiana, the Arab authors, the Arab chroniclers, already are stating in the early eighth century that the Turks on horseback can outride and outshoot Arabs; they are really that good. In 737, the future caliph Marwan leads an army across the Caucasus, defeats the Khazars, and forces a conversion to Islam. We are not sure exactly what this means. Marwan went on to be one of the last caliphs of the Umayyad Dynasty; he actually moved the capital from Damascus to Horan, which is not one of his better moves, though he did build a very nice mosque there that survives in ruins. That defeat and forced conversion was immediately repudiated; and sometime after, at the end of the eighth or the beginning of the early ninth centuries the Khazar court embraced Judaism. Many had accepted for a long time, including myself, the late date of 860; but the discovery of coins, imitative coins—that is, coins issued by the Khazars apparently in imitation of Muslim coins—suggests that the date is a generation or two earlier. These are very rare coins, still to be published fully, found in a hoard in Gotland in Scandinavia, and what they show is a modification of the Arab coin where the [inscription] is substituted with the name Musa, Moses, and there is enough change in the iconography to indicate that the monotheistic religion being proclaimed is not Islam, but Judaism. How did this come about?

One of the great achievements of the Khazars is their promotion of trade; the development of trade along this northern extension of the Silk Road. I mentioned the trade routes skirting the Aral and Caspian Seas and heading to the Greek ports on the Black Sea, bringing in silk and other objects. What was traded in exchange? Not just the products of the Roman world, but also the products of the forest: the amber coming from the Baltic; various types of furs, big trade in furs coming ultimately from the Arctic; but above all slaves, usually Slavic peoples who have been enslaved and are being sold as labor into the Islamic world. Another commodity will be Turks; Turks who are captured in raids, young men between the ages of essentially 14 and 18 who are then sold into the Islamic world to become soldiers. We will discuss the emergence of slave armies when we turn to the caliphate in one of the upcoming lectures. The Khazars exploited all these trade networks.

The movement of goods within the early Islamic Empire was usually in the hands of minorities, especially trade goods across the Mediterranean. Several groups emerged in prominence, foremost the Jews. Jewish bankers and trading houses literally extended from Muslim Spain, across North Africa to

Egypt and Syria. There were big communities in Cordova and Cairo, and we found some remarkable documents—the so-called Geniza documents—in a synagogue in medieval Cairo, in old Cairo, which gives us a sense of the extent and range of Jewish merchandising and banking. They succeeded to the same banking and mercantile practices I described earlier on the Silk Road, and it is almost certain that these Jews were very, very prominent at the Khazar capital at Atil; Muslim sources report them in great numbers. The Khazar khan, probably in the late 700s or early 800s, decided that this was a worthy monotheistic religion. It was not Orthodox Christianity; it was not Islam; it marked the khanate as a separate great state. The court converted to Judaism just as the Uighurs—that is, their eastern kinsmen who established the great khanate in the Mongolian homeland at the time on the eastern steppes—embraced Manichaeism. It was a sensible option.

With the conversion of Judaism came enormous advantages. We have a very, very good account of the journey of a Muslim geographer and historian named Ibn Fadlan who traveled in 921–922 to the Volga. He was really invited there to attend the court of the Bulgar khan of the Volga. These were Bulgar kinsmen of the ones who had settled in the Balkans; they are not to be confused with their kinsmen who eventually become Bulgarians and Orthodox Christians. They were on the Middle Volga; they were subjects of the Khazar khan; and in 921–922 they converted to Islam and they had petitioned the caliph for envoys and for teachers in the new faith. Ibn Fadlan traveled there. He also passed through Atil, the Khazar court, the capital. He makes comment of the numbers of Jews, Christians, and Muslims trading in the city; the fact that there were so many people of these nationalities that special courts had to be set up to adjudicate questions of contract and commerce, and these would be mixed courts. He was also impressed by the extent of the slave trade as well as the powers of the khan, how he ruled as a virtual celestial figure; and he notes the fact that the khanate is a confederation of different tribes and so much wealth is pouring into Atil, the capital, because of the trade connections. This is one of the great geniuses of the Khazar khans: They tolerated all the faiths; they encouraged trade routes; they turned what was originally a tent city, Atil, into a great commercial settlement at the mouth of the Volga, something that really began to resemble a true city.

For all of this success, the question comes up: Where did they go wrong? In my opinion, the Khazar khans had constructed the most successful confederacy on the western steppes until the Golden Horde of the Mongols. It was light years ahead of the Scythians and the Sarmatians, and it was going to be quite far more sophisticated from the Pechenegs and Cumans who would follow them. The problem was that the khans spent so much of their time on trade, commerce, and the benefits of the material culture from the higher civilizations that they failed to enforce their will over the subject tribes. This led to challenges within their own confederacy. There were two tribes who will come to play a very important role in the upcoming lecture. One of them were the Magyars. They are not Turkish speakers; they are actually speaking a language known as Finno-Ugrian, which is a language related to Finnish and Estonian today. They were people of the forests who had moved onto the western steppes and had adopted a pastoral way of life, and they proved very rambunctious and unruly vassals of the Khazar khan. They ended up migrating westward into Eastern Europe, got involved in the Byzantine Bulgarian wars, and were eventually sent ricocheting into Hungary, where they settled and became the Magyars of the Hungarians we know in 897. In the meanwhile, on their route to their final destination, they did quite a job in disrupting the khan's control of his subject tribes.

Another one was the Pechenegs, another unruly group of members of the khanate who came to dominate the South Russian steppes; that is, the areas around the Don and the Dnieper Rivers. The Pechenegs entered into an alliance with a third group of people who were total interlopers. These were the Rus, Scandinavians from Sweden, who since the eighth century had been exploiting the trade route on the Volga and especially were active in the slave trade and were operating as merchant princes by permission in the Khazar khanate. When the Pechenegs in the early ninth century came to dominate the South Russian steppes and were at loggerheads with their overlords the Khazar khans, the Rus or the Scandinavians switched the axis of their trade from the Volga to the Dnieper. They established cities at the future Russian towns of Novgorod and Kiev; they aligned their trade route on Constantinople and entered into alliance with the Pechenegs. This Pecheneg-Rus alliance undermined a good deal of the trade routes that had previously gone to Atil.

Both the Pechenegs and Rus came to see the Khazars as foes; and for various reasons, some of it perhaps religious, the emperor in Constantinople came to prefer the Pechenegs and Rus as allies over the Khazars. In part, the caliphate was in decline; the Khazars were not so important. The Khazars had reconverted to Judaism; and furthermore, the Rus particularly, these Scandinavian warriors who arrived in Constantinople by sea, proved to be excellent soldiers, were recruited into the imperial army as the Varangian Guard, and were receptive to orthodox civilization; the Pechenegs were much closer to the imperial frontier; so these two people essentially replaced the Khazars as the favored imperial allies. Sometime in 965 or 967, the Rus under their leader Sviatoslav and the Pechenegs destroyed the Khazar capital; and the Khazar khanate fragmented shortly after 965.

The Khazars have excited a great deal of imagination, and particularly in various racist and ideological claims and publications of the late 19th and early 20th centuries. There was an argument that was long voiced that the Ashkenazi Jews, the European Jews, were not really Jews, they were not really Hebrews, they were nothing more than wayward Khazars who had been converted in the 9th century and became the origins of the Jewish community of Russia, and therefore they really have no claims to being true Jews. This has turned out to be quite a bogus claim in a number of ways; and for me these claims are generally raised by ideologues who wanted to marginalize or even persecute Jews in Europe. What has been shown by DNA testing is the majority of the Jewish communities across the world have a DNA that confirms what the literary sources have always told us (no surprise to me): that the Jewish communities have a very powerful DNA component that comes out of the Middle East.

What happened to the Khazar Jews? They were only the court and a small aristocracy. After the destruction of their khanate, they probably were absorbed into the later Turkish confederations. Rather than getting involved in all these racist politics of the 20th century, it is better to look at the Khazars for what they had achieved: They had created a great steppe empire based on trade; they had tolerated all the faiths; they had proved immensely successful in defining themselves; and they really provided a model for the next successful rulers of the western steppes and that will be the family of Batu, the grandsons of Genghis Khan, the rulers of the Golden Horde.

Pechenegs, Magyars, and Cumans
Lecture 18

In this lecture, we will complete our exploration of the relationship between the Byzantine world and the nomadic peoples on the Pontic-Caspian steppes. We will look first at the Magyars, who would be assimilated into western Europe as an essentially Christian kingdom and give up their nomadic ways. We will then turn to the Pechenegs, who warred with the Khazars and initially allied with the Rus. These Scandinavians were not steppe nomads, but they played an important role in the reconfiguration of the steppes in the 9th through the 11th centuries. Finally, we'll bring in the Cumans, who fell heir to the western steppes after the Pechenegs and engaged in fighting the Russians throughout the 12th and 13th centuries.

The Magyars

- The Magyars were virtually the only significant nomadic peoples of the Middle Ages who were not Turks; they originated in the forest zones to the northeast of the Urals. Their ancestors clearly go back into the Bronze Age, but at some point between the 5th and 8th centuries, they moved out onto the grasslands and adopted a nomadic way of life. They spoke a Finno-Ugrian language, remotely related to Turkish.

- Once they moved onto the steppes, the Magyars acquired many of the same habits as other steppe peoples. By the early medieval period, they had gained all the trappings of steppe cavalry. They were organized into a loose confederacy, and, initially, they apparently recognized the authority of the Khazar khagan. They were probably regarded as outer tribes of the Khazars.

- Around 850, something put the Magyars in motion, and they began to move to the southwest; they ended up on the south Russian steppes in the valleys of the Don and Dnieper rivers. Very quickly, this new area, just to the north of the Black Sea, was regarded as their ancestral home. They regrouped themselves into a loose confederation of southern tribes and more or less shook off their loyalty to the Khazar khagan.

- The Magyars then started to raid the Balkans, attacking the Bulgars and annoying the Byzantines. In 839, the Byzantine emperor Theophilus sent military engineers and technicians to the khagan of the Khazars to build a fortress on the Don, apparently to inhibit the movement of Magyars eastward into the heartland of the Khazar domains. Islamic sources also confirm that the Magyars and Khazars came to loggerheads.

- In the winter of 895–896, as a result of a diplomatic mistake in a Byzantine-Bulgarian war, the Magyars crossed the Carpathians and settled in their future homeland around Budapest. That is, they took over the Pannonian plains, and starting in 897, they became a nuisance to the western Europeans. Magyars began to raid into Italy and the Holy Roman Empire.

- It isn't until 955, when the Holy Roman Emperor **Otto I** defeated the Magyars at a decisive battle at the Lech, that they were forced to accept boundaries and stop raiding.
  - Within a generation, the Magyars came under strong missionary influence and converted to Latin Christianity. Their king Stephen (r. 1000–1038), often known as Saint Stephen, began the transformation of the Magyars into the Hungarians. Henceforth, these people would play a major role in European history. They forgot their steppe ways and became part of Christendom.

  - In fact, the Hungarian kingdom became the bastion of western Europe against future attacks by nomads to the east, the Penchenegs and Cumans, and would take the full brunt of the Mongol attack in the 13th century.

The Pechenegs and the Rus
- The Pechenegs, known by a variety of names, were Turkish speakers. They were originally part of the coalition of western Gök Turks that was subjected by the Tang emperors, then reasserted its

independence and would clash with the armies of Islam. Sometime in the 9th century, they were pushed west in the typical domino movements by the immediate ancestors of the **Seljuk Turks**, known as the Oghuz or **Ghuzz Turks**.

- About 25 years after the Magyars, the Pechenegs crossed just north of Khazar domains and pushed the Magyars west into central Europe. They then descended into the regions between the Don and the Dnieper. Along the way, the acquired a reputation of being the most pitiless and dangerous of nomadic conquerors. The Byzantine emperors had mixed opinions about the Pechenegs; their horse archers were extremely useful, but they were completely impervious to Christianity.

- The Pechenegs warred with the Khazars, but they reached an agreement with another group of people who were not steppe nomads, the Rus. These were Swedes, Danes, Fins, and other people from Scandinavia who had been trading with the Khazars for at least 150 years.

    o Archaeology indicates that in the beginning of the 8th century A.D., Swedes moved across the Baltic and used the river systems of Russia to reach trade routes along the Volga to the Caspian Sea or routes that led to the Dnieper and, from there, to the Black Sea. These were the same routes that had brought the Goths from Scandinavia onto the steppes in the 3rd century A.D.

    o These Scandinavians had superb merchant ships and warships that could negotiate the rivers of Russia. Initially, in the 8th century and early 9th, the Rus arrived at the Volga with the permission of the Khazar Khagan. But they developed a new route along the Dnieper that took them to Constantinople. Their intention was probably to avoid the taxes imposed by the Khazar middlemen and get directly to the silks and gold of the Byzantine city. To exploit this route, they had to come to terms with the Pechenegs.

- The Rus and the Pechenegs reached an understanding that lasted through much of the 10th century to cooperate in the trade connections to Constantinople. Four times, from 860 to 941, the Rus launched fleets to attack Constantinople, and these extorted commercial treaties out of the emperor. So close was the alliance between the Pechenegs and the Rus that sometime after 965 or 967, they teamed up to sack the city of Atil, the capital of the Khazar khagan.

- A significant change took place in the relationship of the two peoples in 988–989. The then-reigning prince of the Rus, Vladimir, converted to Orthodox Christianity. This was a significant success of Byzantine missionaries and marked a major turning point in the relationship between the Rus (now called Russians) and the Pechenegs.

The conversion of Vladimir to Christianity meant that future Russian princes would look to Constantinople as a model to establish a literate, urban-based civilization in the forest zones of Russia.

  o The Russian princes now ruled as Slavic Byzantine-style kings, that is, Christian monarchs who adopted the laws of Constantinople. As such, they could not sell their Slavic subjects, who were increasingly Christians, as slaves to Turkish nomads.

  o Thus, the slave trade suddenly dried up in the 10th and 11th centuries for the Pechenegs, as well as other nomadic peoples. And the Pechenegs felt free to raid those who would not trade with them.

  o Starting in the 11th century, there was a constant battle along the steppe zone between the Russians and the Pechenegs, with the

Pechenegs trying to capture Slavs to supply the slave markets of the Islamic world.

- Efforts to convert the Pechenegs proved hopeless. Not only were they nomads and, thus, lacked the urban organization necessary for Christianity, but they also fell on the hashish side of the vodka-hashish line. In other words, those who drank vodka tended to become Christian, while those who used hashish were more likely to convert to Islam. This connection was actually noted as one of the ways that the Rus were convinced to adopt the Orthodox Church.

The Cumans

- The Pechenegs now found themselves at odds with the Russian principalities, the Hungarian kings, and the emperors in Constantinople. In 1087, the fighting force of the Pecheneg confederation crossed the Danube and entered imperial territory. The reasons for their movement are a bit uncertain, but in part, they were being pressed by a new group of Turks who were occupying the former domains of the Khazars, the Cumans. They clashed with the Pechenegs over the right to raid Russia for slaves.

- The migration of the Pechenegs into the Balkans was a nightmare for the then-emperor, **Alexius I** (r. 1081–1118), who was desperately trying to hold his empire together. He had lost Asia Minor to the Seljuk Turks, and the Balkan provinces were essentially the only areas he retained. Alexius summoned a huge Cuman army into the Balkans to help defeat this invasion.

- In 1091, a combined Cuman-Byzantine army wiped out the Pecheneg migration, reputedly 80,000 Pechenegs, at the Battle of Levounion, which is near the modern Greek-Turkish border. The Byzantines then replaced the Pechenegs with the Cumans. This was the last success in Byzantine diplomacy because after that, the Byzantine Empire was essentially ruined by the Crusaders and sacked in 1204.

- The Cumans, Turkish speakers, were keen to exploit the slave and fur trade to the Islamic world. In this, they ran up against the Russian principalities, which now assumed the Byzantine role of dealing with Turkish nomads on the steppes. Through much of the 12th century and early 13th, there was constant fighting between the Russians and the Cumans.

- The standoff between the Russians and the Cumans would change dramatically in 1236, when Batu, the grandson of Genghis Khan, swept across the steppes, subjected the Cumans, and plunged into Russia. The full fury of nomadic power would be directed against the kingdom of Hungary and western Europe, and the future of Russia and the western steppes would be decisively altered.

Important Terms

Ghuzz Turks: Speakers of western Turkish or Oghuz languages who emerged on the central Asian steppes between the 9th and 11th centuries. They included Seljuk Turks, Cumans, and Kipchak Turks.

Seljuk Turks: Ghuzz or western Turks who founded the Seljuk sultanate (1055–1194) that revived the power of Abbasid caliphate. Seljuk Turks settled in Asia Minor after the Battle of Manzikert (1071).

Names to Know

Alexius I Comnenus (b. 1056; r. 1081–1118): Byzantine emperor; seized power in the civil war of 1081 and founded the Comnenian Dynasty (1081–1185). He restored imperial power in western Asia Minor by summoning the First Crusade (1095–1099). He allied with the Cumans to destroy the Pechenegs, who had invaded Thrace, at the Battle of Levounion in 1091.

Otto I (b. 912; r. 936–973): Holy Roman Emperor; duke of Saxony and son of Henry the Fowler. Otto was elected king of Germany. In 955, he decisively defeated the Hungarians on the Lech, and his campaigns against the Danes and Slavs secured imperial frontiers. In 962, he was crowned Holy Roman Emperor.

Vladimir (b. c. 958; r. 980–1015): Rus prince of Kiev; he embraced Orthodox Christianity around 989 as part of a marriage alliance with the Byzantine emperor Basil II (976–1025). He founded the royal institutions of the Christian Russian state.

Suggested Reading

Angold, *The Byzantine Empire, 1025–1204.*

Comnena, (Sweter, trans.), *The Alexiad.*

Curta, *Southeastern Europe in the Middle Ages, 500–1250.*

Curta and Kovaley, eds., *The Other Europe in the Middle Ages.*

Dunlop, *The History of the Jewish Khazars.*

Franklin and Sheppard, *The Emergence of the Rus, 750–1200.*

Golden, "The Peoples of the Russian Forest Belt."

Oblensky, *The Byzantine Commonwealth.*

Macartney, *The Magyars in the Ninth Century.*

Vásáry, *Cumans and Tatars.*

Whittlow, *The Making of Byzantium, 600–1025.*

Questions to Consider

1. What accounted for the ease and speed of the migrations of the Magyars and the Pechenegs in the 9th century? Why did they pose such a danger to the Khazar confederation?

2. Why did the Byzantine emperors seek alliances with the Magyars and the Pechenegs? How judicious was their policy? What impact did these new nomads have on Byzantine society? How did the Pechenegs exploit their alliance with the Byzantine emperor?

3. How did the Pechenegs profit from the establishment of Kiev by the Scandinavian Rus in 860? In what ways were the Rus and Pechenegs

allies and trade partners? Why did they desert their alliance with Prince Sviatoslav in 972, after his defeat by the Byzantine emperor John I?

4. How important was the emperor Alexius I in advancing the power of the Cumans? How decisive was the Battle of Levounion 1091?

5. How did the emergence of Christian Hungary and Russia threaten the nomadic peoples of the Pontic-Caspian steppes? How does the epic of Prince Igor reflect the clash between Russians and Cumans on the eve of the Mongol invasion?

Pechenegs, Magyars, and Cumans
Lecture 18—Transcript

In this lecture, I wish to complete the relationship between the Byzantine world and the nomadic peoples on the Pontic-Caspian steppes. We started the discussion of this topic two lectures ago; and we are going a bit beyond chronologically when we dealt with the Chinese and the steppe nomads, and that is to complete the story because two important conclusions come out of this lecture: One is that the Byzantines never really achieve a success in absorbing or converting any of these nomadic peoples to Orthodox Christianity and Byzantine civilization. On the other hand, one of the groups that we are going to talk about, the Magyars, will be assimilated into Western Europe and will become essentially a Christian European kingdom and give up their nomadic ways. In this lecture, I propose to look at first the Magyars and the Pechenegs, two groups that I have discussed previously who are responsible for disrupting the Khazar khanate. In addition, we will be looking at Rus, Scandinavians from Sweden; they are not steppe nomads to be sure, but they play an extremely important role in the reconfiguration of the steppes in the 9th, 10th, and 11th centuries. Furthermore, they will be the Byzantine success. They will convert to Orthodox Christianity and lay the foundations of Russia; and it will be the Russian, in time, starting in the 16th century, who will end the power of the nomadic tribes on the Eurasian steppes, literally from the forest zones of Russia to Manchuria. Finally, we will bring a third group on known as the Cumans, who are Turks, who will close this lecture. We have three nomadic peoples, some wayward Vikings, the Byzantine Empire, the kingdoms of Hungary and Russia, so we have a tall order in this lecture.

Let us turn to the Magyars first. They are significant for several reasons: First, they are not Turkish speakers. They are virtually the only significant nomadic people of the Middle Ages who are not Turks, and they originate in the forest zones, the Taiga as the Russians would call it, more or less to the northeast of the Urals. Their ancestors clearly go back into the Bronze Age, and they dwell in forest areas where they exploited the fur trade, they were involved in fishing and hunting. It is an important point to note that throughout the history of the steppes, there was always this interaction between forest peoples and nomadic peoples; and sometimes forest people become nomads, as in the case of the Magyars. In other cases, there are certain Turkish groups that return to or adopt a forest life. Actually, in his early career, Temujin, the future Genghis Khan, does retreat into the steppes to avoid his enemies and pursues a life that would have been very similar to that of the Magyars.

The Magyars at some point between the fifth and the eighth centuries A.D. moved out onto the grasslands and adopted a nomadic way of life. They did not speak Turkish. They did speak an agglutinative language related to Turkish; it is known as the Finno-Ugrian language. This is a language family that today includes Hungarian, that is, the language of the Magyars; the language of the Finns; the Suomi, as they call themselves; the Lapps to the north; and also the Estonians. It is remotely related to Turkish. Modern Turks would claim that, "Oh, the Magyars speak a form of Turkish"; that is not really quite correct. The Magyars would correct very quickly on that. "We're not a bunch of wayward Turks; we do speak a distinct language," which they have retained, even though they settled in Central Europe and are surrounded by Slavic- and Germanic-speaking peoples.

The Magyars, therefore, are a very good example of how people move between the forest zones and the steppes and will change their lifestyle depending on circumstance. Once they moved onto the steppes, they acquired many of the same habits, the stock raising, the importance of animals. They gained by the early medieval period all of the trappings of steppe cavalry; that is, the horse archer, the types of armaments that we have discussed with the Turks in their clashes with the Tang emperors of China, and the same type of equipment that we discussed with Avars, Bulgars, and Khazars who came into contact with the Byzantines. The Magyars, therefore, in many ways looked like a nomadic people, it is just that their language was somewhat different. They, too, were organized into a very loose confederacy; and initially they apparently recognized the authority of the Ashina khan of the Khazars; that is, they were vassals. They were probably regarded as outer tribes.

Something put them in motion somewhere around the mid-ninth century—we suspect around 850 A.D.; we are drawing this from Byzantine and Arabic sources—and they began to move to the southwest from their original homes and ended up on the South Russian steppes in the valleys of the Don and the Dnieper Rivers. Their migration is very indicative of the structure of these nomadic confederations. Technically, they were vassals of the khan of the Khazars, but apparently this migration was taken on their own initiative, for their own reasons—it could have been simply a matter of finding better pastures—and they move very rapidly. I have mentioned this in previous lectures: When a nomadic group decides to move, they can move great distances very quickly and find new pastures and homelands, and within 15 years that new home has become the ancestral home. Clearly this is what happened with the Magyars. They moved into this zone of Southern Russia, just to the north of the Black Sea, and now regarded that as their ancestral home and regrouped themselves into a loose confederation of seven tribes.

They also more or less shook off their loyalty to the khan of the Khazars and were seen as a very, very difficult and undisciplined group of barbarians who started to raid the Balkans, attacking the Bulgars, annoying the Byzantines, especially their settlement at Cherson. In 839, the emperor Theophilus—one of my favorite Byzantine emperors, by the way—his wife was chosen to him in a bride show compliments of the Khazar court as an inspiration, and Theophilus sent military engineers and technicians to the khan of the Khazars to build a fortress on the Don, Sarkel is its name, and it has apparently been uncovered by Russian archaeologists (or Soviet archaeologists at the time); it was a fortress that was set up to control and inhibit the movement of Magyars eastward into the heartland of the Khazar domains. There are Islamic sources that also confirm that the Magyars and Khazars have come to loggerheads; they are fighting and raiding each other, probably to feed the slave trade and probably to reward their followers. But it is indicative that already in the mid-ninth century the Khazar khanate is under pressure and starting to break up.

The Magyars, therefore, were a new dimension in imperial diplomacy. They ironically get pushed west into their future home of Hungary by a miscalculation in Byzantine diplomacy. They are moved around in the complicated wars between Tsar Symeon, of the Bulgarians at this point, and the Byzantine emperor Leo VI; and they are attacked by another group called the Pechenegs, who are a new Turkish tribe we will introduce in a moment. In the winter of 895–896, because of this diplomatic mistake in a

Byzantine-Bulgarian war, the Magyars cross the Carpathians and settle in their future homeland around Budapest; that is, they take over the grasslands that we have often called the Pannonian plains or sometimes the Hungarian plains, and starting in 897 they become a general nuisance to the Western Europeans. Magyars begin to raid into Italy, into Western Europe. They attack what we call the Holy Roman Empire; that is, the Germanic half of the old Carolingian Empire that has the imperial title of Charlemagne. It is not until 955 when the Holy Roman emperor Otto I defeats the Magyars at a decisive Battle at the Lech and forces the Magyars to accept boundaries and stop raiding.

Within a generation, the Magyars come under very, very strong missionary influence and they convert to Latin Christianity; not to Byzantine Christianity, they embrace the Catholic faith. Their King Stephen, who rules from 1000–1038—very often known at Saint Stephen, as a saintly king— he begins the transformation of the Magyars into the Hungarians, into the Kingdom of Hungary; and henceforth, these people would play a major role in European history. But they have forgotten their steppe ways; they have renounced them; and they have become part of wider Christendom. In fact, the Hungarian Kingdom has become the bastion of Western Europe against future attacks by nomads to the east—Pechenegs, Cumans—and they will take the full brunt of the Mongol attack in the 13th century.

One significant note about the Hungarians: The Hungarians were identified with Huns, Hunoi, by both Byzantine and German chroniclers, and the Hungarians actually like that. Their real name is Magyar, but they are called Huns, which means they are kind of Hungarians, they are Huns; and they claimed some kind of connection to Attila. The later kings of Hungary, the so-called Arpad kings, claim to have the original sword of Attila—which is now in Vienna; it is passed through various families with the marriage alliances of the Hapsburgs—and the name Attila, for instance, is a very common name among Hungarians. In addition, they were apparently regarded as Ogre, Oiagros, various names in Greek and Latin sources from which the word *ogre* comes from, because to the Germans, these people were such violent attackers—they had never witnessed steppe nomads before—they called them "ogres," and that word passed into general European languages.

With the Magyars off the stage as steppe nomads and being turned into Christian Hungarians, let us look at how they got there; and that brings us to the second group of nomadic peoples, the Pechenegs. The Pechenegs are known by a variety of names; I have chosen that one, it is the most common used in Byzantine sources. Patzinaks is another term used for them. They were clearly Turkish speakers; and, in fact, they seemed to speak a Turkish language that would be closely related to modern Turkish in Turkey, Azerbaijani, and the language of Turkmenistan, where some of these other Turkish people such as the Bulgars, the Khazars spoke a distinct leer or western branch of Turkish, which is now largely extinct. In any case, they were pushed west, deliberately left their homelands; they were pushed west because they had dwelled probably just north of the Jaxartes River. They were part of the coalition or confederation of the western Gök Turks going back to that great khanate that was established in the sixth century A.D. that was subjected by the Chinese emperors of the Tang Dynasty; that reasserted its independence; and that will clash with the armies of Islam.

Sometime in the ninth century, they were pushed west in the typical domino movements by a new group of Turks known as the Oghuz Turks, or as they are sometimes called the Ghuzz, which is the Arabic name for them; but Oghuz would be the Turkish name. These are the ancestors, the immediate ancestors, of the Seljuk Turks who will have such an important impact on the Islamic world and medieval history in general. These kinsmen, the Oghuz Turks, dispossessed the Pechenegs of their ancestral lands north of the Jaxartes, around the Aral Sea, and they began to migrate west. They followed the same routes that the Huns would have followed, and probably the Sarmatians before them; and that brought them to the rivers Ural and Volga and into the orbit of the Khazar khans. Again, about 25 years later that the Magyars, less than a generation, they crossed just north of Khazar domains and descended upon the Magyars, and are responsible for dislodging and pushing those Magyars west into Central Europe.

Again, I stress that the Khazar khan had very little control over these people; they were able to move pretty much at will; and it is because these steppe confederations were a loose arrangement of inner and outer tribes, and no khan really exercised authority such as a bureaucratic state in Tang China, the Byzantine Empire, or as we shall see the Abbasid Caliphate. The control was much looser; it involved submissions by the leaders—that is, the lesser khans; the *yabgular* as they would be called in the plural, the *yabgu*—the subordinate rulers to the great khan furnishing tribal armies on request and obeying the general directives. But on a day-to-day basis, these nomadic confederations really did not influence the pattern of life for many of the tribes, and the Pechenegs were happy to move across the domains of the outer tribes of the Khazar khanate and descend into the regions between the Don and Dnieper.

They not only dislodged the Magyars, they got a reputation of being the most pitiless and dangerous of nomadic conquerors, far more dangerous than the Khazars; and the Byzantine emperors had very mixed opinions about them. On the one hand, they were extremely useful; and Pecheneg horse archers appear in imperial armies in the 10th and 11th centuries. They were completely impervious to Christianity; both Western missionaries coming from Germany, Byzantine missionaries had absolutely no success with these people. The best that the emperor in Constantinople could hope for was that his governor at Cherson in the Crimea would attend the traditional festivals of the Pechenegs each spring, watch them string up and slaughter some wolves, and hope that the Pechenegs did not attack imperial territory, particularly in the later 10th century when the Byzantines had regained control of most of the Balkans and had subjected the Bulgarians to their authority.

In addition, the Pechenegs warred with the Khazars; and they came to an agreement with a third group of people who were not steppe nomads but whom I mentioned earlier in this lecture: those are the Rus. These would be Swedes—some Danes, Fins, and other people from Scandinavia—who had been trading with the Khazars for at least 150 years. Archaeology indicates that in the beginning of the eighth century A.D., Swedes moved across the Baltic and used the river systems of Russia to get into contact with either the world of Islam—and that seems to have been the first trade route along the Volga down to the Caspian Sea—or later to take a combination of routes that would lead you to the Dnieper, that great river that now essentially cuts across the Ukraine in a great bend, and then go to the Black Sea and to Constantinople. These trade routes were ancient. They were the same routes that brought Goths from Scandinavia onto the steppes in the third century A.D. and led to that amalgam of Goths and nomadic Sarmatians who had attacked the Roman Empire in the third century and were again reduced to allies of Rome in the fourth century. This represented effectively a second migration out of the Baltic.

In addition, these Scandinavians had superb ships that could negotiate the rivers of Russia, both warships and merchant ships; but in order to negotiate those rivers, they had to come to terms with existing peoples. Initially, in the 8th and early 9th century, these Swedes—collectively known as Rus—arrived as merchant princes, mercenaries, viziers at the Volga at the permission of the Khazar khan. But starting around 860—and we are told this wonderfully fanciful story in the Russian primary chronicle, written in the early 12th century—a Viking warlord named Rurik, perhaps a Slavic rendition of Erik, established a trading post at Holmgard, the future Novgorod, and then his subordinates, his jarls, established another position down at the modern city of Kiev; and they developed a new route along the Dnieper that took them to Constantinople. Their intention was probably to cut out the Khazar middle men and get directly to the silks and gold of Constantinople, whereas with the Khazars they were exporting slaves and furs through Atil and being taxed by the khan. This new route gave the Rus a direct beeline to Constantinople.

However, to exploit this route they had to come to terms with the Pechenegs; and the Pechenegs were happy to do this. They controlled the steppes; all Rus ships would have to navigate very treacherous rapids down at the lower end of the Dnieper River; the boats would have to make portage—that is, they would have to be moved up from the river and moved around—and the Pechenegs controlled this, and if you were not on good terms with these guys they would wipe you out; and as you know, as steppe nomads they were always interested in collecting tableware: the severed heads of their defeated opponents. As a result, there was essentially an understanding between the Rus and the Pechenegs through much of the 10th century to cooperate in the trade connections down to Constantinople. Four times the Rus launched fleets to attack Constantinople starting in 860, the last one was in 941, and these extorted commercial treaties out of the emperor in Constantinople.

They also engaged in slave trading and the fur trade. Furs and slaves were exacted from the Slavic peoples of the forest; and the Rus happily sold these slaves to Pechenegs and other Turkish tribes because that labor was needed in the Islamic world. So close was the alliance that sometime after 965–967, somewhere in there, the Pechenegs and Rus teamed up to sack the city of Atil; that is, the capital of the Khazar khan. The date is a little uncertain, but it probably is before 967 because in that year the Rus prince, his name is Sviatoslav, got it in his head to attack Bulgaria in Constantinople and he was eventually defeated; and he was actually wiped out by his Pechenegs allies on his way back to Russia, and his head got to join the collection of the Pechenegs khan of all the goblets he had collected from his opponents.

There was a significant change in the relationship in 988–989. In that year, the then-reigning prince of the Rus at Kiev named Vladimir, or Valdimar to use his Norse name, converted to Orthodox Christianity. This was the significant second success of Byzantine missionaries. They had converted the Bulgars, turned them into Bulgarians; they now converted the Rus and turned them into Slavic-speaking Russians professing the Orthodox faith and looking to Constantinople as a model to set up a literate urban-based civilization in the forest zones of Russia.

That was a very significant turning point, and it influenced very much the relationship between these Rus—now called "Russians" to designate them as quite distinct from their pagan Scandinavian ancestors—these Russian princes who claimed descent from Rurik, and right down into the end of the 16th century every ruler from the Russian cities was descended from Rurik; nonetheless, they ruled as a Slavic Byzantine-style king, a Christian monarch, who adopted the laws of Constantinople, which is essentially Roman law, who began to build churches in Byzantine fashion, who fortified their posts into insipient cities with stockades. The most significant change is now as Christian monarchs, they could not sell their Slavic subjects, who were increasingly Christians, as slaves to Turkish nomads; that was out. They were only allowed to oppress them as Russian serfs. That meant the slave trade suddenly dried up in the 10th and 11th centuries for the Pechenegs as well as other nomadic peoples. The result was if you were not going to trade, the Pechenegs were going to raid. Starting in the 11th century, you got a constant battle along the steppe zone between the Russians and the Pechenegs; and the Pechenegs are trying to raid and supply the slave market of the Islamic world, and the Russians, of course, wanted to prevent that.

Efforts to convert the Pechenegs, as well as later Turks who come after them, the Cumans, prove hopeless. I always think one of the problems is that not only were they nomads, and Orthodox Christianity requires the cities and urban organizations of essentially a Byzantine style-state, but the Pechenegs, the later Cumans, and even the Mongols when they arrive, they were on the hashish side of the vodka-hashish line. That is, if you live in the Russian steppes and you drink vodka to get through the winter, you are going to go Christian. If on the other hand you are on the steppes and you have your shamans who are in communication with the otherworld—we will talk about why Islam was so impressive to the Turks; they would identify Muslim Sufi mystics as shamans—and they would use a bit of hashish to mount the world tree and get a vision of the mystical world, you are more likely to go over to Islam. It might be something of a silly comparison; yet, on the other hand, this connection is actually made by the Russian primary chronicle as one of the reasons for convincing the Rus, at that point Scandinavians who will then adopt the Orthodox Church and the Slavic rite, for going over to Orthodox Christianity. The result is that the Byzantines have created in the forest zone a set of Russian principalities that in time will play a decisive role in the history of the steppes; but that will come in the 16th century and later.

Meanwhile, the Pechenegs now found themselves at odds with the Russians, the Russian principalities; with the Hungarian kings—there was actually an effort by the Hungarian kings, now Christians, to convert nomadic peoples, that went nowhere—and in addition, with the emperors in Constantinople. In 1087, there was a report that 80,000 Pechenegs, apparently the fighting force of the Pecheneg confederation, crossed the Danube and entered imperial territory. They were pressing in the direction of Constantinople. The reasons for their movement are a bit uncertain; but in part they were being pressed by a new group of Turks who occupied the former domains of the Khazar khan, and they are known as Cumans. They, too, were being forced west—they were Kipchak Turks, as we would call them; Kipchak Turks will play a very decisive role in the Mongol period—and they likewise were being pressed west by the Ghuzz or the Oghuz Turks; that is, the ancestors of the Seljuk Turks. They moved into the domains of the former Khazar khans and clashed with the Pechenegs over the right to raid Russia and collect slaves. In 1087, the Pechenegs decided to migrate into the Balkans.

This was a nightmare for the then-emperor Alexius I, who came to the throne in 1081 and died in 1118; and he was desperately trying to hold his empire together. He had lost Asia Minor to the Seljuk Turks—we will discuss that in a later lecture—and the Balkan provinces were essentially the only areas he still had. Alexius summoned a huge Cuman army into the Balkans to help defeat this invasion because he had visions of the Pechenegs laying siege to Constantinople, contacting the Seljuk Turks, particularly the emir of Izmir named Chaka, and once again Constantinople would be besieged by an army from Asia Minor and a nomadic army from Central Europe. This had happened with the Avars back in 626, they had cooperated with the Persians; the Bulgars had cooperated with the Avars back in 717; and these invasions were warded off by parading the Hodigitria—that is, the icon of Mary Theotokos, the patron of the city—and the Byzantine fleet. To prevent that, he called in a Cuman army; and together a Cuman-Byzantine army in 1091 maneuvered this Pecheneg migration, this reputedly 80,000 Pechenegs, and wiped them out. It took place at the Battle of Levounion; it is near the modern Greek/Turkish border. The result was the Byzantines now replaced the Pechenegs with the Cumans.

It was the last success in Byzantine diplomacy, because after that the Byzantine Empire is essentially ruined by the crusaders and sacked in 1204. The Cumans fall heirs to the western steppes. They are pagans; they are Turkish-speakers; and they are keen in exploiting that slave trade, fur trade to the Islamic world. They run smack up against the Russian principalities, these Byzantine style states in the forest zones that are not going to trade their subjects as slaves to the Cumans. What happens, the Russian states— the various Russian principalities at Kiev, at Suzdal, Chernigov, Novgorod, the Republic of Novgorod, Pskov—they all end up assuming the Byzantine role of dealing with Turkish nomads on the steppes. It ends in essentially equilibrium. Through much of the 12th and early 13th centuries, there was constant fighting going back and forth between the Russians and the Cumans.

The Russians adopted many of the cavalry techniques of the Cumans. We have a remarkable epic, one of the earliest pieces of vernacular Russian, known as the lay of Prince Igor. Prince Igor was apparently a historical figure of the 11th century. It is really in a kind of archaic prose that has the cadence of poetry. It talks of how Prince Igor battles and fights, is captured by the Cumans and eventually escapes. It chides the other Russian princes for not supporting him. It was an important epic revealing the conditions of the fighting between the Russians and the Cumans, and later, of course, it would become a great nationalistic epic in the 19th century and put to music as an opera by Borodin and Rimsky Korsakov. What the epic reveals is this equilibrium between the Byzantine-style Russian principalities and the Cumans, the Turkish nomads on the western steppes; and it is a standoff as the two war with each other, raid with each other.

But that situation will change very, very dramatically in 1236, when Batu, the grandson of the Genghis Khan, will sweep across the steppes, subject the Cumans, and plunge into Russia, and suddenly the full fury of nomadic power will be directed against the Kingdom of Hungary and Western Europe. The future of Russia and the western nomadic steppes will be dramatically, decisively, and abruptly changed.

Maps

Silk Road Routes

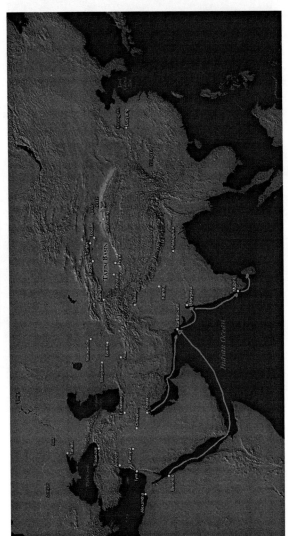

Eurasian Steppes

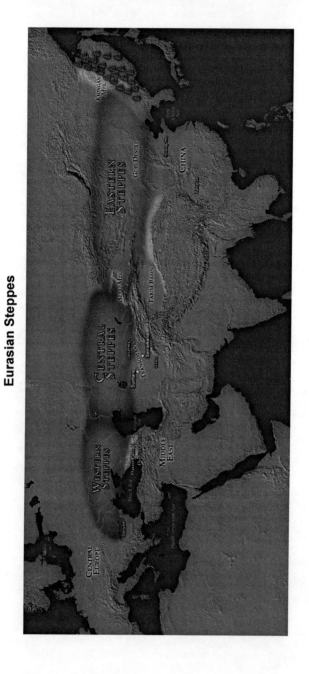

Timeline

Anatolian speakers (Hittites, Luvians, and Palaic speakers) cross the Bosporus and enter Asia Minor

Division of Indo-European languages into centrum and satem branches

First known light chariots in central Asia

2000–1500 B.C. .... Chariots at Nesa (Kültpe) in central Asia Minor

Erlitou culture in the Yellow River valley: origins of Chinese civilization

Andronovo culture in Khazkhstan

Proto-Indo-Iranian speakers migrate to Transoxiana (BMAC)

Domestication of the Bactrian camel

Migrations of Eastern Iranian speakers across Central and Eastern Eurasian steppes

Hattusilis I founds the Hittite Empire in Asia Minor; spread of chariot warfare across the Near East

Migration of Indo-Aryan speakers of Mitanni from Transoxiana into northern Mesopotamia

Shang Dynasty (1600–1046 B.C.): urban, literate civilization in China

1500–1000 B.C. .... Indo-Aryans migrate into northern
India, completing the end of
urban civilization of Meluhha
(Indus Valley civilization)

Introduction of chariot
and horses to China

Collapse of the great states of the
Bronze Age in the Near East and Greece

Zhou Dynasty in China
(1046–256 B.C.)

1000–500 B.C. .... Beginning of widespread
use of iron technology

Migration of Tocharian-speakers
into the Tarim Basin

Earliest mummies of Tarim Basin
(Ur David and Beauty of Loulan)

Spread of cavalry across
Eurasian steppes

Migration of Medes and
Persians into western Iran

Scythians dominate the
Pontic-Caspian steppes

Sacae dominate the central
Asian steppes

Sacae migrate into the Tarim Basin
and upper valley of Yellow River

Cultural exchange between
Iranian nomads and Chinese

Scythians compel Cimmerians to
migrate across the Caucasus

Cimmerians invade Urartu, Phrygia,
and the Assyrian Empire

Life and teachings of Mahavira
Vardhamana, founder of Jainism

Cyrus I (559–530 B.C.) unites Iran
and Transoxiana and conquers
Asia Minor and Babylonia: birth of
Persian (Achaemenid) Empire

King Cyrus slain by Massagetase north
of the Jaxartes River (Syr Darya)

Life and teachings of Siddhartha
Gautama, the Buddha

Reign of Darius I: consolidation
of the Persian Empire

Scythian expedition of King
Darius I of Persia

Founding of the Roman Republic

500–400 B.C. ....Period of Warring States in
China (down to 221 B.C.)

Herodotus visits Olbia and receives
reports about the Scythians

400–300 B.C. .... Alexander the Great conquers
the Persian Empire

Alexander battles the nomadic
Sacae and Dahae across Jaxartes

Greco-Macedonian colonies
founded in Bactria and Sogdia

Diadochoi: wars of successors and
partition of Alexander's empire

Chandragupta (322–298 B.C.) ends
Macedonian rule in northern India

Foundation of Mauyran
Empire (326–187 B.C.)

Seleucus I (312–281 B.C.) establishes
Seleucid Empire (312–63 B.C.)

Hellenization of the Near East
and expansion of the Silk Road

Genesis of Sarmartian tribes on the
steppes between Volga and Ural rivers

300–200 B.C. .... Accession of Ashoka (268–232
B.C.): height of Mauyran Empire

Rome defeats Carthage in
the First Punic War

Conversion of Ashoka to Buddhism

Diodotus of Upper Satrapies
founds Greco-Bactrian kingdom

Third Buddhist Council: division
of Buddhism into Theravada
and Mayahana vehicles

Arsaces I (246–211 B.C.)
founds Parthian kingdom

Unification of China by Qin Shi
Huangdi (246–210 B.C.)

First Chinese empire under the
Qin Dynasty (221–206 B.C.)

Building of the Great Wall
to check the Xiongnu

Touman forges the Xiongnu
confederacy on the eastern steppes

Rome defeats Carthage in
the Second Punic War

Roman conquest of the Mediterranean
world (201–31 B.C.)

Reign of Modu Chanyu
(down to 174 B.C.): Xiongnu
dominate eastern steppes

Emperor Gaozu (206–195 B.C.) founds
Former (Western) Han Dynasty

200–100 B.C. .... Sarmatians subject Scythians and
rule the Pontic-Caspian steppes

Sarmatians impose tribute on
Greek cities of the Crimea

Battle of Magnesia: Romans defeat
Seleucid King Antiochus III

Decline of Seleucid Empire
and rise of Parthians

Reign of Mithridates I: expansion
of Parthian kingdom

Gunchen Chanyu expands
Xiongnu confederation

Yuezhi (Tocharians) driven by
Xiongnu west into Ferghana

Yuezhi drive Sacae into
Sogdiana and Bactria

Reign of Han Emperor Wudi

Mithridates I defeats and captures
Seleucid king Demetrius II

Parthians conquer Media,
Persia, and Mesopotamia

Sacae devastate Sogdiana and shatter
the Greco-Bactrian kingdom

Sacae settle in Drangiana
(Seistan; 140–120 B.C.)

Mission of Zhang Qian to the
Yuezhi (Kushans) and Wusun

War between Han China
and the Xiongnu

Expedition of Antiochus VII
Sidetes against Parthia

Tocharians subject the Greek cities
of Bactria (140–120 B.C.)

Phraates II of Parthia (138–128 B.C.)
defeats and slays Seleucus VII

Sacae and Tocharians invade Media
and defeat and slay Phraates II

Tocharians defeat and slay Parthian
king Artabanus I (128–124 B.C.)

Reign of Mithridates II (123–88 B.C.):
consolidation of Parthian Empire

Construction of Ctesiphon
on the Tigris River

Han armies secure Gansu and the
Tarim Basin (western regions)

Eudoxus of Cyzicus discovers use
of monsoons for sailing to India

Development of trade in the
Erthyraean Sea (Indian Ocean)

War of the Heavenly Horses:
Li Guangli invades Sogdiana

Sogdians render tribute of horses
to Han Emperor Wudi

100 B.C.–1 A.D. .... Roxolani migrate into eastern Rumanian steppes (Wallachia; down to 50 A.D.)

Iazyges migrate into eastern Hungarian steppes

Alans occupy Kuban and steppes north of the Caucasus

King Tigranes the Great of Armenia expels Parthians from Mesopotamia

Outbreak of Third Mithridatic War (74–63 B.C.)

L. Licinius Lucullus defeats Mithridates VI and secures Asia Minor

Battle of Tigranocerta: L. Licinius Lucullus defeats Tigranes the Great

Parthians subject Mesopotamia and Media Atropatene

Pompey the Great (Cn. Pompeius Magnus) imposes Roman suzerainty over Armenia

Pompey secures the Roman frontier on the upper Euphrates

Civil war on the eastern steppes: division into northern and southern Xiongnu

Battle of Carrhae: Parthians
defeat M. Licinius Crassus

Abortive campaign of Mark Antony
in Armenia and Media Atropatene

Octavian, hailed Augustus by the
Senate, establishes the Roman Empire

Augustus imposes settlement
on King Phraates IV

Return of Roman prisoners
and standards of Carrhae

1–100 A.D. .... Wang Mang overthrows
the Han Dynasty

Reforms in China and collapse
of Chinese frontier policy

Reunification of the
Xiongnu confederacy

Guangwu (25–57) founds Later
(Eastern) Han Dynasty (25–220)

Accession of Kujula Kadphises
(30–80): founding of Kushan Empire

Composition of the *Periplus
Maris Erythraei*

War of the Armenian Succession;
Rome opposes King Tiridates

Cn. Domitius Corbulo
campaigns in Armenia

Settlement between Nero and
King Vologeses I over Armenia

Roman governor Tib. Plautius
Silvanus secures the lower Danube
against the Roxolani and Dacians

Alans cross the Caucasus and
ravage the Near East

Han general Bao Chao subjects the
western regions (Tarim Basin)

Dissolution of the northern
Xiongnu confederacy

Reign of Kushan emperor Vima Taktu

Reign of Kushan emperor Vima
Kadphises (down to 127)

Extension of Kushan power
into the Punjab

Introduction of Kushan gold
currency to facilitate trade

Mission of Han envoy Gan Ying
to Kushan Empire and Parthia

Gao Ying receives reports about
Daqin (imperial Rome)

100–200.. Emperor Trajan (98–117)
wages the Parthian War

Roman legions capture and sack
Ctesiphon, the Parthian capital

Trajan crowns Parthamasiris
king of Parthia

Hadrian relinquishes Trajan's
conquests east of the Euphrates

Reign of Kushan emperor Kanishka
I: height of Kushan Empire

Patronage of Iranian and
Hindu gods and Buddhism

Arrian, Roman governor of
Cappadocia, checks attack of Alans

Reign of Kushan emperor Huviskha

War of Marcus Aurelius against Parthia

Roman army sacks Seleucia
ad Tigrim and Ctesiphon

Northern war of Marcus Aurelius
against Germanic and Sarmatian tribes

Reign of Vasuveda I (down to
230): decline of Kushan Empire

War of Septimius Severus
against Parthia

Roman army captures and
sacks Ctesiphon

200–300.. War of Caracalla against Parthia

Life and teachings of Mani,
founder of Manichaeism

End of the Han Dynasty:
political disunity in China

Era of Three Kingdoms
(220–280): Wei, Shu, and Wu

Battle of Hormozgan: Shah Shapur
defeats Parthian King Artabanus V

Shapur I (227–240) founds
Neo-Persian (Sassanid) Empire

Reign of Sassanid Shah Ardashir I

Reforms of Kartir:
codification of Zoroastrianism

War of Ardashir against Roman
emperor Severus Alexander (222–235)

Reign of Sassanid Shah Shapur I

Shapur I invades Mesopotamia:
first war against Rome (242–244)

Gordian III (238–244) marches
east against Shapur I

Goths and Samartians raid
Dacia and Danubian provinces
of the Roman Empire

Death of Gordian III; accession
of Philip I (244–249)

Philip I pays Shapur I 10,000
pounds of gold for peace

Battle of Abrittus: Goths defeat
and slay Trajan Decius

Shapur I invades and sacks Syria:
second war against Rome (253–254)

Shapur I invades Syria: third
war against Rome (256–258)

Expedition of Valerian I
(253–260) against Shapur I

Valerian I captured by Shapur I

Sassanid army ravages Mesopotamia,
northern Syria, and eastern Asia Minor

Rally of eastern Roman army by Prince
Odenathus of Palmyra (260–262)

Battle of Nassius: Claudius II Gothicus
decisively defeats the Goths

Aurelian reunites the Roman
Empire and secures frontiers

Aurelian withdraws Roman garrisons
and colonists from Dacia

Emperor Wu (265–290) reunites China
under the Jin Dynasty (280–420)

Accession of Diocletian (284–305):
imperial reform and recovery

Foundation of the Dominate

Sassanid-Persian War: Caesar Galerius
decisively defeats Shah Narses

Sassanid Shah Narses relinquishes
strategic Mesopotamian provinces

300–400.. Conversion of Constantine I
(306–337) to Christianity

Accession of Shah Shapur II (309–379)

Chandragupta I founds the
Gupta Empire (219–550)

Constantine I campaigns against
the Sarmatians and Goths

Constantine founds
Constantinople (New Rome)

Yujiulu Muglu establishes the Rouran
(Avar) confederacy (330–551)

First migrations of Turkish speakers
into central Eurasian steppes

Shah Shapur II invades
Mesopotamia and sacks Amida

Outbreak of Roman-Persian
War (359–364)

Failure of the expedition of
Julian II against Ctesiphon

Death of Julian II and accession
of Jovian (363–364)

Jovian cedes Mesopotamian
province to Shapur II

Shah Shapur II settles Hephthalites
(White Huns) in Bactria

Hephthalites, as Sassanid allies, secure
northeastern frontier (375–425)

Huns defeat Gothic King
Ermanaric, who commits suicide

Huns subject Goths and Alans on
the Pontic-Caspian steppes

Goths received as federates by
Roman emperor Valens (364–378)

Battle of Adrianople: Goths
defeat and slay Valens

Accession of Theodosius I,
the Great (379–395)

Rome cedes Armenia to
the Sassanid Empire

Uldin, king of the Huns (down to 414)

Theodosius I declares Nicene
Christianity as the empire's official faith

Death of Theodosius I: division of
western and eastern Roman empires

Honorius, western Roman
emperor (395–423)

Arcadius, eastern Roman
emperor (395–408)

Huns cross the Dariel Pass and invade
the Sassanid Empire (395–396)

Daowu (398–409), ruler of the Tuoba,
founds northern Wei Dynasty (398–535)

400–500...Migration of Visigoths
under Alaric into Italy

Germanic tribes migrate into Gaul and
Spain: collapse of the Rhine frontier

Huns migrate into Pannonia: collapse
of the middle Danube frontier

Accession of Theodosius II, eastern
Roman emperor (408–450)

Goths sack Rome

Construction of the Theodosius
Walls of Constantinople

Reigns of Rugila (420–434) and
Octar (420–430) over the Huns

Death of Jin emperor Gong (419–420):
disunity in China (420–581)

Ruglia raids into Thrace and
receives subsidy to withdraw

Reign of Taiwu, emperor of
the northern Wei Dynasty

Construction of colossal
Buddhas at Yungang Caves

Accession of Valentinian III as
western Roman emperor (425–455)

Aetlius, patrician and *magister militum*,
directs western Roman policy

Third Ecumenical Council at Ephesus:
condemnation of Nestorianism

Nestorian Christians establish
churches in Sassanid Babylonia

Accession of Attila (434–453) and
Bleda (434–445) as kings of the Huns

Attila forges a barbarian empire
from the Rhine to the Volga

Attila invades Thrace and
extorts the Treaty of Margus

Annual subsidy (700 pounds of
gold) paid by Theodosius II

Shah Yazdegerd II wages frontier
wars against the Hephthalites

Huns annihilate Burgundians at Worms;
origins of the legend of the Nieblungs

Attila murders Bleda: Attila
sole king of the Huns

Attila devastates the Balkan provinces
of the eastern Roman Empire

Treaty of Anatolus: Attila ends the
Roman frontier on the lower Danube

Accession of Marcian, eastern
Roman emperor (450–457)

Reform of eastern Roman army
and end of subsidies to Attila

Marriage proposal of Honoria to
Attila rejected by the western court

Attila declares war on the
western Roman Empire

Battle of Chalons: Aetius checks Attila

Invasion of northern Italy by Attila

Death of Attila: civil war and
rebellion within the Hun Empire

Battle of Nedao: collapse
of the Hun Empire

Hephthalites defeat, capture, and
ransom Shah Peroz (457–484)

Odoacer deposes last western
Roman emperor, Romulus
Augustulus (475–476)

End of the western Roman Empire

Hephthalites defeat and slay Shah
Peroz and overrun Transoxiana

Wei emperor Xiaowen (471–499)
locates his court at Luoyang

Sinification of the northern Wei Dynasty

Hephthalites subject northern India
and the Tarim Basin (down to 513)

500–550..Construction of the first colossal
Buddha at Bamiyan

Outbreak of Persian–Roman
War (526–532)

Accession of Roman emperor
Justinian (527–565)

Battle of Daras: Belisarius
defeats the Persian army

Timeline

Accession of Shah Khursau I (521–570)

Perpetual peace between
Justinian and Shah Khurau I

Justinian reconquers North Africa,
Italy, and southern Spain

550–600... Bumin overthrows rule of the
Rouran (Avar) khagans

Turks expel Avars and occupy
the Orkhon valley

Establishment of the Gök Turk
khaganate under the Ashina clan

Istami (552–581), brother of
Bumin and *yabgu* of the western
Gök Turks, pursues the Avars and
secures the central and western
Eurasian steppes to the Volga

Accession of Mukan as
khagan of the Gök Turks

Gök Turks subject Tocharian
cities of the Tarim Basin and
control the Silk Road

Construction of the second
colossal Buddha at Bamiyan

Istami, *yabgu* of the western Turks, and
Shah Khosrow attack the Hephthalites

Turks subject Transoxiana

Avars flee into the
Pontic-Caspian steppes

Avar khagan Bayan and Lombard king
Albion (560–572) defeat the Gepidae

Avars occupy the Pannonian grasslands

Khagan Bayan (560–602) rules the
steppes from the Danube to the Don

Avars raid the Byzantine
Balkan provinces

Beginning of migration of Slavs
into the Balkans

Justin II (565–578) receives a
delegation of the western Turks

Lombards migrate into northern Italy

Justin rejects annual
subsidy to Khosrow I

Outbreak of Roman–Persian
War (572–590)

Tiberius II (578–582) allies with
the Avars; collapse of Byzantine-
Turkish alliance; western Turks attack
Byzantine cities in the Crimea

Accession of Tardush as second
yabgu of the western Turks

Emperor Wen (581–604) unites
China and establishes the
Sui Dynasty (581–618)

Death of Taspar Khagan:
civil war between Ishbara
Khagan and Apa Khagan

Tardush asserts de facto
independence of the western
Turks (On Ok, "Ten Arrows")

Division of the Gök Turks into eastern
and western Turkish khaganates

First Persian-Turkish war
over Transoxiana

Vaharam Chobin defeats
the Western Turks

Vaharam Chobin usurps
the Sassanid throne

Khosrow II flees to Constantinople and
receives an army from Maurice Tiberius

Khosrow II (591–626) occupies
Ctesiphon and restores Sassanid rule

Peace between the Byzantine
Empire and Sassanid Persia

Outbreak of civil war in Turk khaganate

600–650.........................Phocas (602–610) overthrows
and murders Maurice Tiberius

Shapur II invades Roman
Mesopotamia and northern Syria

Outbreak of the Byzantine–
Persian War (602–626)

Accession of Sui emperor
Yang (604–617)

Reign of Harsha-Vardhan:
unification of northern India

Accession of Shibi Khan to
eastern (Gök) Turk khaganate

Accession of Heraclius
(610–641) as Byzantine emperor

Shibi Khan defeats Sui emperor
Yang at Yanmen (Shanxi)

Gök Turks raid the northern
frontiers of China

Accession of Tong *yabgu* khagan
(Ziebel) of western Turks (On Ok)

Khazars emerge as dominant
Ashina tribe of On Ok

Emperor Gaozu imposes unity in China
and founds the Tang Dynasty (618–907)

Second Persian–Turkish war; Tong *yabgu* khagan raids to Isfahan

Muhammad (575–632) flees from Mecca to Medina (Hegira)

Heraclius launches his eastern campaigns against Persia (622–626)

Alliance of Heraclius and Tong *yabgu* khagan against Shah Khosrow II

Illig, khagan of eastern Turks, defeats Tang emperor Taizong at Xuanwu Gate

Turks raid northern China to Wei River

Avars and Persians besiege Constantinople

Accession of Tang emperor Taizong (626–649)

Turks under Böri Shad cross the Derbent Gates and devastate Azerbaijan

Tang emperor Taizong promotes rebellions within the eastern Turkish khaganate

Campaign of Li Jing smashes the power of the eastern Turkish khaganate

Gök Turks submit to Tang emperor Taizong

Pilgrimage of Buddhist monk
Xuanzang to central Asia and India

Khazars assert domination over the
western Turkish tribes (down to 670)

Bulgars expel Avars from the steppes
between the Don and Dnieper rivers

Death of Muhammad: election of
Caliph Abu Bakr (632–634)

Death of Abu Bakr: election of
Caliph Umar I (634–644)

Battle of the Yarmuk: Arabic
conquest of Syria

Battle of Kadisiya: Arabs conquer
Iraq and western Iran (639–642)

Arabs conquer Egypt

Death of Heraclius; accession
of Constans II (641–668)
as Byzantine emperor

Fragmenting of the western
Turkish khaganate

Arabs conquer Cyrenaica
and Tripolitana

Election of Caliph Uthman (644–656)

650–700...Khazars repel first Arabic invasion
north of the Caucasus

Accession of Tang emperor
Gaozong (650–683)

Death of Shah Yazdgerd III
(632–651): end of Sassanid Empire

Arab armies reach Merv and
secure Oxus River as a frontier

Mutiny of Arab army in Egypt:
Murder of Caliph Uthman

Egyptian army proclaims
Ali caliph (656–661)

Outbreak of Muslim civil war
between Ali and Muawiya

Arabs raid Mawarannhar (Transoxiana)

Tang emperor Gaozong imposes
hegemony over western Turks

Turgesh emerge as leading
tribe of western Turks

Assassination of Ali; Muwayia
proclaimed first Umayyad caliph

Muwayia (661–680) establishes
Umayyad caliphate at Damascus

Succession of Constantine IV
(668–685) as Byzantine emperor

Khagan Busir Glavan (c. 670–715)
consolidates the Khazar Empire

Ziyad ibn Abihi (670–673),
governor of Iraq, fortifies Merv

Tribal armies settled in Khurasan

First Arabic siege of Constantinople

First revolt of eastern Turks under
Ashina Nishu Beg against Tang rule

Tang general Pei Xingjian
crushes Turkish rebels

Pei Xingjian crushes second Turkish
revolt under Ashinde Wenfu and Ashina
khagan Funian; public execution
of Turkish nobility at Chang'an

Khan Asparuch (681–702) settles
Bulgars in Moesia south of the Danube

Third Turkish revolt under Ashina
Kutlag against Tang rule

Kutlag declared Ilterish khagan
(682–694); end of Tang hegemony

Reestablishment of eastern
Turkish khaganate

Accession of Justinian II
(685–695) as Byzantine emperor

Accession of Caliph Abd
al-Malik (695–705)

Creation of Arabic-Muslim
administration in Umayyad caliphate

Accession of Kapagan
(694–716) to eastern khaganate

Overthrow and exile of
Justinian II to Cherson

Battle of Bolchu: Kapagan
khagan imposes hegemony
over the western Turks

Turks occupy Transoxiana in alliance
with Sogdian cities against Arabs

Arab capture of Carthage

700–750... Qutaibah bin Muslim, governor of Merv

Arab conquest of Transoxiana

Marriage alliance between Justinian
II and Khazar khagan Busir Glavan

Restoration of Justinian II
(705–711) at Constantinople

Khan Tervel of the Bulgars (702–705)
concludes a treaty with Justinian II

Dowager Empress Wu directs
Tang policy (705–712)

Qutaybah ibn Muslim (705–715)
appointed Arab governor of Khurasan

Qutaybah initiates Arab
conquest of Transoxiana

Qutaybah captures Bukhara:
forced conversions to Islam

Arab conquest of Spain (711–713)

Arab conquest of the Sind (711–712)

Accession of Tang emperor
Xuanzong (712–756)

Byzantine–Bulgar treaty: annual tribute
to Bulgars and frontiers confirmed

Tokuz Oghuz Turks, backed by Tang
court, defeat and slay Kapaghan khagan

Kul Tigin and Tonyukuk impose
Bilge as khagan of the eastern Turks

Suluk, khan of Turgesh (716–738),
asserts power over western Turks

Accession of Leo III (717–741),
who founds the Isaurian Dynasty

Byzantine-Khazar alliance against
the Umayyad caliphate

Second Arabic siege of Constantinople

Erection of Turkish monumental
inscription of Tonyukuk
in the Orkhon valley

Arab governor al-Karashi massacres
population of Khujand, Ferghana

General rising of Sogdian cities and
Turkish tribes in Transoxiana

Suluk khagan of Turgesh defeats
Arab expedition ("day of thirst")

Suluk khagan defeats second Arab
expedition into Transoxiana

Byzantine-Khazar marriage alliance

Constantine V marries
Chichek, daughter of Bihar
Khagan of the Khazars

Death of Bilge Khagan; civil wars
in eastern Turkish khaganate

Monumental inscriptions in Orkhon
valley to Bilge and brother Kül Tigin

Arab army under Marwan defeats
Khazars and occupies Balanjar

Khazars compelled to convert to Islam

Assassination of Suluk;
collapse of Turkish resistance
to Arabs in Transoxiana

Nasr ibn Sayyar, Arab governor
of Khurasan (738–748),
secures Transoxiana

Khazar Khagan Bulan renounces
Islam in favor of Judaism

Foundation of new Khazar capital
at Atil on the lower Volga

Rebellion of Uighurs and Karluks:
overthrow of eastern Turkish khaganate

Accession of Umayyad caliph
Marwan II (744–750)

Kurluk Bilge proclaimed first
khagan of the Uighurs

Karluks, vassals of Kurluk Bilge,
secure the central Eurasian steppes

Uighur khagan Bayanchur Khan founds
capital of Baghlasun (Ordu Balik)

Outbreak of rebellion of Arab army in
Khurasan against Caliph Marwan II

750–800...Battle of the Greater Zab: as-
Saffrah defeats Caliph Marwan II

End of Umayyad caliphate

As-Saffrah (750–756) establishes
the Abbasid caliphate

Battle of Talas: Arab-Karluk
army defeats Tang army

Chinese garrisons withdrawn
from the Tarim Basin

Outbreak of An Lushan Rebellion

Uighur khagan Bayanchur Khan
supports Tang court against rebels

Abd ar-Rahman (756–788) proclaims
Umayyad emirate of Cordova

Byzantine emperor wars against Bulgars

Caliph al-Mansur founds Baghdad,
capital of Abbasid caliphate

Uighur khagan Bogu converts
to Manichaeism

Karluks defeat Turgesh and
reorganize the On Ok confederacy

Karluks dominate central Eurasian
steppes as vassals of Uighur khagans

Emergence of Oghuz (Ghuzz)
Turks on the steppes between
the Aral and Caspian seas

Accession of Caliph Harun ar-Raschid
(786–809): height of Abbasid caliphate

Charlemagne, king of the Franks,
smashes the Avar khanate

800–850... Coronation of Charlemagne as
Holy Roman Emperor (800–814)

Magyars migrate into the Pontic-
Caspian steppes (c. 800–830)

Accession of Krum, khan of
the Bulgars (802–813)

Outbreak of Abbasid civil war between
al-Amin and al-Mamun (809–813)

Formation of Turkish bodyguard (*haras*)

Bulgar khan Krum defeats
and slays Byzantine emperor
Nicephorus I at Pliska

Tahir ibn al-Husayn captures
Baghdad: end of Abbasid civil war

Accession of Caliph
al-Mamun (813–833)

Khan Krum defeats Emperor
Michael I at Versinicia

Bulgars devastate the hinterland
of Constantinople

Accession of Leo V (813–820):
extension of Theodosian Walls

Peace between Leo V and the
Bulgar khan Omurtag (814–831)

"Great Fence of Bulgaria"

Ahad obm Asad I appointed Abbasid
governor of Ferghana (819–864)

Foundation of the Samanid
Dynasty (819–1005)

Uighur-Tibetan clash for
control of the Tarim Basin

Caliph al-Mamun appoints
Tahir ibn al-Husayn in Khurasan

Tahirid emirs rule Khurasan
and Transoxiana (821–873)

Pechenegs migrate west from
the central Eurasian steppes

Magyars consolidate power in the
steppes west of the Don (930–895)

Caliph al-Mutasim relocates the
Abbasid capital to Samara

Turkish bodyguard dominates
Abbasid court (836–892)

Caliph al-Mutasim invades Byzantine
Asia Minor and sacks Amorium

Emperor Theophilus wins tactical
victory over Turks at Dazimon

Khazars, with Byzantine
assistance, fortify the fortress
Sarkel against Magyars

Karluks and Krygyz sack Baghlasun:
end of Uighur khaganate

Uighurs migrate into the Tarim Basin

Beginning of migrations of Oghuz
Turks westward (840–925)

Karakhanids dominate central
Eurasian steppes (840–1137)

850–900..Migration of Pechenegs to
steppes west of the Don River

Rurik (Erik) founds Holmgard
(Novgorod) as a Rus settlement

First Rus attack on Constantinople

Saint Cyril fails to convert the
Khazars to Orthodox Christianity

Khan Boris of the Bulgars (852–889)
converts to Orthodox Christianity

Formation of the kingdom of Bulgaria

Tulunid emirs rule over
Egypt (down to 905)

Ahmad ibn Asad ibn Saman appointed
emir of Transoxiana (875–886)

Samanid emirs create the high Persian
culture of eastern Islam (875–1005)

Accession of Oleg (Helgi) as
prince of the Rus (c. 880–912)

Oleg transfers capital to Kiev

Magyars settle on Pannonian grasslands

Accession of Tsar Symeon
of Bulgaria (893–927)

Outbreak of Symeon's first war
against Byzantium (894–897)

Magyars migrate into Pannonian
steppes (Hungary)

Magyars raid into western
Europe (896–955)

900–950... Death of Emperor Li Zhu
(904–909): end of the Tang Dynasty

Period of disunity: Five Dynasties
and Ten Kingdoms (907–980)

Second Rus attack on Constantinople

Abaoji unites the Khitans

Ubaydallah al-Mahdi (909–
934) proclaims the Fatimid
caliphate in North Africa

Accession of Byzantine emperor
Constantine VII (913–959)

Symeon wages second war
against Byzantium (913–924)

Abaoji subjects 16 prefectures and
seizes power of northern China

Abaoji takes Chinese throne
name Taizu (916–926),
establishing the Liao Dynasty

Conversion of Volga Bulgars to Islam

Mission of Ibn Fadlan to the
Bulgars and Khazars

Reign of Khitan emperor
Yelü Deguangr (Taizong)

Ikhshidid emirs rule Egypt and Syria

Accession of Satuk Boghra
Khan (940–955)

Satuk Boghra Khan promotes Islam
among the Karakhanid Turks

Third Rus attack on Constantinople

Khitans conquer Kaifeng

Fourth Rus attack on Constantinople

950–1000................................ Li Xixing (954–967) establishes the Xi
Xia kingdom in the Gansu Corridor

Battle of the Lech: Otto I of
Germany defeats the Hungarians

Zhao Kuangyin seizes power in
Kaifeng as emperor Taizu (960–976)

Taizu establishes Northern
Song Dynasty (960–1127)

Taizu unites southern China
into a Neo-Confucian state

Alp Tigin (961–975) takes over
the town of Ghazna

Establishment of the Samanid emirate

Prince Sviatoslav of Kiev
(965–967) and Pechenegs sack Atil

Collapse of the Khazar khaganate

Pechenegs dominate the
Pontic-Caspian steppes

Prince Sviatoslav of Kiev
invades Bulgaria (967–971)

Reign of Khitan emperor Yelü
Xian (Jingzong; 969–982)

Sinification of Khitan court

Fatimid army occupies Egypt

Prince Sivatoslav overruns
Bulgaria and attacks Byzantium

Battle of Dorostolum:
Byzantine emperor John I
defeats Prince Sviastoslav

Byzantine annexation of
eastern Bulgaria

Pechenegs defeat and slay Prince
Sviatoslav on the Dnieper River

Fatimid al-Mu'izz transfers
the capital to Cairo

Accession of Byzantine emperor
Basil II (976–1025)

Height of Byzantine Empire under
the Macedonian Dynasty

Accession of Song emperor
Taizong (976–997)

Emergence of the Song bureaucratic
state and examination system

Accession of the Samind
emir Nuh II (976–997)

Sebüktigin (977–997) establishes
the Ghaznavid emirate (977–1163)

Reign of Khitan emperor Yelü
Longxu (Shengzong; down
to 1031)

Migration of Seljuk Turks to the
steppes south of Khwarazm

Sebüktigin raids Kabul and
Punjab—domains of the Shahi
Jayapala (964–1001)

Battle of Langhan: Sebüktigin
defeats Shahi Jayapala

Timeline

Conversion of Prince Vladimir of Kiev
(980–1015) to Orthodox Christianity

Foundation of Orthodox Russia

Jiqian of the Xi Xia ends vassalage
to Song and Liao emperors

Sebüktigin and Tafgach Bughra Khan
of the western Karakhanids agreed
to partition the Samanid emirate

Mahmud Ghaznavi (998–1030)
succeeds to the Ghaznavid emirate

Karakhanids occupy Bukhara; Samanid
court flees to Tabaristan (999–1005)

Collapse of the Samanid emirate;
Karakhanids control Transoxiana

1000–1050...................................... Conversion of King Stephen of Hungary
(997–1036) to Latin Christianity

Battle of Peshawar: Mahmud Ghaznavi
annihilates army of Shahi Jayapala

Mahmud raids across the Punjab
and Doab (1001–1024)

Treaty of Chauyuan: Song
emperor Zhenzong (997–1022)
recognizes Khitan control of the
16 prefectures of north China

Mahmud Ghaznavi and Karakhanids
clash along the lower Oxus River

Mahmud Ghaznavi occupies Khwarazm

Mahmud Ghaznavi sacks Somnath,
the sanctuary of Shiva

Tughril Bey and Chagri settle near
Bukhara in Karakhanid service

Mahmud Ghaznavi secures
Khurasan and northern Iran

Mahmud Ghaznavi settles Seljuk
Turks under Tughril Bey in Khurasan

Reign of Yuanhao of the Xi Xia under
the Chinese imperial name Jingzong

Promotion of Buddhism
in Xi Xia domains

Tughril Bey declared sultan at Nishapur

Tughril Bey defeats Ghaznavid
sultan Masud I near Merv

Seljuk Turks conquer cities of
northern Iran (1040–1055)

1050–1100..................................... Tughril Bey and Seljuk
Turks enter Baghdad

Tughril Bey restores the Abbasid
caliphate under Seljuk protection

End of the Macedonian
Dynasty at Constantinople

Timeline

Clash of civil and military aristocracies:
decline of Byzantine power

Accession of Alp Arslan
(1063–1072) as Seljuk sultan

Alp Arslan directs raids
against Byzantine and Fatimid
empires (1063–1071)

Accession of Byzantine emperor
Romanus IV (1068–1072)

Battle of Manzikert: Seljuk sultan Alp-
Arslan defeats Emperor Romanus IV

Seljuk Turks overrun Byzantine
Asia Minor (1071–1081)

Malik Danishmend (1071–1084)
seizes Niksar as Danishmend emir

Cumans migrate west,
attacking the Pechenegs

Accession of Malik Shah
(1072–1092) as Seljuk sultan

Sulayman (1077–1086) seizes Konya
and is proclaimed sultan of Rūm

Accession of King Ladislaus
of Hungary (1077–1095)

Hungarian–Cuman border wars

Accession of Byzantine emperor
Alexius I Comnenus (1081–1118)

Establishment of Comnenian
Dynasty (1081–1185)

Pechenegs migrate into
Byzantine Empire

Battle of Levounion: Emperor Alexius I
and the Cumans destroy the Pechenegs

First Crusade

Battle of Dorylaeum: First
Crusade defeats Sultan Kilij
Arslan I of Konya

First Crusade captures Antioch

First Crusade captures Jerusalem

1100–1150..Accession of Vladimir Monomakh
(1113–1125) of Kiev

Russian–Cuman wars

Wanyan Aguda (1115–1123) unites
the Jurchens in Manchuria

Jurchen rebellion against the Liao
(Khitan) emperor Tianzuo (1101–1125)

Wanyan Aguda assumes Chinese
throne name Taizu of the Jin Dynasty

Alliance of the Sea: Wanyan Aguda and
Song emperor Huizong (1100–1125)
agree to partition the Khitan Empire

Wanyan Aguda conquers the 16
prefectures of China (1121–1123)

Accession of Jurchen emperor
Wanyan Sheng (1123–1135)

Wanyan Sheng ends the
Khitan (Liao) Empire

Yelü Dashi (1124–1143) and the Kara-
Khitans flee to central Eurasian steppes

Yelü Dashi establishes
Kara-Khitan khaganate

Wanyan Sheng conquers from Song the
lower Yellow River valley (1125–1127)

Wanyan Aguda captures
Kiafeng, the Song capital

Gaozong (1127–1162) relocates
the Song capital to Lin'an
(modern Hangzhou)

Beginning of the Southern
Song Dynasty (1127–1279)

Yelü Dashi and the Kara-Khitans
conquer cities of the Tarim Basin

Treaty of Shaoxing:
Song emperor Gaozong
acknowledges loss of north China

Jurchen (Jin) Empire supreme in north
China and eastern Eurasian steppes

Battle of Qatwan: Yelü Dashi defeats
Seljuk sultan Ahmed Sanjar

Kara-Khitans conquer Transoxiana

First reports of legendary Prester
John in western Europe

1150–1200...................................... Collapse of the great Seljuk sultanate

Abbasid caliph al-Muqtafi
asserts independence in Iraq

Birth of Temujin (future Genghis Khan)

Tatars poison Yesugei, father of Temujin

Temujin; his mother, Hoelun;
and siblings live in exile

Ghiyath-ad-Din seizes Ghaznva and
establishes the Ghurid sultanate

Muhammad Ghori as emir directs
Ghurid attacks into India (1173–1192)

Battle of Myricoephalon: Sultan Kilij
Arslan II defeats Emperor Manuel I

Decline of Byzantine
power in Asia Minor

Enslavement and escape of Temujin

Temujin, as ally of Toghrul Khan of
the Keraits, wars against the Merkits

Jamukha and Temujin swear
brotherhood and battle the Merkits

Prithviraj III (1149–1192) of
the Chauhan kingdom builds
the capital at Delhi

Marriage of Temujin and
Börte, birth of Jochi

Clashes between Jamukha and
Temujin; Jamukha allies with
the Merkits and Naimans

Jin emperor Zhangzong
(1189–1208) promotes tribal
wars among the Mongols

Expedition of Prince Igor of Novgorod-
Seversk against the Cumans

Second Battle of Tarain; Muhammad
Ghuri defeats Prithviraj III

Muhammad Ghuri occupies Delhi

Qutb ud-din Aybak directs
Ghurid conquest

Aybak orders the construction of the
Quwwatt-ul Islam mosque complex

Bakhtiyar Khilji, Ghurid general, sacks
Nalanda: end of the Pala kingdom

Aybak orders the construction
of the Qutb Minar

1200–1250...................................... Temujin defeats Jamukha, Naimans,
and Merkits near Khingan Mountains

Muhammad Ghori declared
sultan (1202–1206)

Toghrul Khan allies with Jamukha

Toghrul Khan and Jamukha defeat
Temujin at the Battle of Baljuna

Temujin rallies Mongols and the
kurultai declare war on Jamukha

Temujin wins decisive victory
near Karakorum over Jamukha
and Toghrul Khan

Temujin imposes his authority over
the eastern Eurasian steppes

Kuchlug, prince of Naimans,
flees to Kara-Khitan Gurkhan
Mozhu (1178–1211)

Fourth Crusade sacks Constantinople
and partitions the Byzantine Empire

Accession of Sultan Kay-Khusraw
I (1204–1210) of Konya (Rūm)

Theodore I founds the Byzantine
splinter empire at Nicaea

Seljuk conquest of Anatolia:
subjection of Sivas and Kayseri

The *kurultai* declares
Temujin Genghis Khan

Genghis Khan refuses homage to the
Jin emperor Zhangzong (1189–1208)

Aybak establishes the slave
sultanate of Delhi (1206–1290)

Genghis Khan campaigns against
Xiangzong of the Xi Xia (1207–1209)

Birth of Jalal-ud-din Rumi,
the Mevlana (1207–1273)

Mongol siege of Ningxia;
submission of Xiangzong

Accession of Iltutmish
(1210–1236) as sultan of Delhi

Genghis Khan campaigns
against the Jin Empire

Mongol army conquers the 16
prefectures of north China (1211–1214)

Muhammad Shah of Khwarazm defeats
Gurkhan Mozhu and takes Transoxiana

Kuchlug overthrows Mozhu
and rules the Kara-Khitans

Genghis Khan besieges
Zhongdu (future Beijing)

Jin emperor Xuanzong (1213–1224)
relocates his capital to Kaifeng

Mongol army captures
and sacks Zhongdu

Family of Rumi migrates
from Balkh to Baghdad

Mongol army under Jebe defeats
Kuchlug and ends Kara-Khitan khanate

Mongol conquest of Tarim Basin
and central Eurasian steppes

Muhammad Shan of Khwarazm
provokes war with Genghis Khan

Genghis Khan wages campaign against
Muhammad Shah (1219–1220)

Mongol conquest of Transoxiana;
flight of Muhammad Shah

Genghis Khan sacks Bukhara
and Samarkand

Death of Muhammad Shah in exile

Sübetei and Jebe command Mongol
western expedition (1220–1223)

Siege of Urgench: quarrel
between Jochi and Chagatai

Genghis Khan invades Khurasan;
Mongols sack Merv and Nishapur

Jalal al-Din rallies Khwarazmian
forces in India

Sübetei and Jebe ravage
Armenia and Georgia

Genghis Khan invades India and
defeats Jalal al-Din near Multan

Meeting of Genghis Khan and
Daoist sage Qiu Chuji

Genghis Khan orders Mongol rule
in Khurasan and Transoxiana

Sübetei and Jebe cross the Derbent Pass
and invade the Pontic-Caspian steppes

Genghis Khan withdraws to Mongolia

Sübetei and Jebe defeat the Russian-
Cuman army at the Battle of Kalka

Family of Rumi settles in
Karaman, Anatolia

Death of Jochi; Batu assigned the
Western *ulus* (future Golden Horde)

Death of Genghis Khan: regency
and succession crisis (1227–1229)

Partition of Mongol Empire among
Ögödei, Chagatai, and Batu

Family of Rumi settles in Konya
and establishes medrese

Ögödei (1229–1241) elected
as Great Khan by *kurultai*

Ögödei initiates the conquest of
the Jin Empire (1229–1235)

Rumi succeeds to family medrese
at Konya

Rumi reorganizes Maulawiyah
order (whirling deverishes)

Rumi hailed Mevlana

Beginning of the Islamization
of Anatolia

Ögödei and Song emperor
Ningzong (1194–1224) agree
to partition the Jin Empire

Mongols invade Sichaun (Szechwan)

Ögödei ends the Jin Empire

The *kurultai* approves the
conquest of the west by Batu

Batu subdues the Kipchak
Turks and secures the lower
Volga steppes as his base

Batu subdues the Volga Bulgars

Accession of Sultana Radiyya
Begum (1236–1240) at Delhi

Civil wars in the Delhi sultanate

Accession of Sultan Kaykubad
(1219–1236) of Konya

Height of the sultanate of Konya

Batu invades Russia and sacks
Ryazan and Moscow

Kay-Khusraw II (1237–1246) seizes
the throne of the sultan of Konya

Kay-Khusraw II seeks to subdue the
Turkmen tribes of eastern Anatolia

Batu captures and sacks
Vladimir-Suzdal

Batu defeats and slays
Yuri II of Vladimir-Suzdal
(1212–1238) at the Sit River

Mongol army devastates southern
Russia, sacking Rostov and Yaroslavl

Mongol army subdues the Cumans
and ravages the Crimea (1238–1239)

Turkish tribes rebel under Baba Ishak
(1239–1242) against Kay-Khusraw II

Turkish rebels appeal to Mongol
general Baiju in Iran

Batu captures and sacks Kiev;
Batu declares war against
King Bela IV of Hungary

Mongol army invades Tibet; sack of
Rwa-sgeng and submission of Tibetans

Batu campaigns against
Poland and Hungary

Battle of Chmielik: Mongols
defeat Duke Boleslav V of
Cracow (1243–1279)

Battle of Liegnitz: Mongols annihilate
the army of Duke Henry II of Silesia

Battle of Mohi: Batu defeats
King Bela IV of Hungary

Mongols ravage Hungary and Croatia
and withdraw to lower Volga

Mongols invade northern
India and sack Lahore

Death of Great Khan Ögödei and
regency of Töregene (1241–1246)

Baiju and the Mongol army in
Iran invade eastern Anatolia

Battle of Köse Dağ: Mongol general
Baiju defeats Sultan Kay-Khusraw II

Sultanate of Konya submits to
Mongol rule

Election of Güyük as Great
Khan (1246–1248)

Mission of papal envoy Giovanni
da Plan del Carpini (1246–1247)

Death of Great Khan Güyük:
succession crisis

Regency of Sorghaghtani Beki,
widow of Tolui (1248–1251)

1250–1300...................................... Möngke elected by *kurultai*
as Great Khan

Marco, Niccolo, and Matteo
Polo journey to court of Kublai
Khan (1251–1257)

Kublai Khan, as deputy of Möngke,
conquers the Dali kingdom

King Louis IX of France sends William
of Rubruck as envoy to Khan Möngke

Mongol conquest of Yunnan
and Annan (North Vietnam)

Hulagu and Mongol army invade Iran

Mongol capture and destruction of
Alamut, stronghold of the Assassins

Berke succeeds to the Western
ulus (Golden Horde)

Western Mongols embrace Islam

Möngke and Kublai Khan
invade Song China

Hulagu sacks Baghdad: end
of the Abbasid caliphate

Hulagu conquers the
al-Jazirah and the Levant

Submissions of Prince Bohemond VI of
Antioch and Armenian King Hethoum I

Death of Great Khan Möngke; Arigh
Böke elected Great Khan by *kurultai*

Mongol army in China acclaims
Kublai Khan Great Khan

Outbreak of civil war in the
Mongol Empire (1260–1263)

Kublai Khan appoints Drogön
Chögyal Phagpa "minister of Tibet"

Drogön Chögyal Phagpa commissioned
to create script for Mongolians

Hulagu sacks Aleppo and Damascus

Hulagu retires from Syria to Azerbaijan

Battle of Ain Jalut: Mamluk
sultan Qutuz defeats Mongol
army under Kitbuka

Baybars (1260–1277) murders Qutuz
and is proclaimed Mamluk sultan

Alliance of Khan Berke and
Sultan Baybars against Hulagu

Kublai Khan invests Hulagu with the
ilkhanate in Iran and Transoxiana

Battle of Shimultai: Kublai Khan
decisively defeats Arigh Böke

Surrender of Arigh Böke;
end of Mongol civil war

Kublai Khan reorders the
Mongol Empire (1263–1268)

Death of Hulagu: accession of
Ilkhan Abaqa (1265–1282)

Kublai Khan recognizes Barak
(1266–1271) as Chagataid Khan

War between Barak and Kaidu
over central Asia (1266–1267)

Kaidu, grandson of Ögödei, seizes
power in the Altai Mountains

Kaidu defies Kublai Khan and
Temür Khan (1266–1301)

Barak and Ilkhan Aqaba
(1265–1282) battle for Transoxiana

Kublai Khan invades Song China

Desultory fighting along the
Yangtze River (1268–1273)

Mongols besiege fortresses at
Xianyang and Fengcheng

Kublai Khan claims the
mandate of heaven and takes the
Chinese throne name Shizu

Establishment of the Yuan
Dynasty (1271–1368)

Mongols capture Fengcheng

Fall of Xianyang: collapse of
Song resistance (1273–1275)

First Mongol expedition against Japan

Surrender of Song court at the
capital of Linan (Hangzhou)

Battle of Yamen: defeat
of the Song army

Second Mongol expedition
against Japan

Appointment of Bolad Aqa as
ilkhanate fiscal minister (1285–1313)

Jalal-ad-Din Firuz Shah II (1290–1296)
overthrows the slave sultanate

Establishment of the Khalji
sultans of Delhi

Departure of Marco, Niccole, and
Matteo Polo to ilkhanate court

Mongol invasion of Java (1292–1293)

Death of Kublai Khan; Temür Khan
(1294–1307) succeeds as Great Khan

Temür Khan renounces Yuan
control over the Tarim basin

Ilkhan Mahmud Ghazan
(1205–1304) coverts to Islam

Marco, Niccole, and Matteo
Polo reach Venice

Accession of Ala-ad-Din
Muhammad Shah I (1296–1316)

Height of the Khalji sultanate of Delhi

Marco Polo, in prison, dictates
Livres des merveilles du monde

1300–1350.......................................Malik Kafir commands Khalji
raid into southern India

Accession of Ilkhan Abu
Sa'id (1317–1335)

Transformation of ilkhanate
into a Muslim state

Tughluq seizes power in Delhi;
Ghiyath-ad-Din Tughluq
Shah (1320–1325)

Establishment of the Tughluq
sultanate of Delhi (1320–1414)

Khan Tamashinin (1226–1334)
succeeds to Chagataid khanate

Khan Tamashinin embraces Islam

Death of Ilkhan Abu Sa'id (1317–
1335), last effective ilkhan of Iran

Fragmenting and collapse of the
ilkhanate of Iran (1335–1353)

Birth of Tamerlane (Timur)

Death of Khan Qazan (1343–1346),
last effective Chagataid khan

Division of Chagataid khanate

Tribal warfare on the central Eurasian
steppes and Transoxiana (1347–1370)

1350–1400..Division of the western Mongol *ulus*
into the White and Blue Hordes

Hongwu (1368–1396) captures
Dadu and expels Khan Toghan
Temür from China

End of Mongol rule (Yuan
Dynasty) in China

Emperor Hongwu establishes the
Ming Dynasty (1368–1644)

Tamerlane crowned Great
Emir at Samarkand

Tamerlane subjects Khwarazm

Tamerlane campaigns in Moghulistan
(Chagataid central Asia)

Civil war on the western Eurasian
Steppes (White and Blue Hordes)

Khan Urus expels Tokhtamish

Tokhtamish flees Saray and is
received by Tamerlane

Tokhatmish, with Tamerlane's
assistance, crowned khan
of the White Horde

Tokhatmish unites White and Blue
Hordes into the Golden Horde

Tamerlane sacks the city of
Urganch in Khwarazm

Battle of Kulikovo Field: Grand
Prince Dmitri Ivanovich (1359–1389)
annihilates a Mongol army

Tokhatmish is received as khan of the
western Mongol *ulus* (Golden Horde)

Tamerlane subjects Khurasan
and Afghanistan

Tokhatmish sacks Moscow and Ryazan:
Russian princes submit to Tokhatmish

Tamerlane launches campaign into
Seistan and Kandahar (1383–1386)

Tamerlane sacks Herat

Tokhatmish declares war against
Tamerlane and sacks Tabriz, Iran

Tamerlane initiates campaign to
conquer Iran (1386–1388)

Tokhatmish invades Khurasan, besieges
Herat, and promotes rebellion in Iran

Tamerlane expels Tokhatmish
and sacks Isfahan

Tamerlane crushes revolts in
Khurasan and Moghulistan

Tamerlane leads first campaign
against Tokhatmish

Tamerlane defeats Tokhatmish
at the Battle of Kunduzcha

Tamerlane wages his great
western campaign

Tamerlane overruns Iran and
receives the surrender of Baghdad

Mamluk sultan of Egypt Barkuk
provokes war with Tamerlane

Sultan Barkuk and Tokhatmish
conclude an alliance against Tamerlane

Tamerlane conquers
Armenia and Georgia

Tokhatmish raids into northwestern Iran

Battle of Terek: Tamerlane
decisively defeats Tokhatmish

Tamerlane sacks Saray and
ravages the Golden Horde

Tamerlane celebrates his
triumphs at Samarkand

Ottoman sultan Beyezid I defeats
Crusaders at the Battle of Nicopois

Tamerlane invades northern India

Battle of Delhi; Tamerlane
captures and sacks Delhi

Tamerlane returns to Samarkand
and initiates building program

Tamerlane leads second
western campaign

Ottoman sultan Beyezid besieges
Constantinople (1399–1402)

1400–1450.....................................Tamerlane invades eastern Asia
Minor and sacks Sivas

Tamerlane invades northern
Syria and sacks Aleppo

Tamerlane besieges and
sacks Damascus

Meeting of Tamerlane and
Arab historian Ibn Khaldun

Tamerlane invades Asia Minor

Battle of Angora: Tamerlane defeats
and captures Ottoman sultan Beyezid I

Tamerlane initiates new building
projects at Samarkand

Arrival of Ruy Gonzalez de Clavijo,
ambassador from Castile

Tamerlane declares wars on Ming
emperor Yongle (1402–1424) of China

Tamerlane dies at Otrar on
campaign against Ming China

Western expedition of Ma Huan
and the fleet of Ming China

1450–1500...................................... Ottoman sultan Mehmet II
captures Constantinople

Foundation of the Ottoman
Empire (the Porte)

Grand Prince Ivan III of
Moscow defeats Khan Ahmet
of the Golden Horde

Muscovite army occupies Saray,
capital of the Golden Horde

Ivan III ends the "Mongol yoke"

Birth of Zahir ud-din Muhammad
Bābur, future Mughal emperor

Bābur succeeds as khan of the
Turco-Mongol tribes of Ferghana

1500–1550...................................... Shah Ismail I (1501–1524) founds
the Safavid Shi'ite state in Iran

Muhammad Shaybani of the Uzbeks
defeats Bābur at Samarkand

Bābur secures and rules from Kabul
as a vassal of Shah Ismail I

Shah Ismail I defeats and
slays Muhammad Shaybani
at the Battle of Merv

Ottoman sultan Selim I defeats Shah
Ismail I at the Battle of Chaldarin

Ottoman army occupies Tabriz

Bābur declares war on the Lodi sultan
Ibrahim (1517–1526) of Delhi

First Battle of Panipat: Bābur defeats
Lodi army and occupies Delhi

Foundation of Mughal Empire

Battle of Khanwa: Bābur
defeats the Rajput army under
Rana Sanga (1509–1527)

Death of Bābur; accession of
Humayun (1530–1539; 1555–
1556), as Mughal emperor

Sher Khan defeats Humayun
at the Battle of Chausa

Sher Khan occupies Bengal and
is declared shah of Delhi

Humayun flees to Safavid court

1550–1600..Ivan IV, "the Terrible," conquers the
khanate of Kazan on the middle Volga

Humayun returns to India and
establishes the Mughal Empire

Death of Humayun and accession of
Akbar (1556–1605) as Mughal emperor

Ivan the Terrible conquers
the khanate of Astrakhan

Akbar imposes his authority over
Bengal and northern India

Akbar secures Kabul, and the Panthan
tribes to submit to Mughal rule

1600–1700...................................... Death of Akbar and accession
of Jahangir (1605–1627)
as Mughal emperor

Accession of Shah Jahan as
Mughal emperor (1628–1658)

Aurangzeb overthrows his father, Shan
Jahan, and is declared Mughal emperor

Reign of Aurangzeb (1658–1707);
height of Mughal Empire

Treaty of Nerchinsk; Tsar Peter the
Great (1682–1725) and the Qing
emperor Kangxi of China (1661–1721)
partition the Eurasian steppes

Glossary

Abbasid caliphate: The hereditary dynasty of caliphs (749–1258) established by as-Saffah (r. 750–754) and, from 762 on, resident at Baghdad. Hulagu ended the dynasty with the sack of Baghdad in 1258.

Achaemenid: The royal family of the great kings of Persia (559–329 B.C.).

Ahura Mazda: The supreme god of creation in Zoroastrianism.

airak: Mongolian fermented mare's milk; nomadic beverage of choice.

Alani: Sarmatians who settled on the steppes north of the Caucasus in the 1st century B.C. In A.D. 375, many Alani submitted to the Huns, while others, along with Goths, migrated west. The Alani entered the Roman Empire as allies of the Vandals in 406–407.

Altaic languages: A family of languages with common agglutinative grammar and syntax, vowel harmony, and vocabulary. The major branches are Turkic, Mongolian, and Tungusic; Korean and Japanese may also be branches of this language family.

Amber Road: Overland routes between the lands of the Baltic and the Mediterranean and Black seas since the Bronze Age (2200–1500 B.C.), over which amber and the products of the northern forests and Arctic lands were exported south. Pliny the Elder (23–79) first described the route in his *Natural History*.

An Lushan Rebellion: A rebellion (755–762) raised by the Tang general An Lushan against the emperor Xuanzong (712–756). The revolt, even though it failed, wrought great destruction throughout China and compelled the emperor to withdraw garrisons from the Tarim Basin.

Anatolian languages: The first language family to diverge from Proto-Indo-European (4000–3800 B.C.). Speakers of these languages who migrated into Asia Minor circa 2500–2300 B.C. were ancestors of those speaking Hittite, Luwian, and Palaic.

anda: Sworn brothers in Turkish and Mongolian society.

Arsacid: The royal family of the kings of Parthia (246 B.C.– 227 A.D.).

Aryavarta: The "Aryan homeland," which comprises the lands of the upper Indus and Ganges rivers that are home to the sacred cities of Hinduism.

Aryan: From Sanskrit *arya*, meaning "noble": (1) designation of related languages that has been replaced by Indo-European languages; (2) speakers of Sanskrit who entered India circa 1500–1000 B.C.

Ashina: The royal clan among the Gök Turks; descended from the brothers Bumin and Istami.

atman: In Hinduism, the imperishable soul, subject to reincarnation by the rule of *dharma* until enlightenment, when it achieves union with the universal soul (*brahman*).

Avars: Peoples who founded the first confederation of Turkish-speaking tribes on the eastern Eurasian steppe (330–551). In 551–552, Bumin of the Gök Turks overthrew the Avars, who then migrated west to establish a new khaganate on the Pannonian plains (580–796).

Avesta: The compilation of the sacred texts of Zoroastrianism. The Persian language of the texts, known as Avestan, shares close similarities to the Sanskrit of the Rigveda.

Bactria: Today, northern Afghanistan, this is a fertile region of the upper Oxus River. Its principal city, Bactra, was the nexus of routes of the Silk Road between central Asia and India.

Balghasun: Capital of the Uighur khaganate (744–840). The city was sacked by the rebel Kyrgyz tribes and abandoned in 840.

Bamiyan Buddhas: Two colossal statues (created in 507 and 554) carved out of rock in the Bamiyan valley, 140 miles northwest of Kabul. They were destroyed by the Taliban in March 2001.

bashlyk: The distinctive nomadic felt cap.

BMAC: Bactria-Margiana Archaeological Complex (2300–1700 B.C.); the culture centered on the lower Oxus valley that was likely the common homeland to the Indo-Iranian speakers.

brahman: The universal soul of Hinduism to which the enlightened *atman* will return upon *moksha*.

Brahmi: The oldest alphabetic script employed in India, based on Aramaic scripts of the Near East. The earliest inscriptions date from the reign of Ashoka (268–232 B.C).

Brahmin: In Hinduism, the first or priestly caste; see *varna*.

caliph: Ruler of the Muslim community. In 661, Muawiya established the first line of hereditary caliphs.

caravansary: Walled quarters, stables, and storage rooms constructed and maintained by the Turkish Muslim rulers for the benefit of caravans. The upkeep of the caravansary was paid by the profits of a foundation.

cataphracti: Heavily armored shock cavalry wearing chain mail or lamellar armor. This heavy cavalry, first attested among the Sarmatians, was adopted by the Romans during the reign of Hadrian (117–138).

Cathay: Medieval European name for China; it was derived from a misunderstanding of Khitan, Mongolian-speaking nomadic rulers of northern China who ruled as the Liao Dynasty (907–1125).

centum languages: Western language families that evolved out of Proto-Indo-European in 3000–2500 B.C. These language families shared common changes in sound and morphology. They include the language families of Celtic, Italic, Germanic, and Balkan Indo-European languages (the putative mother language for later Greek, Macedonian, Phrygian, Illyro-Thracian languages, and possibly, Armenian).

Chagatais: Descendants of Khan Chagatai (1226–1242), second son of Genghis Khan; they were rulers of the central Asian steppes and Transoxania.

chanyu: Meaning "son of endless sky," this was the title of the ruler of the Xiongnu reported by Han and Song Chinese sources. In the early 5th century, the title was abandoned, and steppe nomadic rulers henceforth styled themselves as khan.

Chihilgan: Meaning "The Forty," the Turkish military elite who dominated the Delhi sultanate in 1240–1290.

Chingisids: Descendants of Genghis Khan (1206–1227).

Cumans: Western Turkish-speaking nomads and scions of the Kipchak Turks, who migrated from the central Asian steppes into the Pontic-Caspian steppes in the 11th century.

cuneiform: The first writing system, devised by the Sumerians circa 3500–3100 B.C. The wedge-shaped writing was inscribed by a stylus on wet clay.

devsirme: The Ottoman levy of Christian youths who were converted to Islam and enrolled in the Ottoman sultan's corps of Janissaries.

dharma: In Hinduism, the moral law that dictates the cycle of reincarnation.

dhimmi: In Islam, members of protected religious communities of the book, who practiced their faith by payment of a special tax. They were originally Jews and Christians; later, Sabians (polytheists of Harran) and Zoroastrians were so protected.

digvijaya: The ceremonial royal progress made by an Indian maharaja atop an elephant.

Doab: The fertile lands between the Punjab and the upper Ganges and Yamuna rivers; Delhi and Agra are in the Doab.

Fatimid caliphate: Shi'ite caliphs (909–1171) who claimed descent from Fatimah, daughter of the prophet Muhammad and wife of Caliph Ali. In 969, the Fatimid caliphs ruled from Cairo and protected the holy cities of Medina and Mecca.

Finno-Ugric languages: A family of the Altaic languages, which includes Magyar (Hungarian), Estonian, Finnish, and the Samoyedic languages of Siberia.

Five Dynasties; Ten Kingdoms: Rival kingdoms (907–960) ruling in China between the Tang (618–907) and Song (960–1279) dynasties.

foederati: Barbarian military units commanded by their own leaders who fought as allies of the Roman Empire in the later 4th and 5th centuries.

Gansu Corridor: The narrow zone between the Eurasian steppe and the Tibetan highlands that connects China with the Tarim Basin.

ger: Portable home on wheels made of felt stretched over a lattice frame. See **yurt**.

ghazi: The epitome of the heroic nomadic warrior, prized by Turks.

Ghaznavid: A dynasty of Turkish slave emirs (963–1186), who ruled from Ghazna (Afghanistan) over Transoxania and Iran and raided northern India.

ghulam, ghilman (pl.): Arabic word for slave soldiers, usually of Turkish origin. See **Mamluk**.

Ghurid sultans: Leaders (1148–1210) of Iranian origin, who used Turkish Mamluks and tribal regiments to establish the first Muslim sultanate in northern India. They clashed with the rival Khwarezm shahs for control of Transoxania and Iran.

Ghuzz Turks: Speakers of western Turkish or Oghuz languages who emerged on the central Asian steppes between the 9th and 11th centuries. They included Seljuk Turks, Cumans, and Kipchak Turks.

Gog and Magog: Figures (or nations) in the Bible and the Qur'an, whose arrival marked the great wars leading to the final days of the Apocalypse. Since the 5th century, Christian and, later, Muslim writers identified them with the nomadic invaders of the Eurasian steppes.

Gök Turks: The "Celestial Turks" who overthrew the Avar khanate in 551–552. Khan Bumin established the senior Gök Turk khaganate (551–744). His brother Istami (551–575) established the western Turkish khaganate (553–659) on the central and western Eurasian steppe. In 681, after ending Tang Chinese overlordship, the western khaganate was reconstituted as the Confederation of the Ten Arrows.

Golden Horde: The western part of the Mongol Empire (1240–1502), established by Khan Batu; see also **Jochids**.

Gupta Empire: The second great empire of India (320–550), founded by Chandra Gupta I (319–335). The Gupta emperors patronized Sanskrit letters and Hinduism and ended Kushan rule in northern India.

Han Dynasty: Rulers of imperial China as the Former or Western Han (206 B.C.–9 A.D.) and then as the restored Later or Eastern Han (25–220). The usurper Wang Mang, who overthrew the Former Han Dynasty, failed to establish his own Xin Dynasty (9–25).

Hephthalites: The "White Huns" were Tocharian-speaking nomads, driven from the eastern Eurasian steppe by the northern Wei emperors of China and Avar khagans. They founded an empire (408–670) encompassing the western Tarim Basin, Transoxania, and northern India.

Hexi Corridor: See **Gansu Corridor**.

Hinayana Buddhism: The "Lesser Wheel," which includes Buddhist ascetics who rejected the doctrines of Mahayana Buddhism and adhered more closely to the teachings of Siddhartha Gautama (563–483 B.C.).

Huns: Altaic-speaking nomads who conquered the Pontic-Caspian steppes circa 375 and, under Attila, forged a barbarian empire from the Rhine to the Volga that challenged the Roman Empire. The Huns were probably descendants of subject or allied tribes of the northern Xiongnu.

ilkhan: Meaning "loyal khan," the title granted by Kublai Khan to his brother Hulagu in 1260. It was carried by his descendants, the Ilkhanids (1265–1353), who ruled over Iran, Iraq, and Transoxania.

Indo-Scythians: See **Sacae**.

iqta: A military tenure granted to Muslim soldiers by the sultans of Delhi.

Jade Gate: The name for the strategic Yumen Pass on the Silk Road that connected the Tarim Basin to China.

Jazyges: Sarmatians who settled as allies of Rome on the eastern Pannonian grasslands west of Dacia in the mid-1st century.

jihad: In Islam, "holy war."

Jin Dynasty: See **Jurchens**.

jinshi: The highest level of mandarin officials in the Song examination system (960–1279).

Jochids: Descendants of Jochi (1181–1227), the first son of Genghis Khan. Jochi's son Batu founded the western part of the Mongol Empire, or Golden Horde.

Jurchens: Tungusic-speaking peoples of Manchuria who overthrew their overlords and ruled northern China under the Chinese dynastic name Jin, or

"Golden" (1115–1234). The Jurchen emperors exercised a loose hegemony over the Mongol tribes.

Karakhanid: A Turkish confederation on the central Asian steppes that ruled Transoxania from Kashgar and Samarkand (840–1212). They converted to Islam in 934.

Kara-Khitans: Sinicized Khitans (1123–1218) who migrated to the central Asian steppes and, thus, escaped the rule of the Jurchens. In 1141, the Kara-Khitans defeated the Karakhanids near Samarkand—a victory that gave rise to the legend of Prester John. Also called the western Liao; see also **Khitans**.

Karakorum: Located on the Orkhon River, the political capital of the Mongol Empire in 1225–1260.

karma: In Hinduism and Buddhism, the individual merit acquired by an individual through meritorious deeds.

kashuik: The bodyguard of 10,000 of the Great Khan of the Mongols.

khagan: Meaning "khan of khans," a Turkish term denoting a great royal figure ruling over many subordinate khans.

Khalji sultanate: The second Persian-speaking dynasty of Turkish sultans in northern India (1290–1320).

khan: Turko-Mongolian royal title, meaning "king."

Kharoshti: Northern Indian alphabet, based on the Aramaic alphabet of the Near East, used to write Sanskrit and vernaculars of Sanskrit.

khatun: Mongolian queen, meaning "lady."

Khazars: Members of the Ashina clan and western Turkish khaganate, who established their own khaganate (c. 670–967) over the Pontic-Caspian steppes. The Khazar court converted to Judaism in the late 8th century. Circa

965–967, the Khazar capital was sacked by Prince Svyatoslav of Kiev and the Pechenegs.

Khitans: Mongol-speaking conquerors who ruled northern China under the Chinese dynastic name of Liao (907–1125). They were overthrown by their vassals, the Jurchens.

Khwarezm: Fertile delta lands of the lower Oxus River, flowing into the Aral Sea; the land has been home to important caravan cities since the 5th century B.C.

Khwarezmian shahs: Persian-speaking Sunni Muslim rulers appointed as governors of Khwarezm by the Seljuk sultans (1077–1231). After 1156, the Khwarezmian shahs clashed with the Ghurids over domination of former Ghaznavid lands in Iran and Transoxania.

Kipchak Turks: Ghuzz or western Turkish-speaking nomads who dominated the central Asian steppes in the 11th through 13th centuries. They submitted to Mongol Khan Batu in 1238–1241 and constituted the majority of tribes of the Golden Horde.

Kshatriya: In Hinduism, the caste of warriors.

kurgan: A stone-and-earth tumulus raised as monumental grave on the Pontic-Caspian steppes and central Asian steppes from the Bronze Age to the 13th century A.D. The kurgans of Scythians, between the 6th and 4th centuries B.C., have yielded the richest burial goods.

kurultai: The national council of Mongols summoned to elect the khan or to declare war or conclude a peace.

Kushans: Tocharian speakers who forged an empire embracing the central Asian steppes, Transoxania, and northern India (30–230). They promoted Buddhism and trade along the Silk Road. See also **Yuezhi**.

lamellar armor: Armor of overlapping plates sewed together and often worn as a second layer of protection over chain mail armor.

Liao Dynasty: See **Khitans**.

limes: Meaning "path," the word originally designated a Roman military highway. The term came to designate the political and cultural boundary between imperial Rome and the foreign peoples.

magister militum: "Master of the soldiers," the supreme commander of field armies in the Roman Empire. From the reign of Constantine I (306–337), commanders of the cavalry and infantry commanded regional field armies. After 395, their supreme commander was designated *magister militum*, one for the western and one for the eastern Roman Empire.

Magyars: Finno-Ugric nomads who migrated from the Siberian forests east of the Urals to the Pontic-Caspian steppes in the 9th century. In 896, they settled on the Pannonian grasslands in 896; they are the ancestors of the Hungarians.

Mahayana Buddhism: The "Greater Wheel" was the school of Buddhism that emerged in India in the 1st century B.C., stressing the divine status of the Buddha. The schools of Mahayana Buddhism today are in East Asia (Tibet, Mongolia, China, Korea, and Japan).

Mamluk: From the Arabic for "servant": (1) Turkish slave soldier in the Islamic world; (2) dynasty of Turkish slave soldiers that ruled Egypt (1250–1517); (3) dynasty of Turkish slave soldiers that ruled the Delhi sultanate (1206–1290).

Manichaeism: The dualist, monotheistic faith proclaimed by the prophet Mani in Sassanid Mesopotamia. The faith was popular among Sogdian merchants of the Silk Road; the khagan of the Uighurs converted to Manichaeism in 763.

Mauryan Empire: The first empire of India (322–185 B.C.), established by Chandra Gupta (320–298 B.C.). The emperor Ashoka (268–232 B.C.) converted to Buddhism.

Mawarannahr: "Land beyond the river," the Arabic name for Transoxania.

maya: In Hinduism, the illusion of the physical world.

Meluhha: The Sumerian name for the earliest urban civilization of India, known as the Indus Valley civilization (2600–1700 B.C.).

Ming Dynasty: Founded by Emperor Hongwu (1368–1398), who expelled the Mongols, the Ming Dynasty (1368–1644) was the last native dynasty of imperial China.

Mitanni: Indo-Aryan speakers who migrated from Transoxania into northern Mesopotamia in the 16th century B.C., where they established a kingdom over Hurrian- and Amorite-speaking populations. Their language is closely related to Sanskrit and Avestan Iranian.

moksha: The liberation of an enlightened Hindu who is freed from the cycle of rebirths, according to *dharma*.

Mughal Empire: The last Muslim empire (1526–1857) in India; established by Bābur (1526–1530), a descendant of both Genghis Khan and Tamerlane.

muqti: A military governor of the Delhi sultanate who held a military tenure in lieu of a salary.

Nestorian Christianity: The Christian church that followed the teachings of Patriarch Nestorius of Constantinople (429–431), who taught that Mary gave birth only to the man Jesus rather than man and God. The Nestorians, condemned at the Third Ecumenical Council (431), spread their faith across the Silk Road, converting Turkish and Mongol tribes.

northern Wei Dynasty: Sinicized nomadic rulers (386–535) of northern China and the Gansu Corridor. They promoted Buddhism along the Silk Road. They were Turkish-speaking Tuoba, the royal clan of the Xianbei tribes.

oracle bones: Inscribed divination bones of the Shang Dynasty (1600–1046); they are the first examples of Chinese writing.

ordu: Turko-Mongolian army or military encampment.

Orkhon inscriptions: The earliest memorial inscriptions in Turkish (722); written in a distinct runic alphabet.

Parthians: An Iranian-speaking tribe melded into a kingdom, and then a Near East empire of the Arsacid kings (246 B.C.–227 A.D.).

Pechenegs: Turkish-speaking tribes whose confederation dominated the Pontic-Caspian steppes west of the Don River from circa 860 to 1091.

Prakrit: The vernacular language of India that evolved out of Sanskrit after 600 B.C. Buddhist texts were written or translated into Prakrit.

Proto-Indo-European (PIE): The reconstructed mother language of the Indo-European languages, circa 6000–5000 B.C.

Qin Dynasty: The dynasty (221–206 B.C.) founded by Shihuangdi (257–210 B.C.), when he unified China in 221 B.C.

Qing Dynasty: The last imperial dynasty of China, founded by the Manchu conquerors (1644–1911).

Qutb Minar: Built by Sultan Aybak of Delhi in 1198, it is the largest minaret in India.

Quwat ul Islam: Meaning "Might of Islam," the mosque outside of Delhi built from plundered architectural elements of Hindu and Jain temples. It was ordered by Sultan Aybak in 1193.

Rabatak: The site in Afghanistan where a Kushan royal inscription in the Bactrian language was discovered in 1993. The Kushan emperor Kanishka I (127–147) gives his genealogy and names the tutelary gods of the empire.

Rajputs: "Sons of the king"; the Kshatriya or warrior caste who dominated western India between the 9th and 12th centuries. They were later accommodated by the Mughal emperors.

rammed earth: A construction technique using earth, gravel, lime, and clay. The Qin and Han emperors employed this method to build the Great Wall. The construction is simple but labor intensive.

Rashidun caliphs: The first four elected caliphs from among the immediate associates of Muhammad: Abu Bakr (632–634), Umar (634–644), Uthman (644–656), and Ali (656–661).

Rashtrakuta: Prakrit-speaking kings who united most of southern and central India (753–982); they favored Hinduism.

Rigveda: The earliest religious texts of Hinduism. The hymns, written in Sanskrit, have been dated as early as 1500 B.C. and as late as 600 B.C.

Roxolani: Sarmatians who settled on the grasslands between the Carpathian Mountains and the Black Sea in the 1st century.

Sacae: An eastern branch of the Scythians dwelling on the central Asian steppes. In 145–135 B.C., they migrated across Sogdiana and Bactria into the Helmand Valley, then via the Bolan Pass into India in the early 1st century B.C., where they were known as the Indo-Scythians.

Safavids: The dynasty of the Shi'ite shahs of Iran (1501–1732), rivals to the Ottoman sultans.

Samanid: The family of Iranian emirs (819–1005) who ruled from Bukhara, eastern Iran, and Transoxania as the representatives of the Abbasid caliphate. They defined the visual arts and letters of eastern Islam.

sangha: The community of Buddhist believers (laity and ascetics) established by Siddhartha Gautama (563–483 B.C.).

Sanskrit: The sacred literary language of Hinduism.

Sarmatians: Iranian-speaking nomads who succeeded the Scythians on the Pontic-Caspian steppes between the 3rd century B.C. and the 3rd century A.D. The tribes included the Alani, Roxolani, and Jazyges.

Sassanid: The dynasty of Zoroastrian shahs of the neo-Persian Empire (227–651).

satem languages: The eastern branch of language families that evolved out of Proto-Indo-European circa 3000–2500 B.C. The language families share sound changes and morphology. These include the Balto-Slavic and Indo-Iranian language families.

satrapy: A province of the Persian Empire (550–329 B.C.) ruled by a satrap; Darius I (521–486 B.C.) organized the empire into 20 satrapies.

Scythians: The general name applied by classical Greeks to the Iranian-speaking nomads on the Eurasian steppe.

Seljuk Turks: Ghuzz or western Turks who founded the Seljuk sultanate (1055–1194) that revived the power of Abbasid caliphate. Seljuk Turks settled in Asia Minor after the Battle of Manzikert (1071).

Shah-nameh: "*Book of Kings*"; the Middle Persian national epic composed by Abu al-Qasem Mansur (c. 940–1020).

shaman: A mystic prized for insights gained by contact with the spiritual world through trances often induced by hallucinogens, notably hashish.

Shang Dynasty: The first historical dynasty of China (c. 1600–1046 B.C.), centered in the lower and middle Huang He (Yellow River).

Sharia: Muslim religious law based on the Koran.

Shi'ite: The sectarian school of Islam that desired a descendant of Ali (656–661) as the rightful caliph and, thus, upheld the authority of Ali.

Shudra: In Hinduism, the caste of laborers or peasants; see ***varna***.

Silk Road: The network of caravan routes across central Asia that linked China with Europe and the Mediterranean world. The German explorer Ferdinand von Richthofen coined the term in 1877.

Sogdiana: Lands of northern Transoxania and the Fergana Valley; the Sogdians spoke an eastern Iranian language that was long the commercial language of the Silk Road.

Song Dynasty: The Song Dynasty (960–1279) reunited most of China as the successors of the Tang emperors, promoted Confucian traditions, and perfected the bureaucratic state. The Khitans and, later, the Jurchens denied the Song the recovery of northern China.

spolia: Architectural elements or sculpture of older buildings recycled into new buildings.

Strategikon: Byzantine military manual, attributed to the emperor Maurice, with sound recommendations for countering nomadic cavalry.

Sufi: Muslim mystic who follows the Sunni tradition.

Sui Dynasty: The dynasty (581–618) that reunited China and founded the third great imperial order; immediately succeeded by the Tang Dynasty.

Sunni: "The orthodox"; Muslims who accepted the Umayyad caliphate of Muawiya (661–680). The majority of Muslims follow Sunni Islam and the authority of the Qur'an.

suren: The hereditary commander of the Drangiana and Arachosia (today, western Afghanistan and Pakistan). The suren had the right to crown the Arsacid king of Parthia.

sutra: A Buddhist sacred text of aphorisms.

taiga: Forest zones of Siberia.

Tang Dynasty: Founded by Emperor Gaozu, the Tang Dynasty (618–907) represented the greatest imperial family of classical China.

tantric: The higher moral and mystical interpretation of traditional village rites in either Hinduism or Buddhism.

Tarim Basin: An area that encompasses the valleys of the tributaries of the Tarim River between the Tien Shan and the Tibetan highlands. The central zone comprises the Taklamakan Desert, and the eastern end is dominated by the salt depression of the Lop Nur. Today known as Xinjiang or eastern Turkestan, the region was been home to caravan cities on the Silk Road.

Ten Arrows: See **Gök Turks**.

Tengri: The sky god and progenitor of humankind in Turkish and Mongol polytheism.

Three Kingdoms: The period of political division (220–280) in China after the fall of the eastern Han Dynasty.

Tien Shan: "Celestial Mountains" that define the northern boundary of the Tarim Basin (today Xinjiang).

Timurids: Descendants of Tamerlane (1370–1405), who ruled Iran and Transoxania (1405–1506).

Tocharian: The name given to two, possibly three, related Indo-European languages spoken in the Tarim Basin and used to translate Buddhist texts between the 6th and 9th centuries. The ancestors of the Tocharians migrated from the original Indo-European homeland on the Pontic-Caspian steppes to the Altai Mountains and then the Tarim Basin in circa 3700–3500 B.C.

Toluids: Descendants of Tolui (1227–1229), the fourth son of Genghis Khan.

Transoxania: Lands between the Oxus and Jaxartes rivers; in antiquity, known as Bactria and Sogdiana.

Tughluq sultans: Members of the third dynasty of Turkish Muslim rulers in India (1320–1414).

tumen: Mongol military unit of 10,000 soldiers.

tundra: Arctic zones of Siberia.

Tungusic languages: A branch of the Altaic language family, today spoken in Manchuria and eastern Siberia.

türbe: Memorial tomb to a Muslim ruler or mentor.

Uighurs: Turkish-speaking nomads who founded the third Turkish confederation on the eastern Eurasian steppe (744–840). They converted to Manichaeism in 763.

ulema: The religious community of Muslim scholars who interpret Sharia.

ulus: The Turko-Mongolian nation, designating related tribes.

Umayyad caliphate: The first hereditary line of caliphs (661–750), established by Muawiya (661–680) and ruling from Damascus.

ummah: In Islam, the community of believers as proclaimed by the prophet Muhammad (575–634).

Upper Satrapies: The Greek designation of the satrapies of Bactria and Sogdiana (Transoxania) in the Achaemenid Empire of Persia (550–329 B.C.).

Vaishya: In Hinduism, the caste of merchants.

varna: From the Sanskrit for "outward appearance," any one of the original four castes of Indo-Aryan society described in the Rigveda: Brahmins (priests), Kshatriyas (warriors), Vaishyas (merchants), and Shudras (laborers). Only the first three castes were considered twice born; the Shudras represented the subjected populations.

vihara: Meaning "secluded place," the community of Buddhist ascetics.

Vikrama era: The era of reckoning from the year 57 B.C.; widely used by Buddhists in India and Nepal. The year 1 of the era was the accession date of Azes I (57–35 B.C.), king of the Sacae.

Warring States: Kingdoms in the period of political disunity in China following the collapse of effective rule by the Zhou Dynasty (481–221 B.C.).

western regions: Also called Xiyu, the designation by the Han and Tang emperors of their provinces in the Tarim Basin.

White Huns: See **Hephthalites**.

Xi Xia: Sinicized Tanguts who had settled in Gansu and western China in the 10th century as nominal vassals of the Song emperors. With Jingzong (1038–1048), Xi Xia monarchs ruled as Chinese-style emperors who favored Buddhism (1038–1227).

Xia Dynasty: The legendary first dynasty of China (c. 2100–1600 B.C.).

Xinjiang: Eastern Turkestan; see **Tarim Basin**.

Xiongnu: Altaic-speaking nomads who forged the first nomadic confederacy on the eastern Eurasian steppe. In 56–53 B.C., the Xiongnu divided into the southern and northern Xiongnu.

yabgu: The subordinate of a khan or khagan; among the Khazars, the leading commander of the army.

Yassa: Customary Mongol law codified by Genghis Khan; it exalted the authority of the khan over all other legal and religious authorities.

Yuan Dynasty: The Chinese dynasty adopted by Kublai Khan (1260–1294) and his successors who ruled China and Mongolia (1279–1368).

Yuezhi: The Chinese name for Tocharian-speaking nomads who dwelled on the central Asian steppes north of the Tarim Basin. In 155 B.C., the Xiongnu drove the Yuezhi west into Ferghana, where Zhang Qian visited them in 128 B.C. These Tocharian speakers, called Da Yuezhi ("Great Yuezhi") were the ancestors of the Kushans.

yurt: The residence and social bonds of the kinship group of a *ger*. See *ger*.

Zhou Dynasty: The second imperial dynasty of China (1045–256 B.C.), ruling in the early Iron Age. After 481 B.C., Zhou emperors lost control over their vassals, and China lapsed into the period of Warring States.

Zoroastrianism: The monotheistic religion of the Iranians, based on the teachings of Zoroaster, born circa 628 B.C. The Sassanid shahs favored Zoroastrianism as reformed in the 3rd century.

Biographical Notes

Abaoji (b. 872; r. 907–926): Emperor of Liao Dynasty; assumed the Chinese throne name Taizu. He was of the Yila tribe within the confederation of Khitans. In 904, he seized supreme power over the Khitans. In 907, he assumed the name and role of a Chinese emperor, conquering the 16 prefectures in northeastern China and the eastern Eurasian steppe. He established his Sinicized court at Shangjing.

Abd al-Malik (b. 646; r. 685–705): Umayyad caliph who imposed Arabic as the language of administration and forged the first Muslim administrative institutions. He appointed able governors who conquered Carthage in 698 and raided into Transoxania.

Abu Bakr (b. c. 573; r. 632–634): Caliph and friend and associate of Muhammad who succeeded as the first of the Rashidun caliphs after the prophet's death. His reign saw the unification of Arabia under the banner of Islam.

Aetius (d. 454): A *magister militum* (425–454) from a military family in Moesia. By his influence with King Rugila and, later, Attila, Aetius secured Hun *foederati* so that he dominated policy at the court of the western emperor Valentinian III. His policy of alliance with the Huns was ruined by the invasions of Attila in 451–452. In 454, Aetius was executed on grounds of treason.

Ahmad ibn Arabshah (1389–1450): Arabic historian; a native of Damascus who wrote a critical biography of Tamerlane in 1435. He visited the Timurid court at Samarkand, and he consulted Turkish and Persian sources and spoke to eyewitnesses. In his account, Tamerlane is depicted as a savage prince, deformed and spiteful, whose base birth was the reason he committed atrocities.

Akbar (b. 1542; r. 1556–1605): Third Mughal emperor; the son of Humayun. He fiscally and administratively organized the Mughal Empire, laying the foundations of the future British raj. A mystic, he sponsored his own syncretist solar cult of the ruler, Din-i Ilahi ("divine faith"). His personal beliefs and toleration of subjects of all faiths alienated the Sunni *ulema*, and his son and successor, Jahangir (1605–1627), returned to Sunni Islam.

Ala-ad-Din Muhammad Shah I (1296–1316): Khalji sultan of Delhi; greatly extended his sway over the Deccan. Malik Kafur, a Hindu convert to Islam and general, conducted audacious and destructive campaigns into the southern Deccan and Tamil Nadu in 1310–1311. Khalji raids ultimately led to the consolidation of the powerful Hindu kingdom of Vijayanagara (1336–1565) at Hampi.

Ala al-Din Muhammad (r. 1200–1220): Shah of Khwarezm; conquered Iran from the Seljuk Turks in 1205. By 1217, he had secured Transoxania, assumed the title shah, and extended his unwanted protection over the Abbasid caliph al-Nasir. In 1218, he provoked a war with Genghis Khan, who overran the Khwarezmian Empire in 1219–1220. Muhammad Shah died a fugitive on an island in the Caspian Sea near Abaskun.

al-Amin (b. 787; r. 809–813): Abbasid caliph; the unpopular son of Harun al-Rashid. He faced rebellions in Syria and Iraq. In 812–813, the Persian general Tahir ibn al-Husayn besieged Baghdad in the name of al-Mamun (813–833), half-brother of al-Amin. In 813, al-Amin was captured while escaping Baghdad and executed.

Alaric (395–410): King of the Visigoths; served under Theodosius I. Alaric, denied high command by the imperial government, led the Visigoths into Greece in 395–397 and then to Italy in 400–402. Flavius Stilicho checked Alaric until 408. In 410, Alaric sacked Rome in a bid to pressure the emperor Honorius for a command, but he died soon after.

Alexander III, the Great (b. 356 B.C., r. 336–323 B.C.): King of Macedon; son of Philip II (359–336 B.C.) and the Epirote princess Olympias (375–316 B.C.); arguably the greatest commander in history. In 334–329 B.C., he conquered the Achaemenid Empire and defeated the Great King Darius III of Persia (336–329 B.C.). He subdued Bactria and Sogdiana (Transoxania) in 329–327 B.C. and the Indus Valley in 327–325 B.C. Alexander defeated the nomadic Sacae, secured the Upper Satrapies (Bactria and Sogdiana), and established a frontier on the upper Jaxartes. His Greco-Macedonian military colonies in the Upper Satrapies were the basis for the Greco-Bactrian kingdom (c. 250–125 B.C.).

Alexius I Comnenus (b. 1056; r. 1081–1118): Byzantine emperor; seized power in the civil war of 1081 and founded the Comnenian Dynasty (1081–1185). He restored imperial power in western Asia Minor by summoning the First Crusade (1095–1099). He allied with the Cumans to destroy the Pechenegs, who had invaded Thrace, at the Battle of Levounion in 1091.

Al-Hajjaj (b. 661; r. 694–715): Umayyad governor of Khurasan; directed the Muslim conquests of Seistan, Baluchistan, and the Sind.

Ali ibn Abi Talib (b. c. 600; r. 656–661): Fourth of the Rashidun caliphs. Cousin of the prophet Muhammad, Ali married the prophet's only daughter, Fatimah (606–632). Ali was twice passed over for the caliphate. As caliph in 656, he faced opposition from Muawiya in the first Muslim civil war. Ali was slain by sectarian extremists, and in later Shi'ite theology, he was elevated to prophetic status almost on par with Muhammad.

al-Mamun (b. 786; 813–833): Abbasid caliph; son of Harun al-Rashid. In 813, he defeated his half-brother al-Amin and gained the throne. But he surrendered control over Khurasan and the northeastern frontier to Tahir ibn al-Husayn.

al-Mansur (754–775): Second Abbasid caliph; dedicated Baghdad as the new capital in 762 and shifted the locus of Islamic civilization to Iran and Transoxania.

Almish Yiltawar (c. 900–940): Khagan of the Volga Bulgars. Converted to Islam to obtain Abbasid support so that he could renounce his allegiance to the Khazars. In 921–922, he was visited by Ahmad ibn Fadlan, envoy of the Abbasid caliph al-Muqtadir (908–932).

al-Mutasim (833–842): Abbasid caliph. Waged prestige campaigns against the Byzantine Empire. He reformed the army, recruiting a bodyguard of 10,000 Turkish slave soldiers, as well as allied and mercenary Turkish tribal regiments of horse archers.

al-Mustasim Billah (b. 1213; r. 1242–1258): Last Abbasid caliph. Sought to restore the power and authority of the Abbasid state. He blundered into a war against the Mongols. He was slain and his capital, Baghdad, was sacked by the khan Hulagu in February 1258.

Alp-Arslan (b. 1029; r. 1063–1072): Seljuk sultan and nephew of Tughril Beg. Defeated and captured the Byzantine emperor Romanus IV at the Battle of Manzikert. Alp-Arslan opened Asia Minor to settlement by Turkish tribes.

Alp Tigin (961–975): Turkish Mamluk; ruled Ghazna (today Afghanistan) as a vassal of the Samanid emir Mansur I (961–976). He promoted Sunni Islam and raided the Punjab, sacking Hindu temples and Buddhist monasteries. He was succeeded by Ishaq (975–977), and then his son-in-law Sebüktigin (977–997).

al-Tabari (839–923): Persian historian and Qur'anic scholar; was a native of Tabaristan. Tabari wrote in Arabic a universal Muslim history that is the principal source for the Umayyad and early Abbasid caliphates.

Ammianus Marcellinus (c. 325–391): A historian of imperial Rome, a native of Antioch, and a staff officer. He wrote a history of the Roman world from the reign of Trajan (98–117) to Valens (364–378). He provides invaluable information on the Goths, Alani, and Huns, as well as Roman relations with the Sassanid Empire.

An Lushan (c. 703–757): Chinese general of Sogdian-Turkish ancestry. Raised a rebellion against the Tang emperor Xuanzong (712–756). Upon occupying Luoyang, he declared himself the first emperor of the Yan Dynasty. He was murdered by his ministers in January 757, and the rebellion collapsed in 763.

An Shigao (d. 168): Styled a Parthian prince; arrived at the Han court in 148 and translated into Chinese a number of works of the Sarvastivada school of Buddhism. He set the traditions of Chinese Buddhist monasteries.

Antiochus III, the Great (b. c. 241 B.C.; r. 223–187 B.C.): Seleucid king. Restored the power of his empire. In 309–203 B.C., he conducted an eastern expedition and received the homage of the Parthian prince Arsaces II and the Greco-Bactrian king Euthydemus. At the Battle of Panium in 200 B.C., he defeated the Ptolemaic army, conquering Phoenicia, Coele-Syria, and Judaea. He was decisively defeated by the Roman consul Lucius Cornelius Scipio Asiaticus at Magnesia in 190 B.C. Thereafter, the Seleucid Empire fragmented.

Antiochus VII Sidetes (b. c. 158 B.C.; r. 138–129 B.C.): Seleucid king; was crowned after the capture of his brother Demetrius II (146–139 B.C.) by the Parthian king Mithradates I. In 130 B.C., Antiochus recovered Mesopotamia, Babylonia, and Media from the Parthians, but Phraates II decisively defeated and slew Antiochus VII in 129 B.C. and ended the revival of Seleucid power in the Near East.

Antony, Mark (Marcus Antonius) (83–30 B.C.): Roman senator and commander; a member of the Second Triumvirate, along with Octavian and M. Aemilius Lepidus in 43–30 B.C. He was awarded the eastern half of the Roman Empire in 42 B.C., but he steadily broke with his colleague Octavian and allied with Ptolemaic queen Cleopatra VII (51–30 B.C.). In 39 and 37–36 B.C., he waged two unsuccessful Parthian wars. In 31 B.C., he was defeated at the Battle of Actium and subsequently committed suicide.

Arcadius (b. 377; r. 395–408): Elder son of Theodosius I. He was proclaimed Augustus in 383 and, in 395, succeeded to the eastern half of the Roman Empire. He proved a weak-willed emperor, dominated by his ministers, who averted the crisis posed by Alaric and the Visigoths.

Ardashir I (227–240): Shah of Persia; overthrew Parthian rule and founded the Sassanid Neo-Persian Empire. He initiated the first of a series of wars by the Sassanid shahs to conquer the eastern provinces of the Roman Empire.

Arigh Böke (b. 1219; r. 1259–1264): Mongol khan; the fourth and youngest son of Tolui. He was entrusted with the Mongolian homeland by Great Khan Möngke. In 1259, upon the death of Möngke, Arigh Böke was declared Great Khan, but the Mongol army in China acclaimed Kublai Khan. Arigh Böke was defeated in the ensuing civil war in 1260–1254 and forced to abdicate.

Arrian (Lucius Flavius Arrianus) (86–160): Native of Nicomedia (Izmit); a Roman senator and historian who composed a history of Alexander the Great. He also wrote a treatise of his battle line against the Alani in 135, when he was governor of Galatia-Cappadocia.

Arsaces I (246–211 B.C.): Prince of the Iranian-speaking tribe Parni and founder of the Arsacid Dynasty in northeastern Iran. His descendants ruled as the kings of Parthia.

Arsaces II (211–191 B.C.): King of Parthia and a vassal of the Seleucid kings. In 190 B.C., he asserted his independence after the Romans decisively defeated the Seleucid king Antiochus III (223–187 B.C.) at the Battle of Magnesia.

Artabanus II (128–124 B.C.): King of Parthia; the uncle and successor of Phraates II. He was defeated and slain by the Tocharians, ancestors of the Kushans, when they invaded Margiana.

Artabanus V (216–227): King of Parthia; faced an invasion by the Roman emperors Caracalla and Macrinus in 214–218. He was defeated and slain by the Sassanid shah Ardashir I at the Battle of Hormozgan.

Ashoka (b. 304 B.C.; r. 268–232 B.C.): The greatest Mauryan emperor. He ruled most of the Indian subcontinent and published the earliest surviving royal edicts in India that were erected as monumental inscriptions. By 263 B.C., he converted to Buddhism; he promoted the faith throughout India and encouraged Buddhist missionaries on the Silk Road.

as-Saffah (b. 721; r. 749–754): Abbasid caliph; governor of Khurasan who overthrew the Umayyad caliphate in 749–750. He founded the Abbasid caliphate, a Muslim, as opposed to Arabic, state based on the lands of eastern Islam.

Attila (b. c. 410; r. 434–452): Regarded as the second greatest conqueror of the steppes. He and his brother Bleda succeeded their uncle Rugila as joint kings of the Huns. Circa 445, Bleda was murdered by Attila. In 442–443 and 447, Attila launched devastating raids into the Balkans, earning the sobriquet "Scourge of God." In 451, he invaded Gaul and suffered at Châlons a strategic defeat from a Roman-Gothic army under Aetius. In 452, he invaded northern Italy but withdrew due to the intercession of Pope Leo I. Attila died in 452 from overindulgence at his wedding celebrations. The Hun Empire collapsed within two years after his death.

Augustus (Gaius Julius Caesar Octavianus) (b. 63 B.C., r. 27 B.C.– 14 A.D.): Roman emperor; the nephew and adopted son of Julius Caesar (101–44 B.C.). Augustus ended nearly 60 years of civil war and, in 27 B.C., founded the principate.

Aurangzeb (b. 1618; r. 1658–1707): Son of Shah Jahan (1628–1658) and grandson of Akbar. Hailed Alamgir ("world conqueror"), he united nearly all of India under Mughal rule. A zealous Muslim, he alienated his Muslim subjects, and his campaigns in the Deccan exhausted the imperial treasury.

Azes I (c. 58–38 B.C.): Indo-Scythian king, conquered the Indus valley, and was remembered by Buddhists, who took his year of accession as the first year for reckoning by the Vikrama era.

Bābur (Zahir al-Din Muhammad) (b. 1483; r. 1526–1530): First Mughal emperor of India; a descendant of Genghis Khan and Tamerlane. A Timurid prince of Ferghana, he lost his realm in the wars between the Uzbeks and Safavid Iran. In 1504, he seized Kabul and acknowledged the Safavid shah Ismail I as his overlord. In 1526, he invaded India and defeated Ibrahim Lodi, sultan of Delhi, at the Battles of Panipat on April 26, 1526; he then occupied Delhi and founded the Mughal Empire. He composed an engaging autobiography, *Baburnama*, in literary Turkish.

Baiju (d. 1260): Mongol general; appointed by Töregene to the command of Mongol forces in Iran in 1242. He decisively defeated the Seljuk sultan Kay-Khusraw at the Battle of Köse Dag on June 26, 1243. In 1246, Khan Güyük recalled the popular Baiju, but he was restored to his command by Khan Möngke in 1251–1255.

Ban Chao (30–102): Han general who completed the subjection and organization of the western regions in 75–91 and ended the power of the northern Xiongnu.

Baraq, Ghiyas-ud-Din (1266–1271): Mongol khan recognized by Kublai Khan as ruler of the Chagatai khanate in central Asia. He converted to Islam and assumed the Muslim name Ghiyas-ud-Din. He was opposed by rival Khan Kaidu, grandson of Ögödei. In 1267, they concluded a truce so that Kaidu could move against Kublai Khan. In turn, Baraq warred with little success against Ilkhan Abaka (1265–1282) for control of Transoxania.

Batu (b. 1207; r. 1227–1255): Mongol khan; the son of Jochi (the eldest son of Genghis Khan). In 1227, he succeeded to the western *ulus* (the future Golden Horde). He conquered the Cumans in 1235–1236. In 1237–1240, he subdued the Russian principalities. He won a brilliant victory over King Bela IV of Hungary at the Battle of the Mohi on April 11, 1241. The news of the Mongol victory panicked Western Christendom, but in 1242, Batu withdrew to the grasslands of the Volga when he received news of the death of Khan Ögödei. Thereafter, Batu ruled in splendid isolation, professing loyalty to Güyük and Möngke.

Bayan (c. 560–602): Khagan of the Avars; settled his nation on the Pannonian grasslands (eastern Hungary) after defeating the Gepidae in 562. His allies, the Lombards, thereupon invaded Italy, while Bayan raided the Byzantine provinces of Thrace and Moesia in the Balkans.

Bayan (1236–1295): Mongol general; the leading field commander of Kublai Khan in the conquest of Song China. He received the final surrender of the dowager empress Xie Daoqing and the boy emperor Gong (1275–1276) at the Song capital of Linan (Hangzhou).

Bayanchur Khan (747–759): Second Uighur khagan; extended the power of the Uighur khaganate, exploiting Chinese weakness due to the An Lushan

Rebellion (755–763), and welcomed Sogdian merchants from the Tarim Basin to the Uighur capital.

Baybars (1260–1277): Mamluk sultan of Egypt; architect of the victory over the Mongols at Ain Jalut in 1260. Soon afterwards, he seized power in Cairo and reoccupied the Levant. He also claimed to have removed the Abbasid heir from the ruined city of Baghdad to Cairo; thus, he was hailed as the champion of Islam against the Mongols and Crusaders.

Bela IV (b. 1206; r. 1235–1270): King of Hungary; a conscientious ruler who extended royal justice and restored his kingdom after the Mongol invasion. He was, however, decisively defeated by Khan Batu at the Battle of the Mohi on April 11, 1241.

Berke (b. c. 1208; r. 1257–1266): Mongol khan; the son of Jochi and brother of Batu. He succeeded to the western *ulus* of the Mongol Empire (then known as the White and Blue Hordes). He had converted to Islam; thus, he aligned with Mamluk Egypt against his cousin, the ilkhan Hulagu (1256–1265).

Bilge (b. c. 683; r. 717–734): The fourth Ashina khagan of the Gök Turks (or eastern Turks) since the end of the Tang overlordship in 681. The protégé of his *yabgu* and father-in-law Tonyukuk, Bilge restored the power of the Gök Turks on the eastern Eurasian steppe. His deeds are celebrated on the memorial inscriptions in the Old Turkic language in the Orkhon Valley (today Mongolia).

Bleda (434–445): King of the Huns and elder son of Octar. He ruled jointly and clashed repeatedly with his brother Attila, who ordered Bleda's murder.

Bögü Khan (759–780): Uighur khagan; promoted trade and settlements within the Uighur khanate. In 762, he converted to Manichaeism.

Bolad (d. 1313): Mongol chancellor and cultural advisor; served Kublai Khan in 1260–1285. He established a directorate to gather and analyze geographic information and maps. In 1285, he arrived as the Great Khan's envoy and entered into the service of the ilkhans Arghun (1282–1291),

Gaykhatu (1291–1295), and Mahmud Ghazan (1295–1304) as a fiscal expert. He introduced Chinese-style paper money.

Boris I (r. 858–899): Tsar of Bulgaria; converted to Orthodox Christianity in the 860s and, thus, assured the conversion of the southern Slavs. He presided over the conversion of the Bulgar khanate into a Christian Slavic kingdom.

Börte (1161–1230): Principal wife of Genghis Khan. She was affianced to marry him to link their clans, but around 1180, she was abducted by the Merkits; eight months later, she was rescued by Genghis Khan and married. It was widely believed that her first son, Jochi, was the son of Börte's captor, Chilger Bökh. She bore Genghis Khan three sons: Chagatai, Ögödei, and Tolui. Both Genghis Khan and Ögödei valued her for her shrewd judgment.

Buddha: see **Siddhartha Gautama**.

Bumin (546–553): Khagan of the Gök Turks and a member of the Ashina clan. He ruled as vassal king to the Avars over the Turks dwelling in the Altai Mountains. In 552–553, he overthrew his Avar overlord Anagui and established the Gök Turk khaganate on the eastern Eurasian steppe.

Caracalla (b. 188; r. 198–217): Roman emperor; son of the emperor Septimius Severus (193–211). He ruled as co-emperor with his father and, later, his brother Geta (209–212). In 212, he murdered Geta and was remembered as a savage emperor. He waged successful campaigns in Germania, but he was murdered while on campaign against the Parthians (214–217).

Carpini, Giovanni Da Pian Del (1182–1252): Franciscan friar; the envoy of Pope Innocent IV (1243–1254) to the Mongol court in 1246–1247. His party traversed the steppes from Kiev to Karakorum in 106 days. Carpini witnessed the *kurultai* that elected Güyük (1246–1248), and he records important details about the court a generation after the death of Genghis Khan.

Chagatai (b. 1183; r. 1227–1242): Mongol khan; the second son of Genghis Khan and Börte and founder of the Chagatai khanate. In 1227, he was assigned the ulus in central Asia, originally comprising the central Eurasian steppes, Tarim Basin, and Transoxania. He was notorious for his violent temper, but he ruled justly and was praised for his adherence to Mongol traditions. He resented his brother Ögödei, but he supported Töregene as regent in 1241–1242.

Chao Cuo (c. 200–154 B.C.): Han minister and legalist writer; composed a memorandum to Emperor Wen (180–157 B.C.) in which he presented the strategy for battling the Xiongnu. The emperor Wudi (141–87 B.C.) based his strategy on the recommendations of Chao Cuo.

Charlemagne (Charles the Great) (b. c. 747; r. 768–814): King of the Franks; forged the Carolingian Empire. He was crowned Roman emperor in 800, thereby founding the Holy Roman Empire. He built the first effective state in western Europe since the collapse of Roman power. In 791–796, he destroyed the Avar khaganate.

Comnena, Anna (1083–1153): Byzantine historian and daughter of Alexius I; wrote the *Alexiad*, a primary source on the Pechenegs and Cumans of the Pontic-Caspian steppes.

Constantine I, the Great (b. 272; r. 306–337): First Christian Roman emperor; founded New Rome, or Constantinople, in 330 and reorganized the Roman state as an autocracy known as the Dominate. In 323–324, he imposed treaty obligations on the Goths and Sarmatians on the Pontic-Caspian steppes that lasted down to the arrival of the Huns in 375.

Corbulo, Gnaeus Domitius (6–67): Roman senator and consul; a distinguished general under the emperors Claudius (41–54) and Nero (54–68). He commanded the eastern legions in the War of Armenian Succession (54–66), but his success and fame gained him the enmity of Nero, who ordered his loyal commander to commit suicide in 67.

Crassus, Marcus Licinius (115–53 B.C.): Roman senator and consul in 70 and 55 B.C.; a leading commander of the republic and a member of the First Triumvirate. He was defeated and slain by the Parthians at the Battle of Carrhae in 53 B.C.

Cyril (827–869) and **Methodius** (826–885): Fraternal monks, born at Thessalonica. They are hailed "Apostles to the Slavs," converting Moravians, Serbians, and Bulgarians. Cyril devised the Cyrillic alphabet and translated the Bible into Slavic.

Cyrus the Great (b. c. 590 B.C., r. 559–530 B.C.): Achaemenid king; founded the Persian Empire, conquering Lydia in 546 B.C. and Babylonia in 539 B.C. He was hailed in classical sources as the greatest conqueror before Alexander the Great. He was killed in a frontier war against the Massagetai, a Scythian tribe, north of the Jaxartes River.

Darius I (b. c. 550 B.C.; r. 521–486 B.C.): Achaemenid king of Persia; succeeded to the throne during the Great Revolt of 522–521 B.C. He organized the satrapies of the Persian Empire and built the capital of Persepolis. In 515 or 512 B.C., he waged unsuccessful war against the Scythians on the Pontic-Caspian steppes.

Demetrius II Nicator (b. c. 160 B.C.; r. 147–141 B.C., 129–125 B.C.): Seleucid king and son of Demetrius I Soter (161–150 B.C.). This dashing monarch was defeated and captured by the Parthian king Mithradates I in 141 B.C. Demetrius lived in gilded captivity at the Arsacid court and married the sister of Phraates II. In 129 B.C., King Phraates II, at war with Demetrius's brother Antiochus VII, released Demetrius to raise a rebellion in Syria. Demetrius regained his throne but failed to restore Seleucid power.

Diodotus I (250–230 B.C.): Greco-Bactrian king who declared his independence from his Seleucid overlord Antiochus II (261–246 B.C.).

Drogön Chögyal Phags-pa (1235–1280): Fifth leader of the Sakya school of Buddhism in Tibet and the spiritual mentor to Kublai Khan. In 1268, at the behest of Kublai Khan, he devised the Phags-pa script, an adaptation of the Tibetan script, so that all official documents could be published in Mongolian.

Duzong (b. 1240; r. 1264–1274): Song emperor; faced rebellions and a fiscal crisis and, thus, was ill prepared to face the renewed Mongol conquest by Kublai Khan in 1268. In March 1273, the fall of Xianyang, the last strategic fortress on the Yangtze River, signaled the doom of the Song Dynasty, and Duzong died as the Mongol army advanced against his capital in August 1274.

Ermanaric (d. 376): King of the Goths; committed suicide upon the defeat of his people by the Huns. He was remembered in the Norse legend of the Volsungs as the tyrant Jörmunrek.

Eucratides (c. 175–145 B.C.): Greco-Bactrian king; overthrew the royal family of Euthydemus and issued an extensive coinage used along the Silk Road. He lost Herat and other western provinces to the Parthian king Mithradates I.

Eudoxus of Cyzicus (fl. c. 130–90 B.C.): Greek navigator for King Ptolemy VIII (126–116 B.C.); credited with the discovery of the use of the monsoon season to sail the Indian Ocean.

Euthydemus (230–185 B.C.): Greco-Bactrian king who submitted to Seleucid king Antiochus III (223–187 B.C.). His reign witnessed the height of prosperity of the Greek cities of Bactria.

Fadlan, Ahmad ibn (fl. 10th c.): Persian geographer and envoy to the Bulgars in 921–922 who wrote a detailed account of his encounters with the Khazars, Bulgars, and Rus on the Volga River.

Faxian (337–422): Chinese Buddhist monk who visited India in 399–412 and penned an account of his travels.

Ferdowsi (Abu al-Qasem Mansur) (940–1020): Persian poet; wrote the epic *Shah-nameh* (*"Books of Kings"*) in 977–1010. This national epic celebrated Persian historical traditions before the advent of Islam and set the standard of expression in literary Middle Persian.

Galla Placidia (c. 388–450): The daughter of Theodosius I; married to King Ataulphus of the Visigoths in 410–414. In 417, she married the Roman general Constantius III, who was briefly emperor in 421. She acted as the regent for her son, the western emperor Valentinian III.

Gan Ying (fl. 1st c. A.D.): Han envoy; sent by Ban Chao on a mission to contact imperial Rome in 97. He visited Sogdiana, Bactria, Gandhara, and Parthi, and likely reached the shores of the Persian Gulf. He wrote the only Chinese account about the Roman world and gained important new information on the lands of the Near East and Transoxania.

Gao Xianzhi (d. 756): Tang commander of the Four Garrisons (Tarim Basin) and an experienced general of Korean ancestry. He commanded the Tang army that was defeated by the Arabs and Karluks at the Battle of Talas in 751.

Gaozong (b. 628; r. 649–683): Tang emperor of China; ruled in the Confucian tradition. He faced serious rebellions, and in 679–681, the Gök Turks regained their independence. After he suffered a series of strokes, his principal wife and empress took charge of policy and, later, succeeded as regent empress (690–705).

Gaozu (b. 247 B.C.; r. 206–195 B.C.): First Han emperor of China. Overthrew the Qin Dynasty. Born Liu Bang and of humble origin, he preferred negotiation to war with Modu Chanyu after he suffered an embarrassing defeat at Mount Baideng in 200 B.C. Gaozu instituted the tribute system whereby nomadic tribes could be turned into allies dependent on Chinese silk and goods.

Gaozu (b. 566; r. 618–626): Tang emperor of China. One of the greatest soldier-emperors of Chinese history. Under the Sui emperors, Gaozu, or Li Yuan, ruled strategic borderlands in Shanxi. In 618, he seized power. He waged war against the Gök Turks of the eastern khaganate.

Gautama, Siddhartha (563–483 B.C.): The Buddha, a prince of the Kshatriya Shakya clan, was the sage who founded Buddhism. Around 534 B.C., he assumed an ascetic life to achieve understanding of human suffering. In the deer park at Sarnath, he achieved enlightenment and went on to teach the noble truths of the Middle Way, the fundamental tenets of Buddhism.

Genghis Khan (b. 1162 or 1167; r. 1206–1227): Born Temujin, he was the son of Yesugei (d. c. 1171). He was the greatest conqueror of the steppes and founder of the Mongol Empire. In 1180–1204, he defeated his rival,

Jamukha, and united the Mongol tribes. In 1206, the *kurultai* acclaimed Genghis Khan "Universal Lord." In 1209–1210, he compelled the Emperor Xiangzong (1206–1211) of Xi Xia to submit. In 1211–1216, he wrested northern China from the Jin (Jurchen) Empire. In lightning campaigns, he overthrew the empire of Khwarezm in 1218–1223 and, thus, opened the lands of eastern Islam to Mongol conquest. He died while planning his final campaign against the Jin Empire. His generalship and organizational genius place him among the great captains of warfare. By his principal wife, Börte, he had four sons: Jochi, Chagatai, Ögödei, and Tolui.

Ghazan (b. 1271; r. 1295–1304): Ilkhan of Iran; assumed the name Mahmud upon his conversion to Islam. Although he tolerated Buddhism and shamanism, he promoted the high Persian culture of Islam and initiated the first major building program of Muslim monuments at Tabriz.

Guangwu (b. 5 B.C.; r. 25–57 A.D.): Han emperor; restored the Han Dynasty and moved the capital to Luoyang. He pursued a defensive policy against the nomadic tribes, but he reimposed Chinese rule over what is now Korea and Vietnam.

Gunchen (161–126 B.C.): *Chanyu* of the Xiongnu; long abided by treaty arrangements with Han China. Raiding by the Xiongnu and Han retaliatory measures led to the outbreak of war in 133 B.C.

Güyük (b. 1206; r. 1246–1248): Mongol khan; the son of Ögödei and Töregene. The strong-willed Töregene assumed a regency in 1241–1246, until she could arrange for the acclamation of Güyük as Great Khan by the *kurultai*. Güyük, a suspicious ruler and an alcoholic, discredited the house of Ögödei in the eyes of many Mongols. He died while en route to settle scores with his cousin Batu.

Harshavardhana (b. c. 590; r. 606–647): Ruled the Indo-Gangetic Plain from Kannauj. A convert to Buddhism, Harshavardhana maintained the aesthetics and arts of the Gupta Empire. The Chinese pilgrim Xuanzang wrote a description of his court.

Harun al-Rashid (b. 763; r. 786–809): Abbasid caliph; celebrated for his patronage of letters and arts. He proved a foe of Byzantium, and he concluded a treaty with Charlemagne guaranteeing the safety of Christian pilgrims to the Holy Land. With his death, the caliphate experienced civil war and fragmentation.

Heraclius (b. c. 576; r. 610–641): Byzantine emperor and exarch of Carthage; overthrew the usurper Phocas (r. 602–610). Heraclius rescued the eastern Roman Empire from near collapse and transformed it into the Byzantine state. He defeated Shah Khosrow II in 626–628 and recovered the eastern provinces. He nearly succeeded in reconciling the monophysites and Chalcedonians. Incapacitated by illness, the aging Heraclius failed to prevent the loss of Syria and Egypt to the Arab armies in 636–641.

Heraios (c. 1–30): Ruler of the Tocharians and ancestor to the Kushan kings; he is known from his coins, on which he is styled "tyrant."

Herodotus (c. 490–425 B.C.): Known as the father of history. A native of Halicarnassus, he traveled the Persian Empire and the lands around the Black Sea. He wrote his *History* to explain the wars between the Greeks and Persians. He gives a detailed account of the nomadic Scythians on the Pontic-Caspian steppes in the fourth book of the *History*.

Hongwu (b. 1328; r. 1368–1398): Ming emperor of China and the peasant rebel leader and Buddhist monk Zhu Yuanzhang. In 1353–1367, he secured the Yangtze valley and, in 1328, occupied Dadu. He expelled the Mongol emperor Togon-temür (1333–1368) and was hailed emperor of the Ming Dynasty (1368–1644). He razed the Mongol palace and replaced Dadu with the new Chinese city of Beijing.

Honoria (417–454): Daughter of Galla Placidia and Constantius III; created Augusta in 425. Honoria, who despised her brother, the western emperor Valentinian III, precipitated the invasion of Attila in 451.

Honorius, Flavius (b. 384; r. 395–421): Second son of Theodosius I; was created Augustus in 393 and succeeded as western emperor in 395. Real power was in the hands of Stilicho down to 408. Honorius, at his capital at Ravenna from 402 on, witnessed the loss of northwestern and Spanish provinces.

Hulagu (b. 1218; r. 1256–1265): Mongol ilkhan; the son of Tolui and founder of the ilkhanate. In 1256–1260, he waged a war of conquest of the Islamic world, destroying Alamut, the seat of the Assassins, and sacking Baghdad in 1258. He halted his campaign against Mamluk Egypt and withdrew to support his brother Kublai Khan in his civil war against Arigh Böke. Kublai Khan bestowed on Hulagu the rank of *ilkhan*, "loyal khan"—the title held by his successors.

Humayun (b. 1508; r. 1530–1539, 1555–1556): Mughal emperor of India; succeeded his father, Bābur. In 1539, he was expelled from India by Sher Khan, who had rallied the former Lodi mercenary bands of Afghans that had retired to the Bengal after 1527. With Safavid assistance, Humayun reconquered northern India in 1555–1556.

Huo Qubing (c. 140–117 B.C.): Han general; nephew of the general Wei Qing. He distinguished himself as a tactician against the Xiongnu. In 119 B.C., he and his uncle Wei Qing captured Mobei, the encampment of Ichise Chanyu. A favorite of Emperor Wudi, Huo Qubing died prematurely from plague and was honored with a spectacular burial.

Huvishka (147–180): Kushan emperor, succeeded Kanishka I. He consolidated Kushan rule in India and patronized Buddhism and the leading Hindu cults. His coinage reveals that he venerated all the gods of his empire.

Ibn Khaldun (1332–1406): Arab historian; born in Tunis of an Arab family from Andalusia. He wrote the influential *Muqaddimah*, a treatise on the rise and fall of Islamic governments. At the siege of Damascus in 1401, he reportedly met with Tamerlane and conversed on statecraft and proper government.

Ichise (126–114 B.C.): *Chanyu* of the Xiongnu; suffered successive defeats at the hands of Han armies. In 121 B.C., he was driven out of the Gansu Corridor, and he suffered a humiliating defeat and the loss of his capital Modei in 119 B.C. Repeated defeats undermined his authority, and he was assassinated by a disaffected general.

Igor Svyatoslavich, "the Brave" (b. 1151; r. 1180–1202): Prince of Novgorod-Seversky. Led an abortive expedition against the Cumans. He is celebrated in the earliest Russian epic poem.

Illig Khagan (r. 620–630): Ruled over the eastern Turkish khaganate. His raids into northern China precipitated war with the Tang emperor Taizong. In 626–630, the Tang general Li Jing defeated and captured Illig, thereby ending the eastern Turkish khaganate and imposing Chinese overlordship in 630–681.

Ilterish Khagan (682–694): Khagan of the eastern Turks. Ended Chinese rule in 681 and in 682 reestablished the eastern Turkish khaganate.

Iltutmish (r. 1210–1236): Sultan of Delhi; succeeded his father-in-law, Aybak, and reestablished the capital at Delhi. He organized a system of land grants to his emirs and soldiers, but he also co-opted loyal Hindu princes into the military hierarchy.

Ishbara Khagan (650–658): Khagan of the western Turks. Was defeated by a Tang army under Su Dingfang in 657. Henceforth, the western Turks acknowledged as their overlord the Tang emperor Gaozong (649–683).

Isidore of Charax (fl. 1st c. B.C.): Wrote *Parthian Stations*, an itinerary of the Silk Road across the Parthian Empire.

Ismail I (b. 1487; 1501–1524): First Safavid shah of Iran. Founded the Shi'ite state in Iran and revived Iran as one of the great Islamic powers. He fought for Transoxania against Muhammad Shaybani (1500–1510), who had united the Turkish tribes of the central Eurasian steppe as the Uzbek confederation. On December 2, 1510, Shah Ismail decisively defeated and slew Muhammad Shaybani at the Battle of Merv. But Shah Ismail had to confront the Ottoman threat from the west. He was defeated by the Ottoman sultan Selim I (1512–1520) on August 23, 1514.

Istami (553–575): *Yabgu* of the western Gök Turks; brother of Khagan Bumin, who commissioned Istami to pursue the Avars, who had fled west. Istami established western Turks on the central Eurasian steppe. In 557–561, in alliance with Shah Khosrow I, he occupied Transoxania and ended the Hephthalite Empire.

Ivan I Danilovich (b. 1288; r. 1325–1340): Grand prince of Moscow; a loyal vassal of the khan of the Golden Horde (1312–1341). In 1328, the khan rewarded Ivan I with Vladimir and the right to collect from the other Russian princes the tribute due to the Mongols. Ivan, nicknamed Kalita ("Moneybags"), exploited his position to turn Moscow into the premier Russian principality.

Ivan III Vasilyevich (b. 1440; r. 1462–1505): Grand prince of Moscow; renounced his allegiance to the Golden Horde. In 1480, he won a strategic victory over Khan Ahmed (1465–1481) on the Ural River. Vasilyevich secured Saray, capital of the Golden Horde.

Ivan IV (b. 1530; r. 1547–1584): Ivan the Terrible, tsar of Russia. Reformed the Russian army and conquered the khanates of Kazan (1152) and Astrakhan (1556). He ended the Mongol threat, securing the lower Volga valley and, thus, enabling Russian expansion across Siberia.

Jalal al-Din Mingburnu (1220–1231): Khwarezm shah; the son and successor of Muhammad Shah. In 1221, he was forced to retreat across the Hindu Kush into India. In 1224, he returned from exile, but he failed to regain his kingdom.

Jalal al-Din Rumi (1206–1273): Persian mystic and poet; known as Rumi. He was born in Balkh, the son of the Baha al-Din Walad, a celebrated jurist and theologian. His family relocated to Konya in 1228, where Rumi succeeded his father as head of the madrasah in 1232. In 1244, he adopted an ascetic life and founded the Mevlevi mystical order of Sufism. The members of this order, the dervishes, converted the Christians of Anatolia in the 13th and 14th centuries.

Jalal-ud-Din Firuz (1290–1296): Khalji sultan of Delhi; ended the rule of the slave sultans and founded the second Muslim dynasty in India, the Khilji. His talented nephew and successor, Ala-ud-Din Khilji, repelled Mongol attacks and campaigned in the Deccan.

Jamal al-Din (fl. c. 1250–1300): Persian astronomer and native of Bukhara. Entered the service of Kublai Khan circa 1255. In 1285, he presented to Kublai Khan a massive geographical compendium and introduced sophisticated instruments for measuring the earth. He played a pivotal role in the transfer to China of the science of the Islamic world.

Jamukha (c. 1165–1206): Mongol prince; the sworn brother and then rival of Temujin, Genghis Khan. In 1197–1202, he fought against Temujin and Wang Khan and, in 1203, in alliance with Wang Khan, defeated Temujin at the Battle of Baljuna. Temujin, however, later rallied and defeated Jamukha.

Jayapala Shahi (964–1001): Rajput ruler over the Punjab and Kabul Valley. Devoted to Shiva. He was decisively defeated by Sebüktigin at the Battle of the Neelum River in Kashmir in 986. The victory gained Kabul and Peshawar, the future bases for Muslim expansion into India.

Jebe (d. 1225): Mongol general; born as Zurgadai but received his nickname Jebe ("Arrow") when he boldly confessed that he had accidentally wounded Genghis Khan in battle in 1201. He was a trusted field commander and, thus, he shared with Subutai command of the western expedition in 1221–1223.

Jiu Zhuji (1148–1227): Daoist Chinese monk. Was invited to converse with Genghis Khan on matters of immortality and just rule. Jiu Zhuji departed his home in Shandong in 1220 and journeyed west, meeting Genghis Khan at the Mongol camp at the base of the Hindu Kush in May 1222. Even if embroidered, the exchange captures the religious outlook of Genghis Khan.

Jizhu Chanyu (178–154 B.C.): Ruler of the Xiongnu, whose attacks drove the Yuezhi (Tocharian speakers) westward to Ferghana.

Jochi (1181–1227): Mongol prince; the first son of Genghis Khan and Börte, but he was suspected to be the son of the Merkit warrior Chilger Bökh, who had held Börte captive for eight months. Genghis Khan accepted Jochi as his son. Jochi, while personally brave, was perceived as lacking the qualities of a khan. He also had quarreled with his brother Chagatai during the Khwarezmian campaign in 1220. Hence, Genghis Khan decided to assign to

Jochi the western *ulus*. Because Jochi predeceased his father, Jochi's domain (the future Golden Horde) was assigned to his son Batu.

Julian the Apostate (b. 331; r. 360–363): Roman emperor and Neo-Platonic philosopher; nephew of Constantine I. Julian restored the worship of the pagan gods. He waged an unsuccessful campaign against Persia in 363. He failed to capture the Persian capital Ctesiphon, and he was slain in a skirmish in upper Mesopotamia during the retreat of his army.

Justin II (b. c. 520; r. 565–578): Byzantine emperor; nephew and heir of Justinian I. He precipitated a Persian war in 572 and, from 574, because of mental illness, was under the regency of his wife, Sophia (niece of Theodora), and Tiberius II.

Justinian I (b. 482; r. 527–565): Known as Justinian the Great; the greatest emperor since Constantine. He promoted the most talented at his court without regard to birth. He restored imperial rule in Italy and Africa, sought religious reconciliation, and sponsored arts and letters. His most enduring achievements are the Hagia Sophia and the *Corpus Juris Civilis*.

Justinian II (b. c. 669; r. 705–711): The last Heraclian emperor and an unbalanced tyrant. He was overthrown, mutilated (by slitting his nose), and exiled to Cherson. He escaped to the Khazar court and returned with a Khazar army to regain his throne. He was deposed in 711. His foreign policy led to defeats at the hands of the Arabs and exposed Constantinople to a second Arabic siege.

Juvayni (1226–1283): Persian historian and native of Khurasan, served both Khwarezmian shah Jalal al-Din (1220–1231) and the Mongol khans Ögödei (1229–1241) and Hulagu (1256–1625). He wrote his *History of the World Conqueror* based on contemporary sources. He witnessed the sack of Baghdad, and he twice visited the court at Karakorum.

Kaidu (b. 1230; r. 1260–1301): Mongol khan; a grandson of Ögödei with aspirations to the throne of the Great Khan. In the civil war of 1259–1264, he dominated the central Eurasian steppe and clashed with the Chagatai khan Baraq for control of Transoxania. In 1267, he concluded a truce with Baraq and turned against Kublai Khan and his successor, Temür Khan (1294–1307). Based in the Altai Mountains, he waged local rebellion down to his death in 1301.

Kanishka (127–140): Fourth Kushan emperor; revered as convert to Buddhism, although he was more likely a patron who promoted favorable conditions for the spread of Buddhism into central Asia and Han China. He is credited, anachronistically, by a later Buddhist tradition with summoning a Fourth Buddhist Council in 78.

Kartir (fl. 3rd c.): Zoroastrian priest who reformed the monotheistic faith; he was patronized by shahs Ardashir I (227–240) and Shapur I (240–272).

Kay-Khusraw I (1204–1210): Seljuk sultan of Konya (Rūm). United the Turkish tribes in central and eastern Anatolia. He turned Konya into a Muslim capital. He promoted the caravan trade and minted the first Muslim silver coinage in Asia Minor.

Kay-Khusraw II (1237–1246): Seljuk sultan of Konya (Rūm). He failed to maintain control over the Turkish tribes and, thus, faced repeated rebellions. He refused to render homage to the Mongol khan Ögödei (1228–1241). Bayju, the Mongol commander in Iran, invaded Asia Minor and decisively defeated Kay-Khusraw at the Battle of Köse Dag on June 26, 1243. Thereafter, the sultans of Konya, as Mongol vassals, lost control over the emirs and Turkish tribes of Asia Minor.

Khalid ibn Barmak (705–782): Abbasid vizier; first appointed by as-Saffah (750–754). He was descended from the Barmakid family of Balkh, which had converted from Buddhism to Islam circa 670. He patronized scientists, mathematicians, and physicians and promoted the study of Buddhism among Muslim scholars.

Khosrow I (531–579): Sassanid shah; waged two wars against Justinian, emperor of the eastern Roman (Byzantine) Empire, in 530–532 and 550–545. He sought prestige, plunder, or subsidies of gold under treaty from Justinian rather than conquest. In 557–561, he allied with Istami, *yabgu* khagan of the western Turks, to defeat the Hephthalites.

Khosrow II (591–628): Last great Sassanid shah. He gained his throne with the support of the Byzantine emperor Maurice. In 602–628, he waged a war of conquest of the eastern provinces of the Byzantine Empire. In alliance with the Avars, he besieged Constantinople in 626. In 622–628, the emperor Heraclius, along with Turkish nomadic allies, launched offensives in Armenia, Iran, and Mesopotamia that led to the defeat and overthrow of Khosrow II. Heraclius recovered his lost eastern provinces, so weakening the Sassanid state that it fell to Arab armies in 636–651.

Kitbuqa (d. 1260): Mongol general; the leading field commander of Hulagu in 1256–1259. He was defeated and slain by the Mamluk army at the Battle of Ain Jalut on September 3, 1260.

Kokchu (d. 1206): Shaman and advisor to Genghis Khan; credited with great influence over the khan. He was executed on grounds of treachery based on information supplied by Börte, principal wife of Genghis Khan.

Krum (r. c. 803–814): Khan of the Bulgars; defeated the Byzantine emperors Nicephorus I and Michael I. He negotiated the first treaty with Byzantium that delineated the Bulgar state.

Kublai Khan (b. 1215; r. 1260–1294): Mongol khan; the second son of Tolui. Kublai Khan distinguished himself in campaigns against the Jin Empire in 1234–1235 and against Song China in 1257–1259. He was proclaimed khan by the Mongol army in 1260 and defeated his rival brother, Arigh Böke, in the civil war of 1260–1264. In 1268–1279, he completed the conquest of Song China. In 1274 and 1281, he launched two costly, abortive expeditions against Japan. In 1271, he assumed the Chinese temple name Shizu, the first of a new Yuan Dynasty (1271–1368). He founded a new capital, Dadu (Beijing), which Marco Polo called Kanbalu (Xanadu). Kublai Khan ruled through imperial servants of various nationalities rather than the Confucian bureaucratic classes. A convert to Buddhism, he assured the eventual triumph of Buddhism among the Mongol tribes.

Kuchlug (d. 1218; r. 1211–1218): Prince of the Naimans. Refused to submit to Genghis Khan in 1204 and took service with the Kara-Khitan *gurkhan* Mozhu (1178–1211). In 1211, he seized power at Balasagun, deposed the king, and intrigued with Muhammad Shah of Khwarezm against Genghis Khan. A zealous convert to Buddhism, Kuchlug persecuted his Muslim subjects. In 1218, he was overthrown and died an exile when the Mongol army under Jebe invaded the Kara-Khitan Empire.

Kujula Kadphises (30–80): Kushan emperor; crossed the Hindu Kush and conquered Taxila and Punjab. He forged a confederation of the Tocharian tribes in Bactria into a bureaucratic state. He is hailed in the Rabatak inscription as the founder of the Kushan royal family.

Leo I, the Great (b. c. 390; r. 440–461): The first pope of a noble Roman family. Leo upheld papal primacy against the patriarch of Constantinople. He defined the creed of the western church in his *Tome* (449), accepted at the Fourth Ecumenical Council in 451. He won a moral victory by convincing Attila to withdraw from Italy in 452.

Li Guangli (fl. 1st c. B.C.): Courtier and general of Emperor Wudi (141–87 B.C.). Commanded two expeditions to subdue Sogdiana in the so-called War of the Heavenly Horses (104–102 B.C.). In 102 B.C., Li Guangli forced the Sogdians to capitulate and pay a tribute of horses, but he lost most of his army and the horses on his return.

Li Jing (571–649): Tang general and chancellor; proved the ablest commander under emperors Gaozu and Taizong. In 629–630, he defeated and captured Khagan Illig, thereby ending the eastern Turkish khaganate.

Li Shiji (594–669): Tang general; distinguished himself in the campaign against the Gök Turks in 629–630. He pacified the caravan cities of the Tarim Basin and defeated the nomadic Xueyantuo, who occupied the grasslands of eastern Mongolia.

Lizong (b. 1205; r. 1224–1264): Song emperor. He was a noted patron of letters and architecture, but he proved unequal to the task of facing renewed Mongol attacks in 1257. He was saved by the outbreak of the Mongol civil war in 1269–1264.

Lokaksema (b. c. 147): A Kushan from Gandhara and a Buddhist monk at the Han capital of Luoyang. In 178–189, he translated a number of Sanskrit sutras into Chinese. His student Zhi Yao, also styled a Kushan monk, translated a number of Mahayana Buddhist texts in the late 2nd century.

Longjumeau, Andrew of (d. after 1253): Dominican friar. Sent as the envoy of Pope Innocent the IV (1243–1254) to the ilkhanate court in 1245–1247. In 1248–1251, he traveled to Karakorum as the envoy of King Louis IX of France (1226–1270). In 1249, he reached the Mongol Empire after the death of Güyük. The regent Sorghaghtani Beki, although a Nestorian Christian, received the letters and gifts as token of submission by both Pope Innocent IV and King Louis IX.

Lucullus, Lucius Licinius (118–56 B.C.): Consul in 74 B.C.; assumed the command as proconsul against Mithradates VI, king of Pontus, in 73–66 B.C. In 69 B.C., his victory at Tigranocerta over King Tigranes II of Armenia and Mithradates VI made Rome the premier power in the Near East.

Ma Huan (1380–1460): Admiral of Ming China; a Muslim and Arabic speaker. At the command of the Ming emperor Yongle (1402–1424), he set sail with 57 ships in a great expedition to the western lands in 1413. He visited Champa, Java, Sumatra, Malaya, the southern Indian port of Cochin, Hormuz, and ultimately, Mecca.

Mahavira (599–527 B.C.): Sage and teacher; the founder of Jainism. He is hailed as the 24th and last Tirthankara, or teacher, of the Jain faith. Born into a royal family of Bihar, of the Kshatriya caste, he assumed an ascetic life, attained enlightenment, and taught the cardinal principles of a life based on *ahimsa*, or nonviolence, and respect for all living creatures.

Mahmud al-Kashgari (1005–1102): Turkish poet and scholar under the Karakhanids; wrote the first compendium on the Turkish language, *Diwan lughat at-Turk*, and adapted the Arabic-Persian script for writing Turkish. His work contains a wealth of information about early Turkish history and religious traditions. He also drew the first world map showing the location of Turkish tribes.

Mahmud of Ghazni (b. 971; r. 997–1030): Ghaznavid sultan; the son and successor of Sebüktigin. He waged 17 campaigns in northern India, whereby he gained the loot and slaves to sustain his professional army. He clashed with the Karakhanids over Transoxania, and in 1015–1071, he secured Khwarezm. In 1027–1028, he extended his sway over the caravan cities of northern Iran.

Malik-Shah (b. 1055; r. 1072–1092): Seljuk sultan; son of Alp-Arslan. He concentrated on war against the Fatimid caliphate at Cairo, and he faced threats in Transoxania. Independent *ghazi* warriors, who only nominally recognized Malik-Shah, migrated into Asia Minor and established their own states at Konya and Sivas.

Marcus Aurelius (161–180): Roman emperor; considered the last and noblest of the so-called Five Good Emperors of Rome. A Stoic in outlook, he ruled judiciously and waged successful Parthian (161–166) and German (167–180) wars. Merchants, claiming to represent the emperor, are reported to have arrived by sea and were received at the Han court in 166.

Marwan II (b. 688; r. 744–750): Umayyad caliph; moved the capital from Damascus to Harran. In 737, as governor in Armenia, he waged a campaign north of the Caucasus and compelled the Khazars to accept Islam. In 750, he was defeated by as-Saffah at the Battle of the Zab and, later, captured and executed.

Maurice (582–602): Byzantine emperor; waged campaigns against the Avars in the Balkans and ended the Persian war (572–590) by supporting Shah Khosrow II to the Sassanid throne. He is credited with writing the *Strategikon*, a manual of tactics against nomadic horse archers.

Mawlana: see **Jalal al-Din Rumi**.

Meng Tian (d. 210 B.C.): The leading general of the Qin emperor Shihuangdi. In 221 B.C., he led a major expedition against the Xiongnu and established the empire's northern frontier. He directed the construction of the continuous Great Wall of China.

Midas (c. 725–696 B.C.): King of Phrygia. Constructed a great royal tumulus near his capital, Gordion. He was remembered by Greeks for his patronage of the oracle of Delphi. He committed suicide after the Cimmerians, Iranian-speaking nomadic invaders, destroyed his kingdom.

Mithradates I (171–138 B.C.): King of Parthia, defeated and captured the Seleucid king Demetrius II in 140 B.C. and then the Greco-Bactrian king Eucratides. He conquered Media, Persia, Mesopotamia, Margiana, and Aria.

Mithradates II (137–88 B.C.): King of Parthia. Turned the Arsacid state into a Near East monarchy. He founded the capital Ctesiphon.

Mithradates VI Eupator (121–63 B.C.): King of Pontus. Fought three wars with Rome (89–85 B.C., 83–81 B.C., and 74–63 B.C.) for mastery of Asia Minor. He was finally defeated by Pompey the Great, fled to the Tauric Chersonese, and committed suicide.

Modu Chanyu (b. c. 234 B.C.; r. 209–174 B.C.): Succeeded his father, Touman, as *chanyu* of the Xiongnu. He gave the tribal confederation administrative organization and effective leadership in raiding China, and he defeated the army of Han emperor Gaozu at the Battle of Mount Baideng in 200 B.C. Thereafter, he received gifts and silk from the Han court in return for an alliance and sale of horses to the Han armies.

Möngke (b. 1209; r. 1251–1259): Mongol khan and eldest son of Tolui and Sorghaghtani Beki. He proved an intelligent ruler, who commissioned his brother Hulagu to conquer the Islamic world in 1256. In 1257–1259, he along with his brother Kublai Khan, invaded Song China. He died of dysentery while besieging the fortress Diaoyu on the Yangtze River. His death precipitated a civil war.

Montecorvino, Giovanni da (1247–1328): Franciscan missionary; ordained in Cathay in 1307. He had Christian works translated into Uighur. He was credited with converting 6,000 Mongols, including Temür Khan, after 35 years of proselytizing.

Muawiya (b. 602; r. 661–689): Umayyad caliph; general of the Syrian army and father of the Arabic navy. In 656, he refused to accept Ali, the cousin of Muhammad, as the fourth Rashidun caliph because of Ali's implication in the murder of Caliph Uthman (644–656). Muawiya triumphed over the forces of Ali and, thus, founded the first hereditary Umayyad caliphate at Damascus.

Muhammad (570–632): The prophet of God (Allah), he was called to cleanse the religion of Abraham and, thus, founded Islam. His revelations were collected into the Qur'an. Driven from his native Mecca in 622, Muhammad created an *ummah* (community of believers) at Medina that defeated the Meccans. At his death, Muhammad had united all of Arabia under Islam.

Muhammad Ghuri (b. 1150, r. 1202–1206): Ghurid emir; extended the Ghurids into northern India. He conquered the Punjab and Doab in the name of his older brother Ghiyas al-Din (1163–1203). His decisive victory over the Rajput King Prithviraja III (1149–1192) in 1192 gained him control of Delhi. As emir, he entrusted the administration of the Indian conquests to his Turkish general Qutb al-Din Aybak.

Muhammad Shaybani (b. 1451; r. 1500–1510): Khan of the Uzbek confederation, who occupied Bukhara and Samarkand. He clashed with Ismail I, Safavid shah of Iran, and Bābur, who quit his homeland in Ferghana to invade India. On December 2, 1510, Shah Ismail decisively defeated and slew Muhammad Shaybani at the Battle of Merv.

Nasr ibn Ahmad (864–892): Samanid emir; ruled as the Abbasid deputy over Khurasan and Transoxania. Nasr secured the frontier on the Jaxartes and gained wealth from the slave trade with the Turkish tribes. He turned Bukhara into the model of a Muslim city, with its architecture and arts, and sponsored the Persian literary culture of eastern Islam.

Nasr ibn Sayyar (b. 663; r. 738–748): Umayyad governor of Khurasan; completed the conquest of Transoxania. He pursued conciliatory policies toward all religions and reformed taxation and administration.

Nicephorus I (802–811): Byzantine emperor; served as treasurer of the empress Irene (797–802). He was an Arabian by birth and seized power as Irene lost popularity. He suffered humiliating defeats at the hands of the Abbasid caliph Harun al-Rashid. He was defeated and slain by Khan Krum of the Bulgars.

Ningzong (b. 1168; r. 1194–1224): Song emperor of China. Allied with Khan Ögödei to partition the remaining domains of the Jin Empire in 122. But the Song army sought to retake Kaifeng and, thus, precipitated an inconclusive war in 1234–1241.

Octar (c. 420–430): Ruled over the western Huns on the Pannonian grasslands; he was the father of Attila (434–453) and Bleda (434–445). See also **Rugila**.

Octavian: See **Augustus**.

Ögödei (b. 1186; r. 1229–1241): Mongol khan; the third son of Genghis Khan and Börte. Ögödei, popular and affable, was elected by the *kurultai* as successor to Genghis Khan. He ruled directly over the Mongolian homeland, but he was recognized as Great Khan by his brothers Chagatai and Tolui and his nephew Batu. He transformed Karakorum into a capital city and authorized Batu's conquest of the west. His death precipitated the first succession crisis of the Mongol Empire.

Otto I (b. 912; r. 936–973): Holy Roman Emperor; duke of Saxony and son of Henry the Fowler. Otto was elected king of Germany. In 955, he decisively defeated the Hungarians on the Lech, and his campaigns against the Danes and Slavs secured imperial frontiers. In 962, he was crowned Holy Roman Emperor.

Ouyang Xiu (1007–1072): Song official and polymath; rose from obscure origins to high rank through the examination system. He sponsored the literary movement stressing clear expository prose within the tradition of Confucian classics. He epitomized the neo-Confucian scholar-official.

Peroz I (457–484): Sassanid shah; was deposed by his brother Hormizd II. He regained his throne with a Hephthalite army provided by King Khush-Nevaz. Peroz twice waged campaigns against his former ally Khush-Nevaz. In either 469 or 472, Peroz suffered a defeat and had to pay a ransom for his release. In 484, he was slain near Herat, enabling the Hephthalites to raid deep into Iran.

Phraates II (138–128 B.C.): King of Parthia; defeated Antiochus VII Sidetes and ended Seleucid power in the Near East. Phraates, however, was defeated and slain by the Sacae, who had migrated into Aria and Drangiana.

Phraates IV (38–2 B.C.): King of Parthia; negotiated with Augustus the return of the Roman standards and prisoners taken at the Battle of Carrhae in 20 B.C. He recognized Roman hegemony in Armenia—an agreement that lasted down to 54. In turn, Augustus sent the Greek courtesan Musa Urania, who became Phraates's principal wife and mother to his heir, Phraates V (2 B.C.–A.D. 4).

Plautius Silvanus Aelianus, Tiberius (c. 15–85): Roman senator and consul (45 and 74) of patrician lineage. As legate of Moesia in 66–67, he repelled Sarmatian attacks against the Greek cities and secured the lower Danube against nomadic invaders.

Pliny the Elder (23–79): Roman senator, naturalist, and philosopher. He wrote the encyclopedic *Naturalis Historia*, which has a wealth of information on the Amber Road, Silk Road, and trade routes of the Indian Ocean. He died on August 25, 79, while attempting to effect rescues of friends trapped by the eruption of Mount Vesuvius.

Polo, Marco (1254–1324): Venetian adventurer; took service with Kublai Khan as the administrator of the salt monopoly at Yangzhou and as an emissary to the Burmese court. In 1251–1257, Marco Polo, along with his father Niccolò, and uncle Maffeo (who had previously visited the ilkhanate court), journeyed to Dadu. In 1292–1294, the three returned to Venice. In 1298, Marco was captured by the Genoese at the Battle of Curzola. While in prison in 1298–1299, he dictated his adventures of 23 years (1271–1294) to fellow prisoner Rustichello da Pisa, who composed the *Livres des merveilles* *du monde.* Marco's book was an instant success and fired the European imagination and desire to reach Cathay.

Pompey the Great (Gnaeus Pompeius Magnus) (106–48 B.C.): Roman senator and consul (70, 56 and 52 B.C.); a member of the First Triumvirate, along with Gaius Julius Caesar and Marcus Licinius Crassus (59–51 B.C.). He commanded the republican forces against Julius Caesar in the civil war and was decisively defeated at the Battle of Pharsalus (48 B.C.), fled to Egypt, and was murdered on orders of King Ptolemy XIII. In 66–63, Pompey had ended the war against King Mithradates VI of Pontus, reorganized the eastern province, and secured Rome's frontier on the upper Euphrates with an overlordship over Armenia.

Prester John: "Priest John"; a legendary Christian king in inner Asia who would deliver Jerusalem from the Muslims. He was probably inspired by garbled reports about Yelü Dashi (1124–1143), khan of the Kara-Khitans, who had defeated Seljuk sultan Ahmad Sanjar (1118–1153) at the Battle of Qatwan on September 9, 1141. Genghis Khan was later hailed by western European Christians as Prester John or his descendant, David.

Priscus of Panium (c. 410–472): Roman diplomat. Accompanied the mission of the emperor Theodosius II to the court of Attila, king of the Huns, in 441–442. He wrote a perceptive account about the customs of the Huns and the character of Attila.

Procopius (500–565): Byzantine historian and native of Caesarea. He wrote a narrative history of the wars of the emperor Justinian (527–565) and *Buildings* (a monograph of the emperor's building programs). In his *Secret History*, or *Anecdota*, he vents his outrage over Justinian and the empress Theodora. He provides invaluable information on the nomadic peoples of the western and central Eurasian steppes and the Sassanid Empire.

Ptolemy (Claudius Ptolaemeus) (90–168): Mathematician, scientist, and geographer of Alexandria. He composed the *Geographica*, which included a map of the known world to Romans, in the mid-2nd century. He also measured the circumference of the earth and wrote treatises on optics, astronomy, and music.

Qapaghan (694–716): Khagan of the eastern Turks. Restored Turkish power on the eastern Eurasian steppes. He was acknowledged overlord by the western Turks of the Onoq confederacy. He battled both Tang armies and Tibetans for control of the Tarim Basin, and he clashed with Qutaybah ibn Muslim, Umayyad governor of Khurasan, for control of Transoxania.

Qilij Arslan I (1092–1107): Seljuk sultan of Konya (Rūm). Suffered serious defeats at the hands of the First Crusade in 1097. In 1097–1098, the Byzantine emperor Alexius I thus recovered the western third of Asia Minor.

Qilij Arslan II (1156–1192): Seljuk sultan of Konya (Rūm). Defeated the Byzantine emperor Manuel I (1143–1180) at the Battle of Myriocephalon on September 17, 1176. The victory checked the revival of Byzantine power in Asia Minor.

Qutaybah ibn Muslim (b. 699; r. 705–715): Umayyad governor of Khurasan; waged a destructive war against the cities of Transoxania, looting Manichaean, Zoroastrian, and Buddhist sanctuaries. He took Bukhara in 709 and Samarkand in 712. His ruthless efforts to impose Islam galvanized the Sogdian populations to invite Suluk, *yabgu* of the western Turks, to intervene. Qutaybah was executed on grounds of treason on the orders of Caliph Sulayman.

Qutb ud-Din Aybak (1206–1210): Sultan of Delhi; was the leading general of Muhammad Ghuri (1202–1206), who entrusted Aybak with the conquest of the Ganges. In 1206, he made himself sultan of the Turkish slave soldiers and, thus, founded the slave sultanate of Delhi.

Qutlugh Bilge Köl Khagan (744–747): Khagan of the Uighurs; ended the Gök Turk khaganate. He was acclaimed khagan by the *kurultai* of the Uighurs and entered into alliance with Tang China.

Qutuz, al-Muaaffar Sayf al-Din (1259–1260): Mamluk sultan. He refused to submit to Hulagu and planned the campaign of Ain Jalut. He was overthrown and murdered by his leading general, Baybars.

Rashid al-Din (1247–1318): Persian polymath and scholar; was a Jewish convert to Islam and native of Hamadan. At the ilkhanate court, he wrote an encyclopedic history of the Islamic world, *Jami' al-tawarikh*, in which he made extensive use of Chinese sources and the *Secret History of the Mongols*. He also translated Buddhist texts and Chinese works on statecraft into Persian.

Radiyya Begum (b. 1205; r. 1236–1240): Daughter of Iltutmish; was the first Muslim woman to rule in her own right as sultana of Delhi. She failed to win over the Turkish military elite, who were scandalized by her manners and liaisons. Her murder in 1240 marked the end of effective rule by the slave sultans of Delhi.

Romanus IV Diogenes (b. c. 1030; r. 1068–1072): Byzantine emperor; candidate of the officers of the eastern army. He married the empress Eudocia, widow of Constantine X Ducas (1059–1067). Romanus was decisively defeated and captured by the Seljuk sultan Alp-Arslan at the Battle of Manzikert in 1071. In 1072, Romanus was released by Alp-Arslan, but Michael VII ordered him deposed and blinded. Romanus died in exile.

Rubrouck, William of (1220–1293): Flemish Franciscan friar; sent as envoy of French king Saint Louis IX (1226–1270) to the Mongol court in 1253–1255. William of Rubrouck failed in his mission to convert the Mongols, but he wrote a perceptive account on the court of Great Khan Möngke (1251–1259).

Rugila (r. c. 420–434): King of the Huns; ruled over the eastern tribes of the Huns between the lower Danube and the lower Volga. His brother Octar (r. c. 420–430) ruled over the western Huns on the Pannonian grasslands. He was succeeded by his nephews Attila and Bleda.

Salam ibn Ziyad (681–683): First Umayyad governor of Khurasan; conducted raids into Transoxania and settled Arab military colonists on the Oxus River.

Sargon II (722–705 B.C.): Assyrian king; seized the throne in a brief civil war and claimed to be the son of Tiglath-Pileser III (745–727 B.C.). He campaigned against the neo-Hittite and Aramaic kingdoms of the Levant and Babylon. He fell fighting an invasion by the Cimmerians, Iran-speaking nomads from the Pontic-Caspian steppes who had crossed the Caucasus Mountains.

Satuk Bughra Khan (b. 922; r. 934–955): Karakhanid Black Camel khan; ruled the Yaghma Turks in the valley of the Talas River. He had converted to Islam in 934. In 940, he seized power over the Karakhanid khaganate and promoted Islam among the Turkish tribes of the central Eurasian steppes.

Sebüktigin (b. 942; r. 977–997): Ghaznavid emir and sultan; known as the Lion of Ghazni. He was the Turkish commander and son-in-law of Alp Tigin. In 977, he was declared emir by his Turkish soldiers. He forged the Ghaznavid emirate into a Muslim state and conquered the Kabul valley. In 994–999, he secured the Samanid lands south of the Oxus River, while the Karakhanids occupied Transoxania.

Seleucus I Nicator (b. 358 B.C.; r. 312–281 B.C.): Macedonian noble and general. A minor figure in the initial succession wars after the death of Alexander the Great in 323–321 B.C. In 320 B.C., he obtained the satrapy of Babylonia, and between 312 and 281 B.C., he fell heir to the Asia domains of Alexander's empire.

Septimius Severus (b. 145; 193–211): Roman emperor; member of a senatorial family from Leptis Magna in North Africa. He seized the throne in the civil war of 193–195 and founded the Severan Dynasty (193–235). He waged two successful Parthian wars (195–196; 198–201) and organized the Roman province of Mesopotamia in northern Iraq.

Shapur I (240–270): Sassanid shah; waged three major wars against the Roman Empire, in 242–244, 253, and 254–260. In the third war, he took the Roman Valerian captive. His victories are celebrated on the rock reliefs at Naqsh-e Rostam. Shapur failed to conquer Roman territory, and in 262, he faced a counterinvasion by Odenathus, merchant prince of Palmyra and ally of Rome.

Shapur II (309–379): Sassanid shah; waged two wars against the Roman Empire, in 335–350 and 358–363. He repelled the Roman invasion of lower

Mesopotamia led by the emperor Julian II. The retreat and death of Julian enabled Shapur II to conclude a favorable treaty from the new emperor, Jovian, who relinquished the strategic fortresses of upper Mesopotamia.

Sharaf ad-Din Ali Yazdi (fl. c. 1425–1450): Persian historian who served at the Timurid court of Shah Rukh (1405–1447). He wrote a favorable biography of Tamerlane, *Zafernameh.*

Shihuangdi (b. 259 B.C.; r. 246–210 B.C.): Founded the Qin Dynasty and united the warring states of China. He took strong measures against the Xiongnu and ordered the construction of the Great Wall.

Shulu Ping (879–953): Khitan empress of the Liao Dynasty; wife of Abaoji (907–926). She manipulated the court to place on the throne her younger son, Yelü Deguang, who assumed the Chinese throne name Taizong (927–947). She again intrigued in the succession war following the death of Yelü Deguang in 947–950.

Sima Qian (c. 140–86 B.C.): Historian of Han China; wrote a dynastic history in *Shiji* (*Historical Records*). A meticulous scholar, Sima Qian incorporated a number of earlier sources, notably, the account of Zhang Qian about his travels among the Xiongnu and Yuezhi (Tocharians).

Simeon (893–927): Tsar of Bulgaria; second son of Tsar Boris. He had been destined for a religious career, studying at Constantinople. In two wars (894–899; 912–924), he challenged the Macedonian emperors for domination of the Balkans. In 895–896, he courted the Pechenegs as allies against the Magyars, who were allied to the Byzantine emperor Leo VI (886–912). The Pechenegs drove the Magyars, ancestors of the Hungarians, into the Pannonian grasslands.

Sorghaghtani Beki (1204–1252): Kereyid princess and wife of Tolui, son of Genghis Khan, and the niece of Wang Khan. She was the mother of Möngke, Kublai Khan, Hulagu, and Arigh Böke. A Nestorian Christian, she favored her co-religionists at court. In 1248–1251, after the death of Khan Güyük (1246–1248), she secured the support of Batu and the majority in the *kurultai* to elect her son Möngke as Great Khan.

Stein, Sir Aurel (1862–1943): An explorer, archaeologist, and officer of the British army. Stein, born of a prominent Jewish family in Budapest, took British citizenship. He led four archaeological expeditions into the Tarim Basin (1900–1901, 1906–1908, 1913–1916, and 1930). He visited the caravan cities of the Tarim Basin and found the Buddhist cave monasteries at Mogao near Dunhuang.

Stilicho, Flavius (d. 408): *Magister militum* of the western army (395–408); directed the policy of the western court. In 395–397 and in 402–408, Stilicho used the threat posed by Arcadius to secure control over Honorius. Stilicho's policies led to the loss of the northwestern provinces in 406. In 408, he was arrested and executed on grounds of treason.

Strabo of Amaseia (63 B.C.–A.D. 24): Geographer; wrote the definitive account of the geography of the Roman Empire and the surrounding lands. His account includes invaluable information on the trade in the Erythaean Sea and the western routes of the Silk Road.

Stroganov, Anika (1488–1570): Russian merchant prince. A native of Novgorod, who received the right from Ivan the Terrible to develop the fur trade from Solvychegodsk (on the Vychegda River). These rights were confirmed in 1552, 1555, and 1560. The Stroganov family undertook the colonization of Siberia—tundra, taiga, and steppe—establishing trading posts and exacting tribute in furs.

Subutai (1175–1248): Mongol general and early companion of Temujin (the future Genghis Khan); commanded 20 campaigns. He was an expert in strategy and siege warfare. In 1221–1223, he and Jebe conducted a brilliant western campaign that climaxed at the Battle of the Kalka River on May 31, 1223. He distinguished himself in the western campaigns of Batu in 1237–1241 and in the campaign against Song China in 1246–1247.

Suluk (717–738): *Yabgu* of the Turgesh, a leading tribe of the western Turkish khaganate. He waged a brilliant war of attrition against the Umayyad governor in Transoxania.

Sviatoslav (b. c. 942; r. 964–972): Rus prince; son of Prince Igor (914–945) and Queen Olga (Helga), who had embraced Orthodox Christianity in 957. He defeated the Khazars circa 965, but he suffered defeat at the hands of Byzantine armies in Bulgaria (967–971). On his retreat to Kiev, he was defeated and slain by the Pechenegs.

Tacitus, Publius Cornelius (56–117): Roman historian and senator. He wrote two narrative histories, *Annals* and *Historiae*, covering the reigns of Tiberius (14–37) through Domitian (81–96), and the treatises *Germania*, *Agricola*, and *Dialogus*.

Tahir ibn al-Husayn (d. 821): Persian general and emir. Won the civil war of 812–813 for al-Mamun (813–833). He was rewarded with the governorship of Khurasan, which his heirs, the Tahirids, turned into a hereditary emirate.

Taiwudi (b. 408; r. 424–452): Emperor of the northern Wei Dynasty; secured northern China from Avar attacks. A devoted Buddhist, he constructed the five colossal statues of Buddha at Yungang.

Taizong (b. 598; r. 626–649): Tang emperor of China. Defeated the Gök Turks in 629–630 and brought the eastern Eurasian steppe under Chinese rule. His generals Li Jing and Li Shiji subjected the Tarim Basin, defeated the Tibetans, and advanced Chinese influence to the Jaxartes River.

Taizong (b. 939; r. 976–997): Song emperor of China; succeeded his brother Taizu. He is credited with the foundation of the Neo-Confucian bureaucratic state based on the examination system.

Taizu (b. 927; r. 960–976): Song emperor of China; the accomplished general Zhao Kuangyin, who founded the Song Dynasty. In 960, he ended the regional Zhou Dynasty at Kaifeng and then imposed order over the southern Chinese kingdoms. He ruled as the political heir of the earlier Han and Tang dynasties.

Tamerlane (b. 1336; r. 1370–1405): "Prince of Destruction"; regarded as the third greatest conqueror of the steppes (after Genghis Khan and Attila). He was the heir to the Mongol military tradition, recruiting professional regiments of cavalry based on loyalty and rewards. Tamerlane, emir of the Turko-Mongol Barlas tribe, emerged as the leading emir in the tribal wars in Transoxania in 1360–1370. In 1370, Chagatai khan Suurgatmish (1370–1384) named Tamerlane grand emir. Tamerlane also married Saray Mulk Khanum, a descendent of Genghis Khan. From his capital, he waged six campaigns of conquest between 1381 and 1401, in which he conquered most of the western half of the Mongol Empire. In 1391–1392 and 1393–1396, he defeated Tokhtamysh and broke the power of the Golden Horde. He won his greatest victories near Delhi over the Tughluq army in 1398 and at Angora over the Ottoman army of Bayezid Yildirim in 1402. Yet neither campaign resulted in territorial expansion. In February 1405, he died en route to his seventh campaign against Ming China. His exploits inspired legends; he is credited he with writing the flattering *Memoirs of Temur*.

Tardu (581–602): Succeeded Istami as *yabgu* of the western Turks (575–581). In 581, he assumed the title khagan and established the western Turkish khaganate.

Temujin: See **Genghis Khan**.

Theodosius I, the Great (b. c. 346; r. 379–395): The son of Count Theodosius, a leading general of Valentinian I, Flavius Theodosius rose to high command under Gratian. In 379, as Augustus of the east, Theodosius restored order, granting a treaty to the rebellious Goths, who henceforth served as *foederati*. In 395, he was succeeded by Arcadius and Honorius, his sons by his first wife, Aelia Flacilla.

Theodosius II (b. 401; r. 408–450): Flavius Theodosius, the son of Arcadius and Eudocia (daughter of the Frankish general Bauto); succeeded as a minor. The emperor was directed by his ministers and his older sister, Aelia Pulcheria. Theodosius agreed to humiliating treaties dictated by Attila the Hun in 443 and 447.

Tiridates (r. 53–c. 75): Arsacid king of Armenia and brother of King Vologeses I of Parthia. He was received by the Armenian nobility and refused to acknowledge the suzerainty of Rome. In 38–59, the Roman commander Gnaeus Domitius Corbulo expelled Tiridates from Armenia and crowned Tigranes V (60–62). Vologeses I intervened on behalf of Tiridates, but he was checked by Corbulo. In 64, a diplomatic settlement was reached whereby Tiridates regained the Armenian throne, but he was required to journey to Rome and receive his crown from Nero in 66.

Todar Mal (d. 1589): The Hindu finance minister of Akbar (1556–1605); of the Kshatriya caste. He entered the service of Akbar in 1560 and managed the mint, introduced a census, and reformed the system of taxation.

Togon-temür (b.1320; r. 1333–1368): Last Mongol khan and Yuan emperor; ruled China under the throne name of Huizong. He ruled as a figurehead, and in 1358, he fled from Dadu to Mongolia, where he died in exile in 1370.

Tokhtamysh (d. 1406; r. 1376–1395): Khan of the Golden Horde. Fled to Tamerlane in 1376 after he failed to unseat his uncle Urus Khan (1361–1375). With the support of Tamerlane, he was received as khan of the Golden Horde. In 1382, he avenged the Mongol defeat at Kulikovo Field by sacking Moscow and forcing Grand Prince Vasily to return to his Mongol allegiance. In 1395, Khan Tokhtamysh blundered into a war with his overlord Tamerlane (1370–1405), who ruthlessly sacked Saray and appointed as his vassal a new khan, Temür Kutlugh (1395–1401). Tokhtamysh died in exile in 1406.

Tong Yabgu (618–630): Khagan of the western Turkish khaganate. Ended civil war and reorganized the tribes into the Confederacy of the Ten Arrows. In 626, he allied with the Byzantine emperor Heraclius against the Sassanid shah Khosrow II and, thus, regained the cities of Transoxania.

Tonyukuk (646–726): A *yabgu* of the eastern Turkish khaganate and advisor to Bilge Khan (717–734). He restored the power of the khaganate after the end of the Tang overlordship in 681. In 716, he erected a memorial inscription of his deeds and his advice in the Old Turkic language at Bayn Tsokto in the Orkhon Valley (today Mongolia).

Töregene (c. 1185–1248): Naiman princess; married Ögödei in 1204. In 1241, upon the death of her husband, she assumed the role of Great Khatun (regent) and arranged for the election of her son Güyük as Great Khan in 1246. She directed imperial affairs and appointed ministers at court and generals. She retired from the regency in 1246 and died out of favor with her son.

Touman (c. 220–209 B.C.): First known *chanyu* of the Xiongnu; organized the first nomadic confederation on the eastern Eurasian steppe. He warred with the Qin emperor Shihuangdi and with the rival Yuezhi (Tocharians) for control of the Gansu Corridor.

Trajan (b. 53; r. 98–117): Roman emperor; hailed the best of emperors (*optimus princeps*). He conquered Dacia (101–106) and waged a successful Parthian war (114–117). Trajan briefly occupied Mesopotamia and appointed his own Arsacid king, Parthamaspates (116–118). His successor, Hadrian (117–138), withdrew from Trajan's conquests.

Trajan Decius (b. 201; r. 249–251): Roman emperor; seized the imperial throne with support of the legions of the Danube frontier. He and his son Herennius Etruscus were defeated and slain by the Goths at the Battle of Abrittus. He also initiated the first empire-wide persecution of Christians in 250–251.

Tughluq, Ghiyas-ud-Din (1320–1325): Sultan of Delhi; a leading Khalji general of mixed Turkish and Jat descent. He seized power and established the third line of Muslim sultans at Delhi, the Tughluqs (1320–1412).

Tughril Bey (b. 999; r. 1037–1063): Seljuk sultan; restored the power of the Sunni Abbasid caliphate at Baghdad. In 1025, Tughril Beg and his brother Chaghri had settled their Ghuzz Turks in Khurasan as vassals of Sultan Mahmud of Ghazna. In 1030–1037, Tughril Beg conquered Transoxania and took the title sultan. In 1040, he defeated the Ghaznavid sultan Masud (1031–1041) and conquered the former Ghaznavid domains in northern Iran. In 1055, he entered Baghdad and was received as great sultan by Caliph al-Kasim (1031–1075).

Uldin (r. c. 395–412): King of the Huns. Directed attacks of the Huns into the Balkans to extort subsidies and trading privileges from the eastern Roman emperor Arcadius. He commanded Hun contingents sent on request of the western Roman emperor Honorius in 406.

Umar I (b. 584; r. 634–644): Second of the Rashidun caliphs; was elected in preference to Ali. He directed the conquests of Byzantine Syria, Egypt, and Libya and the Sassanid Empire of Persia.

Uthman (b. 577; r. 644–656): Third of the Rashidun caliphs; was elected in preference to Ali. He headed the powerful Umayyad clan but personally lacked the will to govern effectively from Medina. He was slain by mutinous soldiers of the Egyptian army, who then offered the caliphate to Ali.

Valentinian III (Flavius Placidius Valentinianus) (b. 419; r. 425–455): Son of Galla Placidia and Constantius III. As western Roman emperor, Valentinian lost the remaining provinces in Spain and North Africa. His mother, who directed affairs of state, clashed with the powerful *magister militum* Aetius. Valentinian III, murdered by a clique of senators, left no heirs; thus, the western Roman Empire disappeared within 20 years of his death.

Valerian (b. c. 193; r. 253–260): Roman emperor; waged two Persian wars. He was captured by Shah Shapur I and died ignominiously in captivity. As a result of Valerian's defeat and capture, Shah Shapur ravaged Roman provinces in eastern Asia Minor and northern Syria in 260. He ordered the second empire-wide persecution of Christians in 258–260.

Vasily I Dmitriyevich (b. 1371; r. 1389–1425): Grand prince of Moscow; the grandson of Ivan I. He defeated a Mongol army of 35,000 on Kulikovo Field on September 8, 1380. In 1382, Khan Tokhtamysh invaded and stormed Moscow and sacked the city, forcing Grand Prince Vasily to return to his Mongol allegiance.

Vasudeva I (190–225): The last effective Kushan emperor; witnessed the fragmenting of the Kushan state. His heirs ruled as vassals of the Sassanid shahs of Iran.

Vespasian (b. 23; r. 69–79): Roman emperor; established the Flavian Dynasty of Rome. He proved a practical emperor who corrected a fiscal crisis and secured imperial frontiers. Vespasian commenced the construction of the *limes* (highways and fortifications) on the upper Euphrates.

Vima Kadphises (105–127): Kushan emperor; received envoys from the Roman emperor Trajan. He extended Kushan domains in India and introduced gold coinage.

Vima Taktu (80–105): Kushan emperor; the son and successor of Kujula Kadphises. He is known from the Rabatak inscription and minted an extensive coinage but without the royal name.

Vladimir (b. c. 958; r. 980–1015): Rus prince of Kiev; he embraced Orthodox Christianity around 989 as part of a marriage alliance with the Byzantine emperor Basil II (976–1025). He founded the royal institutions of the Christian Russian state.

Vologeses I (51–78): Arsacid king of Parthia. Supported his brother Tiridates to the throne of Armenia in a war against Rome. In 66, he concluded a peace with the emperor Nero, whereby Tiridates retained the Armenian throne but recognized the hegemony of Rome.

Wang Khan (d. 1203; r. c. 1175–1203): Khan of the Keraits. His personal name was Toghrul; in 1197, he received the Chinese title Wang ("King") from the Jin (Jurchen) emperor Zhangzong (1189–1208). The sworn brother of Yesugei, the father of Temujin, he received Temujin into his service in 1180. He supported Temujin against Jamukha, but in 1203, he switched his loyalty to Jamukha. Temujin captured the Kerait encampment, and Wang Khan fled and was slain by the Naimans.

Wang Mang (b. 45 B.C.; r. 9–23 A.D.): Usurper who overthrew the Former Han Dynasty and issued sweeping reforms. He failed to maintain the northern frontier against the Xiongnu.

Wanyan Min (b. 1068; 1115–1123): Jurchen emperor of the Jin Dynasty; assumed the Chinese throne name Taizu. He united the Jurchens and overthrew the Khitan Empire. In 1121, he concluded with Song emperor Huizong (1100–1125) the so-called Alliance of the Sea that called for the partition of the Khitan Empire.

Wanyan Sheng (b. 1075; r. 1123–1135): Jurchen emperor of the Jin Dynasty; assumed the Chinese throne name Taizong. He succeeded his brother Wanyan Min and completed the conquest of the Khitan state. In 1127, he captured Kaifeng and the Song court, including the retired emperor Huizong. The new Song emperor Gaozong (1127–1162) agreed to cede northern China to Wanyan Sheng.

Wei Qing (d. 106 B.C.): Han general of imperial descent; the strategic genius behind the victories over the Xiongnu. He and his nephew Huo Qubing captured the Mobei, the tent capital of Ichise Chanyu. Thereafter, he retired from active service and served as strategic advisor to Emperor Wudi.

Wen (b. 541; r. 581–604): Sui emperor; reunited China under the Sui Dynasty (581–618). He promoted Buddhism, secured the northern frontiers by reconstructing the Great Wall, and initiated the Grand Canal.

Wudi (b. 157 B.C., r. 141–87 B.C.): Han emperor; presided over the territorial expansion of China. In 133 B.C., Wudi initiated war against Gunchen, *chanyu* of the Xiongnu. By campaigning across the Gobi in 127–119 B.C., his general broke the power of the Xiongnu. In 121–115 B.C., Wudi's armies imposed Han suzerainty over the western regions (Tarim Basin). His wars, however, proved costly and nearly bankrupt the imperial treasury.

Xuanzang (596–664): Buddhist monk and Chinese pilgrim; wrote an account of his travels in the western regions and India in 629–645. He visited the court of Harsha Vardhana (606–647) at Kannauj on the Ganges. He revealed the international network of Buddhist monasteries in central Asia and India on the eve of the Islamic conquests.

Xuanzong (712–756): Tang emperor of China, who had to evacuate the western regions (Tarim Basin) soon after the defeat at the Battle of Talas (751) to face the An Lushan Rebellion (754–763). He was noted for his taste in exotic luxury items and musicians arriving on the Silk Road.

Yangdi (b. 569; r. 604–618): Sui emperor; reorganized the imperial army, recruiting Turkish cavalry. He initiated the conquest of what is now Vietnam, but expeditions against Korea proved costly failures. His assassination precipitated a brief civil war, whereby the general Li Yuan seized the throne as Gaozu, first emperor of the Tang Dynasty.

Yazdegerd III (632–651): Last Sassanid shah and grandson of Khosrow II; lost his empire to the Arab armies. In 636 (or 639), the Arabs occupied his capital Ctesiphon after their victory at the Battle of al-Qadisiyyah. In 642–651, Yazdegerd failed to check the Arab advance into Iran and was murdered near Merv. His son and heir, Peroz, died an exile at the Tang court.

Yelü Chucai (1190–1244): Khitan minister; a noted scholar of Buddhist and Confucian classics. He served under the Jin (Jurchen) court, but in 1218, he entered the service of Genghis Khan and, later, of Ögödei. He was credited with admonishing Ögödei that China was won on horseback, but it could not be ruled from horseback.

Yelü Dashi (b. 1087; r. 1124–1143): Kara-Khitan khan; a descendant of Abaoji who refused to accept Jurchen rule. In 1130–1131, he led a migration of Khitans into the Tarim Basin; in 1137, he overthrew the Karakhanid khaganate and founded a new Kara-Khitan Empire in central Asia. On September 9, 1141, Yelü Dashi decisively defeated the Seljuk sultan Ahmet Sanjar (1118–1153) at the Battle of Qatwan—the event that gave rise to the legend of Prester John. The victory delivered Transoxania to the Kara-Khitans.

Yelü Deguang (b. 902; r. 927–947): Khitan emperor of the Liao Dynasty; assumed the Chinese throne name Taizong. He proved a valiant warrior-emperor who conquered the lower Huang He valley and occupied Kaifeng. His premature death plunged the Khitan Empire into a succession crisis in 947–950.

Yelü Longxu (b. 972; r. 982–1031): Khitan emperor of the Liao Dynasty; assumed the Chinese throne name Shengzong. He presided over the transformation of the Khitan Empire into a Chinese bureaucratic state. In 1005, he concluded the Treaty of Chanyuan with the Song emperor Zhenzong (997–1022), who recognized the Khitan Empire and agreed to pay an annual subsidy.

Yuri II (b. 1189; r. 1212–1238): Prince of Vladimir-Suzdal; campaigned against the Volga Bulgars and Russian rival princes. In 1238, Batu captured Vladimir. Yuri II escaped, but his capital was sacked and the population slaughtered. On March 8, 1238, he and his army were annihilated by the Mongols at the Battle of Sit River.

Yusuf Khass Hajib (1019–1085): Turkish poet and native of Balasagun; composed *Kutadgu Bilig* for the Karakhanid prince of Kashgar. The work is a guide to proper rule, combining Turkish martial traditions with Islamic political and religious ideals.

Zhang Qian (200–114 B.C.): Official of the Han court. Sent by emperor Wudi as envoy to the Yuezhi (Tocharians) to form an alliance against the Xiongnu in 137–125 B.C. Zhang Qian failed in this mission; twice he was captured by the Xiongnu. His account of the western regions is an invaluable source on the customs of the Xiongnu and the reigns of the *chanyus* Gunchen (161–126 B.C.) and Ichise (126–114 B.C.). His account was incorporated into the *Shiji* ("*Historical Records*") by the historian Sima Qian in the 1st century.

Zhu Xi (1130–1200): Neo-Confucian philosopher and philologist of the Song Dynasty who edited the Confucian classics and wrote commentaries. He also wrote the *Daxue* (*Great Learning*), a moral guide for the Mandarin scholar class.

Ziyad ibn Salih (748–751): Arabic governor of Khurasan who commanded the Arabic-Turkish Karluk army that defeated the Tang army at the Battle of Talas in 751.

Ziyad ibn Abi Sufyan (d. 673): Umayyad governor of Basra (664–673) who commanded Arab expeditionary forces in Iran. In 670–673, he ordered the fortification of Merv as a military base on the northeastern frontier.

Bibliography

Agusti, Alemany. *Sources on the Alans: A Critical Compilation*. Leiden: Brill Academic Publishers, 2000.

Alam, Muzaffar, and Sanjay Subramanyam, eds. *Mughal State, 1526–1750*. Oxford: Oxford University Press, 2011.

Allsen, Thomas T. *Culture and Conquest in Mongol Eurasia*. Cambridge: Cambridge University Press, 2001.

———. "Mongols as Vectors of Cultural Change." In *Cambridge History of Inner Asia: The Chinggisid Age*. Edited by Nicola di Cosmo, Allen J. Frank, and Peter B. Golden, pp. 135–156. Cambridge: Cambridge University Press, 2009.

Ammianus Marcellinus. *The Later Roman Empire (A.D. 354–378)*. Translated by Walter Hamilton. New York: Penguin Classics, 1986.

Angold, Michael. *The Byzantine Empire, 1025–1204: A Political History*. London: Longman, 1984.

Anthony, David W. *The Horse, the Wheel, and Language: How Bronze Age Riders from the Eurasian Steppes Shaped the Modern World*. Princeton: Princeton University Press, 2007.

Bachrach, Bernard S. *A History of the Alans in the West from Their First Appearance in the Sources of Classical Antiquity through the Early Middle Ages*. Minneapolis: University of Minnesota Press, 1973.

Barfield, Thomas J. *The Perilous Frontier: Nomadic Empires and China, 221 B.C. to A.D. 1757*. Oxford: Blackwell, 1989.

Bosworth, C. E. *The Ghaznavids, 994–1040*. Edinburgh: Edinburgh University Press, 1998.

Brian, Michael. "The Mongols of Central Asia from Chinggis Khan's Invasion to the Rise of Temür: The Ögedeid and Chaghandaid Realms." In *The Cambridge History of Inner Asia: The Chinggisid Age*. Edited by Nicolas di Cosmo, Allen J. Frank, and Peter B. Golden, pp. 46–66. Cambridge: Cambridge University Press, 2009.

Braudel, Ferdinand. *Civilization and Capitalism, 15th–18th Century.* Vol. I: *The Structure of Everyday Life.* Berkeley: University of California Press, 1992.

——. *Civilization and Capitalism, 15th–18th Century.* Vol. II: *The Wheels of Commerce.* Berkeley: University of California Press, 1992.

——. *Civilization and Capitalism, 15th–18th Century.* Vol. III: *The Perspective of the World.* Berkeley: University of California Press, 1992.

Brook, Levin Alan. *The Jews of Khazaria.* 2nd ed. New York: Rowman and Littlefield, 2009.

Bulliet, Richard W. *The Camel and the Wheel.* New York: Columbia University Press, 1990.

——. *Cotton, Climate and Camels in Early Islamic Iran: A Moment in World History*. New York: Columbia University Press, 2009.

Burns, T. R. *A History of the Ostrogoths*. Bloomington: Indiana University Press. 1984.

Cahen, Claude. "The Mongols and the Near East." In *A History of the Crusades*. Edited by Kenneth W. Setton, vol. II, pp. 715–734. Madison, WI: University of Wisconsin Press, 1969.

——. *Pre-Ottoman Turkey: A General Survey of the Material and Spiritual Culture and History, c. 1071–1330.* Translated by J. Jones-Williams. London: Sidgick and Jackson, 1968.

————. "The Turkish Invasion: The Selchukids." In *A History of the Crusades*. Edited by Kenneth W. Setton, vol. I, pp. 135–176. Madison, WI: University of Wisconsin Press, 1969.

Canepa, Matthew P. *The Two Eyes of the Earth: Art and Ritual Kingship between Rome and Sasanian Iran*. Berkeley: University of California Press, 2009.

Chang, Kwang-Chih. *Shang Civilization*. New Haven: Yale University Press, 1980.

Comnena, Anna. *The Alexiad*. Translated by E. R. A. Sweter. New York: Penguin Books, 1960.

Cribb, Joe, and Georgina Herrmann, eds. *After Alexander: Central Asia before Islam*. Oxford University Press, 2007.

Crone, P., and G. M. Hinds. *God's Caliph: Religious Authority in the First Centuries of Islam*. Cambridge: Cambridge University Press, 1980.

Curta, Florin, and Roman Kovaley, eds. *The Other Europe in the Middle Ages: Avars, Bulgars and Cumans: East Central and Eastern Europe in the Middle Ages, 450–1450*. Leiden: Brill, 2007.

Curta, Florin, *Southeastern Europe in the Middle Ages, 500–1250*. Cambridge: Cambridge University Press, 2006.

Curtis V. S. S., and Sarah Stewart, eds. *The Age of the Parthians*. London: I. B. Tauris, 2007.

Dale, Stephen F. *The Muslim Empires of the Ottomans, Safavids, and Mughals*. Cambridge: Cambridge University Press, 2010.

————. "The Later Timurids, c. 1450–1526." In *Cambridge History of Inner Asia: The Chinggisid Age*. Edited by Nicola di Cosmo, Allen J. Frank, and Peter B. Golden, pp. 199–220. Cambridge: Cambridge University Press, 2009.

Daryaee, Touraj. *Sasanian Persia: The Rise and Fall of an Empire.* New York: J. B. Taurus & Co., Ltd., 2009.

Debevoise, N. C. *A Political History of Parthia.* Chicago: Chicago University Press, 1938.

Donner, Fred M. *The Early Islamic Conquests.* Princeton: Princeton University Press, 1981.

Dunlop, D. N. *The History of the Jewish Khazars.* Princeton: Princeton University Press, 1954.

Elverskog, Johan. *Buddhism and Islam on the Silk Road.* Philadelphia: University of Pennsylvania Press, 2010.

Ferrill, Arther. *The Fall of the Roman Empire: The Military Explanation.* London: Thames and Hudson, 1986.

Foltz, Richard. *Religion of the Silk Road: Premodern Patterns of Globilization.* 2nd ed. New York: Palgrave Macmillan, 2010.

Fowden, Garth. *From Empire to Commonwealth: Consequences of Monotheism in Late Antiquity.* Princeton: Princeton University Press, 1993.

Franke, Herbert. "The Forest Peoples of Manchuria." In *The Cambridge History of Early Inner Asia.* Edited by Denis Sinor, pp. 400–423. Cambridge: Cambridge University Press, 1990.

Franklin, Simon, and Jonathan Sheppard. *The Emergence of the Rus, 750–1200.* New York: Addison Wesley Longman, 1996.

Frye, Richard N. *The Heritage of Central Asia: From Antiquity to the Turkish Expansion.* Princeton: Markus Wiener Publishers, 1998.

———. *The Heritage of Persia.* New York/London: Mentor Books, 1966.

Fuller, J. F. C. *The Generalship of Alexander the Great*. New York: Minerva Books, 1960.

Golden, Peter B. *Central Asia in World History*. Oxford: Oxford University Press, 2011.

―――. "Inner Asia, c. 1200." In *The Cambridge History of Inner Asia: The Chinggisid Age*. Edited by Nicolas di Cosmo, Allen J. Frank and Peter B. Golden, pp. 9–25. Cambridge: Cambridge University Press, 2009.

―――. "The Karakhanids and Early Islam." In *The Cambridge History of Early Inner Asia*. Edited by Denis Sinor, pp. 343–370. Cambridge: Cambridge University Press, 1990.

―――. "The Peoples of the Russian Forest Belt." In *The Cambridge History of Early Inner Asia*. Edited by Denis Sinor, pp. 230–255. Cambridge: Cambridge University Press, 1990.

―――. "The Peoples of the South Russian Steppes." In *The Cambridge History of Early Inner Asia*. Edited by Denis Sinor, pp. 246–284. Cambridge: Cambridge University Press, 1990.

―――, et al., eds. *The World of the Khazars*. Leiden: Brill, 2007.

Goldsworthy, A. K. *The Roman Army at War, 100 B.C.–A.D. 200*. Oxford: Oxford University Press, 1996.

Gonzalez de Clavijo, Ruy. *Embassy to Tamerlane, 1403–1406*. Translated by Guy Le Strange with revised introduction by C. Sonte. The Roan, Scotland: Hardinge Simpole Ltd., 2009.

Gordon, C. D. *The Age of Attila: Fifth-Century Byzantium and the Barbarians*. Ann Arbor, MI: University of Michigan Press, 1972.

Graff, David A. *Medieval Chinese Warfare, 300–900*. London/New York: Routledge, 2002.

Gupta, Parmeshwari Lal, and Sarojini Kulashreshtha. *Kuṣāna Coins and History*. Delhi: D. K. Printworld, Ltd., 1994.

Hansen, Valerie. *The Silk Road: A New History*. Oxford: Oxford University Press, 2012.

Harl, Kenneth W. *Coinage in the Roman Economy, 300 B.C.–700 A.D.* Baltimore: Johns Hopkins University Press, 1996.

Headrick, Daniel R. *The Tools of Empire: Technology and European Imperialism in the Nineteenth Century*. Oxford: Oxford University Press, 1981.

Herodotus. *The Histories*. Translated by A. de Selincourt. Rev. ed. New York: Penguin, 1972.

———. *The Histories*. Rev. ed. Translated by J. M. Marcincola and Aubery de Selincourt. New York: Penguin, 2003.

Hildinger, Erik. *Warriors of the Steppe: A Military History of Central Asia, 500 B.C. to 1700 A.D.* Cambridge, MA: Da Capo Press, 1997.

Hill, John E. *Through the Jade Gate to Rome: A Study of the Silk Routes during the Later Han Dynasty, 1ˢᵗ to 2ⁿᵈ Centuries C.E.* Charleston, SC: Book Surge Publishing, 2009.

Hirth, F. *China and the Roman Orient: Researches into Their Ancient and Medieval Relations as Represented in the Old Chinese Records*, Chicago: Ares Press, 1975; reprint of Shangai–Hong Kong, 1885.

Holt, Frank L. *Alexander the Great and Bactria: Formation of a Greek Frontier in Central Asia*. Leiden: E. J. Brill, Mnemosyne Supplement, 1988.

Hopkirk, Peter. *The Great Game: The Struggle for Empire in Central Asia*. New York: Kodansha America, 1990.

Hucker, Charles. *China's Imperial Past: An Introduction to Chinese History and Culture*. Stanford: Stanford University Press, 1995.

Isaac, Benjamin. *The Limits of Empire: The Roman Army in the East*. 2nd ed. Oxford: Clarendon Press, 1993.

Istvan, Vasary. *Cumans and Tatars: Oriental Military in the Pre-Ottoman Balkans, 1185–1365*. Cambridge: Cambridge University Press, 2005.

———. "The Jochid Realm: The Western Steppes." In *The Cambridge History of Inner Asia: The Chinggisid Age*. Edited by Nicolas di Cosmo, Allen J. Frank, and Peter B. Golden, pp. 67–88. Cambridge: Cambridge University Press, 2009.

Jackson, Peter. *The Delhi Sultanate: A Political and Military History*. Cambridge: Cambridge University Press, 1999.

———. "The Mongol Age in Eastern Inner Asia." In *The Cambridge History of Inner Asia: The Chinggisid Age*. Edited by Nicolas di Cosmo, Allen J. Frank, and Peter B. Golden, pp. 26–45. Cambridge: Cambridge University Press, 2009.

———. *The Mongols and the West, 1221–1410*. New York: Pearson Longman, 2005.

Keay, John. *India: A History*. New York: Grove Press, 2000.

Kelenkna, Pita. *The Horse in Human History*. Cambridge: Cambridge University Press, 2009.

Kennedy, Hugh. *The Armies of the Caliphate: Military and Society in the Early Islamic State*. New York/London: Routledge, 2001.

———. *The Great Arab Conquests: How the Spread of Islam Changed the World We Live In*. Philadelphia: Da Capo Press, 2007.

————. *The Prophet and the Age of the Caliphates: The Islamic Near East from the Sixth to the Eleventh Century*. 2nd ed. London: Pearson Longman, 2006.

Khodarkovsky, Michael. *Russia's Steppe Frontier: The Making of a Colonial Empire, 1500–1800*. Bloomington, IN: Indiana University Press, 2002.

Kinoshita, Hiromi, and Jane Portal. eds. *The First Emperor: China's Terracotta Army*. London: British Museum, 2007.

Kuhn, Dieter. *The Age of Confucian Rule: The Song Transformation of China*. Cambridge, MA: Harvard University Press, 2009.

Lange, Christian. The *Seljuqs: Politics, Society, and Culture*. Edinburgh: Edinburgh University Press, 2012.

Lewis, Mark E. *China between Dynasties: The Northern and Southern Dynasties*. Cambridge, MA: Harvard University Press, 2009.

Li, Rongxi, trans. *The Great Tang Dynasty Record of the Western Regions*. Berkeley: Numata Center for Buddhist Translation and Research, 1995.

Lieu, Samuel N. C. *Manichaeism in the Roman Empire and Medieval China*. Tubingen: J. C. R. Mohr, 1992.

Lincoln, W. Bruce. *The Conquest of a Continent: Siberia and the Russians*. Ithaca, NY: Cornell University Press, 1994.

Liu, Xinbu. *The Silk Road in World History*. Oxford: Oxford University Press, 2010.

Macartney, C. A. *The Magyars in the Ninth Century*. Cambridge: Cambridge University Press, 2008; reprint of 1930 edition.

MacKerras, Colin. "The Uighurs." In *The Cambridge History of Early Inner Asia*. Edited by Denis Sinor, pp. 317–342. Cambridge: Cambridge University Press, 1990.

Magdalino, P. *The Empire of Manuel I Komnenos, 1143–1180.* Cambridge: Cambridge University Press, 1993.

Mallory, J. P. *In Search of the Indo-Europeans: Language, Archaeology, and Myth.* London: Thames and Hudson, 1989.

Mallory, J. P., and Victor H. Mair. *The Tarim Mummies: Ancient China and the Mystery of the Earliest Peoples from the West.* London: Thames and Hudson, 2000.

Manz, Beatrice F. *The Rise and Rule of Tamerlane.* Cambridge: Cambridge University Press, 1989.

———. "Temür and the Early Timurids to c. 1450." In *Cambridge History of Inner Asia: The Chinggisid Age.* Edited by Nicola di Cosmo, Allen J. Frank, and Peter B. Golden, pp. 182–198. Cambridge: Cambridge University Press, 2009.

Marozzi, Justin. *Tamerlane: Sword of Islam, Conqueror of the World.* Cambridge, MA: Da Capo Press, 2004.

Meaenchen-Helfen, Otto J. *The World of the Huns: Studies in Their History and Culture.* Edited by Max Knight. Berkeley: University of California Press, 1973.

Melyukova, A. I. "The Scythians and Samartians." In *The Cambridge History of Central Asia,* edited by D. Sinor, pp. 97–117. Cambridge, 1990.

Millar, Fergus. *The Roman Near East, 31 B.C.–A.D. 337.* Cambridge, MA: Harvard University Press, 1993.

Mote, F. W. *Imperial China, 900–1800.* Cambridge, MA: Harvard University Press, 1999.

Narain, A. K. "Indo-Europeans in Inner Asia." In the *New Cambridge History of Inner Asia.* Edited by Denis Sinor, pp. 151–176. Cambridge: Cambridge University Press.

Oblensky, Dimitri. *The Byzantine Commonwealth: Eastern Europe, 500–1453*. Crestwood, NY: St. Vladimir's Seminary Press, 1982.

O'Flynn, John Michael. *Generalissmos of the Western Roman Empire*. Edmonton: University of Alberta Press, 1983.

Okladnikov, A. P. "Inner Asia at the Dawn of History." In *The Cambridge History of Inner Asia*. Edited by Denis Sinor, pp. 41–96. Cambridge: Cambridge University Press, 1990.

Ostrer, Harry. *Legacy: A Genetic History of the Jewish People*. Oxford: Oxford University Press, 2012.

Peacock, Andrew, and Sara Nur Yildez, eds. *The Seljuks of Anatolia: Court and Society in the Medieval Middle East*. London: I. B. Tauris, 2012.

Piggott, Stuart. *The Earliest Wheeled Vehicles from the Atlantic Coast to the Caspian Sea*. Ithaca, NY: Cornell University Press, 1983.

Polo, Marco. *The Travels of Marco Polo, the Venetian*. Translated and edited by Thomas Wright. London: George Bell and Sons, 1907.

Pourshariati, Parvaneh. *Decline and Fall of the Sasanian Empire: The Sasanian-Parthian Confederacy and the Arab Conquest of Iran*. New York: J. B. Taurus, 2008.

Ratchnevsky, Paul. *Genghis Khan: His Life and Legacy*. Oxford: Blackwell Publishing, 1999.

Reder, Ellen, and Michael Treiser. *Scythian Gold*. New York: Harry N. Abrams, 1999.

Rice, Tamara Talbot. "The Scytho-Sarmatian Tribes of South-Eastern Europe." In *The Roman Empire and Its Neighbors*, by Fergus Millar, 2nd ed., pp. 281–294. New York: Holmes & Meier, 1981.

———. *The Seljuk Turks*. London: Thames and Hudson, 1961.

Richards, John F. *The Mughal Empire*. Cambridge: Cambridge University Press, 1996.

Rossabi, Morris. *Kublai Khan, His Life and Times*. Berkeley: University of California Press, 2006.

———. *The Mongols and Global History*. New York: W. W. Norton and Company, 2011.

Runciman, Stephen. *A History of the First Bulgarian Empire*. London: G. Bell and Sons, 1930.

Saunders, J. J. *A History of Medieval Islam*. London: Routledge and Kegan Paul, 1965.

———. *The History of the Mongol Conquests*. Philadelphia: University of Pennsylvania Press, 1971.

Shaban, M. A. *The Abbasid Revolution*. Cambridge: Cambridge University Press, 1970.

Shavegan, M. R. *Arsacids and Sasanians: Political Ideology in Post-Hellenistic and Late Antique Persia*. Cambridge: Cambridge University Press, 2011.

Sinor, Denis, ed. *The Cambridge History of Early Inner Asia*. Cambridge: Cambridge University Press, 1990.

———. "The Establishment and Dissolution of the Türk Empire." In *The Cambridge History of Early Inner Asia*. Edited by Denis Sinor, pp. 285–316. Cambridge: Cambridge University Press, 1990.

———. "The Hun Period." In *The New Cambridge History of Inner Asia*. Edited by Denis Sinor, pp. 177–205. Cambridge: Cambridge University Press, 1990.

Skaff, Jonathan K. *Sui-Tan China and Its Turko-Mongol Neighbors: Culture, Power, and Connections, 580–800.* Oxford: Oxford University Press, 2012.

Sulimirski, T., and T. Taylor. "The Scythians." In *The Cambridge Ancient History.* Vol. III, part 2. Edited by John Barodman et al.. pp. 547–590. Cambridge: Cambridge University Press, 1991.

Szádeczky-Kardoss, Samuel. "The Avars." In *The Cambridge History of Early Inner Asia.* Edited by Denis Sinor, pp. 206–228. Cambridge: Cambridge University Press, 1990.

Tacitus. *Annals of Imperial Rome.* Translated by Michael Grant. New York/London: Penguin Books, 1975.

Tarn, William Woodthorpe. *The Greeks in Bactria and India.* 3rd ed., rev. by Frank L. Holt. Chicago: Ares Publishers, 1984.

Thapar, Romila. *A History of India.* Vol. I. New York/London: Penguin Books, 1966.

Thompson, E. A. *The Huns.* Oxford: Blackwell Publishers, Ltd., 1996.

Vásáry, István. *Cumans and Tatars: Oriental Military in the Pre-Ottoman Balkans, 1185–1365.* Cambridge: Cambridge University Press, 2009.

Veith, Veronika. "The Eastern Steppe: Mongol Regimes after the Yuan (1368–1636)." In *Cambridge History of Inner Asia: The Chinggisid Age.* Edited by Nicola di Cosmo, Allen J. Frank, and Peter B. Golden, pp. 157–181. Cambridge: Cambridge University Press, 2009.

Vyrnos, Speros. *The Decline of Medieval Hellenism in Asia Minor and the Process of Islamization from the Eleventh through the Fifteenth Century.* Berkeley: University of California Press, 1964.

Waldron, Arthur. *The Great Wall of China: From History to Myth.* Cambridge: Cambridge University Press, 1990.

Watt, W. Montgomery. *Muhammad, Prophet and Statesman.* Oxford: Oxford University Press, 1975.

Weatherford, Jack. *Genghis Khan and the Making of the Modern World.* New York: Three Rivers Press, 2004.

Whitby, Michael. *The Emperor Maurice and His Historian Theophylact Simocattta on Persian and Balkan Warfare.* Oxford: Clarendon Press, 1988.

Whittlow, Mark. *The Making of Byzantium, 600–1025.* Berkeley: University of California Press, 1996.

Yarshater, E., ed. *The Cambridge History of Iran.* Vol. III: *Seleucid, Parthian, and Sasanian Periods.* Cambridge: Cambridge University Press 1983.

Ying-shi Yu. "The Hsiung-nu." In *The Cambridge History of Inner Asia.* Edited by Denis Sinor, pp. 118–150. Cambridge: Cambridge University Press, 1990.

———. *Trade and Expansion in Han China: A Study in the Structure of Sino-Barbarian Economic Relations.* Berkeley: University of California Press, 1967.

Zakaria, Rafiq. *Razia, Queen of India.* Oxford: Oxford University Press, 1966.

Notes

Notes

Notes

Notes

Notes

Notes

The Barbarian Empires of the Steppes

Kenneth W. Harl, Ph.D.

THE
GREAT
COURSES

PUBLISHED BY:

THE GREAT COURSES
Corporate Headquarters
4840 Westfields Boulevard, Suite 500
Chantilly, Virginia 20151-2299
Phone: 1-800-832-2412
Fax: 703-378-3819
www.thegreatcourses.com

Kenneth W. Harl, Ph.D.
Professor of Classical and Byzantine History
Tulane University

Professor Kenneth W. Harl is Professor of Classical and Byzantine History at Tulane University, where he has taught since 1978. He earned his B.A. from Trinity College and his M.A. and Ph.D. from Yale University.

Professor Harl teaches courses in Greek, Roman, Byzantine, and Crusader history from freshman to graduate levels. A recognized scholar of coins and classical Anatolia, he also takes students to Turkey on excursions and as assistants on excavations of Hellenistic and Roman sites.

Professor Harl has published numerous articles and is the author of *Civic Coins and Civic Politics in the Roman East, A.D. 180–275* and *Coinage in the Roman Economy, 300 B.C. to A.D. 700*. His current work includes publishing the coin discoveries from the excavation of Gordion, Turkey, and a new book on Rome and its Iranian foes. Professor Harl also serves on the editorial board of the *American Journal of Archaeology* and is a fellow and trustee of the American Numismatic Society.

Professor Harl has twice received Tulane's coveted Sheldon Hackney Award for Excellence in Teaching (voted on by both faculty and students) and has received the Student Body Award for Excellence in Teaching on multiple occasions. He was also the recipient of Baylor University's nationwide Robert Foster Cherry Award for Great Teaching. In 2007, he was the Lewis P. Jones Visiting Professor in History at Wofford College.

Professor Harl's other Great Courses include *Alexander the Great and the Macedonian Empire*, *The Fall of the Pagans and the Origins of Medieval Christianity*, *The Era of the Crusades*, *Origins of Great Ancient Civilizations*, *The World of Byzantium*, *Great Ancient Civilizations of Asia Minor*, *Rome and the Barbarians*, *The Peloponnesian War*, and *The Vikings*. ∎

Table of Contents

Table of Contents

The Barbarian Empires of the Steppes

Scope:

Our study begins with a description of the sack of Baghdad by the Mongols under Hulagu, grandson of Genghis Khan, in 1258. The Mongols ended the Abbasid Caliphate—a major shock to the Islamic world. To this day, Muslims regard this event as a catastrophe and a turning point in their history. The incident sums up popular images and stereotypes about the fierce steppe nomads. The course will examine the relationship of the barbarians of the Eurasian steppes with the sedentary civilizations of Europe, the Middle East, India, and China.

Lecture 2 starts with the peopling of the steppes in the Bronze Age, the domestication of the horse and camel, the invention of wheeled vehicles, and the spread of Indo-European speakers (Iranian and Tocharians) over the steppes—and then into Europe, Iran, and India. This was the first major movement on the steppes, and it went from west to east.

Then, we begin to explore the steppe nomads and their interaction with the urban civilizations and each other from about 600 B.C. to 600 A.D. We start with the eastern steppes, discussing Han China and the nomads. Wars and migrations led to the first travels across the steppes from east to west, thus influencing the central and western steppes. The last players in these migrations were the Huns and Hephthalites, the foes of Rome and Sassanid Iran, respectively. These nomads helped to bring a close to antiquity.

Lectures 14 to 25 deal with the steppes in the early Middle Ages, from about 600 to 1200 A.D., that is, before the Mongols. Again, we start in the east, with Tang China and the Turks who emerged on the eastern steppes and spread dramatically across Eurasia, displacing and assimilating Tocharian and Iranian speakers. The Turks apparently devised the stirrup and the composite bow to become dreaded horse archers. We will also deal with the Turkish nomads and Constantinople; these khaganates anticipated the later Golden Horde and played a decisive role with Byzantium and the caliphate.

In Lectures 19 to 25, we concentrate on the relationship between the Turkish-speaking nomads, or Turkmen, and Islam. Once the Turks embraced Islam and entered the Middle East, they assumed the dominant military role ever after and carved out new Islamic worlds in Anatolia and India. In time, Turkish dialects won out over other languages in the cities of Transoxiana. The Battle of Talas in 751 was pivotal, bringing together the Turkmen, Tang China, and the Abbasid caliphate. The Turks, who henceforth dominated the steppes (even under the Mongols), for the first time saw Islam rather than China as the most powerful civilization—a major change.

Lectures 26 to 35 explore the impact of the Mongols. We start with the Chin Dynasty in northern China (the typical Manchurian-Chinese frontier state) and Sung China, scrupulously posing as the heir to Confucian traditions and the Han Empire. This division was exploited by Genghis Khan, who rapidly expanded across the whole of the steppes, and his heirs, notably, his grandsons Khubilai Khan and Batu, who subjected the urban civilizations of Christian Russia, Muslim Iran and Transoxiana, and Sung China. This Pax Mongolica had a major cultural and technological impact. Ironically, it led to the spread of gunpowder that produced the first cannons and handheld firearms, which, when perfected by Christian Europe, put the steppe nomads out of business.

The Russians, starting with Ivan the Terrible, expanded across the steppes and ended the power of nomadic armies. But in the Islamic world, the Ilkhans converted to Islam, and the heirs of Genghis Khan, notably the conquerors Tamerlane and Baybur, ruled two of the great Muslim empires of the early modern age.

We close our course with the end of steppe power after 1500, notably with Ming China, Safavid Iran, and czarist Russia. Yet today, the steppes have again emerged as strategic, especially as the Soviet Union has fragmented and with prospects of separatist movements in Xinjang. ∎

Islam and the Caliphate
Lecture 19

In this lecture, we will shift back to the middle regions of the steppes and the associated civilizations in what we would today call the Middle East and India. That requires us to refocus our attention on the urban literate civilizations that had such a significant impact on nomadic peoples in the early Middle Ages. The effects of the caliphate and Islam were probably as far ranging and important as the impact of Buddhism and Chinese civilization had been on the nomads of the eastern steppes. Indeed, Islam defined the nomadic peoples of the western steppes far more profoundly than either western or Orthodox Christianity.

The Prophet Muhammad

- **Muhammad** is regarded by Muslims as the last and the greatest of all of God's prophets. He received his revelations in Mecca, probably when he was around the age of 40. The verses that came to him—suras—were later written down and codified into the Qur'an. This text is believed to be the uncreated word of God.

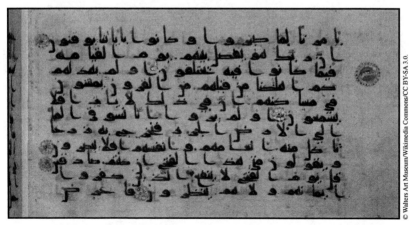

The Qur'an is considered the uncreated word of God, which means that it can't be translated; the best one can do is to translate the meaning of the Qur'an.

○ Muhammad's strictures were rather simple; the first and most important principle was to submit to the will of Allah. Thus, the religion came to be known as Islam, "submission." Those who practiced the religion, Muslims, were those who had submitted. From the start, Muslims accepted much of the testimony and prophecies of the Jews and Christians and saw themselves as direct heirs of the religion of Abraham.

○ Muhammad called for a new community of believers who were bound up in this new faith and recognized the importance of almsgiving and making a pilgrimage at least one time to Mecca. This preaching brought Muhammad directly in conflict with the ruling clans of his native city of Mecca.

• Mecca had been an important caravan city, and its rival city was Medina. These cities had long been linked to the Roman world and had been subject to influence by missionaries and merchants carrying both Judaism and various forms of Christianity. Muhammad's teachings required the end of idol worship and animal sacrifice, which had characterized Arabian cults since time immemorial. That led to conflict with the leading families, who objected on both business and religious grounds.

• In 622, Muhammad and his followers removed themselves to the rival city of Medina. That year is taken as the year of the flight and became year 1 in the new Islamic world. In Medina, Muhammad accepted Medinan merchants and others into the faith; those who believed became members of an *ummah*, a single community. Questions of clan, tribe, and family no longer mattered so much as the union of one faith.

• By the time of his death in 632, Muhammad had recovered Mecca and united the Arabian tribes under the banner of this new faith. The close followers of Muhammad who succeeded to his traditions then directed a spectacular conquest. In less than three generations, the Muslims ripped away the southern and eastern provinces of the Roman Empire and overthrew the Sassanid state.

Muslim Conquests

- A succession of able Arab generals, men who had trained in Byzantine and Sassanid armies, led Bedouin regiments across the frontiers and won stunning victories. For instance, at the Battle of Yarmouk, Khalid ibn al-Walid, known as the Sword of Islam, annihilated the Byzantine army in Syria, and in the next several years, all the Syrian possessions fell.

- Probably in the year 639, at the Battle of al-Qadisiyyah, another force of Arabs, some 20,000 strong, defeated the field army of the then-reigning Sassanid shah, **Yazdegerd III**. The Sassanid Empire collapsed over the next several years. By 651, Arab armies had reached the Amu Darya, the traditional boundary between Iran and Transoxiana.

- In the west, the conquest of Syria opened up Egypt in 641. Egypt was disaffected from imperial rule and welcomed the Arab conquerors. In 642, Arab armies began a relentless march across North Africa. By 698, the city of Carthage had fallen, and the Arabs continued to the Strait of Gibraltar. In 711, Arab forces and their Berber allies (desert nomads of North Africa) overran most of Spain. At the same time, an extraordinary feat of arms was carried out when yet another Arab army crossed the Makran desert and conquered the lower Indus Valley.

- Within less than 100 years, a new imperial power stretched from the Atlantic to the Hindu Kush. The Arabs, themselves desert nomads, had up until this point played a limited role among the civilized states of the Middle East and North Africa. Now, they were conquerors and rulers of a world empire.

Rise of the Umayyad Caliphs

- This great world empire put stress on the original community as Muhammad had conceived it. First, there was a question of authority. Three times in the 7th century, in the early stages of the Islamic Empire, a college of six electors met to choose a caliph ("successor"). In 632, the choice was obvious; the office went to

Abu Bakr, the second convert after Muhammad's wife. When he died, a man named **Umar** was elected.

- Umar was an accomplished general and presided over the spectacular conquests from 634 to 644. When he died, a man named **Uthman**, from the prominent Umayyad family, was elected. All three elections frustrated **Ali**, who was the cousin of Muhammad and saw himself as the natural successor.

- In 656, the Arab army in Egypt mutinied over various grievances, marched to Medina and Mecca, slew the caliph, and offered the throne to Ali, who instantly accepted. Objections were raised across the Islamic world, particularly by **Muawiya**, the governor of Syria, who was related to the deceased caliph. A civil war ensued. Ali was killed by a group of extremists, and Muawiya was acclaimed caliph in 661. He and his descendants would henceforth rule over **Sunni** Islam (Orthodox Islam) from Damascus as the Umayyad caliphs. The partisans of Ali, known as the Shi'a, went underground; today, we call them **Shi'ites**.

Empire of the Abbasids

- The Umayyads were responsible for many of the initial conquests, but by the end of the 7th century, they had suffered some serious reverses. They had been defeated by the Byzantines at Constantinople, were thwarted by the Khazars along the Caucasus, and were locked in difficult fighting with Turks over Transoxiana. As a result, shortly after 700, the caliphate began to come under severe fiscal and military pressures.

- The Arab tribal regiments that garrisoned the military towns in this expanding empire became increasingly independent and rapacious. Many of them harbored sympathies for Ali; others, for Shi'a. Southern and northern Arabs were also often engaged in fighting each other. The military governors spent much of their time trying to focus the efforts of these regiments on conquering new territory for Islam, rather than killing each other.

- In 749, the governor in Merv rebelled against the Umayyad caliphs. His mixed army of Arab tribal regiments and Persian converts swept west and defeated the Umayyad forces. By 750, the Umayyad Dynasty had been overthrown and a new dynasty, the **Abbasid caliphate**, was proclaimed.

- In the process of taking power, the Abbasids alienated a number of their allies. Many Shi'a and Alids (followers of Ali) had joined the so-called Abbasid revolution to overthrow the hated Umayyad caliphs. But they now found themselves saddled with an Abbasid caliph who was studiously and carefully Sunni in his religious beliefs. All the animosity that these groups once had against the Umayyads was transferred to the Abbasids.

- The Abbasids proved to be the most successful of the medieval dynasties. Several significant points about this caliphate dictated the future relationships between the emerging Islamic world and the nomadic peoples of the steppes.
  - The second caliph, al-Mansur, moved the capital from Damascus to Baghdad. That move announced that this new line of caliphs had no interest in conquering Constantinople or becoming heir to the Roman Empire. The Abbasid caliphs adopted much of the high culture of Sassanid Persia.

  - Further, they turned their empire from an Arabic empire into a Muslim empire. Something like 34 of the 37 Abbasid caliphs were the sons of non-Arab slaves, most of them Persians. They appreciated the Persian converts who provided infantry, administrators, and thinkers who were responsible for the flowering of Islamic civilization.

Weaknesses and Rivalries
- Of course, the Abbasid state had certain weaknesses. It faced opposition from Shi'ites and other extremists. In addition, the unity of the Abbasid state was always questionable. Half the dynasty was made up of the former Roman Empire in North Africa and Spain, along with Arabia. The other part was the eastern or Iranian

half. Over the course of the 8th through 10th centuries, the Abbasid state fragmented.

- The prime group that was the real danger to the Abbasid caliphs was the Alids. They could penetrate the guilds and trade networks across the Abbasid Empire. The Alids pulled off some successes, including one in 909, when an Alid pretender organized the Berber populations into an effective tribal army, swept across North Africa, and occupied Egypt.

- This group established the rival **Fatimid caliphate**, with its capital at Cairo. The Fatimids occupied Mecca and Medina and took over the cities of the Levant. They were hailed by Shi'ites across the Islamic world. They also entered into an alliance with the resurgent Byzantine state, which was on the move against the Sunni emirs on its eastern frontier.

- Baghdad looked to be in real trouble. It seemed as if a Fatimid army would cross the Fertile Crescent and occupy Baghdad, ending the Abbasid caliphate in favor of a Shi'ite caliphate. This didn't happen because out of the steppes of central Asia came a new people, the Seljuk Turks. Their leader, Tughril Bey, entered the city of Baghdad in 1055 and restored the power of the Abbasid caliph, along with the power of Islam itself.

Important Terms

Abbasid caliphate: The hereditary dynasty of caliphs (749–1258) established by as-Saffah (r. 750–754) and, from 762 on, resident at Baghdad. Hulagu ended the dynasty with the sack of Baghdad in 1258.

Fatimid caliphate: Shi'ite caliphs (909–1171) who claimed descent from Fatimah, daughter of the prophet Muhammad and wife of Caliph Ali. In 969, the Fatimid caliphs ruled from Cairo and protected the holy cities of Medina and Mecca.

Shi'ite: The sectarian school of Islam that desired a descendant of Ali (656–661) as the rightful caliph and, thus, upheld the authority of Ali.

Sunni: "The orthodox"; Muslims who accepted the Umayyad caliphate of Muawiya (661–680). The majority of Muslims follow Sunni Islam and the authority of the Qur'an.

ummah: In Islam, the community of believers as proclaimed by the prophet Muhammad (575–634).

Names to Know

Ali ibn Abi Talib (b. c. 600; r. 656–661): Fourth of the Rashidun caliphs. Cousin of the prophet Muhammad, Ali married the prophet's only daughter, Fatimah (606–632). Ali was twice passed over for the caliphate. As caliph in 656, he faced opposition from Muawiya in the first Muslim civil war. Ali was slain by sectarian extremists, and in later Shi'ite theology, he was elevated to prophetic status almost on par with Muhammad.

Abu Bakr (b. c. 573; r. 632–634): Caliph and friend and associate of Muhammad who succeeded as the first of the Rashidun caliphs after the prophet's death. His reign saw the unification of Arabia under the banner of Islam.

al-Mansur (754–775): Second Abbasid caliph; dedicated Baghdad as the new capital in 762 and shifted the locus of Islamic civilization to Iran and Transoxania.

Muawiya (b. 602; r. 661–689): Umayyad caliph; general of the Syrian army and father of the Arabic navy. In 656, he refused to accept Ali, the cousin of Muhammad, as the fourth Rashidun caliph because of Ali's implication in the murder of Caliph Uthman (644–656). Muawiya triumphed over the forces of Ali and, thus, founded the first hereditary Umayyad caliphate at Damascus.

Muhammad (570–632): The prophet of God (Allah), he was called to cleanse the religion of Abraham and, thus, founded Islam. His revelations were collected into the Qur'an. Driven from his native Mecca in 622, Muhammad created an *ummah* (community of believers) at Medina that defeated the Meccans. At his death, Muhammad had united all of Arabia under Islam.

Umar I (b. 584; r. 634–644): Second of the Rashidun caliphs; was elected in preference to Ali. He directed the conquests of Byzantine Syria, Egypt, and Libya and the Sassanid Empire of Persia.

Uthman (b. 577; r. 644–656): Third of the Rashidun caliphs; was elected in preference to Ali. He headed the powerful Umayyad clan but personally lacked the will to govern effectively from Medina. He was slain by mutinous soldiers of the Egyptian army, who then offered the caliphate to Ali.

Yazdegerd III (632–651): Last Sassanid shah and grandson of Khosrow II; lost his empire to the Arab armies. In 636 (or 639), the Arabs occupied his capital Ctesiphon after their victory at the Battle of al-Qadisiyyah. In 642–651, Yazdegerd failed to check the Arab advance into Iran and was murdered near Merv. His son and heir, Peroz, died an exile at the Tang court.

Crone and Hinds. *God's Caliph.*

Donner, *The Early Islamic Conquests.*

Kennedy, *The Armies of the Caliphate.*

———, *The Prophet and the Age of the Caliphates.*

Shaban, *The Abbasid Revolution.*

Watt, *Muhammad, Prophet and Statesman.*

Questions to Consider

1. What accounted for the rapid conquests of the Rashidun and Umayyad caliphs? What was the nature of this early Islamic Empire? How was religious and political authority exercised by the caliph? How was this

Lecture 19: Islam and the Caliphate

Islamic state perceived by the subject peoples and the nomads of the Eurasian steppes?

2. How did Muhammad, as prophet and statesman, establish the precedent for the authority of the caliphs? How would the religious and political authority of the caliphs eventually be adapted by Turkish steppe nomads?

3. What accounts for the prosperity and cultural achievements of the Abbasid caliphate in the 9th and 10th centuries? How would the subject peoples and nomads of the Eurasian steppes view this new Islamic civilization? In what ways did Turkish tribes profit from the Abbasid caliphate?

4. What accounted for the widespread use of Turkish slave soldiers and mercenaries in the Islamic world from the early 9th century? What were the broader implications of this shift in military power in the Islamic world?

Islam and the Caliphate
Lecture 19—Transcript

In this lecture, I want to shift us back to the middle regions of the steppes, and also the associated civilizations in what we would today call the Middle East and India; and that requires us to refocus our attention on the urban literate civilizations that have such an important impact on nomadic peoples in the early Middle Ages. That civilization that exercised such influence on Turkish speaking nomads of the central steppes is Islam.

Islamic civilization—or to use the term *caliphate*, which refers to the entire institutional arrangements of Islam under the caliphs, the successors of Muhammad—that institutional Islam, the folk faith of Islam, and the culture that becomes associated with Islam, which is largely a Persian high culture; that whole package of Islam has a profound effect on the nomadic peoples. Its effects are probably as far ranging and as important as the impact of Buddhism, which had been received on the Silk Road, and the impact of Chinese civilization on the nomads of the eastern steppes; so Islam becomes in effect the third great religious cultural force transforming and defining the nomadic peoples in a far more profound way than either western or Orthodox Christianity did among the nomads of the western steppes.

To address this issue, it is necessary to give some background of the emergence of the Caliphate, the teachings of Muhammad, and why this Muslim civilization that emerged—really had burst—upon the scene in the seventh century A.D. very, very dramatically in some of the most spectacular world conquests of any time, how did this civilization emerge and come to play such an important role among the Turkish-speaking peoples of the Eurasian steppes? That requires us to back up a bit and look at a little of the career of Muhammad, the creation of the Caliphate, its divisions, and above all how the creation of a Muslim capital at Baghdad, and then associated cities starting in the eighth century and ninth century, exercised a very, very important influence because of trade connections. It is through the trade connections in the end that the nomads will receive Islam.

First, Muhammad is regarded as the last and the greatest of all of God's prophets, Allah. You have to remember that Muhammad had his revelations in Mecca, probably starting at the age of 40; he essentially was a prophet and statesman at the same time. These suras, these verses, which came to him were later written down, codified, and put together into the work known as the Koran, which Muslim theologians in the ninth century, especially in the city of Baghdad, determined was the uncreated word of God; that God had spoken directly through Muhammad in Arabic. You really cannot translate the Koran; the best you can do is translate the meaning of the Koran.

Muhammad's strictures were rather simple, just as in the case of the Revelations of Siddhartha Gautama, the Buddha; and fundamentally, the first and most important call was the principle to submit to the will of God, Allah in Arabic. The religion came to be known as Islam, "submission"; and those who practiced the religion, Muslims, were those who had submitted to the fact that God had sent Muhammad, late in life—according to the accounts we have in his sura, biography, and the early traditions, the Hadith, he may have been close to 40 years of age when he had these revelations—to recognize the oneness of God and to return to the purity of the faith as it had once been preached by earlier prophets. These earlier prophets included the prophets of Israel, above all Moses or Musa; also Jesus, Isa as he is called in Arabic, was recognized as a prophet; and from the very start, the Muslims did accept much of the testimony and prophecies of the Jews and the Christians and saw themselves as direct heirs of the religion of Abraham, or Ibrahim as he would be called in Arabic. Muhammad called for a new community of believers that were bound up in this new faith, submitting to the will of God, recognizing the importance of almsgiving, attempting to make a pilgrimage at at least one point in life to Mecca (we will discuss that later on); and these preachings brought Muhammad directly in conflict with the ruling clans of his native city of Mecca.

Mecca had been an important caravan city, an oasis city, and its rival city was Medina. These cities had long been linked to the Roman world. They had been subject to influence by missionaries and merchants carrying both Judaism and various forms of Christianity. Muhammad's teachings required the ending of idol worship and animal sacrifice, which had characterized Arabian cults since times in memorial. That led to conflict with the leading families that objected to this on grounds of loss of business as well as pious reasons; and in 622, Muhammad and his followers had removed themselves to the rival city of Medina. That year, 622, is taken as the year of the migration of the flight, usually abbreviated as AH, the *anno hegirae*, the Latin rendition; and it becomes year one in this new Islamic world.

Muhammad in Medina took a very important step. He had accepted Medinans—a number of merchants who had actually invited him to come to their city—and henceforth, those who believed became members of an *umma*, of a single community. Some scholars have noted that Muhammad's background as a merchant, particularly on camel caravans, was behind part of his thinking. It was almost a contractual sense coming out of commerce that all believers, all Muslims, whether they are from Medina, whether they are from Mecca, certainly questions of clan and tribe and family no longer mattered so much as the union of one faith. Eventually Muhammad, by the time of his death in 632, had recovered Mecca and united the Arabian tribes under the banner of this new faith.

It is a question as to how many of the Arabian tribes really understood what their monotheism meant; that is a small consequence. Clearly, the close followers of Muhammad, who succeeded to his traditions, were convinced monotheists; they had accepted this new faith. It was they who directed the spectacular conquests, which in less than three generations ripped away the southern and eastern provinces of the Roman Empire and overthrew the Sassanid state. The conquests are still studied from a military viewpoint. Arab chroniclers writing long after the initial conquests saw these victories as manifestations of the favor and will of Allah; and from their viewpoint, that was well taken. The victories of the seventh century A.D. confirmed Islam in the eyes of many—not just of the insipient Muslim community, but even of many of the foes who would in time convert—that this was a religion of victory; this had some sort of power that other religions might have been lacking.

The conquests were really the result of the armies commanded by the first three caliphs. *Caliph* was a term that means "successor"; and the caliph combined both the qualities of a statesman as well as the director of the religious community, the *umma*. A facile statement is often made that the caliphs were essentially emperor and pope together, and that is a bit more distorting than helpful. But whatever the case, a succession of able Arab generals, men who had actually trained in Byzantine and Sassanid armies, led these Bedouin regiments across the frontiers and won stunning victories. At the Battle of the Yarmouk, Khalid ibn al-Walid, known as the "Sword of Islam," annihilated the Byzantine army in Syria, and in the next several years all of those possessions fell. Probably in the year 639—the date is debated—at the Battle of Qadisiyya, another force of Arabs, some 20,000 strong, defeated the field army of the then-reigning Sassanid shah, Yazgerd III. That army went down in defeat in a great three-day battle in which a sandstorm actually interrupted the battle and threw the Persians in disorder. The Sassanid Empire effectively collapses over the next several years. The shah retreats east; he is eventually murdered quite ignominiously in an obscure village out in the region of Khurasan. He had attempted to get assistance from the emperor Heraclius in Constantinople, from Taizong, the Tang emperor; none of that materialized. By 651, Arab armies had reached the Oxus, the Amu Darya, the traditional boundary between Iran and Transoxiana.

In the west, the conquest of Syria opened up Egypt in 641. An army crossed the Sinai, invaded Egypt. Egypt was disaffected from imperial rule, welcomed the Arab conquerors, and in the following year, in 642, Arab armies began a relentless march across North Africa. In 642, the cities of Libya submitted, the old Roman provinces of Cyrenaica and Tripolitania. By 698, the city of Carthage had fallen to Arab arms and the Arabs swept across North Africa, reached the Straits of Gibraltar; and in 711, Arab forces and now their Berber allies—that is, the desert nomads of North Africa—crossed into Spain, smashed the Visigothic kingdom, and overran most of Spain. At the same time, an extraordinary feat of arms was carried out when yet another Arab army crossed the Makran Desert—that horrible Gedrosian desert that gave Alexander the Great so much trouble—descended into the lower reaches of the Indus Valley, and conquered the lower Indus Valley up to the city of Multan, a spectacular conquest indeed. Within less than 100 years, approximately three generations, a new imperial power stretched from the Atlantic to the Hindu Kush. The Arabs, themselves desert nomads, had up until this point played a very limited role among the civilized states of the Middle East and North Africa; now they were conquerors and rulers of a world empire.

This great world empire put great stress on the original community as Muhammad had conceived it. As I said, Muhammad had many visions, he had many—these are called sura—insights into how to organize this new community; but within a very rapid time, his first three successors, the Rashidun or the rightly-guided caliphs, were now saddled with a major problem of running a world empire, and a world empire that comprised largely of people who were non-Muslims: Christians, Jews, Zoroastrians, as we shall see later Buddhists, Manichaeans, and others.

There was also a question of authority: Who was to follow the prophet? Three times in the seventh century, at the early stages of the Islamic Empire, a college of six electors met to choose a successor, a caliph. In 632, the choice was pretty obvious; it went to the senior colleague, the second convert after Muhammad's wife, Abu Bakr (who was also a part-time camel herder). He directed the initial conquest. When he died, the college then elected a man called Umar. Umar presided over the spectacular conquest from 634–644; he was an accomplished general. When he died, mortally wounded by a slave who was outraged over the victories over the Persians (the slave was of Persian origin), Umar directed a third election which elected a man named Uthman from a very, very prominent family, the Umayyad family, which had extensive contacts in the Arab leadership, and many of the important governorships were in the hands of this family, particularly the governor of Syria based in Damascus, a man named Muawiya.

In all three of these elections that occurred—and that would have been in 632, again in 644, and above all that final election that put Uthman on the throne—all of those elections on three occasions, Ali was frustrated. Ali was the first cousin of Muhammad. His father Abu Talib had essentially reared Muhammad. He was married to the only daughter of the prophet, Fatimah, and he saw himself as the natural successor. In the year 656, the Arab army in Egypt mutinied over various grievances including lack of back pay, marched on to Medina and Mecca, slew the caliph, and then offered the throne to Ali, who instantly accepted. The result was objections across the Islamic world, particularly by Muawiya, the governor of Syria, who was related to the deceased caliph. A civil war ensued, and Muawiya won. Actually Ali was done in by a group of extremists in 661, Kharijites, who mean "those who go out," and these were fundamentalist Muslims who did not want to have anything to do with either side, and a plague on caliphs and anything that even smacked of monarchy. They did in Ali but missed Muawiya; and Muawiya, in 661, was acclaimed caliph by the majority of the Muslims. He was seen as a legitimate successor of Muhammad, and he and his descendants would rule henceforth from Damascus as the Umayyad caliphs over Sunni Islam; that is, Orthodox Islam.

The defeated did not give up. The partisans of Ali, known as the Shi'a, went underground; today we would call them Shi'ite's. There were actually several different types of dissident groups. Some were strictly Aliad's; they wanted to put a descendent of Ali and Fatimah on the throne. Others were Shi'ite's and related groups who wanted not only to overthrow the caliph, but they saw this as part of the opening of a cosmic struggle, almost a Muslim apocalypse. All of these groups were in opposition and constantly being suppressed by the Umayyad government and later by the Abbasid caliphs.

The Umayyads were responsible for a lot of the initial conquests, but by the end of the seventh century the Umayyad caliphs located in Damascus had suffered some serious reverses. They had been defeated by the Byzantines at Constantinople; they were thwarted by the Khazars along the Caucasus; and as we shall see in an upcoming lecture, they were locked in very difficult fighting with Turks over Transoxiana and that northeastern frontier that gave so much trouble to the Sassanids. As a result, the Umayyad caliphate, shortly after 700 A.D., began to come under severe fiscal and military pressures. It could not keep up the pace of conquest. In addition, the Arab tribal regiments that garrisoned the military towns in this expanding empire—outside of Tunis at Fustat or Old Cairo; in the cities of lower Iraq, such as Basra, Wasit; and above all, the Arab army stationed in Merv on the Oxus, that old important caravan center going back really to antiquity—all of those forces became increasingly independent and rapacious. The Arab tribal regiments were very difficult to control. Many of them harbored sympathies for Ali, others were Shi'a. Also, it took a lot of effort on the part of Arab governors of these military forces to keep the Arab regiments focused on fighting the foes rather than fighting each other, because they were all tribal regiments with all sorts of blood feuds and personal quarrels between southern and northern Arabs. This constantly meant that any of these military governors spent more of his time trying to keep the tribes from killing each other and trying to focus their efforts on conquering new territory for Dar al-Islam—that is the heartland of Islam, house of Islam—from the infidels, the unbelievers, who dwelled in Dar-al-Harib, or the abode, the house of war. There was this notion of the Islamic world as opposed to the non-Islamic world, which emerged very quickly in the Umayyad caliphate.

The Umayyad caliphate is eventually overthrown; and the overthrow came from the east, significant so, in the region known as Khurasan. I have mentioned it before; that is Eastern Iran, on the border of the caravan cities. In 749, the governor in Merv raised the black flags of rebellion against the Umayyad caliphs. This man is later known as as-Saffah, "the Bloodthirsty" is the title he will take. His mixed army of Arab tribal regiments and Persian converts, *mawali* as they were called—the Persians had come to provide the bulk of the infantry for the eastern army, and that has become very evident when we discuss the difficulty of fighting the Turks and bringing Transoxiana under control—this army swept west and defeated the Umayyad forces; and by 750, the Umayyad Dynasty had been overthrown and a new dynasty was proclaimed. This is the Abbasid state. The new caliph made the claim he was descended from Abbas, the uncle of the prophet; and the Abbasid caliphs insisted that they had this connection going back to the prophet. In the process of taking power, they had alienated a number of their allies. Many Shi'a and Alids joined the so-called Abbasid Revolution to overthrow the hated Umayyad Caliphs only to find them saddled with yet another monarchy, an Abbasid caliph who was studiously and carefully Sunni in his religious beliefs. All of the animosity that these groups once had against the Umayyads was now transferred again to the Abbasids.

The Abbasid proved to be the most successful of the medieval dynasties. They were the third and greatest line of caliphs; they would be eliminated by the Mongol sack of Baghdad in 1258. Several significant points about the Abbasid caliph dictate the future relationships between this emerging Islamic world and the nomadic peoples of the steppes. The second caliph, al-Mansur, moved the capital from Damascus to Baghdad. That was a very significant move; it announced that this new line of caliphs really had no interest in conquering Constantinople and becoming heir to the Roman Empire. Instead, they created a capital very close to the ancient city of Ctesiphon where the Parthians had once ruled and the Sassanid Persians, and that new capital put the new Muslim dynasty essentially in a Persian cultural world. The Abbasid caliphs, in effect, adopted much of the high culture of Sassanid Persia. Many of their political institutions and pretentions really can be traced back to the shahs of Sassanid Iran. Furthermore, they turned their empire from an Arabic empire into a Muslim empire. Something like 34 of the 37 Abbasid caliphs were the sons of slaves, non-Arab slaves, most of them Persians; and they appreciated above all the Persian converts, who not only provided infantry but a lot of the administrators, and as we shall see in an upcoming lecture many of the thinkers who were responsible for the flowering of Islamic civilization in the reign of Harun ar-Rashid. He rules from 786–809. He is the caliph known to most westerners in the *Tales of the 1001 Arabian Knights*. His reign is seen as the apex of Abbasid civilization; of a Muslim empire as opposed to just an Arabic empire where only Arabs had privileged positions; an empire where all who served the caliph and who professed the true faith were welcomed. It is this vision of this great, tolerant, powerful empire that influences many calls back to traditional Islam that are made today; and in order to understand that current politic ideology, you have to have some understanding of how they view the Abbasid state.

This Abbasid state has certain weaknesses. For one, there were still the rival opponents; mostly Aliad and Shi'ite opponents, there were other extremists. They went underground and they opposed the caliph in Baghdad. In addition, the unity of the Abbasid state was always questionable from the start. It really comprised two halves. It comprised the former Roman Empire in North Africa, the east, and Spain; in fact, the Abbasid caliph ruled more of the former Roman Empire than the emperor in Constantinople did. So that was one half; and then there was Arabia, the homeland; and then there was the eastern or Iranian half. These two parts eventually went their separate ways, with the Abbasid caliphs ruling from Baghdad, which had been really the capital from at least 762; it was the main mint, it was where most of the activities of the caliph and his administration were centered. What happened over the course of the 8th, 9th, and 10th centuries is the Abbasid state fragmented. Various powerful men—and we will meet some of them in the upcoming lectures, particularly in Iran and Transoxiana, which slowly came under Islamic rule—known as emirs, governors, styled themselves as agents of the caliph, obtained what is called a *firman*, and ruled in his name.

This political fragmenting began after the death of Harun ar-Rashid. His death marked a great civil war; a civil war that pitted his two sons, al-Amin and al-Mamun—Al-Mamun, who was actually the son of a Persian concubine slave won; but he won with the help of the eastern army in Khurasan, particularly from members of what were known as the Tahirid family—and they set themselves us as essentially independent emirs. They in turn gave way in Khurasan to a new group of rulers, again Persian converts. We know them as the Samanid emirs. They represented converts to early Islam; the founder of this group, and he was given in effect a *firman* in 813, was a perfectly good Sunni emir. His name was Ahmad. He claims descent from his grandfather Saman; therefore we call it the Samanid emirs. They would rule from Bukhara and played a very, very important cultural role in the development of Islam in Iran and Transoxiana, the very Islamic culture that was carried to the nomads of the steppes. By the early ninth century, the Abbasid state was politically breaking up. All of these Sunni emirs recognized the caliph in Baghdad, who was increasingly a religious figure; but they had become, in effect, independent rulers.

At the same time, there were other would-be rivals to the Abbasid caliph. These represented various dissident groups. Some of them have been traced back to pre-Islamic apocalyptic groups. You got some rather colorful figures revolting against the Abbasid authority in the early ninth century; one of my favorite ones was the so-called Green Prophet who had all sorts of bizarre millenarian visions. The prime group that was the real danger to the Abbasid caliphs were the Alids; that is, those groups who had organized themselves in cells and wanted to overthrow Abbasid authority. These groups could penetrate the guilds, could penetrate the trade networks across the Abbasid Empire—and we will be discussing the important role of trade in the Abbasid Empire in an upcoming lecture; a very, very important set of connections that linked the Islamic world to the various Turkoman tribes—and these Alids pulled off some successes.

The most notable one was in 909, when one of these Alid pretenders who claimed to be a descendent of Fatimah, the daughter of Muhammad, came out of hiding. He was a hidden imam—these are hidden prophets in the Shi'a tradition—and he organized the Berber populations of North Africa into a very, very effective tribal army, and Fatimid armies swept across North

Africa. In 969, they entered the Nile valley, occupied Egypt. The capital of the Fatimid caliphs was transferred to Cairo. They occupied Mecca and Medina, the holy cities. They took over the cities of the Levant—that is, the eastern shore of the Mediterranean—and they established a counter caliphate. They were hailed by Shi'ites across the Islamic world, particularly one Sectarian group, the Nizarites, who are better known by the name "Assassins." They get that name from hashish because their hit squads, who were primarily aimed to take out Sunni rulers—emirs, and if they could the caliphs themselves—were hyped up on hashish when they committed their assassinations. They hailed them, and they were located in remote mountain fortresses in Iran and elsewhere.

The Fatimids, however, saw themselves very quickly as the rivals to the Abbasids. To the disappointment of many of the extreme sectarians, the later caliphs at Cairo—we call them Shi'ite, or better yet I think Alid is a better term—they saw themselves as the rival to Baghdad. As a result, the caliph of Cairo and the caliph of Baghdad now disputed authority over the Islamic world. The Fatimids enjoyed a number of advantages. They had the holy cities. They entered into alliance with the Byzantine emperor, a resurgent Orthodox Byzantine state that was on the move against the Sunni emirs on their eastern frontier. Baghdad looked in real trouble. Baghdad looked like its days were numbered; that a Fatimid army would cross the Fertile Crescent and occupy Baghdad and end the Abbasid caliphate in favor of a Shi'ite caliphate.

But it did not happen, because out of the steppes of Central Asia came a new people, Oghuz Turks of the family of Seljuk; and these Turks, under their leader Tughril Bey, entered the city of Baghdad in 1055, restored the power of the Abbasid caliph, attacked the Fatimids, and the Seljuk Turks would not only restore the power of the Abbasid caliph, but the power of Islam itself. The role that they would come to play was a result of the interaction on that northeastern frontier between the caliphate and the Turkish tribes of the central steppes, and that is the next chapter in the history of the empires of the steppes.

The Clash between Turks and the Caliphate
Lecture 20

This lecture looks in more detail at the initial contact between Islamic civilization and the people of the central Eurasian steppes. This requires us to look at the wars waged between the early caliphs, before the Abbasid caliphate, and the Turkish tribes. The lecture will end with a rather peculiar battle in 751, the Battle of Talas, which is seen as a turning point in this relationship. It's a battle that evokes a great deal of controversy and, in some ways, is remembered for the wrong reasons. Before we get to that battle, however, we need to understand how the Islamic armies came to fight on such a distant frontier, close to the borders of the Tang Empire.

Arabs on the Northeastern Frontier

- The **Rashidun** and Umayyad caliphs fell heir to the Sassanid Empire's northeastern frontier. Those regions had largely fallen into the hands of subordinate Turkish tribes who acknowledged the authority of the khans of the western Gök Turks. The cities there were ruled by different merchant princes speaking Sogdian and Tocharian languages. When the Arab armies had defeated the shah's army, they moved into Iran and reached the Oxus frontier around 651.

- From the start, the Arab armies realized that this region was unlike anything they were familiar with in the Byzantine and Roman worlds. Known to us as Transoxiana, the region beyond the Oxus had an extremely diverse religious and linguistic background. Excavations have revealed opulent houses of great merchant princes, and the decorations indicate that the occupants were familiar with Buddhism, Nestorian Christianity, and Manichaeism. Languages spoken included Sogdian, Aramaic, and Tocharian.

- This region was a formidable one for the Arabs to take on. There was no central and imperial power to defeat but, instead, a constellation of city-states.

- o Well beyond the knowledge of the Arabs in 651 was the Jaxartes River. This had been the boundary between Transoxiana and nomadic peoples, who had longstanding trade connections.

- o Within Transoxiana itself were settled smaller groups of nomads, who interacted with the agriculturalists in the cities.

- o Thus, Transoxiana was, in many ways, something of an urban extension of the central Eurasian steppes. Once the caliphs reached this frontier, they weren't quite sure what to do with it.

- About 671, a permanent camp was built at Merv, an old caravan city. From there, in the late 7th century and early 8th, Arab forces crossed the Oxus at different points and raided the cities of Transoxiana, such as Bukhara and Samarkand. The riches acquired on these massive raids were brought back to Merv, but there was no thought of conquest—of bringing these regions into the House of Islam.

- The Umayyad caliphs grew suspicious because the governors commanding in Merv had enormous military power. They controlled some of the best Arab regiments in the empire. Further, they recruited large numbers of Persians, who were converted to Islam, served as infantry, and were often given grants of land.

Conquest in Transoxiana

- The situation began to change at the opening of the 8th century. The powerful caliph **Abd al-Malik** (r. 685–705) reorganized the administration of the empire and the frontier provinces, particularly the eastern province in Transoxiana. In 705, a new governor arrived, **Qutaybah ibn Muslim**, who had been assigned to begin the conquest north of the Oxus.

- Qutaybah served as governor in Merv for some 10 years and launched a methodical set of campaigns intended both to net loot to satisfy the Arab tribal regiments and to begin the conversion of the area. We have reports from the city of Bukhara, for example, that the Buddhist temple there was leveled and replaced by a mosque. Further, the locals were rounded up to attend services.

- These attempts by Qutaybah to force Islam on the great caravan cities provoked a reaction. The cities resisted more seriously against the Arabs and called in their allies, the Turkish nomads. The man who responded to the call was a colorful figure known as **Suluk**. He was a brilliant campaigner, and in the clashes between the Arab and Turkish armies, especially in the 720s, it became clear that the Turks could outride and outshoot the Arams on the steppes of central Asia.

- Between 718 and 722, many of the cities in Transoxiana that had submitted to Abbasid rule declared their independence or went over to the Turks. The caliphs' frontier essentially fell back to the Oxus. But in 722, Suluk was killed, and the resistance to the Arabs fell apart. Succeeding governors began to come to terms with the cities of Transoxiana. By 750, they had more or less delivered the region to the control of the caliphs in Damascus.

- This piecemeal conquest of Transoxiana posed something of a religious crisis in the early Islamic community.
  - The initial conquests of the Arabs had been of areas occupied primarily by Christians and Jews, people of the book. Although they were not treated as equals and had to abide by certain restrictions, they were allowed to maintain their religious institutions.

  - With the conquest of Persia, the Arabs incorporated a region, particularly Iran, that was Zoroastrian. Although this religion wasn't referenced in the Qur'an, the Zoroastrians were essentially lumped together with Christians and Jews as protected people.

  - Crossing the Oxus, however, brought into the power of the caliph all sorts of people who practiced religions with which the Arabs had absolutely no familiarity: Buddhism,

Manichaeism, various pagan cults, Iranian cults, and so on. In time, the Islamic government would have to come to terms with these groups. By 750, Transoxiana was under the control of the caliph, but it was hardly an Islamic land.

The Battle of Talas

- The Arab armies were now on the western fringe of the power of the Tang emperors of China. In July or August of 751, a major battle took place between these two armies. On the Arab side was an experienced governor named **Ziyad ibn Salih**. The Tang general was **Gao Xianzhi**, who had ruled the western regions of the Tarim Basin. Both of these governors commanded important provincial armies, but both also depended heavily on Turkish allies, primarily, the Karluk Turks.

- The Battle of Talas was not actually planned. It resulted from the exiles of client rulers of both great powers. Those rulers appealed to Ziyad and Gao Xianzhi for help in regaining their thrones. Of course, both commanders were also aware of the strategic importance of Transoxiana and of the trade routes over the Pamirs. Undoubtedly, as they assembled their armies, these were considerations for backing the exiles' claims. The idea was to put in power local rulers who would favor either the Tang emperor or the Abbasid caliph.

- In 751, the armies moved into position and encountered each other at the Talas River. We have both Chinese and Arabic accounts of the battle. Perhaps some 30,000 to 35,000 men were marshaled on both sides. The key players in the battle would be the Karluk cavalry.

- The Chinese had at least 10,000 imperial forces, including excellent crossbowmen. But they had also recruited large numbers of Turkish cavalry, perhaps 20,000. Ziyad fielded perhaps 10,000 to 15,000 tribal Arabic regiments and Persian infantry. At least half, if not the majority, of his army was made up of Turkish allies, mostly Karluks who were fighting on both sides.

© Thermokarst/Wikimedia Commons/Public Domain.

The precise location of the battlefield along the Talas River is unknown; it is clear that the Chinese and Muslim armies maneuvered for several days before they came into contact with each other.

- The two armies came into contact somewhere on the Talas River. What decided the battle was the desertion of the Karluks on the Chinese side to the Muslim side. We don't know the reason for this defection.
  - For the first five days of the encounter, Ziyad was reluctant to commit his Arab and Persian forces to an assault across the river directed at Chinese infantry supported with crossbows. The Arabs may not have had much contact with the Chinese, but they quickly understood the power of the Chinese infantry in a fortified position.

  - Once the Chinese lost their supporting flanks of cavalry, then Ziyad could launch an attack against the infantry in the center, and his Turkish allies would eventually encircle and reduce the Chinese. This is apparently what happened.

- The Arabic cavalry ran into tough professional Chinese infantry. The Chinese general Gao Xianzhi rallied his forces and held the center. His subordinate officers fought an excellent holding action, and 2,000 of the Chinese managed to break out of the encirclement and escape, including most of the senior officers who wrote memoirs after the battle.

- Many of the Chinese soldiers fought on until they surrendered on terms. The Arab sources speak of taking many captives.

- Neither the Chinese emperor nor the Abbasid caliph pushed the battle. The Chinese emperor had problems with rebellions at home, and the caliph was dismayed by the success of both his governor and the Turkish allies. Thus, both empires accepted the battle as a draw. The Talas River would represent the boundary between them.

- The Chinese emperor withdrew his forces, and Chinese influence in the western regions lapsed; it would not return until the Ming emperors. Meanwhile, the Islamic empire did not gain any real estate. In fact, the Karluk Turks ended up being the beneficiaries. They now dominated the central steppes. Soon, these Turks would construct new confederations, embrace Islam, and invade the Muslim world.

Important Term

Rashidun caliphs: The first four elected caliphs from among the immediate associates of Muhammad: Abu Bakr (632–634), Umar (634–644), Uthman (644–656), and Ali (656–661).

Names to Know

Abd al-Malik (b. 646; r. 685–705): Umayyad caliph who imposed Arabic as the language of administration and forged the first Muslim administrative institutions. He appointed able governors who conquered Carthage in 698 and raided into Transoxania.

Gao Xianzhi (d. 756): Tang commander of the Four Garrisons (Tarim Basin) and an experienced general of Korean ancestry. He commanded the Tang army that was defeated by the Arabs and Karluks at the Battle of Talas in 751.

Qutaybah ibn Muslim (b. 699; r. 705–715): Umayyad governor of Khurasan; waged a destructive war against the cities of Transoxania, looting Manichaean, Zoroastrian, and Buddhist sanctuaries. He took Bukhara in 709 and Samarkand in 712. His ruthless efforts to impose Islam galvanized the Sogdian populations to invite Suluk, *yabgu* of the western Turks, to intervene. Qutaybah was executed on grounds of treason on the orders of Caliph Sulayman.

Suluk (717–738): *Yabgu* of the Turgesh, a leading tribe of the western Turkish khaganate. He waged a brilliant war of attrition against the Umayyad governor in Transoxania.

Ziyad ibn Salih (748–751): Arabic governor of Khurasan who commanded the Arabic-Turkish Karluk army that defeated the Tang army at the Battle of Talas in 751.

Suggested Reading

Graff, *Medieval Chinese Warfare, 300–900.*

Kennedy, *The Great Arab Conquests.*

———, *The Prophet and the Caliphates.*

Questions to Consider

1. Why drove the Rashidun and Umayyad caliphs to conquer eastern Iran and Transoxiana? How foreign and daunting were the peoples and cultures of these lands? Why did the Arabic conquest take more than a century?

2. How effective were the frontier armies of the Umayyad caliphs? What problems of discipline and motivation inhibited Arab success? How did

polices of the Arab governors alienate Sogdian and Bactrian cities and Turkish tribes alike? How did they perceive the Arabs?

3. Why did the Turks under Suluk rally so successfully? How did the succession of defeats suffered by the Arabs change their views and stereotypes of the steppe nomads?

4. Why did the Umayyad and Tang armies clash at the Battle of Talas in 751? In what ways was this battle decisive? How did the Turkish combatants fare in this battle? What lessons did the Turks draw from this Arabic victory?

5. Why did the Abbasid caliphs halt Islamic expansion? What were the consequences for this change in Muslim policy for the Turkish nomadic tribes?

The Clash between Turks and the Caliphate
Lecture 20—Transcript

In this lecture, I want to address in more detail the initial contact between Islamic civilization and the people of the Central Eurasian steppes who were Turkish speakers. This requires us to look at the conflicts, the wars, waged between the early caliphs, before the Abbasid caliph came into power, and eventually the Turkish tribes. This lecture will end on a rather peculiar battle in 751, the Battle of Talas, which is seen as a turning point in this relationship. It is a battle that evokes a lot of controversy and in some ways is remembered for the wrong reasons. But until we get to that battle, we need to explain how did the Islamic armies, largely Arabic-speaking at this point, come to fight a battle on a distant frontier, really on the borders of Kazakhstan today, close to the borders of the Tang Empire of China?

That gets us to the fact that the caliphs, the Rashidun—that is, the first four caliphs—and the Umayyad caliphs ruling from Damascus down to 750 fell heir to the Sassanid Empire's northeastern frontier. That was two issues: First was the region of Transoxiana, where the Caribbean cities are and that were outside of the power of the shah at the time of the Arab invasions. If you recall, those regions had fallen largely into the hands of Turkish tribes; that is, Turkish tribes that acknowledged the authority of the khans of the western Gök Turks. These were generally subordinate tribes. The cities were ruled by different merchant princes speaking Sogdian and Tocharian languages; and so when the Arab armies had defeated the shah's army, they had moved into Iran and they reached the Oxus frontier. At that point, in 651, the Arabs were really at the limit of effective Sassanid power. The river beyond was quite a different matter. It represented a whole different world, quite unusual, and a world that most Arabs would have found extremely unfamiliar. From the start, when the Arab armies reached the Oxus River, today the Amu Darya, they called the region to the north Transoxiana as "those regions that were beyond the river"; and that Arabic expression leads to the Islamic name for that region, which you find in later Islamic accounts, and it is known as Mawarannahr, "the area beyond the river." From the very, very start, the Arab armies realized that this was a region that was not at all like what they were familiar with in the Byzantine and Roman world.

Furthermore, the world beyond the Oxus represented a world that was very, very different to anything they had experienced in the Fertile Crescent; and we have to also adjust our perceptions of that world. This region—which we like to call Transoxiana; and I have tended to use that term because it is generally recognized by most Westerners—is usually thought of as the home of fabled cities; all sorts of silly orientalizing movies, nostalgia have been made about it, novels; Samarkand; they conjure up images of great mosques and minarets. You have to delete all of that. The great monuments in Bukhara and Samarkand are really the work of the Samanid emirs of whom we will speak later, and later still of the conqueror Tamerlane. Those did not exist.

In 651, the Arabs looking across the Oxus saw a very, very different world. It was extremely diverse in its background; and some sense of this diversity has been captured by archaeology in the excavations of a town in Tajikistan that is known as Panjakent. It is on the caravan route from Samarkand to Kashgar. The city apparently sprang into action sometime in the fourth century A.D. and persisted into the ninth century A.D. Excavations have revealed opulent houses of great merchant princes. The decorations indicate that clearly these occupants were familiar with Buddhism, Nestorian Christianity, Manichaeism; it is undoubtedly in villas such as these where Sogdian merchant princes welcomed Buddhist monks, the elect of the Manichees, where probably learned discussions took place. The objects that have been found in excavation indicated imported goods across the full extent of the Silk Road. This one town—and the town goes into decline in the ninth century and is essentially abandoned—is a glimpse into what all of the cities of Transoxiana and the Tarim Basin must have looked like on the eve of the Arabic conquest. There were Zoroastrian fire altars; Buddhist monasteries, the *vihara*; places of worship for the Manichees; Nestorian churches; Jewish synagogues. It was a very diverse religious area. Furthermore, many languages were spoken in these cities, primarily the merchant languages of Sogdian; of Aramaic, which is also the liturgical language of the Christians in these cities; and above all, Tocharian was still spoken. In fact, the region around Balkh, ancient Bactra, on the Oxus River—it was just outside of Arabic control initially—that area was known to the Arabs essentially as Tocharian land. They called it "Tokharistan," indicating that that ancient Indo-European language was still spoken and the majority of people there were Buddhists. This would be the kingdom where the great Bamiyan

Buddhas were, which were destroyed by the Taliban extremists by blowing them up in a way to renounce the fact that many of their ancestors had once been Buddhists before the Arabic conquest.

This entire region was a formidable region for the Arabs to take on. There was no central and imperial power to defeat; it was not convenient; you just did not knock off the army of the shah and then a whole empire fell to you with its administrative apparatus. The same thing had happened in the Roman provinces in Syria, Egypt, and North Africa. There were a constellation of city-states beyond the Oxus; well beyond the knowledge of the Arabs in 651 was the great river Jaxartes. The Jaxartes had been the boundary between Transoxiana and the nomadic peoples, and there dwelled various Turkish-speaking tribes; Turkish-speaking tribes that had long been in association with the cities of Transoxiana through caravan connections, trade connections. Many of the Turks had hired themselves out as guards to caravans. Others had served as ethnic regiments to the Sogdian merchant kings or the Tocharian princes who ruled the cities of Transoxiana. Within Transoxiana itself were settled smaller groups of nomads, clans, and families who interacted with the agriculturalists in the cities; had worked out a very sophisticated pattern of life. So Transoxiana was in many ways something of an urban extension of those central Eurasian steppes when the Arabs came on the scene. The only reason the Arabs got to the Oxus River initially was they were afraid that the last shah Yazdgerd III might rally support in the east and challenge Arab control of Mesopotamia and Syria. That did not happen.

Once on that frontier, initially the caliphs were not quite sure what to do with it. It was not until about 671 when a permanent camp was built at Merv. Merv is the old caravan city known as Margiana in Classical sources. It represented the outpost of Arab power; and again, what was quartered there were three different Arab regiments, and these Arab regiments proved extremely unruly to keep in line. What happened was very quickly the Umayyad governors assigned to Merv kept their tribal regiments occupied by crossing the Oxus and raiding. In the late seventh century and early eighth century, Arab forces crossed the Oxus at different points based at Merv, crossed into the cities of Transoxiana, they hit Balkh to the east on the upper Oxus; they went against the cities of Bukhara and Samarkand. Samarkand is probably the extreme end of their activities. None of these were permanent conquests; these were rather raids, massive raids, to pay the Arab tribal regiments. We have an account, for instance, of the looting that went on when an Arab force took the city of Bukhara in 709. The looting was on an unimaginable scale. The Arabs broke into the city; they sacked the Buddhist monasteries, damaged the stupa; but above all, they carried off enormous numbers of religious objects in silver and gold. All of these riches were brought back to Merv, brought back to the Abbasid Empire, and many of the silver objects were actually melted down and coined into Sassanid-style dirhams, silver coins, which were used to pay these tribal armies.

That meant that the raids maintained a sort of security on the frontier, but there was no thought of conquest; there was no thought of actually bringing these regions within Dar Islam; it was rather a way of keeping your Arab regiments occupied. The Umayyad caliphs grew suspicious because the governors commanding—and they had good reason—in Merv had enormous military power. They controlled some of the best Arab regiments in the empire. Furthermore, they recruited large numbers of Persians who served as the infantry; and these Persians were often given grants of land, they were converted to Islam, they were classified as *mawali*, and served side by side with the Arab tribal regiments.

The situation began to change at the opening of the eighth century. First, there was a powerful caliph on the throne by the name of Abd al-Malik. Abd al-Malik was really a pivotal caliph in the Umayyad Dynasty. He ruled from 685–705. He may have expended most of his efforts on trying to capture Constantinople, which failed; but he carried out the reorganization of the administration of the empire. It was with him that the first Islamic coins were issued; where Arabic was made the administrative language of the empire—that is, Greek and Persian were no longer used; for the first three generations, you were essentially using non-Arab bureaucrats—but he carried out significant reorganization of the frontier provinces, above all that eastern province in Transoxiana. In 705, a new governor arrived there, a very important man, and his name was Qutayba ibn Muslim. Qutayba took on the job of not only conducting raids, but he was given the go ahead to begin the conquest north of the Oxus.

He was governor in Merv for some 10 years and launched a methodical set of campaigns that were not only intended to net loot to satisfy the Arab tribal regiments, but also to begin the conversion of the area. To be sure, the attacks to some extent resembled earlier Arab attacks. They were attacks on livestock, on the pastures, the agricultural basis to the cities; and there is no doubt that the Arab tribesmen were intent on gaining loot. But there were also significant efforts on his part to convert the population. We have several reports, particularly in the city of Bukhara, when that city was captured by the armies of Qutayba, that the great Buddhist temple was leveled and a Friday mosque was built there; that is, a mosque for the great Friday prayer. Furthermore, the locals were rounded up to attend the services. The services were read out in Persian, not in Arabic, because it was probably a version of Sogdian. There are also anecdotes reported in later sources that soldiers were sent out into the countryside to round up the peasants so you had a proper congregation. Very often these Arab soldiers were greeted by jeers and stones and refusals on the part of the local population to give up their ancestral religion and embrace this new faith. From 705–715, this governor, Qutayba, tried to ram down Islam on the great caravan cities.

This provoked a reaction. In part, cities resisted far more seriously and fervently against the Arabs; and above all, they called in allies. The obvious allies to call in were Turkish nomads. This is where Arab armies and large Turkish tribal regiments began to clash over the traditional battlefields of Transoxiana in the early eighth century. The man who responded to the call was a colorful figure. He is sometimes called a khan; he more likely had a lesser title of *yabgu* khan, and he is remembered in the sources as Suluk. He turned out to be a brilliant campaigner; and in the clashes between the Arab and Turkish armies, especially in the 720s, it became very, very clear in Transoxiana and on the steppes of Central Asia, the Turks could outride and outshoot the Arabs. The Arabs had now run into a mounted opponent who could fight them to a draw; in fact, they could possibly outfight them. Between 718 and 722, Suluk reversed the situation. Many of the cities in Transoxiana that had submitted to Ummayad rule declared their independence or went over to the Turks. The Turks were seen actually more in the lines as allies; maybe not so much liberator, but at least a people that was understood in the caravan cities with whom they had long dealings, whereas to them the Arabs represented the interlopers bringing a new religion and attacking the various shrines and looting the various shrines and their cities. The result was, up until 722 the position was reversed and the caliph's frontier essentially fell back to the Oxus.

However, in 722, Suluk was killed. The resistance to the Arabs fell apart; and the succeeding governors were not nearly as fervent as the previous one and they began to come to terms with the cities and began a piecemeal conquest of Transoxiana, which within a generation, by 750, more or less delivered the great cities of Transoxiana to the control of the caliphs ruling in Damascus. This was a different type of conquest. The very conquest of Transoxiana posed something of a religious crisis to the early Islamic community. When Muhammad had preached original jihad, a holy war, which led to the initial conquest of the first three generations, most of the areas that fell under the control of the Arabs, at least initially, were occupied by Christians and Jews. These people were *dhimmi*, "people of the book"; they were protected people; they did have prophets accepted in Islam. Christians and Jews would be tolerated in the true sense of the word from its Latin origin: They were "suffered to exist"; they were allowed to maintain their religious institutions, Christians and synagogues. They were no way treated as equals; that was not at all in the meaning of the word. They would be represented through their religious leaders; they had to wear certain dress; they could not ride horses; they were not supposed to practice the use of arms; they paid a head tax to practice their faith, which, of course, Muslims did not pay. There were a number of disabilities. On the other hand, the caliphs were more than content to leave their Christian and Jewish subjects unmolested; so long as they were loyal, there was no problem.

By the conquest of Persia, the Arabs incorporated a region that was Zoroastrian, particularly Iran. There were some Christians in Persian Mesopotamia, but Iran was essentially a Zoroastrian world. This religion posed a bit of a problem; there really were not any references to it in the Koran. In fact, Muhammad had probably no direct experience really with Zoroastrians. Already in the time of Abd al-Malik, it was clear that you had to come to some kind of accommodation with all these Persians; and so the Zoroastrians were now lumped together with Christians and Jews as protected people. Crossing the Oxus, however—especially starting in 705 and going down to 750, in that little over a generation—the battles across the traditional fields of Transoxiana, that brought into the power of the caliph all sorts of peoples who practiced religions with which the Arabs had absolutely no familiarity: Buddhism, Manichaeism, various pagan cults, Iranian cults. In time, the Islamic government would have to come to terms with these groups as well because many of them had surrendered on terms. By 750, Transoxiana was under the control of the caliph. It was hardly an Islamic land; and that is going to bring a process we will examine in an up and coming lecture.

By 750, the armies of the caliph had reached the limits of their power just about. They were now on the very, very western fringe of the power of the Tang emperors of China. In July, 751, a major battle took place between the armies of the caliph and the armies of the Tang emperor. When the battle took place, probably sometime in July, perhaps in August of 751, the main fighting was done by governors. The main Arabic governor was a fellow by the name of Ziyad ibn Salih; he had been an experienced governor. He was actually in many ways an appointment of the Umayyad caliphate, and when the battle was fought it was fought actually under the first Abbasid caliph; that is, As-Saffah, who had overthrown the Umayyads. On the other hand, the Tang general who represented the emperor was a man by the name of Gao Xianzhi, a very experienced commander; a man who had ruled what the Chinese would call the western regions, [Anxi]; it is an odd Chinese rendition of Arsacid, some vague memory of the fact that the Parthians may have once been in that vicinity. It was the western regions of the Tarim Basin, which had been organized as the Four Garrisons by Tang armies back in the 650s and 660s. Both of these governors commanded important provincial armies, but both of them also depended very heavily on Turkish allies. Those were primarily Karluk Turks, a tribe of the Western Turkish confederation, which were recruited by both sides. The Karluk Turks, in the end, were going to decide the battle.

How this battle came about was really a set of accidents. It was not planned. It was not part of a strategic design on the part of Baghdad to expand into the Tarim Basin. It certainly was not an effort on the part of the Tang emperor to try to take back or try to expand into regions where once there was some kind of Han influence; not at all. This was a dispute that actually blew up because client rulers of both great powers in the complicated fighting that went on as the Arabs reasserted their authority in Ferghana resulted in exiles at the courts of the two governors. There was a ruler of Shash, Tashkent today, who fled to Samarkand and appealed to Ziyad, the Muslim governor, that he needed help to regain his throne. On the other hand, there were other refugees, Sogdian princes, who would come to the court of the Tang military governor Gao Xianzhi with the same kind of appeals. They needed assistance to regain their thrones because their towns had been captured by the Arabs. It was really the appeal of the subordinate allies that drew the two imperial armies into a showdown. Both governors were not unaware of the strategic position of Transoxiana, particularly the Jaxartes valley and Ferghana, the source of all those wonderful horses. They were also quite aware of the importance of the trade routes and the strategic routes over the Pamirs. Undoubtedly, as they assembled their armies, these were considerations for backing these clients. The idea was to put in power local rulers who would favor either the Tang emperor or the Abbasid caliph.

In 751, the armies moved into position to march and they encountered each other at the Talas River. We have both Chinese and Arabic accounts of the battle. The best Islamic account comes from a much later source from a fellow named Tabari, who is a Persian writer; but he based his accounts on eyewitness' accounts. He apparently read accounts by Arab generals who actually fought there; he drew upon earlier works no longer available. The Chinese were always very good at recordkeeping, especially in matters of statecraft and overall strategy. The Chinese generals who fought in this battle, particularly the subordinate officers as well as Gao Xianzhi, later wrote up memorandums to the emperor to explain what happened. This was customary in the Tang army; its part of the collective knowledge of the Tang military to find out what went wrong and what can be corrected later, and this is classic within Tang military writing.

We have some sense of the size of each army. The accounts, of course, exaggerate the size of the opponents. The Chinese, in part, explain that "We were just overwhelmed by numbers"; and the Arabs say, "Well, we won despite the overwhelming Chinese numbers." The best guess is some 35,000–30,000 men were marshaled on both sides; and the key players in this battle would be the Karluk cavalry. The Chinese had imperial forces, compliments of Xuanzong, the emperor back in Chang'an; they were actually imperial-level Chinese divisions there, at least 10,000 strong, including excellent crossbowmen. But they had also recruited large numbers of Turkish cavalry; some would put it at 20,000. Ziyad on the other side, Ziyad ibn-Salih, fielded tribal Arabic regiments and Persian infantry. They, too, may have been on the order of 10,000 or 15,000; but at least half, if not the majority, of his army were also Turkish allies, mostly Karluks who were fighting on both sides.

The two armies came into contact somewhere on the Talas River. The precise location of the battlefield is unknown; we have some speculation. What is clear is the armies maneuvered for several days, maybe a much as four or five days, before they actually came into contact with each other. What decided the battle was the desertion of the Karluks on the Chinese side who went over to the Muslim side; this will happen in other battles later on in this course where Turks made common cause with each other. What the reasons were for this defection we do not know. What we do know is for the first five days, Ziyad was very, very reluctant to commit his Arab and Persian forces in an assault across the river at Chinese infantry supported with crossbows. They may not have had much contact with the Chinese, but they quickly understood the power of what Chinese infantry could do in a fortified position. Once those Chinese lost their supporting flanks of cavalry, then Ziyad could launch the attack against the Chinese infantry in the center and his Turkish allies in overwhelming numbers would eventually encircle and reduce the Chinese army in a great battle of encirclement; and this is apparently what happened.

However, the fighting was ferocious. The Arabic cavalry ran right into tough professional Chinese infantry. The Chinese general Gao Xianzhi rallied his forces and held the center. His subordinate officers fought an excellent holding action, and 2,000 of the Chinese managed to break out of the encirclement and escape, including most of the senior officers who wrote memoirs after the battle. Many of the Chinese soldiers fought on until they surrendered on terms. The Arab sources speak of taking many, many captives. There is a later fanciful story that these captives introduced block printing into the Islamic world.

What were the results of this great battle, the first great battle ever to be fought between Muslims and Chinese? It is hard to say. Neither emperor pushed the battle. The emperor in China did not want to avenge the defeat. He had more problems with rebellions back at home, especially the An Lushan Rebellion. The new caliph in Damascus, the Abbasid caliph, really was dismayed by the success not only of his governor, but of all these Turkish allies who proved to be decisive in the fighting. So what happened is both empires accepted the battle as a draw; and the Talas River, in effect, represented the boundary between the two empires.

However, the battle did decide something: The Chinese Emperor eventually had to withdraw his forces to meet rebellions, and Chinese influence in the western regions lapsed and would not return until the Ming emperors. In the meanwhile, the Islamic Empire did not gain any real estate in this; in fact, the Karluk Turks ended up being the big beneficiaries. They now dominated the central steppes; they were big players in the Tarim Basin. But what the battle did establish was that Islam was a religion of victory, for it had been a Muslim victory. It established the frontiers of the Caliphate, and the Turks were now left undisturbed controlling those steppes. There, they would construct new states, new confederations; they would embrace Islam; and they would soon invade the Muslim world.

Muslim Merchants and Mystics in Central Asia
Lecture 21

In the last lecture, we ended with the Battle of Talas, in which Islamic and Chinese armies fought themselves to a strategic draw, even though the Muslims had clearly won the battle. The result of that battle was essentially to halt Islamic political and military expansion for the next 300 years. The achievements of Islam at this time can instead be found in the creation of a cultural synthesis, a whole new civilization across the former Near East, the Persian Empire, and parts of the former Roman world. It was this Islamic synthesis that proved to be so important for the peoples of the Eurasian steppes.

Emergence of a New Civilization

- As mentioned earlier, the Abbasid caliphs had shifted the locus of their power to Baghdad, which became the intellectual and economic center of the Islamic world. This great city became the model for the lesser provincial cities of the Islamic world in terms of letters, architecture, aesthetics, and visual arts.

- The success of the Abbasid civilization rested not only in the caliphs but also in the early viziers, or chief ministers. These were men who often came from the Barmakid family, known to be great patrons of scholarship and familiar with Buddhism.

- Most of the people creating this Islamic civilization in Baghdad were not Arabic but came from a variety of backgrounds. In addition, various types of writers in Aramaic, Persian, and Greek were encouraged. These included Christians, Jews, and Zoroastrians, who began the process of translating early literary traditions into Arabic. Great strides were made in medicine and mathematics.

- In the process of synthesizing earlier intellectual and literary traditions into a wider world, the Arabic language itself was enriched and transformed, both in its poetry and its ability to express intellectual and mathematical ideas. Numerous loan words were taken from both Greek and Persian, and the language was refined to be more than just the revealed word of God through the prophet. By 800, Arabic was now a literary language in its own right.

- An important political change accelerated this process. In 813, **al-Mamun** became the new caliph, and he looked to Persia for his cultural background. He also took over the role once performed by viziers of sponsoring poets and intellectuals. This became a major activity of the Abbasid caliphs throughout the 9th and into the 10th centuries.

  o Al-Mamun increasingly modeled his court on the old Sassanid court, incorporating harems and eunuchs, Persian ministers, and a high degree of opulence and ceremony.

  o Further, the empire became studiously Muslim. Administrative posts were staffed by men loyal to the caliph, many of whom were Persian. Arab military regiments were increasingly replaced with Turkish mercenaries and slave soldiers. The latter were excellent warriors who had been pulled from their families and were devoted to the caliph.

Contributions of the Samanids

- In addition to changes in aesthetics and letters, there were also important changes in architecture. The **Samanid** emirs, for example, on the eastern frontier, took it upon themselves to sponsor arts and architecture, and they set the model for other emirs. From the 9th to the early 11th centuries, the wealthy Samanid emirs poured their money into monuments, essentially creating the high Persian culture of Islam.

  o Such monuments included mosques; medreses, that is, religious schools with minarets; and *türbes*, roughly translated as "memorial mausoleums." In some ways, these were the most important monuments for the Islamisation of the landscape.

  o The *türbe* of Ahmad, which survives in Bukhara, is a gem of tile construction and the early use of the dome. It set the tone

The basic architectural forms worked out by the Samanid emirs, as seen in the türbe at Bukhara, were adopted by later Turkish rulers.

for the architectural development of eastern Islam from the 9th to the 11th centuries.

○ In addition to the *türbes*, we cannot underestimate the importance of medreses. These were theological schools where **Sharia**, the law of Islam, was studied. All medreses usually had attached kitchens, hospices, and various types of institutions to carry out charitable work. They were founded in cities and supported by merchants and other pious Muslims. In some ways, they filled the social and economic roles of Buddhist and Christian monasteries that had long been established in the cities of the Silk Road.

○ This development on the part of the Samanid emirs was a gradual process, taking place over perhaps 200 or 300 years.

- The Samanid emirs were also behind the promotion of Persian as a literary language. In Baghdad, all the disputation over the Qur'an, as well as the medical and mathematical texts, were being written in Arabic. But the Samanid emirs, themselves descended from Iranian converts, wanted to use the literary language of Persian.
    - Significant Persian literary works were produced in the 9th and 10th centuries. Perhaps the best one known is the ***Shah-nameh***, written by **Ferdowsi**, which became the national epic of Persia.

    - This epic not only preserves earlier national tales before the Arabic conquest, but it also shows that Persian was recast into a literary language. It was now written in the Arabic script and had been enriched by loan words. It was not the dialect spoken in the various cities of Transoxiana.

- When the Turks entered Transoxiana, they were, at best, practicing folk Islam, but they saw the Persian Muslim culture of Transoxiana and eastern Iran as a model for themselves. They would essentially follow the path of the Samanid emirs and devise their own distinct architecture. They would adapt their language to the Arabic script and record their ancient traditions, creating an ethnic identity that was both Muslim and Turkish.

Spread of Islam on the Steppes

- How did Islam reach the people of the steppes? Part of the answer is that the nomads inevitably would have had contact and trade with the caravan cities and would have seen their marvelous architecture. But the interchange was far more significant and long term than just being impressed by the new face of caravan cities.

- Merchants in the Abbasid Empire, especially starting in the 8th century, began to convert to Islam in fairly large numbers for a number of reasons. First, by 700, Arabic was supplanting other languages as a commercial language. Second, members of the *ummah* were seen as representatives of a powerful ruler; this was especially true for merchants engaged in trade outside the limits of the Abbasid caliphate. Therefore, they carried with them the implicit protection of Muslim law.

- In the course of the 8th century, many people converted to Islam and began to learn Arabic. Of course, they traded among the nomadic peoples of the Eurasian steppes and made contact with the Turks. In addition, merchant caravans traveled with religious figures and teachers, including **Sufi** mystics.
  - o Sufi mystics were not members of the theological schools that were studying the Qur'an or perfecting Sharia. They were popular mystics and inspired figures. They impressed the Turkish nomads with their contact with the other world.

  - o Sufis were nominally part of Sunni Islam, but they didn't operate within the Sunni institutional apparatus, which made them ideal traveling companions for merchants on the Silk Road.

  - o These mystics stressed prayer, dance, trances, and songs, leading them to achieve an ecstatic state. To the Turks, they looked like shamans—inspired teachers with some sort of insight into the other world.

- In time, the Sufi mystics would convince many Turks to convert to Islam, although these conversions were often less than complete. When later strict theologians of the religious schools traveled among the Turks, they discovered that their converts were still carrying out animal sacrifice, consulting shamans, and invoking ancient gods and goddesses. This is typical of how nomads assimilated and adapted religions to their own existing structures.
  - o One such adaptation can still be seen today in the invocation of the mother goddess, Umay, by women in childbirth in the Turkish world. Umay came to be identified with Mary, the mother of Jesus, who is the prophet Isa to the Muslims.

  - o The persistence of these traditional habits and beliefs can be seen in the tsarist government's and, later, the Soviet government's attempts to identify the Muslim population on the steppes. The tribes' varied practices prevented any kind of census based on religion, and officials ultimately had to catalogue these people based on tribal identities rather than religious identities.

- Still, these conversions to Islam were important because they made the tribes on the Eurasian steppes part of the wider *ummah*. The Turks were seen as ruthless and, in many instances, cruel, but they were accepted as Sunni Muslims and now had the opportunity to enter a literate, urban civilization.
  - Earlier empires, such as the Han, the Byzantine, and the Roman, saw only two ways to deal with nomads: either assimilate them or expel them.

  - But the in case of the Muslim world, the Turks—although they were outlanders—were now Sunni Muslims. As such, they would turn themselves into the military elite of the Islamic world, conduct a new era of Islamic expansion, and create their own version of Turkish Islamic civilization.

Important Terms

Samanid: The family of Iranian emirs (819–1005) who ruled from Bukhara, eastern Iran, and Transoxania as the representatives of the Abbasid caliphate. They defined the visual arts and letters of eastern Islam.

Shah-nameh: "*Book of Kings*"; the Middle Persian national epic composed by Abu al-Qasem Mansur (c. 940–1020).

Sharia: Muslim religious law based on the Koran.

Sufi: Muslim mystic who follows the Sunni tradition.

türbe: Memorial tomb to a Muslim ruler or mentor.

al-Mamun (b. 786; 813–833): Abbasid caliph; son of Harun al-Rashid. In 813, he defeated his half-brother al-Amin and gained the throne. But he surrendered control over Khurasan and the northeastern frontier to Tahir ibn al-Husayn.

Ferdowsi (Abu al-Qasem Mansur) (940–1020): Persian poet; wrote the epic *Shah-nameh* (*"Books of Kings"*) in 977–1010. This national epic celebrated Persian historical traditions before the advent of Islam and set the standard of expression in literary Middle Persian.

Suggested Reading

Bulliet, *Cotton, Climate and Camels in Early Islamic Iran.*

Elverskog, *Buddhism and Islam on the Silk Road.*

Foltz, *Religions of the Silk Road.*

Golden, *Central Asia in World History.*

Hansen, *The Silk Road: A New History.*

Questions to Consider

1. Why did the Umayyad armies fail to win over large numbers of converts in Transoxiana and among the Turkish tribes of the Eurasian steppes? What were early Muslim attitudes toward the diverse faiths they encountered in these regions? How did the Arab Muslims initially view the Turkish nomads?

2. How did the recruitment of Turks into Abbasid armies change attitudes toward Islam among the nomadic peoples? Why did the Persian culture of the Abbasid caliphate impress the nomadic peoples? What was the role of the Samanid emirs in transmitting both Islam and the Persian civilization of Abbasid Baghdad to the Turkish tribes?

3. What were the appeals of Islam to the merchants in the cities of the Silk Road or among the Turkish tribes? Why was it so easy to identify Sufi

Lecture 21: Muslim Merchants and Mystics in Central Asia

mystics with Turkish shamans? How did the Turks combine Islam with their folk beliefs?

4. How did writers play such an important role in defining the Turkish identity within the wider Islamic world? Why could the Turks maintain their language and identity and still be members of a wider Islamic civilization?

5. Why did merchants and the expansion of the caravan trade prove decisive in the conversion of Turkish tribes to Islam from the 10th century? Why did Buddhism steadily give way to Islam at the same time?

Muslim Merchants and Mystics in Central Asia
Lecture 21—Transcript

In the last lecture, we ended with the climactic Battle of the Talas River in which essentially Islamic and Chinese armies fought themselves to a strategic draw, even though the Muslims had clearly won the battle. The result of that battle was essentially to halt expansion by the Abbasid caliphate. Starting with the first caliph, as-Saffah, particularly his son and successor al-Mansur who built the city of Baghdad starting early in his reign (and by 762 the court is in Baghdad), the Abbasid caliphs were content to consolidate rather than to conquer. That fact underscores a very important point that is at odds with usual popular perceptions in the West: Islam was always a religion of conquest, of jihad, religious war; that vast numbers of people in the early Islamic period, in the early Middle Ages, were converted by the sword, that is, either you accept Islam or you will be slain. Some such acts were committed in the conquest of Transoxiana, especially in the early eighth century, and there are several governors in Merv who carried out such conversions. But really, that is not how to characterize the Abbasid state after 750. In fact, Islamic political and military expansion stopped for the next 300 years; and instead, the achievements of Islam were creating a cultural synthesis, a whole new civilization across the former Near East, the Persian Empire, and parts of the former Roman world, and it was this Islamic synthesis that proved so important for the peoples of the Eurasian steppes.

There are several reasons why this came about under the Abbasid caliphs. As I mentioned earlier, the Abbasid caliphs shifted the locus of their power to Baghdad. The construction of Baghdad was important because it became the intellectual and economic center of the Islamic world, drawing in talent, merchants, and all sorts of people into this great center. Baghdad would prove the model for the lesser provincial cities of the Islamic world to model themselves in terms of letters, in terms of architecture, aesthetics, and visual arts; and Baghdad, while it is today in Iraq, is really part of the Persian world and is the Muslim successor to the ancient cities of Ctesiphon and [Seleucia on the Tigris]. The Abbasid Caliphs, therefore centered in Baghdad, promoted cultural activities that produced the brilliant court culture that owed a great debt to Persian civilization.

The success of the Abbasid civilization rested not only in the caliphs but in unusual successors of early viziers—viziers would be the chief ministers—and these were men who came from what is often known as the Barmakid family. They were descended from a fellow named Barmak who apparently was an early convert to Islam; it was his descendent Khalid ibn Barmak, who served as vizier under the first caliph of the Abbasid caliphate as-Saffah. He was a staunch supporter of the new regime; and what was more important, he apparently knew Sogdian or Tocharian, whatever the language was that was being spoken in the city of Balkh, and his ancestors had administered a very important Buddhist sanctuary outside of Balkh. They had for centuries been engaged in supporting monks, in carrying out theological debates, patronizing the copying of Buddhist texts. Khalid's family, really up until 803 when the family fell from favor in the reign of Harun ar-Rashid, they turned out to be great patrons of all types of scholars operating at Baghdad. These were not just Arab writers; in fact, far from it. Most of the people operating in Baghdad creating this Islamic civilization were not Arabic. They came from different backgrounds. In the case of Khalid and his family, they were already familiar with Buddhism; at least some members of the family retained ties with those members of the family who had not converted. It was only in the eighth and ninth centuries where Arab writers actually became familiar with the stories of the Buddha and some of the teachings of the Buddha, because previously rude tribal armies, tribal warriors, sacking cities would have just seen what they called idols—that is, images of the Buddha—and they were simply there to be melted down.

In addition, various types of writers in both Aramaic and Persian and in Greek were encouraged. These included Christians, Jews, Zoroastrians; they came and began the process of translating the early literary traditions into Arabic. This saw great strides in certain realms of endeavor. One was in medicine. The Aristotelian texts, texts of Hindu medicine—that is, texts that had come through Prakrit, Tocharian, or Sogdian languages, ultimately Hindu in origin—these texts became available. There was a great deal of activity; and we know that the physician Abu Musa Jabir was a court physician. He was actually introduced to the court by the Barmakid emir, and he began a very important translation of medical texts into Arabic. There was a great deal of mathematical work that was initiated, even though the great achievements would not come until later in the 9th and 10th centuries, which would see the birth of algebra, the invention of algebra; and that was because Greek mathematics and Indian mathematics were now available, a proper notation system was evolved, and translations in Arabic provided Muslim scholars with the information to make strides in mathematics. Therefore, the court at Baghdad really became a brilliant center for the synthesis of earlier intellectual and literary traditions into a new wider world of belles lettres. In the process, the Arabic language itself was enriched and transformed, both in its poetry and its ability to express intellectual and mathematical ideas. Numerous loan words were taken from both Greek and Persian, and the language was refined to be more than just the revealed language of the prophet, the revealed word of God through the prophet; it was now a literary language in its own right by 800 A.D.

There was an important political change that accelerated the process. I mentioned that Harun ar-Rashid, who was seen as the greatest of the Abbasid caliphs, died in 809 after a very, very glorious reign; but within several years of his death in 811, a civil war broke out between his two sons. Al-Mamun was supported by the eastern army, particularly the army in Khurasan; the elder brother, al-Amin, controlled Baghdad; and the war ended in 813 with the victory effectively of the Persian party. Caliph Mamun was very, very inclined to look to Iran, to look to Persia, for his cultural background; his mother was of Persian origin. Furthermore, he took over the role once performed by viziers of sponsoring different poets and intellectuals; and that became a major activity of Abbasid caliphs the whole 9th into the 10th centuries. They took a keen interest, many of them, in the intellectual life of their city, which marked Baghdad really as the great capital of the Islamic world.

He undertook two other important measures: One was to turn to a Persian state graph; to model the court increasingly after the old Sassanid court. This is where the classic harem emerges, the use of eunuchs to protect the harem, the use of Persian ministers; all of the opulence and ceremony we associate with the great Islamic courts is really devised in the ninth century and owes its origin largely to Persian traditions. In addition, this empire was studiously, even painfully Muslim. The administrative posts were staffed by men loyal to the caliph. Many of them were non-Arab, many of them were Persian; and above all, the Arab military regiments were increasingly replaced with Turkish soldiers. They were either mercenaries and allies that are hired right off the steppes, or they are slave soldiers, often called by terms such as *mamluk* or *ghilman*, the Arabic term. We will be revisiting this issue when we look at the emergence of the Turkish power on the steppes; but large numbers of young men, Turks, were sold into slavery into the Islamic world to be recruited into the bodyguard and elite units of the Abbasid caliph because they would be loyal. They were deracinated; they were pulled up from their background; they were taught essentially Arabic; they were converted to Islam. They had no ties to family; they were outsiders; and they were devoted, excellent warriors. It was the need for slave soldiers that became one of the major reasons for the expansion of trade between the Eurasian steppes and the Abbasid caliphate.

In addition to the changes in aesthetics and letters, there were also important changes in architecture. As I mentioned in the previous lecture, many of our visions of what the early Islamic urban landscape looked like really have to be eliminated because you are dealing in a world that was still largely non-Muslim. A consequence from that civil war was increasingly entrusting power to local rulers. These men styled themselves as emirs. One of the big winners of that was the Tahirid family. Tahir, the man who founded that dynasty, had really won the victory that put al-Mamun on the throne. He was rewarded with the control of Khurasan; that is the strategic eastern frontier that guarded the borders of Iran and also gave them access to the caravan cities of Transoxiana. These rulers took it upon themselves to sponsor arts and architecture, and they set the model for other emirs.

The most important of these emirs were the Samanid emirs. It is difficult to exaggerate the importance of this family, particularly its greatest representative, Nasr ibn Ahmad, who ruled from 864–892. The Samanid emirs dominated the cultural world of Iran and Transoxiana through the 9th, 10th, even into the early 11th century; the dynasty was finally overthrown in 1003. Its influence was far greater than its political and military influence. What the Samanid emirs did was create essentially the high Persian culture of Islam, which defines eastern Islam thereafter. To be sure, the Abbasids played an important role—they were sponsoring all the intellectual activity, the translations, the debate over the nature of the Koran, an authoritative text to the Koran—but the Samanid emirs were directly hooked up with trade;

they had lots of money, it was coming in from the slave trade and other activities; and this money was poured into monuments.

The monuments were of different types: First and foremost was the mosque, obvious, but above all *medreses*; *medreses* were religious schools with minarets. Then, another monument that is easy to overlook but in some ways was the most important monument for Islamisizing the landscape, and that is the *türbe* or the *tekke*, roughly translated as the "memorial mausoleum." Such buildings are not really tombs in a Christian sense; in the Muslim tradition, the body is wrapped up in a simple shroud and put in the earth. The *türbe* and *tekke* are memorial mausoleums above that simple burial. The one of Ahmad, which survives in Bukhara, is a gem of architecture, a gem of tile construction and early use of dome construction; and it really sets the tone for the architectural development of eastern Islam through the 9th, 10th, and 11th centuries. It is those basic architectural forms worked out by the Samanid emirs that are then later adopted by the Turkish rulers, by the conqueror Tamerlane; and so it is only in the 8th and 9th centuries that the cities of Transoxiana began to assume a real Muslim face.

Besides the *türbe* and *tekke*, you cannot underestimate the importance of *medresses*. *Medresses* were important for several reasons. In some ways, they provided the functions of a Buddhist monastery or a Christian monastery; the so-called Buddhist *vihara*. *Medresses* were theological schools. It was where Sharia, the law of Islam was studied. All *medresses* usually had attached to them kitchens, hospices, various types of institutions to carry out charitable work. They were founded in the cities and supported by merchants and other pious Muslims an act of their piety; and the medresses in some ways came to replace the social and economic role of Buddhist monasteries and Christian monasteries that had long been established in the cities of the Silk Road. This is a gradual process. The Samanid emirs did not simply outlaw Christian and Buddhist monasteries and sanctuaries and say, "No, no, no it's got to be Islamic." Instead, they patronized these institutions, which gained increasing visibility in the cities; and as more and more merchants and other prominent members of the upper class converted to Islam, they put their money into building programs, and gradually over a 200 or 300 hundred year period, the cities of Transoxiana began to assume the urban landscape that is conjured up in popular images.

The Samanid emirs also were very much behind the promotion of Persian as a literary language; and that is a point that is difficult to overstress. In Baghdad, all of the disputation over the Koran, all of the medical and mathematical texts, were being written in Arabic. To be sure, they were drawing on Persian, Greek, and Aramaic sources. But the Samanid emirs themselves descended from Iranian converts; they wanted to use the literary language of Persian. It is in the 9th and 10th centuries that significant Persian literary works are produced. Perhaps the best one known is the so-called heroic epic the *Shah-nameh*, which becomes the national epic of Persia. That was composed by a very important poet, Ferdowsi. That epic is not only important because it preserves all these earlier national tales before the Arabic conquest, it also shows that Persian had now been recast into a literary language. It was now written in the Arabic script, not in the old Pahlavi script of the Sassanid period, which is what the Avesta was originally written in. No, they were now using an adaptation of the Arabic script; the Kufic script, actually, to be precise. In addition, the language had been enriched by loan words, and it was a literary Persian; it was not the dialect spoken in the various cities of Transoxiana. In fact, some scholars would argue that the literary Persian of the great epics that were being produced at the Samanid court would be difficult to be understood by many merchants unless they had obtained the requisite training to read those texts.

The Samanids themselves were behind some of the intellectual achievements in, for instance, medicine and mathematics; they were known to support physicians and mathematicians as well. But their real impact was in creating literary Persian and the architectural forms of eastern Islam. The Turks, when they entered into Transoxiana, they had at best a very, very little understood notion of Islam—they were at best practicing a folk Islam—but they see in the Persian Muslim culture of Transoxiana and eastern Iran a model for themselves; and the Turks will follow essentially the path of the Samanid emirs and they will devise their own distinct architecture, Islamic to be sure, but architecture patronized by Turkish rulers. They would take the Persian route of adapting their language, Turkish, to the Arabic script recording their ancient traditions and essentially creating a national or better yet an ethnic identity that was both Muslim and Turkish. The Samanids really set a very, very important example for the later Turks who would arrive and take over the political legacy of the Samanids; these Turks would also adapt the cultural legacy.

How did Islam get out to the people of the steppes? I mentioned that when the Turks do enter, particularly the Seljuk Turks—and they are going to be the subject of the next lecture—they arrive; they are nominally Sunni Muslims. They arrive in the 11ᵗʰ century; they had been exposed to Islam at least a century earlier. Part of it is that the nomads inevitably would have contact and trade with the caravan cities; they would see all these marvelous buildings going up, *medresses*, *türbe*, mosques, and the like. But the interchange is far more significant and far more long-term than just being impressed by the new face of caravan cities. For one, merchants in the Abbasid Empire, especially starting in the 8ᵗʰ century, began to convert to Islam in fairly large numbers. There were a number of practical reasons for doing this. One is that by 700 A.D., Arabic was supplanting other languages as a commercial language. Second, by becoming members of the *ummah*, and especially for merchants engaged in long-distance trade outside the limits of the Abbasid Caliphate, they were seen as representative for a very, very powerful ruler; and therefore, they carried with them the implicit protection of Muslim law, the protection of the caliph. In the course of the 8ᵗʰ century, many *mawali*— that is, converts—began to embrace Islam and learn Arabic. Of course, they traded among the nomadic peoples of the Eurasian steppes; and so the Turks came into contact with these merchants, again trading for the traditional goods, but also with an appetite for that slave trade, which is a subject of an upcoming lecture.

In addition, with the merchants on these caravans traveled religious figures, aesthetics, and teachers. This was inevitable; we discussed this on the earlier Silk Road that Buddhist monks followed merchants on caravans, the Manicheans, the Christians, all went along the different routes. First and foremost among the Muslims were the Sufi mystics. Sufi mystics were not members of the theological schools that are studying in the *medresses*, who are reading the Koran, perfecting Sharia; far from it. They were popular mystics and inspired figures. They got their name *Sufi* from *suf*, which means either a white woolen or linen garment, a very, very simple garment that they wore; and they impressed the Turkish nomads with their mysticism and their contact with the other world. These Sufis, these mystics, would be nominally part of Sunni Islam—they were seen as within the Sunni Islamic tradition—but they did not need the institutional apparatus to operate. They did not need the *medresses*; they did not need all of the facilities that urban Islam would need; and therefore, they were ideal to travel along with merchants on the Silk Road to enter into the Eurasian steppes.

When the Turks met these people, they were impressed. For one, Sufi mystics put stress on prayer, but also on dance; on trances, sometimes induced by hashish; on song; on all sorts of activities that would lead the Sufi mystic to achieve an ecstatic state. To Turks, this looked like shamans; we have guys like this all the time. These are, to use the modern Turkish term, *hoca*. They were inspired ones; they were teachers; they had some sort of insight into the other world; and therefore the Sufi mystics increasingly took the place of former Buddhist and Nestorian monks, or the elect of the Manichees. In time, the Sufi mystics would convince many of these Turks to start going over to Islam. Very often, these conversions were less than complete. Large numbers of Karluks converted to Islam, probably at the end of the eighth, the beginning of the ninth centuries. These are the descendents of the fellows who fought at the Battle of Talas. When later Muslim teachers—strict theologians of the religious schools—traveled among these guys, they found them hopelessly heterodox. They were carrying out animal sacrifice; the women were still running off and consulting shamans; and there were a whole bunch of practices, social practices and religious practices, which were not really strictly Islamic. It was typical of how the nomads assimilated these religions, adapted these religious, to their existing structures.

One of those adaptations can still be seen today. Many times, women in childbearing in the Turkish world—not only the Republic of Turkey, but today in the Central Turkish Republics such as Uzbekistan—would invoke the mother goddess, Umay as she would be called in various Turkish languages. Umay gets to be identified with Mary, the mother of Jesus; that is, Isa. Isa is a prophet to the Muslims. What often happens, especially in modern Turkey today, is that to invoke Mary, the mother of Isa, Turks will tie little pieces of white ribbon or paper on shrubbery around a sanctuary, originally a Christian sanctuary to the Virgin Mary, and this is a throwback to older shamanistic traditions of invoking the mother goddess in childbearing, which has survived down to this day in the Turkish Republic.

In addition, the persistence of these traditional habits and beliefs can be seen in the way the Tsarist government and later the Soviet government handled most of the nomadic steppe peoples. Catherine the Great attempted to win the loyalty of the ever more Muslim subjects under Moscow by establishing Islam as a favored, respected religion, essentially following the old Islamic tradition of it is a protected community, they are subjects of the Tsar or Tsarina, they should be allowed to practice undisturbed. In the 19th century, when they tried to extend this system and start counting all of the tribes on the steppes, they were really hard put where to put many of those tribes. Are they really Muslims or not, given their basic practices? They do not really look very Islamic. Ultimately, the Tsarists officials gave up in frustration and eventually catalogued all these people based on language and customs; that is, by tribal identities rather than by religious identities. It is a powerful explanation, an example, of how those traditional Turkish customs and identities persist even though they are now a part of the wider Islamic world. When the Soviets took over, when Lenin held a great conference in 1920 to order the Central Asian Republics, which became independent after 1991, they followed the same definition: They divided the people up along ethnic and linguistic lines, not along religious lines. Again, it underscores that the Turks came to Islam on their own terms.

Nonetheless, it is important that they had converted, because by converting to Islam the tribes on the Eurasian steppes were now part of the wider *ummah*. They got, in effect, a pass when they entered the Islamic world. To be sure, the Turks would be seen as ruthless and harsh masters, in many instances as cruel. You will encounter in Arabic accounts admiration for Turkish martial abilities, and at the same time deploring the Turks as rapacious, difficult to appease, really not much better than the barbarian opponents such as the Franks or even later the Mongols. But they were Muslims; and as such, when they entered the Islamic world, they were accepted as Sunni Muslims and that gave them an ability to enter in a way that all previous steppe nomads had not entered a literate, urban civilization. Think back for a moment in some of the previous lectures. The Chinese attitude was well summed up by the various envoys of the Han court. The Xiongnu are barbarians. There is only one of two ways to deal with them: either you assimilate them or you expel them. The Romans were not that much different, particularly in their dealings with Attila the Hun. It had to be a bit moderated when you had

Byzantine emperors or in marrying into the Khazar court, members of the Khazar court; but on the whole the Roman attitude is not too different from the Chinese attitude, probably not too different from the Sassanid attitude.

But in the case of the Muslim world, the Turks who arrived, to be sure, they were in many ways outlanders; but they would arrive as Muslims and above all—and this is what is most important—as Sunni Muslims, and therefore as agents of the caliph of Baghdad. In that capacity, they would turn themselves into the military elite of the Islamic world; they would conduct a new era of expansion of Islam, and they would create their own version of Turkish Islamic civilization.

The Rise of the Seljuk Turks
Lecture 22

In this lecture, we will follow up on some of the implications of the previous two lectures. As you recall, we discussed the clash between the armies of the caliphate and the western Turks that ended in the Battle of Talas. Then, we talked about the dissemination of Islam onto the western steppes through trade connections. Those issues lead directly to the subject of this lecture, which is a series of Turkish migrations that resulted in the formation of new powers on the steppes. We will discuss three states in particular: the Karakhanids, the Ghaznavids, and the Seljuk Turks, who represented the greatest of these new Turkish political organizations.

The Aftermath of Talas

- The Battle of Talas marked, in some ways, the beginning of a new wave of migrations across the central Eurasian steppes. We might think that the Karluks, the Turkish allies who deserted from the Chinese to the Muslims, would go on to dominate the central steppes, but that did not happen. The Karluks represented a loose confederation; they fell to fighting among themselves and got swept up in the slave trade.

  o In addition, the Karluks were vassals of the Uighur khagan, who exercised a nominal hegemony over the central steppes of Eurasia. But the Uighur khagans were defeated in an uprising of their subject peoples in 840. The khaganate broke up, and many of the Uighurs migrated to the caravan cities of the Tarim Basin. Their homeland, the Orkhon valley, was never reoccupied by Turks.

  o In the wake of the Uighurs, the Karluks never imposed any kind of authority over the central Eurasian steppes. As a result, there were more migrations of Turks from east to west into the central and western steppes.

- The Abbasid caliphate and the Samanid emirs ruling in Bukhara were not displeased by the new wave of migrations on the steppes, because they played directly into one of their greatest needs: the slave trade.
  - From the very start of the Abbasid caliphate, the caliphs distrusted their Arab tribal regiments—and with good cause. The Arabs were rapacious and unruly, difficult to discipline, and many were infected with Shi'a, Alid, or Umayyad sympathies.

  - For this reason, the Abbasid caliphs began to replace their Arab soldiers with professionals, including Persians, Armenians, Kurds, and above all, Turks. Large numbers of Turks were hired as mercenaries or recruited as allies to fight in the armies of the great caliphs. In addition, the caliphs began to recruit a Turkish bodyguard, the *haras*.

  - The bodyguard was composed of slave soldiers. These were generally young men, around the ages of 14 or 15, who had been taken in tribal wars and sold as slaves. They were educated in religious schools, converted to Islam, and drilled to be elite soldiers.

  - The Islamic world came to depend on the manpower of the Eurasian steppes, and the disorder on the steppes—the failure of the Karluks to construct a new confederacy and the collapse of the Uighur khaganate—was to the advantage of the Abbasid caliphs and the Samanid emirs.

- In time, however, merchants operating on the Eurasian steppes began to introduce Islam. Turkish tribes began to understand the religion and gain more organization. We have reports of massive tribal converstions in the 10th century. Several important political orders grew out of these new conditions.

The Karakhanid Turks
- The **Karakhanid** Turks were ruled by the Kara khans, or "black khans." The confederation was divided into a western and an

Kashgar boasts some of the earliest Islamic monuments found in Central Asia, especially monumental mausoleums.

eastern half. The eastern half would have been east of Kashgar on the steppes around the Altai Mountains, and the western tribes were north of the Jaxartes and came to control Kashgar.

- The Karakhanids began to convert to Islam starting in the mid-10th century and styled themselves as both Turkish rulers and patrons of Muslim civilization. Indeed, Kashgar emerged in the 10th and the 11th centuries as one of the first centers of a distinct Turkish Islamic civilization. The khagans there patronized poets and scholars, and it was in Kashgar and the associated towns involved in the Silk Road trade where Turkish was adapted to the Arabic script.

- A number of figures came to define this Turkish civilization, including the writer **Mahmud al-Kashgari**, whose career spanned most of the 11th century.

- Mahmud recorded many of the Turkish heroic and epic traditions in something called a *diwan* ("compendium"). This work is the first comprehensive discussion of the Turkish language, and it cites many early oral poems and other traditions. Mahmud also appended maps to his work, showing the positions of the various Turkish tribes on the Eurasian steppes.

- Mahmud was a pivotal figure in turning Turkish into a literary language. Henceforth, the Turks as a whole would embrace Islam, but they would do so on their own terms. Turkish would become one of the three great languages of the Islamic world, along with Arabic and Persian.

- When the Turks entered the wider Islamic world, they would not be assimilated in the way many other nomadic peoples had been. The Turks acquired a cultural-religious identity, one that was Islamic but also distinctly Turkish.

- As mentioned earlier, starting in the mid-10th century, the rulers of the Karakhanids began to convert, bringing with them whole tribes. These conversions gained pace throughout the 10th and 11th centuries and were different from the individual conversions won by merchants and Sufi mystics or the conversions of slaves brought into the Islamic world. The Karakhanids emerged as one of the great political powers out of this interaction between the steppes and the Islamic world.

The Ghaznavid Sultans

- Another great political order emerged as a product of the slave system; these were the rulers who are known as the **Ghaznavid** sultans. They were essentially a succession of slave soldiers, or **Mamluks**, who had started out in the employ of the Samanid emirs of Bukhara.

- The founder of this dynasty, **Alp Tigin**, had been exiled to the remote town of Ghazna, which is in Afghanistan today. He took over the town and turned it into a successful frontier post. His power was eventually transmitted to his son-in-law, **Sebüktigin**.

- Sebüktigin took over the Ghaznavid emirate probably in the year 977 and, in some ways, pointed the Turks and Islam in the direction of India. He repeatedly invaded the Punjab, plundering Hindu temples and Buddhist monasteries. He also depended heavily on slave troops that had been recruited from the steppes, and above all he used Persian administrators. Sebüktigin may have been Turkish in origin, but culturally, he was a product of high Persian-Iranian culture.

- Later Ghaznavid sultans, especially Sebüktigin's son **Mahmud**, carried out some extraordinary raids into India. In 1024, Mahmud descended through the Khyber Pass into Gujarat and sacked the great temple of Shiva at the city of Somnath.

- As the Ghaznavids emerged as the power of eastern Islam, they ran up against the Karakhanids, with both states squeezing out the Samanid emirs. Eastern Islam was partitioned between the two powers, with the Oxus River again accepted as the boundary. The city of Balkh fell into the hands of Mahmud. The Karakhanids were content with the cities of Transoxiana.

- It seemed as if Mahmud and his successors would go on to unite eastern Islam, but that didn't happen because a third group suddenly intervened and knocked out both contenders—the Seljuk Turks.

The Seljuk Turks
- The ancestors of the Seljuk Turks, the Oghuz or Ghuzz Turks, had settled in the Jaxartes valley, the lands around the Aral Sea. They entered the Islamic world in the 10th century. The founder of this tribe, Seljuk, moved into the region known as Khurasan, an important border area that is in eastern Iran and parts of Afghanistan and Turkmenistan today. The Seljuks were military colonists and seem to have been involved in camel breeding.

- The grandsons of Seljuk, particularly **Tughril Bey** and his brother Chagri Bey, took power over these tribes and exploited the clash between the Karakhanids and the Ghaznavid sultans. In the 1030s, the Seljuks swept through many of the cities of eastern Iran. Tughril Bey was careful to ensure that his soldiers represented themselves as agents of the caliph in Baghdad. In 1037, he had himself proclaimed sultan ("guardian") at Nishapur.

- On May 23, 1040, in the vicinity of Merv, Tughril Bey won a major victory over the Ghaznavid army. It was a classic victory of Turkish cavalry over an army that had come to depend heavily on Indian forces. The Ghaznavid sultan had brought up infantry and even war elephants from India. He did not have access to the same number of cavalrymen, and the battle proved decisive. The Ghaznavids were forced to retreat into India, and the Karakhanids were then pushed back to the Jaxartes.

- All of Transoxiana fell into the hands of Tughril Bey, and the Turkish armies began to march relentlessly across northern Iran. They arrived at all the great caravan cities not as nomadic barbarians or conquerors but as Sunni Muslims and agents of the caliph. In 1055, Tughril Bey entered Baghdad itself, and his position as sultan was confirmed by the caliph. He married a daughter of the caliph, and henceforth, the Abbasid caliphate would be directed by a Turkish sultan.

- The victory of Tughril Bey was spectacular and unexpected. In capturing Baghdad, the Seljuk sultan and his successors found that they now had a problem of meeting foes on numerous frontiers. The Karakhanids were still in the northeast, and the Ghaznavids in India could always mount a comeback, but above all, the Seljuks now assumed the commitment of dealing with the Shi'a caliphs of Cairo and their Christian allies, the Byzantine emperors of Constantinople.

Ghaznavid: A dynasty of Turkish slave emirs (963–1186), who ruled from Ghazna (Afghanistan) over Transoxania and Iran and raided northern India.

Karakhanid: A Turkish confederation on the central Asian steppes that ruled Transoxania from Kashgar and Samarkand (840–1212). They converted to Islam in 934.

Mamluk: From the Arabic for "servant": (1) Turkish slave soldier in the Islamic world; (2) dynasty of Turkish slave soldiers that ruled Egypt (1250–1517); (3) dynasty of Turkish slave soldiers that ruled the Delhi sultanate (1206–1290).

Names to Know

Alp Tigin (961–975): Turkish Mamluk; ruled Ghazna (today Afghanistan) as a vassal of the Samanid emir Mansur I (961–976). He promoted Sunni Islam and raided the Punjab, sacking Hindu temples and Buddhist monasteries. He was succeeded by Ishaq (975–977), and then his son-in-law Sebüktigin (977–997).

Mahmud al-Kashgari (1005–1102): Turkish poet and scholar under the Karakhanids; wrote the first compendium on the Turkish language, *Diwan lughat at-Turk*, and adapted the Arabic-Persian script for writing Turkish. His work contains a wealth of information about early Turkish history and religious traditions. He also drew the first world map showing the location of Turkish tribes.

Mahmud of Ghazni (b. 971; r. 997–1030): Ghaznavid sultan; the son and successor of Sebüktigin. He waged 17 campaigns in northern India, whereby he gained the loot and slaves to sustain his professional army. He clashed with the Karakhanids over Transoxania, and in 1015–1071, he secured Khwarezm. In 1027–1028, he extended his sway over the caravan cities of northern Iran.

Sebüktigin (b. 942; r. 977–997): Ghaznavid emir and sultan; known as the Lion of Ghazni. He was the Turkish commander and son-in-law of Alp Tigin. In 977, he was declared emir by his Turkish soldiers. He forged the Ghaznavid emirate into a Muslim state and conquered the Kabul valley. In 994–999, he secured the Samanid lands south of the Oxus River, while the Karakhanids occupied Transoxania.

Tughril Bey (b. 999; r. 1037–1063): Seljuk sultan; restored the power of the Sunni Abbasid caliphate at Baghdad. In 1025, Tughril Beg and his brother Chaghri had settled their Ghuzz Turks in Khurasan as vassals of Sultan Mahmud of Ghazna. In 1030–1037, Tughril Beg conquered Transoxania and took the title sultan. In 1040, he defeated the Ghaznavid sultan Masud (1031–1041) and conquered the former Ghaznavid domains in northern Iran. In 1055, he entered Baghdad and was received as great sultan by Caliph al-Kasim (1031–1075).

Suggested Reading

Bulliet, *Cotton, Climate, and Camels in Early Islamic Iran.*

Bosworth, *The Ghaznavids, 994–1040.*

Cahen, "The Turkish Invasion: The Selchukids."

Elverskog, *Buddhism and Islam on the Silk Road.*

Jackson, *The Delhi Sultanate.*

Golden, "The Karakhanids and Early Islam."

Keay, *India: A History.*

Questions to Consider

1. What accounted for the migrations of Turkish tribes westward in the 9th and 10th centuries? What was the impact of these migrations? Why did a powerful khaganate fail to emerge that could have united the steppes?

2. How did Abbasid caliphs and Samanid emirs exploit the disunity among the Turkish tribes? What was the long-term impact of the slave trade on the nomadic peoples?

3. What was the nature of the Karakhanid confederation? Why did these Turkish tribes convert to Islam in the 10th century? How did conversion change the relationship between nomads and sedentary peoples?

4. What accounted for the success of the Ghaznavid sultans? To what degree was the state simply the personal achievement of Sebüktigin and Mahmud? Why did the Ghaznavids fail to defeat the Seljuk Turks?

5. How much did Seljuk success depend on Tughril Bey? What advantages did the Seljuk Turks enjoy? Why were they so readily accepted as defenders of Sunni Islam? Why did the occupation of Baghdad pose a crisis of policy for Tughril Bey and his successors?

The Rise of the Seljuk Turks
Lecture 22—Transcript

In this lecture, I wish to follow up on some of the implications of the previous two lectures. As you recall, we talked about the clash between the armies of the Caliphate and the western Turks, notably the Karluks, ending in the great Battle of Talas; and then we spent some time talking also about how Islam was disseminated onto the western steppes through trade connections. We should keep those changes in mind as we turn to this subject, which is going to deal with the implications of both of those two previous issues; and those issues lead directly to the subject of this lecture, which is a series of Turkish migrations that lead to the formation of new powers on the steppes. We will be talking about three states in particular; those states are going to be the Karakhanids, the sultans of Ghazni or Ghazna—sometimes it is spelled with an un-dotted "I" at the end, sometimes an "A"; we call them the Ghaznavid sultans or the Ghaznavid emirs—and then finally the Seljuk Turks, who will enter at the end of this lecture and represent the greatest of these new Turkish political organizations.

To understand this, we need to go back to the Battle of Talas and look at the two centuries after that battle that are really rather curious in several ways. The Battle of Talas witnessed in some ways the beginning of a new wave of migrations across the Central Eurasian steppes. You would think that the winners of the battle, the real winners of the battle, were not the Muslim or the Chinese armies—even though those governors, Ziyad al-Salih in particular, the Abbasid governor won an extraordinary victory tactically—it was the Karluks; it was the Turkish allies who eventually deserted from the Chinese side over to the Muslim side that tipped the balance.

The Karluks were western Turks. They were members of the western Gök Turk khanate that had often reconfigured itself as the On Ok, the Ten Arrows; that is, the Ten Inner Tribes. You would think that the Karluks would go on to dominate the central steppes of Eurasia, but that did not happen. That did not happen for several reasons: For one, it was a very, very loose confederation. The tribes fell out among themselves fighting, and also they got swept up in the slave trade, which we will discuss. In addition, they were also vassals of the Uighur khan; and as you recall, the Uighur khans ruled the eastern steppes of Eurasia and exercised a nominal hegemony over the central steppes of Eurasia. The Uighur khans suddenly were defeated by an uprising of their various subject peoples in 840. That resulted in rather wild Turkish tribes occupying the forest zone; they were in the Yenisei River basin, the upper basin. They descended upon the Uighur capital, Balasagun, which is very close to the later capital of Genghis Khan, Karakorum, and sacked it in 840. The result was the Uighur khanate broke up immediately. Many of the Uighurs migrated to the caravan cities of the Tarim Basin, some went into Gansu, others were actually received into the Chinese Empire; and the Uighur khanate essentially collapsed. That political fragmentation was very significant. As a result of the loss of their homeland—and the Uighurs essentially just decamped, many of them heading to the caravan cities and the steppes just north of the Xiaoshun—that homeland was never reoccupied by the Turks. That would be the Orkhon valley, the Selenge Valley; there is a series of sacred mountains in the area; it is where the earliest Turkish inscriptions were found. Henceforth, that area would become home in time to a new people, the Mongols.

What happened after the time of the Battle of Talas in 751, the Uighur khanate in less than a century fragmented; broke up. The Karaluks never really imposed any kind of authority on the Central Eurasian steppes; and as a result, there were more migrations of Turks from east to west into the central and western steppes. This was very disruptive. There was also a second factor that played upon these changes; and this had to do with the Abbasid caliphate, and then starting in the ninth century with the representatives of the Abbasid caliph; that is, the Samanid emirs ruling in Bukhara. Whether you are talking about the Abbasids or the Samanid emirs, you are still talking about representatives of a very powerful, literate Muslim civilization.

The Abbasid caliphs and later the Samanid emirs were not so displeased by the conditions on the steppes, this new wave of migrations, because this played directly into one of their biggest needs, which I alluded to in the past lecture, and that was the slave trade. The slave trade turned out to be extremely important. It was important to essentially fuel—or, I should say, supply—the armies of the caliphate as well as the armies of the Samanid emirs. Already, at the very start of the Abbasid caliphate—particularly the second caliph al-Mansur, who established the city of Baghdad—the Abbasid caliphs distrusted their Arab tribal regiments, with good cause. The Arab tribal regiments had repeatedly proved rapacious and unruly; they were difficult to discipline; they often fought among themselves over issues of blood feud and honor. Furthermore, many of them were infected with Shi'a or Aliad, or even worse, Umayyad sympathies. It was really the Arab army in Spain that received the Umayyad prince who essentially was able to create his own caliphate, or actually first called himself emir in 756 at Cordova, and breakaway from the Abbasid state. The Abbasid caliphs began to replace their Arab soldiers with professionals. These included Persians, Armenians; also Kurds, warlike races within the empire; but above all, they came to appreciate the Turks.

As I mentioned in the fighting that culminated in the Battle at Talas in 751, the caliphs were well aware that a Turkish cavalry was the best cavalry anyone could hire. Large numbers of Turks were hired as mercenaries or recruited as allies to fight in the armies of the great Caliphs; Harun ar-Rashid, for one, the man whose reign represents the pinnacle of the Abbasid state. He used large numbers of Turks in his prestige campaigns; that is campaigns he waged against the Byzantine emperor where he postured as the defender of Islam and waged in jihad. The best forces there were generally Turks. In one such campaign later by his successor al-Mu'tasim in 838, 10,000 Turkish cavalrymen almost wiped out the army of the emperor Theophilus at the Battle of Dazimon; it was almost a prelude in the Battle of Manzikert in 1071. In addition to the allies and mercenaries, the caliphs began to recruit a Turkish bodyguard. This goes back to that civil war I mentioned that erupted in 811, which essentially pitted the two sons of Harun ar-Rashid against each other; and the winner, al-Ma'mum, went out of his way to create this special Turkish bodyguard, the *haras*.

These were slave soldiers. Initially, there were 4,000 of them in Baghdad. It eventually grew, and they essentially became the Praetorian Guard of the Abbasid Caliphate; that is one comment about them. They were often known as *Mamluk* or a *ghulam*, which is the Arabic term. These are terms to indicate young men, usually between the ages of let us say around 14, 15, maybe as old as 18 who had been taken in these tribal wars and sold as slaves. They arrived in the Islamic world; they were put under generally the religious schools, sometimes Sufi mystics; they were converted to Islam, and drilled to be elite soldiers. They already had the skills as cavalrymen; and as a result, starting in the ninth century, the military power of the Islamic world rested in its Turkish slave soldiers, its Turkish professional mercenaries and allies, even before the Turks had entered the Islamic world. The Islamic world had come to depend on that manpower on the Eurasian steppes; and the disorder on the Eurasian steppes, the failure of the Karluks to construct a new confederacy, the collapse of the Uighur khanate in 840, all of that was to the advantage of the Abbasid and later Samanid emirs. That meant there was lots of tribal warfare and lots of slaves available.

These conditions did not last forever, because in time merchants operating on the Eurasian steppes began to introduce Islam. The fighting along the borders, particularly along the Upper Jaxartes River valley, the regions around the Aral Sea—on the southern shores of the Aral Sea were the very wealthy cities of Kwharyzm, which were important caravan cities—in all of these areas, Turkish tribes came into contact with the Islamic world and they began to gain more organization, some of them began to understand Islam, and by the 10th century we get the reports of the first massive tribal conversions; that is, whole tribes going over in large numbers to Islam.

Several important political orders came out of these new conditions starting essentially in the 10th century. The first of those political orders I want to look at are the Karakhanid Turks. They take their name—it is a kind of artificial name—it has been coined out of the writings of a very important figure who wrote at Kashgar. His name is Mahmud ibn Husayn, which means "son of Husayn," al-Kashgari, which means "from Kashgar." As you recall, Kashgar was that crucial city on the caravan route that linked Transoxiana, especially the caravan city of Samarkand, to Khotan, Turfan, the various cities of the Tarim Basin. These tribes were ruled by the Kara Khans, the "Black Khans." Why black, we are not sure; it was probably some sort of color involved with their banners and their horse tail insignia. Furthermore, the confederation was divided into a western and eastern half. The eastern half of the confederation, which would have been east of Kashgar on the steppes around the Altai Mountains, they were known as the Arslan Kara Khans, which means the "Lion Black Khans." The western tribes, which were north of the Jaxartes and came to control Kashgar, they were known as the Bughra

Kara Khans; that is, the "Black Camel Khans." The Black Camel and the Black Lion apparently referred to totem animals of the leading clans.

They had a very complicated political organization—a lot of sub-commanders, sub-clans—but what was important about the Kara Khans is they began to convert to Islam starting in the mid-10th century. Particularly those Black Camel Kaghans, the Bughra Kara Khans, they styled themselves as not only Turkish rulers, but patrons of Muslim civilization. Kashgar emerged in the 10th and the 11th century as one of the first centers of really a distinct Turkish Islamic civilization. The khans there patronized poets and scholars. It was in Kashgar, in the associated towns that are involved in the trade of the Silk Road, where Turkish was adapted to the Arabic script. It was not a direct adaptation of the Arab script; it was actually using the Middle Persian version of Arabic writing. That was the Arabic script that was used by the Samanid emirs and other emirs in Eastern Iran to create the Middle Persian literature that flourished starting in the 9th century; that was what they were taking as their model. In addition, you see efforts at adapting Samanid architectural forms, and Kashgar boasts some of the earliest Islamic monuments in Central Asia to this day, especially those monumental mausoleums.

There were a number of figures that came to define this Turkish civilization, but the one I want to talk about is Mahmud al-Kashgari. His career spanned most of the 11th century. He was given an extraordinary life, thought to be born around 1005 or thereabouts; died shortly after 1102 in his 90s. He was the son of a rather minor family of officials who had served at the court; but what is significant about him is that he recorded many of the Turkish heroic traditions and epic traditions in something called a *diwan*, which is a compendium; *diwan* or divan, both forms of the word are found in Islamic countries. It has different meanings; it is also a point where judgment is rendered by later Mogul emperors or Ottoman sultans. But in this sense, it is a compendium; it is a rendering of judgment on the Turkish language and grammar, and it is the first comprehensive discussion about the Turkish language. Furthermore, he cites many early oral poems and other traditions, especially the ancient heroes. He links the Kara Khans—that is, the Black Khans—with the Ashina clan; that is, that remote clan of Turks that were responsible for the Gök Turk khanate. A lot of information we have about the early Turks ultimately comes back to his writings. He also appended an extraordinary map. It is very, very schematic; but the map nonetheless shows the position of the various Turkish tribes on the Eurasian steppes. This work has survived in many later editions. The Ottoman sultans loved it, and the best manuscripts are now in Istanbul because the sultans saw that as essentially their origins. Mahmud is also hailed today by various republics in Central Asia; Kyrgyzstan, Kazakhstan, the Uighurs in Chinese Turkistan all claim him as a national hero; they have all sorts of modern bronze statues to him.

But he is a pivotal figure that turns Turkish into a literary language. There were other writers at the same time putting down the epics, their scholarly pursuits. But this was a very, very significant turning point because it means that the Turks as a whole will embrace Islam, but on their own terms; and they will turn their language into one of the languages, really one of the three great languages, of the Islamic world, of the medieval Islamic world and even down to this day. Some would say that you use Arabic for writing theology and serious mathematical works; you use Persian for literature and poetry; and you use Turkish to talk to horses and soldiers, in that order (I am paraphrasing Frederick the Great about German). That represents the prejudices probably of the Persian elite; but nonetheless, despite these prejudices, Turkish now emerged as a legitimate literary language. It had a life of its own, and that means when the Turks entered into the wider Islamic world, they would not be assimilated the way many nomadic peoples were. That was the feature we saw, particularly with the Chinese Empire; it was what we saw with the Bulgars and Magyars in Europe where they were assimilated into the wider Christian populations. In this case, the Turks have now required a cultural religious identity. It was Islamic, but it was also distinctly Turkish.

We have a wonderful story about the conversion of one of the khans, the initial conversion, Satuk Khan, he was actually the Black Camel Khan, and that conversion is attributed to his contract with a Sufi mystic when he was a young boy and the family was visiting Bukhara; and then when he overthrew the pagan ruler—that is, of Kashgar—he began building mosques and he promoted Islam. The story has a great deal of retelling behind it; but nonetheless, the point of that story was that the rulers starting in the mid-

10th century among these tribes of the Karakhanids began to convert, and in doing so they took over whole tribes. We have a report from around the mid-10th century of 50,000 Turkish tents converting following the example of Satuk, who when he became the Black Camel Khan in Kashgar brought over the whole town to Islam. These conversions gained pace through the 10th and the 11th century—the ancestors of the Oghuz Turks undoubtedly converted at this time; these will be the direct ancestors of the Seljuk Turks—and these conversions are very, very different from the individual conversions won by merchants and Sufi mystics or the conversions of slaves who had been bought on the slave markets and brought into the Islamic world. The Karakhanids then emerged as one of the great political powers out of this interaction between the steppes and the Islamic world.

The second one that emerged was really a product of the slave system. That involves the rulers that came to be known as the Ghaznavid sultans. They were essentially a succession of slave soldiers, *mamluks*. They had started out in the employ of the Samanid emirs of Bukhara. The founder of this outfit, a fellow by the name of Alp Tigin—and you have to remember these "g's" and "gh's" that you often see in Turkish names are really more of a glide, they are almost a "y" sound; in modern Turkish they are known as *yumusak ge*, and both conventions are used to render Turkish names and sometimes they are a little bit confusing when you see them; it is one of the few exceptions in the modern Turkish alphabet that is a bit bewildering to Westerners—anyway, Alp Tigin, he tried to play kingmaker at Bukhara; and what they did with him is send him off to a remote province at the time, and that was the town of Ghazni or Ghazna, which is today in Afghanistan, and that was on the borders of India. He took over the town, turned it into a successful frontier post, and then eventually power was transmitted—his son did not last very long—to his son-in-law, a very important man known as Sebüktigin.

Sebüktigin took over power of the Ghaznavid Emirate—it would have been called an emirate at this point—probably in the year 977; and he turned that Amerid into a bastion that in some ways pointed the Turks and Islam in the direction of India. He is often known as the Lion of Ghazna or Ghazni. He repeatedly invaded the Punjab, plundering Hindu temples and Buddhist monasteries to support his armies with plunder. He depended very heavily on slave troops that had been recruited from the steppes, also from Iranians, from Khurasan; and above all, he used Persian administrators. Sebüktigin may have been Turkish in origin—he was a slave who rose to a high military post—but culturally he was a product of that high Persian-Iranian culture. In some ways, Sebüktigin and his successors—and that would be especially his son Mahmud and then his grandson Masud—they really were models for the later Mogul emperors of India; that is, combining Persian administrators, Turkish nomadic cavalry, and Islam as the basis of setting up a very, very effective state.

The Ghaznavid sultans carried out some extraordinary raids into India. Mahmud particularly, in 1024 conducted a raid that was just off the charts militarily. His army came out of the Thar Desert—that is, they descended through the Khyber Pass, out of the Thar Desert—into Gujarat and sacked the great temple of Shiva at the city of Somnatha, a great shrine. The lingam of Shiva was turned over and hammered into bits, and all the wealth was taken back to Ghaznavid and used to decorate a new Friday mosque in his capital. The Ghaznavids emerged as the power of eastern Islam; and they ran smack up against the Karakhanids because both of these states—one based on slave troops, the other based on a tribal confederation—squeezed out the Samanid emirs. By 1030, the Samanids were finished—they actually escaped off to a lonely exile on an island in the Caspian Sea, which is an exile place for a lot of ex-rulers, as we will see in the Mongol period—and the result was eastern Islam was partitioned between the Ghaznavid sultans and the Karakhanids. The Oxus was accepted again as the boundary; that is, the Amu Darya, a classic boundary. Balkh fell into the hands of Mahmud; the Karakhanids were content with the cities of Transoxiana.

It looked like Mahmud and then his successors would go on to unite eastern Islam. The next step was Baghdad to get a *firman* from the caliph directly. It did not happen; and that is because a third group suddenly intervened and knocked out both contenders, and those were the Seljuk Turks. The Seljuk Turks's ancestors were known as Oghuz Turks, or Ghuzz Turks as they would be called in Arabic; and the Oghuz Turks had settled in the Jaxartes valley, the lands around the Aral Sea. They were responsible for kicking out the Pechenegs in the 9th century. They entered into the Islamic world in the 10th century and the founder of this tribe, known as Seljuk, who gave his name to the whole tribe, moved into the region known as Khurasan; that is Eastern Iran today, it is also part of Afghanistan and Turkmenistan. It was an important border area with the great cities of Nishapur; it had close connections with the city of Merv; and so in Khurasan the Turks arrived as settlers. They were military colonists. There is also a thesis that has been advanced that they were very big on the Silk Road because they provided the camels. I mentioned in an earlier lecture that there was a crossbreeding of the dromedary from Arabia with the two-humped Bactrian camel to create a camel in Central Asia that was still able to handle the cold winters, but had the advantages of the Arabian breed with greater staying power, better conservation of water. The Seljuk Turks seem to have been involved in that breeding; they were supplying the caravans with the camels. There was a major expansion of the caravan trade in the 10th century, particularly in cottons and linens; that is, the Samanid emirs really were very, very assiduous in promoting different plantation systems across Northern Iran to supply the growing markets of Baghdad, but also the cities of Northern Iran, Transoxiana, and even India. The Seljuk Turks arrived as colonists. They were settled, in part, because of their military abilities. They were in essentially a frontier zone. Furthermore, they were involved in the caravan trade, and there was always a need for nomads in Khurasan and Transoxiana because there was a close association with people tending flocks and herds with supplying the agriculturalists and the cities.

The grandsons of Seljuk and the oldest one, the most important one, Tughril Bey, and his brother Chagri Bey, they took power over these tribes and they exploited the clash between the Karakhanids and the Ghaznavid sultans. They were settled in the area of Bukhara around 1025 by the Karakhanids. They went over to Mahmud when he occupied the city, and then they went into business for themselves. In the 1030s, they swept through many of the cities of Eastern Iran, and Tughril Bey was very, very careful. He imposed discipline on his soldiers. They were not only excellent nomadic warriors, but they represented themselves as agents of the caliph in Baghdad; they were Sunni Muslims. In 1037, he had himself proclaimed sultan at Nishapur. That is a very important title that gains currency in the 11th century. It means "guardian"; that is, you are the guardian of the interests of the Abbasid caliphs, the then-reigning Ghaznavid ruler Masud was using the same title.

On May 23, 1040, in the vicinity of Merv, Tughril Bey won a major victory over the Ghaznavid army. It was a classic victory of Turkish cavalry over an army that had come to depend very, very heavily on Indian forces. Masud had brought up infantry and even war elephants from India; he did not have access to the same number of cavalrymen; and the battle proved decisive. In 1040, the Ghaznavids essentially were forced to retreat into India. The Karakhanids were pushed back to the Jaxartes. All of Transoxiana fell into the hands of Tughril Bey, and the Turkish armies began to march relentlessly across Northern Iran, being received at all the great caravan cities, Hamadan, Rav, Tabriz; and again, they arrived not as nomadic barbarians, not as conquerors, but as Sunni Muslims, as agents of the caliph. In 1055, Tughril Bey entered Baghdad itself. At that point, he had reached the pinnacle of his power because his position as sultan was now confirmed by the caliph. He henceforth ruled as the guardian, the sultan of the caliph al-Hakim. He married a daughter of the caliph who entered the harem; and henceforth, the Abbasid Caliphate was going to be directed by a Turkish sultan.

The victory of Tughril Bey was spectacular, unexpected. But in capturing Baghdad, the Seljuk sultan Tughril Bey and his successors found that they now had a problem of meeting foes on all sorts of frontiers. There was still the Karakhanids to the northeast; the Ghaznavids who were always in India could mount a comeback; but above all, they now assumed the commitment of dealing with the Shi'a caliphs of Cairo and their Christian allies, the Byzantine emperors of Constantinople.

Turks in Anatolia and India
Lecture 23

As we've seen in previous lectures, for nearly 300 years during the Abbasid caliphate, the political and military expansion of the Islamic world had halted. During that same period, Abbasid caliphs and various emirs ruling in the name of the caliph came to depend on Turkish military power. Once the Seljuk Turks emerged as a major factor in eastern Islam, they were responsible for conquering two new regions: Anatolia, often referred to as Asia Minor, and northern India, particularly the region around Delhi known as the Doab. This lecture will compare these conquests.

The Problem of Cairo

- As mentioned in the last lecture, in 1055, Tughril Bey, leader of the Seljuk Turks, entered the city of Baghdad. From that point forward, Tughril Bey and his successors were confronted with running a vast empire, far larger than any Turkish ruler had yet administered.
  - They could now tap into the wealth of a good portion of the Silk Road, but they also faced a series of commitments that strained Seljuk resources.

  - The Karakhanids were still present to the east and might contest Transoxiana. The Ghaznavids and their vassal allies could come out of India and the borderlands of Afghanistan. And above all, the western frontier posed challenges.

- The Fatimid caliphs had resided in Cairo since 973. They represented a counter-caliph to the Sunni caliph in Baghdad, in whose name Tughril Bey and the Seljuk Turks fought. Knocking out these sectarian rivals, who posed a challenge to the authority of the Abbasid caliphate and the Seljuk sultan, became a priority.

- Further, in 1055, after the Seljuk withdrawal from Baghdad, rebels in the city called in a Fatimid army, and Baghdad was occupied for

40 days. Tughril Bey appeared and chased out the Fatimid army, but he was henceforth committed to a war against Cairo.

- The Fatimid caliphs had come to an agreement with the Orthodox emperors of Constantinople. At the time, the Byzantine state was deeply divided between two factions: a civil elite in the capital that wanted to slash military expenditures and a military elite based in Anatolia that put priority on containing the frontiers. The civilian group came to dominate politics in Constantinople, a fact that had dire consequences for the military budget and the efficiency of the Byzantine army.

- Up until the arrival of the Seljuk Turks, an agreement existed between the Byzantines, who controlled northern Syria, and the Fatimids, who controlled southern Syria and the rest of the Levant, to protect Christian pilgrimage routes to Jerusalem. This agreement had two important consequences for Tughril Bey and his Seljuk Turks.
  - First, Tughril Bey turned his Turkish regiments on the Byzantine Empire to keep the Byzantine emperors distracted. At the same time, he concentrated the bulk of his forces to take Syria and Jerusalem, then hold Mecca and Medina, and lastly take Cairo. As a direct consequence of this fighting, which disrupted the pilgrimage routes, Pope Urban II preached the First Crusade in 1095.

  - Second, the emirs of Tughril Bey began to attack Asia Minor and found no resistance. In Byzantine Anatolia, they found cities to sack but also grasslands that were similar to their homeland in central Asia. Further, this region was not occupied by Muslims but by Christians. The soldiers could fight as *ghazi* warriors in the name of **jihad**. This was an ideal place for Turkish expansion.

The Battle of Manzikert
- Starting in 1055, Turkish tribal armies began to raid across Anatolia, and the Byzantine state reacted ineptly. In 1068, a new emperor came to the throne, **Romanus IV Diogenes**, whose job was to

reckon with the Seljuk Turks. Romanus inherited a treasury that had been bankrupt by 50 years of incompetence and an army that was in a poor state. He tried to bring the raiders to bear, but it was difficult because the Turks had learned the various routes across Asia Minor.

- The fighting climaxed in August of 1071 when Romanus marched a large field army west and encountered the new sultan, **Alp-Arslan**, the nephew of Tughril Bey, at the town of Manzikert. The town was on grasslands that were ideal for the Turkish cavalry.

- Romanus is often criticized for ineptitude, but he actually did a credible job. He drew up his army immediately to the west of the modern town, which still has heavy fortifications built from the Byzantine age. He put his infantry in the center, arranged the usual flanking forces with archers, and held his cavalry in reserve.
  - Romanus fought the sort of battle that would have been recommended by both Byzantine authors and Tang generals, but he also commanded an army that had no sense of unity. He held his own over the course of the day. At the end of the day, he called his forces together and told them to fall back to camp because they could not bring the Turks to battle.

  - The infantry wheeled around and opened up gaps that Alp-Arslan was able to exploit. The army was thrown into confusion. Rumors flew that the emperor had been killed. The cavalry, particularly the forces in the rear that were supposed to prevent such an occurrence, defected.

  - Actually, Romanus had fallen into the hands of the sultan. He was later released and received the standard Byzantine imperial retirement package: He was blinded and left in a monastery.

The Crusades

- In the wake of the victory at Manzikert, independent bands of Turks moved into Asia Minor and carved out their own principalities. Within a decade, most of Asia Minor had fallen into the hands of

Turkish adventurers, technically professing to be the emirs of the Turkish sultan in Baghdad but actually independent operators.

- The Byzantine emperors had no choice but to take Asia Minor back. In 1081, a successful general, Alexius I Comnenus, battled his way to the throne and decided to call in western Europeans as mercenaries to beat back the Turks and retake Asia Minor. That appeal was interpreted by Pope Urban II as a call to liberate Jerusalem, and thus, the First Crusade was launched. Between 1097 and 1099, more than 50,000 western Europeans streamed across Asia Minor toward Jerusalem.

- The result was a seesaw struggle across Asia Minor among Byzantines, Crusaders, and Seljuk Turks. Initially, the Crusaders won stunning victories over the Turks. Western and coastal regions of Asia Minor fell back under Byzantine control. But the Byzantine emperors could never drive the Turks off the plateau. The Turkish tribes settled in significant numbers, came to terms with the Christian agriculturists, and began to create a Turkish heartland in this peninsula.

- The fighting also played into the hands of the Seljuk Turks. It broke down Byzantine institutions, cities, and road systems, resulting in conditions that favored the nomadic way of war. Large parts of Asia Minor passed out of agricultural use into grasslands, and steadily, the balance shifted in favor of the Turks. Two events confirm this shift.
  - In 1176, the emperor Manuel I was decisively beaten at the Battle of Myriocephalon. That battle marked the end of Byzantine efforts to expel the Seljuk Turks from Asia Minor.

  - In April of 1204, members of the Fourth Crusade stormed into the city of Constantinople and sacked it. Byzantine power was finished. The political and, ultimately, the cultural destinies of Asia Minor shifted decisively to the Seljuk Turks settled in Anatolia, who would turn that region into a new Turkish-speaking, Muslim land.

Conquests into India

- At the same time that the Seljuk Turks were winning victories in the west, there were also significant battles taking place on the eastern frontier. India at this time was divided into a number of competing kingdoms, vying for control of the **Aryavarta**, the Aryan homeland. This region essentially encompassed the Indus Valley, the **Doab**, and the Ganges. When a Hindu king gained ascendency over his opponents, he didn't build great bureaucratic structures but attempted to control this region.

The crucial victories that opened northern India up to Muslim conquest were won by the Ghaznavid sultans, using combined Turkish, Arab, and Persian forces.

- As a result of different dynasties vying for control, there was no organized resistance when the Ghaznavid sultans began to raid into India, even before the Seljuk Turks were on the scene. In addition, the Ghaznavid sultans increasingly realized that they couldn't take back their domains in Iran or contend for the cities of Transoxiana; thus, they began to take over the regions of India. In this regard, the conquest was very different from that in Asia Minor.

- In 1192, at the Battle of Tarain, just north of Delhi, the nomadic cavalry of the Ghaznavid sultan **Muhammad Ghuri** crushed the most effective state in northern India, that of Prithviraj III. In the next year, his forces took Delhi. Those victories, combined with earlier ones by the sultan Mahmud, collectively had the impact of Manzikert in Asia Minor, opening northern India to Muslim conquest and settlement.

- However, in the 11th and 12th centuries and even into the 13th, the Turkish conquest of northern India was much more a military occupation than a settlement. This is quite different from the situation in Asia Minor, where perhaps 500,000 nomads settled in the wake of Manzikert and, in time, would create a new Turkish identity.

○ In contrast, with his victory in 1192, Muhammad Ghuri gained control of Delhi and faced a population 10 times that of Asia Minor. Further, he was dealing with 2 million square miles on the subcontinent, as opposed to 300,000 square miles in Asia Minor. Above all, in India, the Turkish Muslim conquerors ran into the power of caste, *varna*, and the traditions of Indian civilization in a terrain and a climate that did not permit the settlement of nomads. In fact, it wasn't even conducive to horses.

○ From the start, then, the sultans ruling in Delhi faced a very different situation than their contemporaries did in Konya in Asia Minor. As a result, two distinct Turkish Muslim civilizations came out of these two conquests: a Turkish civilization in Anatolia and a ruling elite in Delhi.

Important Terms

Aryavarta: The "Aryan homeland," which comprises the lands of the upper Indus and Ganges rivers that are home to the sacred cities of Hinduism.

Doab: The fertile lands between the Punjab and the upper Ganges and Yamuna rivers; Delhi and Agra are in the Doab.

jihad: In Islam, "holy war."

Names to Know

Alp-Arslan (b. 1029; r. 1063–1072): Seljuk sultan and nephew of Tughril Beg. Defeated and captured the Byzantine emperor Romanus IV at the Battle of Manzikert. Alp-Arslan opened Asia Minor to settlement by Turkish tribes.

Muhammad Ghuri (b. 1150, r. 1202–1206): Ghurid emir; extended the Ghurids into northern India. He conquered the Punjab and Doab in the name of his older brother Ghiyas al-Din (1163–1203). His decisive victory over the Rajput King Prithviraja III (1149–1192) in 1192 gained him control of Delhi. As emir, he entrusted the administration of the Indian conquests to his Turkish general Qutb al-Din Aybak.

Romanus IV Diogenes (b. c. 1030; r. 1068–1072): Byzantine emperor; candidate of the officers of the eastern army. He married the empress Eudocia, widow of Constantine X Ducas (1059–1067). Romanus was decisively defeated and captured by the Seljuk sultan Alp-Arslan at the Battle of Manzikert in 1071. In 1072, Romanus was released by Alp-Arslan, but Michael VII ordered him deposed and blinded. Romanus died in exile.

Suggested Reading

Cahen (Jones-Williams, trans.), *Pre-Ottoman Turkey*.

———. "The Turkish Invasion: The Selchukids."

Elverskog, *Buddhism and Islam on the Silk Road*.

Jackson, *The Delhi Sultanate*.

Keay, *India: A History*.

Magdalino, *The Empire of Manuel I Komnenos, 1143–1180*.

Rice, *The Seljuk Turks*.

Vyrnos, *The Decline of Medieval Hellenism in Asia Minor and the Process of Islamization from the Eleventh through the Fifteenth Century*.

Questions to Consider

1. What reasons compelled Turks to invade both Anatolia and India? How did these two conquests differ? In what ways were they similar?

2. Why did the Battle of Manzikert in 1071 prove so decisive in its results? Why did the Turks settle so successfully in Asia Minor? Why did the Comnenian emperors and the Crusaders fail to expel the Turks from Asia Minor? How did the desultory fighting between 1097 and 1176 ultimately benefit the Seljuk Turks?

3. What was the political, religious, and cultural order in northern India in the 11th century? Why did the leading Indian kingdoms fail to unite against the Turkish invaders?

4. How were the careers of Mahmud of Ghazvi and Muhammad Ghuri decisive for the future of Muslim India? How did the Indian populations react to the widespread destruction of Hindu temples and Buddhist monasteries?

Turks in Anatolia and India
Lecture 23—Transcript

In this lecture, I wish to deal with the implications of the rise of the Seljuk Turks. The Seljuk Turks are responsible for conquering really two new regions to the Islamic world. As I mentioned in the previous lectures, particularly with regard to the Abbasid Caliphate, for nearly 300 years the political and military expansion of the Islamic world had halted. During that same period, Abbasid caliphs and various emirs ruling in the name of the Abbasid caliph came to depend on Turkish military power.

Once the Seljuk Turks emerged as a major factor in eastern Islam, they were responsible for conquering two new regions that were not previously part of Dar al-Islam: Anatolia, often referred to as Asia Minor; the modern Turkish name is Anadolu, but it really is a Greek word. That would be today the Asiatic portions of the Republic of Turkey. The second area that the Seljuk Turks were responsible for, kind of indirectly, was Northern India; particularly the region around Delhi, the so-called region the Doab, that strategic zone, that very fertile zone that essentially links the upper tributaries of the Indus, the Punjab, the Land of the Five Rivers with the Upper Ganges and forms the center of any imperial power on the Indo-Gangic plain in the subcontinent. Both of these areas, Northern India and Anatolia, were directly or indirectly brought into the Islamic world by the power of Seljuk Turks or people who had been pushed into India fighting the same way, notably the Ghaznavids, who were also depending on Turkish power.

This lecture is a lecture of comparative conquests. Let us first turn to the west and to the Seljuk Turks directly. I mentioned last time that in 1055, Tughril Bey, the leader of the Seljuk Turks, self-styled sultan, had entered the city of Baghdad. That represented the pinnacle of his military achievement since 1037 when he had essentially proclaimed himself sultan; and henceforth, Tughril Bey and his successors—his nephew Alp-Arslan and eventually the third Seljuk sultan, Malik-Shah—they were confronted with running a vast empire far greater than any Turkish ruler had yet administered. They had perfected the technique of using Persian administrators; they, of course, obtained the bureaucratic structures of Baghdad; they had now the wealth of a good chunk of the Silk Road to tap into; but on the other hand, they now faced a series of commitments that really strained Seljuk resources from the very start. I mentioned that there was still the Karakhanids to the east who might contest Transoxiana. There were also the Ghaznavids and their various subordinate vassal allies who could come back out of India and the borderlands of Afghanistan; but above all, it was the western front that was important.

In Cairo, since 973, resided the Fatimid caliphs. As I had mentioned, they represented a counter-caliph to the Sunni caliph in Baghdad. Tughril Bey and his Seljuk Turks professed Sunni Islam, they fought in the name of the caliph, and therefore they were now stuck with the problem of dealing with Cairo; and that was now the priority: not the access to the Eurasian steppes, not even so much the Silk Road, but knocking out the sectarian rival who really posed a challenge of authority to the Abbasid caliphate as well as to the sultan. Furthermore, in 1055 it became clear very quickly that Tughril Bey had to have a reckoning with the government in Cairo. The Seljuk Turks, once they had occupied Baghdad, withdrew. There were reasons for this. Large numbers of nomadic warriors, Ghazi warriors as they are usually called, annoyed the urban population. They may have been Sunni Muslims; but in day-to-day transactions with the urban population of Baghdad, there were the usual clashes between rude nomadic warriors. The best thing was to get these guys out of Baghdad, send them up to Azerbaijan, or try to settle them on the al-Jazirah, the grasslands between the Euphrates and Tigris Rivers. These areas were at least conducive to the Turks; they had grasslands. The Seljuk Turks had brought their families; they could find pasture and water for their horses, and they would be out of the hair of the urban population of Baghdad.

When the Seljuk army had essentially withdrawn, there was a revolt in Baghdad. A number of the chief ministers around the caliph subverted the Turkish bodyguard; those were the slave troops, the *haras*. They had been the effective power for a long time, really since the early ninth century, and they staged a revolt and called in a Fatimid army, which occupied Baghdad for 40 days. During those 40 days, at the Friday prayer at midday, the name of the Fatimid caliph was announced in Baghdad as a mark of loyalty, not the Abbasid caliph. This was intolerable. Tughril Bey appeared immediately, chased out the Fatimid army; everyone involved in the conspiracy was arrested; that Turkish bodyguard was finally disbanded; and the result was Tughril Bey was henceforth committed to a war against Cairo. All the Turkish resources had to be put on Cairo; the eastern and northeastern fronts could wait for later.

I had mentioned in passing in the previous lecture that the Fatimid caliphs of Cairo had come to an agreement with the Orthodox emperors of Constantinople. The Byzantine emperors at this time, in 1055, were representatives of the old Macedonian Dynasty; actually the Macedonian dynasty died out in 1055–1056, and the Byzantine state was deeply divided between two factions: a civil elite in the capital that wanted to slash military expenditures, and a military elite based largely in Anatolia with the states who, of course, put priority on the frontiers. Very, very quickly it was a civilian group that came to dominate politics in Constantinople, and that had dire consequences for the military budget and the efficiency of the Byzantine army. In 1059, the civilian elite put their guy on the throne, a man named Constantine Ducas, Constantine X.

The Byzantine emperors also had an accommodation with the Fatimid caliphate. The government in Cairo and the government in Constantinople had, up until the arrival of the Seljuk Turks, an understanding that the pilgrimage routes across the Byzantine Empire into the Fatimid Empire would be protected; that Christians had rights to the access of Jerusalem. There was a famous treaty signed in 1001 that guaranteed this. The Byzantines, who controlled Northern Syria, the Fatimids, who controlled Southern Syria and the rest of the Levant, they provided the opportunity for Christian pilgrims from Western Europe to come in increasing numbers to Jerusalem.

This had two important consequences for Tughril Bey and his Seljuk Turks. First, he turned his Turkish regiments on the Byzantine Empire to keep the Byzantine emperors distracted. At the same time, he concentrated the bulk of his forces to take first Syria and Jerusalem, then the holy cities Mecca and Medina, and finally Cairo. This fighting disrupted the pilgrimage routes; and as a direct consequence, Pope Urban II was going to preach the First Crusade in 1095. It also had another important consequence, and that is not the sultan's armies initially, but his subordinates, his emirs, began to attack Asia

Minor and found no resistance. In Byzantine Anatolia, they found cities to sack, but also grasslands very similar to their homeland in Central Asia, areas that they could exploit; they knew how to exploit. Furthermore, this region was not occupied by Muslims; it was occupied by Christians. You could fight as a Ghazi warrior in the name of jihad, holy war. This was an ideal place for Turkish expansion. Starting in 1055, Turkish tribal armies started to raid across Anatolia. The Byzantine state reacted very ineptly, especially under Constantine X; the army was not up to the job. There was a political struggle in Constantinople. In 1067, the emperor Constantine X died. His widow Eudoxia briefly ruled on her own. The military elite forced the empress to marry a general, a man called Romanus IV Diogenes, and Romanus gets his job as emperor to reckon with the Seljuk Turks. Unfortunately for Romanus, he inherited a treasury that had been bankrupt by 50 years of incompetence, particularly by the empresses Zoe and Theodora, the high-maintenance empresses of the 11th century. He also inherited an army that was in a very, very poor state. It comprised largely of mercenaries; it did not have a sense of victory; it was not a uniform force.

Romanus tried to bring the raiders to bear, but it was difficult because the Turks instinctively had learned the various routes across Asia Minor. They knew where to enter the passes, where to cross the Taurus. They had essentially blitzed Armenia, seized the cities of Ani and Kars, which they were using as bases. The fighting climaxes in the year 1071 when Romanus the IV marches a large field army east and encounters the new sultan, Alp Arslan, the nephew of Tughril Bey, who had come to the throne in 1063. In August, 1071, the two armies encountered each other at the distant town of Manzikert, which is today in Eastern Turkey. It is on grasslands that are ideal to the Turkish cavalry, and Romanus is lured into a battle. He is usually criticized for ineptitude, particularly by some of the contemporary sources, notably Michael Psellos (but if you believe Psellos, you will believe anything); actually, Romanus did a very credible job. He drew up his army immediately to the west of the modern town, which still has heavy fortifications built from the Byzantine age; there is still an Ottoman fortress built on top of it. He put his infantry in the center. He had the usual flanking forces with archers. His cavalry was in reserve. He fought a classic battle; the sort of battle that would have been recommended by Byzantine authors as well as Tang generals. The problem was he was betrayed. He also commanded an army that really had no sense of unity that had been put together for this expedition. He held his own over the course of the day and then as they marched and countermarched. At the end of the day Romanus called his army together, called a halt, and informed his army that they would fall back to the camp because they could not bring the Turks to battle.

His army was perhaps 35,000; they Turks may have been around 20,000. The infantry wheeled around and, given their inexperience, they opened up gaps that Alp Arslan exploited. The army was thrown in confusion. The rumor goes out that the emperor was killed; actually it was not true, actually the emperor fell into the hands of the sultan. The cavalry, particularly the forces in the rear that were supposed to prevent this, defected. Notably, the forces of Andronicus Ducas, who was related to the empress—I believe he was the empress's nephew—he galloped off along with most of the other cavalry because they were going to seize power in Constantinople, and when Romanus was finally released he got the general Byzantine retirement package: He was blinded and dumped in a monastery and a new emperor was put on the throne, Michael VII, a totally unfit ruler.

The victory at Manzikert was stunning. It is usually dated to the 19th of August, 1071. It is still celebrated as a great event in Turkey today. You can go there and see these remarkable monuments, these twin pillars; they look like something out of *2001: A Space Odyssey*. Nonetheless, the battle opened up Asia Minor to settlement by the Seljuk Turks. As I said, the main effort was fighting the Fatimid caliphs; and therefore independent bands of Turks moved into Asia Minor and carved out their own principalities. Foremost was Konya, the ancient city of Iconium. Also, the Danishmend emirs seized the region around Nicaea and Amasia in Northeastern Turkey. Within a decade, most of Asia Minor had fallen into the hands of Turkish adventurers, technically professing to be the emirs or the sultans, the subordinates of the Turkish sultan in Baghdad—and after 1072, that was Malik Shah—but really they were independent operators; and this added to the confusion and disruption of the peninsula.

The Byzantine emperors had no choice but to take Asia Minor back. They had stupidly allowed the peninsula to fall into the hands of the Seljuk Turks, and in 1081 a very successful general battled his way to the throne. His name was Alexius I Komnenos, and he decided to call in Western Europeans as mercenaries to beat back the Turks and retake Asia Minor. That appeal is interpreted by Pope Urban II as a call to arms to liberate Jerusalem, and presto, Alexius I did not get 2000 mercenaries but the First Crusade, as over 50,000 Western Europeans between 1097 and 1099 streamed across Asia Minor, making a beeline to Jerusalem. This battle among—really it is a three-sided struggle—Byzantines, Crusaders, and Seljuk Turks resulted in a seesaw struggle across Asia Minor over the course of the 12th century. Initially, the Crusaders won stunning victories over the Seljuk Turks, in part, the novelty of Western European cavalry took the Turks by surprise. Kilij Arslan, the Sultan of Konya, was decisively defeated at the Battle of Dorylaeum; Western Asia Minor and the coastal regions of Asia Minor fall back under Byzantine control. However, the Byzantine emperors could never drive the Turks off the plateau because the Turkish tribes settled in significant numbers, came to terms with the Christian agriculturists, and began to create a Turkish heartland in this peninsula. As I have said many times, the peninsula of Asia Minor is essentially a fragment of Central Asia that has been thrust into a Mediterranean peninsula; and the Turks are able to bring in their herds, their people, their families, and establish a Turkish society on the plateau. The Christian agriculturalists there living in the river valleys came to terms with them, very well-documented by all the rock cut churches that date from this period where the Christians who are no longer under Byzantine rule pay a tribute to the Seljuk Turks. Eventually at Konya, a Seljuk Turkish civilization will emerge.

The fighting also plays into the hands of the Seljuk Turks. It was a desultory war over the borders, which sees the breakdown of Byzantine institutions and cities, the road system; all of this results that the conditions in Asia Minor favor the Turkish way of war, the nomadic way of war, large parts of Asia Minor pass out of agricultural use into grasslands, and steadily the balance shifts in favor of the Turks. Two events confirm this: In 1176, the emperor Manuel I was decisively beaten at the Battle of Myriocephalon. That marks the end of Byzantine efforts to expel the Seljuk Turks out of Asia Minor. On 13–15 April, 1204, members of the Fourth Crusade stormed into the city of Constantinople and sacked it. Byzantine power was finished. The political and ultimately the cultural destinies of Asia Minor had now shifted decisively to the Seljuk Turks settled in Anatolia who would now turn that region into a new Muslim Turkish-speaking land. That will be the subject of an upcoming lecture.

While the Seljuk Turks were winning these victories in the west, there were significant battles going on on the eastern frontier; and I want to turn for a moment to look at some of the parallel conquests going on conducted by various Turkish generals into India. When we look at Northern India at the time, it is important to get a couple of points straight. India at this point was divided among a number of competing kingdoms. In the Modern Nationalist literature of India today, these kings are often severely criticized for not joining together and meeting the Turkish threat. Primarily it was Turkish cavalry—there would be Arabs and Persians as well—but what was invading India were Turkish cavalry, both tribal regiments as well as slave soldiers. That is an unfair criticism, because at this point there really was no United India. The last man to rule over United India was the king Harsha Vardhana, who ruled from approximately 606, I believe, to 647; he was in the seventh century. His capital was at Kannauj, very close to where Delhi is today. He controlled the sacred cities of India, notably Varanasi. That state, which was a successor state to the Gupta Empire, had collapsed in the mid-seventh century; and since then you had a competing set of kingdoms trying to gain control of what in the Hindu text is known as *arya-varta*; that is the Aryan homeland. When I use the term *Aryan*, I am using it in the Indian context. It means "people who speak a language based off Sanskrit," or if they speak Dravidian languages, they accept the Sanskrit texts, the Rig Vedas, the Upanishads, the Mahabharata, the stories of Rama. They were devoted to the reorganized Hindu cults as they had emerged in the first century B.C., notably to Shiva and Vishnu. The Brahmins were the religious elite who administered the rites. So Aryan means or Aryan civilization, the adoption of that whole higher Hindu culture and cults associated with the Sanskrit text and the primacy of caste, Varna, with the Brahmins taking center stage, particularly in Southern and Central India; the Shastra caste, that is, the warrior royal caste, now occupying a second position; and that is what we refer to when we talk of *arya-varta*.

That region essentially encompasses the Indus valley, the Doab, the regions around Delhi today, and also the Ganges, the Ganga, the Great River; the mother goddess that springs from the Himalayas, particularly from Mount

Kailash, the home of the god Shiva. The effort of the Hindu kings was to control this region. When a Hindu king in particular gained ascendency over his opponents, he did not build great bureaucratic structures, he did not try to rule all of India the way the Mauryan emperors had tried in the third century B.C. or even the Gupta emperors, instead he accepted the submission of other kings, of other rajs; and he would often conduct a royal progress, which was known as a *digvijaya*. It was a progress of the four points of the compass around all of the kingdoms that were under your authority; you received submissions; you were in a sense the ruler of the four quarters of the Hindu world; you controlled the mother river Ganga; you would draw her sacred waters up in containers as symbolic of that. It was not an effort to organize an effective kingdom, a bureaucratic kingdom, as we would understand it.

As a result, in the 11th and early 12th centuries, there were a series of competing kingdoms. In the Bengal, there were the Pala kings. They actually favored Buddhism, and their great monastery was at Nalanda. In the northwest, in the Punjab and parts of Afghanistan where the Khyber Pass was, the strategic pass into India, that was in the hands of devotees of Shiva. They ruled as the Shahi kings, the Shahi Rajas, actually taken from the Old Persian term *shah*. Central India, in the Doab, that was a real free for all with different dynasties vying for control of the *arya-varta*; and as a result, there was no organized resistance when the Ghaznavid sultans had begun to raid into India even before the Seljuk Turks were on the scene. The crucial victories that opened Northern India up to Muslim conquest were won by the Ghaznavid sultans, particularly Sultan Mahmud, the man who sacked the Great Temple in 1024. He waged repeated wars against the Shahi rulers in the Khyber Pass who broke through. He captured the city of Lahore, which gets turned eventually into a base for Muslim expansion. He still primarily thought in terms of plunder; but nonetheless, he had opened the main routes into India for future Muslim conquerors basing their armies on steppe cavalry.

The other important feature that developed in the 11th century was that the Ghaznavid sultans increasingly realized that they really could not take back their domains in Iran or contend for the cities of Transoxiana unless they began to settle, expand, and take over the regions of India. In this regard, the conquest was very different from Asia Minor from the very start, starting with Mahmud, the Ghaznavid sultan, down to Muhammad Ghori. Muhammad Ghori was actually a Ghaznavid general who went into business for himself around 1173; and he was responsible for entrenching Muslim power in Northern India. In 1192, in a very, very important battle at Tarain, just north of Delhi, his nomadic cavalry crushed the most effective state in Northern India. This was the state of Prithviraj III, who controlled most of Rajasthan, Ajmer, Delhi; those were the important cities in the Doab. In the next year, in 1193, his forces took Delhi. Those victories in 1192–1193, as well as the victories of Mahmud, collectively had the impact of Manzikert in Asia Minor: It opened Northern India to Muslim conquest and settlement.

However, there were very, very significant differences between the two conquests. To be sure they were contemporary; to be sure both in Asia Minor and Northern India, nomadic cavalry had proved its worth. They were able to defeat far superior armies depending on infantry; and in the case of India, large numbers of elephant corps, especially in 1192. When they defeated the armies of Prithviraj III, there were at least 200 elephants on the opposing side, the Hindu side, which were lined up with the infantry. Again, the swift cavalry managed to encircle and destroy that army, and the unfortunate raj ended up being target practice for the Seljuk Turks after he surrendered. Militarily, in both instances, nomadic cavalry proved that they could conquer; they could defeat the far larger armies of urban, literate civilizations.

On the other hand, there were some very significant differences. The Turks, as well as their associated allies, largely from Khurasan—Persians from Khurasan who acted as administrators and Afghans who were incorporated as part of the cavalry—they encountered in India a very different world from Asia Minor. This was not at all conducive to the settlement by Turkish tribes. Furthermore, the conquest itself had been conducted by men who depended heavily on slave soldiers, those *mamluks*, rather than tribal regiments; and so from the start, it could be argued that in the 11th and 12th centuries, even into the 13th century when we look at the sultans of Delhi after 1206, to a large extent the Turkish conquest of Northern India was much more a military occupation rather than a settlement. This is quite different from Asia Minor. We do not have the large numbers of people moving in and settling into India, the large number of Turks.

Let us take a couple of statistics to bear that out. The best guess is that in 1071, when Alp Arslan won the Battle of Manzikert, Anatolia had some 12–15 million residents, Greek- and Armenian-speaking for the most part. The best guess over the course of the 11th, 12th, and 13th centuries, 500,000 nomads—men, women, and children—moved into Asia Minor and settled there. In time, they would assimilate the Greek, Christian, and Armenian Christian populations; the majority of them would become Turkish speakers, and you would create a new Turkish identity in Asia Minor. Contrast that with what Muhammad Ghori got after his victory in 1192 at Tarain. He gained control of Delhi; in fact, the sultans would make Delhi the great city of India (it was really a rather minor city up until that point). Nonetheless, he had essentially a military force. Even if the migration of Turks was anything on the order of what we know in Asia Minor, he was facing a population 10 times the size of Asia Minor; Hindus mostly, but also Jains and Buddhists. Furthermore, you were dealing with 2 million square miles on the subcontinent as opposed to 300,000 square miles in Asia Minor; and above all, in India the Turkish Muslim conquerors ran into the power of caste, *Varna*; into the great traditions of Indian civilization in a terrain, in a climate, that did not permit the settlement of nomads. In fact, it was not even conducive to horses. One of the reasons that the Turks could win over the Indian armies is they had the same advantage that steppe nomads had over Chinese armies: Horses were not readily bred in the climates of India. There were just too many parasites, inadequate farmland, grasslands; and India depended not on horses and camels but on excruciatingly slow bullocks, ox carts, with largely infantry armies and elephants.

From the start, the sultans who came to rule in Delhi faced a very, very different situation than their contemporaries did in Konya in Asia Minor. As a result, two different distinct Turkish Muslim civilizations came out of these two conquests, which in some ways bear similarities in their initial stages, but will produce a Turkish civilization in Anatolia and a ruling elite in Delhi, and it could even be argued to some extent Islam and the Turks were absorbed into greater India as just one more religion in a subset of caste.

The Sultans of Rūm

Lecture 24

This lecture looks at how the Seljuk Turks of Asia Minor made use of their victories in the 11th and 12th centuries to construct a new Turkish civilization in Asia Minor. Up until 1204, it was unclear what would happen in the struggle between Byzantines and Turks for possession of Anatolia. When the Turks succeeded, Konya emerged as the center of this new Muslim Turkish civilization. In this lecture, we'll look at the attempts of the sultans in Konya to forge a wider unity once it was clear that there would be no Byzantine reconquest of Asia Minor.

Errors of the Byzantines

- In the struggle for control of Anatolia with the Turks, the Byzantines made two fatal miscalculations. The first was calling in the western Europeans, who would turn their arms against the Byzantines rather than fighting the Muslim foe. A second, deeper miscalculation was born of previous Byzantine experience with nomadic peoples.

  o Both the Bulgars and the Magyars had been successfully converted to Orthodox Christianity, and the emperors in Constantinople believed that the sultans of Konya and the Danishmend emirs of Niksar (in northeastern Turkey) could eventually be brought under the Christian umbrella, as well.

  o What they didn't understand was that when the Turks entered Asia Minor, they had already turned themselves into a distinct Muslim ethnicity that had married the Turkish language, traditions, and values to a kind of folk Islam.

  o In 1204, after Constantinople was sacked by the Fourth Crusade, no Byzantine emperor was ever in a position to conduct a serious effort to convert the Seljuk Turks.

- Konya emerged as the center of Asia Minor and, therefore, the center of a Muslim Turkish civilization.

The Rise and Fall of Konya

- Starting in the early 13th century, a succession of talented sultans in Konya managed to expand control over the peninsula. Most of Asia Minor was eventually put together as a single sultanate recognizing the authority of Konya. The fact that the sultans were able to reign in the various nomadic tribes and join rival cities into a single state was a considerable achievement.

- The pivotal ruler in this was **Kay-Khusraw II**. He came to the throne after a series of civil wars fought with his half-brothers over the succession.
  - Kay-Khusraw managed to eliminate the collateral lines, but one of his half-brothers had appealed to both nomadic tribes and Mongols. Kay-Khusraw refused to submit to the great khagan, Ögödei, the son of Genghis Khan.

  - In 1243, the Mongol governor in Tabriz, Bayju, decided to intervene in Asia Minor. His army smashed the forces of Kay-Khusraw, who managed to escape. He went on to rule as a Mongol vassal for another three or four years.

- This defeat at the hands of the Mongols essentially ended the political power of Konya. By the early 14th century, the various Muslim states in Asia Minor again fragmented into a constellation of lesser states and political powers. That situation would remain in Asia Minor down to the reign of Mehmed II, the Ottoman sultan who would reunite the region as part of the Ottoman Empire.

Cultural Achievements in Konya

- In political terms, the sultans of Konya did not do particularly well in establishing a wider political unity. After 1309, Konya was, in many ways, finished as a political center, although it would survive as a religious and cultural center.

- In the 12th century, the sultans of Konya had scored a major success in transforming Asia Minor culturally and religiously. The courts at Konya and lesser cities, such as Sivas, Amasya, and Niksar, all favored the high Persian culture of eastern Islam. Persian was the literary language used at court, and Persian poets and scholars were appreciated.

- The Turkish-dominated cities of Asia Minor became linked to the caravan trade even more intimately, and greater numbers of Muslims from the wider Islamic world settled in these cities. The administrative and cultural talent that came into Asia Minor was used to construct Turkish civilization.

- In addition, the Mongol conquests of the 13th century drove increasing numbers of Turkish tribes and Muslims out of central Asia and Iran westward into the Seljuk domains. That brought many more Turkish settlers, who reinforced the Turkish component on the peninsula, but it also brought mystics, scholars, poets, craftsmen, and, above all, architects.

- In the early 13th century, several significant developments allowed the sultans of Konya to undertake a massive reworking of the urban landscape of previously Christian Byzantine cities in Asia Minor.
  - One example can be found in eastern Turkey, in the city of Divriği. In 1229, a wonderful mosque-hospital complex was built there, and it remains virtually untouched. The plain exterior is nicely contrasted with the doors and portals that feature elaborate carving. The interior is inviting, with a good deal of prayer space opened by columns. Early mimbars (wooden pulpits) survive that show marvelous carving from nomadic traditions.

  - Medreses were also built across eastern Turkey, and several can be seen today.

  - Steadily over the 13th century, the skylines of cities in Turkey were transformed into Muslim skylines, with medreses, minarets, and mosques. These were the first significant buildings in Asia Minor in more than 150 years. The money for

A great deal of money came into the sultanate through caravansaries—way stations for merchants along the Silk Road.

this construction came from the successful consolidation of the power of the sultans of Konya and the Silk Road.

- Another monument that came to characterize Seljuk Asia Minor was the **caravansary**, essentially a rest stop along the Silk Road. Caravans could stop there for up to three days to rest while their goods were securely stored. Some caravansaries included chapels for Islamic worship. The caravansaries were supported by endowments and were under the protection of the sultan, which meant that the caravans that used these facilities could be taxed.

- In the countryside, yet another architectural feature that points to the transformation of Asia Minor into a new Seljuk homeland are the memorial tombs, or *türbes*.
  - At least 3,500 of these have been counted as having been constructed in the 13th and early 14th centuries. Many of them

were memorials to *hocas* ("holy men") or Sufi mystics. Three have survived in Divriği in a wonderful state of preservation.

○ The *türbes* served to attract Christian agriculturalists to Islam. They replaced, in effect, the traditions of the saints in the Christian tradition and played an important role in the gradual conversion of Asia Minor to Turkey.

The Power of Sufi Mystics

- One final ingredient in the Islamization of Asia Minor was the power of Sufi mystics. As mentioned in an earlier lecture, these Muslim holy men were, in many ways, unconventional in their religious beliefs. They were not always well-versed in Sharia or the Qur'an per se. Instead, their communication with God was often more personal and direct. This aspect of the Sufis coincided with the Turkish reverence for *hocas*.

- At the same time, in the fighting that had raged over Asia Minor in the course of the 11th and 12th centuries, Christian institutions had been severely disrupted. Monasteries were particularly targeted and repeatedly sacked. And even if the churches themselves were respected, many of the bishops decamped to Constantinople.

- Many of the Greek churches fell under the control of priests who were generally ignorant of scripture, and increasingly, the Christian community became disoriented; certainly by the 13th century, Christian spiritual life was quite impoverished. Thus, the Christian population was ideally suited for proselytizing by Sufi mystics.

- Foremost among these mystics was **Jalal al-Din Rumi**, known to us as the poet Rumi. He came from a fine, literate family, and his father was a *hoca* and teacher. In 1228, his family moved to Konya at the invitation of the sultan. Rumi succeeded to the school of his father, then in 1244, underwent a conversion, in which he became an aesthetic. He and his followers, popularly known as dervishes, made a decisive difference in the conversion of Christians.

- Rumi was convinced that the oneness of God was all-important and that God could be reached through poetry and dancing, especially mystical dancing. These beliefs led to the so-called whirling dervishes, who use their bodies as the vehicle for communication with the divine.

- Rumi and his followers were seen as great teachers and holy men who could perform miracles. We have large numbers of stories written by his followers in the generations after him that report mystical conversions carried out among Christian populations.

- To the Christian populations, such mystics presented a powerful image. The Christians had not had bishops and monks for generations. Now, these Sufi mystics came into their villages and offered a vision of the divine that had long been lacking.

- Steadily, as a result of this contact, the countryside was won over. By 1350, the population had decisively tipped toward Islam and was completely Turkish speaking. The political failure of Konya was a moot point because by 1350, the Seljuk sultans had set in motion a transformation of the peninsula into a new Islamic land.

Important Term

caravansary: Walled quarters, stables, and storage rooms constructed and maintained by the Turkish Muslim rulers for the benefit of caravans. The upkeep of the caravansary was paid by the profits of a foundation.

Names to Know

Jalal al-Din Rumi (1206–1273): Persian mystic and poet; known as Rumi. He was born in Balkh, the son of the Baha al-Din Walad, a celebrated jurist and theologian. His family relocated to Konya in 1228, where Rumi succeeded his father as head of the madrasah in 1232. In 1244, he adopted an ascetic life and founded the Mevlevi mystical order of Sufism. The members of this order, the dervishes, converted the Christians of Anatolia in the 13th and 14th centuries.

Kay-Khusraw II (1237–1246): Seljuk sultan of Konya (Rūm). He failed to maintain control over the Turkish tribes and, thus, faced repeated rebellions. He refused to render homage to the Mongol khan Ögödei (1228–1241). Bayju, the Mongol commander in Iran, invaded Asia Minor and decisively defeated Kay-Khusraw at the Battle of Köse Dag on June 26, 1243. Thereafter, the sultans of Konya, as Mongol vassals, lost control over the emirs and Turkish tribes of Asia Minor.

Ögödei (b. 1186; r. 1229–1241): Mongol khan; the third son of Genghis Khan and Börte. Ögödei, popular and affable, was elected by the *kurultai* as successor to Genghis Khan. He ruled directly over the Mongolian homeland, but he was recognized as Great Khan by his brothers Chagatai and Tolui and his nephew Batu. He transformed Karakorum into a capital city and authorized Batu's conquest of the west. His death precipitated the first succession crisis of the Mongol Empire.

Suggested Reading

Cahen (Jones-Williams, trans.), *Pre-Ottoman Turkey*.

———, "The Turkish Invasion: The Selchukids."

Lange, *The Seljuqs: Politics, Society, and Culture*.

Peacock and Yildez, eds., *The Seljuks of Anatolia*.

Rice, *The Seljuk Turks*.

Vyrnos, *The Decline of Medieval Hellenism in Asia Minor and the Process of Islamization from the Eleventh through the Fifteenth Century*.

Questions to Consider

1. Why did the 13th century prove so decisive for the genesis of an Islamic Asia Minor? Why did the Seljuk Turks ultimately reject assimilation into the Byzantine cultural commonwealth?

2. How did border warfare shift the military balance in favor of the Seljuk Turks by the early 12th century? How did the migration of Turkish tribes in the 13th century contribute to the spread of the Turkish language and nomadic material life among the Christian sedentary populations?

3. How effectively did the sultans of Konya impose their authority over the emirs and *ghazi* lords of Anatolia? Why did the sultans Kay-Khusraw I and his heirs make Konya the arbiter of Muslim Anatolia? Why did the sultanate fragment?

4. What enduring Muslim political, administrative, and cultural institutions were forged by the sultans of Konya? What was their debt to the Samanid emirs of Transoxiana? How much did they owe to their traditions brought from the Eurasian steppes?

5. How did the sultans of Konya promote trade in the 13th century? What was the cultural and economic impact of making Anatolia an integral part of the wider Silk Road? How did the network of caravansary promote prosperity and Islam?

6. What factors led to the conversion of Christians to Islam? What was the role of the Jalal al-din Rumi? How did the promotion of Muslim arts and monumental buildings by the sultans contribute to the process?

The Sultans of Rūm
Lecture 24—Transcript

In this lecture, I want to look at how the Seljuk Turks of Asia Minor made use of their victory—or victories really—in the 11th and 12th centuries to construct a new Turkish civilization in Asia Minor. This is going to be followed by a parallel lecture dealing with how Turkish Muslim rulers in Delhi at the same time in the late 11th, 12th, and 13th centuries, attempted to construct a new Muslim order in Northern India. In effect, we are going to look at: How well did the conquerors use their victory?

In the case of Asia Minor, I mentioned that up until 1204, it was really unclear what would happen in the struggle between Byzantines and Turks for possession of Anatolia. I think, in part, the Turks succeeded because there were a number of factors in their favor; not only military factors, but the way Anatolia was conducive for them to settle in large numbers and to create a sort of nomadic society in Asia Minor, which would, of course, supply the military with lots of horse archers. There was also another factor in the fighting, and that was the Byzantines themselves. I think they made two fatal miscalculations. The first was calling in the Western Europeans. This is well known ever since the magisterial work of Steven Runciman on the history of the Crusades. There is a whole tradition of Western scholarship criticizing the crusaders for turning their arms against the Byzantines rather than fighting the Muslim foe. Also, it could be argued that the Crusaders distracted Christian efforts to Jerusalem rather than centering on the real issue, which was to take back Asia Minor for the emperors in Constantinople. Some of these criticisms are really a bit beyond reasonable given the political perceptions and values of the time; but there was a deeper miscalculation besides bringing in western co-religionists; and that was born of previous Byzantine experience with nomadic peoples.

They had successfully converted the Bulgars who had settled in the Balkans. They had made attempts to convert the Pechenegs, not with great success. The Magyars had been converted by Western European missionaries; and for the longest time the emperors in Constantinople thought that the sultans of Konya, the Danishmend emirs of Niksar, which is out in Northeastern Turkey, that they could be courted; that they could eventually be brought into the umbrella of Orthodox Christian civilization. What they did not understand is that when the Turks entered Asia Minor, they had already turned themselves into that distinct Muslim ethnicity that was Turkish in speech and in values; that had the traditions of the Ghazi warrior; and that these were married with the folk Islam, a dedication of jihad, even if jihad in many times is nothing more than an excuse to plunder the Christian neighbors or to attack monasteries and churches for the goodies. Nonetheless, I think the Byzantines miscalculated here. In 1204, after Constantinople was wrecked by the Fourth Crusade, no Byzantine emperor was ever in a position to conduct anything like a serious effort to convert the Seljuk Turks.

That means Konya emerged as a new capital on the plateau. Given the fighting that had raged for some 200 years over that peninsula in the 13th century, Konya emerged as the center of Asia Minor and therefore the center of a Muslim Turkish civilization. There are two points I want to look at, and that is: How did the sultans in Konya attempt to forge a wider unity once it was clear that there would be no Byzantine reconquest; because Asia Minor was a kaleidoscope of various different competing Turkish powers, local emirs and sultans, it was by no means sure that Konya would be the power? Then the second question is: How well did the sultans in Konya succeed in creating a new Turkish civilization?

Starting in the early 13th century, a succession of very, very talented sultans in Konya managed to expand control over the peninsula. The first of these fellows was by the name of Kay-Khusraw I. He happened to rule at the beginning of the 13th century when Constantinople was defeated; and down to his successor, Kay-Khusraw II—and there is a succession of different sultans of Konya, and he dies in 1246; he had the mistake of running into the Mongol army in 1243 that we will get into—most of Asia Minor was eventually put together as a single sultanate recognizing the authority of Konya. This was a considerable achievement that the sultans in Konya were able to reign in the various nomadic tribes; they were able to join rival cities such as Sivas, Niksar, Konya, into a single state.

The pivotal ruler in this was Kaykhusraw II. He came to the throne under some rather difficult circumstances. As I have mentioned before, the Seljuk Turks, being very, very good nomads, practiced lateral succession. When his father died, Kayqubad, in 1236, there was the usual dispute of exactly who got the throne; Kay-Khusraw II had to deal with various half-brothers who thought of themselves as also entitled. As a result, there were several significant civil wars that were fought across Asia Minor, and it ended in the unification under Kay-Khusraw II and eliminating those collateral lines. However, in the course of the fighting, the emir in Erzincan—which is today actually on the main earthquake fault, it is always being rattled by earthquakes; it really is on the northern route leading out of Asia Minor— his half-brother complicated the succession by appealing to various nomadic tribes, his name was Izz ad-Din, and also appealing to the Mongols. At this point, the Mongols were the major power in Asia—we will be discussing that—and Kay-Khusraw II had the misfortune that various insurgents sought refuge with the Mongols. Kay-Khusraw II refused to submit to the Great Khan; that, at the time, would be Ögedei, who was the son of Genghis Khan. In 1243, the Mongol governor in Tabriz, and his name was Bayju, decided to intervene in Asia Minor. A Mongol army came rushing into Asia Minor, and near the modern city of Zara at a very strategic pass known as Köse Dağ, the Mongol army smashed the army of the Seljuk sultan. Kay-Khusraw II escaped. He went on to rule as a Mongol vassal for another three or four years; he died in 1246.

But that defeat at the hands of the Mongols essentially ended the political power of Konya. By the early 14th century, the various states in Asia Minor, the Muslim states, again fragmented into a whole constellation of political powers, we usually call them the *beylikler*—*beylik* means a domain ruled by a bey; *beylikler* are the *beylicks*, that is, these lesser states—and that will be the situation in Asia Minor really down to the reign of Mehmed II, the great Ottoman sultan who will reunite Asia Minor as part of the Ottoman Empire. In political terms, the sultans of Konya did not do particular well in waging a wider political unity. To some extent, there was never really a danger from the Byzantines—they had been destroyed by the Crusaders—and the effort to put together a fragile, effective central state among the various Turkish nomadic peoples in Asia Minor failed. It in part failed because the institutions were not there; and furthermore, the Mongols decisively intervened and essentially smashed a Seljuk power. Konya, in many ways after 1309, was finished as a political center. It would survive as a religious and cultural center, which we will be getting to in a moment.

On the other hand, the sultans of Konya, in the 12ᵗʰ century when they were still fighting the Byzantines and then again in the 13ᵗʰ century, did score a major success in transforming Asia Minor culturally and religiously. That came in several forms. First and foremost was architecture. Here, the sultans of Konya had several advantages. When they arrived in Asia Minor, they already were heirs to the tradition started with Tughril Bey, the first great sultan back in the 11ᵗʰ century, of employing Persian administrators. The courts at Konya and the lesser cities such as Sivas, Amasya, Niksar—which were either ruled by cadet members of the family at Konya or earlier by independent emirs—all favored the high Persian culture of Eastern Islam. Persian was the literary language that was used at the courts; Persian poets and scholars were appreciated. At the same time, they sought out architects and craftsmen from the wider Islamic world. Because they were Muslims and not just nomads who had settled in Asia Minor, these cities, the Turkish-dominated cities of Asia Minor, became linked to the caravan trade evermore intimately, and more and more Muslims from the wider Muslim world settled in the cities and brought their skills and expertise. These were especially architects and craftsmen. There was an administrative and cultural talent that came into Asia Minor that could be used to construct Turkish civilization.

In addition, the Mongol conquests—and they are going to form a whole separate part of the course—in the 13ᵗʰ century, starting with the conquest of Khurasan by Genghis Khan, clearly one of the great military campaigns of all times, drove increasing numbers of Turkish tribes and Muslims out of Central Asia, out of Transoxiana, out of Iran westward into the Seljuk domains. That brought many more Turkish settlers—those included tribesmen; they reinforced the Turkish component on the peninsula—but it also brought mystics, scholars, poets, and above all architects.

In the early 13ᵗʰ century, there were several significant developments now that allowed the sultans of Konya to undertake a massive rewrite of the urban landscape of previously Christian Byzantine cities of Asia Minor. Konya became a showplace for Seljuk architecture. There had been also earlier achievements of Seljuk architecture, particularly in the eastern cities today: in Erzurum, the ancient city of Theodosiopolis, in Sivas, in the city of Tokot today, and in Niksar—these are cities that are in Northeastern Turkey— the small caravan town of Divriği. We see some of the earliest efforts at an independent Turkish architecture. In part, it represents the architecture of the Samanid emirs; but it also has distinctly Turkish elements. Take, for example, one of my favorite cities to visit in Eastern Turkey: Divriği, Byzantine Tephrike. It is actually on an old caravan route, which now is no longer paralleled by the highway system; there is a new highway system, so it is a little bit out of the way. In 1229, there was a wonderful mosque-hospital complex built there that is virtually untouched; there is no later building. It is an early 13th century Turkish monument; it is a gem. You have a tradition of a long hall incorporated with early efforts at domes; what is known as a squinch dome. Furthermore, the plain exterior is very, very nicely contrasted with the doors and the portals that show this elaborate sculptured, almost like a scalloped, carving; these pillars. This is all out of Turkish woodwork and textiles; and so you get the interplay of these elaborately carved doors and windows against the simple surface of the masonry outside. Then when you walk in, it is an extremely inviting and pleasing mosque with lots of prayer space opened up by columns. There are early *mimbars* that survive—that is, the wooden pulpits in the Islamic religion—that show marvelous carving, again out of the nomadic traditions. You can see these *mimbars* at not only Divriği but also in the museum at Sivas. A number of these Turkish *mimbars* have survived from the 13th and 14th centuries. You get the construction of complexes like this.

Medreses, religious schools: They, too, were built across Eastern Turkey. Çifte Medrese; there is one both in Sivas, another in Erzurum. Gök Medrese: It only survives with its minarets today; the building was very damaged and they are doing some heavy-handed restoration. Nonetheless, steadily over the 13th century, the skylines of cities in Turkey are transformed into a Muslim skyline with *medreses*, with minarets, with mosques, and these are the first significant buildings in Asia Minor in over 150 years. The money for this was coming from the successful consolidation of the power of the sultans of Konya, and also the Silk Road.

Another monument that comes to characterize Seljuk Asia Minor is the caravansary. The caravansary is a camel rest stop, as it is sometimes called. They come in three forms: the deluxe, the medium, and the kind of cheap version. The deluxe version is the sultan Hans. There is a wonderful one outside of Aksaray today, and that is a very, very pleasing building. Again, it is essentially a simple fortification. It has a chapel—a *meçit* as it would be called in modern Turkish—for Islamic worship in the center of this courtyard. There is plenty of storage area. Roman arches have been deployed in a brilliant way to provide accommodations for camels and other types of beasts of burden. These caravansaries were set up at crucial points along the way on what the Turks would call the İpek Yolu, the Silk Road. Caravans could stop there for up to three days, rest. They were supported by endowments—*vafik* is the Turkish rendition of that; that was usually Christian agriculturalists—and that meant the caravans had security. They could put their goods behind walls; they could not be attacked by brigands; they were under the protection of the sultan; and that meant caravans arrived regularly and the sultan could tax them. Lots of money came in there.

The sultans also got access to silver and they coined the first significant silver coinage in Asia Minor, a very distinctly Seljuk silver coinage, which began to replace Byzantine money. In the course of the 13th century, economically, socially, architecturally, the peninsula was being rewritten into a new cultural landscape, and the sultans in Konya were presiding over it.

In the countryside, there is another architectural feature that points to how Asia Minor was being transformed into a new Seljuk homeland. These are the memorial tombs, mausoleums, very, very simple, known as either a *tekke* or *türbe*. There is a great deal of debate as to the origins of these; I have mentioned them in conjunction with the Samanid emirs. You will see them again in the time of Tamerlane, at Samarkand; and the climax of great memorial commemorations to rulers, of course, will be the vast building programs in Mogul India. The *tekke* and *türbe* in Asia Minor are very, very simple. Some would say they look like little mini Christian domes; others would argue they were off the traditions of tents and stone. Whatever the traditions were, there are at least 3,500 that have been counted as having been constructed in the 13th and early 14th centuries, and they were Islamisizing the countryside. They were memorials to *hojas* and Sufi mystics; Muslim holy men or particularly pious individuals—at my favorite city of Divriği, there are three of them that are survived and they are in a wonderful state of preservation—and those were places where Christian agriculturalists would be attracted by the religion. They replaced, in effect, the traditions of the saints in the Christian tradition; and, again, they represent a wonderful and ingenious variation of religious architecture by the Seljuk Turks and they play a very, very important role, in my mind, in the gradual conversion of Asia Minor over to Turkey. The visual arts give us one dimension into this, and they were being sustained by a very, very successful exploiting of the resources of Asia Minor, and above all the profits of the Silk Road.

There is one final ingredient in the Islamization, and we will be investigating this issue in India in the next lecture where again Islam was brought in by Turkish conquerors; why did Islam remain a minority religion in India whereas it won out in Asia Minor and became the overwhelmingly majority religion in the peninsula of Asia Minor? This had to do with the power of the *hoja* or the Sufi mystics; I mentioned them in connection with the initial conversions of Turks on the Eurasian steppes. Muslim holy men were in many ways unconventional perhaps in their religious beliefs. They were not always well-versed in Sharia—that is, the religious law—or the Koran per se. Their communication with God was often more personal and direct, at least many who came into contact with the Turks on the steppes. In Asia Minor, there was therefore this reverence for a *hoja*, for a holy man who had communication with the divine.

At the same time, in the fighting that had raged over Asia Minor in the course of the 11th and 12th centuries, Christian institutions had been severely disrupted. The sultans in Konya as just Muslim rulers followed the Islamic traditions of respecting the Christians as *dhimmi*; that is, peoples of the book. Their prophet Isa, Jesus, was accepted in the Islamic tradition, the same was accorded to Jews; and they were not to be violated. But the fighting had been particularly violent, and the clashes between Byzantine armies and Turks, crusading armies and Turks, this led to a great disruption of the Greek Orthodox religious institutions. Monasteries were particularly targeted and sacked repeatedly in the 11th and 12th centuries, and I think instinctively Turks understood that the monasteries were really the bastions of Christianity in Asia Minor. It was to monks and aesthetics that most Christian peasants would turn to for intercession with God. The churches themselves, even if they were respected, many of the bishops decamped to Constantinople. Very good studies of the episcopacy—that is, the senior prelates of the Orthodox Church—reveals that the Byzantine emperor and the patriarch in Constantinople recognized all these bishops of ancient cities of Asia Minor.

Let us take, for instance, a city such as Cotiium: There was a continual succession of bishops of Cotiium through the whole of the 13th, 14th, and 15th centuries; except Cotii was now Turkish Cutaya, the bishop did not bother to go out there. He simply held the title, but remained in Constantinople.

Many of the Greek churches fell under the control of priests who were not very literate, generally ignorant of scripture; and increasingly, the Christian community over the course of the 12th and 13th centuries became more and more disoriented, their Christianity became less and less important. Many of the rock-cut churches, which are today premier tourist sites in Asia Minor, there is a tradition of trying to argue that many of those rock-cut churches—and they have wonderful frescoes that are painted—were done by Christians in this period as part of the representation or part of the policy of the sultans' toleration. That is wrong; except for four churches, the last one is the Saint George in the Peristrema Valley, probably finished around 1294, all of those churches were done before the Turks arrived, and therefore the Christian spiritual life, in my opinion, certainly in the 13th century, was quite impoverished.

That meant the Christian population was ideally suited for prosthelytizing by Sufi mystics. Foremost among them was one man. He is now today revered as the Mevlana. He was born in either 1206 or 1207, in Iran actually, in Balkh. He died in 1273. His prime language of communication was Persian. His name at his birth was Jalal-ad-Din, and he later became Jalal-ad-Din Rumi; that is, the "Jalal living in Rome, Asia Minor." His father was a *hoja* and teacher; and he came from a very, very fine and literate family. Rumi himself—we often refer to him as Rumi— was a poet of great power. The family had fled Balkh because of the Mongol invasions. His father, Baha al-Din Walad, took the family to Karaman, which is in Southeastern Turkey today; it was the ancient city of Larande. Then in 1228 they moved to Konya on the invitation of the sultan. Rumi succeeded to the school of his father; and then in 1244 underwent a remarkable conversion, a transformation in which he becomes aesthetic.

He and his followers, who are now popularly known as dirvishers, were mystics who made the difference in the converting of Christians. Rumi was convinced that the oneness of God was all important, and that God could be reached through poetry and through dancing, especially mystical dancing; this leads to the so-called Whirling Dervishers. Any of you who have ever seen that dancing can see that the dervisher is supposed to point to heaven, point to the ground; his body in effect becomes the vehicle for the communication of the divine with the mundane. Furthermore, Rumi and his followers were seen as great teachers and holy men who could conduct miracles. We have large numbers of stories written by his followers, particularly Eunice and others in the generations after him, reporting these types of mystical conversions that were carried out among Christian populations.

It is easy to miss how important these experiences were in winning over Christians. The experience is incredibly personal, and yet awesome at the same time. Personally, I have observed not Rumi's group, it is a different order, they are known as the [Naqshbandi]. It is an order that emerged in the 13th and 14th centuries in Central Asia. In 2010, I and a former student of mine went to the town of Mengal in Eastern Turkey—that would be close to the current tourist attraction of Nemrut Dağ—and we happened to witness the prayers conducted by this order in their mosque. Furthermore, this was what is called a Summer Mosque in which the roof is rolled away at the evening prayer and the firmament comes into view. When you stand in a situation like that, you are in the presence of earliest and purest Islam, praying directly to God; and you feel as if you are with early Arab and Turkish nomadic warriors where they just threw a prayer rug on the ground and offered up their evening prayer. Each of the mystics there is in his own state, in his own prayer with God. He goes into his own trance, his own experience, and when he comes out of it he is finished and he walks away.

Very much, this is what prayer, dance, all of these means of communicating with the divine represented; and to the Christian populations, this was a very, very powerful image. They had not had bishops and monks for generations, and now these Sufi mystics came into their villages, came into their towns, offered a vision of the divine that had long been lacking; and steadily, as a result of this contact, the countrysides were won over, *türbler*, *tekkler* (that is, the plural for *türbe* and *tekke*) were constructed across the landscape, and by 1350 the population had decisively tipped. It was going over to Muslim; it was completely Turkish-speaking; it was now an independent

Islamic Turkish civilization. The political failure of Konya is a moot point, because by 1350 the Seljuk sultans had set in motion a transformation of this peninsula into a new Islamic land; and perhaps their greatest achievement was to patronize the Mevlana. The Mevlana and his *türbe*, which was constructed after his death in 1273 in Konya, is today the most sacred city for Muslims in Turkey.

The Sultans of Delhi
Lecture 25

In this lecture, we'll look at the results of the conquests of northern India by Turkish nomadic warriors in the early 13th century. This lecture runs parallel to what we just discussed on the Turkification and the Islamitization of Asia Minor. Why did the sultans ruling at Delhi fail to forge a wider imperial unity? They ran into some of the same problems as the sultans of Konya. On the other hand, what were their successes, and what were the limitations in creating a Muslim civilization in India? At the end of the lecture, we'll examine the question of whether the Muslim conquest of northern India was more of a military occupation than a real settlement.

Aybak's Rule in Northern India

- In 1192, Muhammad Ghuri had gained control of northern India, but he was distracted by events in central Asia. He entrusted the running of his conquests to subordinate generals—Mamluk slave soldiers. In particular, a general named **Qutb ud-Din Aybak** was essentially left on his own to direct various campaigns.

- Those campaigns saw the consolidation of a kingdom in and around Delhi with a much looser confederacy across the Indo-Gangic plain. From the start, power rested in the hands of nomadic steppe warriors and slave soldiers. In 1206, when Muhammad Ghori died, Aybak essentially became an independent ruler. He assumed the title sultan, ruled from Delhi for the next four years, and transmitted power through his family.

- From the start, Aybak realized that he couldn't depend solely on tribal regiments and slave soldiers. He began to give out essentially endowments or fiefs (*iqta*) to leaders (*muqtis*), who would then use this land to support military units that would be the basis of power for the sultan. Some of these commanders were quite independent. The **Khalji** family, for instance, essentially carved out its own independent operation. This would be a problem repeatedly in dealing with *muqtis*. Nonetheless, Aybak set the basis for political control of Delhi and the Doab.

Challenges for Iltutmish

- Aybak was succeeded by his son-in-law **Iltutmish**, who ruled from 1210 to 1236. He, too, originated as a military commander, but he owed his position on the throne to the fact that he had married Aybak's daughter and was absolutely trusted.

- Iltutmish proved to be a very able ruler. He extended the use of endowments. He campaigned prodigiously and extended the influence of the Delhi sultanate across the Indo-Gangic plain. But from the start, he was concerned about a succession because the state was potentially unstable; his conquests were quite tentative.

- Already in Iltutmish's reign, it was clear that a ruler in India would have to co-opt members of the Kshatriya caste, that is, the warriors and princes, if any kind of meaningful political order was to be constructed. The ruler would have to come to terms with that Hindu ruling class even though he might raid and dispossess them in some areas. On the other hand, the only way for this to work would be to start building a wider network of alliances.

- Furthermore, the ruler in India would have to satisfy the *muqtis*, who formed essentially an inner council of the sultanate, usually known as the Forty. They could pass judgment on a number of issues, including the succession to the various fiefs. They were rewarded with an *iqta* that involved a governorship or the profits of some kind of concession or monopoly. This was the way to maintain a large standing army.

- In addition, Iltutmish was concerned about his family. He had several sons whom he didn't trust and groomed his daughter to succeed him. This was **Radiyya Begum**, who came to the throne in 1236, when her father died.

Radiyya and the Deterioration of the Dynasty

- Radiyya was clearly an able ruler, but she violated numerous social conventions. She wore the trousers of the steppes, was a great equestrian, and knew how to fight. She ruled successfully down to 1240 but was then overthrown by a coalition of *muqtis*.

- For the *muqtis*, not only was Radiyya a woman, but she also represented a centralizing tendency of the court. She intended to rule through her agents and to rein in the *muqtis* so they wouldn't become so independent. She and her husband were captured in a major battle outside of Delhi on October 12, 1240, and eventually she was executed. The dynasty deteriorated after that point.

- Radiyya was followed by a succession of weak rulers until the family was overthrown by the Khaljis in Bengal. Radiyya's reign proved a turning point for at least two reasons.
  - The efforts of the dynasty to centralize and rein in the independent commanders had failed.

  - In each of the two succeeding dynasties, the Khalji Dynasty and the Tughluq Dynasty in the late 13th and early 14th centuries, the founders attempted to forge a wider unity by conquering regions to the south of Delhi, notably, the northern districts of the Deccan and farther south. Those efforts ultimately failed, as well.

The Khalji and Tughluq Families

- The Khalji family came to power in 1296. The second sultan of this dynasty, Muhammad ala-ad Din, took it upon himself to direct major campaigns into southern India. This was the first time that Muslim forces really crossed the boundary line that runs along the Narmada River and essentially cuts northern India from southern India. Muhammad ala-ad Din was well served by Malik Kafir, or Kafur, a general who was actually a Hindu convert.

- This general commanded successive invasions into central and southern India, resulting in the destruction of major temple complexes. The armies penetrated deep into southern India and raged farther east, again, targeting temples known for their wealth, yet these conquests failed to net ala-ad Din territorial acquisitions because they were vast raids. The Muslim armies rounded up captives and plunder, then retreated.

- This dynasty ran into the same problem of trying to reconcile central control with the *muqtis*, and when the raids began to come to an end in 1320, it was overthrown by a new family, the Tughluqs. Muhammad Tughluq, the most prominent of this family, likewise conducted similar types of operations against various Hindu kingdoms. Ultimately, these efforts to bring the Hindu kingdoms to heel failed.

- Muslim attacks of Hindu kingdoms led to the consolidation of southern India around the city of Hampi. There, two brothers, who were reputed to have initially submitted to the sultan of Delhi, established a Hindu kingdom known as Vijayanagara ("Victory City"). In the mid-14th century, this kingdom acted as a check on further Muslim advances into central and southern India.

Building Programs in Delhi
- By the middle of the 14th century, there was a political standoff between the Muslim kingdoms consolidated in central and southern India and the sultans of Delhi. From a political standpoint, the sultans were somewhat successful. They retained their thrones and resisted the Mongols, but they never quite had the prestige in the Islamic world for their military and political achievements as the Mamluks of Egypt.

The Qutb Minaret, built by the early sultans of Delhi, soars 240 feet high and served as a symbol of both victory and the Islamic faith.

- The sultans of Delhi, just like their counterparts at Konya, carried out an active building program to promote both Islam and their own position in the Islamic world. The Qutb complex south of Delhi is an example that can still be seen today. In the early 13th century, these buildings came to symbolize the power of the sultans of Delhi.

- The complex is named after Qutb ud-Din Aybak, the first of the so-called slave sultans who took power in 1206. It was completed by Aybak's son-in-law and successor, Iltutmish. The complex features the **Qutb Minar**, the largest minaret in the Islamic world at the time, and a major mosque. It was expanded by Iltutmish and, later, the Khalji and **Tughluq sultans**.

- The mosque as we know it today is called **Quwat ul**, meaning "Might of Islam." It is an impressive building constructed of brick and *spolia*—material seized from older buildings. The mosque has a great open courtyard, an *avlu*, where the faithful gather to pray; in the middle is the fountain, necessary for ablutions. Gates, memorial tombs, and subsidiary buildings were added over the course of the next 200 years. In size and audacity, the mosque at the Qutb complex dwarfs anything built by the Seljuk sultans of Konya.

Results of the Conquest

- The building programs of the sultans transformed Delhi into a great city, the center of Muslim power in northern India. The military operations from this city were far ranging and daring, yet Islam always remained a minority religion. The question of what the occupation of the sultans brought to India remains a matter of great debate, with Muslims stressing the power of the Turkish horse archers and cavalry and Hindu nationalists deploring the destruction of their shrines.

- From about 1192 to 1707, we have about 500 good texts documenting the Muslim targeting of specific temples for destruction. Sometimes, they were driven to loot them to pay the army; other times, they clearly targeted these temples to break resistance. This is not nearly the thousands of temples and thousands of Brahmins killed suggested by other sources.

- The impact of these first 250 to 300 years of Muslim rule in India on Buddhism and Hinduism has also been studied. Buddhism had begun to retreat into Tibet and was essentially finished off by the Muslim invasions. In terms of the Hindu populations, however, Islam ran up against a powerful hierarchy and caste system.
  - Hindu worship centers on great temples that were ill-suited for conversion into mosques, requiring the Muslims to construct new mosques.

  - Further, the great cults of India were linked with the worship of the villages of India, associated with the so-called practices of tantra; that is, the notion that there's a higher allegorical, spiritual meaning behind all the simple rites practiced in the villages across India. These rites were almost family and village worship and were not dependent on the support of the Brahmins and the temples.

  - Thus, Islam encountered an institutional religion that had far greater resources and strength behind it than the Turks did in Asia Minor.

- As a result, by 1350, where Asia Minor was being converted into an Islamic land, the sultans of Delhi were ruling over a set of Muslim cities in a largely Hindu countryside. They faced powerful Hindu kingdoms to the south and to the east. In some ways, the Indians came to view the newcomers, the Turkish invaders, not so much as invaders and conquerors but as a subset of caste, and Islam, in many ways, became much more an Indian religion rather than the Indians becoming Muslims.

Important Terms

iqta: A military tenure granted to Muslim soldiers by the sultans of Delhi.

Khalji sultanate: The second Persian-speaking dynasty of Turkish sultans in northern India (1290–1320).

muqti: A military governor of the Delhi sultanate who held a military tenure in lieu of a salary.

Qutb Minar: Built by Sultan Aybak of Delhi in 1198, it is the largest minaret in India.

Quwat ul Islam: Meaning "Might of Islam," the mosque outside of Delhi built from plundered architectural elements of Hindu and Jain temples. It was ordered by Sultan Aybak in 1193.

spolia: Architectural elements or sculpture of older buildings recycled into new buildings.

Tughluq sultans: Members of the third dynasty of Turkish Muslim rulers in India (1320–1414).

Names to Know

Iltutmish (r. 1210–1236): Sultan of Delhi; succeeded his father-in-law, Aybak, and reestablished the capital at Delhi. He organized a system of land grants to his emirs and soldiers, but he also co-opted loyal Hindu princes into the military hierarchy.

Qutb ud-Din Aybak (1206–1210): Sultan of Delhi; was the leading general of Muhammad Ghuri (1202–1206), who entrusted Aybak with the conquest of the Ganges. In 1206, he made himself sultan of the Turkish slave soldiers and, thus, founded the slave sultanate of Delhi.

Radiyya Begum (b. 1205; r. 1236–1240): Daughter of Iltutmish; was the first Muslim woman to rule in her own right as sultana of Delhi. She failed to win over the Turkish military elite, who were scandalized by her manners and liaisons. Her murder in 1240 marked the end of effective rule by the slave sultans of Delhi.

Suggested Reading

Elverskog, *Buddhism and Islam on the Silk Road*.

Jackson, *The Delhi Sultanate*.

Keay, *India: A History*.

Thapar, *A History of India*, volume I.

Zakaria, *Razia, Queen of India*.

Questions to Consider

1. What were the achievements of Qutb ud-Din Aybak and Iltutmish, the founders of the sultanate of Delhi? How did they transform Delhi into a Muslim capital? What was the impact of their building programs in northern India?

2. What accounted for the later political instability of the sultanate? Why was the reign of Radiyya Begum a turning point? What were institutional and military limitations of the sultanate? What was the impact of the Mongol attacks after 1220?

3. Why did the Khalji and Tughluq sultans of Delhi fail to forge a more effective imperial state? What was the Hindu response to the repeated attacks by the sultans of Delhi in the 14th and 15th centuries?

4. What were the appeals of Islam to the diverse peoples of India in the 13th and 14th centuries? Why did the majority of Hindus and Jains remain loyal to their ancestral worship? What role did the Turkish conquest play in the demise of Buddhism in India?

5. What were the interactions between Turkish and Persian Muslim conquerors and the populations of India? How were Islam and Islamic civilization transformed in India?

The Sultans of Delhi
Lecture 25—Transcript

In this lecture, I plan to look at the results of the conquests of Northern India by Turkish nomadic warriors in the early 13th century. This is a lecture that is parallel to what we just discussed on the Turkification and the Islamicization of Asia Minor. It requires us to look at some of the same features; that is, why did the sultans ruling at Delhi fail to forge a wider imperial unity? They ran into some of the same problems as the sultans of Konya. On the other hand, what were their successes and what were the limitations in creating a Muslim civilization in India? As I mentioned in passing in a previous lecture, sometimes the Muslim conquest of Northern India in the 13th and 14th centuries is really compared to a military occupation rather than a real settlement. We will want to examine that question a bit at the end of this lecture. That requires us to look at two aspects of Muslim India in the 13th and 14th centuries: First is the whole political success. The second will be the cultural and religious issues.

Let us start with the year 1206, when Muhammad Ghori died. He had carried out some of the most successful campaigns against Hindu opponents ever. In 1192, I mentioned he won that decisive battle at Tarain, north of Delhi; that delivered him control of Northern India, at least the Doab, the upper reaches of the Ganges, and the Punjab. He, however, was distracted by events in Central Asia and to him India was a source of revenues; and so he really entrusted the running of his conquests to his subordinate generals. These, again, were Mamluks; they were slave soldiers. The most important of these fellows was a fellow by the name of Aybak. Actually, Aybak's full name is Qutb-ud-din Aybak. He was commissioned with directing the conquests in Northern India, especially after 1197 when Muhammad Ghori was really more involved in dealing with the Kara-Khitans and eventually the ramifications of the Mongol invasions, or what led to the Mongol invasions; he was clashing with the shahs of Khurasan. Aybak was essentially left on his own to direct various campaigns. Those campaigns in 1190 saw the consolidation of a kingdom in and around Delhi with a much looser confederacy across the Indo-Gangic plain.

From the start, power rested in the hands of these nomadic steppe warriors plus slave soldiers. In 1206, when Muhammad Ghori died, Aybak essentially became an independent ruler. He assumed the name sultan, and he ruled for the next four years from Delhi and then transmitted power in his family. The sultanate is often called the slave sultans of Delhi, and that is a bit deceptive. This is a false analogy to the Mamluk sultans of Egypt who were also slave sultans. In Egypt, there was a consortium of the leadership of the different military regiments in the Mamluk army. They would decide who would be sultan and they did not pay attention to hereditary succession. Aybak, on the other hand, established a sultanate in which power was transmitted through the family. They just happened to be Mamluks in origin; and so the term "slave sultans of Delhi" is a bit deceptive. Furthermore, from the start, Aybak realized you could not just depend on tribal regiments and slave soldiers. There was the problem of obtaining horses, and he began to give out essentially endowments or fiefs—*iqta* is the technical term—and these were handed out to *muqtis*, to leaders, to commanders, who would then use this land to support military units that would in turn be the basis of power for the sultan.

Some of these commanders were really quite independent. The Khalji family, for instance—and they would eventually come to displace the so-called slave sultans; that is, the family of Aybak—they were given the commission to conquer Bengal. The founder of that family, his name is Muhammad Khalji—the name comes from where they originated back in Afghanistan—they overran the lower Ganges; he sacked the great Buddhist sanctuary at Nalanda; and essentially finished the Palas kingdom in the Bengal, which was the only significant kingdom in India that was still supporting Buddhism. That family essentially carved out an independent operation. This would be a problem repeatedly in dealing with your subordinates, your *muqtis*: that they could not conquer a region in India that was so wealthy that it could support their own court and their own army. A saying that comes down from the Mughal period is very relevant to the whole of the history of Muslim India. It was stated by the Rajputs in Rajasthan at their city of Udaipur in Northern India. "Udaipur is far from Delhi"; that is, "We might recognize the authority of the sultan in Delhi"—when that phrase was coined, it was the Mughal emperor—"but what really goes on in our city has very little to do with what the sultan in Delhi is concerned about."

Nonetheless, Aybak set the basis for the political control of Delhi and the Doab. He was killed in a curious freak accident in that bizarre polo game that is played on the steppes, and he was succeeded by his son-in-law, a man known by his Turkish name, Iltutmish. Iltutmish came to the throne, and he ruled for a long time, from 1210–1236. He really was not a slave sultan in the sense of the Mamluks. He, too, originated as a military commander as a very young boy; he had been sold into military service. But he owed his position to the throne because he had married the daughter of Aybak and was absolutely trusted. He proved a very, very able ruler. He extended the use of endowments. He campaigned prodigiously, and extended the influence of the Delhi sultanate across the Indo-Gangic plain. Both he and his predecessor Aybak would be very important in the construction of architecture to magnify the glory of this regime; we will be talking about that later.

From the start, he was concerned about a succession because the state was potentially unstable. Again, I must stress that while you can draw a map showing the extent of Iltutmish's conquests, those conquests were really very tentative. The state still thought in terms of having a large area that it could raid from which it could exact tribute, and in some ways the sultan of Delhi was not too different from a Hindu raj who would perform the traditional progress of receiving submissions. Already in Iltutmish's reign, it was clear that in order to rule India successfully, you were going to have to start coopting members of the Kshatriya caste—that is, the warriors and princes; particularly the Rajputs, the Jats in Northern India; later, kingdoms down on the Deccan and even farther south—if any kind of meaningful political order was to be constructed; and therefore you would have to come to terms with that Hindu ruling class even though you might raid and dispossess them in some areas. On the other hand, the only way for this to work was to start building a wider network of alliances. This is something that the Seljuk Turks in Asia Minor never had to do. For them, it was a clear contest: Byzantines on one side, Turks on the other.

Furthermore, you had to satisfy the *muqtis*, and they formed essentially a governing inner council of the sultanate. They are usually known as the Forty. They could pass judgment on a whole bunch of issues, including the succession to the various fiefs. They were rewarded with an *iqta* that would involve a governorship; it might involve the prophets of some kind of concession or monopoly; but usually it was land. This was the way to maintain a large standing army.

In addition, Iltutmish was concerned about his family. He had several sons; especially his older son who he did not trust with good cause, and he groomed his daughter to succeed him. This was a remarkable event; in fact, as far as I know, it was the first time that a female would rule as sultan (not feminine sultana, but a sultan in her own right). The lady's name was Radiyya Begum—again in that *yumusak* "ğ"—and she came to the throne in 1236 when her father died. She clearly was an able ruler. She was not a great ruler, but she was certainly above average, and certainly light years ahead of the later sultans of the family that followed. She, however, violated a lot of social conventions, at least in a strictly Islamic context. For one, she liked riding elephants. She also put on the trousers of the steppes. She was a great equestrian. She knew how to fight. In some ways, scholars see her as not only just unconventional, but a woman who comes off the steppes; that is, that tradition that you could already detect among the Scythians and Sarmatians that women of high rank might end up ruling, they might actually end up being warrior princesses, and so some would argue that the tradition was really a recovery of this older steppe nomadic tradition in India. Others might argue that in part it was influenced by the role that queens had played traditionally in India before the advent of the Muslims; that they could rule independently in some kingdoms, they could wield great power. Whatever the case might be, she did rule successfully down to 1240, and then she ran into difficulty.

The *muqtis*, the governing body of the Forty, in effect carried out a coup; more than a coup, they staged a full-scale rebellion. There were rumors that the sultan had been consorting with one of her viziers of low origin; there were other rumors that she had dishonored various *muqtis*; they were outraged. The religious community, the ulema—that is, the theologians of the Islamic *medreses*—they, too, found her objectionable on a number of grounds. As a result, she faced very, very serious opposition and was eventually overthrown by a coalition of these *muqtis*; and part of their problem for her was not only that she was a woman, but she also represented a centralizing tendency of the court. She intended to rule through her agents and to reign in the *muqtis* so they would not become so independent. The result was that she was captured in a major battle; she and her new husband were seized; they were defeated outside of Delhi on October 12, 1240; and eventually she was executed. The result was the dynasty deteriorated after that point. Radiyya was followed by a succession of weak rulers until the family was overthrown by one of those *muqti* families, the Khaljis in Bengal.

Her reign proved a turning point for several reasons. One, the efforts of the dynasty to centralize and to bring in the independent commanders had failed. The council of the Forty had essentially won by defeating her efforts to centralize the state. Second, the two succeeding dynasties—the Khalji Dynasty, and then another dynasty that follows them, the Taluk Dynasty, in the late 13th and early 14th centuries—in each of those dynasties, the founders attempted to forge a wider unity by conquering regions to the south of Delhi, notably the northern districts of the Deccan and farther south. All of these efforts ultimately failed. The first family, the Khalji family, came to power in 1296; and the second sultan of that hereditary dynasty in Delhi, who was known by the name of Ala ad-Din Muhammad, took it upon himself to direct major campaigns into Southern India. This was the first time that Muslim forces really crossed this boundary line that runs along the river that essentially cuts Northern India from Southern India, including the Deccan in the far south.

He was well served by a general who was actually a Hindu convert. His name is Malik Kafur. He probably was a low-caste Hindu. He may have been captured in a war and enslaved; he had risen to high rank under the Khalji Dynasty. He commanded successive invasions into Central and Southern India. These resulted in destructions of major temple complexes, particularly very well-known temples of the Hoysala kingdom; one of the great temples at Belur, for instance, was attacked and sacked. The armies penetrated deep into Southern India, into the Dravidian-speaking regions. The temples at Madurai were sacked; this was very, very far south in the Pandya kingdom. Furthermore, Muslim armies raged farther east, again targeting major temples that were known for their wealth, their pilgrimage; yet these conquests failed to net Ala ad-Din territorial acquisitions because they were vast raids, they rounded up captives, they rounded up plunder, and then the Muslim armies retreated.

This dynasty, too, ran into the same problem of trying to reconcile central control with the *muqtis*. When the raids started to cease—that is, the plunder, the loot was not coming in—in 1320, this second dynasty of Delhi was overthrown, and it was overthrown by a new family, the Tughluq family. Muhammad Tughluq, the most prominent of this family, likewise conducted similar types of operations against various Hindu kingdoms; but ultimately, these efforts to bring the Hindu kingdoms to heel failed. It certainly enraged many of the Brahmins who saw their temples sacked; and above all, it led to the consolidation of Southern India around the city of Hampi, where two brothers who were actually reputed to have initially submitted to the sultan of Delhi established a great Hindu kingdom that we know by the name of Vijayanagara, which essentially means "victory city." This kingdom in the mid-14th century—somewhere between 1335 and 1345; there is now a reassessment over the time—consolidated and acted as a block, a check, on further Muslim advance into Central and Southern India. It was, in effect, a reaction to the attacks by the sultans of Delhi. By the middle of the 14th century, you had, in effect, a political standoff between the Hindu kingdoms consolidated in Central and Southern India and these sultans of Delhi. As I said, to some extent, the sultans of Delhi largely ruled by permission of their *muqtis*, that consortium of Forty that exercised a great deal of influence in policy and even sometimes in selecting the sultan.

On the political scale, the sultans of Delhi were somewhat successful. They did retain their thrones; they did resist the Mongols, but that would turn out more to be accidental; and they never quite had the prestige in the Islamic world for their military and political achievements as the Mamluks of Egypt, who in 1260 at Ain Jalut would defeat the Mongols. None of the sultans at Delhi could claim that; far from it: The Mongols would repeatedly ravage the Muslim cities of Northern India from the 1220s on. On the other hand, the sultans of Delhi, just like their counterparts at Konya, carried out a very, very active building program; and that is seen in Delhi today. To some extent, the building program was to promote Islam, but it was also to promote their own position within the Islamic world. Their armies were not ethnic tribal armies as you had in Asia Minor. Many of their forces were mercenaries; they were a composite group of different tribes. They still depended on slave soldiers. They were terribly tied, very, very much dependent, on the trade bringing in horses from Central Asia. In order to promote an image of imperial power, building programs were the way to go. The buildings of the sultans of Delhi turned out for their period to be some of the largest buildings in the entire Islamic world; and they were a way of showing that Islamic power now rested in Delhi.

If you go to Delhi today, you have to go south, and you go to a region that is known as the Qutb complex. That is named after Qutb-ud-ala-din Aybak, the first of the so-called slave sultans, who took power in 1206 and died in 1210. He commissioned a major building program in this area. His successor, his son-in-law Iltutmish, completed it. These buildings in the early 13th century came to symbolize the power of the sultans of Delhi; they were comparable to the building programs that were going on in Konya at the same time. One of them, for instance, is the great, we would call it "minaret," it is however called the Qutb Minaret, or Minar; that would be the rendition in India, the word *minaret*. It is an enormous minaret; it is, in fact, the largest in Islam at the time. It is a brick building that soars 240 feet high; it has I believe five or six galleries to it; and it was a symbol of victory as much as it was for the Islamic faith. He also began the construction of a major mosque complex right next to that. That complex was really not finished until his successors, especially Iltutmish expands that mosque; then there were later additions by the Khalji and even the Tughluq sultans; and I think there may even be some additions if I remember correctly in the 15th century before the Mongols.

This is a great victory mosque; it is significant for several reasons. One is the mosque as we know it today is by the name of Quwwat-ul, it means the "Might of Islam." When you go there, it is an impressive building constructed of brick as well as spolia. "Spolia" refers to any kind of material that you have seized from older buildings. It is a term that is used quite often in conjunction with ancient buildings, and it applies here as well. The great mosque ordered by Aybak and completed by successors is built in part from the spolia—that is, the debris, pieces—of some 27 Jain and Hindu temples. If you go there today, you stand in a great open courtyard, an *avlu* in the Islamic tradition, and that is where the faithful will gather to pray. The *avlu*, the open area, is actually partially enclosed by these colonnades and, of course, the side facing Mecca is where you direct your prayer; and those colonnades are built from all sorts of pieces of sculpture taken from Hindu and Jain temples. You can see that it is essentially a memorial complex at the same time that it is an Islamic shrine. In the middle, of course, is the fountain, the çheşme, necessary for ablutions for the faithful. Later gates were added to the far end of the complex and mausoleums (that is, memorial tombs) and subsidiary buildings were added over the course of the next 200 years.

The central mosque itself, next to the great minaret in the Qutb complex, announced the victory of Islam; and it is an extraordinary set of monuments. In size and audacity, it dwarfs anything being built by the Seljuk sultans of Konya. Furthermore, in the middle of that *avlu*, that open courtyard, is the iron column of a Chandragupta; not the famous one of the Mauryan dynasty, a later one of the Gupta period of the fourth century. It is a great Hindu monument that had been put in the middle of the *avlu* to show it was now good taste; it had now been incorporated as a decorative piece in a Muslim mosque. One wonders what the majority of the Hindu population made of it, because this mosque was built with *corvee* labor—that is, large numbers of Indians worked on it—and it must have been something of an humiliating job to dismantle your own temples and then use them to build the mosque of the victors.

The building programs of the sultans transformed Delhi into a great city. Delhi previously had been a minor city in India; it now became the city of Muslim power in Northern India, the natural center of any imperial order—any raj, as it was later called—that would base itself on the traditional power of the Punjab, the Ganges, and the Doab.

The building programs were spectacular; the military operations were far-ranging and really daring; yet Islam always remained a minority religion. This has caused great excitement, great discussion, as to what did the conquest or the occupation of the sultans of Delhi bring for India? This is now clouded with all sorts of nationalist opinions; Muslims always stressing the power of the Turkish horse archers and cavalry, Hindu nationalists deploring the destruction of their shrines. There has been a very good scholarly study on this, and it is an analysis of all the literary reports of temples that were sacked by Muslim armies, essentially running from the time of Muhammad Ghori; that is, let us say from 1192 down to about the death of the Mughal emperor Aurangzeb, and he died in 1707. In that period, there are only really 500 good documentations of the Muslims targeting specific temples to destroy.

Sometimes they were driven to loot them to pay the army, other times they clearly targeted these temples because they were breaking resistance, either a foe or a rebel; but it was not nearly as many as the texts would suggest where thousands of temples, thousands of Brahmins were killed. There was an awful lot of exaggeration. Yet, on the other hand, let us not make a mistake here, too: The destruction of temples, yes, it occurred when Hindu rulers fought with each other, but it was not supposed to happen. It is quite different when an outside conqueror comes and destroys your religious shrines.

It has also been studied very carefully how much impact these first 250–300 years of Muslim rule in India had on the religions. Buddhism essentially was finished off by the Muslim invasions. The great sanctuary of Nalanda was sacked by armies really of Muhammad Ghori led by one of his subordinates in 1197; but Buddhism was already on the retreat. There were very, very few Buddhist monasteries left, only the Pala kingdom had supported it; and Buddhism had begun to retreat into Tibet in Central Asia, so at most the Turks delivered the coup-de-grace. But in terms of the Hindu populations, there Islam ran up against a powerful hierarchy, a powerful caste system, which is reciprocal; which defines peoples' lives, their place in society, dharma, their destiny; and also the notion of karma, the good acts that will lead the believer to breaking the cycle of rebirths, the cycle of lives, and achieving nirvana (or actually to be more accurate, *moksha* in the Hindu tradition); liberation from the pattern of life where your atman, your soul, will rejoin the world's soul.

Those sorts of traditions behind Hinduism had long crystallized, and Hindu worship centered around great temples. These temples were really ill-suited to be converted into mosques; Muslims had to build mosques anew. This is quite different from Christian churches that could easily be modified into a mosque. A Hindu temple is essentially the sanctum of the God; it is very, very small, the inner sanctum. They are massive buildings with marvelous decoration; decoration that the Muslims often mistook as erotic and as somehow evil. Really what the sculptural programs on high Hindu mosque temples represent is the mundane world, the world of Maya, illusion, which is distinct from the real world of the God in the sanctum. If anyone has traveled in India, they would have seen this type of relief sculpture on the outside of the temple. The temples at Khajuraho are particularly telling of this. Muslim soldiers encountering this type of sculpture would have found it anathema; they would have seen it as the idol worship that Muhammad had abolished in Mecca. Nonetheless, it was integral to understanding the message of the Hindu cults, the cults of Shiva and Vishnu; and furthermore, the great cults of India were also linked with the worship of the villages of India. That is associated with the so-called practices of tantra; that is, the notion that there is a higher allegorical spiritual meaning behind all the simple rites practiced in the villages across India. These rites were almost family and village worship and were not dependent on the support of the Brahmins and the temples; and so Islam encountered an institutional religion that had far greater resources and strength behind it than the Turks did in Asia Minor.

As a result, by 1350, where Asia Minor was being converted into an Islamic land, the sultans of Delhi were ruling over a set of Muslim cities in a largely Hindu countryside. They face powerful Hindu kingdoms to the south and to the east; and in some ways the Indians came to view the newcomers, the Turkish invaders, not so much as invaders and conquerors, but as a subset of caste, and that Islam in many ways became much more an Indian religion rather than the Indians became Muslims.

Manchurian Warlords and Song Emperors
Lecture 26

In this lecture, we will move away from the Islamic world and return to the eastern steppes and China. In China, in the year 907, the Tang Empire collapsed. The Great Wall was no longer an effective barrier—political, moral, or cultural. As a result, nomadic peoples moved into northern China. In this lecture, we'll discuss three of those groups: Khitans, Jurchens, and Xi Xia. By studying their interaction with the restored Chinese Song Dynasty in the 10th and 11th centuries, we will come to understand why the Mongols emerged and had such a dramatic impact on the 13th century.

The Khitans

- The **Khitans** were not technically steppe peoples; they were originally from the Manchurian forest, and they learned nomadism through contact with the ancestors of the Mongols and Turks. They came to dominate parts of northern China in the early 10th century and eventually ruled as Chinese-style emperors.

- The Khitan state was established in the early 10th century by **Abaoji**. In 907, he overthrew his master, carved out a state in northern China, and began to rule in the manner of a Chinese emperor. Abaoji, whose throne name was Taizu, initiated the conquest of strategic Chinese provinces, later known as the 16 prefectures.

- While the Khitans had authority over other nomadic tribes, they

To their nomadic allies and vassals, the Khitans projected the image of great warriors; for their Chinese subjects, they modeled a traditional imperial administration.

also ruled many Chinese subjects—estimates run from 10 to 15 million just in the 16 prefectures alone. That meant they had to control a loose confederation of nomadic peoples and devise a government by Chinese officials to manage this area. From the start, this empire had a dual administration.

- Furthermore, Abaoji wanted to pass power within his family, father to son, as a Chinese emperor would: the system of primogeniture. Nomadic peoples, on the other hand, practiced lateral succession.

A Dual Administration
- From the start, the royal family in the Khitan Empire was torn between the desire to become Chinese emperors or retain strong ties with the steppes. Increasingly, over the 10th and 11th centuries, they opted for the Chinese model.

- The emperor Shengzong, whose Khitan name was **Yelü Longxu** (r. 982–1031), completed the process of turning the Khitan Empire of the steppes into a Chinese bureaucratic state. However, the Khitan emperors, who adopted the Chinese dynastic name Liao, still tried to project the image of being nomadic conquerors to the tribes.

- They cemented ties with various tribes, which involved overtures of hospitality, marriages, celebration of events, and traditional rites. On the other hand, they also ruled as Chinese emperors; that is, they cultivated Chinese bureaucrats.

Treaty with the Song Dynasty
- The Khitan Empire came into conflict with the Song emperors of southern China, and in 1005, they signed a treaty with the Song emperor Zhenzong that arranged a partition between the Khitan state and the restored empire of China to the south.

- For the Khitans, this was a major triumph. It established the Khitan state as heir to the northern Chinese traditions of the Tang. The Song emperors, however, were furious. They did everything in their power to undermine the Khitan state.

- This treaty also recognized the independence of the **Xi Xia**—Tangut-speaking people who embraced Buddhism and who would maintain the Silk Road. The Xi Xia also proved to have an essential skill: They had adapted Chinese characters to write their own version of a script. They would, in time, provide many of the translators, ministers, and merchant princes who would advise the Mongol court in the 13th century.

Aguda

- The Song emperors believed that they were the heirs to the Han Dynasty. It was unacceptable to have any part of China under the control of barbarians. To destroy the Khitans, they brought in another barbarian: **Wanyan Min**.

- Wanyan Min, or Aguda, who was the khagan of the people dwelling on the northern reaches of the Amur River, had a personal quarrel with the Khitan emperor. He was more than willing to accept subsidies and technical advisors, especially Chinese military advisors, to wage war against the Khitans.

- This alliance was called the Alliance of the Sea because the only way to exchange envoys was to go by water to get around the territories controlled by the Khitan emperors. **Jurchen** warlords rallied around Aguda, who launched a major campaign into the Khitan territories and drove the Khitan emperor farther south, right into the hands of the Song armies.

- Aguda conquered much of the Khitan kingdom. The Song, however, were far less effective in reclaiming their territories from the Khitans.

The Jin Dynasty

- **Wanyan Sheng**, the new ruler of the Jurchens and the brother of Aguda, took a high-sounding Tang throne name, Taizong. He continued to press south. As a result, the Song court found that its new ally-turned-rival captured the northern Tang capital city of

Kaifeng in 1127. The Jurchens also captured the court, including the retired emperor Huizong.

- The Song Dynasty then relocated further south. A younger son, Gaozong, took power and established a capital at the modern city of Hangzhou.

- The entire lower and middle Huang He valley was now in the hands of the Jurchen emperors, who styled themselves as the Jin— the Chinese term for "gold." The Golden emperors now ruled a large section of northern China, perhaps 30 to 40 million Chinese subjects, and controlled a nomadic confederacy stretching to the Altai Mountains.

- Over time, the Jin emperors would become too distant from their nomadic allies and vassals. This allowed for the emergence of the Mongols.

Song Rule

- Why was the Song court incapable of driving out the Khitans and then the Jurchen invaders? The Song could not extend their control back over the western districts that had brought in revenue from the Silk Road.

- The Song controlled southern China from 960 to 1279, when their dynasty was destroyed by the Mongols. The Song ruled about two-thirds of the Chinese population. The dynasty was founded by an accomplished general, Zhao Kuangyin, who seized power and united a number of smaller kingdoms in the mid-10th century.

- The new dynasty projected itself as a Confucian dynasty. Confucian texts were widely read by the upper classes. This had been assisted by the invention of block printing. Many of the cultured and administrative elite had relocated south to escape attacks from the northern barbarian states.

A Successful Bureaucratic State

- The Song emperors instituted a new way of recruiting officials: a standard examination to recruit scholars rather than recommendations or dependence on the military elite.

- The future bureaucrat went through a series of exams. A total of 300,000 might take the exam, but only 300 would get the *jinshi*—the highest degree that allowed admittance into the top ministerial classes. The examination system ensured continuity in the members of the upper classes. They had a shared culture of the classics.

- These classics were important because they were read for their moral precepts and to gain an understanding of the duties of the government. This inculcated in the court and the administration a sense of professionalism that transcended the individual emperor.

- As a result, the Song Empire was perhaps one of the most successful bureaucratic states ever created. It maintained a cultural coherence and continuity that persisted from the 10th century to today.

Economic Development

- In addition, as part of their role as Confucian emperors, the Song emperors sponsored enormous economic development. The Song Empire exploited the invention of the blast furnace for iron technology and encouraged massive production of ceramics. Silk-linen production became a state-regulated industry, and these products were exported far outside the Song Empire. Chinese merchants traveled to Indonesia, the Chola kingdom in India, and to Fatimid Cairo.

- Thus began the rage for Chinese porcelains. Iron technology proved a boon to agriculture. Rice production expanded because of the availability of iron tools. The Song also expanded the use of money and were the first to use a kind of paper money.

- The Song Empire was extremely successful except in one area. The Song had to accept the fact that they had lost their northern zones and that their military was largely defensive and could no longer take on the job of expelling the barbarians. As a result, the Song court invariably resorted to diplomacy.

Kara-Khitans

- In the fighting that led to the overthrow of the Khitan Empire, one figure, **Yelü Dashi**, stands out. Yelü Dashi was a Khitan prince who refused to accept the loss of Khitan power. He took 10,000 warriors and went west.

- Yelü Dashi evaded the armies of the Jin emperors, who now ruled northern China. He attacked the Karakhanid Turkish tribes centered on the Jaxartes and the steppes just north of the Tarim Basin.

- This invasion was a shock to the Islamic world. This group of Khitans, who called themselves the **Kara-Khitans**, overwhelmed the Turkish confederation. In 1141, they inflicted a decisive defeat on the Seljuk Turk Ahmad Sanjar at a battle called Qatwan. The Kara-Khitans crossed the Jaxartes, overran Transoxania, and took over the great caravan cities. Their victory toppled the Seljuk sultanate in Baghdad.

Repercussions in the Islamic World

- The caliph of Baghdad was delighted because the Arab caliphs were fed up with the Turkish sultans. The victory in 1141 had major repercussions in the Islamic world. Many Muslims were shocked that a pagan army had overthrown an Islamic army.

- With the Seljuk Turks off the map, politically, the Abbasid caliphs were able to reassert themselves as a regional power. But for many Muslim authors and intellectuals, and certainly for the religious community, this was not supposed to happen.

- What they did not realize is that the Kara-Khitan invasion was nothing more than a dress rehearsal for the Mongol conquest.

jinshi: The highest level of mandarin officials in the Song examination system (960–1279).

Jurchens: Tungusic-speaking peoples of Manchuria who overthrew their overlords and ruled northern China under the Chinese dynastic name Jin, or "Golden" (1115–1234). The Jurchen emperors exercised a loose hegemony over the Mongol tribes.

Kara-Khitans: Sinicized Khitans (1123–1218) who migrated to the central Asian steppes and, thus, escaped the rule of the Jurchens. In 1141, the Kara-Khitans defeated the Karakhanids near Samarkand—a victory that gave rise to the legend of Prester John. Also called the western Liao.

Khitans: Mongol-speaking conquerors who ruled northern China under the Chinese dynastic name of Liao (907–1125). They were overthrown by their vassals, the Jurchens.

Song Dynasty: The Song Dynasty (960–1279) reunited most of China as the successors of the Tang emperors, promoted Confucian traditions, and perfected the bureaucratic state. The Khitans and, later, the Jurchens denied the Song the recovery of northern China.

Xi Xia: Sinicized Tanguts who had settled in Gansu and western China in the 10th century as nominal vassals of the Song emperors. With Jingzong (1038–1048), Xi Xia monarchs ruled as Chinese-style emperors who favored Buddhism (1038–1227).

Abaoji (b. 872; r. 907–926): Emperor of Liao Dynasty; assumed the Chinese throne name Taizu. He was of the Yila tribe within the confederation of Khitans. In 904, he seized supreme power over the Khitans. In 907, he assumed the name and role of a Chinese emperor, conquering the 16 prefectures in northeastern China and the eastern Eurasian steppe. He established his Sinicized court at Shangjing.

Wanyan Min (b. 1068; 1115–1123): Jurchen emperor of the Jin Dynasty; assumed the Chinese throne name Taizu. He united the Jurchens and overthrew the Khitan Empire. In 1121, he concluded with Song emperor Huizong (1100–1125) the so-called Alliance of the Sea that called for the partition of the Khitan Empire.

Wanyan Sheng (b. 1075; r. 1123–1135): Jurchen emperor of the Jin Dynasty; assumed the Chinese throne name Taizong. He succeeded his brother Wanyan Min and completed the conquest of the Khitan state. In 1127, he captured Kaifeng and the Song court, including the retired emperor Huizong. The new Song emperor Gaozong (1127–1162) agreed to cede northern China to Wanyan Sheng.

Yelü Dashi (b. 1087; r. 1124–1143): Kara-Khitan khan; a descendant of Abaoji who refused to accept Jurchen rule. In 1130–1131, he led a migration of Khitans into the Tarim Basin; in 1137, he overthrew the Karakhanid khaganate and founded a new Kara-Khitan Empire in central Asia. On September 9, 1141, Yelü Dashi decisively defeated the Seljuk sultan Ahmet Sanjar (1118–1153) at the Battle of Qatwan—the event that gave rise to the legend of Prester John. The victory delivered Transoxania to the Kara-Khitans.

Yelü Longxu (b. 972; r. 982–1031): Khitan emperor of the Liao Dynasty; assumed the Chinese throne name Shengzong. He presided over the transformation of the Khitan Empire into a Chinese bureaucratic state. In 1005, he concluded the Treaty of Chanyuan with the Song emperor Zhenzong (997–1022), who recognized the Khitan Empire and agreed to pay an annual subsidy.

Suggested Reading

Barefield, *The Perilous Frontier*.

Elverskog, *Buddhism and Islam on the Silk Road*.

Franke, "The Forest Peoples of Manchuria."

Kuhn, *The Age of Confucian Rule*.

Mote, *Imperial China, 900–1800*.

Saunders, *The History of the Mongol Conquests*.

1. Why did the Khitans and Jurchens establish such successful Sinified empires? How were these states models for later Mongol organization? What accounted for the failure of the Khitan emperors of the Liao Dynasty?

2. What role did the Xi Xia emperors play by controlling the Gansu Corridor? What lessons in administration did they provide for the later Mongol khans?

3. Why did the heirs of the Song emperors Taizu and Taizong fail to reunify China? How did the Song creation of a Neo-Confucian bureaucratic state and culture hinder the defense of this very state against the northern barbarians?

4. Why did the Jurchen emperors of the Jin Dynasty fail to maintain order on the Eurasian steppes? What dangers were posed to China by the incessant tribal warfare of the 12th century?

5. What was the impact of the Kara-Khitan invasion into the eastern Islamic world? How did their migration and conquest anticipate the Mongol invasions?

Manchurian Warlords and Song Emperors
Lecture 26—Transcript

This lecture begins the last third of the class. We are going to deal with the rise and impact of the Mongols. In some ways, the Mongols represent the climax and the epitome of all of the different steppe confederations and empires; and in other ways, they are a remarkable exception. This requires us to go back to the eastern steppes; to move away from the Islamic world where we have been discussing the interaction between Turkish speakers and Islamic civilization, and return to the eastern steppes and also to China. Perhaps it is best to start with something of an update of what has been going on in China from the 10th through the 11th centuries, which is simultaneous with events that had been going on in the Islamic world where we discussed the impact of the Turks on the wider Islamic world, their conquests in Anatolia and India, and the great extension of Islamic civilization compliments of the Turks.

Let us think back again to the year 907. In that year, the Tang Empire essentially collapsed. A general deposed the last Tang emperor, declared himself an emperor, Taizu, taking a throne name that is that of an early Tang emperor, and attempted to rule from the Yellow Valley as the new Tang emperor. But actually the empire had fragmented into a number of rival kingdoms; Later Confucian scholars referred to this period from 907–960 as the Five Dynasties in the Ten Kingdoms. This, again, was the conceit that China should always be unified; that there was never really an outside influence; that disunity was an aberration, and a single dynasty with the Mandate of Heaven was the norm. In many ways, the Tang Empire had really ceased to be an effective state ever since the An Lushan Rebellion back in the mid-8th century. Furthermore, the breakup of the Tang Empire in the early 10th century resembled in some ways the breakup of the Han Empire after 220. That meant that the fortifications along the northern frontiers, the Great Wall—and again I stress, do not think of the current Great Wall, that great Ming structure, the masonry architecture that is a 14th and 15th-century construction; the Great Wall was much simpler, it was made of rammed earth and wooden palisades, it was not a continuous fortification—nonetheless, the wall was seen as a political, moral, and cultural barrier; and that moral barrier collapsed after 907.

As a result, new peoples, nomadic peoples, moved into Northern China. In this lecture, we are going to discuss three of them. The first group is the Khitans. They were not really steppe peoples, they were originally forest people from the Manchurian forest; and they learned nomadic techniques from contact with the ancestors of Mongols and Turks. It is still a debate as to precisely what language they spoke: Is it Mongolian or Proto-Mongolian? Is it more Turkish, or is it a related language family known as Tangut? Whatever their language was, they came to dominate parts of Northern China in the early 10th century and eventually ruled as Chinese-style emperors. In addition, we will talk about two other peoples. Those are going to be the successors to the Khitans; those are the Jurchens, also coming from Manchuria, and even regarded by the Chinese as wilder, if you can believe that, than the Khitans were initially. They will take over especially between 1123 and 1127; they will essentially overthrow the Khitans and construct a very large North Chinese state. The final group we will mention in passing is a group that may have also been Tangut speakers, and those are known in Chinese sources as the Xi Xia. They would occupy the Ordos triangle, the Gansu, some of the steppe zones that linked the Tarim Basin to Western China.

These are the three players we are going to look at; and, of course, we are going to revive the Chinese empire under the great Song emperors. It is a tall order in this lecture; but I think by looking at the interaction of these three new nomadic peoples and the restored Chinese empire of the Song in the 10th and 11th centuries, we will understand why the Mongols emerged and had such a dramatic impact on the 13th century.

Let us first turn to our Khitans. This state was established in the early 10th century by a fellow by the name of Abaoji. He was a leading khan, if you will, of his tribe and he carved out a state in Northern China. Abaoji also took a Chinese throne name, Taizu; that name linked him with the ancient Tang emperors. Initially, he was a lower level khan of a lesser tribe. He overthrew his master in 907 and began to rule like a Chinese emperor—the term in Chinese would be Huangdi—and he conquered or initiated the conquests of certain strategic Chinese provinces. This was not completed until his successors, but those provinces were later known as the 16 prefectures. It represented sections of Northern China, around Beijing today: densely populated; extremely wealthy with agriculture, especially millet, towns; and that small North Chinese possession was actually economically and fiscally the most important part of this emerging Khitan Empire.

In addition, Abaoji and his successor extended their authority over the other nomadic tribes. They put together a rather loose confederation because they depended on the military power of the horse archers. That meant that from the start, the Khitan emperors were sort of ambiguous as to exactly how they should style themselves. To their nomadic allies and vassals, they were to be great warriors, in some ways like the Tang warrior emperors or certainly the early Xiongnu; one extracted silk, silver, other types of goodies from the Chinese, distributed it among the tribes. That sustained both honor and life. On the other hand, they also ruled many Chinese subjects—estimates run from 10–15 million just in the 16 prefectures alone—and that meant they would have to devise an administration by Chinese officials to run this area. From the start, this empire was a dual empire in that sense; it had a dual administration.

Furthermore, Abaoji wanted to pass power within his family, father to son, as a Chinese emperor would—that is, we would call it a system of primogenitor; that would be the English term—and this would encounter with the notions of lateral succession that characterized nomadic peoples. As I said, the Khitans were originally a forest people, but they had learned nomadic ways, probably by contact with ancestors of the Mongols and the Turks. Therefore, Abaoji wanted his older son to succeed, a fellow by the name of Yelü Bei. He was given a fine Chinese education and he comported himself too much like a Chinese emperor; and when Abaoji died, this whole arrangement was set aside, largely by the intrigues of his wife, Shulu Ping, a rather remarkable and formidable lady who comes down through the sources under a number of names such as the Empress of the Earth. She was actually to join her husband in death, which was an old-style custom that the consort would be buried with the khan. She chopped off her right hand and did a token burial and managed to manipulate the succession for the next three reigns through the various intrigues and eventually got on the throne a son of hers who represented much more the old-time nomadic values. His name was Yelü Deguang, and he followed in the tradition of the nomadic warrior fighting to extend territory in China to exact money out of the Chinese kingdoms.

From the start, the Khitan Empire had this instability within the royal family. What direction do we go? Do we become Chinese emperors or do we retain the ties with the steppes? Increasingly, over the 10th century and 11th century, more and more emperors opted for the Chinese model. The emperor Yelü Longxu—that is his Khitan name; he ruled under a Chinese name, which is probably better known, as Shengzong, from 982–1031—he really completed the process of turning this empire of the steppes into a Chinese bureaucratic kingdom. The Khitan emperors, who took now the Chinese dynastic name Liao, they still tried to project the image of being nomadic conquerors to the tribes; but they had a complicated progress where they went around to a number of different cities, there were five major capitals, they spent time cementing ties with the different tribes. This involved, for instance, ties of hospitality, marriages, celebration of events, traditional rites. But on the other hand, they also ruled as Chinese emperors—that is, they needed Chinese bureaucrats; they set up a court—and they also came into conflict with the Song emperors of Southern China; and in 1005, they signed a treaty with the Chinese emperor, and his name was Zhenzong, which essentially arranged a partition between the Khitan state and the restored empire of China to the south. That treaty in 1005 was renegotiated on a number of occasions. That specifies the payment of silk; silver in the form of ingots weighed by the tael, which is the Chinese ounce; also bronze coins, the so-called cash coins. Those treaties revealed that one bolt of silk was equal to one ounce of silver, which was equal to 1,000 of the copper cash coins; and the Song had the money to pay this. For the Khitans, this is a major triumph. It establishes the Khitan state as heir to the Northern Chinese traditions of the Tang. The Song emperors however were furious. The Song court never really accepted it and would do everything in their power to undermine this state; and that is how we would get eventually to the Jurchens who take over. They were essentially called in by the Song to wipe out the Khitans.

This treaty also recognized the independence of that other group I mentioned briefly at the start, the Xi Xia; that is, the Tangut-speaking people who would embrace Buddhism and who really maintained the Silk Road. That small kingdom, which through the 10th and 11th centuries ruled as essentially an independent Chinese-style kingdom, really was able to exist because of the conflict between the Khitan emperors who called themselves the Liao Dynasty in Chinese terms, and the Song emperors. The Xi Xia proved to be very important in one regard: They had adapted the Chinese characters to write their own version of a script, and they were on good terms with the Uighurs of the Tarim Basin. This kingdom in time would provide many of the translators, ministers, and merchant princes who would advise the Mongol court in the 13th century.

To get back to the Song and to our second major nomadic people who had an impact in China at this point, let us return to that treaty of 1005 briefly and look at it from the Chinese viewpoint. The Song emperors—and we will be talking about the Song a bit more in detail to explain their policy concerns—always postured that they were the heirs to the Han Dynasty; and to them, the Great Wall was a moral, political boundary. Any part of China, even just the 16 prefectures, in the hands of barbarians was always unacceptable. The ideology is very clear through the Song texts that they were the Han emperors; they had the Mandate of Heaven; that the emperor, the Huangdi, represented the true way, the Dao, as it would be called in Daoist text; and therefore driving the Khitans out was their policy, except the Song army just was not up to it, as we shall see.

The way to destroy a barbarian was to summon in another barbarian, and they had someone on hand. His name was Wanyan Aguda. He was the khan of the people to the north dwelling on the northern reaches of the Amur River, largely a forest people who engaged in hunting and fishing, but also had learned the techniques of cavalry and were vassals of the Liao Dynasty; that is, the Khitan emperors. Wanyan Aguda had a personal quarrel with the Khitan emperor, and he was more than willing—actually the quarrel had something to do with the fact that he had to perform some sort of ignominious dance when the Khitan emperor was visiting his territory as part of the imperial progress—but in any event, Wanyan Aguda was more than happy to accept subsidies, technical advisors, especially Chinese military advisers, to wage war against the Khitans. This alliance, sometimes colorfully called the "Alliance on the Sea"—because the only way to exchange envoys was essentially to go by water to get around the territories controlled by the Khitan emperors—ended up in a joint effort to overthrow the Khitan Dynasty. That meant the Jurchen warlords rallied around Aguda, who launched a major campaign into the Khitan territories and drove the Khitan emperor farther south, right into the hands of the Song armies who were making their efforts to make a comeback and retake the 16 prefectures. The result was the Khitan state found itself between these two opposing forces.

Wanyan Aguda conquered much of the Khitan kingdom. The Song, however, did not do such a good job; and they were far less effective in reclaiming their territories from the Khitans. The new ruler of the Jurchens, the brother of Aguda, took the throne; his name was Wanyan Sheng, and he took, again, a very high-sounding Tang throne name, Taizong, the great Tang emperor who won great victories over the nomads. This new Taizong, or Wanyan Sheng, decided that "It was nice to take the Khitans; we have the nomadic power, we have the tribes on our side," and he continued to press south. The result was that the Song court found itself in the embarrassing situation that this new ally turned rival overran Northern China, the North Chinese plain, the Yellow River, captured the northern Song capital city of Kaifeng in 1127; they also captured the court, including the Emperor Huizong who was at this point in retirement in the home court, and the emperor and his court were taken off and died in captivity. The result was the Song dynasty relocates south. A younger son by the name of Gaozong took power. He established a capital at the modern city of Hangzhou today, then called Lin'an, and he consolidated the Song Empire on the Yangtze or Yangzi, and eventually the Song emperors had to come into accommodation with these new invaders; new treaties were concluded; new subsidies were paid at very, very high cost in terms of silver and silk. The best analysis by scholars is that overall the payment of tribute was probably cost effective. The Song presided over an impressively expanding economy, and these payments could easily be sustained by the Song treasury, except it was humiliating.

The entire Lower and Middle Yellow River Valley was now in the hands of the Jurchens emperors who styled themselves as the Jin; that is, the Chinese term for "gold." They were the Jin emperors, the Golden emperors; and they now ruled a big section of Northern China—perhaps 30–40 million Chinese subjects—and they also had a confederacy, they exercised control over a nomadic confederacy, stretching at least to the Altai Mountain range; that is, more or less the same dimensions as the old Xiongnu confederacy. The Jin emperors controlled perhaps a third of the Chinese population; many of the cities; certainly the heartland of Chinese civilization; as well as great nomadic power. In time, the Jin emperors would become far too distant from their nomadic allies and vassals, they would lose touch with them; and in so doing, this would allow for the emergence of the Mongols because in the case of the Jin emperors, unlike their predecessors the Liao or Khitan emperors, they were ruling as a very small minority, no more than several hundred thousand over 30 or 40 million Chinese subjects; and so the Jin court very quickly assumed the façade of a Chinese court.

Meanwhile, what was going on in Southern China? Why was the Chinese emperor, why was the Song court not capable of driving out first the Khitans and then the Jurchens invaders? Furthermore, the Song court could not extend its control back over those western districts that had been traditionally so important for the Silk Road for revenues coming into the court. We have talked about how Han and Tang emperors expended so much effort, military and diplomatic, to secure the caravan routes, at least to Kashgar. That comes down to the nature of the Song Dynasty and what the revival of imperial power meant in the 10th century.

The Song, who controlled Southern China from 960 down to 1279 when the dynasty was finally knocked out by the Mongols, came to rule perhaps two-thirds of the Chinese population. The dynasty was founded by a general, a very accomplished general, by the name of Zhao Kuangyin, who seized power and united a number of smaller kingdoms in the mid-10th century, and he centered his power initially at Kaifeng in the Yellow River valley; that was the capital later lost in 1127 when the dynasty had to relocate south to the Yangtze. Initially, this succession of Song emperors looked really good. They were going to retake all of the traditional borderlands; they were going to restore the empire to its original extent. The new dynasty also projected itself very much as a Confucian dynasty.

That meant several significant differences from the previous dynasties, the Han and the Tang. Chinese scholars today see the Song as a cultural turning point that really defines classical China down to, some would argue today, and some would even argue that Mao Zedong was the last emperor as conceived by the Song Confucian gentry class. One of the most important changes in the Song Empire was its own identification and understanding of what it meant. The Confucian texts were now widely read by the upper classes;

this had been assisted by the invention of block printing. Furthermore, the Song emperors imposed a new way of recruiting officials. This had been used earlier, but they created a standard examination across the country to recruit scholars rather than using recommendation and depending on the old military elite, which had characterized the Sui and Tang dynasties. In fact, most of that military elite had happily killed itself on fighting these civil wars between 907 and 960. To some extent, the Song emperors had to seek out new talent to run the empire.

In addition, many of the cultured and administrative elite had relocated south to the Yangtze or the Yangzi. There was a shift of Chinese population to the southern regions as a result of the attacks and successes of those northern barbarian states. As a result, a new way of defining a scholar bureaucrat was based on an examination system. You went through a series of exams; there were actually three levels. You might start out with 300,000 taking the exam and you would end up with only 300 who get the *jinshi*—that is, the highest degree that gets you into the top ministerial classes—but that examination system ensured a continuity in the upper classes. They had a shared culture of the classics; and these classics were important because they were read for their moral precepts, for understanding the duties of the government, and it inculcated in the court and the administration a sense of professionalism that transcended the individual emperor. This is best seen in the career of one of these men; in fact, one of the men responsible for really defining what these classics represented. His name was Ou-yang Hsiu. He lived from 1007–1072. He rose from a relatively obscure position to a position in the high court where he defined what was necessary to become a gentleman. How do you take these examinations? Why is it that these texts train men in order to run the Chinese Empire? As a result, the Song Empire was perhaps one of the most successful bureaucratic states ever created. It gave a cultural coherence and continuity that would persist from the 10th century really down to today.

In addition, the Song emperors sponsored, as part of their role as Confucian emperors, enormous economic development. The Song Empire seized the invention of the blast furnace for iron technology. It seized massive production of ceramics. Silk linen production became a state-regulated industry; and furthermore, these products were exported far outside the Song Empire. We know of Chinese merchants going to Indonesia, to the

Chola kingdom in India, to Fatimid Cairo. Chinese porcelains were sent across Asia; that began the rage for Chinese porcelains. Iron technology was impressive. Ironically, it was never really applied as successfully to the military, but it certainly improved agriculture; it saw a great expansion of rice production because of the availability of iron tools. The Song extended the use of money. They were the first people to know of to use a kind of paper money; that is, letters of credit. On the whole, the economic development of the Song Empire was impressive. The consolidation of the bureaucratic class was also astonishing. The achievements and aesthetics belong more to a course in Chinese civilization; but the Song Empire was incredibly successful except in one area: They had to accept the fact that they had lost those northern zones and that their military was largely defensive and could no longer take on the job of expelling the barbarians. The result was the Song court invariably resorted to diplomacy.

In the fighting that led to the overthrow of the Khitan Empire, one figure, his name is Yelü Dashi—Yelü Dashi was a Khitan prince who refused to accept the decision of the loss of Khitan power—took 10,000 warriors and went west. He fled the Jin emperors, the Jurchens, who were now ruling Northern China. He evaded their armies and eventually ended up attacking the Karakhanid Turkish tribes centered on the Jaxartes and the steppes just north of the Tarim Basin. This invasion was a shock to the Islamic world. This was totally unexpected; and it fell, however, very well within the tradition of what we have been talking about: Major political changes on the eastern steppes vis-à-vis the Chinese Empire generally had a domino effect that sends tribes moving west. This group of Khitans, who called themselves the Kara Khitans—and realize they were not Turks, they are not to be confused with the Karakhanids; that is, that Turkish confederation on the central steppes—they overwhelmed the Turkish confederation, and in 1141 they inflicted a decisive defeat on the then-Seljuk Turk, Sanjar (Ahmad Sanjar, to give his full Islamic name) at a battle called Qatwan in which the Kara Khitans overran Transoxiana; that is, they crossed the Jaxartes, they took over the great caravan cities, it toppled the Seljuk sultanate in Baghdad. The caliph was delighted because the Arab caliphs were fed up with their Turkish sultans. They had been trying for years to clean these guys up by teaching them proper manners and governance; and while the Turkish soldiers were excellent, great to use against the Fatimids and the Byzantines, they were extremely unruly and very, very difficult to manage.

The victory in 1141 had major repercussions in the Islamic world. Many Muslim writers are shocked that a pagan army—the term would be *gâvur*; that would be a common Arabic Turkish word today, "heathens"—had overthrown an Islamic army. The Abbasid caliph was not so disappointed that the Seljuks were off the map politically, and the Abbasid caliphs were able to reassert themselves as a regional power; but for many Muslim authors and intellectuals, and certainly for the religious community, this was not supposed to happen. These nomads who now entered Dar al Islam, they were not at all Muslims. What they did not realize is that the Kara Khitan invasion was nothing more than the dress rehearsal for the Mongol conquest.

The Mongols
Lecture 27

In this lecture, we'll explore who the Mongols were at the time Temujin—Genghis Khan—was born, around 1162. The Mongol Empire was largely the creation of Genghis Khan and his successors. It was Genghis Khan who united the various Mongol tribes into a new confederation and launched a remarkable career of world conquest. He occupies a special position in the gallery of great commanders.

The Tatars

- The Tatars were subjects of the Khitan emperors and, later, the Jin emperors. When Temujin was born in 1162, the Mongols shared the eastern steppes with a group of neighboring tribes, some speaking Mongol, others speaking Turkish.

- At the time of Temujin's birth, the most important tribe was the Tatars. They were better known by a corruption of that name, Tartars, which Christian authors used to describe them when the Mongols invaded Russia in 1236 and overran eastern Europe.

- The Tatars spoke a version of Turkish and dwelled in the steppes to the west of the Mongols. They were in close contact with the Jin emperors and Chinese officials. They were connected by trade routes and most likely could field the largest nomadic cavalry on the steppes.

- The Tatars represented a major power. They had 70,000 warriors in a population of 150,000 to 200,000 people, since almost every male from birth to the age of 60 could ride. Furthermore, the Tatars were extremely aggressive and fought for control of the Kerulen River valley, a valley sacred to both the Mongols and Tatars.

- The Tatars had long been in association with China. They had received silks and various gifts from the Chinese empires, first the

Song and, later, the Jin. The Tatars represented one of the most civilized tribes on the eastern steppes.

Merkits, Oirats, Naimans, and Keraits

- To the northeast of the Mongols was another important tribe, the Merkits. They were regarded as some of the best warriors on the steppes. They were not as numerous as the Tatars, but they were notorious for stealing wives and horses. In fact, they stole the wife-to-be of Genghis Khan early in his career.

- The Merkits, too, were nomads and kept their flocks around the great glacial body of water Lake Baikal. The Merkits followed shamans. They had not been exposed as much to Chinese civilization although, later on, many became Nestorian Christians.

- The Oirats dwelled on the western steppes, and farther west were the Naimans. The Naimans were perhaps the second most important tribe in Mongolia in 1162. The Naimans and the Tatars would both oppose the unification of the tribes by Genghis Khan.

- Because of their location, which put them north of the Tarim Basin, the Naimans had been visited by many Uighur merchants, and they were familiar with Buddhism. They may have had an early written script. They also were extremely aggressive and drove the Keraits east to become the immediate neighbors of the Mongols.

- The Keraits had originally dwelled in the Altai Mountains, regions that were once home to the Turks. The Naimans pushed the Keraits up against the Mongols. The Keraits were mainly Nestorian Christians, and there was much intermarriage between them and the Mongol tribes.

An Unstable Political Situation

- All these tribes were loosely affiliated. They spoke Mongol languages or Turkish languages with a heavy Mongol component. They all had been in contact with the Chinese world to some degree.

- Politically, the situation was very unstable. Both Jin emperors and Song emperors wanted to incite wars among the tribes and keep them all weak. This allowed the Jin emperors to posture as masters of the steppes.

- But actually what the Jin emperors did—in significant contrast to the Khitan emperors—was to create the conditions that would allow for someone like Genghis Khan to emerge. He would come forward to unite the tribes engaged in incessant tribal warfare provoked by subsidies and alliances of the Jin emperors.

The Secret History of the Mongols

- Scholars have a number of sources about the life of Genghis Khan. *The Secret History of the Mongols*, written shortly after his death in 1227, was a significant work that presented much valuable information about the early life of the great conqueror. It was a long narrative account written from a nomadic perspective.

- Another important work was from the Muslim polymath **Rashid al-Din**. He wrote at the court of Hulagu, a grandson of Genghis Khan, and his work was based in large part on the *Secret History*. He also interviewed eyewitnesses about later Mongol history.

- Another key source was **Juvayni**, a native of Khurasan, or eastern Iran. Juvayni wrote a universal history and was an eyewitness to the sack of Baghdad in 1258.

The Yassa

- A significant work put together in Genghis Khan's own time was the codification of Mongol customs, known as the **Yassa**. This crucial work would have major ramifications for the Islamic world on questions of religious, as opposed to political, authority.

- The Yassa comprised rulings that Genghis Khan dictated later in life that came to synthesize political customs and traditions of the Mongols. These rulings reveal the very pragmatic and meticulous mind of Genghis Khan and give us insight into the Great Khan who would command expeditions that required remarkable strategic and logistical preparation.

Genghis Khan: Personal Life

- During his difficult formative years, Genghis Khan came to trust people based on their talent and their loyalty to him. His commanders and officers were great generals—the so-called Four Dogs of War. None of them gained his position based on his ethnicity or religion. What mattered was loyalty to the khan and clan.

- Genghis Khan was clearly personally brave, receiving wounds during sieges. He led by example, inspiring the tribes to follow him on wild, bold, and daring—even foolhardy—expeditions.

- In personal habits, he was quite modest. He shared the hardships of his men, and he enriched them with gifts: brides from foreign conquests, bolts of silk, silver, horses. Genghis Khan saw such patronage as simply a way to power. He never made the mistake of confusing the trappings of power with the reality of power.

- He lived in a simple tent. Although there were reports of his keeping huge harems, those conquered brides were just political tools. The only woman who really mattered to him was his first and only wife, **Börte**, a clever girl and the mother of his four sons. Overall, he was a conqueror, a ruler, whom the great tribes could admire and follow.

Genghis Khan: Political Life

- To his rivals, Genghis Khan was a terror. They saw him as the fearsome embodiment of the barbarian of the steppes. He terrorized his rivals with deliberate and calculated atrocities.

- These atrocities had a strategic goal: to confuse the enemy and frighten cities into immediate submission. Even by the standards of the rules of war during the 13th century, Genghis Khan, his sons, and grandsons waged war on a scale hitherto unseen. He terrorized the Chinese, the Muslim, and the Christian worlds.

- Genghis Khan also created a vision of world conquest by the time of his death. He was able to transmit this vision to his sons and grandsons, who proved very worthy successors.

Early Life of Genghis Khan
- When Temujin was born in 1162, in the Mongol heartland, his father, Yesugei, was a minor leader of a clan, probably a vassal of the Jin emperor. He arranged for a marriage for Temujin with a girl named Börte, who represented an important political alliance in the clan.

- Temujin's father was subsequently poisoned by the Tatars. When his father died, his clan forced the family into the forest. In those dire circumstances, Temujin learned resourcefulness—and he never forgave the Tatars.

- He gained a reputation as a great leader and began to raid the flocks and horses of Tatars and other tribes. By around 1180, when he was about 18, he had gathered around him a number of young Mongols who admired and followed him.

- That brought Temujin to the attention of the leader of the Keraits, **Wang Khan**, who took Temujin in as his subordinate and commander. Temujin also cemented relations with another important Mongol prince, **Jamukha**, and together they began to raid and attack opposing tribes in the late 1190s.

- A Merkit tribe kidnapped Börte. In fact, Temujin and Börte's first son, **Jochi**, is thought to have been the son of a Merkit prince, fathered when Börte was in captivity. Genghis Khan, however, accepted this boy as his firstborn.

Decisive Early Battles
- Temujin won great acclaim by bringing back his wife and by challenging the Merkits. In the ensuing tribal wars between Temujin and the other tribes on the Eurasian steppes, Jamukha became increasingly jealous, and the two friends fell out.

- That rift climaxed in a battle fought on the eastern steppes in 1230, in which the Tatars and their allies were decisively defeated. Temujin massacred the Tatars.

- Thereafter, Temujin and his patron, Wang Khan, fell out, and Wang Khan allied with Jamukha. There was a second great battle in which Temujin was defeated. However, he managed to rally in late 1203 and defeat and capture Jamukha, whom he executed.

The Great Khan

- By 1203–1204, these victories had cemented Temujin's domination on the steppes. To the Jin and Song emperors, this was just the usual tribal warfare. What they did not realize was that the victories of Temujin put in power a man who was without a doubt a military genius.

- In 1206, among the sacred mountains of central Mongolia, Temujin summoned a great assembly, known as the *kurultai*. The kurultai

The *kurultai*—an assembly of tribal leaders—was held near the sacred mountains of central Mongolia; there, Temujin was proclaimed "Universal Lord": Genghis Khan.

was a significant religious event that gathered all the leading men of the tribes and clans.

- The representatives of all the tribes now proclaimed Temujin as Genghis Khan, or "Universal Lord." This marked a major milestone; Genghis Khan now had not only the power of the tribes of the Eurasian steppes but also the vision and the means to organize these tribes into an effective imperial army and undertake world conquest.

Important Terms

kurultai: The national council of Mongols summoned to elect the khan or to declare war or conclude a peace.

Yassa: Customary Mongol law codified by Genghis Khan; it exalted the authority of the khan over all other legal and religious authorities.

Names to Know

Börte (1161–1230): Principal wife of Genghis Khan. She was affianced to marry him to link their clans, but around 1180, she was abducted by the Merkits; eight months later, she was rescued by Genghis Khan and married. It was widely believed that her first son, Jochi, was the son of Börte's captor, Chilger Bökh. She bore Genghis Khan three sons: Chagatai, Ögödei, and Tolui. Both Genghis Khan and Ögödei valued her for her shrewd judgment.

Jamukha (c. 1165–1206): Mongol prince; the sworn brother and then rival of Temujin, Genghis Khan. In 1197–1202, he fought against Temujin and Wang Khan and, in 1203, in alliance with Wang Khan, defeated Temujin at the Battle of Baljuna. Temujin, however, later rallied and defeated Jamukha.

Jochi (1181–1227): Mongol prince; the first son of Genghis Khan and Börte, but he was suspected to be the son of the Merkit warrior Chilger Bökh, who had held Börte captive for eight months. Genghis Khan accepted Jochi as his son. Jochi, while personally brave, was perceived as lacking the qualities of a khan. He also had quarreled with his brother Chagatai during the

Khwarezmian campaign in 1220. Hence, Genghis Khan decided to assign to Jochi the western *ulus*. Because Jochi predeceased his father, Jochi's domain (the future Golden Horde) was assigned to his son Batu.

Juvayni (1226–1283): Persian historian and native of Khurasan, served both Khwarezmian shah Jalal al-Din (1220–1231) and the Mongol khans Ögödei (1229–1241) and Hulagu (1256–1625). He wrote his *History of the World Conqueror* based on contemporary sources. He witnessed the sack of Baghdad, and he twice visited the court at Karakorum.

Rashid al-Din (1247–1318): Persian polymath and scholar; was a Jewish convert to Islam and native of Hamadan. At the ilkhanate court, he wrote an encyclopedic history of the Islamic world, *Jami' al-tawarikh*, in which he made extensive use of Chinese sources and the *Secret History of the Mongols*. He also translated Buddhist texts and Chinese works on statecraft into Persian.

Wang Khan (d. 1203; r. c. 1175–1203): Khan of the Keraits. His personal name was Toghrul; in 1197, he received the Chinese title Wang ("King") from the Jin (Jurchen) emperor Zhangzong (1189–1208). The sworn brother of Yesugei, the father of Temujin, he received Temujin into his service in 1180. He supported Temujin against Jamukha, but in 1203, he switched his loyalty to Jamukha. Temujin captured the Kerait encampment, and Wang Khan fled and was slain by the Naimans.

Suggested Reading

Golden, "Inner Asia c. 1200."

Jackson, "The Mongol Age in Eastern Inner Asia."

Mote, *Imperial China, 900–1800.*

Ratchnevsky, *Genghis Khan: His Life and Legacy.*

Rossabi, *The Mongols and Global History.*

Saunders, *The History of the Mongol Conquests.*

Weatherford, *Genghis Khan and the Making of the Modern World.*

1. How did the Mongols transform themselves into nomads? In what ways did they live a typical nomadic way of life? In what ways were they exceptional?

2. What are the sources on Genghis Khan? What are their limitations and virtues? What are the images about Genghis Khan that emerged from these accounts?

3. What were the political, social, and economic conditions in Mongolia at the time of the birth of Temujin? How did these conditions allow for the unification of the nomadic tribes? How important were the policies of the Jurchen emperors of the Jin Dynasty in this process?

4. How did his early life of survival and adventure hone the skills of Temujin as a great leader? At what point did Temujin emerge as the khan who could unite the tribes? What advantages did he and the Mongols possess in 1206 so that they could wage campaigns of world conquest?

The Mongols
Lecture 27—Transcript

In this lecture, I want to pick up where we left off, and that is to bring on the Mongols. They will occupy center stage now for really most of the rest of the course. As I mentioned at the start of previous lectures, the Mongols in some ways were extraordinary; in other ways, they were more typical nomads pursing the same type of life and also the same nomadic way of war. We should start looking at who these people were at the time that Temujin— and that was the personal name of Genghis Khan—united the different Mongol tribes into a new confederation and launched a remarkable career of world conquest.

The Mongols spoke a distinct agglutinative language that is part of that Altaic language family, which takes its name from the Altai Mountains where supposedly the Turks, the Mongols, Tanguts, and others descended from; anyway, that is what comes through the legendary history. The language is distinct; it is distinct enough from Turkish that it represents a separate language group. It shows a lot of the same features as Turkish. For one, everything is done with suffixes in order to indicate grammar; various functions in Indo-European languages that would be done by prefixes, prepositions, it is done by suffixes. In addition, it shows the same principles of vowel harmony. There are a lot of loan words that have been taken from Turkish that have entered into the Mongolian languages, and these loan words indicate that Mongols and Turks have long been in association with each other. They were both nomadic peoples, so many of the same ideas were passed from the Turks to the Mongols. Some Turks today would essentially regard the Mongols as nothing more than cousins speaking a language that is almost Turkish, not quite there. However, there are features in the language that suggest that it has closer affiliations with Chinese Tibetan languages; and some scholars would go so far as to argue that Mongolian speakers had a common parent language in the distant past with, say, Japanese and Korean.

What is significant, though, is that by the time Temujin was born—and that would be around 1162; we are not quite sure of his birthdate, there are several possibilities, but 1162 is a good guess—when he was born, the Mongols had long since adopted a nomadic way of life. They had a very, very clear sense of who they were. There was a long legendary history that was known by the time of Temujin's birth, and this history or these legends of a mythical ancestor sprung from a wolf and a doe—that complete mismatch that created a heroic eponymous hero who founded the Mongol race and had valiant children and all of these legends—these came out of the stories preserved in what is known as *The Secret History of the Mongols*, a work that was written shortly after the death of Genghis Khan. We will discuss that work in greater detail, but it preserves many, many ancient traditions even though the work is later; it was actually redacted and edited in the reign of the second Khan, Ögedei, who came to the throne in 1229.

We also have large numbers of inscriptions that have come down from the reign of Kublai Khan, who ruled from 1260–1294 and conquered China. He made sure that a distinct script was devised so that Mongolian could be put up as an administrative and commemorative language in China, no doubt to the great ire and discontent to the Confucian scholar class, the so-called *shi* who had gone through the examination system. The Mongols had a very, very distinct language; they had a very distinct sense of themselves. They also had rather limited contact with the Chinese civilization, as far as we can see. They were subjects of the Khitan emperors and then later of the Jin emperors. When Temujin was born in 1162, there would have been very little notice taken of the Mongol tribes because Temujin's tribe and clan were rather minor. The Mongols shared the eastern steppes with a group of neighbors, other tribes, some of them speaking Mongol, others of them speaking Turkish; and very often they are simply lumped together as Turko-Mongolian speakers because the connections are so close.

At the time of Temujin's birth in 1162, the most important tribe would have been the Tatars. The Tatars are better known by a corruption of that name, Tartars; and that is the name that Christian authors use for them. When the Mongols invaded Russia in 1236 and they blitz the Russian cities and overrun Eastern Europe, they broke into Central Europe and that was a misunderstanding of the name. The Tatars are really a distinct different people. They spoke probably a version of Turkish and they dwelled in the steppes to the east of the Mongols and probably represented the most powerful tribe on the steppes in 1162. They were in close contact with the Jin emperors, and Chinese officials knew about them; they would have been connected by trade routes; and they could field probably the largest nomadic cavalry on the steppes at the time of Temujin's birth. The Tatars—or under their misnomer, the Tartars in the Western sources; and that is because they were associated with Tartarus, hell, in the Classical sources—they represented a major power. The Tatars were essentially dwelling south and west of the Mongols, and they were reckoned to have something like 70,000 warriors; and by calculating the numbers you are looking at a population of maybe 150,000–200,000 people, since almost every male from the age of 0–60 could ride.

Furthermore, the Tatars were extremely aggressive and they fought for control of the Kerulen River valley, which is regarded as a sacred valley to the Mongols and the Tatars both. They had been in long association with China. They had received silks and various gifts from the Chinese emperor—first the Song, later the Jin emperors—and therefore the Tatars represented perhaps one of the most civilized tribes on the eastern steppes, and really ones that could be taken seriously by the Chinese, either the Jin or Song emperors. To the northeast of the Mongols was another important tribe known as the Merkits. They were regarded as some of the best warriors on the steppes. They were not as numerous as the Tatars, but they were notorious for stealing wives and horses; in fact, they would end up stealing the wife-to-be of Genghis Khan early in his career. They, too, were nomads, and they centered their flocks around that great glacial lake known as Lake Baikal; that would today be in Russian Siberian possessions, which contained something like 20 percent of the world's fresh water in that one place. The Merkits followed shamans. They had not been exposed as much to Chinese civilization; although later on we find a number of them were Nestorian Christians.

On the western steppes were the Oirats. They dwelled in a forest steppe zone; regarded as great hunters as well as herders. Further west were also the Naimans. The Naimans were perhaps the second most important tribe in Mongolia in 1162. The Naimans and the Tatars would both oppose the unification of the tribes by Genghis Khan, or Temujin to use his name; they were Buddhists. Because of their location, which put them north of the Tarim Basin, they had been visited by many Uighur merchants. They were familiar with Buddhism; they may have had an early written script. They certainly had close contacts with the Chinese Empire, and the Song and Jin emperors both courted the Naimans as potential allies. They also were extremely aggressive, and they drove a tribe known as the Keraits east to become the immediate neighbors of the Mongols. The Keraits had originally dwelled in the Altai Mountain region, the regions that had once been the home of the Turks; and they ended up being pushed smack up against the Mongols compliments of the Naimans, and that explains why the Keraits and Mongols came together very closely. They were largely Nestorian Christians, and there would be a great deal of intermarriage between that tribe and the Mongol tribe proper.

All of these tribes were loosely affiliated. They spoke Mongol languages or Turkish languages with a very heavy Mongol component. They all had been to some degree in contact with the Chinese world. The situation politically was very unstable; and this is because both Jin emperors and Song emperors wanted to incite wars among the tribes and keep them all weak. This allowed the Jin emperors to posture as masters of the steppes; but actually what the Jin emperors did—and this was a significant contrast from the Khitan emperors—the Jin emperors created the conditions that would allow for someone like Genghis Khan to emerge to unite the tribes who were engaged in constant tribal warfare, egged on by subsidies and alliances of the Jin emperors.

This gets us to Genghis Khan himself, and exactly what made the difference with his birth in 1162. We have a number of sources about him. These sources above all include the *Secret History*. *The Secret History of the Mongols*, I mentioned to you earlier, was a very important work. It was written shortly after his death in 1227; it was later edited. It is known in a lot of Chinese versions, actually. That work gives us a great deal of information about the early life of Genghis Khan. It is the basis for many of the popular histories that have circulated, and there are several very good ones out there right now; and they draw that information out of the *Secret History*, the very turbulent and adventurous life that Genghis experienced from about age 9 to age 18.

We have other important works from the Muslim world. One of them is the great polymath, his name was Rashid ad-Din. He wrote at the court of

Hulagu, who was a grandson of Genghis Khan; and his work was based in large part on the *Secret History*. He also interviewed eyewitnesses about the later Mongol history, because Rashid ad-Din wrote essentially a universal history ending with the great Mongol conquest; and his information, we are able to use to check against the *Secret History*. One other important source is a fellow by the name of Juvaini or Ata al-Malik Juvaini. He was a native from Khurasan; that is, eastern Iran, which is the center of so much of Iranian civilization. Again, he wrote another one of these universal histories. He was an eyewitness, by the way, to the sack of Baghdad in 1258, which we started this course with. These sources give us an unusual amount of information on Genghis Khan, as well as for the first time a long narrative account written from a nomadic perspective, and that is the *Secret History*. We also have a painting, a portrait of Genghis Khan that has come down to us, which is a lifetime portrait done in his life by probably a Chinese artist. The information we have on Genghis Khan gives us an insight to the man that we do not have for previous steppe conquerors. This would include figures such as Attila the Hun or Modu Chanyu, the great leader of the Xiongnu. We have just very, very brief character sketches of these rulers written by essentially hostile sources.

We have another important work that, again, was put together in Genghis Khan's own time; that was the codification of Mongol customs, known as the *yassa*. There are several names it was known by. This work was very, very important. It would have major ramifications especially for the Islamic world on questions of religious as opposed to political authority. These were rulings that Genghis Khan dictated later in life that came to synthesize the various political customs and traditions of the Mongols, and you can see in the rulings and the way they were organized the very pragmatic and meticulous mind of Genghis Khan. It gives us an insight into the Great Khan who would command expeditions that required remarkable strategic and logistical preparation. That same mind is at work in putting together the legal traditions of the *yassa*.

Chinese, Muslim, Christian sources give us more information; clearly the Mongols had an immense impact. These sources tend to be largely hostile; they came through various chronicles, universal histories. We will have accounts later, after Genghis's death, from different Western envoys arriving from the papacy trying to convert the Mongols; the most important one will be Giovanni Carpini and then a fellow named William of Rubruck, who was actually sent by Saint Louis the Pious of France. We have an unusually excellent set of sources, and we got a portrait of what the man looked like.

Genghis Khan was without a doubt, in my opinion, a genius; or at least a military genius, let us qualify a bit. Many scholars might find this a bit unsettling, especially putting stress on social and wider events. I conclude this by looking at the sources that Genghis Khan really made the difference and was responsible for the exceptional role played by the Mongols, and he was followed by remarkable sons and even more brilliant grandsons. I could be accused a bit of hero worship or even being an apologist, just as one could say of a figure like Alexander the Great; but there is no way of disputing the fact that the Mongol Empire was largely the creation of Genghis Khan and his family. To be sure, they would commit atrocities on a scale that is really quite unimagined; the same could be said of Alexander the Great and other great conquerors. But looking at what he had and what he achieved, you have to grant him that special role, that special position, in the gallery of great commanders. He inspired his men. This came from a very, very difficult life where he came very, very quickly in those formative years to trust people based on their talent and their loyalty to him. He always selected his commanders and officers, his great generals, the so-called "Four Dogs of War," of which probably the best was Subutai. These were men personally loyal to Genghis Khan—Temujin in his earlier career—and none of them gained their position based on necessarily their ethnicity, their religion, or anything else. What mattered was loyalty to the khan; and clan and other considerations overrode that.

He was clearly personally brave. The Persian author Giovanni reports of his bravery in the campaign against Khurasan from 1219–1220 when Genghis Khan himself excelled in the fighting. There are repeated reports of him receiving wounds during sieges; one very important one in 1215 when he attacked the Jin Empire. He followed by example and inspired the various tribes to go with him on these wild and some would say daring, even bold and foolhardy, expeditions.

In personal habits, he was really quite modest. He shared the hardships of his men and he enriched them with all sorts of gifts. These included various brides from foreign conquests, bolts of silk, silver, horses taken in the early thefts against other tribes. In that sense, Genghis Khan saw wealth as simply a way to power. He himself never made the mistake—which some of his successors did, particularly his son Ögedei—of confusing the trappings of power with the reality of power. He lived in quite a simple tent. Yes, there are reports of him keeping huge harems—all these wagons going across the steppes with the conquered brides—those were political; they really meant very little. The only woman that really mattered to him was his first and only real wife, Börte, a very, very clever girl and the mother of his four sons. Overall, he was a conqueror, a ruler, whom the great tribes could just admire and follow.

To his rivals, he was a terror. They saw him as the absolute embodiment of the barbarian off the steppes. He terrorized his rivals with deliberate and calculated atrocities; we will talk about some of these in great detail. At times, you get the impression that Genghis Khan was looking for excuses to destroy cities, particularly in the Muslim world. There were several instances of this happening in the conquest of Transoxiana where the death of a favorite grandson, a son-in-law, or a favorite general was an excuse to essentially level the city and kill every living creature in it. To be sure, these atrocities had a strategic goal: to terrorize, confuse the rivals; to frighten many cities into submission immediately. But on the scale of the rules of war of the period of the 13th century—and believe me, there was no set of Geneva rules of convention—even by the tough set of rules of the 13th century, Genghis Khan, his sons, and grandsons waged war violently on a scale that really hitherto had not been seen and certainly terrorized the Chinese, the Muslim, and the Christian worlds.

Even so, these tribes, the Mongols and the Turks, saw Genghis Khan as essentially the favorite of Tengri; that is, the God of Heaven, the universal god in the shamanist tradition who ruled over all. He was seen to have that favor; it would be the equivalent to the Mandate of Heaven to the Chinese emperor, except it was won by ferocious ability on the battlefield and personal bravery. He also created a vision of world conquest by the time of his death, and this vision he was able to transmit to his sons and grandsons, who proved very, very worthy successors.

This man whom we can reconstruct, we can actually get a sense of what he was like from the *Secret History* and from the other sources, really was someone who quite by chance ended up uniting the tribes. When he was born in 1162 in the Mongol heartland, his father was a rather minor leader of a clan and not particularly well known, Yesugei was his name. He had probably been a vassal of the Jin emperors. He arranged for a marriage for Temujin very, very early in Temujin's life with a girl called Börte who represented a very important political alliance in the clan. When he went to cut the deal with the local clans, he left Temujin there to be reared by his future in-laws. He returned to his clan, and enroute he fell in with some Tatars or Tartars who poisoned him—actually they administered a slow poisoning—and by the time he returned home, he was fast dying and summoned Temujin to his deathbed. Temujin arrived; he was probably around age nine at the time when this happened. When his father died, the clan essentially set the interests of Temujin and his siblings aside; and so the widow, Hoelun, and her children were forced into the forest and living really on small mammals and fish for the formative years, for the next eight or nine years.

Temujin in that situation learned resourcefulness. He never forgave the Tatars for this. He gained a reputation as a great leader and began to raid the flocks and the horses of Tatars and other tribes. Around 1180, when he was about 18 years of age, he was such an impressive figure he had collected around him a number of young Mongols who knew that if they hung out with Temujin their position was assured. That brought Temujin to the attention of the leader of the Keraits—those are the neighbors to the Mongols; and the ruler of the Keraits styled himself with a Chinese title, Wang Khan, but he was better known by his personal name, Toghrul Khan—and he took Temujin in as essentially his subordinate and commander. Temujin also cemented relations with another important Mongol prince, Jamukha, and together they began to raid and attack in the late 1190s the opposing tribes. One was to take back Temujin's wife-to-be, Börte. When Temujin came to the attention of Toghrul Khan, the marriage was to be celebrated. In the course of going back to celebrate the marriage, a bunch of Merkits descended on the train. Börte told Genghis Khan or Temujin, "Get out of here, you can always come back and rescue me later." He did so with the help of Jamukha and the Keraits, and apparently the first son to the couple, Temujin and Börte, the first son named Jochi, is thought to have been actually the son of a Merkit prince when Börte was in captivity; and the name literally means "guest." Genghis Khan, however, accepted this boy as the firstborn, as his own, although there was always the sort of sense that Jochi's parentage was in question; and his interest would be set aside later in the succession in 1227 in favor for one of the younger sons who clearly was the son of Börte and Temujin.

Temujin won by great credit by bringing back his wife, by challenging the Merkits; and in the ensuing tribal wars between Temujin and the other tribes on the Eurasian steppes, Jamukha became increasingly jealous. The two friends fell out; and in 1202, Temujin and Toghrul Khan had to face a coalition not only of the other tribes, but of disaffected Mongols who are following Jamukha. That climaxed in a great battle fought somewhere on the eastern steppes in 1203 in which the Tatars and their various allies were decisively defeated. Temujin made sure to punish those Tatars. There was a massacre conducted of the soldiers who were captured; the women were clearly taken over. It was sort of a preview as to the type of massacres that would be committed by the Mongol armies. It was more than just an issue of tribal warfare; there was a strong sense of vengeance. These guys had poisoned dad and now they were going to pay for it. Temujin never forgot or forgave an insult or any ill action committed against the imperial family.

However, very quickly, Temujin and his patron Toghrul Khan fell out. Toghrul Khan allied with Jamukha. There was a second great battle in which Temujin was defeated; but he managed to rally in late 1203, defeat Jamukha, capture Jamukha, who eventually was taken before Temujin and in the end executed, even though Temujin was really, really close to forgiving his old comrade in arms. These victories, by 1203–1204, had cemented Temujin's domination on the steppes. To the Jin emperors and even the more remote and distant Song emperors, these were just another set of a bunch of tribal warfare. It did not really matter much who controlled what tribe over another. This fellow Temujin, the Mongols, and the Keraits had now knocked out the Tatars and other tribes, the Merkits, we can do business with this new group.

What they did not realize was that the victory of Temujin had put in power a man in his mid 40s who was without a doubt a military genius. In 1206, at the great valleys—the Selenge Valley and the Onon Valley where there are very sacred mountains; this is in Central Mongolia today—Temujin summoned a great assembly. This is known in the Mongol texts as the *kurultai*. The *kurultai* was not a democratic assembly; it was an assembly of all the leading princes, the great men of the tribes and the clans. They came together. There was a celebration of ancestral rites, sacrifices; generally animal sacrifices to the spirit of the ancestors. There was the drinking of *kumis*, or *qumish* in the Turkish form of the word, which is the fermented mare's milk. Temujin, in effect, presided over this great religious event; and the assembly of Mongols, the representatives of all the tribes, now proclaimed Temujin as Genghis Khan, or universal lord, or as they liked to say the universal lord of all those who dwell within the felt tents. This marked a major departure because Genghis Khan now had not only the power of the various tribes of the Eurasian steppes, but also the vision and the means to organize these tribes into an effective imperial army and undertake world conquest.

Conquests of Genghis Khan
Lecture 28

In this lecture, we will turn to the events in Genghis Khan's career after the *kurultai* of 1206, when Temujin was declared Genghis Khan, universal lord of the nomads. At this time, he was about 44 years old. He had attained a primacy on the Eurasian steppes not seen since the Xiongnu, when Modu Chanyu had united the tribes, and then again when Bumin, the first of the Gök Turk khagans, created his vast empire.

The Shaman Tradition

- Throughout his life, Genghis Khan took great care to consult the shamans. He was attended in 1206 by a very important shaman, **Kokchu**, who actually predicted the universal domain of Genghis Khan.

- Kokchu, as many shamans, was believed to enter trances in which he would mount a world tree and have visions of the future. These notions were ancient and characteristic of the steppe nomads. Even when they had embraced religion, such as Buddhism, Christianity, or Islam, many Mongol and Turkic peoples always had an underlying trust in shamans.

- Genghis Khan was a pragmatist in religious matters—again, characteristic of the steppe peoples. He treated all holy men— Nestorian Christians, Islamic imams, Sufi mystics, and Daoist monks—as if they were shamans.

- Whoever had access to or contact with the divine powers should be paid attention to and should be respected, he believed. That was one of the peculiarities about the Mongol conquest. Although there was wholesale looting of religious shrines, at the same time, there was deep respect paid to holy men as legitimate representations of divine power.

Reorganization of the Army

- In 1206, Genghis Khan was in a position to carry out a reorganization of his army. By this time, he had under his control most of the tribes of the eastern steppes.

- Genghis Khan organized his army by divisions of 10. This was an old system that went back at least to the Xiongnu. Units were built on multiples of 10, 100, 1,000; and the key unit was the 10,000 unit known as the **tumen**.

- The tumen was a military formation that some would compare to Napoleon's corps or to a Roman legion. It was a military force capable of operating as an independent unit, as a small army. The Turkish Mongolian word for army is ***ordu***, from which we get the word *horde*.

The Mongols and the Turks saw Genghis Khan as essentially the favorite of Tengri, the universal god in the shamanist tradition who rules over all.

- Importantly, the Mongol hordes referred to separate tumens in which the men were recruited based on their loyalty, their ability, and their courage—not on clan and tribal affiliations. This was a significant distinction.

- Genghis Khan replaced the loyalty based on ethnic ties with a new loyalty: All these men were now *anda*, or sworn brothers to the Great Khan. The officers knew that promotion meant distinction on the battlefield and loyalty to the khagan.

- By 1227, literary sources tell us that there were 129 tumen—more than a million who acknowledged Genghis Khan as their lord.

Keys to Military Success

- In 1219, Genghis Khan waged his most ambitious war of conquest against the shah of Khurasan, **Ala al-Din Muhammad**, or Muhammad Shah. This was a battle for control of Iran and Transoxania. The action entailed moving a large army from the tent city of Mongolia, **Karakorum**, to the banks of the Jaxartes—about 3,500 miles across the steppes.

- Genghis Khan organized this march meticulously. Three columns swept across the steppes, which were cleared of all tribes and animals, leaving plenty of fodder. The army moved out in early spring. Every warrior had 5 to 10 extra horses as remounts. The army appeared much larger than it was. The Mongol main force, a tumen, could cover 40 miles in a day or more; it was a spectacular cavalry.

- More than any other world conqueror, Genghis Khan had access to enormous amounts of information. All this was used for planning, logistics, strategy, and movement of forces. For example, the best mapmakers in 1227 were found in Karakorum.

Control of the Tarim Basin

- In the course of fighting the Xi Xia in the Tibetan highlands, Genghis Khan learned to appreciate the importance of siege warfare. In fact, there were a couple of embarrassing setbacks; the Xi Xia diverted a river that almost flooded out Genghis Khan's camp.

- After that, he saw the need for engineers and began to recruit northern Chinese engineers into a corps of 1,000 that would accompany the army wherever it went.

- The war with the Xi Xia concluded with a treaty. The Xi Xia agreed to pay tribute, and they became a crucial component in providing translators and administrators for the emerging Mongol Empire. That gave Genghis Khan control of the caravan routes into the Tarim Basin.

Control of Northern China

- Genghis Khan's next objective was the Jin Empire. He wanted to control the regions of Manchuria and the northern Chinese provinces, which were extremely valuable not only for their millet production but also for the industrial manufacture of armaments.

- The result was another war. From 1212 to 1215, the Mongols carried out a methodical conquest of the northern domains of the Jin emperor. What was really important was the siege of the future city of Beijing.

- The capture of the Jin capital essentially sealed Genghis Khan's control of northern China. The Jin were no longer a serious threat, and the Song emperors had neither the means nor the inclination to contest the conquest of northern China and the western areas. Genghis Khan now controlled the key borderlands of China.

At the Threshold of the Islamic World

- Genghis Khan also controlled the trade routes through which silk would move and bring in profits. He did, however, have to clean up the western steppes. Various Mongol dissidents had fled into the Kara-Khitan Empire and had carried out raids against the Mongol domains.

- Pacifying the area and bringing it under control required a Mongol force under **Jebe**. This effort was aided by the fact that the Mongols who had taken over the Kara-Khitan Empire proved very unpopular rulers. They had become enthusiastic Buddhists and had persecuted the Muslim populations, particularly in the Tarim Basin.

- That victory, in 1218, brought the Mongol Empire to the central steppes. Genghis Khan now stood at the threshold of Transoxania, in the Islamic world.

Muhammad Shah

- At that time, Transoxania and Iran were ruled by Muhammad Shah. An ill-advised incident broke out that involved a Mongol caravan. Muhammad Shah's agents arrested several merchants as spies. Genghis Khan then wrote to Muhammad Shah.

- Muhammad Shah essentially treated Genghis Khan as a subordinate, as some sort of local barbarian ruler, and dismissed the incident altogether. However, he was perfectly aware that Genghis Khan was gaining control of the steppes.

- Muhammad Shah depended on Mamluks, largely recruited from different Turkish tribes, but the Mongol khagan was set to interrupt the flow of recruits. A conflict was probably inevitable, and this incident gave Genghis Khan an excuse to mobilize the Mongol army.

Invasion of the Islamic World

- In 1219, Genghis Khan set out on his most important campaign, which was a turning point: the invasion of the Islamic world. It was the largest display of nomadic power ever seen on the steppes—to be repeated a few times thereafter.

- Even though Muhammad Shah had a large army, he lacked the same kind of cavalry, and he made the mistake of dispersing his forces. The Mongol forces converged on the city of Otrar and savagely sacked it. The population was massacred.

- The army of Muhammad Shah was just not up to the task. His field forces were swept away, and in 1219–1220, the campaigns quickly become a war of sieges. Genghis Khan then made a beeline to Bukhara, also taken in a ruthless sack.

- Samarkand, which was held by a Turkish garrison, was captured, as well. The civilian population was largely massacred; craftsmen and others that were selected for serving the Mongol khagan were sent back to Mongolia.

- From 1219 to 1220, the caravan cities of Iran, Transoxiana, and into Afghanistan fell into the hands of the Mongol armies. Muhammad Shah fled west and eventually died in exile on an island in the Caspian Sea.

Genghis Khan's Successor: Ögödei

- Genghis Khan detached two tumen, 20,000 men, to pursue the remnants of the army of Khurasan. They carried out campaigns into Russia and eventually circled back and brought information of the lands of the west.

- The son of Muhammad Shah fled to India and tried to raise forces, but Genghis Khan's army decisively defeated his army on the Indus.

- By 1221, the lands of eastern Islam had been ransacked and leveled by the Mongol army. It was a stunningly quick and incredibly savage conquest. The result was that the Mongols had burst into the Islamic world as an absolute terror, and the Islamic world was shocked.

- In the meantime, Genghis Khan was able to make his way back to Mongolia. In the course of the campaign, he had decided that the succession would fall to his third son, Ögödei, who had distinguished himself in the campaigns.

- When Genghis Khan died in 1227, he ruled a far greater empire than any other steppe conqueror. He had created a vast imperial army and, above all, left a clear vision of world conquest that was now transmitted to his sons and successors.

Important Terms

anda: Sworn brothers in Turkish and Mongolian society.

Karakorum: Located on the Orkhon River, the political capital of the Mongol Empire in 1225–1260.

ordu: Turko-Mongolian army or military encampment.

tumen: Mongol military unit of 10,000 soldiers.

Names to Know

Ala al-Din Muhammad (r. 1200–1220): Shah of Khwarezm; conquered Iran from the Seljuk Turks in 1205. By 1217, he had secured Transoxania, assumed the title shah, and extended his unwanted protection over the Abbasid caliph al-Nasir. In 1218, he provoked a war with Genghis Khan, who overran the Khwarezmian Empire in 1219–1220. Muhammad Shah died a fugitive on an island in the Caspian Sea near Abaskun.

Jebe (d. 1225): Mongol general; born as Zurgadai but received his nickname Jebe ("Arrow") when he boldly confessed that he had accidentally wounded Genghis Khan in battle in 1201. He was a trusted field commander and, thus, he shared with Subutai command of the western expedition in 1221–1223.

Kokchu (d. 1206): Shaman and advisor to Genghis Khan; credited with great influence over the khan. He was executed on grounds of treachery based on information supplied by Börte, principal wife of Genghis Khan.

Suggested Reading

Brian, "The Mongols of Central Asia from Chinggis Khan's Invasion to the Rise of Temür."

Golden, "Inner Asia c. 1200."

Ratchnevsky, *Genghis Khan: His Life and Legacy.*

Rossabi, *The Mongols and Global History.*

Saunders, *The History of the Mongol Conquests.*

Weatherford, *Genghis Khan and the Making of the Modern World.*

Questions to Consider

1. What was the symbolic and practical significance of the election of Temujin as Genghis Khan by the *kurultai* in 1206? How did the peoples of the eastern Eurasian steppes perceive this act? What were the perceptions of the emperors of the Xi Xia, Jin Empire, and Song China?

2. In what ways did Genghis Khan innovate in the nomadic way of war since the 6th century A.D.? What were the crucial elements that accounted for the success of Mongol armies in the 13th century? How much did Mongol success owe to the genius of Genghis Khan?

3. Why was Genghis Khan determined from 1210 to conquer the Jin emperors of Jurchen? How were his aims in northern China comparable to those of previous conquerors of the steppes? What accounted for his success in winning over Turkish and Khitan tribes?

4. How did the war against Muhammad Shah in 1219–1221 transform the Mongol Empire? What were the aims of Genghis Khan and his heirs upon their return to Karakorum in 1225?

5. What was the situation of the Mongol Empire on the death of Genghis Khan in 1227? In what ways was this new empire of the steppes exceptional from previous such empires? Was the rapid expansion of the empire after 1227 inevitable given the army, imperial organization, and vision Genghis Khan gave to his heirs?

Conquests of Genghis Khan
Lecture 28—Transcript

In this lecture, I want to pick up from our previous lecture; that ended in the spring of 1206, when Temujin was declared Genghis Khan, universal lord of all those nomads who dwelled within the felt tents. This was ratified effectively by a national assembly, the so-called *kurultai*. They met at the Onon River in view of a set of sacred mountains, the Khenti Mountains, which we regarded as the home of Tengri, the universal sky god.

At this point, our best guess is Genghis Khan—and we will refer to him now by his title universal lord—was somewhere around the age of 43 or 44. He had attained a primacy on the Eurasian steppes that no one had ever seen really since the Xiongnu, when Modu Chanyu had united the various tribes and then again when Bumin, the first of the Gök Turk khans, had created this vast empire. Considering the turns of events, the adventures, the difficulties of attaining that position, especially all the fighting in the 1180s and 1190s, most men would have been satisfied with that proclamation of universal lord and would have been content to rule over this great confederacy. Genghis Khan seemed so inclined, at least at the festivities. There was great consumption of mare's milk, the fermented mare's milk, the *kumis*. This was drunk by all the officers and commanders who in effect became an *anda*. An *anda* was a sworn brother; and Genghis Khan—before he was Genghis Khan, as Temujin—had actually exchanged *kumis* with Jamukha, his sworn brother and originally ally, later rival, hence the great reluctance on his part to order his execution when he finally defeated his old friend. What Genghis Khan did at the celebrations after his proclamation was to extend that idea of sworn brotherhood to all of his followers: the officers, known as *noyans* in Mongol, and even to the various members of the tribes who would serve in the reorganized Mongol army. That is because Genghis Khan put loyalty at a premium. He expected success and loyalty; fighting and dying in battle due to incompetence from mistakes was acceptable. He expected his officers to win. He expected his men to exert themselves the same way that he would have exerted himself. The punishments in the Mongol army were as harsh as could be. On the other hand, the awards were immense. The rewards could involve all sorts of advantages through conquests in the forms of silk and in the forms of horses, brides from foreign nations; all of this was the great loot that would come to the soldiers serving with Genghis Khan.

The ceremonies were also sanctified by various rites I discussed, by shamans. Genghis Khan throughout his life really took care to consult the shamans. He was attended in 1206 by a very important shaman who had actually served his dad, Kokchu. Kokchu actually predicted at the time of the proclamation the universal domain of Genghis Khan. Kokchu, as many shamans, was believed to enter trances in which he would mount a world tree on some kind of gray horse, have visions of the future. These types of notions were very ancient on the steppes. They characterized the belief of most Mongol and Turkic peoples, even when they had embraced religion such Buddhism, Christianity, or Islam. There was always this underlying trust in shamans. Kokchu made the mistake of trying to plot against Genghis Khan soon after the events of 1206. He was seized and executed; and when you execute a shaman or anyone of rank, the usual way of doing that was to roll the guy up in a carpet and then have the Mongol cavalry ride over you and essentially trample you to death. This was a punishment give to many defeated foes. The Mongols were very superstitious that if a man had great sacral power, contact with the other world, shedding his blood might be a pollution, might bring on bad luck or an evil eye—as modern Turks would say, katugas—and therefore this was the ceremonial punishment for trampling defeated foes who were usually rulers, who were regarded as some kind of sacral position or any kind of shamans who had crossed you.

Genghis Khan was also a pragmatist. In religious matters, this is again characteristic of the steppes. The various holy men he came into contact with, he treats them as if they were shamans. Nestorian monks, Islamic imams, Sufi mystics; there was even a report of him having a conversation with a Daoist monk when he was coming back from India after he had danced on the army of Jalal al-Din, the son of Muhammad Shah. All of this was part of the pragmatic outlook of any of the nomadic peoples of the steppes that whoever had access or contact with the divine powers should be paid attention to and should be respected. That was one of the peculiarities about the Mongol conquest: the wholesale looting of religious shrines, Christian, Buddhist, or Islamic; and yet, at the same time, respect paid to those shamans, Sufi mystics, monks who presented themselves at court and were received by the Mongol khan as a legitimate representation of divine power. It is a very, very curious aspect about the religious and political outlooks of all the Mongol khans.

Genghis Khan was also in a position in 1206 to carry out a reorganization of his army. These changes were probably already going on earlier; but in 1206, he had under his control most of the tribes of the eastern steppes. There were still some holdouts who had run into the Gök khan of the Kara Khitans far to the east; but we will take care of those guys later. With the various tribes, Genghis Khan made an important break. He organized his army by decimals of 10. This was an old system, it goes back at least to the Xiongnu; that is, units were built on multiples of 10, 100, 1000, and the key unit was the 10,000 unit known as the *tumen*. The *tumen* was a military formation that some would compare to Napoleon's corps or to a Roman legion. It was a military force capable of operating as an independent unit, as a small army. The Turkish Mongolian word for army is *ordu*, hence we get the word *horde*; the Mongol hordes really refers to separate army corps, a *tumen* of 10,000 men, or to use the Turkish plural the *tumenler*. That *tumen* was based on military units in which the men were recruited based on their loyalty, their ability, and their courage. They were not based on clan and tribal affiliations. This was a significant difference.

All of these early steppe nomadic empires as far as we can tell are built on the building blocks of ethnic units, clan units, or family, the assumption being that they fight under their ancient totems, they follow their particular leaders and shamans, and that was an almost indestructible unit. Genghis Khan now replaced that with a new loyalty; that is, all these men are now *anda*, they are sworn brothers to the great Khan, they have accepted their salt from Genghis Khan. That is an expression that comes into use in the 13th century: Any man who accepted the salt—a very valuable commodity, almost invariably obtained in trade with the sedentary civilizations—that was a way of saying that "I have accepted my service." It is a term that was used across the steppes. It survives actually in Mogul India as late as the 18th century as far as I know. The drinking of the fermented mare's milk, the accepting of salt, all of that bound together his soldiers.

The soldiers, therefore, were an imperial army, and they were recruited without regard to language, nationality, religion; Genghis Khan had no concern about that. He also formed the best men into a bodyguard; it was called the *kashik*. That bodyguard was more than just the 10,000 best Mongol warriors; that bodyguard was also the training ground for all of his generals and his officers at all levels. The Mongol army in some ways was very traditional; but in its organization, its discipline, and ethos, it was professional and imperial. The officers in general saw their loyalty to Genghis Khan. They knew that promotion meant distinction on the battlefield, loyalty to the khan. This made the difference, the reorganization of this army. By 1227, we are told by our literary sources that there were 129 *minghan*—that is, that tactical unit of 1,000 men—and if so, there may have been somewhere around a million or 750,000 peoples on the steppes who acknowledged Genghis Khan as their lord.

With this army, Genghis Khan, as I said, was quite satisfied. He had control of the steppes. In the course of time, as he moved beyond the steppes and encountered different foes, he would add to this army. Chinese engineers: When he ran into fighting cities in Northern China starting in 1209 and ending really in 1215; there were a number of important sieges, especially against the Jin emperors, and that meant he needed Chinese engineers to capture cities. He gained in his understanding of logistics, which also premised his strategies; his ability to move large numbers of men across the steppes. Again, that was that meticulous mind we see in his legal rulings, the *yassa*. In 1219, he waged his most ambitious war of conquest against the shah of Khurasan—his name was Muhammad Shah—and that was a battle for really control of Iran and Transoxiana. To move a great army from the tent city of Mongolia (that is, Karakorum) to the banks of the Jaxartes was about 3,500 miles across steppe. Genghis Khan organized this march meticulously. Three columns swept across the steppes. The steppes were cleared of all the tribes and animals so there was plenty of fodder. The army moved out early in spring. Every warrior had either 5 or 10 extra horses as remounts; and so the army looked much bigger than it actually way. That type of organization meant there were never problems of supply. There was always lots and lots of water available. Furthermore, the Mongol main force, a *tumen* maybe could cover maybe 40 miles in a day. Lead elements are known to have gone as fast as 50 miles or more to secure advanced positions. The Mongol army could literally outride and bewilder any opponent probably riding two to three times faster than the best Turkish cavalry, Mamluk slave troops, or tribal regiments in the employ of any Islamic ruler. It was just a stunning cavalry in that regard.

Furthermore, Genghis Khan knew that he could trust his officers, particularly Jebe and Subutai and then later his sons, above all the second son and the third son; that would be Ögedei, the third son who eventually got to be the next khan who was regarded as perhaps the most judicious. The oldest son, who was not really Genghis Khan's son, Jochi, showed a sort of inaction that eventually ruled him out as khan. The grandsons of Genghis Khan, especially Hulagu and Kublai Khan whom Genghis really marked out as his potential successors—even though the sources may be a little distorted here—all of these sons and grandsons, Genghis paid very close attention to see if they had the stuff to lead the army in the same fashion that he did. We now had a steppe army that was on a whole other level of organization and ethos that no previous conqueror of the steppes ever had commanded.

With this army, what are you going to do with it? Genghis Khan as a steppe conqueror could not just remain satisfied with ruling the largest confederation since the second century B.C. You have to remember, as I stated in an earlier lecture, that from Genghis Khan's viewpoint the world was not oriented on the map as we think of it: north, with the map being conveniently pointing to the Arctic Circle. He was standing at effectively the roof of the world looking out; that is, Mongolia was in the center of a much wider-spreading world, the Chinese Empire was to the southeast, the Islamic world to the southwest, to the far west ruled those pale Christian monarchs, you got reports about them in the trade. Genghis Khan, more than any other world conqueror, had access to enormous amounts of information. His success had brought all sorts of caravans, envoys from the Jin emperor, from the Song emperor; and the Mongols were extremely good in collecting information. They probably had more information on the wider world, they had a better sense of their world, than any other people in the sedentary civilizations. All of this was used by Genghis Khan and his successors for planning logistics, strategy, movement of forces; they knew where their armies could move, and it was only when they got beyond that realm—when they pushed into China, into Western Europe, or into the Levant—that they outran not only the steppes, but really their sources of information. But up until that point they had an extraordinary amount of information; and some scholars would say if you were looking for the best mapmakers in 1227, you would find them at Karakorum, the tent capital of Genghis Khan.

In 1206, Genghis Khan therefore looked south and east to the world of China; and in a series of campaigns, he smashed those northern rival kingdoms ruled by Tangut speakers in Western and Northern China. In the spring of 1209, his army came out of the steppes and crossed the Gobi Desert to descend on the Gansu corridor; and there his army invaded that small kingdom of the Xi Xia, who had control of the Silk Road. They were nomadic peoples from the Tibetan highlands who had ruled independently, this semi-Chinese kingdom. In the course of the fighting there, Genghis Khan learned to appreciate the importance of siege warfare. In fact, there were a couple of embarrassing setbacks, including the Xi Xia diverting a river that almost flooded out Genghis Khan's camp. He saw the need for engineers after that and began to recruit largely North Chinese engineers into a corps of 1,000 strong that would accompany the army wherever he went. This war concluded with a treaty. The Xi Xia essentially agreed to pay tribute, and as I said they become a very, very important component in providing translators and administrators for the emerging Mongol Empire.

That gave Genghis Khan control of the caravan routes into the Tarim Basin. His next objective was the Jin Empire, and he had two reasons for doing this. First, it was personal. His father had apparently been a vassal of the Jin emperor, and the Jin court was very, very impatiently waiting for the proper submission from the newest barbarian on the steppes. There was an acrimonious exchange of envoys, and this broke down essentially into a declaration of war in 1211. But besides the personal matter, there was also the simple matter that Genghis Khan wanted to control the regions of Manchuria and above all those North Chinese provinces that were very, very valuable, not only for the millet and the foodstuffs, which sustained the peoples on the steppes, but also of all the industrial production going on in those cities including armaments. The result was another war, starting really in 1212 when Genghis Khan really took the field. The fighting in 1211 was rather desultory; various Turkish tribes who were allied to the Jin emperor defected over to the Mongol side. The whole system of the Great Wall, not that it was much in place anyways, collapsed; and from 1212–1215, the Mongols carried out a methodical conquest of the Northern Chinese domains of the Jin emperor. There was a change of ruler, a usurper, which complicated the situation. The Jin court essentially checked out to Kaifeng on the lower Yellow River and gave up the control of most of its northern domains and survives as a rump state. What was really important was the siege of the future city of Beijing, which would have been called Zhongdu at the time. In that siege—and it lasted from 1214–1215—Genghis Khan really came to appreciate the need for engineers. Some scholars would date that it was at this point that the regular corps of Chinese engineers was recruited in 1215 after the capture of that Jin capital.

The capture of the Jin capital essentially sealed Genghis Khan's control of North China. The Jin were not a serious threat. They were at Kaifeng; they were just a rump state. The Song emperors had neither the means nor the inclination to contest the conquest of Northern China and the western areas. Genghis Khan now controlled the key borderlands of China; and he was satisfied with that. He probably would have been more than content—maybe he wanted to take out the Jin emperor—but he would have been more than content with this arrangement because it gave him an absolutely overwhelming position vis-à-vis both the Jin and Song emperors. They did not have the horses to mount serious cavalry forces. Genghis Khan now controlled the trade routes through which silk would move and bring in profits to the Song emperors. He could have been very, very satisfied with this arrangement that he could exact tribute and reward all of his followers indefinitely.

He did have to clean up the western steppes a bit; there were some unruly tribes right after the victories over the Jin. Mongol armies moved west, secured the central steppes. Above all, they occupied the Kara Khitan Empire, or at least its eastern sections. That was because, in part, various Mongol dissidents had fled into the Kara Khitan Empire and had focused discontent against Genghis Khan and carried out raids against the Mongol domains. It required a Mongol force to come in under Jebe to pacify and bring the area under control. It was helped by the fact that the Mongols who essentially took over the Kara Khitan Empire had proved very unpopular rulers. They had become enthusiastic Buddhists and had persecuted the

Muslim populations, particularly in Kashgar, Khoton, the city in the Tarim Basin. The Mongols were essentially welcomed by the majority of the Kara Khitans as fellow nomads who were of a great lord and certainly to be preferred to the Mongol exiles who were trying to put together some sort of state in the Kara Khitan khanate.

That victory in 1218 brought the Mongol Empire to the central steppes. It brought it almost to the shores of the Aral Sea, to the upper reaches of the Jaxartes River. That meant Genghis Khan now stood at the threshold of Transoxiana. The advance here was really taken largely for cleaning up; the steppes brought dissident tribes under control. It was not part of a planned world conquest—"We got North China, let's check the western steppes next"—but those victories, that advance, brought Genghis Khan smack into the Islamic world. At the time, the Jaxartes River was a political boundary; and as we have seen, it was never really a very good political boundary because nomadic peoples always were crossing the Jaxartes, they were moving into the caravan cities, some of them hooked into Iran, some of them hooked into India. That was a natural set of routes. But at the time, in 1218, Transoxiana and Iran were ruled by a man named Muhammad Shah. He ruled based on the cities of Khurasan. Khurasan was the lower delta region of the Oxus River, the Syr Darya; and those cities had prospered since antiquity, at least since the fourth century B.C. They were on the caravan route; they were very, very prosperous. There was actually silk production there because mulberry trees had been introduced from China. Furthermore, Muhammad Shahj saw himself as the heir of all the lands of eastern Dar al-Islam, the lands of Islam; and his idea was to bring the Abbasid Caliphate back under his control and essentially play the role that the Seljuk Turks had played in the 11th and early 12th centuries. (By the way, the Abbasid caliph in Baghdad was not keen on this idea; so initially he was probably not too distressed that the Mongols came in and knocked out Muhammad Shah.)

A stupid incident broke out; it involved a caravan. Muhammad Shah's agents at the city of Otrar or Utrar impounded a Mongol caravan; they arrested a bunch of merchants. There was an envoy from the Great Khan apparently to the court of Muhammad Shah, and he took it upon himself, this magistrate, to claim that all these guys were spies, and they were executed. Actually, it was probably a plausible suspicion—Genghis Khan and his successors were not above slipping in all sorts of spies, envoys, embassies, merchants—but it gave a great excuse for Genghis Khan to write to Muhammad Shah, we have two versions of the letter, and Muhammad Shah wanted to know, "Who is this barbarian?" He looked like some kind of weird Kara Khitan; he did not take him seriously. The sources stress that Muhammad Shah—this comes especially from Juvaini—really treated Genghis Khan as a subordinate, as some sort of local barbarian ruler, and just dismissed it altogether.

Behind this was a greater issue. Muhammad Shah was perfectly aware— even though he was haughty and proud overall—that Genghis Khan was gaining control of the steppes, and that would shut down his military forces. Muhammad Shah depended on Mamluks, slave soldiers, largely recruited from different Turkish tribes—particularly Kipchaks, but others—and the Mongol kaghan was going to control all these routes and interrupt the flow of recruits. The second point is Muhammad Shah was more than aware that this newest barbarian was a formidable foe and naturally would look south of the Jaxartes River to those caravan cities. A conflict was probably inevitable, and this incident gave an excuse for Genghis Khan to mobilize the Mongol army.

In 1219, Genghis Khan set out on his most important campaign, which was a turning point. This was his invasion of the Islamic world. Again, I mentioned he had to move some 3,000–3,500 miles across the steppes to reach the Jaxartes River. He divided his army into three columns. It was the biggest display of nomadic power ever on the steppes, and only to be repeated a couple of times thereafter. The armies moved in three great columns. Muhammad Shah, even though he had a large army, lacked the same kind of cavalry. He made the mistake of dispersing his army to defend the various cities, and the result was the Mongol forces converged on the Jaxartes—they actually converged on the city Otrar where the incident took place—and they just savagely sacked the city. The official had molten silver poured down his throat; the population was massacred. The army of Muhammad Shah was just not up to the task. The field forces were swept away, and the campaigns in 1219–1220 very quickly became a war of sieges. Genghis Khan made a beeline to Bukhara, the former Sumatic capital, home to all the great *medreses*. Bukhara was taken in a ruthless sack. All people who were of skills, craftsmen, and all good looking girls, they got shipped off to Mongolia. The rest of the population was recruited essentially into the Mongol army and marched to Samarkand where they were used as targets for the garrison's archers or to advance and fill in the moats and obstacles; and, of course, this means the civilian populations took enormous losses. Samarkand, which was held by a Turkish garrison, was too captured. Again, the similar atrocities that you encountered in other cities along the route were enacted. The civil population was largely massacred; craftsmen and others that were selected for serving the Mongol khan were sent back to Mongolia.

What is remarkable is how quickly these sieges took place. Because of the Chinese engineers, Mongol armies could move up to the cities. They would use the captured population and the cities would be methodically taken and sacked. From 1219–1220, all of the caravan cities of Iran, Transoxiana, and into Afghanistan fell into the hands of the Mongol armies. Muhammad Shah fled west; he eventually died in exile on an island in the Caspian Sea. Genghis Khan detached two *tumen*—that is, 20,000 men—under Jebe and Subutai to pursue the remnants of the army of Khurasan across Iran, and they would carry out very important campaigns into Russia and eventually circle back and bring information of the lands of the west. Genghis Khan also destroyed any attempts at a revival of the power of Khurasan. The son of Muhammad Shah fled to India. He tried to raise forces. Genghis Khan's forces descend—his name was Jalal al-Din—and his forces were decisively defeated on the Indus.

By 1221, the lands of Eastern Islam had been ransacked and leveled by the Mongol army. It was a stunning conquest in its speed. It was an incredibly savage conquest. Muslim chroniclers report pyramids of heads of the civilian population; bleached bones and decaying bodies over the centuries. Several cities were singled out for particular destruction. Above all, the city of Bamiyan, where the great Buddhas were, we discussed it was on the Silk Road; that city had killed, I believe, one of the favored grandsons of Genghis Khan, he had fallen in the siege, and the city was essentially obliterated. The result was that the Mongols had burst into the Islamic world as absolute terror, and the Islamic world was shocked. If you thought the Kara Khitans were shocked, they never quite recovered from the impact of these invasions.

In the meanwhile, Genghis Khan was able to make his way back to Mongolia. In the course of the campaigning, he had come to decide that the succession would fall on his third son Ögedei, who had distinguished himself in the campaigns. When he died in 1227, he now ruled a far greater empire than any other steppe conqueror; he had created a great imperial army; and above all, he left a vision of world conquest that was now transmitted to his sons and successors.

Western Mongol Expansion
Lecture 29

In this lecture, we explore Mongol expansion to the western steppes, the Russian forest zone, and even into Hungary and Poland. These areas came under Mongol attack in 1220, 1223, and again in the great campaign of Batu, lasting from 1236 to 1242. Batu was the son of Genghis Khan's oldest son, Jochi. When Genghis Khan was planning his succession, he knew that Jochi did not have the ability to hold together the vast Mongol confederation. The third son, Ögödei, would succeed as Great Kahn. Because Jochi predeceased his father by several months, his domains went to his son Batu, who proved to be one of the great successes of the Mongol Empire.

Ögödei as the Great Khan

- When Genghis Khan died, most likely in August 1227, there was again an assembly of all the princes, the *kurultai*. There was a delay of about 18 months before Ögödei was elected the new Great Khan. The proclamation of Ögödei, however, was unanimous.

- In 1229, Ögödei became the Great Khan. He faced some daunting challenges, one of which was administrative. Already the Mongol Empire extended farther than any previous steppe empires. Genghis Khan had carried out a military conquest of the Islamic world, but he still intended to rule that empire from his capital in Mongolia.

Ögödei, the third son of Genghis Khan, was the best available successor to the Great Khan; he could keep his other brothers in line and focus the family on conquest rather than infighting.

- The Great Khan would rule not only all the steppe lands but also great urban centers. That meant hiring administrators to run the northern Chinese provinces that had been conquered from the Jin, the 16 prefectures, the regions of the Tarim Basin, and the caravan cities in Transoxania and Iran.

- With Ögödei, we see the first efforts to switch from a tribute-based empire to a tax-based empire. This experiment was first carried out in the northern Chinese regions. Ögödei also had ambitions to the west; he wanted to bring the western Eurasian steppes under his control and rule over all the tribes.

Partitioning of the Empire

- In his final missives, Genghis Khan had loosely divided up his empire. It was understood that Ögödei would rule the whole of the empire as Great Khan; that Chagatai, the second son, would rule the central steppes, the regions that had been conquered from the Kara-Khitans; and that Tolui would handle the homeland.

- **Batu**, the son of Jochi, was given the commission to go west and conquer all the lands to the far western ocean. It was very much in the interest of both Ögödei and Batu to conduct a western campaign. Batu was highly ambitious; if he wasn't sent west, he might have challenged Ögödei back at home.

- As soon as the Jin Empire was conquered in 1234, plans were made to carry out the conquest of the western steppes. This would be another ambitious imperial campaign. Ögödei not only gave the commission to Batu, but he also assigned his most experienced commanders to the mission. Among them was **Subutai**, who had distinguished himself in an earlier campaign to pursue Muhammad Shah.

Veteran General Subutai

- In the earlier campaign, Jebe and Subutai had not only pursued Muhammad Shah, but they had also discovered the grasslands of Azerbaijan in northwestern Iran, which were ideal grazing lands for Mongol cavalry horses. They attacked the Christian kingdoms of Georgia and the Caucasus and won stunning victories, mortally wounding King George IV of Georgia.

- In a daring winter campaign in 1222–1223, they crossed from Azerbaijan over the Caucasus Mountains, and in the spring, they descended on the south Russian steppes. They swept aside all resistance and sent the Cuman army running. The Cuman khan Köten fled to the Russian prince of Novgorod to raise a coalition of Russian princes and Cumans to oppose the Mongol invasion.

- This army met the Mongol army on the banks of the Kalka River on May 31, 1223. In a classic use of tactics, the Mongol army encircled and smashed the coalition of Cuman and Russian princes. More than 10,000 Russians fell. Russian chroniclers were staggered at the defeat.

- That victory on the banks of the Kalka River completely changed the image of the Mongols in the minds of western Europeans. Initially, reports of battles from central Asia had led Christian Europe to think that the Mongols were somehow associated with the legendary kings **Prester John** and David.

- The victory on the Kalka River revealed that these people were not the followers of Prester John; they were the Tartars, from Tartarus, or hell, in classical mythology. And they retreated just as mysteriously as they came.

Launch of the Western Campaign

- Subutai was a veteran general who knew the Russian steppes. He and his experienced soldiers were assigned to Batu as part of the invasion force in 1236 that would move west.

- Ögödei made sure that every major figure in the imperial family accompanied this expedition, including two future khans: **Möngke**, the son of Tolui, and Ögödei's own son **Güyük**.

- It was an all-star cast of the Mongol imperial family in an all-star army. Some scholars argue that as many as 75,000 Turks and Mongols rode west in 1236 on an expedition of both exploration and conquest.

Yuri II and the Russian Defeat

- The campaign opened with a sweep of the western steppes. These were largely occupied by **Kipchak** Turks, or Cumans, who readily submitted. By 1236, all the tribes to the Ural Mountains had submitted to Genghis Khan. Many of the Kipchaks were recruited into the imperial army and eventually became the mainstay of the western khaganate of Batu, which was later known as the Golden Horde.

- Late in 1236, Batu, who had excellent information about the political divisions among the Russian princes, conducted a winter campaign. The army crossed the Volga in force. Subutai led a column north to ravage the lands of the Bulgar khagans; the main force entered onto the south Russian steppes.

- The leading prince at the time was **Yuri II**, who ruled the city of Vladimir-Suzdal, the forerunner of Moscow. In November 1237, the Mongol offenses opened up against the Russian cities. Yuri unsuccessfully tried to raise a coalition of other Russian princes.

- In 1238, Batu's army ran through the Russian army, put Vladimir-Suzdal under siege, and slaughtered the city. Yuri fought a second battle, but he was wiped out in early March of 1238.

- Then, from 1238 to 1239, the Mongol army systematically destroyed virtually every major Russian city. There was little opposition. The princes all defended their own towns, but there was no concerted effort to meet the Mongols in open battle.

The Sack of Kiev

- Batu then retired to the south Russian steppes. At this new encampment, he began to collect information about what was farther west. He had now brought all the steppes under his control and thoroughly sacked the Russian cities. At this point, Batu had under his command more than 150,000 men. He decided to move next into central Europe.

- The first goal, however, was to carry out a pacification of the last Russian city: Kiev. Kiev was the only city that had not fallen into Mongol hands, and it was on the main route leading into Galicia, or southern Poland. The city of Kiev was put under siege and sacked, and the population was massacred.

- Kiev had been regarded as the most beautiful city in Russia. The princely families of Kiev had intermarried with many of the European nobility and royal families. Most of central Europe was linked in some way to the city. The sack was seen as a shock and a warning about what might come next.

Campaign in Poland
- With Kiev captured, Batu gained reinforcements from the east. He refitted his army and, in 1241, launched an invasion into Europe itself. Two great attacks were envisioned.

- The first one, given to Subutai, was an attack into southern Poland, or Silesia, and ultimately into Germany and central Europe. The mission was to prevent the Teutonic knights from joining up with **Bela IV** in Hungary. The second objective was to defeat King Bela.

- In February 1241, Subutai crossed the frozen Vistula and entered Poland. The Mongol army completely outmaneuvered its opponents, and Krakow was abandoned and torched.

Battle with Bela IV of Hungary
- Subutai crossed over the mountains of Galicia and descended into Hungary from the north. Meanwhile, Batu had set in motion the main Mongol army in four major columns. It crossed into Hungary, King Bela IV was taken by surprise, and the Mongol forces swept across the Pannonian grasslands in Hungary.

- In April 1241, the Hungarian army of Bela and the Mongol army under Batu took up positions alongside the Sajo River. Batu's forces surprised the Hungarian camp, and a ferocious battle ensued.

- The Hungarian knights distinguished themselves. Bela IV and his forces eventually broke out and fled to Buda and points west. The Mongols slaughtered many of the Hungarian infantry in heavy fighting.

Beyond the Steppes
- Mongol losses at the Sajo River were significant; furthermore, Batu encountered something that he had not seen before as the Mongol army moved west across the Hungarian plains: fortified masonry castles.

- Batu had outrun not only his geographic knowledge but his logistical limits. For Batu to move forward into central Europe, he would need a different kind of army, with large numbers of infantry and engineers who had the expertise to take masonry castles.

- In effect, central Europe posed the same problem that Song China had posed. The Mongols had outrun the steppe zones. Batu was at a loss for what to do next. However, that problem was solved for him.

- In 1242, after ravaging Hungary for most of 1241, Batu pulled his army back to the lower Volga because he heard news that his uncle Ögödei had died. That meant a new election.

- Batu was keen to be in on the election of the next khan. For the first time—but not for the last—the political dynamics and succession issues at the Mongol court would drive world events.

Important Term

Kipchak Turks: Ghuzz or western Turkish-speaking nomads who dominated the central Asian steppes in the 11th through 13th centuries. They submitted to Mongol Khan Batu in 1238–1241 and constituted the majority of tribes of the Golden Horde.

Batu (b. 1207; r. 1227–1255): Mongol khan; the son of Jochi (the eldest son of Genghis Khan). In 1227, he succeeded to the western *ulus* (the future Golden Horde). He conquered the Cumans in 1235–1236. In 1237–1240, he subdued the Russian principalities. He won a brilliant victory over King Bela IV of Hungary at the Battle of the Mohi on April 11, 1241. The news of the Mongol victory panicked Western Christendom, but in 1242, Batu withdrew to the grasslands of the Volga when he received news of the death of Khan Ögödei. Thereafter, Batu ruled in splendid isolation, professing loyalty to Güyük and Möngke.

Bela IV (b. 1206; r. 1235–1270): King of Hungary; a conscientious ruler who extended royal justice and restored his kingdom after the Mongol invasion. He was, however, decisively defeated by Khan Batu at the Battle of the Mohi on April 11, 1241.

Güyük (b. 1206; r. 1246–1248): Mongol khan; the son of Ögödei and Töregene. The strong-willed Töregene assumed a regency in 1241–1246, until she could arrange for the acclamation of Güyük as Great Khan by the *kurultai*. Güyük, a suspicious ruler and an alcoholic, discredited the house of Ögödei in the eyes of many Mongols. He died while en route to settle scores with his cousin Batu.

Möngke (b. 1209; r. 1251–1259): Mongol khan and eldest son of Tolui and Sorghaghtani Beki. He proved an intelligent ruler, who commissioned his brother Hulagu to conquer the Islamic world in 1256. In 1257–1259, he along with his brother Kublai Khan, invaded Song China. He died of dysentery while besieging the fortress Diaoyu on the Yangtze River. His death precipitated a civil war.

Prester John: "Priest John"; a legendary Christian king in inner Asia who would deliver Jerusalem from the Muslims. He was probably inspired by garbled reports about Yelü Dashi (1124–1143), khan of the Kara-Khitans, who had defeated Seljuk sultan Ahmad Sanjar (1118–1153) at the Battle of Qatwan on September 9, 1141. Genghis Khan was later hailed by western European Christians as Prester John or his descendant, David.

Subutai (1175–1248): Mongol general and early companion of Temujin (the future Genghis Khan); commanded 20 campaigns. He was an expert in strategy and siege warfare. In 1221–1223, he and Jebe conducted a brilliant western campaign that climaxed at the Battle of the Kalka River on May 31, 1223. He distinguished himself in the western campaigns of Batu in 1237–1241 and in the campaign against Song China in 1246–1247.

Yuri II (b. 1189; r. 1212–1238): Prince of Vladimir-Suzdal; campaigned against the Volga Bulgars and Russian rival princes. In 1238, Batu captured Vladimir. Yuri II escaped, but his capital was sacked and the population slaughtered. On March 8, 1238, he and his army were annihilated by the Mongols at the Battle of Sit River.

Suggested Reading

Istvan, *Cumans and Tatars*.

———, "The Jochid Realm."

Jackson, *The Mongols and the West, 1221–1410*.

Rossabi, *The Mongols and Global History*.

Saunders, *The History of the Mongol Conquests*.

Questions to Consider

1. What were the strategic objectives of the expedition of Subutai and Jebe in 1220–1223? What did this expedition reveal about Mongol military organization and logistics? What was the impact of the Battle of the Kalka River in 1223?

2. Why did Ögödei and Batu agree to the conquest of the far west? How did this expedition figure in overall Mongol aims of world domination?

3. How did Batu exploit the political weaknesses of his foes, the terrain and weather, and tactical discipline of his army to achieve such spectacular victories over Cumans, Russians, Poles, and Hungarians in

1237–1241? How did the Mongols acquire such accurate information of their opponents?

4. What was the role of terror inflicted by Batu in demoralizing foes? How did western Europeans receive the news of the sacks of Vladimir-Suzdal and Kiev?

5. Why did the Mongols win the battles of Leignitz and Mohi in 1241? Did these victories open central Europe to Mongol conquest? Why did the succession crisis forever end Mongol western expansion?

Western Mongol Expansion

Lecture 29—Transcript

In this lecture, I want to look at Mongol expansion to the west, and by the west I mean primarily the western steppes and the Russian forest zone and even into Central Europe, that would be Hungary and Poland. These areas came under Mongol attack in 1220–1223 and again in the great campaign of Batu, lasting from 1236–1242. He was the grandson of Genghis Khan; he was the son of the oldest son of Genghis Khan, Jochi, who was thought not actually really to be Genghis's son but was the son of Börte by a Merkit prince who had captured her in that early raid.

To start this lecture off, let us recall what Genghis had achieved when he returned home from his conquests of Khorasam and Eastern Islam. He did not really make it back to his homeland until 1223; and already that campaign had led him to decide who was to succeed him. He knew that he was aging. He still planned to conquer what was left of the Jin Empire; that was a matter to settle. He died in 1227 before he could carry out that campaign, and it was left to his successor Ögedei to extinguish the Jin Empire, which was essentially the rump state on the Lower Yellow River centered on the city of Kaifeng; and that capitulated in 1234.

Genghis Khan already was planning his succession, and he knew that the oldest son, Jochi, just did not have the ability to hold together this great confederation. It really came down to sons number two and three. Tolui was regarded as too young, and furthermore he was only so-so in his campaigns. From an early age, he did not quite distinguish himself as much as the second and third sons did. Chagatai was already known to be hotheaded but incredibly brave. He had shown, however, bad judgment at the strategic level. Ögedei, the third son, was usually agreed to be the one that everyone could accept. He could keep his other brothers in line and focus the family on conquest rather than fighting over who should get what once dad was gone. So it was clear in the final days of Genghis Khan that the third son Ögedei was to succeed as Great Khan. Ögedei had his virtues as well as his vices. For one, he did love very much pomp and circumstance, and he would start turning Khwarazm, the tent city, into something of a regular settlement; and he liked all the Chinese symbolism, all the Chinese ceremony. Furthermore, he was notoriously a heavy drinker, apparently experimented with hashish as well; and that would also be true of his son and successor Güyük. Ögedei was on good terms with the older brother Jochi and the family of Jochi who came to rule the western steppes known as the Golden Horde; whereas the family of Chagatai sort of held the balance and the family of Tolui, which eventually succeeded as Great Khans—that would be Möngke and Kublai Khan—they represented the youngest branch, and in the end they were the branch to take over the position of Great Khan. Jochi predeceased his father by several months. He died in 1227; and therefore his domains, his commands, went to his son Batu, who proved to be one of the great successes of Genghis Khan.

When Genghis Khan died, probably in August of 1227, there was again an assembly of all of the princes; but for almost 18 months, there was a delay in the *kurultai* meeting and electing Ögedei the new Great Khan. There was not any question who was supposed to be elected, but it took time for all the khans, all the tribes, the various electors to arrive; and furthermore, you have to think of these elections as not a knocked out, dragged out debate followed by a vote. This would characterize a democratic or a republican type of constitution; instead, the Mongols liked to reach a consensus so that whoever was the Great Khan, or if it was a matter of war and peace, there was a declaration, more or less a uniform declaration without the kind of debates in voting that you would associate with either a democratic or republican constitution. This is very traditional for these types of hierarchical societies. So it took time to canvas among the voters and the electors, Ögedei was the one to go with; and when he was proclaimed, he was proclaimed unanimously. In that interval, Tolui, the youngest brother, actually acted as sort of a regent. This again was common. The youngest son usually got the homeland, usually got the traditional grazing lands, where the older sons were given khanates in the conquests. Tolui was in a very, very good position to make sure that his sons—and there were four of them—had an advantage in future elections because they were closely connected with the homeland as opposed to the new conquest areas.

In 1229, Ögedei was now the Great Khan, and he faced some daunting challenges. One was administrative. Already, this empire was far beyond any kind of conceptions of previous steppe empires. You have to remember that

Genghis Khan carried out a military conquest of the Islamic world. He still intended to rule that empire from his capital in Mongolia. Previous steppe conquerors usually raided into the settled areas exacted tribute, took captives and plunder; or whole tribes migrated into the sedentary civilizations and created empires in the sedentary civilizations with some contact with the steppes. This was a case where the Great Khan was going to rule not only all the steppe lands, but also great urban centers, which were now tributary and subordinate to a khan who resided on the great Eurasian steppes. This was quite a difference. That meant hiring the talent to run these places; run the northern provinces that had been conquered from the Jin, the Northern Chinese provinces, the 16 prefectures; run the cities of the Tarim Basin that had submitted very early in the reign of Genghis Khan; and above all what do you do with all those caravan cities that you so methodically sacked in Transoxiana and Iran? With Ögedei you see the first efforts to switch the empire from a tributary-based empire, where you exact tribute or you plunder, to a tax-based empire. It was first carried out in the Northern Chinese regions, especially after 1234 when Ögedei conquered the Lower Yellow River valley and ended the Jin Dynasty.

Ögedei also had ambitions to the west. He wanted to bring the Western Eurasian steppes under his control; that is, all of the tribes. Genghis Khan, in his final missives and reports to his sons, had loosely divided up the empire. It was understood that Ögedei would rule the whole of the empire as Great Khan; that Chagatai, the second son, would rule the central steppes, the regions that had been conquered from the Kara Khitans; that Tolui would handle the homeland; but Batu, the son of Jochi, was given the commission to go west and to actually conquer all the lands where the Mongol hooves would trample, would march, to the far western ocean. It was very much in the interest of both Ögedei and Batu to conduct a western campaign. Batu expected to get his khanate, and that was in the west and still largely to be conquered. Chagatai had his. Of course, Ögedei was the Great Khan. Tolui was going to command the homeland. So Ögedei had to provide for the grandson of technically the son of the oldest brother; actually the oldest grandson of the Genghis Khan. Batu was also ambitious, and if you did not send him west then Batu might challenge Ögedei back at home.

As soon as the Jin Empire was conquered in 1234, plans were put afoot to carry out the conquest of the western steppes. That was another ambitious campaign. It was going to be conducted on the order of the conquest of Khwarazym, that great campaign by Genghis Khan in 1219–1220, and it was also going to be an imperial campaign. Ögedei not only gave the commission to Batu, he also assigned his most experienced commanders to go with him. This included the commander Sübedei. Sübedei had distinguished himself in an earlier campaign in the west; and I want to just back up for a moment and refer to that earlier campaign of Genghis Khan. I had mentioned in passing that when Genghis Khan returned to the homeland he had detached his two best generals, Jebe and Sübedei, to pursue Muhammad Shah. They not only pursued Muhammad Shah, they moved west across Iran. They discovered the grasslands of Azerbaijan, in Northwestern Iran today, which were ideal for Mongol cavalry to graze. Then they took it upon themselves to attack the Christian kingdoms of Georgia and the Caucasus and won stunning victories, mortally wounding King George IV of Georgia and essentially forcing the Georgians and the Armenians to submit to the will of the Great Khan, Genghis Khan at the time. Then in a daring winter campaign in 1222–1223, they crossed from Azerbaijan over the Caucasus Mountains in a brutal crossing of the Derbent Pass in the snows, and in the spring of 1223 descended on the South Russian steppes. They swept aside all resistance; the Christian Alans, various Georgian peoples known as the Lazians were routed. They sent the Cuman army running. The Cuman khan Koten fled to the Russian princes to the north. He made his way to the city of Novgorod and he convinced the prince of Novgorod, Mstislav, to raise a coalition of Russian princes and Cumans to oppose the Mongol invasion.

This army met the Mongol army on the banks of the Kalka River on May 31, 1223. In a classic set of tactics, the Mongol army encircled and smashed the coalition of Cuman and Russian princes. Over 10,000 Russians fell. The army was panicked. The Russian chroniclers were stunned at the defeat. The Russians had been fighting Cumans for 150 years, and these were pretty much even matches. They had no idea what they were going to encounter in a Mongol army, and it was not the full Mongol army; it was only two *tumen* that had been detached from the main Mongol force. The chronicles speak of where these people come from we do not know, but they were clearly here to punish the sins of the Russians; and the monks delighted enlisting all the sins, because to be that badly defeated the Russians had to be really bad. Then just as mysteriously, these people left.

That victory on the banks of the Kalka River really changed the image of the Mongols in the minds of the Western Europeans. Initially, reports of battles from Central Asia had led Christian Europe to think that the Mongols were somehow these legendary kings, Prester John and David. These are reports that go back to the 1140s; probably garbled reports that had reached Western Europe when the Kara Khitans had defeated the Seljuk sultan Sanjar in 1141. Pope Alexander III actually sent letters in Latin off to this mysterious king; of course, the envoys disappeared, never heard of again. The attacks of Genghis Khan into the Islamic world, these were hailed as perhaps this legendary Christian king. No, it was not. The victory on the Kalka River revealed that these people were not the followers of Prester John; they are the Tatars; that is they were from Tatarus, the hell in Classical mythology, and they retreated just as mysteriously as they came. Sübedei was a veteran general. He knew these lands; he knew the Russian steppes. He was aware of the Russian cities; he had had some sense. He and his veteran soldiers were, of course, assigned to Batu as part of the invasion force in 1236 that was going to move west.

In addition, Ögedei made sure every major prince in the imperial family was going to go along on this expedition; and that included two future Khans: Möngke, the son of Tolui and a future khan; and Ögedei's own son, Güyük, who went along as subordinate commanders; as well as the various brothers of Batu; and the grandsons of Ögedei and Tolui were also along. It was an all-star cast of the Mongol imperial family and an all-star army. The size of this army is difficult to estimate, but some would argue as many as 75,000 Turks and Mongols rode west in 1236 on an expedition of both exploration and conquest. In addition, the Chinese engineers went along, as well as a number of various vassal peoples providing technical assistance; Persians and Muslims were particularly appreciated for their engineering skills.

In 1236, the campaign opened with a sweep of the western steppes. These were largely occupied by Kipchak Turks—that is, Cumans—and they quickly submitted. By 1236, all the tribes to the Ural Mountains had submitted to Genghis Khan. Many of the Kipchaks were now recruited into the imperial army and they eventually became the mainstay of the western khanate, the khanate of Batu, which is later known as the Golden Horde. Late in 1236, Batu, who had excellent information about the political divisions among the Russian princes, conducted a winter campaign. The army crossed the Volga in force. Sübedei led a column north to ravage the lands of the Volgar khans; that is, Volgar, those Turks on the middle Volga who had converted to Islam back in 921–922. The main force entered onto the South Russian steppes; it crossed the Volga, made a beeline for the Don, and began to sweep aside all resistance.

At this point, the Russian princes were really stunned; they were not sure what to make of this. Initially, they allowed the Mongols the freedom to ravage those eastern steppes, those South Russian steppes. Furthermore, their memories of the defeat of the Kalka River had apparently faded. The leading prince at the time was a man named Yuri II who ruled the city of Vladimir-Suzdal; and that principality was effectively the forerunner of the later principality of Moscow. Initially, Yuri II kind of looked with some favor upon the fact that the Cumans were being wiped out on the South Russian steppes in 1236; but that situation changed in the next year. In that year, in the late autumn/early winter of 1237, the Mongol armies now turned their attention north against the Russian cities, which were largely in the forest zone. As I stressed, the Russian cities were in the taiga, the forest zone, where they had built settlements. They had adopted Orthodox Christianity. The steppes were still largely in the hands of Cumans. There was very little Russian settlement there; we did not have any Cossacks yet. Those people, the Cumans, had submitted to the power of Batu and were now providing forces as well as information about the Russian cities because the Cumans and Russians had constantly been battling along that zone, the famous Vodka-Hashish zone I talked about.

In November, 1237, the offenses were now opened up against the Russian cities. The first Russian city to get hit was the city of Ryazan, and Ryazan was fortified with a wooden palisade. The Mongols brought up their Chinese engineers; they stormed into the city on December 21, and burned it to the ground. These Russian cities, once they were torched, they went up immediately because it was largely timbered construction, and the only major buildings were the Orthodox churches, which were an adaptation of

Byzantine art. At that point, Prince Yuri II realized these guys were not in for just attacking the nomads, this was a serious invasion. He tried to raise a coalition of other Russian princes; and as in all Russian coalitions, the vast majority of the princes decided to sit it out, defend their own towns, and let Yuri do most of the fighting. Yuri suffered two major embarrassing defeats, the first one on the last day of lent in 1238. Batu's army just ran through the Russian army. They showed up at Vladimir-Suzdal; they put the city under siege. It was captured and slaughtered; most of the royal family went down. Yuri tried to rally his army; he fought a second battle. He was wiped out in early March, 1238; and then, starting from that point on—from 1238 running into 1239—the Mongol army reduced and destroyed virtually every major Russian city.

There was very little opposition. The princes all defended their own towns. There was no effort to meet the Mongols in open battle; that was seen as suicide, but equally insane was trying to defend the cities individually because Batu just brought up the Chinese engineers, the cities were immediately reduced, and the populations were slaughtered. The medieval chronicles speak of repeated massacres of populations; some deportation of artisans, some of the female population, but on the whole, the cities of Russia suffered a major destruction, and most of the early churches built in the aftermath of the conversion of Christianity were essentially gone.

Batu then retired to the steppes that he had conquered, the South Russian steppes, and he found the region of the Lower Volga particularly congenial. As you recall, this was the nucleus of the earlier Khazar khanate; it was probably the nucleus of a number of Cuman tribes. In time, Batu's heirs would settle and build a new city, a tent city that emerges into a settlement, on the Volga known as Saray, which is the Turkish Mongolian word for "palace." At this new encampment, Batu began to collect information about what was farther west. He had now brought all of the steppes under control, probably everything up to certainly the Dnieper, probably the Dniester River. The Russian cities had been thoroughly sacked. The only cities to escape were Novgorod and Pskov, which were so far north in the swamps, the winters, and the forests that they were not even worth going after at this point and they could essentially be safely ignored.

At this point, historians question: What were Batu's motives next? He had conquered the western steppes; he had his khanate. We are not really told exactly what Batu had in mind; this has to be inferred from the sources, and most of these are straightforward narrative. At this point, Batu had under his command probably over 150,000 men. He could put together field armies of 20,000 or 30,000 for fast-moving columns. Batu took it upon himself to move next into Central Europe. Again, I think this was just part of his carrying out the commission to extend Mongol power as far west as the hooves of the Mongolian horses would ride. His knowledge of what went beyond those Russian steppes was probably pretty vague. He did know there was a Christian Europe; he had probably reports of something like a pope, whom he thought was sort of like the strange Western version of the Chinese emperor with the Mandate of Heaven. But the immediate cause came down to Cumans who had escaped into the kingdom of Hungary and into Galicia, which today would be Southern Poland and Southwestern Russia, and had found refuge particularly with King Bela IV of Hungary. This was the excuse to push west; it was a pretext.

The first thing that Batu did was carry out a pacification of the last Russian city, Kiev. That city was the only city that had not fallen into Mongol hands, and it was on the main route leading into Galicia (that is, Southern Poland). The city of Kiev was put under siege; the garrison appealed to help. It was actually a possession of a fellow called Daniel of Galicia Duke; he was not able to support the city. Assistance was summoned from King Bela of Hungary; he was too busy with his own problems. The result was Kiev fell; there was another massacre and sack. Kiev was regarded as the most beautiful city in Russia, the mother of Russian cities. The princely families and the great families of Kiev had intermarried with many of the European nobility and royal families; most of Central Europe was somehow linked to the city. It was seen as a shock and a warning as to what was to come next.

What came next was, again, the typical Mongol winter campaigns. With Kiev captured, Batu gained forces from other tribes; more forces arrived from the east. He refitted his army, and then he was ready in 1241 to launch an invasion into Europe itself beyond the steppe zone. Two great attacks were envisioned. The first one was an attack into Southern Poland that would lead the Mongol armies into Silesia and ultimately into Germany and Central

Europe. That command was given to Sübedei with various Mongol princes, and its mission was to prevent the forces of Poland, of Silesia, the Teutonic knights, from joining up with King Bela in Hungary. The second objective was, of course, King Bela of Hungary.

In February, 1241, Sübedei crossed the frozen Vistula and entered into Poland. The Mongol army split up into columns, completely outmaneuvered its opponents. One force led by (a lovely name) his name was Duke Boleslav "the Chaste" of Krakow, his army was essentially wiped out. Krakow was abandoned and torched. The other army was commanded by Duke Henry II, Henry "the Pious" of Silesia; he ran smack into a Mongol army at the city of Liegnitz, by its German name Liegnitz, which is in Silesia, today its part of Poland. That army was decisively defeated in April, 1241. It was a total romp on the part of the Mongols. King Henry was actually thrown from his horse; his head was cut off. Nine sacks of ears were collected to count the dead. Essentially, Sübedei and those princes had done their job: They had neutralized any kind of support from Poland and the eastern nobles of the Holy Roman Empire. The result was Sübedei crossed over the mountains of Galicia and descended into Hungary from the north.

Meanwhile, Batu had set in motion the main Mongol army in four major columns. It crossed into Hungary, King Bela was taken by surprise, and the Mongol forces swept across the Pannonian steppes or grasslands. They found most of Hungary really very congenial; it was essentially grasslands, there were no real fortresses. The Mongol army concentrated at a tributary ultimately of the Tisza River that flows into the Danube called the Sajo River; and in April, 1241, the Hungarian army of Bela IV and the Mongol army under Batu camped across this river and took up positions for a great battle. Bela IV fortified his camp near the modern city of Mohi, or Muhi as it is sometimes pronounced in modern Hungarian. Sometimes it is called the Battle of the Mohi, other times it is called the Battle of the Sajo River or the Sajo Bridge. What happened is Bela IV tried to secure the strategic bridge by a night maneuver on the night of April 10 and 11 in 1241. His forces secured the bridge, but they alerted the Mongol army and Batu moved up quickly, drove the garrison off the bridge on the dawn of April 11, and then the army marched five miles to surprise the camp of Bela IV, who was still readying his army thinking that he had control of the bridge and he could march his army out, cross the bridge, and fight the Mongols on the east bank of the river. The result was an absolutely ferocious battle. The Hungarian knights distinguished themselves. Bela IV fought on; eventually they broke out and fled to the city of Buda and points west. The Mongols slaughtered a good deal of the Hungarian infantry that panicked, but the fighting was heavy.

Mongol losses were very significant; and furthermore, Batu encountered something that he had not really seen before: As the Mongol army moved west across the Hungarian plains, they ran into fortified masonry castles. Batu had just outrun not only his geographic knowledge, but his logistical limit. That meant that for that Mongol army to move forward into Central Europe, you were going to need a very different kind of army. You were going to need more than just some Chinese engineers; you were going to need large numbers of infantry, and you were going to need engineers who had the expertise to take masonry castles. In effect, Central Europe, medieval Europe, posed the same problem that Song China posed: You had outrun the steppe zones; if you were going to conquer this sedentary civilization, you needed to create a new and different army that could operate in tandem with the Mongol forces.

Batu really was at a loss, probably, of what to do next. What happened is the problem was solved for him: In 1242, after having ravaged Hungary for most of 1241, Batu pulled his army back to the Lower Volga because he heard news that his uncle Ögedei had died on a hunting expedition on December 11, 1241. That meant a new election, and Batu was very keen to be in on the election of the next khan. He was not on the best of terms with some of his relatives, and he wanted to make sure he had a decisive voice in the upcoming election. For the first time, but not for the last, the dynamics, the politics, at the Mongol court would determine expansion and Western Europe was essentially spared a return of the Mongol army because of the succession issues at the Mongol court.

Mongol Invasion of the Islamic World
Lecture 30

I n this lecture, we will examine the Mongol invasions into the Islamic world. In the previous lecture, we saw how dynastic politics back at Karakorum, the Mongol capital, had halted Batu's invasion of central Europe. We will see the same dynamic here. The planned invasion of the Islamic world by Hulagu was also cut short by dynastic politics that would plunge the Mongol Empire into its first civil war.

The State of the Islamic World
- When Genghis Khan returned home to his capital at Karakorum, he left behind a largely devastated Islamic world. Impressed by Islamic teachers, Genghis Khan was not necessarily hostile to Islam as a religion, so long as it knew its place as one of many faiths within the Mongol Empire.

- Genghis Khan left little in the way of an administration in the Islamic world. There was no real effort to revive the cities or to put agricultural land back under production. There had been widespread devastation in some of the cities.

- What's more, there were counter-authorities in the Islamic world that were perceived as dangers to Mongol rule. That included the Abbasid caliphs in Baghdad, who were a strong regional power; the Assassins, the infamous Ishmaelite sect at their fortress Alamut; and above all, the Mamluk, or the slave sultans of Egypt.

The Election of Güyük
- In 1241–1242, the Mongol Empire was in a crisis brought about by the death of Ögödei. Because the nomadic peoples practiced lateral succession, the choice of the next Great Khan was by no means assured.

- In 1242, there were several candidates, including Güyük, the son of Ögödei, who had a reasonable claim to the throne, and Batu, the son of the oldest son of Genghis Khan. Other possible candidates were the sons of Tolui, the youngest son.

- Tolui died in 1232, but he and his wife had four sons, all capable of obtaining the khaganate: Möngke, Hulagu, Kublai (later Kublai Khan), and **Arigh Böke**. It was not until 1246 that the electors decided to go with Ögödei's son Güyük, who was elected the Great Khan.

Rivalry and Political Instability
- That change in leadership also brought about a change in policy, because the new khan was hostile to Batu. Güyük did not want to renew the western campaigns because doing so would bring distinction to Batu.

- Batu, therefore, aligned himself with the widow of Tolui: **Sorghaghtani Beki**. Sorghaghtani Beki was probably the favorite daughter-in-law of Genghis Khan; she favored her sons Hulagu and Kublai, the future Kublai Khan.

- Batu threatened civil war at one point, and these machinations underscored the instability of the nomadic tradition of lateral succession. There was intense rivalry in the third generation after Genghis Khan because all the cousins had equal claim to be the Great Khan. If they did not get the position of Great Khan, they expected to get an *ulus*—a huge area with nomadic tribes and military power.

- This political instability would eventually break out into civil war and, in time, would lead to the unraveling of the empire of Kublai Khan.

The Election of Möngke
- A second important election came on July 1, 1251, after the death of Güyük; the Mongols elected Möngke as the new khan. That meant

that the power of the Great Khan now passed from the Ögödei family to the Tolui family.

- That was an important change because Möngke was a very different ruler than Ögödei and Güyük. He had none of the pretentions of being a Chinese-style monarch. He was a Mongol ruler, much more in the manner of Genghis Khan.

- He was modest in his appearance and manners. He was committed to new expansion to sustain the monarchy. The flow of treasure, silk, and captives was crucial to keeping loyal followers.

Möngke followed the policies of his grandfather, Genghis Khan, in restructuring the upper levels of his military and focusing on the expansion of his empire.

- Möngke carried out important changes in the military, purging the officer corps of those loyal to the house of Ögödei and replacing them with his own men. By the second or third year of his reign, he was ready to expand his empire.

Assumption of Power in a New Generation

- Batu, the cousin out on the western steppes, was essentially confirmed in his position as ruler of the Mongols and Turks of the far west. That *ulus* eventually evolved into the Golden Horde. The khans ruling in the western steppes in time evolved into independent rulers; they also eventually adopted Islam.

- The family of Chagatai was rewarded with control of the central steppes. The **Chagataid** khans had claim over Transoxania and the cities of the Tarim Basin.

- The most important commissions were given to the two younger brothers of the new khan. Kublai Khan was commissioned with the eastern steppes and given the charge to conquer China. Hulagu was ordered to return to the Islamic world and take out any opposition to Mongol control of the eastern lands of Islam.

Elimination of the Assassins

- Möngke had good reasons for his move in the Islamic world. For one thing, the Abbasid caliph in Baghdad represented a counter-authority. Further, the Mamluk sultans of Egypt, or the slave soldier sultans, were on the rise and had an excellent army.

- Above all, there was a secretive group—an extreme Shi'ite cabal based in Alamut that had cells across the Islamic world—known as the Assassins.

- Hulagu was given the greater part of the field army. It was now transferred from the western steppes to the central steppes to invade the Islamic world. This campaign would perhaps be the most impressive since those of Genghis Khan. Hulagu had an enormous army; estimates run from 80,000 to 200,000.

- The army left Karakorum in 1253, moved across the Eurasian steppes, and reached Samarkand in 1255. It was a display of Mongol power never seen before. The army swept into Iran, crossing the Oxus near the city of Merv, and moved across northern Iran. By 1257, most of the fortresses of the Assassins had fallen.

- The last grand master at Alamut was just a young boy; he surrendered the fortress and allowed the Mongols to occupy it. Because the Assassins were seen as a political danger, the Mongols burned all their libraries—an inestimable loss for future generations of scholars. The Assassins were finished.

Destruction of Baghdad

- Hulagu then moved against his next opponent: the caliph of Baghdad. For this operation, he needed reinforcements from the eastern Christians, including Antioch and the Armenian kingdom of

Cilicia. These two Christian states sent forces and fought with the Mongols down to 1260.

- After the usual exchange of envoys, the caliphs simply dismissed the Mongols. That was a mistake: War was declared, and Hulagu planned an extremely ambitious campaign.

- In January 1258, Mongol columns moved out of the grasslands of Azerbaijan and converged on Baghdad. They ravaged the lands and slaughtered upward of 800,000 people. Hulagu's expert Chinese engineers moved their artillery up to the walls of Baghdad and pounded them to dust.

- The sack of Baghdad was seen by many in the Islamic world—and even beyond—as the height of Mongol atrocities. The caliph watched his own family humiliated and executed. The citizens were marched out on the plains of Iraq and beheaded.

Across the Al-Jazirah

- The destruction of Baghdad gave Hulagu control of the religious, political, and commercial center of eastern Islam. It also destroyed the authority of Sunni Islam because only the caliph could give legitimacy to the various rulers of the Islamic world. The sack of the city was a religious and political disaster as much as a demographic and economic one.

- In 1259, after retiring to Azerbaijan during the winter and refitting his army, Hulagu launched a new campaign and swept across the region that we call the Al-Jazirah: the grasslands between the upper Euphrates and Tigris.

- At this time, the area was populated with Turkish and Arab speakers who practiced nomadism. It was also an area dotted with caravan cities ruled by Ayyubid emirs, members of the family of the great conqueror Saladin.

- The Mongol army made short work of the area. They sacked a number of famous cities, and Damascus simply surrendered—not about to take on the Mongol army.

- Hulagu's general **Kitbuqa** actually sent lead elements as far south as Gaza. The Mongol army had reached the Mediterranean shores. At that point, it looked as if there was no stopping the Mongols— except that Hulagu had run to the end of his logistical capability. He would need a fleet.

- While Hulagu was planning his next move, he received news that Möngke had died and that his younger brother Arigh Böke had been elected the new khan. That meant that Hulagu had to suspend operations, retire to Azerbaijan, and await instructions.

- He left a small force to secure his western frontier. This force comprised largely Turkish elements, as well as Christian allies— Armenians and knights from the principality of Antioch. It was entrusted to the senior commander Kitbuqa.

Decline of Mongol Power in the West
- Meanwhile, in Cairo, the sultan was busy putting together forces to intervene and defeat the Mongol force that was stationed in the Beqaa valley, in today's Lebanon.

- **Qutuz**, the Mamluk sultan, put together an army and crossed the Sinai. At Ain Jalut, the Mamluk army set up positions, and the Mongol army moved out of the Beqaa valley, taking the bait. On September 3, the two armies agreed to fight. The real architect of victory was not the sultan, but his leading emir, **Baybars**.

- The Mongol army went down fighting. Although many of the soldiers were Turks and allies, not full imperial Mongol forces, the Mongols had been defeated in an open battle for the first time. Sultan Qutuz got the credit and was immediately assassinated by Baybars.

- Baybars became the new sultan, and the Mamluk army briefly reoccupied Baghdad. They found a supposed member of the old Abbasid family, brought him back to Cairo, and claimed that the caliphate had been restored. Cairo henceforth emerged as the new power of the Islamic world.

- This battle marked the end of Mongol power in the Islamic world. Kublai Khan, who eventually succeeded as Great Khan of the Mongol Empire, went on to accomplish the unthinkable: a nomadic conquest of the ancient Middle Kingdom.

Important Terms

Chagatais: Descendants of Khan Chagatai (1226–1242), second son of Genghis Khan; they were rulers of the central Asian steppes and Transoxania.

ulus: The Turko-Mongolian nation, designating related tribes.

Names to Know

Arigh Böke (b. 1219; r. 1259–1264): Mongol khan; the fourth and youngest son of Tolui. He was entrusted with the Mongolian homeland by Great Khan Möngke. In 1259, upon the death of Möngke, Arigh Böke was declared Great Khan, but the Mongol army in China acclaimed Kublai Khan. Arigh Böke was defeated in the ensuing civil war in 1260–1254 and forced to abdicate.

Baybars (1260–1277): Mamluk sultan of Egypt; architect of the victory over the Mongols at Ain Jalut in 1260. Soon afterwards, he seized power in Cairo and reoccupied the Levant. He also claimed to have removed the Abbasid heir from the ruined city of Baghdad to Cairo; thus, he was hailed as the champion of Islam against the Mongols and Crusaders.

Kitbuqa (d. 1260): Mongol general; the leading field commander of Hulagu in 1256–1259. He was defeated and slain by the Mamluk army at the Battle of Ain Jalut on September 3, 1260.

Qutuz, al-Muaaffar Sayf al-Din (1259–1260): Mamluk sultan. He refused to submit to Hulagu and planned the campaign of Ain Jalut. He was overthrown and murdered by his leading general, Baybars.

Sorghaghtani Beki (1204–1252): Kereyid princess and wife of Tolui, son of Genghis Khan, and the niece of Wang Khan. She was the mother of Möngke, Kublai Khan, Hulagu, and Arigh Böke. A Nestorian Christian, she favored her co-religionists at court. In 1248–1251, after the death of Khan Güyük (1246–1248), she secured the support of Batu and the majority in the *kurultai* to elect her son Möngke as Great Khan.

Suggested Reading

Cahen, "The Mongols and the Near East."

Hildinger, *Warriors of the Steppe.*

Mote, *Imperial China, 900–1800.*

Saunders, *A History of Medieval Islam.*

———, *The History of the Mongol Conquests.*

Questions to Consider

1. How successful was Ögödei in imposing peace and order on the Muslim lands of Iran and Transoxiana that had been devastated by Genghis Khan in 1219–1221? How did the generals with a permanent Mongol army in Azerbaijan keep order?

2. How important were dynastic politics at the Mongol court and the succession crises in dictating Mongol expansion?

3. What were the threats posed to Mongol rule by the Assassins, the Abbasid caliphate, and the Mamluk sultans of Egypt? How important were the caravan cities of Iran and Transoxiana as sources of Mongol revenue?

4. How skillfully did Hulagu conduct his campaigns in 1258–1260? If a succession crisis had not arisen due to the sudden death of Möngke,

could Hulagu have conquered Egypt, or had the Mongol army reached its logistical limits?

5. What were the long-term consequences for the Islamic world of the invasion of Hulagu? How did it decisively shift the axis of Islamic civilization?

Mongol Invasion of the Islamic World
Lecture 30—Transcript

In this lecture, I plan to look at the Mongol invasions into the Islamic world. We are going to concentrate on the campaigns of Hulagu, who was the brother of Kublai Khan; actually the older brother of Kublai Khan. I want to make two important points to tie this lecture to the previous lecture. In the previous lecture, we discussed how Batu, the grandson of Genghis Khan, had commanded a great army that overran the western steppes and invaded Russia, Hungary, and Poland. That invasion had been cut short by really dynastic politics back at Karakorum, the Mongol capital in the homeland. On December 11, 1241, the Great Khan Ögedei died and that resulted in Batu halting his invasion; and I mentioned that for the first time dynastic politics influenced imperial policy. This lecture will show the same feature. When we discussed the Mongol invasion of the Islamic world—and the decision was taken as early as 1253; the main conquest occurred between 1257 and 1260—the ultimate plan of this invasion, which was to take Cairo, was also cut short by dynastic politics. That actually plunged the Mongol Empire into the first civil war.

In addition, both campaigns bear another important resemblance that you should keep in mind as we discuss the operations in the Islamic world. In both Central Europe—in Hungary and Poland—as well as in the Middle East in this upcoming lecture, the Mongols essentially hit their logistical limit. They moved into areas where they would have to alter their way of warfare, devise new strategies, new logistics, and literally create a new army to accompany the traditional steppe cavalry if they were to operate in Egypt or in Central Europe. They would face the same barriers when they tried to conquer China. They overcame the barriers in China; but they never had the time or the opportunity to do so to return to the Middle East and to Central Europe. It is important to keep both of these thoughts in mind about the dynastic politics, the limits of Mongol logistics, strategy, and even knowledge in waging the war against the eastern lands of Islam.

Let us back up a moment and recall what the situation was at the death of Genghis Khan in 1227. Genghis Khan had carried out one of the remarkable invasions of all time by the nomadic armies of the steppes. He had planned an audacious campaign that had swept through the cities of Transoxiana and Iran, had overthrown the empire of Khorasan, had literally hunted and hounded down that ruler Muhammad Shah, who died a miserable exile on an island in the Caspian Sea. The victories were spectacular, but so were the atrocities and the massacres that accompanied the conquest; and the result was when Genghis Khan slowly returned home to his capital at Karakorum, he left behind him a largely devastated Islamic world. There are many anecdotes indicating that on his return, Genghis Khan was rather impressed by Islamic teachers, imams. He is credited with making favorable comments about Sufi mystics, although this idea of a pilgrimage to Mecca completely escaped him, he always thought, "Mongol law, the *Yassa*, the traditional customs, trumped everything"; but he was not necessarily hostile to Islam as a religion so long as it knew its place, which was as one of many faiths within the Mongol Empire.

He left little in the way of an administration. There was no real effort to revive the cities, to put agricultural land back under production; there had been widespread devastation in some of the cities. It really was Ögedei, the second khan, who began to put in a rudimentary administration. That largely was stationing a Mongol army at Tabriz in the region today known as Azerbaijan. As I mentioned, Azerbaijan was part of a set of steppes in Northwestern Iran that was very congenial to Mongols and Turks. It provided grasslands; it had historically been attractive to nomads. The Mongol military force—and most of those guys were actually Turks, they were not Mongols—were stationed there to provide protection for the regions of Iran and Transoxiana, which had been brought under Mongol control. It was that army in 1243, shortly after Ögedei's death, that invaded Asia Minor and clobbered the sultan of Konya and brought most of Asia Minor under the tutelage of the Mongol khan. Ögedei had died; that was actually during the regency of this very, very formidable lady known as Töregene who was actually the widow of Ögedei.

The situation in the Islamic world was really one of no functioning Mongol administration, a great deal of devastation. On the other hand, there were counter authorities in the Islamic world that were perceived as dangers to Mongol rule. That included the Abbasid caliphs in Baghdad, who were a powerful regional power; the Assassins, that famous Ishmaelite sect at their fortress Alamut, the so-called Eagles Nest; and above all the Mamluk, the slave sultans of Egypt.

In 1241–1242, as I mentioned, the Mongol Empire was in a crisis; and this was brought about by the death of Ögedei. Hostile sources say that Ögedei drank himself to death; he was known for his indulgence, extravagant expenditures. He was not popular in his later years. That death, which occurred on December 11, 1241, was quickly communicated by the courier system across the Eurasian steppes to Batu where the majority of the Mongol nation was battling in Hungary. Batu knew early in 1242 there would be a new election. As I mentioned before, the nomadic peoples practiced what is called lateral succession. It was by no means assured who was going to be elected the next khan or to be more accurate, the Great Khan; that is, who would succeed to the position of Genghis Khan. In 1242, there were two candidates. The leading candidate was Güyük, the son of Ögedei, who had a reasonable claim to the throne. Furthermore, his interests were pushed by his mother, the widow of the Great Khan, Töregene, and she was a powerful and formidable lady who was going to put her son on the throne. There were other candidates; Batu himself was a potential candidate. He, after all, was the son of the older son of Genghis Khan, who had died in 1227, months before Genghis. Then there was the family of the second son of Genghis Khan, the family of Chagatai. There was also the family of the youngest son, Tolui; Tolui had died in 1232.

There were a number of candidates available. In 1242, only one of the four sons of Genghis Khan was still alive. That was Chagatai who ruled the central steppes. He had a number of sons. He was too old. He was an important elector in the events, but he himself was not a candidate. The other candidates came down to Batu, who was in the west with a majority of the army; but as you recall, his father Jochi was not really Genghis Khan's son. He was probably a son by a Merkit prince and the wife of Genghis Khan, Börte, when she was in captivity, although Genghis had always treated him as a son. Batu had a lot to recommend him. He had command of the western armies. The other possible candidates were the sons of Tolui, the youngest son. Tolui had died in 1232, but he and his wife had four sons, all capable of obtaining the khanate; and that included the eldest, Möngke, who eventually would become khan, and then his brothers Hulagu, Kublai, the later Kublai

Khan, and the youngest brother, a fellow by the name of Arigh Böke; so there were plenty of candidates.

The election did not take place until years after the death of the Great Khan. It was not until 1246 when the electors decided to go with Ögedei's son Güyük, who was elected the Great Khan and acclaimed by all the peoples who dwelt within the felt tents. The reason for the delay was not communications, but maneuvering the electors to come to that consensus at the assembly, at the *Kurultai*; and as I mentioned, this was not a democratic assembly where you debated and voted. Everyone more or less knew who was supposed to be elected; it would be an acclamation and a great religious event.

That change in leadership also changed policy, because the new khan, Güyük, was very, very hostile to Batu; there were rumors that he wanted to poison Batu; and furthermore, Güyük did not want to renew the western campaigns because that would bring distinction to Batu. Batu, therefore, aligned himself with the widow of Tolui, the youngest son of Genghis Khan, and his cousins. Those four sons had a just as domineering and powerful and remarkable mom as Güyük did. Her name was Sorghaghtani Beki. Sorghaghtani Beki was probably the favorite daughter-in-law of Genghis Khan, and her two sons that were the apple of her eye—that was the second and third, Hulagu and Kublai, the future Kublai Khan—they were also favorite grandsons of Genghis Khan. Eventually, they would get their day in 1248 when Güyük died prematurely; and the eldest of those four brothers, Möngke, would be elected khan.

These machinations—and they were really lurid politics; there was accusations of poisoning, Batu threatened civil war at one point— underscored the instability of nomadic traditions of lateral succession, and also the rivalry in the third generation from Genghis Khan. All of these cousins had equal claim to the Great Khan, and if they did not get the job Great Khan, they expected to get an *ulus*; that is, a people. *Ulus* is still an important word in both Mongolian and Turkish; that is a huge area with nomadic tribes and military power and, in addition, either the commission to attack a sedentary civilization that would provide tribute or control of an area that had already been conquered such as the Russian principalities, Northern China, or Transoxiana. This basic instability would eventually break out into civil war and in time would lead to the unraveling of the empire of Kublai Khan.

The second important election came on July 1, 1251, when again the Mongols decided to choose a new khan; and that was Möngke, the eldest son of Tolui. That meant that the power of the Great Khan, the position of the Great Khan, now passed from Ögedei's family—and Ögedei was the third son of Genghis Khan—to the family of the youngest son, Tolui. That was an important change, because Möngke cut a very, very different image from his cousin and from his uncle; that is Ögedei and Güyük. For one, he had none of these pretentions of being a Chinese-style monarch. He was a Mongol ruler, much more in the manner of his granddad Genghis Khan. He was rather modest in his appearance and his manners; he was accessible and affable. He was supported by three very capable brothers; and those four brothers—until Möngke's death, and the youngest one precipitated a civil war—generally operated very well as a unit; Mom made sure of that. In addition, Möngke was committed to new expansion. Expansion was necessary to sustain the monarchy; it was important to providing the booty, the silk, the captives that were so important in winning followers. He carried out important changes in the military. He purged the officer corps of those people who had been previously loyal to the house of Ögedei, replaced them with loyal men. In this way, he was following very much the policy of his granddad, Genghis Khan. By the second or third year of his reign, he was ready to go.

Batu, the cousin out on the western steppes, was essentially confirmed in his position as ruler of the Mongols and Turks of the far west; and that *ulus* eventually evolved into the Golden Horde. Batu did very well. He transmitted his position to his younger brother Böke; and those khans ruling in the western steppes eventually evolved into independent rulers. They would adopt Turkish and eventually adopt Islam, and they would go their separate way. The family of Chagatai was rewarded with control of the central steppes. The various sons of Chagatai would rule these regions, although they had covetous eyes for Transoxiana and the cities of the Tarim Basin and there would always be dispute whether the Chagataid—that is, the descendants of Chagatai—khans had claim over those two key urban areas.

The really important commissions were given to the two younger brothers of the new khan. Kublai Khan was commissioned with the eastern steppes, was given the commission to conquer China—we will get into that in the next lecture—and Hulagu, the second brother, was told, "Return to the Islamic world, put some kind of order in those conquests, and also take out any opposition to Mongol control of the eastern lands of Islam," and Möngke had very, very good reason to do this. For one, the Abbasid caliph in Baghdad represented a counter authority. The Mongols always were not quite sure what the caliph's authority was. He looked sort of like a weird Chinese emperor, the Son of Heaven. They had the same problem with the Pope and the Holy Roman Emperor; they never quite understood what the arrangement was between the Pope and particularly Frederick II (and, in fact, most Western Europeans did not know what the arrangement was between Frederick II and the papacy). In any case, that was a possible counter authority. The other was the rising Mamluk sultans of Egypt who depended on Turkish slave soldiers that were actually sold from the steppes into service and transported compliments of Venice to Cairo so that the Mamluk sultans, which means the slave soldier sultans, had an excellent army. Above all, this secretive group, this extreme Shiite group led by a grand master living in Alamut—that great fortress in the Elburz Mountains—and with cells across the Islamic world known as the Assassins; that was their popular name, they were better known as Ishmaelites. They had set out hit squads to take out Mongol governors; there was apparently one reputedly that was sent after Möngke. These guys all had to be removed in the minds of the Great Khan and his brothers.

Hulagu was given the bulk of the field army; it was now transferred from the western steppes to the central steppes to invade the Islamic world. It was perhaps the most impressive campaign since Genghis Khan. Hulagu had an enormous army; estimates run from 80,000–200,000. Clearly, when that army moved across the Eurasian steppes—and it left from Karakorum in 1253; it did not reach Samarkand until 1255—it was a display of Mongol power that had never been seen before. That army swept into Iran, crossing the Oxus near the city of Merv—one of the few cities that had not be trashed in the earlier campaigns; it had been smart enough to surrender immediately—and began to move across Northern Iran. In 1257, most of the fortresses of the Assassins had fallen.

The last Grand Master at Alamut was a young boy and really did not have any stomach for this; he just surrendered the fortress on terms and allowed the Mongols to occupy it. The Mongols went through these fortresses burning various libraries because the Assassins were seen as a political danger. Scholars wonder how much damage was done by this particular act of destruction because the Assassins kept large libraries on all sorts of information, particularly about their political opponents; and that meant this was an inestimable loss for later scholars and future generations. Nonetheless, most of the Muslims, at least the Sunni Muslims, applauded the destruction of the Assassins, who were regarded as political terrorists. In the campaigns of 1256–1257, Iran was secured; the Assassins were eliminated.

That meant Hulagu was ready to move against the next opponent, and that was the caliph of Baghdad. For this operation, Hulagu needed reinforcements; he needed local allies; and local forces were provided particularly by some of the Eastern Christians client rulers. This included the king of Cilician Armenia, King Hethum, who compromised his kingdom later with the Muslims; Bohemond VI, the Prince of Antioch. These two Christian states sent forces and they fought with the Mongols down to 1260. The rest of the [Christian princes] were far less eager to get involved in this struggle and more or less sat on the sidelines. The target was Baghdad and there was the usual exchange of envoys; the caliphs simply dismissed the Mongols: "I'm the caliph of the Islamic world and Sunni Islam will rally to me." That was a mistake; and the result was war was declared and Hulagu planned a very, very ambitious campaign.

He timed his invasion early in the year 1258; and in January, 1258, Mongol columns moved out of the grasslands of Azerbaijan, they avoided the heat of the summer, and they converged on Baghdad. They ravaged the lands; they drove the population into the city. Clearly the city was swollen with numerous refuges; and the reports are that 800,000 would eventually be slaughtered. Hulagu also had with him expert Chinese engineers as well as all sorts of allied kingdoms, and they were able in early February to move their artillery up to the walls of Baghdad and begin pounding the walls. It was clear that the mud brick walls were not going to hold up to Chinese engineers; their artillery was just too formidable. On February 10, the caliph, al-Musta'sim, decided to negotiate. He negotiated a surrender and the terms are unclear; but because he had defied the Mongol initially, when the Mongols actually occupied the city some three days later, Hulagu's attitude was, "All bets are off, you still had defied us." He allowed the Mongol army to sack the city thoroughly.

That sack, which we used as the opening of this course, was seen by many in the Islamic world, and even beyond the Islamic world, as perhaps the height of Mongol atrocities. The caliph, of course, watched his own family be destroyed, humiliated, and executed. The citizens were marched out on the plain of Iraq. The men, women, and children were ceremoniously beheaded. Piles of skulls were seen on the plains. The bodies and the bones were still to be seen years later. The only people to escape destruction were the Nestorian Christians, a small community, because Hulagu himself was married to a Nestorian wife, although he-himself believed in the ancient gods of the Mongols—Tengri, the god of the sky—and he consulted shamans. According to the accounts, the Tigris ran first black with ink. So many manuscripts were tossed in the Tigris and destroyed as wanton acts of destruction that the libraries were essentially gone. Mosques, *medreses*, the hospitals, the markets that sustained these Islamic institutions, they were all thoroughly ransacked and then destroyed. Then the Tigris ran red with blood as the population was herded out and slaughtered. We do believe that craftsmen, particularly good-looking girls and boys, and some experts were saved and deported to be used in the Mongol court back in the homeland. But on the whole, it was a pretty thorough and shocking destruction of a civilian population.

Baghdad was a city on a whole other order in size from the caravan cities such as Samarkand and Bukhara. The figure of 800,000 or a million residents is certainly plausible. It is still not known whether Hulagu was influenced by his Nestorian wife or perhaps by his favorite general, Kitbuka, who was also known to be a Nestorian and no friend of Islam; but the action was seen as a deliberate and savage act of terrorism, and this atrocity sent shockwaves through the Islamic world. The destruction of Baghdad gave Hulagu control of the religious, political, and commercial center of Eastern Islam. It also destroyed the authority of Sunni Islam, because only the caliph could give a *firman*, which would give legitimacy to the various rulers of the Islamic world. This sack of the city was a religious and political disaster as much as a demographic and economic disaster.

In 1259, after retiring to Azerbaijan during the winter and refitting his army, the next year after the capture of Baghdad, Hulagu launched a new campaign and swept across the region that we call the al-Jazirah. The al-Jazirah is the grasslands between the Upper Euphrates and Tigris. They had traditionally been home to nomads. At this time, there were many Turkish speakers and Arab speakers who practiced a nomadic life. It was also an area dotted with caravan cities ruled by petty emirs, Ayyubid emirs; that is, members of the family of the great conqueror Salidan. The Mongol army made short work. They sacked a number of famous cities, particularly the city of Horan. It was noted for its ancient mosque going back to the Umayyad caliphs. The city never recovered; it is still in ruins. One emir by the name of al-Kamil was seized and tortured brutally; he was forced to eat his own flesh. There were other acts of atrocity committed at the Syrian cities of Aleppo, lesser Syrian cities in the Orontes Valley. Damascus simply surrendered; they were not about to take on the Mongol army. Kitbuka actually sent lead elements as far south as Gaza. The Mongol army had reached the Mediterranean shores.

At that point, it looked like there was no stopping the Mongols, except, again, Hulagu had run into the end of his logistical line to invade Egypt. He would need a fleet. He would need cooperation of Venice and the Crusaders. He would need all sorts of new logistics. While he was planning his next move, he received news that on August 11, 1259, Möngke had died and that his younger brother, Berke, was elected the new khan. That information meant that Hulagu had to suspend operations, retire to Azerbaijan, and wait upon events. He left a small force to secure his western frontier. This force comprised of largely Turkish elements. It also had some Christian allies, notably Armenians and Christian knights from the principality of Antioch. This force was entrusted to the senior commander Kitbuka, and he was given the go ahead to consolidate this area.

Meanwhile, in Cairo, the sultan of Cairo was not slack. He was putting together forces and ready to intervene and defeat that Mongol force that was stationed in the Beqaa Valley, very close to the ancient city of Baalbek, Heliopolis. Qutuz, who was then the Mamluk sultan—and the sultan was chosen by a consortium of various emirs, that is, slave soldier commanders—he put together an army, he swiftly crossed the Sinai, he got a benevolent neutrality out of the Crusader princes, and in early September his army reached the Galilee at the location of Ain Jalut. At Ain Jalut, the Mamluk army set up positions, and the Mongol army moved out of the Lebanon, out of the Beqaa Valley, and took the bait of a major battle. On September 3, the two armies agreed to fight. The real architect of victory was not the sultan but his leading emir, Baybars, who went on to overthrow his master. Baybars set up a battle line that lured the Mongol cavalry to attack in the center, drew them up the hill and then sprang a trap, a concealment on the flanks, and the Mongol army went down fighting; and again, most of these were Turks and allies, not really full imperial Mongol forces. Nonetheless, the Mongols had been defeated in an open battle for the first time. Sultan Qutuz got the credit, and then was immediately done in by his leading emir and Baybars became the new sultan; and the Mamluk army actually briefly reoccupied Baghdad, found a supposed member of the old Abbasid family, brought him back to Cairo, and claimed that the caliphate had been restored. Cairo henceforth emerged as the new power of the Islamic world, compliments of Baybars and his success at the Battle of Ain Jalut.

This battle marked the end of Mongol power in the west, in the Islamic world, and it revealed the same weaknesses we saw in Central Europe. Kublai Khan, who would succeed eventually as Great Khan of the Mongol Empire, faced the same problems when he undertook his conquest of China. But in his case, he solved those problems and pulled off the unthinkable: a nomadic conquest of the ancient middle kingdom.

Conquest of Song China
Lecture 31

In this lecture, we'll explore the last of the Mongol campaigns: Kublai Khan's conquest of Song China. This was perhaps the greatest of the Mongol military achievements. Song China posed immense logistical, political, and military problems for a force based on horse archers. To conquer China, Kublai Khan had to devise a new kind of army. Although previous Mongol campaigns had been characterized by terror and violence, Kublai Khan succeeded in winning over the Chinese population. By 1271, he ruled as a Chinese-style emperor, taking the name Yuan for his dynasty. As the Roman historian Livy stated, "It is not only important to know how to win victories, it is also important to know how to use them."

Background to the Song Invasion

- Why did Kublai Khan and Möngke depart from the policy of the earlier khagans and decide to take on the Song Empire in China?

- At his death in 1227, Genghis Khan had achieved most of what he wanted territorially. He had unified the central and eastern steppes. He controlled the rich cities of the Tarim Basin, the Gansu Corridor, and most of northern China.

- The Song court had had close dealings with Genghis Khan and his various successors; in fact, they had been criticized by their people for not taking stronger measures against the Mongols. From the Song viewpoint, however, the Mongols did not offer much of a threat.

- On the other hand, the Mongols were not in much of a position to invade south into the Yangtze valley and take on the Song fortifications. Furthermore, the emperors of the Song Dynasty were served by able generals and capable bureaucrats who were loyal to the throne.

- These bureaucrats may not have been skilled in warcraft, but they understood statecraft. They had read the Chinese classics on strategy and on wider diplomatic policy, and they had a good sense of the political situation on the steppes.

Commission to Conquer China
- From the Mongol viewpoint, conquering the Song Empire was a daunting task that required a dynamic and energetic khagan. When Möngke was confirmed as khan in 1251, he appointed his brother Kublai as master of the eastern armies and commissioned him to go south.

- The youngest brother, Arigh Böke, was given nominal control of the heartland; he stayed in Karakorum. That position allowed him to amass important political support.

- Kublai Khan was ideally suited for the commission to conquer China. He had not had much training in the western domains and knew very little about the Islamic world. However, he knew a great deal about the Mongolian homeland and, above all, the Mongolian domains in northern China.

© Anige of Nepal/Wikimedia Commons/Public Domain.

Kublai Khan gained expertise in his initial campaigns against the Song Empire, developing logistical systems and making use of Chinese forces to augment the Mongols.

- In some ways, Kublai Khan, more than any of his brothers, appreciated the importance of China. He was brave, excelled in hunting and horsemanship, and possessed all the qualities of a Great Khan. Möngke knew that Kublai Khan had the intelligence to develop the logistics and strategy to undertake the conquest of China.

Operations in Tibet and Yunnan

- The war began with operations to secure the western approaches to the Song Empire, which would eventually become the southern frontiers of the Mongol Empire. In 1258, Kublai Khan led an expedition of more than 650 miles across the rugged terrain of Tibet and into the current province of Yunnan in southwestern China.

- This campaign was significant, largely because it was a war of sieges and logistics. Kublai Khan perfected the logistical system to provide the fodder, water, and food to support a cavalry army in a landscape inhospitable to the type of nomadic warfare that was the hallmark of Mongol armies.

- Kublai also recruited many more Chinese infantry to garrison cities, which would relieve the Mongol forces to carry out field operations, maneuvers, stealth operations, and battles of encirclement.

- The Tibetans had paid homage to Möngke—an important connection, because he allowed Tibetan **tantric** Buddhism to flourish. Buddhism eventually became the preferred religion of Kublai Khan and his successors, the **Yuan** emperors.

Böke as Great Khan

- Once the western areas had been secured, in 1259, Möngke and Kublai moved south to the Yangtze River. The Song army was huge—perhaps 600,000 men—but it was weak in cavalry. The region north of the Yangtze was thick with Song fortifications; the river was patrolled by flotillas.

- Kublai knew that the Mongols would have to gain those fortresses along the Yangtze. That would mean gaining control of the waterways and the canal systems. In the initial expedition by Möngke and Kublai, the Mongol army got bogged down in a war of sieges along the Yangtze.

- On August 11, 1259, Khan Möngke died of cholera. Initially, Kublai continued fighting, but then he got word that his younger brother,

Arigh Böke, had summoned a rump session of the *kurultai* and had himself proclaimed khan.

Civil War in the Mongol Empire

- Both Hulagu and Kublai refused to recognize the election. Eventually, Kublai held his own *kurultai*, in inner Mongolia, the first time the Mongols had ever met in assembly outside the homeland. They proclaimed Kublai the Great Khan.

- In early 1260, we see two Great Khans and, for the first time, a civil war. Hulagu from the start supported Kublai. The result was that the majority of the military force was in the hands of Kublai Khan. In 1261, his field army knocked out the forces of Arigh Böke, who retreated west into the central steppes.

- Kublai Khan won the civil war easily. He cut off food shipments to Mongolia. The population of Karakorum had swollen to somewhere between 30,000 and 50,000 permanent residents. It had to be supplied by foodstuffs brought in from the Chinese provinces, and Kublai Khan controlled those routes.

- A particularly severe winter drove the point home: Whoever controlled China controlled the Mongol Empire.

Rule of the Mongol Empire

- Kublai Khan had gained the empire—but at a price. In order to achieve the position of Great Khan, he had to agree that he would conquer China and incorporate it into a great eastern khaganate.

- There were four other *ulus*. The western reaches, or the Golden Horde, were ruled by the descendants of Batu. The Chagataid rulers controlled the central steppes. In Iran and Transoxania, Kublai Khan recognized the son of Hulagu, who became the next ilkhan.

- Kublai Khan, in effect, partitioned the Mongol Empire not only along cultural lines but also along the geographic lines of the steppes.

War against the Song

- In 1268, Kublai Khan reopened the war against the Song court. He amassed a great army, including the core of the operations: the esteemed cavalry forces of Mongolia. He also chose the most capable generals. His finest general was **Bayan**, who was entrusted with the final mopping-up operations after 1273. Kublai Khan also recruited large numbers of Chinese infantry. Above all, he expanded the engineering corps.

- His nephew, the ilkhan of Persia, had sent Muslim engineers and technicians to build superior engines of war, especially artillery. Certain Song generals defected to Kublai Khan at the start of the campaign, especially in 1268–1269. They not only brought valuable information but also explained the fortification systems along the Yangtze.

- Importantly, these Song defectors understood incendiaries, which were ignited by gunpowder. These included primitive grenades or iron bombs that exploded and fire lances that could ignite the Chinese fortified cities, which were largely wooden palisades on top of **rammed-earth** platforms.

- Kublai Khan had the best of expertise and, above all, large numbers of ships that were used to isolate the crucial fortresses along the lower Yangtze. Those fortresses were the scene of major sieges. The fortress of Fengcheng was brutally sacked, and that led to the surrender of other fortresses. At that point, the Song court knew that the war was over.

A Chinese-style Emperor

- In addition to the war of sieges and the successes along the Yangtze, Kublai Khan departed from the usual policy of Mongol conquerors. On the whole, the conquest of Song China was not accompanied by the traditional massacres and atrocities. From the start, Kublai Khan intended to win over the Chinese people as subjects; already by 1271, he presented himself as a Chinese-style emperor.

- He intended to win the war politically, as well as militarily. By December 1272, when the main fortresses had been battered down, it was clear that the war was over. Kublai Khan retired to his capital in the north, Dadu, or Xanadu, which was later Beijing. There was a major ceremonial surrender in 1276; Gong abdicated.

- Kublai Khan had conquered Song China and, with it, all the administrative apparatus to run it. The Confucian scholars, or Mandarin gentry class, realized it was time to come to terms with Kublai Khan. To a certain degree at least, Kublai Khan respected Chinese civilization.

Logistical Overreach

- Kublai Khan also fell heir to some of the territorial ambitions of the Chinese. This led him to make two ill-advised naval invasions of Japan. Both of these campaigns were failures.

- Large numbers of Chinese were drafted into both invasions, while the number of Mongols involved was low. The smaller expedition, in 1274, was an invasion of the island of Kyushu. Because of storms, much of the fleet was destroyed and nearly half the men never returned. A larger expedition with two great flotillas was sent in 1281. That, too, failed; the army was caught on the beaches by a typhoon.

- The failure of both expeditions in Japan represented, again, the limit of Mongol logistics and military power. Kublai Khan had overreached. Despite the embarrassment of the Japanese expeditions, however, they certainly did not endanger the throne or Mongol control of China.

Important Terms

rammed earth: A construction technique using earth, gravel, lime, and clay. The Qin and Han emperors employed this method to build the Great Wall. The construction is simple but labor intensive.

tantric: The higher moral and mystical interpretation of traditional village rites in either Hinduism or Buddhism.

Yuan Dynasty: The Chinese dynasty adopted by Kublai Khan (1260–1294) and his successors who ruled China and Mongolia (1279–1368).

Name to Know

Bayan (1236–1295): Mongol general; the leading field commander of Kublai Khan in the conquest of Song China. He received the final surrender of the dowager empress Xie Daoqing and the boy emperor Gong (1275–1276) at the Song capital of Linan (Hangzhou).

Suggested Reading

Barefield, *The Perilous Frontier*.

Mote, *Imperial China, 900–1800*.

Polo (Wright, ed. and trans.), *The Travels of Marco Polo, the Venetian*.

Rossabi, *Kublai Khan, His Life and Times*.

Saunders, *The History of the Mongol Conquests*.

Questions to Consider

1. How did Genghis Khan view the Song Empire? What was the policy and ultimate aim of Ögödei in his campaigns again the Jin and into Tibet? What limitations did Ögödei face if he were to undertake a conquest of China?

2. What were the strengths and weaknesses of the Song Empire in the 13th century? How effective were the courts of emperors Lizog and Duzong in confronting Kublai Khan?

3. In what ways did Kublai Khan display strategic and logistical genius in his conquest of China? How important was his generalship in achieving victory? What other factors accounted for Mongol victory in 1279?

4. Why was Kublai Khan compelled to invade Japan in 1274 and 1281? What accounted for Mongol failure to conquer Japan? How did these amphibious landings mark the limit of Mongol military power?

5. How does the conquest of Song China by Kublai Khan compare to the campaigns of Batu (1236–1242) and Hulagu (1257–1260)? What lessons did Kublai Khan learn from these earlier campaigns and apply to his conquest of China?

Conquest of Song China
Lecture 31—Transcript

In this lecture, I want to deal with the last of the great Mongol conquests, and that is the conquest of Song China. This was largely the achievement of Kublai Khan. Some scholars would argue it is perhaps the greatest of the Mongol military achievements.

Song China posed logistical, political, and military problems that could have stumped the Mongol army, which was basically a steppe army based on horse archers. To conquer China, Kublai Khan literally had to invent a new army. It is also a major question why Kublai Khan—and actually his predecessor, his elder brother Möngke—decided to depart with the policy of the earlier khans and actually take on the Song Chinese Empire. Genghis Khan, for all of his successes, was really rather traditional in his dealings vis-à-vis the Song court.

At his death in 1227, Genghis Khan had achieved most of what he wanted territorially. The conquests of the Islamic lands in Iran and Transoxiana were arguably something of a fluke. It was not intended; he was drawn into it by border conflicts by the proud and haughty exchanges with Muhammad Shah. But otherwise, Genghis Khan had achieved pretty much what most steppe conquerors would want. He had the central and eastern steppes unified under his sole authority. He had at his disposal something like 150,000, maybe 200,000 nomadic cavalry, Turks, and Mongols. He also controlled those key border areas vis-à-vis the Chinese Empire. The rich cities of the Tarim Basin; largely populated by Uighur speakers now, who provided his ministers, his translators, his interpreters. He controlled the Gansu corridor, a corridor that linked those cities to Northern China. He controlled most of Northern China. He did not control the Lower Yellow River valley or the peninsula of Shandong; that was still in the hands of the Jin emperors. But otherwise, he had pretty much what he needed. His attitude towards the Song court would also be traditional. You exchange embassies; perhaps you could extort gifts and tribute. You would get recognition that you were deserving of an imperial marriage. In this sense, Genghis Khan vis-à-vis Song China was probably quite traditional in his policies.

He did intend to conquer what was left of the Jin Empire; he had to do that. The city of Kaifeng was targeted, and it was really left to his son Ögedei to complete that conquest in 1234–1235. But otherwise, the Song court could probably rest at ease that the Mongols posed no immediate threat. Ögedei, of course, fell heir to the campaign against the Jin. Genghis Khan had actually planned a campaign before he died in August, 1227. There was the usual delay over the election—it was not until 1229—and actually Ögedei went out of his way to contact the Song court and agree to a partition of the former Song domains. This was also in keeping with previous policies. You remember how the Song court had approached the Jurchens who had overthrown the Khitan or Liao emperors and also agreed to some kind of partition between Northern and Southern China. Ögedei was quite content to knock out the Jin, occupy Kaifeng, and leave it at that. It was the Song court that attempted to take back Kaifeng; that was the emperor Lizong's policy. The Chinese army was driven back. That provoked retaliatory raids into the western frontiers of China into the region that would be known as Sichau. There were acrimonious exchanges of embassies. But in part, Ögedei was responding to this Song posturing that those cities of the Lower Yellow River valley really belonged to China, they were really part of China; and whatever agreements that were made to take out the Jin were vitiated by the Song sense that we have to gather all of the Han people back under our control. Even so, Ögedei did not decide to follow up with this; he had no intentions of waging a war against Song China. His interests were west; he was sending most of his army west with his nephew Batu who could carry out the conquest of the Western steppes in Russia.

The Song court, which has sometimes been criticized—particularly the emperor Ningzong, who had had close dealings with Genghis Khan and his various successors—for not taking stronger measures against the Mongols. But really, from the Song viewpoint, the Mongols did not offer all that much of a threat. They were far away, they were remote; and furthermore, the Song had very, very good reasons to trust to their army and to their traditional sense of strategy. To be sure, they were not able to take back the northern regions. They were frustrated in 1235; by that, their army could not penetrate and drive out the Mongols. On the other hand, the Mongols were not in much of a position to invade south into the Yangtze or the Yangzi River valley and take on the Song fortifications. Furthermore, the emperors of the Song Dynasty may not have commanded armies on the battlefield; they were not in the manner of the great Tang emperors; but they were served by able generals and able bureaucrats. One aspect about the Song examination system in the Confucian state that was constructed in the 10th century is those Mandarin bureaucrats had a real sense of loyalty to the throne. Sure, they may have been bureaucrats and they may not have been soldiers by training, but they understood statecraft; they had read the Chinese classics on statecraft, on strategy, on wider diplomatic policy, and they had a very, very good sense of the steppes and they had a long tradition of previous emperors, Han and Tang particularly, in manipulating the tribes. Every time there was a succession crisis in the Mongol Empire—such as in 1242, or again in 1248, and above all during the civil war that resulted in the suspension of operations against the Song in 1259–1263—the Song court could probably rest assured that this Mongol confederation would break up and go away as many previous Mongol confederations had.

From the Mongol viewpoint, conquering the Song Empire was an awesome and daunting task; and it really required a dynamic and energetic khan to conduct this. Neither Ögedei nor Güyük, in my opinion, had the personality and the training to do it. But Möngke and Kublai Khan, they did. Möngke was confirmed as khan in 1251 after the usual maneuvering, and he appointed his brother Kublai Khan as master of the eastern armies. The youngest brother, the fourth one in the group, Arigh Böke, is given the kind of nominal control of the heartland and he talks to the shamans and hangs out at Karakorum. That was actually an important position because it allowed him to mass important political support. But it is clear that Möngke had Kublai Khan designated with the commission "Go south," while the other brother, the second brother Hulagu, went west into the Islamic world.

Kublai Khan was ideally suited for this task. He had not had much training in the western domains. He did not serve in Batu's army, for instance; Möngke did. So he had very little experience with Cumans, Russians, and Kipchak Turks; he knew very little about the Islamic world; but he did know a great deal about the Mongolian homeland, and above all about the Mongolian domains in Northern China. In some ways, Kublai Khan, more than any other of those four brothers appreciated the importance of China; and that would become evident in the civil war and then in the way how he conducted his own conquests when he was khan and reopened that war and carried out the final conquest of the Song Empire. He clearly was brave. He had all the qualities of a Great Khan. There were stories of how Genghis Khan admired this grandson, particularly on the return march from Khorasam. Kublai Khan excelled in hunting and horsemanship; so did Möngke. The two brothers—and those would be the first and third brother in the set of four— were unusually close, and Möngke knew that Kublai Khan had the smarts to develop the logistics and strategy to undertake the conquest of China.

The war opened up with actually operations that were peripheral to the conquest of China, and that was to secure the western approaches to the Song Empire; they eventually became the southern frontiers of the Mongol Empire. In 1258, Kublai Khan led an expedition over 650 miles across the rugged terrain of Tibet into the current province of Yunnan in Southwestern China, which was then an independent kingdom with its capital city at Dali; and these were non-Chinese people who had converted to Buddhism and were ruled by a sort of Chinese-style monarchy. They were known as the Bai people.

This campaign was significant, largely because it was a war of sieges and logistics. Kublai Khan perfected the logistical system to provide the fodder, the water, the food to support a cavalry army in a landscape that was really quite inhospitable to the type of nomadic warfare that was the hallmark of Mongol armies. Kublai also recruited many more Chinese infantry. They always used Chinese engineers; from the very start, they understood that these guys could knock down walls and take cities. But Kublai Khan realized already—and I should not call him Kublai Khan, he was still Kublai; he was not the Great Khan—Kublai recognized the need to have Chinese infantry in large numbers; they could take cities, they could garrison cities, and that would relieve the Mongol forces to carry out field operations of maneuvers, surprise, stealth, and battles of encirclement. These expertises were gained in these initial campaigns. Those campaigns also resulted in Mongol expeditions into Tibet. The Tibetans essentially paid homage to Möngke; and that is a very important connection, because under a sort of Mongol protection Tibetan tantric Buddhism flourished and eventually became the preferred religion of Kublai Khan and all of his successors who would rule as Chinese-styled emperors known as the Yuan emperors. Therefore, once

237

those western areas had been secured in 1259, Möngke and Kublai moved south against the Yangtze River.

The Song army was large. We have all sorts of estimates how big it was, 600,000 men. They certainly were weak in cavalry; they did not have access to the horses. Whatever cavalry force they could put in the field, it was clearly outclassed by the Mongol army, especially being led by two of the grandsons of Genghis Khan, who brought the majority of the Mongol field forces with them. On the other hand, the whole of the regions on and just north of the Yangtze bristled with fortifications. The river was patrolled by flotillas. There was a navy that secured the coastal zones, particularly the capital city Lin'an, which was on the shore, on the sea—I guess it would be the South China Sea—and it was also at the head of the Grand Canal.

Immediately, Kublai knew that they would have to gain those fortresses along the Yangtze; that would mean gaining control of the waterways, the canal systems. In the initial expedition by the two brothers, Möngke and Kublai Khan, the Mongol army got bogged down in a war of sieges along the Yangtze. On August 11, 1259—and I referred to that earlier in the lecture with Hulagu—the khan, Möngke, probably died of cholera while besieging one of the supporting fortresses near the city of Hochwan, which is one of the strategic cities that had to be taken on the Yangtze. It took several weeks for the news to get out to his brothers. Initially, Kublai thought, "Let's keep pressing operations"; he tried to continue fighting in the early fall of 1259. Then the news got back to Kublai that dear younger brother back at Karakorum had been palling around with the shamans and the various tribal leaders, had summoned a rump session of the *kurultai*, the national assembly, and had himself proclaimed khan. Kublai was taken aback. He was commanding in China with the bulk of the Mongol nation fighting with him, and his brother—the second brother of the four, who was actually older than Kublai—was fighting of course in the west. He was going to zero in and knock out the Mamluks. Both of those brothers were taken aback. This was not apparently agreed upon; and furthermore, the election was very, very much unrepresentative because the vast majority of Mongols were not in the homeland. That meant both Hulagu and Kublai refused to recognize the election.

Berke had to his advantage the fact that he had been ratified at the traditional meeting place close to the sacred mountains in the Onan Valley. Clearly all the proper rites had been performed; there was the usual feasting. But the majority of the Mongols did not accept this; and eventually Kublai held his own assembly, his own *kurultai*, in Inner Mongolia, and it was the first time the Mongols had ever met in assembly outside the homeland. They proclaimed Kublai the Great Khan. In early 1260, you had two Great Khans; and, for the first time, civil war. Hulagu from the start supported brother Kublai. We do not know whether that was because of personal reasons, or because he banked on the fact that Kublai could win. Furthermore, Kublai, Hulagu, and Hulagu's sons—and those would be Kublai Khan's nephews— they always seemed to be on particularly close terms, as I mentioned; and the result was the majority of the military force was in the hands of Kublai Khan. Furthermore, he had another advantage: Not only could he invade the homeland, in 1261 the field army just knocked out the forces of Böke with very little trouble. Böke retreated west into the central steppes. He tried to contact his relatives, especially the family of Batu, the Chagataid khans ruling on the central steppes; he was trying to marshal support among other houses of the family of Genghis Khan. But the real advantage that Kublai Khan had was the wealth and the resources of China.

He won the civil war very easily. He cut off food shipments to Mongolia. The development of the Mongolian Empire—the development of Mongolian settlements in the homeland, particularly at the capital, Karakorum—meant that these settlements were now dependent not only on just the luxuries and the tribute of an empire, but also for basic foodstuffs. The population of Karakorum had swollen to 30,000 or 50,000 permanent residents; it had to be supplied by tribute foodstuffs and other goodies brought in from the Chinese provinces, and Kublai Khan controlled it. There was very little chance that the tribes would not go over to Kublai Khan. He was helped by a particularly severe winter that drove home the fact that the guy who controlled China controlled the empire, and certainly controlled the homeland. This was a major revelation; it showed essentially a reversal of the position. Yes, Mongolia provided the cavalry that conquered the world empire, but China provided the resources that sustained that homeland. Therefore, Arigh Böke, in a very, very tearful reunion, surrendered in 1263. He was retired; he was pensioned off; he died several years later. There are some rumors of murder; but fundamentally, Kublai Khan had gained the empire.

But he had gained it at a price. In order to achieve that position of the Great Khan, he had to agree that he would rule the Mongolian homeland and he had the right to conquer China and incorporate that into a great eastern khanate. There were three other *ulus*—that is, peoples of the Mongols—and that included the western reaches; the so-called Golden Horde, as it is known later. That was ruled by the descendants of Batu, and a grandson of Batu was appointed as khan. He ruled at Saray—that is, the palace settlement built on the Lower Volga—and henceforth the khans of the Golden Horde were essentially a bunch of independent rulers. He also had to recognize the right of the Chagataid family—that is, the descendants of Chagatai, the second son of Genghis Khan—to control the central steppes, although it was open question as to who got the Tarim Basin and who got Transoxiana; and that became the cockpit of a number of family quarrels and wars, especially in the 14th century. Nonetheless, the central steppes too broke away into an independent *ulus*. It acknowledged those Chagatai khans; acknowledged the authority, the prestige of Kublai Khan; but they were essentially on their own, and they, just as the khans of the Golden Horde, eventually adopted Turkish as their language and embraced Islam.

In Iran and Transoxiana, Kublai Khan recognized the son of Hulagu; that is, his nephew Abaqa. He became the next Ilkhan. That was a title awarded Hulagu for supporting Genghis Khan in the civil war; it meant the "obedient khan." The family of Hulagu would continue to rule in Iran, Azerbaijan, Iraq; it would claim control of Transoxiana and that would change hands repeatedly between these Ilkhans ruling at Tabriz and their kinsmen ruling on the central steppes. But the Ilkhans, while they had close collaboration with the Great Khans of the east, nonetheless, they too were independent. Kublai Khan, in effect, recognized the partition of the Mongol Empire; a partition that in some ways very much approximated not only cultural lines, but also the geographic lines of the steppes, which I mentioned at the start of this course.

In 1268, Kublai Khan reopened the war against the Song court. He amassed a great army. He had access to the great cavalry forces of Mongolia; that was without question the core of his army. He also had the best generals; particularly his finest general, a man named Bayan who was entrusted with the final mopping up operations after 1273. He also recruited large numbers of Chinese infantry; and above all, he expanded the engineering corps. His nephew, the Ilkhan of Persia or Iran, had sent all sorts of Muslim engineers and technicians. They could build superior engines of war, especially artillery. These would be trebuchets that could fire with deadly accuracy and at great range. Various Song generals defected to Kublai Khan at the start of the campaign, especially in 1268–1269. They brought not only valuable information, but also explained the fortification systems along the Yangtze; and in addition, they included many subordinate officers who knew the incendiaries, which were ignited by gunpowder. These included primitive grenades or iron bombs that exploded. Once they were shot by these torsion engines of war, trebuchets. It also included things known as fire lances that were apparently ignited by the gunpowder, which would then burn the Chinese fortified cities, which were largely wooden palisades on top of rammed earth platforms. So Kublai Khan had the best of expertise; and above all, he had great river flotilla. These were large numbers of ships that were used to isolate the crucial fortresses along the lower Yangtze; and this was something that had been missing in that earlier campaign with his brother back in 1259: how to take the great Song fortresses.

These fortresses checked the advance of the Mongol army. The fortresses included several important cities. They were on the Lower Yangtze River and they protected the Song capital Lin'an. Those fortresses were really the scene of major sieges between the start of the war in 1268, and they only finally capitulated in 1273. The fortress of Fengcheng was actually brutally sacked, and that led to the surrender of the other fortresses. At that point, the Song court knew that it was over.

In addition to the war of sieges and the successes along the Yangtze, Kublai Khan departed from the usual policy of Mongol conquerors. One or two fortresses were singled out because they had defied the Great Khan; but on the whole, the conquest of Song China was not accompanied by the traditional massacres and atrocities we have seen in the Islamic world or on the western steppes and in Russia and Central Europe. From the start, Kublai Khan intended to win over these Chinese people as subjects, and already by 1271 he was styling himself as a Chinese-style emperor. He was going to win this war politically as well as militarily. By December, 1272, when the Persian engineers who had designed these expert machines had battered down the main fortresses, it was clear that the war was over and Kublai Khan could retire to his capital in the north, a city called Dadu, later Beijing—and actually that city is known in western sources as Xanadu—and he could entrust the final pacification to his leading general Bayan.

The Song court just surrendered. There was very little reason to continue fighting. The grand dowager empress led the young boy emperor out; there was a major ceremonial surrender in 1276. Gaozong essentially abdicated. He was pensioned off. He was treated actually quite well by Kublai Khan. There were loyalists who fought for another couple of years, but by 1276 it was over. Kublai Khan had Song China, and with it all of the administrative apparatus to run it; because in the final stages of the campaign, not only many generals, but large numbers of Confucian scholars—people who represented the [Mandarin gentry scholar class] as it was sometimes awkwardly described—they realized it was time to come to terms with Kublai Khan. He did seem to respect, at least to a certain degree, Chinese civilization; and so when the final boy emperor abdicated in 1276, Kublai Khan already was heir to the administration in the traditions of the Song court.

He also fell heir to some of the territorial ambitions. This led him to make two ill-advised invasions of Japan; these were naval invasions. Again, he was following probably in the footsteps of the Tang emperors; and both of these campaigns really went very, very badly. For one, it required the building of large numbers of horse transports, largely done by the Koreans; large numbers of Chinese were drafted into both invasions. The number of Mongols who were involved was very few. The smaller expedition occurred first in 1274. It landed on the island of Kyushu. It quickly got into trouble because of storms, and much of the fleet was destroyed. Close to half of the expedition did not come back. A larger, probably twice as large, expedition with two great flotillas was sent in 1281. That, too, failed. The fleet was large and especially the army was caught on the beaches by a typhoon. This is the famous kamikaze that the Japanese remember ever after. The failure of both expeditions in Japan represented again the limit of Mongol logistics and military power. Kublai Khan had gone too far. He had reached too far.

However, both expeditions were really rather minor in comparison to the conquest of China; and while it was an embarrassment, it certainly did not endanger the throne or Mongol control of China.

What did these great conquests represent? We spent three lectures dealing with the conquest of the west, the conquest of the Islamic world, the conquest of China. All of these were conducted by the grandsons of Genghis Khan. Each one of them can be studied from a strategic and logistical viewpoint that shows that these grandsons were almost on the par of granddad. They certainly all three belong in the hall of great generals, or great captains if you will. The campaigns of Batu and Hulagu were characterized with the kinds of massacre and terrors that was seen in the campaigns of Genghis Khan. Kublai Khan made a significant difference here. He did not engage in that type of terror. He made an attempt to win over the Chinese population and as a result, by 1271 he was able to rule as a Chinese style emperor and he took the name for his dynasty, the Yuan; in fact, the technical name is Da Yuan, which means the Great Yuan. It comes from the *Book of Changes*, a very important Confucian text. It means that they were the great originators. It was an impeccably Chinese name; and Kublai Khan realized a very, very important lesson once stated by the Roman historian Livy: "It is not only important to know how to win victories, it's also important to know how to use them."

Our next two lectures are going to turn to that very question. Whatever the success is, whatever the cost of the Mongol conquest, what did those conquests mean for the greater Eurasian steppes and the sedentary civilizations? Was there really a Mongol peace or was this more of an illusion?

Pax Mongolica and Cultural Exchange
Lecture 32

In this lecture, we will examine the consequences of the great Mongol conquests. On the one hand, an enormous number of people died as a result of the Mongol campaigns. It has been estimated that at least 500,000 Russians died as a result of Batu's campaigns over the course of five years; a similar number was slaughtered in the northern Chinese areas. The destruction wrought against the Islamic world was colossal. On the other hand, scholars have argued that once the conquests were over, the Mongols imposed peace and stability—certainly on the Eurasian steppes. Let's look at what constituted this *Pax Monogolica*, or "Mongol peace."

Population Movements

- Following their conquests, the Mongol khagans quickly set up courts and built capitals that attracted not only trade but numerous specialists. At all the Mongol courts, interpreters, translators, and administrators were in high demand.

- Muslims, Christians, Buddhists, and others participated in Mongol society. In addition, Mongol courts were sustained by captives. In many cases, craftsmen were spared and sent to the Mongol capital or to devastated lands in northern China. For example, Muslims brought in the cultivation of fruit trees, particularly lemon and other citrus.

- There was a significant movement of population across Eurasia because of the policies of the khans. Chinese were sent west and posted on the Iranian frontier. Alani, who were Christians of the Caucasus, were sent to China. This movement of populations led to cultural exchange.

- Of course, some of these population movements were forced. Numerous Turks and Muslims fled out of central Asia and Transoxania into Delhi and Konya to reinforce the Muslim civilizations there. The ancestors of the Ottoman sultans traced their descent from tribes that fled west from the Mongol conquerors.

Spread of Religion

- The movement of these peoples also allowed for the spread of religions. Initially, all faiths were tolerated in the Mongol Empire. Genghis Khan ruled on this in his Yassa, although each of the four *ulus* had a different response.

- For instance, the Golden Horde embraced Islam. In contrast, the ilkhans of Persia maintained a cosmopolitan court. There are cases of Muslim ilkhans supporting Buddhist monasteries. Even in Iran, a number of stupas and Buddhist monasteries were built. The Chagataid khagans of central Asia were tolerant of most religions.

- Kublai Khan himself embraced Buddhism. He was also respectful of Daoism and the Neo-Confucian traditions. He knew he needed the services of the Chinese administrative class, but he always interacted with Muslims, with Uighurs, and with adventurers from the west—including Marco Polo.

- Kublai Khan preferred the Sakya form of Buddhism, a prominent school in Tibet. He sponsored monasteries. He used the Tibetan monks to create a new, distinctly Mongolian script that was non-Chinese—no doubt to the dismay of the Confucian scholar class.

Travel and Trade

- The Mongols also promoted travel and trade, particularly along the Silk Road and the complementary sea and ocean routes. Missions were sent by western Europeans to the Great Khan's court.

- The earliest one recorded is from 1246. **Giovanni Da Pian Del Carpini**, a Franciscan friar, was sent by Pope Innocent IV to witness the enthronement of Güyük. He traveled for about 110 days, some 3,000 miles. Some years later, another Franciscan, **William of Rubrouck**, was sent as the envoy of the Crusader king Louis IX.

- The prosperity on the Silk Road increased once the Mongol peace was imposed. The upsurge in trade was also evident in the development of sea routes that moved goods around the Indian Ocean to the South China Sea. An example was the dissemination of Chinese porcelains across the Islamic world.

- **Marco Polo** returned home after 23 years in **Cathay** at the court of Kublai Khan by taking the sea route. The trip was quite an adventure. The travelers were shipwrecked and took two years to get back to Venice. They eventually landed in Iraq and took caravans to Trebizond; from there, they found passage on ships back to Venice. Both sea routes and the Silk Road prospered under the Mongol khans.

Technology Transfer

- There were four major areas of cultural exchange and technology transfer during this time. First was in the area of astronomy and mathematics. Genghis Khan and most of the other khans, especially Kublai Khan, were keenly interested in these subjects.
  - Mathematics, which had been perfected in Baghdad in the 10th century when Muslim scholars invented algebra, was brought to China to improve the calculations of astrology. Astrology was connected to both the Daoist and the shamanistic traditions.

  - This exchange brought Muslim science to the attention of the Chinese, and in turn, Chinese calculations were sent back. Rashid al-Din, the scholar in residence at the ilkhan court, played an important role in that exchange.

- Another area of exchange was in geography, cartography, history, and mapmaking. There was, again, an exchange between the two great Mongol courts in Iran and China. Rashid al-Din was at the forefront of this. He demonstrated a range of interest in geography, mathematics, and even anthropology. This meant that both the Chinese and Muslim worlds had extremely accurate information for mapmaking.

- A famous **Ming** admiral, **Ma Huan**, set out in 1413 on a voyage of discovery and exploration in the South China Sea. He reached India and even all the way to Baghdad. Although he was a subject of the Ming emperor of China, he also spoke Arabic and was a Muslim.

  - He clearly had maps that were far superior to those of the great navigators of the period of European discovery, starting with Christopher Columbus.

- Information related to medicine, food, and plants was also exchanged. Grapes and fruit trees were brought by the Muslim world to China. In turn, various luxury items that were well known in Chinese cuisine, such as tea, black pepper, and cinnamon, became available in the Islamic world—and both worlds improved their diet and cuisine substantially. Major translations of works on cultivation, aromatics and spices, and medicines were completed. The Mongol conquest brought together two of the greatest medical traditions at the time: the Chinese and the Islamic.

- Finally, block printing and paper were devised by the Chinese and were perfected in the Song period; subsequently, block printing became available in the Islamic world. The ilkhans of Tabriz used block printing to issue paper money, an imitation of the Song paper money and letters of credit. This experiment was abandoned after 1353, but it was a highly significant and interesting trial of the use of fiduciary currency.

Gunpowder

- A technology exchange of particular significance was gunpowder. Gunpowder went back as early as the Han period in China. The Mongols encountered it in the incendiaries used against them in the great sieges on the Yangtze River, and black gunpowder was also spread across the Eurasian steppes.

- However, it is curious that this was probably the only significant transfer of technology received by the Europeans. The western

Europeans were fascinated with it. Already in 1346, King Edward III of England had cannons.

- The Europeans managed to enclose the gunpowder into tubes and create artillery. The Mongols, Chinese, and the Muslim world never hit on this innovation. One speculation is that the European smiths were familiar with bronze and brass casting methods.

- Thus, by the middle of the 14th century, the Europeans were casting guns and beginning to create artillery that could knock down walls. What's more, the Europeans then created handheld firearms and mounted artillery on oceangoing vessels.

Ottoman sultans, Mughal emperors, and Chinese rulers developed cannons after the Europeans, probably using knowledge provided by Jesuits.

- From the end of the 15th century on, western Europe, with those military advantages, essentially conquered the world. One could argue that the expansion of European imperialism came thanks to the gunpowder received from the Mongols—under the Mongol peace.

Marco Polo

- There were many travelers to the Mongol courts, but Marco Polo occupies a special position. He wrote a work titled *Livres des merveilles du monde*—usually known as *The Travels of Marco Polo*—that chronicled 23 years of service at the court of Kublai Khan.

- Some doubt Marco Polo existed or even went to China. He may have run a salt monopoly; at any rate, he was a minor official. He had joined his father and uncle, who had made an earlier trip to the

Mongol court to represent the commercial interests of the Republic of St. Mark, or Venice.

- When he returned to Italy in 1298, he was captured in a naval battle and languished in a Genoese prison. There, he dictated his account. Whatever the actual details of Marco Polo's career, they pale in comparison to the significance of what he wrote.

- We are not sure how much of this account was altered, edited, or embroidered, but it was an instant commercial success. It was translated into many languages. Although there were many questionable aspects of his account, it nonetheless replaced all the previous fanciful notions of the Far East, of India, and even of the Islamic world with a wealth of information.

- Before Marco Polo, Christian Europe had very little information outside of its immediate area. Much of it consisted of wild tales from classical antiquity, legends, and stories of Prester John. These were now replaced with actual descriptions of a real kingdom, Cathay, and a real capital, Xanadu.

- These fantastical places were goals for the Europeans to seek out. In fact, it was Marco Polo's work, according to Christopher Columbus, that inspired him to make his great first voyage of discovery. Besides gunpowder, perhaps the second greatest gift from the Mongol peace to the Europeans was this vision of Cathay. Europeans set out in search of this vision and carried out one of the greatest expansions of all time—the great imperial expansion across the oceans of the globe.

Important Terms

Cathay: Medieval European name for China; it was derived from a misunderstanding of Khitan, Mongolian-speaking nomadic rulers of northern China who ruled as the Liao Dynasty (907–1125).

Ming Dynasty: Founded by Emperor Hongwu (1368–1398), who expelled the Mongols, the Ming Dynasty (1368–1644) was the last native dynasty of imperial China.

Carpini, Giovanni Da Pian Del (1182–1252): Franciscan friar; the envoy of Pope Innocent IV (1243–1254) to the Mongol court in 1246–1247. His party traversed the steppes from Kiev to Karakorum in 106 days. Carpini witnessed the *kurultai* that elected Güyük (1246–1248), and he records important details about the court a generation after the death of Genghis Khan.

Ma Huan (1380–1460): Admiral of Ming China; a Muslim and Arabic speaker. At the command of the Ming emperor Yongle (1402–1424), he set sail with 57 ships in a great expedition to the western lands in 1413. He visited Champa, Java, Sumatra, Malaya, the southern Indian port of Cochin, Hormuz, and ultimately Mecca.

Polo, Marco (1254–1324): Venetian adventurer; took service with Kublai Khan as the administrator of the salt monopoly at Yangzhou and as an emissary to the Burmese court. In 1251–1257, Marco Polo, along with his father Niccolò, and uncle Maffeo (who had previously visited the ilkhanate court), journeyed to Dadu. In 1292–1294, the three returned to Venice. In 1298, Marco was captured by the Genoese at the Battle of Curzola. While in prison in 1298–1299, he dictated his adventures of 23 years (1271–1294) to fellow prisoner Rustichello da Pisa, who composed the *Livres des merveilles du monde*. Marco's book was an instant success and fired the European imagination and desire to reach Cathay.

Rubrouck, William of (1220–1293): Flemish Franciscan friar; sent as envoy of French king Saint Louis IX (1226–1270) to the Mongol court in 1253–1255. William of Rubrouck failed in his mission to convert the Mongols, but he wrote a perceptive account on the court of Great Khan Möngke (1251–1259).

Suggested Reading

Allsen, *Culture and Conquest in Mongol Eurasia.*

————, "Mongols as Vectors of Cultural Change."

Jackson, *The Mongols and the West.*

Polo (Wright, ed. and trans.), *The Travels of Marco Polo, the Venetian.*

Rossabi, *The Mongols and Global History.*

Saunders, *The History of the Mongol Conquests.*

Questions to Consider

1. How destructive were the great Mongol conquests on cities, trade, and civilization in the first half of the 13th century? Did the Mongol invasions have a catastrophic impact on Russia, the Islamic world, and China?

2. In what ways did the Mongols contribute to the transmission of technology and the arts of civilization across Eurasia? In what ways did the Mongols promote trade and prosperity in the later 13th century?

3. What accounted for the popularity of Islam among the Mongols? Why did the ilkhans, the Chagataid khans of central Asia, and the khans of the Golden Horde embrace Islam? How did the Mongol peace and the accompanying trade lead to the Islamization of the cities of the Tarim Basin?

4. What was the appeal of Buddhism for the Yuan emperors of China and the Mongols of the homeland? Why did Buddhism prevail over the other religions on the eastern Eurasian steppes?

5. What was the impact on Europeans of the reports of missionaries and envoys sent to the Mongol court? Why were the Mongols so unimpressed by Christianity as presented by the missionaries from western Europe? What was the impact of the journeys of Marco Polo on exciting the imagination of Europeans that led to the Age of Discovery?

Pax Mongolica and Cultural Exchange
Lecture 32—Transcript

In this lecture, I want to deal with the results and consequences of the great Mongol conquests. We spent considerable time on the conquests of Genghis Khan and then of his three grandsons. Those lectures revealed a Mongol army of extraordinary ability and the question I posed was: What were the results and the benefits, as well as the costs, of this conquest? Scholars have sometimes spoken of a *Pax Monogolica*—that is, a "Mongol peace"—that was imposed across the steppes and the related sedentary civilizations that came under Mongol control. On the other hand, there is also a great deal of images, and these images come especially out of popular literature as well as nationalist histories, of a Mongol yoke. This is particularly true of Russian historians who in many ways would argue that the whole development of Russia was, in effect, perverted by the long tributary status of the Russian cities to the khans of the Golden Horde resident at the palace city of Saray. Both images have foundations in reality, and this lecture is not intended to take a position on one case or the other; it intends to present the facts, present what we do know about Mongol rule in the 13th and early 14th centuries.

Let us look on the costs. We have mentioned them in passing with the campaigns; various reasons why these actions of terror, these atrocities were committed. It is difficult to estimate how many people were killed or died as a result of the Mongol campaigns, the great Mongol conquests. Numbers run up to fantastic levels, far beyond what we suspect the population of the world was at the time. There are comparisons, sometimes very facile comparisons, which are made literally to the scientific genocidal extermination of populations by the Nazis or by Stalin with the great purges and the collectivization. Again, the Mongols never practiced slaughter quite on that level, and a term such as *holocaust* can be essentially belittled by calling every massacre atrocity a holocaust. The Holocaust, in my mind, is really quite exceptional among all atrocities.

On the other hand, we do have some potential numbers of what the destruction involved. For instance, it has been estimated that at least 500,000 people, Russians, died as a result of the campaigns of Batu over a course of about five years. Many of these were killed in the sacks of Russian cities;

many more probably died of exposure, starvation, and the privations that followed after a Mongol army had swept through, burned all the villages and fields, had turned agriculture to pasture. Again, there are suspicions that there were very high losses of population in the Northern Chinese areas, regions that had been under the Jin emperor, the so-called 16 prefectures; that Genghis Khan's campaigns that climaxed in the conquest of the Jin capitals of Northern China in 1215 had a similar destructive level on Northern China as Batu's campaigns in Russia. All agree that the destruction wrought against the Islamic cities in Transoxiana by Genghis Khan, later by Hulagu, the destruction of Baghdad, those are colossal numbers of destruction. Hundreds of thousands were slain and died in the aftermath of those destructive invasions. Last but not least, we do have information on the kingdom of Hungary; that was the campaign in 1241. After defeating the Hungarian army, Batu's soldiers seized the royal treasury and the seal; and the Mongols through the whole of the summer of 1241 sent out letters that resulted in the surrender of cities, and towns and huge numbers of captives were rounded up, large numbers that are exaggerated in the medieval chronicles. Then, in 1241, when Batu had to return to Saray and get involved in that election of the new Great Khan, these captives were slaughtered; and again, we get fantastic numbers of Hungarians slain in the retreat by the Mongol army.

We have a lot of anecdotal material about the destruction of cities. Perhaps one should suffice; and that is the former capital of Muhammad Shah, near the Aural Sea at the lower Oxus River. That capital, the city of Urgench, was put under siege by Genghis Khan's sons and the city was essentially leveled. The course of the river was changed in order to undermine the walls, and as a result, the Oxus River actually flowed into the Caspian Sea for the next couple of hundred years. The city lost its water supply; everything was chopped down, the mulberry trees for silk; the irrigation ditches were deliberately destroyed; and the city was turned into a desert and ruins and was never rebuilt.

Those types of actions can be added up, but it is still difficult to get the full cost of the Mongol conquest; and I do not want to minimize it. We are subject to what our sources tell us, and yes there is a lot of exaggeration; but there is little doubt that the Mongol conquest exacted a heavy cost on the conquered. On the other hand, scholars could also argue that once the conquests were over, the Mongols imposed peace, certainly on the Eurasian steppes. This is clear with Genghis Khan and his sons, and there are a number of ways of testing what this *Pax Mongolica* represented. One way is to look at the cultural exchange and the prosperity. What I want to do in the bulk of this lecture is turn to those questions. What benefits came from the Mongol conquests without minimizing the horrendous costs that were paid by the subject peoples, especially in the initial stages of the conquest? For one thing, the Mongol khans quickly set up courts: Karakorum in the Mongolian homeland; the Ilkhans, the family of Hulagu, resided at the city of Tabriz; Saray was built on the Volga by Batu; and then only the family of Chagatai that controlled the Central Asian steppes did not really have a capital. But the others did build great capitals, and these became markets; they attracted not only trade, but numerous specialists. At all of the Mongol courts, interpreters, translators, administrators were in high demand. Muslims, Christians, Buddhists, all sorts of people appeared at the Mongol court. In addition, these courts were sustained by the deportees; that is, the captives taken in the great conquest. We have a number of anecdotal cases of people being removed far from their homeland to serve the khans in some capacity. I mentioned that at both Bukhara and Samarkand apparently craftsmen were spared and those Muslim craftsmen were sent to the Mongol capital. We have reports of numerous Muslims being settled to restore the devastated lands in Northern China; that is, the former Jin regions. These Muslims brought in the cultivation of fruit trees, particularly citrus and the use of lemon. We know of garrisons being recruited among the subject peoples. There was a case of 1,000 Chinese who were recruited and sent very far west; they were posted off on the Iranian frontier. There was another Chinese group that was actually set up in a town. It is on the shores of Lake Urmia today, and that was virtually a Chinatown into the 14th century; that is, the Chinese continued to maintain their own traditions and language. We know of Christians sent to China. These included Alans who were Christians of the Caucasus descended from those Iranian nomads back in antiquity; so there was a major movement of population across Eurasia because of the policies of the khans.

Some of these movements were forced and certainly not planned. Many of them represented part of the cost of the Mongol conquests. For instance, I mentioned that the Mevlana—that is, Jalal-ad-Din Rumi, the great Sufi mystic in Turkey—his family moved from Balkh to Konya because of the Mongols; they were fleeing in terror. Numerous Turks and Muslims fled out of Central Asia and Transoxiana into Delhi and Konya to reinforce the Muslim civilizations there. The ancestors of the Ottoman sultans traced their descent to tribes that fled west before the Mongol hordes.

This movement of population led to all sorts of exchange, and there are a number of individuals that you can look to study at it. One of them is the important scholar Rashid al-Din, and he lived from 1247–1318. He dominated the later 13th century; and Rashid al-Din wrote one of the important works that we use to consult about the life of Genghis Khan. He knew Persian and Chinese. He served at the Ilkhan court n Tabriz, and he took it upon himself to translate many works on Chinese statecraft into Persian. He also set a standard for literary Persian. So in these exchanges, it was not all just captives; it was not all just hardship. Although I do not want to minimize that: I can say in any of these deportations, the older and the younger ones clearly suffered and died in great numbers. Having evacuated from the city of New Orleans in the so-called evacuation from Hurricane Katrina, I have direct experience with what any "evacuation" means. The deportations of the Mongols were probably on a whole other order.

The movement of these people, the imposing of an imperial peace on the steppes, also allowed for the spread of religions. Initially, the Mongols were very tolerant. I mentioned that all of the khans initially were very pragmatic; that all faiths were tolerated. Genghis Khan ruled on this in his *yassa*, although each of the four *ulus* took a different turn on this. For instance, the Golden Horde, the successor to Batu, Berke, he embraced Islam and he became a pretty strong convert to Islam. He had contempt for the Russian principalities in Christianity, and the court at Saray became pretty strongly Muslim at the end of the 13th century and really aligned itself with the Mamluk sultans of Cairo. On the other hand, their cousins ruling in Iran— that is, the Ilkhans of Iran, the family of Hulagu—they, too, would eventually embrace Islam. On the other hand, the Ilkhans of Persia always maintained a cosmopolitan court. There are cases of Muslim Ilkhans supporting Buddhist monasteries. Hulagu and his initial heirs—and it took a long time for the Ilkhans to go over to Islam; it was not until the end of the 13th century—they actually sponsored a revival of Buddhism across Central Asia; and even in

Iran there were a number of stupas and Buddhist monasteries built. These would decline after 1353 when the Ilkhanate fell and a series of petty Muslim states emerged in the former Ilkhan domains. But the Ilkhans pursued a very, very tolerant policy towards religions; and that was in keeping with the policies of Genghis Khan

Likewise, their cousins, who battled for control of Transoxiana and eventually got it away from the Ilkhans—those would be the Chagatai khans of Central Asia; in fact, they were in general suspicion of cities anyway, they loved to tax caravans but they did not hang out at courts—but they, too, were tolerant of most religions; and above all Kublai Khan. Kublai Khan embraced Buddhism. He was respectful to Daoism and the neo-Confucian traditions. He knew he needed to use the Chinese administrative class, but he always supplemented with Muslims, with Uighurs, with adventurers from the West, including that figure Marco Polo who we will be talking about later in this lecture. In particular, Kublai Khan fell in the tradition of many conquerors of the steppes who have occupied parts of China, and that is the favoritism is to Buddhism, which was an international faith; it was not just Chinese. Kublai Khan preferred the Sakya form of Buddhism; that is, a very important school in Tibet. He sponsored monasteries. He used these Tibetan monks to create a new Mongolian script, very, very distinct, which was non-Chinese. Monuments were put up in Kublai Khan's domains that were both in this peculiar Mongolian script as well as Chinese characters, no doubt to the dismay of the Confucian scholar class. Kublai Khans's policies resulted in the spread of Buddhism increasingly across the eastern steppes.

When the Mongol Empire essentially broke up and went its separate ways in the 14th century, the religious policies had caused the great what I would call religious and cultural divide in Central Asia. Tibet, parts of China, the eastern steppes would fundamentally go to Buddhism. The old shamanistic religions would lose out; Nestorianism, Manichaeism, they would lose out. The Tarim Basin, the cities of Transoxiana, the central and western steppes, those eventually folded back into Islam and actually represented expansion of Islam, particularly on the western steppes and in the Tarim Basin. The Tarim Basin was turned into essentially Eastern Turkistan as the Uighurs abandoned Buddhism and embraced Islam in the course of the 13th, 14th, and 15th centuries, in part imitating their Mongol masters, the Chagataid khans.

The one interesting development in all this is in Iran, the later Ilkhans, even the Muslim Ilkhans, were particularly tolerant, particularly of Shi'a Sufis. It was in the 14th century that Shi'a Islam began to make its first inroads in Iran; and in time, after the Ilkhans were gone and Tamerlane were gone in the 15th and 16th centuries, Iran would be turned into a Shi'a state, which was a very, very significant transformation in Islam because up until this point Iran had been really regarded as part of the Sunni heartland of Islam.

Religious proselytizing, religious change is one way of measuring the Mongol success; and some of these changes would not have occurred without the imposition of that Mongol peace. The Mongols also promoted travel and prosperity, particularly trade along the Silk Road and the complementary sea and ocean routes. You can get some sense of the speed and security by the missions that were sent by Western Europeans to the Great Khan's court. There are several of them recorded. The earliest one we have is 1246 when a fellow called Giovanni Carpini, a Franciscan friar, was sent by Pope Innocent IV and he made a journey of some 3,000 miles across the steppes, actually in time to witness the enthronement of Güyük. He did that probably on an average of 40 miles a day. There were all sorts of exchanges and swapping of horses; and he traveled about 110 days, some 3,000 miles. Some years later—I believe in 1253–1254; it was over the winter—another Franciscan, a fellow by the name of William of Rubruck who was from Flanders, was sent as the envoy of the Crusader king Louis IX who was hanging out in Cyprus and getting ready to invade Egypt; and he, too, made the same distance in about the same amount of time. These are extraordinary distances and both envoys report the relay systems, the security with which caravans could travel. No caravan would do these distances of 40 miles a day, but caravans could travel with some sense of security. They could move from station to station, from city to city; they could conduct business. Again, this was a feature of the later 13th and early 14th century; the fighting, especially in the early conquests, would have disrupted this whole caravan network, but the Silk Road did make a significant comeback. The prosperity on the Silk Road increased once the Mongol peace was imposed.

This upsurge in trade can also be examined by archaeological finds and literary sources by the development of sea routes. There were those complementary sea routes that moved goods around the Indian Ocean to the

South China Sea. They were never competitive to the Silk Road; they were always complementary, they went back to the second century B.C. This trade, too, expanded. This was shown by the dissemination of Chinese porcelains across the Islamic world; they became the rage of collecting, later by Mogul emperors, by Safavid shahs of Iran, and the Ottoman sultans. Marco Polo, his dad, and his uncle, Niccolo and Matteo; they actually returned home after 23 years in Cathay—that is, at the court of Kublai Khan—by taking the sea route. It was quite an adventure; they were shipwrecked. I think it took them from 1292–1294 to get back to Venice. They eventually landed in Iraq and took caravans to Trebizond, ships from there back to Venice. But it is to stress the fact that both sea routes and the Silk Road prospered under the Mongol khans.

This situation led to some very important transfers: cultural transfers and transfers of technology. What I would like to do is zero in on that aspect of cultural and technological changes, because these had wide-ranging implications, whatever we decide about the cost of the Mongol conquest and how valid the notion of a Mongol peace really is. I see four major areas where there were important exchanges. First, is the area of astronomy and mathematics; and this starts with Genghis Khan, and most of the khans, especially Kublai Khan were interested in these subjects. One would wonder why. In part, the use of Arabic mathematics and Muslim mathematics, which had been perfected in Baghdad back in the 10th century where Muslim scholars invented algebra, this was all brought to China to improve the calculations of astrology because astrology was used to calculate marriages, all sorts of events. It was connected in both the Daoist tradition and even the shamanistic tradition; so there was a practical concern here, it was not just a dispassionate interest in math and science. Nonetheless, this exchange brought Muslim science to the attention of the Chinese, and in turn Chinese calculations in science were sent back. In this exchange, the court of Kublai Khan at Dadu, the future city of Beijing, and the Ilkhan court were all important. That fellow Rashid al-Din, the scholar in residence at the Ilkhan court played a very important role in that exchange. He was involved in using a number of these sources.

Another area of exchange was in geography, cartography, history, and mapmaking. There was, again, an exchange between the two great Mongol courts in Iran and China. Rashid al-Din was in the forefront of this. He wrote that universal history that contains a lot of information out of the secret history of the Mongols; that is, the quasi-biography of Genghis Khan. That indicates that Rashid al-Din had translators; that he was able to consult some of the originals. He also had access to all sorts of Hindu works because he had information on India that is quite good. In addition, he shows a range of interest in geography, mathematics, subjects that we today would call anthropology, that was astonishing; far beyond the narrow kind of chronicles that you got in the early Islamic period that simply reported victory after victory, the expansion of Dar al-Islam, temporary setbacks but always great victories. This was serious work. The geography meant that both the Chinese and the Muslim world had very, very accurate information on mapmaking and cartography.

There was a famous Ming admiral, his name was Ma Huan. He set out in 1413 in sort of a voyage of discovery and exploration down the South China Sea. He got to India; he actually got all the way to Baghdad. He was the subject of the Ming emperor of China, but he also spoke Arabic and he was a Muslim. He clearly had maps, far superior than most maps that the great navigators of the period of European discovery had, starting with Christopher Columbus. It was extraordinary how good their mapmaking was; and that was a result, again, of that interchange between the Mongol courts where the Chinese and the Muslim world came into contact, two of the great civilizations on the Eurasian land mass.

Another area of exchange was in all sorts of information about medicine, about food, plants. I mentioned some of this was practical; that is, grapes and fruit trees were brought by the Muslim world to China. In turn, various items that were well known in Chinese cuisine such as tea, black pepper, cinnamon—these were real luxuries—they became available in the Islamic world, and both worlds improved their diet and cuisine substantially. There were major translations done on works on cultivation and all sorts of information on aromatics, on medicines and spices; and what happens is the Mongol conquest put together two of the great medical traditions at the time, the Chinese and the Islamic, and the Islamic is really, really quite sophisticated; and the result is improvement on both ends.

Finally, there is the matter of technology. (I should mention in passing: The idea that pasta went from China to Europe compliments of Marco Polo is a total myth. The pasta was known in Europe in the ninth century; that was devised in the Islamic world. You should really delete that one from the categories.) On the other hand, the last area I want to talk about is technology. In that area, there was a very, very curious exchange. One of the biggest items is block printing and paper. This was devised by the Chinese, it was particularly perfected in the Song period; and block printing became available in the Islamic world. Actually, the Ilkhans of Tabriz used it to issue paper money in imitation of the Song paper money and letters of credit. This was an experiment that was abandoned after 1353, but was a very significant and interesting experiment in fiduciary currency.

The final one, and the one that everyone knows, is gunpowder. Gunpowder goes back as early as the Han period. The Mongols encountered it among the incendiaries used against them in the great sieges on the Yangtze River, and black gunpowder was also spread across the Eurasian steppes. However, it is very curious that this was probably the only significant transfer of technology or culture received by the Europeans. The Western Europeans were fascinated with this. Roger Bacon in his *Opus Majas* makes reference—it is probably one of the earliest references to gunpowder—and already in 1346, King Edward III of England had early cannons. For some reason, the Europeans managed to enclose the gunpowder into these tubes, these early bombards, and create artillery. The Mongols, the Chinese, the Muslim world never came up with this. One speculation—and again, it is a bit fanciful—is that the European smiths were familiar with casting bronze and brass bells. You could kick a bell over, you got an early bombard; that is, cannon. Whether it is true or not, we do not know; but in the 14th century, by the middle of the 14th century, the Europeans were casting early guns and were beginning to create artillery that could knock down walls. Most of the rest of the Eurasian rulers like cannons—the Ottoman sultans, the Mogul emperors, eventually the Chinese even get them (compliments of the Jesuits)—and they knocked down walls and destroyed nobles and obnoxious people you wanted to bring under your control. On the other hand, it was the Europeans who then took gun powder and created handheld firearms and mounted this artillery on oceangoing vessels; and starting really from the end of the 15th century on, with those military advantages essentially conquered the world. One could argue that sees the expansion of European imperialism complements of the gunpowder they received from the Mongols, probably the only significant thing the Europeans learned under the Mongol peace.

Another and final note I want to end with is Marco Polo. There were a lot of travelers to the Mongol courts, a lot of tales, but Marco Polo occupies a special position. Some even doubt he existed or even went to China. The work he wrote *Le Livres des Merveilles du monde*, the *Marvels of the World*, usually translated as *The Travels of Marco Polo*, chronicled 23 years of service at the court of Kublai Khan. We cannot pin him to any name in Chinese sources; there have been a couple of identifications. He may have run a salt monopoly. He clearly was a minor official and exaggerated his role. He hooked up with his father and uncle, who had done an earlier travel to the Mongol court to represent the commercial interests of the Republic of Saint Mark; that is, Venice.

Whatever the actual details of Marco Polo's career really pale in the fact of what he wrote. We actually have to thank the Genoese for this because when he returned he got captured in 1298 in a naval battle and languished in a Genoese prison and dictated his account. We are not so sure how much of this account was altered, edited, embroidered; it was actually published by a fellow prisoner, Rustichello of Pisa, who wrote it in French because French was widely well-known in Europe as a commercial and as a crusading language and it was an instant success. It was translated into all sorts of vernaculars; and there are a lot of fanciful tales, and clearly Marco was not above exaggerating his role. There are many questionable aspects of it. Nonetheless, this account replaced all the fanciful notions of the East, the Far East, of India, and even of the Islamic world. Christian Europe had very little information outside of its immediate area. Much of it were wild tales from classical antiquity, legends, the stories of Prester John; that was now displaced by a description of a real great kingdom in Cathay, a real capital Xanadu, and these became goals for the Europeans to seek out. It was Marco Polo's work, according to Christopher Columbus, that inspired him to make his great first voyage of discovery. So besides gunpowder, perhaps the second greatest gift from the Mongol peace to the Europeans was this vision of the Far East of Cathay, because Europeans set out in search of this image and then carried out one of the greatest expansions of all time: the great imperial expansion across the globe's oceans.

Conversion and Assimilation
Lecture 33

In this lecture, we will study the passing of the Mongol peace and the Mongol Empire. The process was not so much decline and fall as conversion and assimilation. The four *ulus* underwent changes and fell away from the Mongol imperial legacy. Those four *ulus* included the domains of Kublai Khan, which comprised the Mongolian homeland in Tibet and China; the central steppes in the Tarim Basin, controlled by the Chagataid khagans; Transoxania, controlled by the ilkhans of Persia under the family of Hulagu; and the Golden Horde, controlled by the descendants of Batu, ruling the western steppes, with hegemony over the Russian Orthodox principalities in the forest zones.

Reign of Kublai Khan

- In China, Kublai Khan inherited a policy from his uncle Ögödei. An important minister who had served the Jin emperor warned Ögödei, "You may conquer China from horseback, but you cannot rule it from horseback." From the start, Kublai Khan made an effort to win over the Confucian scholar classes.

- He spared most of the Chinese populations. He did not reenact the massacres that characterized the brutal conquest of the Islamic world, Russia, and Hungary. On the other hand, Kublai Khan did not use the Song examination system; he retained the right to select his ministers personally based on their loyalty and usefulness to the khan. Buddhism was the religion of choice.

- Kublai Khan feared that if he put himself too much in the hands of the bureaucrats, ultimately, his rule would be undermined. Assimilation was always a danger. If the Mongols became too accustomed to Chinese ways and luxuries, they would lose their military edge.

- The numbers told the story. The Song Empire and the former Jin Empire together were estimated to be 120 million strong, most of them in south China. The number of Mongols and Turkish tribes Kublai Khan commanded did not reach 1 million. This led to a basic tension.

Waning Control in the *Ulus*

- As Yuan emperor, Kublai Khan built his own capital, Dadu, which is today the modern city of Beijing. It was reported in Marco Polo's account as the fabled city of Xanadu. The capital was far enough north that it allowed Kublai Khan to stay in touch with the steppe peoples.

- Although the system succeeded in the time of Kublai Khan, his successors were not as strong and powerful. From the start, they received, at best, provisional cooperation from the Confucian scholar class.

- Furthermore, Mongol control of the other *ulus* started to wane after 1294. The other three khaganates went their separate ways, and all eventually embraced Islam. That would act as a divide between them and the Great Khan ruling in China and the Mongolian heartland.

Zhu Yuanzhang

- The later Yuan emperors made high demands on the military. The emperors were accused of neglecting not only the Dao and the Confucian traditions but also the management of the empire itself. Events came to a head in 1351.

- Zhu Yuanzhang, a peasant leader who proved a highly capable opponent to the Yuan emperors, headed up a dissident group known as the Red Turbans. He actually spent most of his time fighting other dissident groups. By 1356, however, he controlled most of southern China and brought these other groups into alliance.

- In 1368, this man was able to proclaim himself the first Ming emperor, **Hongwu**. He sent an expedition north against the Mongol capital. The reigning Yuan emperor, a young man, fled back to Mongolia and gave up the heritage. Henceforth, the Mongols would never again rule China.

Overthrow of the Ming

- The reoccupation of China by the Ming armies was a significant turning point. The Mongol capital was leveled, and a new city called Beijing was built on top of it.

- In addition, the Ming emperors ordered the reconstruction of the old Han and Tang walls. Earlier, this boundary had consisted of a set of fortresses, signal towers, and monitoring stations, but the Ming emperors now ordered the construction of masonry walls.

- It is ironic, however, that the Ming emperors failed to guard against their most dangerous threat. That came from the forest of Manchuria, when, in 1644, the Manchus entered China and overthrew the Ming Dynasty.

In some ways, the construction of the Great Wall was a psychological response to the humiliation of Chinese rule by outsiders—the Mongols.

Chagataid Khans

- Meanwhile, in central Asia, the Chagataid khans were able to prosper off the Silk Road. The khaganate extended from the regions around the Aral Sea, the upper Jaxartes, and east to the Altai Mountains. On those steppes were various Turkish and Mongol tribes who had preserved the traditions of Genghis Khan.

- They followed the notions of the Yassa—that is, the authority of the khan overrode all religious law and other customs. They were proud of their steppe heritage and claimed to be the true Mongols, even though most of them spoke Turkish.

- The region also included the Tarim Basin and the caravan cities, which steadily adopted Islam. The great Buddhist monasteries in the area gradually passed out of existence.

Ilkhans of Persia

- The ilkhans of Persia ruled one of the most prosperous of the *ulus*, second only to China. They were engaged in trade and cultural exchange. Hulagu and his successors long maintained a cosmopolitan court and were enthusiastic sponsors of Buddhism. Some of the greatest thinkers and scholars in the cultural exchange worked at Tabriz.

- We can get a sense of the cultural diversity and intellectual achievement among the ilkhans by looking at the people they patronized. In addition to the earlier scholar Rashid al-Din, there was a Mongol prince who had served in the court of Kublai Khan, **Bolad**. He had been trained in Chinese and the Confucian classics and supervised the improvement of agriculture and streamlined the Yuan bureaucracy.

- In 1285, Bolad was sent as an envoy by Kublai Khan to the reigning ilkhan of Tabriz. Bolad decided to stay at Tabriz and offer his services to the ilkhanate court. He spent the rest of his career carrying out important translations of Chinese works into Persian. He introduced court ceremony, dress, taste, and aesthetics from China.

- The exchange enriched the high culture of eastern Islam, or Persian culture. This culture became the basis for the three great Muslim empires of the early modern period, often called the gunpowder empires: the Ottoman sultanate, the **Safavid** shahs of Iran, and the Mughal emperors of India.

The Golden Horde

- The Golden Horde was led by the family of Batu. Batu had transferred his power to his brother, **Berke**, a devout Muslim. He came to the throne in 1227 and aligned himself with the Mamluk sultans of Cairo. He furnished slave soldiers, mostly Kipchak and Cuman Turks, to the Mamluks.

- The later khans embraced a simpler Islam that was appropriate to nomadic peoples, emphasizing Sufis and mystics. Many of the tribes in the confederation were quite unconventional in their Islamic beliefs.

- This khaganate also exercised control over the Russian principalities, a result of the victories of Batu. The Russian princes who cooperated with the khagans at Saray prospered. One of the most important was **Ivan I Danilovich** of Moscow.
  - Ivan proved a very loyal vassal of the Golden Horde. In 1328, the ruling khagan entrusted Ivan with the collection of tribute from the Russian princes and gave him important cities, such as Vladimir.

  - The result was that Moscow emerged at the nexus of the river routes that linked up the systems of the Don, Dnieper, and Volga. Ivan I Danilovich gained a key principality and enriched himself as the collection agent for the Mongol khagans.

Battle of Kulikovo

- However, the khagans of the Golden Horde quickly came to realize their vulnerability vis-à-vis the Russian princes. This was dramatically revealed in 1380 in the Battle of Kulikovo.

- The then-reigning prince of Moscow, **Vasily I Dmitriyevich**, put together a coalition of Russian princes, marched the army to the Don, and surprised a Mongol force. In a hard-fought battle, in which they mounted heavy cavalry, the Russians won. For the first time, the Russians had defeated a Mongol army.

- Khan **Tokhtamysh** immediately summoned his protector, Tamerlane, and vast numbers of forces descended from central Asia. Vasily I Dmitriyevich and the other princes immediately gave their loyalty back to the Mongol khagan. It would be another 120 years before that kind of overlordship would end.

- The battle, however, was a significant turning point. It proved that the Russians could mount armies that could defeat the Mongols.

Russian Power

- Two important events occurred that tipped the balance in favor of the Russians. By 1500, the princes of Moscow—now the tsars of Russia—began a march to conquer the steppes.

- The first to fall was the Golden Horde, which broke up into a series of competing khaganates. They came to depend on the Ottoman sultan for military support, technical advice, and money.

- Meanwhile, the grand princes of Moscow embraced the new military technology of handheld firearms and artillery. In 1480, **Ivan III Vasilyevich** engaged the Mongol army on a tributary of the Volga.

- From there, he and his successor, **Ivan IV** (Ivan the Terrible), went on to conquer the Eurasian steppes. Through the fur trade, the influx of military colonists armed with firearms, and incursions of Cossacks (the Russians' response to Mongol cavalry), Russia was able to expand its power across the tundra, the taiga, and the steppe zones.

- The success of the Russians was symbolized by the Treaty of Nerchinsk in 1689. This was an agreement between the young Tsar

Peter the Great (and his brother, Ivan) and the **Qing** court—the Manchu emperors of China who had overthrown the Ming.

- The partition outlined in the treaty meant that the steppes fell into the hands of the Russians and the Chinese. The Russians got most of the steppes and Transoxania. The Chinese got Tibet, the Tarim Basin, and inner Mongolia. The Mongolian heartland was preserved as a buffer between the two empires. This division has dictated politics and geopolitics ever since.

Important Terms

Qing Dynasty: The last imperial dynasty of China, founded by the Manchu conquerors (1644–1911).

Safavids: The dynasty of the Shi'ite shahs of Iran (1501–1732), rivals to the Ottoman sultans.

Names to Know

Berke (b. c. 1208; r. 1257–1266): Mongol khan; the son of Jochi and brother of Batu. He succeeded to the western *ulus* of the Mongol Empire (then known as the White and Blue Hordes). He had converted to Islam; thus, he aligned with Mamluk Egypt against his cousin, the ilkhan Hulagu (1256–1265).

Bolad (d. 1313): Mongol chancellor and cultural advisor; served Kublai Khan in 1260–1285. He established a directorate to gather and analyze geographic information and maps. In 1285, he arrived as the Great Khan's envoy and entered into the service of the ilkhans Arghun (1282–1291), Gaykhatu (1291–1295), and Mahmud Ghazan (1295–1304) as a fiscal expert. He introduced Chinese-style paper money.

Hongwu (b. 1328; r. 1368–1398): Ming emperor of China and the peasant rebel leader and Buddhist monk Zhu Yuanzhang. In 1353–1367, he secured the Yangtze valley and, in 1328, occupied Dadu. He expelled the Mongol emperor Togon-temür (1333–1368) and was hailed emperor of the Ming

Dynasty (1368–1644). He razed the Mongol palace and replaced Dadu with the new Chinese city of Beijing.

Ivan I Danilovich (b. 1288; r. 1325–1340): Grand prince of Moscow; a loyal vassal of the khan of the Golden Horde (1312–1341). In 1328, the khan rewarded Ivan I with Vladimir and the right to collect from the other Russian princes the tribute due to the Mongols. Ivan, nicknamed Kalita ("Moneybags"), exploited his position to turn Moscow into the premier Russian principality.

Ivan III Vasilyevich (b. 1440; r. 1462–1505): Grand prince of Moscow; renounced his allegiance to the Golden Horde. In 1480, he won a strategic victory over Khan Ahmed (1465–1481) on the Ural River. Vasilyevich secured Saray, capital of the Golden Horde.

Ivan IV (b. 1530; r. 1547–1584): Ivan the Terrible, tsar of Russia. Reformed the Russian army and conquered the khanates of Kazan (1152) and Astrakhan (1556). He ended the Mongol threat, securing the lower Volga valley and, thus, enabling Russian expansion across Siberia.

Tokhtamysh (d. 1406; r. 1376–1395): Khan of the Golden Horde. Fled to Tamerlane in 1376 after he failed to unseat his uncle Urus Khan (1361–1375). With the support of Tamerlane, he was received as khan of the Golden Horde. In 1382, he avenged the Mongol defeat at Kulikovo Field by sacking Moscow and forcing Grand Prince Vasily to return to his Mongol allegiance. In 1395, Khan Tokhtamysh blundered into a war with his overlord Tamerlane (1370–1405), who ruthlessly sacked Saray and appointed as his vassal a new khan, Temür Kutlugh (1395–1401). Tokhtamysh died in exile in 1406.

Vasily I Dmitriyevich (b. 1371; r. 1389–1425): Grand prince of Moscow; the grandson of Ivan I. He defeated a Mongol army of 35,000 on Kulikovo Field on September 8, 1380. In 1382, Khan Tokhtamysh invaded and stormed Moscow and sacked the city, forcing Grand Prince Vasily to return to his Mongol allegiance.

Suggested Reading

Allsen, *Culture and Conquest in Mongol Eurasia.*

Elverskog, *Buddhism and Islam on the Silk Road.*

Khodarkovksy, *Russia's Steppe Frontier.*

Lincoln, *The Conquest of a Continent.*

Mote, *Imperial China, 900–1800.*

Rossabi, *The Mongols and Global History.*

Veith, "The Eastern Steppe."

Questions to Consider

1. Why did Kublai Khan and his successors choose to rule as Chinese-style emperors of the Yuan Dynasty (1271–1368)? What were the strengths and weaknesses of this policy? How well did they succeed in winning over their Chinese subjects? How did the Neo-Confucian Mandarins view Yuan rule? What accounted for the overthrow of Yuan rule in 1368 and the establishment of the native Chinese Ming Dynasty?

2. Why did the Yuan emperors favor Buddhism? Why did the Mongols turn to Buddhism, received from Tibet in the 14th and 15th centuries?

3. In what ways did the Chagataid khans maintain best the Mongol military and political traditions? How did the adoption of Islam and the Turkish language transform the Chagataid court and society? How much did the later conquerors Tamerlane and Bābur owe to their Chagataid predecessors?

4. What was the contribution of the Mongol ilkhans at Tabriz for the future political, cultural, and religious evolution of Iran?

5. Why did the khans of the Golden Horde and its successor states fail to appreciate the danger posed by the grand princes of Moscow? What developments ended the power of steppe nomads in the 16th century?

Conversion and Assimilation
Lecture 33—Transcript

In this lecture, I want to look at essentially a passing of the Mongol peace and the Mongol Empire. We really cannot study the Mongol Empire as a decline and fall the way some have done with the Roman Empire; in effect, we look at issues of largely conversion and assimilation. This lecture builds on the lecture that dealt with the Mongol peace, the prosperity, the cultural exchange, and the dissemination of religions across Eurasia in the 13th and 14th centuries.

What I want to achieve in this lecture is some understanding how the four *ulus*—that is, the domains of Kublai Khan at his death in 1294 that embraced the Mongol homeland, essentially Tibet and China; the middle *ulus*, the central steppes in the Tarim Basin in the hands of the Chagatai rulers, the Chagatai khans, the Ilkhans of Persia and Transoxiana; the family of Hulagu; and finally the so-called Golden Horde, the descendants of Batu ruling the western steppes with the hegemony over the Orthodox Russian principalities in the forest zones—how did these four areas change? How did they fall away from the Mongol imperial legacy? In effect, how and even did they fall in any kind of meaningful sense?

It is best to look at China first. As I have stated throughout, the events on the eastern steppes and its interaction with Chinese civilization have for so long dictated so much of the history on the Eurasian steppes and its wider ramifications for Eurasian civilizations. Let us go back to Kublai Khan and look at his situation in 1271 when he had essentially proclaimed himself emperor and had taken that Chinese dynastic name the Yuan family, a name that would resonate with Confucian scholar class, the so-called *shi*. Those would be the men who had gone through the imperial examination system as it had been formalized by the Song emperors. They knew their Confucian classics; they engaged in calligraphy; they understood all of the aesthetics and the moral qualities of the canon of Confucian text. That was a direct appeal to this group.

Kublai Khan inherited a policy that was attributed actually to his uncle Ögedei. There was a very important minister of Genghis Khan and Ögedei.

He had actually served the Jin emperor; his name was Yelü Chucai. He was a high official at the Jin court. He went over to Genghis Khan early on and he served with Ögedei. As Ögedei conquered the remnants of the Jin Empire, this minister warned Ögedei, "You may conquer China from horseback, but you cannot rule it from horseback"; and that image I have used repeatedly in dealing with several of the nomadic conquerors, notably, for instance, the Parthians, who tried to rule Iran from horseback.

It does not work. In the case of Kublai Khan, from the start he made an effort to win over the Confucian scholar classes. He spared most of the Chinese populations; we did not reenact the massacres that characterized the brutal conquest of the Islamic world, Russia, and Hungary. On the other hand, it was always tentative. There were several important provisions about this. Kublai Khan was ever a pragmatic grandson of Genghis Khan. He did not use the Song examination system; far from it. He retained the right to select his ministers personally, and this was based on loyalty and usefulness to the khan. This was a major departure from the Song policy. By the time Kublai Khan did this—it had been several hundred years—this class had come to expect that it dominated the running of the middle kingdom (that is, China); and it would be premised on those men who had the proper expression, who understood calligraphy, the canon, who had the moral character who understood the way, the Dao as it would be said in the Daoist traditions, and above all who would represent the emperor and his Mandate from Heaven. Kublai Khan feared that if you put yourself too much in the hands of these bureaucrats, ultimately it would undermine his rule; and assimilation was always a danger. If the Mongols became too accustomed to Chinese ways and luxuries, they would lose their military edge; and the numbers really told in this. The Song Empire and the former Jin Empire together were estimated to be 120 million strong, most of them in South China. The number of Mongols and Turkish tribes Kublai Khan commanded did not reach a million. From the start, Kublai Khan had to use all sorts of outsiders—Uighurs, Buddhists from Tibet, Muslims from Transoxiana and Iran, Western adventurers such as Marco Polo—to staff various administrative posts. This led to a basic tension, even under the best of arrangements between Kublai Khan and the Confucian scholar class. To be sure, Kublai Khan and his successors, the later Yuan emperors, they patronized arts; they were very, very active in Buddhist sanctuaries in China. There was quite a continuity in letters and aesthetics among the Chinese educated classes. There was not a suppression of Chinese expression. However, Kublai Khan himself did not engage in this; it was always done at a distance. The religion of choice was Buddhism.

Kublai Khan also built his own capital, Dadu, which is today the modern city of Beijing; it means "the capital." It came down through Marco Polo's account as the fabled city of Xanadu. There was a Chinese-style palace built there as well as a Chinese-style city, but it also was the capital of the Great Khan. He chose what institutions to patronize, who would be admitted to court; and the capital was far enough north that it allowed Kublai Khan to stay in touch with the steppes as well as run his Chinese domains. I mentioned one example of that was creating a Tibetan-inspired script, which was used in all the monumental architecture; it was not Chinese characters. We can document going all the way back to the Xiongnu that almost all the nomadic peoples on the eastern steppes use the Han, the Chinese characters, to write their own language. This was an adaptation; they wanted their script to look Chinese, therefore it would be elevated. This was not the case with the Mongols. The Yuan emperors used their own script, undoubtedly much to the dismay of the Confucian scholar class.

The system succeeded in the time of Kublai Khan, but his successors were not as strong, not as powerful; and from the start, they did face an at best provisional cooperation from the Confucian class. Furthermore, Mongol control—that is, the control of the great khan of the other *ulus*—started to wane after 1294. Those other three khanates went their separate ways; they would all eventually embrace Islam. That will act as a divide between those three khanates, as well as the Great Khan ruling in China and in the Mongol heartland.

Furthermore, the later Yuan emperors made high demands. They made high military demands because there were rebels to crush; there were abortive expeditions, some of them sent into Indo-China; there were vast building programs; there was the endowment of Buddhist monasteries. The Yuan emperors were accused of neglecting not only the way, the Confucian traditions, but also the management of the empire itself, above all the canal systems. There were reports of repeated flooding, ruining of crops and silk production. All of these led to very heavy combinations of the Buddhist apocalypse with traditional opposition to emperors who had lost the Mandate of Heaven, and it exploded in 1351.

A peasant leader—who proved to be a very, very capable opponent to the Yuan emperors; his name was Chu Yuan-chang—headed up various dissident groups loosely labeled the Red Turbans. He actually spent more of his time defeating other dissident groups. By 1356, he controlled most of South China and then brought these other groups into alliance. In 1368, this man was able to proclaim himself the first Ming emperor. He sent an expedition north against the Mongol capital—that is, the former palace of Kublai Khan—and the then-reigning Yuan emperor, a young man, essentially fled back to Mongolia and gave up the heritage; that is, henceforth the Mongols would never again rule China.

The reoccupation of China by the Ming armies was a significant turning point. It led to the expulsion of the Mongols forever; and the Ming emperors carried out several important policies to demonstrate this. First and foremost, that Mongol capital was leveled and a new city called Beijing was built on top of it. Beijing was commenced in 1403. It was completed in the reign of the emperor Yongle, including the famous Forbidden City. The later Mings actually made their capital at Beijing, which had initially been just a military base, in order to drive home the message to the descendants of Kublai Khan that the Mongols would never again be able to mess with the Chinese emperor; he was vigilant on that northern frontier.

In addition, the Ming emperors ordered the reconstruction of the old Han and Tang walls. I described that those earlier walls were really a set of fortresses, signal towers, monitoring stations. They did not represent the Maginot mentality that early scholars attributed to them. The walls that exist now are the masonry walls ordered by the Ming emperors, and this was more of an emotional, psychological response to the humiliation that China had been once ruled by Mongols, by nomads, by people who were not of the Han peoples, and this would never happen again. It is ironic that in moving their capital to Beijing, to expending enormous amount of efforts on building the Great Wall, that the Ming emperors failed to guard against the threat they did not see, and that again came from the forest of Manchuria when in 1644 a new people, a people of the forest, the Manchus, entered

China, overthrew the Ming dynasty and ruled in the fashion of a sanified set of conquerors. You never are overthrown by the threat you guard against, it is always the one you do not expect. The Ming emperors learned that lesson to their dismay and grief.

The situation in China differed from the other three *ulus*. In Central Asia, the Chagataid khans were able to prosper off the Silk Road, and they ruled a very odd khanate in the 14th century that really had three components. One of those components and perhaps the most important were the central steppes; we have talked about them before. They were essentially extending from the regions around the Aral Sea, the Upper Jaxartes; they moved east to about the Altai Mountain range. On those steppes were various Turkish and Mongol tribes, and they preserved the traditions of Genghis Khan. They followed the notions of *yassa*; that is, the authority of the khan overrode all religious law, all other customs. They also were proud of their steppe heritage. They did not want to live in cities; they were very disdainful of cosmopolitan cities. They essentially claimed to be the true Mongols, even though most of them spoke Turkish; and the region is often known as Moghulistan or Mughalistan, "Mongol area," from which the later Mughal emperors of India took their name (and we will talk about that in a later lecture). They also included the Tarim Basin, the caravan cities; these cities steadily went over to Islam. They steadily adopted the Uighur Turkish; and by the opening of the 15th century, Buddhism had passed. The great Buddhist monasteries in cities such as Turfan, Dongwan had all passed out of existence, and instead you had a Turkish-speaking Uighur population tied to the nomads of the central steppes and to the caravan cities of Transoxiana. That was the third component.

Other great cities we have talked about so much, Samarkand, Bukhara; those were a point of contention between the Chagataid khans ruling on the central steppes with their kinsmen, the Ilkhans of Persia. Eventually, the Ilkhans would lose out; and when their khanate fragmented in 1353 into competing states, Transoxiana was then again part of that central *ulus*. In that region, the population went Islamic; but there are two important points I wish to stress: The Chagataid khans never pursued their Islam rigorously or zealously. They tolerated other faiths. Furthermore, they always kept touch with the steppe traditions and the importance of *yassa*; that is, the law of the khan. These two concepts will prove extremely important because the successor of this tradition would turn out to be a down, out of luck descendent of both Tamerlane and Genghis Khan called Babur. He would take these traditions over the Hindu Kush and use them to construct the Mughal Empire, the great imperial order of India, the predecessor of the Raj; but the birth of that Raj owed a great deal to that steppe tradition passed through the Chagataid khans and going back to Genghis Khan.

Let us look at the Ilkhans of Persia. They ruled the second most prosperous of the *ulus*, second to China. They were certainly engaged in all of the trade and the cultural exchange we talked about. Hulagu and his successors long maintained a cosmopolitan court. They were great sponsors of Buddhism. Some of the greatest thinkers and scholars in the cultural exchange worked at Tabriz. Conversion to Islam did not result in the Ilkhans embracing Islam to the disadvantage of the other faiths. I had mentioned that Buddhist monasteries still flourished into the early 14th century. The situation would change in the 14th century. Islam would mount a recovery. The later Ilkhans would be more orthodox in their beliefs. After the fall of the Ilkhans family—it was essentially finished in 1353—Buddhism lost all patronage and essentially disappeared in Iran and Transoxiana after that brief revival.

You can get some sense of the cultural diversity of faiths and of intellectual achievement among the Ilkhans by looking at some of the people they patronized. I mentioned, of course, that earlier scholar Rashid al-Din who was very important; but there was another one. He was a Mongol prince who had served in the court of Kublai Khan. His name was Bolad Aqa, and he had been in the forefront of a number of important administrative tasks entrusted to him by Kublai Khan. He, for instance, had been trained in Chinese and the Confucian classics. He supervised translations of agricultural works. He supervised the improvement of agriculture in the reign of Kublai Khan; streamlined the Yuan bureaucracy; devised a system of appointments and recommendations that Kublai Khan liked. Then, in 1285, he was sent as an envoy by Kublai Khan to essentially Kublai Khan's nephew, the then-reigning Ilkhan of Tabriz. Because of wars on the steppes, temporary civil war, Bolad decided to stay at Tabriz and offer his services to the Ilkhanate court. He spent the rest of his career carrying out important translations of Chinese works into Persian. He introduced a lot of court ceremony, dress, taste, and aesthetics from China. He epitomized the type of exchange that went on between these two courts and had far wider ramifications than just what happened at the courts because it enriched the high culture of Eastern Islam, that Persian culture; it introduced the court at Tabriz to Chinese porcelains and silks, all sorts of ritual and protocol; and it became the basis for the great three Muslim empires of the early modern period, often called the gunpowder empires—the Ottoman sultanate, the Safavid shahs of Iran, and the Mughal emperors of India—that cultural mix that was shared by those three great states before the coming of the Europeans, the European impact on the Islamic world, goes back really to these achievements of the Ilkhanate court; that is, the family of Hulagu, a man who had been no friend to Islam and had cut wide swathes of destruction in his conquest of Iran and Iraq.

Therefore, the Ilkhanate court, in a way, was converted and assimilated into the wider Islamic world. But that Islamic world owed a great debt to the Ilkhans for its enrichment and its revival of Islamic architecture, in Islamic intellectual activities. To me, the Ilkhanate court was the intellectual and cultural success of the whole Mongol Empire. Whatever Kublai Khan achieved in China ended up being expelled; it was short-lived. The Chagataid khans and the Khans of the Golden Horde never played that same cultural role, but the family of Hulagu gets high marks in my mind for what they achieved in the rebirth of Islamic civilization in the lands of Eastern Islam.

Finally let us turn to the last *ulus*. That is popularly known as the Golden Horde, it was known under a number of names; and this is the family of Batu. Batu transmitted power to his brother, Berke. I mentioned that Berke proved a very devout Muslim. He came to the throne in 1227 and he had, however, converted earlier to Islam under the impact of a Sufi mystic. Berke was the first of the Mongol rulers that we know who put religion as a loyalty above kinship. Berke aligned very quickly with the Mamluk sultans of Cairo. He was furnishing the slave soldiers, mostly Kipchak and Cuman Turks who had been enslaved in tribal warfare and who were being sold through the Genoese colony of Kaffa or later the Venetian colony at Taman, which is just at the mouth of the Kuban River. These were two great slave *entrepots*. The Venetian and Genoese carried these slaves, who became the basis of Mamluk power. Berke was not displeased when he heard the news of the defeat of his cousin's army, Hulagu, at the Battle of Ain Jalut.

Furthermore, these later khans, at their palace city of Saray, pursued a policy similar to their kinsmen in Central Asia. They were standoffish about urban civilization. They embraced Turkish. They liked the simpler Islam that was appropriate to nomadic peoples, particularly of Sufis and of mystics. Many of the tribes in the confederation were quite unconventional in their Islamic beliefs. I mentioned that in an earlier lecture in the questions of conversion; that when the Russians came to later catalog these tribes—Were they Islamic, were they Christian, were they Buddhist?—Russian census takers became very frustrated and essentially cataloged them by ethnicity and language because the Islamic religious practices were so unconventional and looked so un-Muslim to the Russians.

This khanate also exercised control over the Russian principalities. That was a result of the victories of Batu. The Russians have an historical memory that has been augmented by national histories that they suffered under the Tatar yoke, and that Tatar yoke really hamstrung or perverted Russian development. That is a simplification; the Russian princes were never agreed on anything. They always fought each other quite happily. But the Russian princes who played ball with the khans at Saray, they prospered very well; and one of the most important ones was Prince Ivan of Moscow. He proved a very loyal vassal of the Golden Horde. He proved loyal in a very important civil war; and in 1328, the then-ruling khan Özeg entrusted Ivan with the collection of tribute from the Russian princes that was owed to the khan. This was a great deal for Moscow. The khan also threw in some important cities like Vladimir and others; and Moscow emerged at the nexus of the river routes that linked up the whole systems of the Don, the Dnieper, and the Volga. They gained a very, very important principality by 1328, and they also are the collection agency for the Mongol khans. This Ivan is remembered affectionately as "Ivan the Moneybags," "Ivan Kalita" in Russian; and that is because he amassed resources and money at the expense of his fellow princes in paying off the khans.

There is, however, an important point to note. The khans of the Golden Horde very quickly came to realize their vulnerability vis-à-vis the Russian princes. This was dramatically revealed in 1380. This battle, the Battle of Kulikovo—which occurred on September 18, 1380, and is still celebrated as a great heroic event in Russia—by no means ended the Mongol yoke; but it did point out that the Mongol army could be defeated. The then-reigning prince of Moscow, Vasili I, put together a coalition of Russian princes, and this army marched to the Don and surprised a Mongol army on the Don in September. They came out of the mists; they were unexpected. The Mongols were raiding for reinforcements; and in a very, very hard fought battle in which the Russians mounted heavy cavalry European style, the Russians won. A number of the princes fell mortally wounded; but for the first time, the Russians beat a Mongol army.

This was a significant event. It did not, however, lead to the overthrow of Mongol rule. The khan, Toktamish, ruling at Saray, immediately summoned his protector, Tamerlane; vast numbers of forces came from Central Asia, and very quickly Vasili of Moscow and the other princes were brought back to heel, they immediately gave their loyalty back to the Mongol khan. It would be really another 120 years before that kind of overlordship would end. The battle was a significant turning point. It proved that Mongol cavalry could be defeated and that the Russians were getting better and better at mounting the sort of armies that could defeat the Mongols, and they had access to the Western technology.

Two important events occurred that tipped the balance in the course of the 14th century; and by 1500, the princes of Moscow had turned themselves into the tsars of Russia and were on the march to conquer the steppes. The first was the Golden Horde itself. It broke up into a series of competing khanates: the khanate of the Crimea, the khanate of Astrakhan, the khanate of Kazan. All of these states engaged in the slave trade, and starting in 1453 supplied slave soldiers and slaves to the court of the Ottoman sultan. They came to depend on the Ottoman sultan for military support, technical advice, and even money. The Golden Horde, in effect, fragmented and became clients of the Ottoman sultan in Constantinople.

Meanwhile, the grand princes of Moscow were not idle. They embraced the new military technology of handheld firearms and artillery. That included the primitive firearms known as the arquebus, the disciplined infantry that could fire them, and above all field artillery. In 1480, Prince Ivan III decided to engage the army of the khans, and there was a battle on a tributary of the Volga, a very important battle sometimes known as the Battle of the Ugra

River, in which the Russian army lined up on one side, the Mongols on the other; and the Mongols were very, very hesitant—and for Mongols read largely Turks or Tatars—to attack the Russian army. As the river froze in December, the Mongols retreated into the steppes. Ivan, kind of ridiculously, declared a victory.

But, in effect, it was a victory. From there, he and his successor, the famous Ivan the Terrible, went on to conquer Kazan and Astrakhan. They gained control of the Volga. The khans of the Crimea lingered on as vassals of the Ottoman sultan, but the steppes were now in the hands of the princes of Moscow who turned themselves into the tsars of Russia. They had the firearms and the artillery to conquer the Eurasian steppes as well as the incentive. Starting from 1500 on, the tsars entrusted to the Stroganov family the right to collect the furs of Siberia. It was the fur trade and the colonization by military colonists armed with firearms and backed up by Cossacks starting in the 17th century who were the Russians response to Mongol cavalry, which led to the rapid expansion of Russian power across the tundra, the taiga, and the steppe zones.

The result is that the movement that had for so long been from east to west now went from west to east. The success of the Russians was symbolized at the Treaty of Nerchinsk in 1689. That was an agreement by the then very, very young tsar Peter the Great and his brother, Ivan, with the then Ch'ing court—that is, the Manchu emperors of China who had overthrown the Ming—and that partition has been essentially redone several times, but that partition essentially resulted in the steppes falling into the hands of the Russians and the Chinese. The Russian tsar got most of the steppes and Transoxiana. The Chinese eventually got Tibet, the Tarim Basin; Inner Mongolia and the Mongolian heartland were preserved as a buffer between the two empires. This division has dictated politics and geopolitics ever since. It is ironic to me that the Golden Horde, which in some ways was the greatest military force in 1294, resulted in galvanizing the Russian princes, the tsars of Moscow, to adopt the military technology that they had gained under the Mongol peace to march across the steppes, conquer those steppes, and forever end the military power of nomadic horse archers.

Tamerlane, Prince of Destruction
Lecture 34

<hr>

In this lecture, we will explore the career of Tamerlane, whose nickname was the Prince of Destruction. His given name was Timur, and he was called Timur the Lame because he was wounded early in his career. Tamerlane had a mixed career. On the one hand, he was hailed as the Sword of Islam—the heroic Muslim conqueror. On the other hand, accounts of him are filled with tales of atrocities. Muslim scholars saw him as a barbarian conqueror with only a marginal claim to being the Sword of Islam. In fact, most of the fury of Tamerlane's army was directed against his Muslim opponents.

An Astute Commander

- **Tamerlane** had the same powerful, charismatic personality that we saw in Genghis Khan and his successful grandsons. He also relished terror in the extreme.

- Tamerlane was the quintessential barbarian conqueror, a child of the steppes who was released on the Muslim world. He was born outside of the city of Samarkand into a relatively unimportant tribe, the Barlas. His father was a minor emir, at best, and Tamerlane grew up close to the urban civilization of Transoxania and its high Persian culture.

Tamerlane revived the imperial military organization imposed earlier by Genghis Khan; his men were promoted based on ability and loyalty to their commander.

- He was greatly influenced by the political and legal traditions of the Mongol Empire, particularly the Chagataid khaganate, of the central steppes. By the time Tamerlane was born, it had divided into two competing khaganates, eastern and western, that battled for control of the cities and trade routes.

- It was in these wars that Tamerlane proved to be an astute commander. He had a many of the qualities of Genghis Khan, but he could never aspire to be a khan: He didn't have the bloodlines. He was not really a Mongol but a Turk.

- Starting in 1361, Tamerlane positioned himself as the agent of a legitimate Chagataid khan: Tughluq Temür. Tughluq Temür empowered Tamerlane as the emir of the Barlas. Tamerlane used that position to secure Transoxania and eventually, in 1370, to create his own khan—a figurehead—in Samarkand.

Tamerlane's Early Career

- Tamerlane held the rank of grand emir. He was the commander-in-chief of a Mongol army primarily composed of Turkish tribes from the central Eurasian steppes.

- In the 1360s, when he received both his wound, as well as lessons in statecraft and military training, Tamerlane returned to Genghis Khan's method of organization for his army. He divided the army into the tumen—the 10,000-man units—all of whom swore oaths of loyalty.

- He came to rule an imperial-style army that eventually numbered at least 10 tumen—more than 100,000 mounted warriors drawn from the central and western steppes. Although not a descendant of Genghis Khan, this Turkish general was, in many ways, heir to the earlier conqueror's military and political legacy.

- By the time of Tamerlane, there was no longer any great Mongol khagan. He had been deposed in 1368 when the Ming emperor of China chased the Mongols out of China forever. Tamerlane was on his own to carve out a career as a great conqueror.

Seven Major Campaigns

- Between 1381 and his death in 1405, Tamerlane conducted seven major campaigns. By 1381, he had established his position in Samarkand after 10 or 11 years of harsh fighting. His was an extraordinary career, both in time and in geography.

- Starting in 1381, Tamerlane opened up a series of campaigns that swept across the traditional caravan cities of Iran. He consolidated the domains of the old ilkhans of the house of Genghis Khan. The battles and campaigns were characterized by extraordinary devastation; the civilian population was slaughtered and great mounds of skulls were piled on the plains.

- These campaigns alarmed Tokhtamysh, khan of the Golden Horde, who crossed the Caucasus and invaded Azerbaijan. This was a strategic region, particularly Tabriz, where Tamerlane wintered his army when he was on western campaigns.

- Tamerlane beat back the invasion; he blitzed Georgia and Armenia, Christian kingdoms that were nominal allies of Tokhtamysh. Further, he singled out for destruction Muslim cities that had in any way supported his rival. The fighting in the early 1380s was particularly bitter because Tamerlane had earlier supported Tokhtamysh in a civil war.

Clashes with the Golden Horde

- Tamerlane singled out the Golden Horde for defeat. In 1391, he led a massive army across the steppes north of Samarkand in a huge sweep west. He went 700 miles north and 1,000 miles west, caught the army of Tokhtamysh, and crushed it.

- Tokhtamysh retreated westward onto the southwestern steppes, and Tamerlane decided to pull back to Samarkand—he was beyond his supply systems. He returned to Samarkand and plotted a second war, a second strategic invasion against the Golden Horde, across the Caucasus.

- That invasion involved Tamerlane in some complicated campaigns in Syria, especially fighting against the Mamluk sultans, who were trying to put a puppet sultan on the throne of Baghdad.

- In 1395, Tamerlane crossed the Derbent Pass, entered the Kuban steppes, maneuvered the army of Tokhtamysh into a decisive battle, and defeated them. The Kipchak Turks who were fighting in the ranks of Tokhtamysh defected to Tamerlane in the course of the fighting.

- The victory over Tokhtamysh, this second campaign, was absolutely extraordinary. As a result, Tamerlane now had his own vassal on the throne of the Golden Horde, and he could boast that he gathered together the three *ulus* of Genghis Khan: the western steppes, the central steppes, and the ilkhanate.

Ottoman and Mamluk Sultans

- The victory over the Golden Horde meant that Tamerlane was bound to clash with the Ottoman sultan and the Mamluk sultan of Egypt, who were long allied to the Golden Horde and dependent on the slave soldiers exported through the Genoese and Venetian ports in the Crimea.

- Before that final reckoning, Tamerlane—for reasons still uncertain—took a timeout and decided to invade India. His real target was the Tughluq sultan of Delhi. That resulted in a great victory in December 1398 outside of Delhi. Delhi was sacked, Lahore was sacked, and a number of Hindu temples were reduced to rubble.

- Tamerlane made his way back to Samarkand. He then moved west to reckon with both the sultan of the Ottomans and the sultan of Egypt. From 1399 to 1402, he conducted a series of complicated campaigns across the Middle East.

- In 1400, Tamerlane's forces swept into Asia Minor, spreading terror everywhere. In 1401, he returned to Baghdad. In the course of the fighting, Baghdad exchanged hands four times and was sacked twice.

- In 1402, at the climax of the campaign, Tamerlane decided to take out the Ottoman sultanate, to go after the then-ruling Sultan Bayezid (the Thunderbolt), one of the great sultans of early Ottoman history. Bayezid marched to the vicinity of Angora, and on July 20, 1402, Tamerlane fought perhaps his greatest battle.

- His engineers diverted the water supply before the actual fighting took place. He had brought an elephant corps from India. He had a superior cavalry and, perhaps, superior forces; the result was the Ottoman army went down in its first serious defeat. The sultan was captured.

Campaign to Ming China

- By the time Tamerlane returned to Samarkand, he had built an extraordinary career. He had defeated Mamluk armies, the Ottomans, the sultan of Delhi. He had overthrown the Golden Horde, and all the tribes of western and central Asia were in his employ.

- In 1405, he set out on a final expedition to reckon with Ming China. Still uncertain what his goals were, at best, he might have surprised the Chinese army in the Tarim Basin. Since 1368–1370, Ming Chinese armies had reoccupied that area.

- It was the first time Tamerlane had planned a winter campaign, however, and it was too much for him. He contracted an illness and died in February 1405.

Bābur

- In some ways, Tamerlane's career was on a level with that of Attila the Hun or even Genghis Khan. However, his empire fragmented immediately—also true of Attila the Hun's. There are several significant reasons that this empire failed to last.

- First, Tamerlane never was khan; he never ruled the Mongol nation. There was never an assembly, a *kurultai*, that could give him the tribal authority that all the Mongol khans had enjoyed. He was, after all, nothing more than the emir of the legitimate khan in Samarkand.

- Second, Tamerlane could not aspire to religious authority. That was in stark contrast to the successor states that arose after Tamerlane.

- The Ottoman sultans, who recovered from the Battle of Angora, eventually became the caliphs of Sunni Islam—a position they held until 1924. **Ismail I**, the shah who built the Iranian state, turned Iran into the Shi'ite Islamic society we see today.

- The real successor to Tamerlane was his descendent Bābur, who built the great Mughal Empire in India, a precursor to the British raj. Although Bābur was a descendent of Tamerlane, he was also a direct descendent of Genghis Khan—and that counted for everything.

Names to Know

Bābur (Zahir al-Din Muhammad) (b. 1483; r. 1526–1530): First Mughal emperor of India; a descendant of Genghis Khan and Tamerlane. A Timurid prince of Ferghana, he lost his realm in the wars between the Uzbeks and Safavid Iran. In 1504, he seized Kabul and acknowledged the Safavid shah Ismail I as his overlord. In 1526, he invaded India and defeated Ibrahim Lodi, sultan of Delhi, at the Battles of Panipat on April 26, 1526; he then occupied Delhi and founded the Mughal Empire. He composed an engaging autobiography, *Baburnama*, in literary Turkish.

Ismail I (b. 1487; 1501–1524): First Safavid shah of Iran. Founded the Shi'ite state in Iran and revived Iran as one of the great Islamic powers. He fought for Transoxania against Muhammad Shaybani (1500–1510), who had united the Turkish tribes of the central Eurasian steppe as the Uzbek confederation. On December 2, 1510, Shah Ismail decisively defeated and slew Muhammad Shaybani at the Battle of Merv. But Shah Ismail had to confront the Ottoman threat from the west. He was defeated by the Ottoman sultan Selim I (1512–1520) on August 23, 1514.

Tamerlane (b. 1336; r. 1370–1405): "Prince of Destruction"; regarded as the third greatest conqueror of the steppes (after Genghis Khan and Attila). He was the heir to the Mongol military tradition, recruiting professional regiments of cavalry based on loyalty and rewards. Tamerlane, emir of the

Turko-Mongol Barlas tribe, emerged as the leading emir in the tribal wars in Transoxania in 1360–1370. In 1370, Chagatai khan Suurgatmish (1370–1384) named Tamerlane grand emir. Tamerlane also married Saray Mulk Khanum, a descendent of Genghis Khan. From his capital, he waged six campaigns of conquest between 1381 and 1401, in which he conquered most of the western half of the Mongol Empire. In 1391–1392 and 1393–1396, he defeated Tokhtamysh and broke the power of the Golden Horde. He won his greatest victories near Delhi over the Tughluq army in 1398 and at Angora over the Ottoman army of Bayezid Yildirim in 1402. Yet neither campaign resulted in territorial expansion. In February 1405, he died en route to his seventh campaign against Ming China. His exploits inspired legends; he is credited he with writing the flattering *Memoirs of Temur*.

Suggested Reading

Golden, *Central Asia in World History*.

Gonzalez de Clavijo (Le Strange, trans.), *Embassy to Tamerlane, 1403–1406*.

Jackson, *The Mongols and the West, 1221–1410*.

Manz, *The Rise and Rule of Tamerlane*.

———, "Temür and the Early Timurids to c. 1450."

Marozzi, *Tamerlane: Sword of Islam, Conqueror of the World*.

Saunders, *The History of the Mongol Conquests*.

Questions to Consider

1. What accounts for the different images of Tamerlane as a conqueror? Does he deserve either the title of Prince of Destruction or Sword of Islam?

2. What accounted for Tamerlane's early successes? How did Tamerlane exploit the civil wars and succession crises within the Chagataid khanate to become the great emir at Samarkand in 1370?

3. In what ways was Tamerlane a worthy successor to the military traditions of Genghis Khan and the Mongol Empire? How did Tamerlane display his strategic genius in his campaigns against the Golden Horde, against the sultanate of Delhi, and the Ottoman and Mamluk sultanates? How were his battles at Delhi and Angora tactical masterpieces?

4. How did Tamerlane promote the high Persian culture of Islam? How was Samarkand transformed into a great capital?

5. Why did Tamerlane's empire fail to survive his death? Why did Tamerlane fail to forge the institutions that would have preserved an imperial unity? Would Tamerlane's successful invasion of China have compromised his empire?

Tamerlane, Prince of Destruction
Lecture 34—Transcript

In this lecture, I plan to open up with the career of Tamerlane, or Timur, his actual name. Tamerlane and Babur, who was a descendent of Tamerlane, will form the last two narrative lectures of this course. They were both great conquerors of the steppes; they were both heirs to the Mongol legacy; and as we will see in this lecture and the next lecture, they represent an important contrast as to what is the standard for a successful conqueror to get in that gallery with Attila the Hun and Genghis Khan. Tamerlane is probably a distant third of the great steppe conquerors. He is not recognized as quickly as Attila the Hun and Genghis Khan; yet, for my money, he has one of the best titles: He was usually called "Prince of Destruction." He would have preferred the name "Sword of Islam," but he really shed too much Muslim blood and sacked too many Muslim cities to deserve that title.

As a result of his career—and it is a very mixed career, as we shall see— Tamerlane has really two faces, two portraits that have come down to us in the contemporary literature. On the one hand, he is hailed as that Sword of Islam; that great heroic Muslim conqueror. That comes through in a history that was written shortly after his death by a Persian historian, Sharaf ad-Din Ali Yazdi, and he penned an account in which Tamerlane was a great noble Muslim prince; he was almost in the guise of the great defenders of Islam who fought the Crusaders. This work has come down to us with a great deal of details about the reign, particularly Tamerlane's earlier career: how he got the name "Tamerlane" or "Timur the Lame," Timur the Lame because he was wounded very early in his career in his hip and that resulted in the conqueror having a limp throughout his life; that was in the fighting in the 1360s where he established himself as the effective ruler of Samarkand. On the other hand, we have a number of stories about his atrocities and that has led to a very different picture. We have accounts of shortly after his death discussing how he had been a brutal conqueror; that yes, he was interested in talking to Muslim theologians. There is even a story about him meeting the famous historian Ibn Khaldūn, very, very well-known for his account of Muslim dynasties, usually looked upon as one of the great historians of traditional Islam. This occurs at the siege of Damascus and it is something of a conceit. Even so, the accounts shortly after his death are filled with pages about massacres and brutalities; atrocities really on the order of the worst atrocities committed by Genghis Khan, Hulagu, and Batu.

In this way, Tamerlane presents us a very, very mixed picture. His contemporaries were often shocked by his brutality. Muslim authors saw him as really very often a barbarian conqueror with only a marginal claim to being the Sword of Islam. Anyway, that was a title he picked up while he was battling in India where he sacked some Hindu temples, and later when he destroyed churches in Georgia and Armenia. Most of the fury of Tamerlane's army was really directed against Muslim opponents. We have some colorful incidents about him, and several facts become clear from both accounts and they agree on this one point; that is, both the negative and the positive accounts on Tamerlane: He had that same powerful, charismatic personality that we had seen in Genghis Khan and in his successful grandsons.

He also relished terror on an order that is really quite extraordinary; and sometimes these acts of terror, which were again within the Mongol tradition of demoralizing your foes, seemed to be almost gratuitous and almost experimental. For instance, on several occasions he ordered great towers of skulls of the decapitated prisoners to be piled up on the plain. There are accounts where garrisons surrendered and Tamerlane promised, "I'm not going to shed any of your blood," and then had these poor guys inured in walls; he did that on several occasions both in Iran and in Asia Minor. On the eve of one of his greatest battles, outside of Delhi in 1398—really in December, under very, very dark skies, threatening rain—he was fearful that the numerous Hindu captives he had taken, and they were destined for the slave markets of Samarkand, they might revolt. He ordered an absolute massacre before the battle to make sure that there was no danger of them ever acting up in the course of the fighting.

Tamerlane really comes down as the quintessential barbarian conqueror; a child of the steppes who was released on the Muslim world. There are several points to keep in mind about this image. First, Tamerlane was actually born outside of the city of Samarkand among a rather unimportant tribe, the Barlas tribe. His father was a minor figure, a minor emir at best; and Tamerlane grew up close to the urban civilization of Transoxiana, and that included all that high Persian culture. We will find later in his reign, after

1370 when he has essentially established himself as the Grand Emir, that he was a patron of Persian culture for Samarkand, for his capital. In addition, he drank very heavily from the political and legal traditions of the Mongol Empire, particularly of the Chagataid khanate. As you recall, that was the khanate of the central steppes. That went to the second son of Genghis Khan, and that family from Chagataid ruled over the central steppes, over Transoxiana, over the cities of the Tarim Basin. By the time that Tamerlane was born, it had divided into two competing khanates, the so-called eastern and western khanate. The khans were largely figureheads, although they were descendants of Genghis Khan through Chagatai; and many of the emirs who battled for control of the cities and trade routes did so in the name of the Chagatai khan. That was a very important political fiction: These tribal leaders who took the old Islamic title emir usually postured as agents of the legitimate Mongol khan, whether he be in the east or the west.

It was in these wars, in this fighting, that Temür, the future Tamerlane, grew up; and he proved to be a very, very astute commander. He had a lot of the qualities of Genghis Khan. He learned to trust only those men loyal to him. He had an extremely adventurous career, and he also understood how to exploit his position. He could not ever aspire to be khan; he did not have the bloodlines. He was not really a Mongol, he was a Turk. Later stories that put out he was descended from Genghis Khan are all fabrications. Starting in 1361, Tamerlane learned that the best thing to do was to posture as the agent of a legitimate khan, a Chagatai khan. The first was a fellow called Tughluq Temür, and he empowered Tamerlane as literally the emir of his family tribe, the Barlas. Over the course of a decade in the 1360s, Temür used that position to secure Transoxiana, and eventually in 1370 to create his own khan in Samarkand, a descendent of Genghis Khan, who acted as a figurehead. Throughout his career, starting from 1370 on, Tamerlane was never khan. He held the rank of Grand Emir. He ruled from Samarkand. He very much embraced the high Persian culture of Eastern Islam; and if you said you were khan or you were aspiring to be Great Khan, of course he would deny it: "No, no, I am simply the emir of the legitimate Mongol khan at Samarkand." This had advantages and also disadvantages; and you have to keep in mind that throughout his career, Tamerlane was essentially just the commander in chief of a Mongol army, which happened to be composed mostly of Turks, Turkish tribes from the Central Eurasian steppes.

In that pivotal decade, in the 1360s, where he received both his wound as well as lessons in statecraft and military training, Tamerlane went back to the army of Genghis Khan. One of the features of the Chagatai khanate had been to go back to tribal and clan organizations; that was one reason why these khans were so powerless. Tamerlane went back to the imperial organization devised by Genghis Khan after 1206; and that is, men were promoted by ability and loyalty to Tamerlane. He again organizes the army into the *tumen*, that is, the 10,000-man unit. All of these men swear oaths of loyalty. That tradition of receiving one's salt is imposed by Tamerlane among his various supporters. He came to rule an imperial-style army that eventually was perhaps at least 10 *tumen*, over 100,000 mounted warriors drawn from the central and then later the western steppes. This army was in many ways a replica of the imperial armies that we saw in the 13th century commanded by Genghis Khan and his grandsons, except now they were being commanded by a Turkish general, emir, who had really no connection to the family of Genghis Khan but was very, very much the heir to the military and political legacy of Genghis Khan.

In that capacity, starting in 1370, Tamerlane probably saw himself as the heir to the Ilkhanate of Iran—that is, that Mongol state that had been constructed by Hulagu—as well as to the central steppes and the old khanate of Chagatai and his family. Starting in the 1370s, he waged a series of campaigns to bring these areas under control. He was assisted by the fact that there really was now no longer any great Mongol khan; he had been deposed in 1368 when the Ming emperor of China chased the Mongols out of China forever. Therefore, Tamerlane was pretty much on his own to carve out a career as a great conqueror.

Between 1381 and his death in 1405, there were seven major campaigns; and it is a little artificial in the way these campaigns are divided, but there are seven major campaigns that are recorded to us in the accounts in which Tamerlane embarked on an extraordinary career of conquest. Perhaps the last one, where he died—he died during his last campaign early in 1405 in an expedition to conquer Ming China and we will talk about that later on—that may well have been a rather foolish venture, and some would argue he was saved from defeat by dying of illness in February of 1405. What do we make out of these campaigns?

The best way to understand them is to see them in several phases. By 1381, he essentially had established his position in Samarkand; that is, after about 10 or 11 years of harsh fighting. He had his position among the tribes; he had created this army; and his first objective was essentially to secure those domains that represented the old Ilkhanate and the Chagataid khanate. There was a great deal of important campaigns across Iran and Transoxiana. There was an important turning point, however, during those campaigns, and that occurred in the campaign starting in 1381 and running to 1384, which is often called the First Great Campaign depending on how you count these things. In that campaign, he clashed with the khan of the Golden Horde, Toktamish. That battle, that fighting, actually eventually turned out to be a very important shift in his policy, and that led eventually to a series of campaigns to destroy the Golden Horde. The Golden Horde represented the only real *ulus* still surviving from Genghis Khan. Toktamish was a direct descendent of Genghis Khan, and furthermore had been a protégé of Tamerlane and eventually had a falling out with him; and so from especially the campaign of 1391–1392, Tamerlane targeted the Golden Horde. That first campaign directed solely against the Golden Horde was very much in the guise of Batu; and when that did not succeed, he waged a new war in which he followed the route used by Subutai in 1221–1223 and invaded the Golden Horde from the south over the Caucasus Mountains to win a really important and decisive victory. That meant the Golden Horde was out of commission. It was essentially destroyed. It never recovered; it fragmented and it fell prey to the Russian tsars after 1480.

He took an extended timeout from these campaigns in 1398–1399. He invaded India, probably for the hell of it; that is what a Mongol conqueror should do, and anyway you make an enormous amount of booty to pay that huge army that had accepted a salt from him. But the success in demolishing the Golden Horde meant that Tamerlane now had as his enemies two important Muslim powers: One was the Mamluk government in Cairo; the other was the Ottoman Sultanate. Both of those drew Tamerlane into an important war in the west from 1399–1402. It would result in the greatest victory of Tamerlane at Angora where he defeated the Ottoman army; but it really ended up being a hollow victory because there was really no follow up. Tamerlane found that he hit the end of his logistical system. He did not have a navy; he could not destroy Ottoman power in Europe; he could not invade Egypt.

For whatever reason, he turned his attention after his successes in this great western campaign to an expedition against China, and he died enroute to that Chinese expedition. You keep these campaigns in mind; they were absolutely far ranging. They spanned the whole of the Central and Asian steppes; they involved Iran, Transoxiana; with invasions into India, in Asia Minor; a planned invasion into Egypt. These represent most of this man's lifetime from his mid-30s until he died somewhere around the age of 68. It was an extraordinary career, both in time and in geography.

Let us look at some of the fighting in the initial phases, in those early campaigns. Those campaigns were directed largely to secure Iran. Starting in 1381, he opened up a series of campaigns that swept across the traditional cities of Iran—the great caravan cities such as Rayy and Hamadan—and those campaigns lasted from 1381–1384, where he essentially consolidated the domains of the old Ilkhans of the House of Genghis Khan. The battles and campaigns were characterized by extraordinary devastation; cities were blockaded; irrigation ditches were destroyed. That is where we get a number of accounts that any city that rebelled could expect to have its civilian population slaughtered and great mounds of skulls piled on the plain to send a warning never to rebel.

In these wars, Tamerlane was very much operating in the guise of Hulagu. The wars, of course, shocked much of the Islamic world. It gained him the enmity of both the Ottoman sultan and the Mamluk sultan; and furthermore, it alarmed Toktamish who ruled the Golden Horde, and Toktamish took it up himself to cross the Caucasus and invade Azerbaijan. I mentioned earlier that Azerbaijan had been the cockpit of fighting between the Ilkhans of Persia and the khans of the Golden Horde. It was a strategic region, particularly Tabriz. That was generally where Tamerlane wintered his army when he was on the western campaigns; they always would retreat to Tabriz. Eventually Tabriz would be the center of the Safavid shahs who would unite Iran after Tamerlane and really create the traditional Shi'a state we think that Iran should be. At this period, in the 14th century, Iran was still largely Sunni Muslim. In any case, that provoked an attack into Azerbaijan.

Tamerlane reacted promptly. He beat back this invasion. He blitzed Georgia and Armenia, the Christian kingdoms that were nominal allies of Toktamish. Furthermore, he took it upon himself to single out Muslim cities for destruction that had in any way supported this rival.

The fighting in the early 1380s was particularly bitter because Tamerlane had earlier supported Toktamish in a civil war. You will recall back in 1380 that the Russian princes in September, 1380 on the banks of the Don had smashed an army of the Golden Horde under a coalition of princes led by Dmitri Ivanovich. That defeat put Toktamish in a real danger. It was with forces from Tamerlane that Toktamish eventually won back his position. Tamerlane also backed him in a civil war against an uncle whereby Toktamish united the various hordes—which is essentially a Mongol Turkish word for "army," *ordu* today in modern Turkish—and ruled the Golden Horde without any kind of opposition. The fighting in the 1380s over Azerbaijan changed the strategic aims of Tamerlane. He was no longer content to be the heir to the Ilkhanate in the steppes of Central Asia. He singled out the Golden Horde for defeat.

In 1391, in the spring—and Tamerlane always launched spring campaigns; he did not do the Mongol winter campaigns, he was never brought up on the steppes to do that—he led a huge army of conquest across the steppes north of Samarkand in a huge sweep west. He went 700 miles north, 1,000 miles west, and he caught the army of Toktamish unaware on a tributary of the Volga and clobbered it. But Toktamish retreated westward onto the southwestern steppes, and Tamerlane decided maybe it was better to pull back to Samarkand; he was beyond his supply systems; he was really very, very far from his capital. He returned to Samarkand and then plotted a second war, a second strategic invasion, against the Golden Horde; and this is the one that came over the Caucasus. That invasion involved Tamerlane in some very, very complicated fighting in Syria, in Transoxiana—that is, Georgia and Armenia—especially fighting against the Mamluk sultans who were constantly trying to put a puppet sultan on the throne of Baghdad.

In 1395, after he had cleared up that mess, he crossed the Derbent Pass, entered the Kuban steppes, and he maneuvered the army of Toktamish into a decisive battle on April 15, 1395. This battle decided the issue. Many of the

Kipchak Turks who were fighting in the ranks of Toktamish defected; they went over to Tamerlane in the course of the fighting. The army just scattered; and after that Toktamish was in exile and simply escaped onto the distant steppes, and eventually dies a rather obscure death after living a rather obscure life in 1406, shortly after Tamerlane's own death a year before. The victory over Toktamish was awesome. This second campaign was absolutely extraordinary; and as a result, Tamerlane had put a vassal on the throne of the Golden Horde and he could posture that he had now gathered together the three *ulus* of Genghis Khan: the western steppes, the central steppes, and the Ilkhanate.

That success meant he was bound to clash with the Ottoman sultan and the Mamluk sultan of Egypt, who were long allied to the Golden Horde and dependent on all those slave soldiers exported through the Genoese and Venetian ports in the Crimea. Before that final reckoning, Tamerlane, for still uncertain reasons, took a timeout and decided to invade India. His real target was the Tughluq sultan of Delhi. That resulted in a great victory in December, 1398, outside of Delhi under very, very cloudy skies; that was where he massacred the captives in advance. He lined up his army to cope with the elephant army and infantry of the Delhi sultan, and his soldiers were taught to shoot the mahouts and then stampede the elephants into the Tughluq army; and it was a tremendous victory. Delhi was sacked, Lahore was sacked; and a number of Hindu temples were sacked along the way so you could claim that you were the Sword of Islam, but really the brunt of the destruction was taken by the Muslim cities.

Tamerlane made his way back to Samarkand. He ordered another great building program, which eventually culminated in his great mausoleum. Samarkand was transformed into a beautiful city again after it had been so thoroughly destroyed back in 1220, and most of the monuments in the city today were built by Tamerlane from the loot of his Indian invasion particularly. Once back in Samarkand, the man took no timeout, no rest; he immediately moved west to reckon with both the sultan of the Ottomans as well as the sultan of Egypt.

From 1399–1402 were a series of complicated campaigns across the Middle East. Again, Tamerlane was based in Azerbaijan. His forces in

1400 swept into Asia Minor, following that traditional route, the so-called North Anatolian fault line. He swung through Sivas; he attacked a number of eastern cities of Asia Minor spreading terror everywhere. Again, as I said, some of the acts of terror seem to be a bit gratuitous. The garrison at Sivas—a very, very beautiful Seljuk city still boasting of some of the finest Seljuk monuments of the 13th century—the garrisons surrendered, some 3,000 of them, and Tamerlane said, "I won't shed your blood," and, of course, he inured them in a tower. There was almost a sadistic pleasure particular to Tamerlane in the way he treated the defeated. In 1401, he turned on Syria and he returned to Baghdad. In the course of the fighting, Baghdad exchanged hands four times, was sacked twice. By the time the fighting was over, Baghdad was a wreck of a city. It had never recovered from the sack of 1258, and its only importance thereafter was it had once been the center of the caliphate. That was why the Ottomans and the Iranians later fought over it simply for its symbolic value. Tamerlane's army twice did a job on sacking the city and committing the usual atrocities against the civilian population.

In 1402, the climax of the campaign, Tamerlane decided to take out the Ottoman sultanate; to go after the then-ruling sultan, Bayezid the Thunderbolt. Bayezid the Thunderbolt was one of the great sultans of early Ottoman history. He won the Battle of Blackbirds—that is, the Battle of Kosovo—that essentially smashed Serbia. At the time, he was besieging the city of Constantinople. The army of Tamerlane appeared in Asia Minor out of nowhere. Bayezid had to raise the siege, and he marched to the vicinity of Ankara to the town of Angora—incidentally, that is where we get the term "Angora wool"—and on July 20, 1402, Tamerlane fought perhaps his greatest battle. His engineers diverted the water supply, the river, before the actual fighting took place. He had brought an elephant corps from India. He had a superior cavalry, perhaps superior forces. The result was the Ottoman army goes down in its first serious defeat. Furthermore, the sultan was captured. Later legends say that Bayezid was taken to Central Asia in a golden cage to amuse Tamerlane, but that is a legend. Actually the Sultan died enroute back to Samarkand. By the time Tamerlane returned to Samarkand, he had amassed a career that was extraordinary. He had defeated Mamluk armies, Ottoman armies. He had smashed the armies of the sultan of Delhi. He had overthrown the Golden Horde; all of the tribes of Western and Central Asia essentially were in his employ. In 1405, he set out on a final expedition to reckon with Ming China. Still uncertain what his goals were; at best he might have surprised the Chinese army in the Tarim Basin since 1368–1370 Ming Chinese armies had reoccupied the basin. It was the first time Tamerlane had planned a winter campaign and it was too much for him. He contracted an illness and died in February, 1405.

What do we make out of this extraordinary career? In some ways, as I say, many would put him up on level with Attila the Hun or even Genghis Khan. However, his empire fragmented immediately, and that was true also of Attila the Hun. But there are several significant reasons why this empire failed to be long-lasting. First, Tamerlane never was khan. He never ruled the Mongol nation. There was never an assembly, a *kurultai*, which could give him authority; the great tribal authority that all the Mongol khans had enjoyed. That did not exist; he was after all nothing more than the commander, the emir, of the legitimate khan in Samarkand. The second point about that, he also could not aspire to religious authority. He was, again, simply an emir; and while he liked the idea of *yassa*—that is, Mongol customary law that exalted the ruler—he could not aspire to any kind of religious symbolism. This is an important point and it stands in contrast to the three successor states, in my opinion, which came out of the career of Tamerlane. The Ottoman sultans, who recovered from the Battle of Angora, they eventually became the caliphs of Sunni Islam, and they held that position down to 1924. Ismail I, the shah who rebuilt an Iranian state, was a mystic and cloaked himself in the symbols of Shi'a Islam and turned Iran into the Shi'a Islamic society we see today.

The real successor to Tamerlane was his descendent Babur. He conquered the empire in India, the so-called Mughal Empire. Babur did not use the religious symbols that either the Ottoman sultan or the Safavid shahs of Iran did; he did not need them because while he was a descendent of Tamerlane, he was also a direct descendent of Genghis Khan. That counted for everything in the difference in the careers between Tamerlane and Babur. Babur would go on to build the great Mughal Empire, which ultimately ended up being the anticipation of the British raj.

Bābur and Mughal India
Lecture 35

In this lecture, we will look at the last descendent of Genghis Khan and the last great conqueror from the steppes, who would have a major impact on world history. His full name was Zahir al-Din Muhammad. Bābur ("Tiger") was a name he adopted for his memoirs. In 1526, he invaded India, occupied Delhi, and founded the Mughal Empire—an empire that endured up to the arrival of the British and was the model for the British raj.

Early Career of Bābur

- Born into a Turkish-speaking family, Bābur was the great-grandson of Tamerlane. In the 10th generation, through his mother, he counted himself a descendent of Genghis Khan. Even more important, Bābur was a product of the political and military traditions of the Mongol Empire and the **Timurid Empire**: the empire of Tamerlane and his successors.

- He was conscious of the position and authority of any ruler who could base his authority on Yassa, which Tamerlane never had. Bābur followed the traditions of the steppes, including dependence on the traditional nomadic cavalry, as well as tolerance and a pragmatic attitude toward religion. It was only his great-grandsons who returned to true Sunni Islam.

- His early career was rather lackluster. He got swept up in the turbulent politics of late Timurid Iran, which saw the emergence of two new powers: the Uzbek Turks, who would eventually come to dominate the central steppes, and the Safavid Dynasty in Tabriz.

- In the course of his battles, Bābur became a vassal of the shah of Iran and was entrusted with the control of Kabul. Kabul, in today's Afghanistan, was a strategic region, with access to the Khyber Pass that linked the region from northern India to the central Asian steppes to Transoxania and points farther west.

- With control of that pass, Bābur held an important strategic position. He nominally accepted Shi'ite Islam. He rendered homage to Ismail I and was able to amass warriors to follow him in battle. These were the traditional steppe nomads, the horse archers with a component of heavy cavalry.

Defeat of the Sultanate and the Rajputs

- By fighting in the armies of Ismail I, Bābur acquired new techniques, which included early handheld firearms and field artillery and the use of infantry to anchor two powerful wings of nomadic cavalry.

- With his forces and resources from the shah, in 1526, Bābur crossed the Hindu Kush, went through the Khyber Pass, and descended into India with the intent of claiming his heritage. Bābur did not intend to simply sack India and leave. He planned to overthrow the Lodi sultanate and rule India.

- The Lodi sultanate, at this point, was the last of a series of families that had ruled Delhi. They had all the classic problems in northern India of a Muslim administration over a large Hindu population. The sultan, Ibrahim Lodi, marched out with a large army to oppose Bābur at the town of Punjab on April 15, 1526.

- Bābur had a smaller force, but with the technology of handheld firearms and artillery, he defeated the traditional Indian army based on infantry and elephants. He then defeated the **Rajputs**, the Hindu warrior caste who ruled western India and had kept the Muslim sultans of Delhi in check.

- Bābur came to control most of the strategic regions of the Punjab. He realized that to run this area, he would need the cooperation of the existing Muslim population, as well as the Hindus. From the start, he pursued a policy of religious tolerance, which would characterize the reigns of his son and grandson and would culminate in the administrative reforms of **Akbar**.

Humayun

- However, in one way, Bābur was too much a child of the steppes. He practiced lateral succession and divided his state—which included not only India but also significant regions in Afghanistan and Transoxania—among his sons.

- The eldest son, **Humayun**, took over the Indian possessions in 1530 at the death of his father but did not hold them for long. Within a couple of years, he was opposed by Afghan mercenaries and tribal forces settled in Bengal, who followed Sher Khan. Control of Bengal was always a problem for the Mughal emperors because Bengal was a wealthy area. Any lord assigned there by the Mughal emperor or any previous sultan of Delhi could always evolve into an independent ruler.

- Humayun then went to the ruling shah of Iran to obtain money and forces to return to India. His army was successful, and by January 1556, when Humayun died, Delhi had been reoccupied and the nucleus of a great Indian empire was passed to Humayun's son Akbar.

Akbar: An Administrative Genius

- Ruling from 1556 to 1605, Akbar proved to be an administrative genius. He retained many of the steppe traditions. He understood that the power of this emerging state depended on the steppe cavalry and, above all, Persian administrators—the educated and experienced officials and scholars who could run the empire in India.

- In addition, Akbar was heir to the steppe tradition of the Yassa: the notion that the ruler is the supreme authority. Therefore, he did not have to assume a religious authority, and his court was tolerant of all faiths.

- The administration built by Akbar transformed the state from a nomadic one to a bureaucratic one. The hierarchy of the state was remarkably diverse and adopted a professional attitude toward administration and military service.

- Under Mughal auspices, large sections of the Ganges areas were brought under cultivation and turned into irrigated farms and fields. The Rajputs and Jats, the Hindu military castes, which made up at least 25 percent of the Mughal aristocracy by 1605, had been co-opted into the Mughal elite. They were not required to convert to Islam. Their hereditary lands could not be taken from them. This won over very powerful and important Hindu support. So long as the Mughal emperors could retain that support, they could rule effectively and expand their control over Hindu India.

Fiscal Organization

- Another important feature of Akbar's empire was its fiscal organization. Paper and block printing were introduced into India by Akbar. That made it possible to keep the records to tax and administer an Indian state.

- Akbar's administration was characterized by improved land measurements, standard weights and measures, and new currency based on the mohur, a gold coin, and the rupee. Much of this was the work of Hindu bureaucrats, as well as scribes and tax collectors.

- In addition, there is now increasing evidence that under the Mughal emperors, a good deal of the banking and trade throughout the Mughal Empire and into Iran came into the hands of Hindu and Jain moneylenders and bankers.

The Mughal Empire

- The result was that the Mughal Empire turned out to be a highly successful bureaucratic state. It drew on all sorts of nationalities and races to administer the vast empire. By the time of Akbar's death in 1605, there were perhaps 1.5 million Muslims running an empire of at least 120 million Indians, who followed either Hinduism or Jainism.

The finest expression of the Indo-Islamic style is the Taj Mahal, built by Akbar's grandson.

- This was an extraordinary achievement and quite in contrast to the other two states that arose out of the Tamerlane tradition: the Ottoman Empire and the Safavid shahs of Iran. In the case of the Ottoman sultan, almost all the ministers were slaves. Initially, the elite forces were Janissaries, which was a kind of slave soldier.

- The Mughal state brought in many features of the high Islamic culture from Iran and popularized them among the upper classes of India. Rajputs and Jats, in particular, embraced much of the architecture, especially the use of tile and decoration. Marvelous palaces were built by the Hindu vassals of the early Mughal emperors that imitated the architecture of eastern Islam to create a unique Indo-Islamic style.

A Syncretic Solar Religion
- Akbar's religious leanings went perhaps a bit too far, however, at least in the eyes of the orthodox Sunni Muslims, particularly the religious schools in Delhi and Agra.

- Akbar experimented with a kind of syncretic solar religion. It is still unclear exactly what he intended by it. We have various visual arts that suggest that this was some combination of different types of religious views. Akbar was known to have debates with all sorts of mystics, starting with the Sufis and bringing in Hindus, Jains, and others.

- This religion left a peculiar legacy. There were a number of gold coins issued by Akbar, later in his reign, that showed the signs of the zodiac. This was a curious and unusual use of figural art in Islamic coinage. Whatever this experiment was, it passed with his death.

Bābur's Ultimate Successor
- Akbar's successors proved to be ever more strict Muslims. Jahangir went back to Sunni Islam, and his great-grandson, **Aurangzeb** (r. 1658–1708), proved to be a zealous Muslim.

- Not only was Aurangzeb a great warrior, but he departed dramatically from the policy of accommodation of Hindus and other faiths. He spared no Hindu temples in his conquests. Although he brought the empire to its height territorially, he also ensured the seeds of its destruction.

- After his death in 1707, the later Mughal emperors lost the support of their Hindu subjects. They drove the Sikhs into opposition, they lost the Rajputs, and they saw the emergence of a new Hindu opposition group, the Maratha confederacy.

- The Mughal Empire had shrunk to a mere north Indian state. However, it had passed on its institutions. The ultimate successor of Bābur and the early Mughal emperors would not be the Hindu rulers; it would be a new invader who would, unexpectedly, come by sea: the British.

Rajputs: "Sons of the king"; the Kshatriya or warrior caste who dominated western India between the 9th and 12th centuries. They were later accommodated by the Mughal emperors.

Timurids: Descendants of Tamerlane (1370–1405), who ruled Iran and Transoxania (1405–1506).

Names to Know

Akbar (b. 1542; r. 1556–1605): Third Mughal emperor; the son of Humayun. He fiscally and administratively organized the Mughal Empire, laying the foundations of the future British raj. A mystic, he sponsored his own syncretist solar cult of the ruler, Din-i Ilahi ("divine faith"). His personal beliefs and toleration of subjects of all faiths alienated the Sunni *ulema*, and his son and successor, Jahangir (1605–1627), returned to Sunni Islam.

Aurangzeb (b. 1618; r. 1658–1707): Son of Shah Jahan (1628–1658) and grandson of Akbar. Hailed Alamgir ("world conqueror"), he united nearly all of India under Mughal rule. A zealous Muslim, he alienated his Muslim subjects, and his campaigns in the Deccan exhausted the imperial treasury.

Humayun (b. 1508; r. 1530–1539, 1555–1556): Mughal emperor of India; succeeded his father, Bābur. In 1539, he was expelled from India by Sher Khan, who had rallied the former Lodi mercenary bands of Afghans that had retired to the Bengal after 1527. With Safavid assistance, Humayun reconquered northern India in 1555–1556.

Suggested Reading

Alam and Subramanyam, eds., *Mughal State, 1526–1750.*

Dale, *The Muslim Empires of the Ottomans, Safavids, and Mughals.*

———, "The Later Timurids, c. 1450–1526."

Richards, *The Mughal Empire.*

1. How did the rapid collapse of the empire of Tamerlane lead to the emergence of new political orders in the 15th century? What accounted for the success of the Shayanid khans of the Uzbeks and the Safavid shahs of Iran?

2. What led Bābur to conquer India in 1526–1530? Why did Humayun nearly lose the Indian empire? What accounts for Mughal military success?

3. What traditions and institutions of the Mongol empire did Akbar (1556–1605) adapt to his Indian empire? How important were these policies in ensuring the success of Mughal rule? Why would Mughal emperors never be able to Islamize the Indian subcontinent?

4. How did the Mughal Empire compare to the contemporary Muslim states of the Ottoman Empire and Safavid Iran? How did the Mongol legacy give the Mughals an advantage in ruling their empire?

5. What lessons did the British learn from the Mughals to construct their own imperial order in the India, the raj?

Bābur and Mughal India
Lecture 35—Transcript

In this lecture, I want to look at the last descendent of Genghis Khan who would have a major impact on world history and really represents the last great conqueror from the steppes. His full name was Zahir ud-din Muhammad Bābur. Bābur was actually a name he took in his memoirs; he tells us that it means "tiger," and it referred to his determination as well as his ferocity on the battlefield.

Bābur was both a descendent of Tamerlane as well as Genghis Khan, and he is a very, very significant figure. He essentially lost his kingdom in Ferghana where he grew up—that is, close to the Central Asian steppes—but eventually conquered an empire in India, and an empire in India that endured really down to the arrival of the British and acted as the model for British rule. In addition, he built the most successful empire, he and his descendants, which had ruled India really since Ashoka, the great emperor of the third century B.C. who had embraced Buddhism. The Mughals to this day are still remembered as great rulers by Hindus, by Sikhs, by Muslims; it represented a heyday, especially the early Mughal Empire of the 16th and 17th centuries, and we will see what that is true.

He, again, came from a relatively obscure background such as his ancestor Tamerlane. He was technically the great-grandson of Tamerlane. He was born of a Turkish-speaking family. The Mongol blood in him was rather diluted; the family had intermarried with various Turks. He spoke a form of Turkish very closely related to the Uzbek Turkish today as well as the literary Persian of Eastern Islam. In the 10th generation, through his mom, he counted himself a descendent of Genghis Khan. But even more important, Bābur was a product of the political and military traditions of the Mongol Empire and the Timurid Empire; that is, the empire of Tamerlane and his successors, and his successors were usually called the Timurids, meaning the "descendants of Timur," the actual name of Tamerlane. Bābur was very conscious of this. He was also very conscious of the position and authority of any ruler who could base his authority of *yassa*—that is, traditional Mongol law—something that ancestor or great-granddad Tamerlane never had. In addition, he would fall heir to other traditions of the steppes. That included the dependence on the traditional nomadic cavalry as well as a toleration and pragmatic attitude toward religion, which will characterize Bābur and his descendants, at least his son and grandson. In fact, his grandson Akbar went off creating virtually his own kind of solar monotheism peppered with a lot of stuff out of the zodiac. It was only his great-grandsons who really returned to a true Sunni Islam: Jahangir, Shah Jahan, and above all Aurangzeb, the later Mughal emperors.

His biography is peppered with a lot of the same stories we encounter of any conqueror. They foretell the greatness, his archery, his ability with horsemanship, his commanding background; and again, a lot of this is stock praise, but it was written by Bābur himself in his biography written late in life, and that biography shows a real mastery of high literary Persian. He was a cultured man. In reading through the biography as well as the contemporary accounts, while he practiced the harsh rules of nomadic warfare—and that meant punishing rebels severely; once you get India the Mughals picked up a new way of punishing relatives, rebels, and problem relatives, and that was having them trampled by elephants, which was sort of an update on using the horsemen riding over the fellow in a carpet—there were such executions and there were a number of massacres, but you do not get the sense of the kind of wholesale destruction that had characterized Tamerlane or some of the more remote Mongol ancestors of Bābur. That, again, came into play in constructing the basis of a great Mughal Empire in India.

His career started off really as a rather lackluster career. He got swept up in the rather turbulent politics of late Timurid Iran, which saw the emergence of two new powers: the Uzbek Turks on the steppes, who would eventually come to dominate the central steppes and create a great khanate that really had no affiliation with the Mongol Khanate directly, although the Uzbeks to this day like to claim Genghis Khan as one of theirs; it also saw the emergence at Tabriz of a powerful dynasty, we call it the Safavid Dynasty, the Safavid shahs. They took the old Persian title "shah" deliberately to link themselves with the traditions of the Sassanid Empire, as well as promoting Shi'a Islam. The founder of this dynasty was a man named Ismail I. He went a great way to restoring a distinctly Shi'a Iranian state, which is the basis of modern Iran today.

Caught among these battles, Bābur ended up becoming a vassal of the Shah of Iran—the same thing happened to his son when he was in exile—and Bābur was entrusted with the control of Kabul. Kabul has always been a strategic region; today it is in Afghanistan. From this course, you realize that Kabul is the access to the Khyber Pass and the Khyber Pass has always linked Northern India to the Central Asiatic steppes to Transoxiana and points farther west. With control of that pass, Bābur had a very strategic importance to the Shah. He nominally accepted a Shi'a Islam; he rendered homage to Ismail; and with that position he was able to amass followers, warriors, who would follow him in battle. These, again, were the traditional steppe nomads, the horse archers, with a component of heavy cavalry; the armies that had always dominated the battlefield, really since the Scythians came up with horseback riding back in the early Iron Age. In addition, by fighting in the armies of his master Ismail, he learned new techniques that had been perfected by the Ottoman sultans, particularly Selim I, and that included early matchlocks, early handheld firearms; and field artillery; and the use of infantry to anchor two powerful wings of nomadic cavalry that would do the encirclement in a classic battle of annihilation. That was a tactic that had been turned on the Iranians by Selim I at a very famous battle known as Chaldiran, August 23, 1514; regarded as one of the decisive battles of the early modern Middle East.

With that sort of forces and money from the Shah and his blessings, in 1526 Bābur crossed the Hindu Kush, went through the Khyber Pass, and descended into India with the intent of claiming his heritage. In part, Bābur postured as an heir to Genghis Khan as well as Tamerlane. Both of those conquerors had invaded India, but it was nothing more than sacks of mosques and Hindu temples for booty. Bābur, on the other hand, intended to stay. Bābur did not intend to simply sack India and leave. That may have been what many of his Uzbek allies in particular wanted; he was going to overthrow the Lodi Sultanate and rule India. The Lodi Sultanate, at this point, was the last of a series of families that had ruled Delhi. They had all the classic problems of a Muslim administration in Northern India over a large Hindu population. The then-ruling sultan, a man named Ibrahim, was forced to march out with a large army to oppose the army of Bābur at the town of Panipat. That was on April 15, 1526. Actually, it was just before the monsoons; really, Bābur was cutting it close, the monsoons could have drowned his army out. The Battle of Panipat turns out to be that second decisive battle in the early modern Islamic period.

Bābur adopted the same formations that the Ottomans had used against the Safavid army. He had a laager of carts in the center where his artillery and his matchlock infantry were stationed. They just ripped holes in the elephant charge of the Lodi army, the infantry supported by elephants; the elephants, again, panicked, there were like 300 of them. They stampeded into the center of the opposing army, and then the flanks swung in with the nomadic cavalry. Numbers at the Battle of Panipat are difficult to come up with. The Lodi army was numbered at like 130,000, 140,000. Bābur supposedly commanded only 12,000; these are clearly undercounted. But the fact is that with the significantly smaller force that now matched the new technology of handheld firearms and artillery with nomadic cavalry, Bābur was able to defeat the traditional Indian army based on infantry and elephants. He then defeated the Rajputs, the important Hindu warrior caste—the princes who ruled Western India and really kept the Muslim sultans of Delhi on their best behavior because without an alliance with the Rajputs, no Muslim ruler in Delhi could really rule for very long. In the next year, the Rajput army was defeated, and very, very quickly Bābur came to control most of the strategic regions of the Punjab with its capital at Lahore; Delhi, the so-called Doab; and the Upper Ganges.

It was a stunning success; and from the start, Bābur realized that to run this area—to run the nucleus of an incipient Indian Empire—he would need to cooperation of the existing Muslim population as well as the Hindu population. He pursued from the start a policy of religious toleration of all the faiths, which would characterize the reign of his son and his grandson particularly, and will culminate in the administrative reforms of Akbar. However, in one way Bābur was too much a child of the steppes. He practiced lateral succession and he divided his state, which included not only India but significant regions in today Afghanistan, and so access to that steppe cavalry among his sons.

The eldest son, Humayun, got the Indian possessions. He took them over in 1530 at the death of his father, and he did not hold them for very long. Within a couple of years, he was opposed by Afghan mercenaries and tribal forces settled in the Bengal. These Afghans had been brought in by the Lodi sultan. They followed a fellow known as Sher Khan, and that Afghan army mounted a comeback. This was always a problem for the Mughal emperors, controlling Bengal, because Bengal was a very, very wealthy area; and any lord assigned there by the Mughal emperor or any previous sultan of Delhi could always evolve into an independent ruler. This would happen later in the 18th century when the rulers of Bengal essentially ran their own show and paid no attention to what was going on in Delhi or the court at Agra, which was one of the later Mughal capitals. Agra and Delhi could say what they wanted; the rulers in Bengal were essentially on their own. Therefore, Humayun found himself an exile back in the hometown, Kabul. He had to go to the then-ruling Shah of Iran, promise to become a Shi'a Muslim, get money and forces, and beg his way back to India with a borrowed army. But he had learned his lessons well from dad; that army was equipped similarly to the invasion force of 1526, and they won a similar set of astounding victories, largely due to the effort of Humayun's generals rather than Humayun himself, but it did not matter. By the time of January, 1556 when Humayun died, Delhi had been reoccupied and Northern India and Delhi— the nexus of the Ganges and the Indus, which are the two great rivers that form the sort of crescent across Northern India; we call it the Indo-Gangetic plain—that was the basis for any imperial order in India ever since really the third century B.C. That empire, that nucleus of a great Indian Empire, was passed to Humayun's young son at age 12 who came to the throne under the name Akbar.

Akbar proved to be an administrative genius. He ruled from 1556–1605. He was an extremely curious ruler. There is a lot of speculation that he was probably dyslexic. He certainly seemed to have a very limited knowledge of reading and writing. He could not put out the kind of high Persian autobiography that his grandfather could. He also still retained a lot of the traditions of the steppes. He knew that the power of this emerging state depended on the steppe cavalry and above all Persian administrators; that is, educated, talented officials and scholars who could run the empire in India. They were the only kind of administrative staff really available in Eastern Islam. There are also stories that he, just like his grandfather Bābur, longed for the melons of Central Asia; and this is a conceit in all of the Mughal poetry, the early accounts. The Mughal emperors never quite forgot the fact that they came from Central Asia, and that was where you can really get the delicious melons; you really cannot grow them in India, it is just too humid. Part of that was a posture of that Central Asiatic tradition, and it was very real because the Mughal emperors, the early Mughal emperors, always fought to retain control of Kandahar, of Kabul, and access to the military forces of the central steppes as well as the Persian administrators. The loss of those areas eventually would prove a real setback for later Mughal emperors.

In addition, Akbar was heir to two other very important traditions: the notion that the ruler is the supreme authority under *yassa*; and therefore he did not have to cloak himself necessarily in the religious symbols of Islam or even pay heed, as the Shi'a Shahs eventually have to do, to a religious community of experts who would hold the ruler to account to Sharia, traditional Islamic law. That meant, in tandem with it, toleration of various types of subjects; that would Muslims, Jains, Hindus, and Sikhs, this new sort of form of reform movement of monotheistic Hinduism that emerged in the Punjab in part as a response to the Muslim impact in India. That meant that the administration and army built by Akbar had two important features: First, it essentially transformed a state that at the accession of Akbar was still largely a nomadic state transplanted to India into a great bureaucratic state. In the end, by the time Akbar died in 1605, he transmitted to his family a truly bureaucratic Indian state. There were elements of the old nomadic traditions that were very, very important in the formation of that state and certainly the conquest; but it was now really a quintessentially Indian state.

The second point is that the administration and the army created for that, the hierarchy, was remarkably diverse. It consisted of two levels: There was a lower rung of the imperial aristocracy of bureaucratic servants and officers, people who were ruling the countryside and provide military forces, and those were the *mansabdars*. The *mansabdars* could be of any kind of background. Many of them were Muslims; but in time they came to include Rajputs, Jats, another important Kshatriya subcaste that claimed descent from the Sakai, those fellows who had invaded back in the second century B.C. It also include later Sikhs, who when they become militarized as possible members of the lower rungs of the aristocracy. Above them was a higher rung known as the *mansabs*. They represented the elite; they would actually provide the generals, the ministers, many of the top officials for the

Mughal state. They all depended on the revenues and support of the Mughal emperor because this aristocracy maintained itself on grants; we could call them infiefments. It was really more the income of a property and it did not necessarily have to be real estate; but it could be, it usually was. That was known as a *jagir*; and the *jagir* represented the income necessary for say *mansab* to support himself and the obligations owed to the Mughal emperor. Very often the Mughal emperors styled themselves as *padishahs* or *padshahs*, which means "great shahs," that old Persian title; it essentially was a revival of that notion of Shah of Shahs, King of Kings.

That meant this imperial aristocracy was well-rewarded and they took a very professional attitude either towards administration or military service. There have been calculations on the size of this aristocracy and the number of military retainers that could be provided, and the numbers are really quite impressive; they ran up to at least 150,000. Furthermore, *mansabs* could be transferred from place to place and they often were. This infiefment was not hereditary. One could be promoted or even demoted in the imperial hierarchy. On the other hand, they were given every incentive to develop their *jagirs*, and it was really under Mughal auspices that large sections of the Ganges especially were brought under cultivation and turned into the irrigated farms and fields that we see today; and this was, again, to advantages in meetings one's obligations to the Mughal emperors.

There was an important twist or an exception in this: The Rajputs and Jats, the Hindu military castes, they perhaps comprised at least 25 percent of the Mughal aristocracy by 1605. They had been co-opted into the Mughal elite, and they were not required to convert to Islam. Their hereditary lands were made exceptions; that is, they could not really be transferred from them, they could still remain in their homeland, they owed the military service. This won over very, very powerful and important Hindu support. So long as the Mughal emperors could retain that support, they could rule effectively and expand their control over greater Hindu India because this was not an exclusively Muslim imperial administration; everyone could see that.

Another important feature was in the fiscal organization; and here, Akbar owed something to the cultural exchange that occurred under the Mongol peace. Paper and block printing was introduced into India by Akbar essentially. That meant you could keep the kind of records to tax and administer an Indian state that had not been available beforehand. All earlier Indian states had depended on this stuff called palm leaf paper; and if you ever look at it, this stuff is extremely fragile and can disintegrate on you without any trouble. That meant that henceforth the various tax collectors, the local officials—and they were all known as zamindars, who were at the local level with scribes—and even down to the headmen and the councils at the village levels could keep a set of records that would allow Akbar to tax his empire and gain the revenues at a rate that probably no previous Indian ruler ever had.

There were introductions of improved land measurements; standard weights and measures; a new currency based on the so-called mohur, the gold coin, and the rupee. A lot of this was really the work of Hindu bureaucrats and scribes, tax collectors, and in particular one important figure known as Tal Mahal. He was a Hindu by birth, was never required to convert, and he was the man who really put together the tax and administrative system of the Mughal Empire and is a testimony to the fact that men of all sorts of faiths and backgrounds were welcome in the service of the Mughal emperor. In addition, there was now increasing evidence that under the Mughal emperors a good deal of the banking and trade throughout the Mughal Empire, and even beyond into Iran, came into the hands of Hindu and Jain moneylenders and bankers who were very, very important behind the whole financing of the Mughal administration.

The result was the Mughal Empire turned out to be a very, very successful bureaucratic state. It drew on all sorts of nationalities and races in order to administer this vast empire. By the time of Akbar's death in 1605, you were looking at perhaps a million, a million and a half Muslims running an empire of at least 120 million Indians who either followed Hinduism or Jainism; Buddhism had largely declined starting in the 13th and 14th centuries. It is an extraordinary achievement and quite in contrast to the other two states that came out of the traditions and the impact of Tamerlane's state: the Ottoman Empire and the Safavid shahs of Iran. There, service was all done by either loyal Muslims or by various slaves. In the case of the Ottoman sultan, almost all the ministers were slaves. Initially, the elite forces were Janissaries, which was a style of slave soldiers.

This success allowed the Mughal state to really bring in many features of the high Islamic culture from Iran and popularize them among the upper classes of India. Rajputs and Jats particularly embraced a lot of the architecture; the use of tile in decoration. If one, especially today, travels in Rajasthan amongst cities such as Jodhpur, you see marvelous palaces built by the Hindu vassals of the early Mughal emperors that really imitate that architecture of eastern Islam. It was merged with Indian traditions to create a unique Indo-Islamic architecture, and the best expression of that would be built by Akbar's own grandson, the Taj Mahal; the Taj Mahal that was built after Shah Jahan's favorite wife who had died in childbearing (I think this was like child number 13 or 14 when she died).

The success of the Mughal Empire was extraordinary, and it ultimately rested in part on that Mongol legacy: on the use of the military forces to capture the empire, to defeat the Lodi sultans; to make that comeback that was done by Humayun, who could have easily ended up in obscure exile on the frontiers of Iran. Above all, it was symbolized by the success of Akbar. Akbar and his policies perhaps went too far, at least for the tastes of the Orthodox Sunni Muslims, and particularly the religious schools in Delhi and Agra, the great capitals of Akbar. Akbar experimented with what some would call a syncretist—*syncretist* meaning "a mixing together"—a syncretist solar religion. It is still unclear exactly what he intended by it; did he intend to see himself as a divine voice as speaking the word of God, or was he more interested in divine status? We have various visual arts that suggest that this was some kind of rare combination of different types of religious views. Akbar was known to have debates with all sorts of mystics, starting with Sufi mystics but then bringing in Hindus, Jains, and others. This religion, which left its legacy in a very peculiar way—there were a large number of coins, gold coins issued by Akbar later in his reign that showed the signs of the Zodiac; and this was a very, very curious and unusual use of figural art in Islamic coinage—but whatever this experiment was, an experiment to create a religious authority peculiar to the Mughal emperor and therefore separate from Sharia and giving the Mughal emperor both a spiritual as well as the customary *yassa* as his two pillars for authority, it passed with his death.

His successors proved to be evermore strict Muslims. Jahangir went back to Sunni Islam, and his great-grandson Aurangzeb, who ruled from 1658–

1707 and spent over 40 years campaigning through India, proved to be a very zealous Muslim. Not only was he a great warrior, but he departed dramatically from the policy of accommodation of Hindus and other faiths. He spared no Hindu temples in his conquests. While he brought the empire to its height territorially, he also insured the seeds of its destruction, because after his death in 1707, the later Mughal emperors lost the support of their Hindu subjects; they drove the Sikhs into opposition; they lost the Rajputs; they saw the emergence of a new Hindu confederation, the so-called Maratha Confederacy; and the Mughal Empire shrunk into a North Indian state. However, it had passed on institutions to the successor states, and ultimate successor of Bābur and the early Mughal emperors would not be the various Hindu rulers, but would be a new invader, an invader who would come from the sea unexpectedly: the British.

Legacy of the Steppes

Lecture 36

In this course, we have covered some 6,000 miles and 6,000 years. In our final lecture, we will explore two key issues. The first is why, by the year 1500, the nomadic peoples of the Eurasian steppes ceased to play a decisive military role and declined as a force of cultural exchange, trade, and prosperity in the civilizations of Eurasia, the Mediterranean world, the Near East, India, and China. The second issue is to examine what the legacy of the empires of the steppes means to us today.

Advances in Military Technology

- In the 15th and 16th centuries, a revolution in military technology took place, originating in northwestern Europe: the introduction of handheld firearms, the use of artillery on the battlefield, and the European mastery of oceangoing vessels that could mount artillery.

- Ironically, this revolution was possible, in part, because of the Mongol peace that had allowed dissemination of the knowledge of black gunpowder to the West during the 14th century.

- The advances in military technology meant that the horse archers, who were clearly the premier warriors since the early Iron Age, now had to face forces that could annihilate them on the battlefield at a capacity hitherto unknown.

New Political Orders

- In addition, new political orders had emerged that would restrict the migration of nomadic peoples and would begin to encroach on the Eurasian steppes.

- The states in the Islamic world were the Ottoman Empire and Safavid Iran, both of which had remote connections to the nomadic traditions. In each case, the dynasties traced their descent to Turkish conquerors going back to the 11th and 10th centuries.

- The other two great powers were the Russians and the Chinese, who in effect partitioned the steppes in the Treaty of Nerchinsk. That partition then gave later tsars the opportunity to expand into Transoxania.

- In the 19th century, the tsars crossed the Jaxartes and conquered the great caravan cities of Transoxania. These regions were forced to submit to the Russian Orthodox tsar. That situation persisted up to 1920, when Lenin eliminated the emirs. Those regions became independent republics after 1991.

- Another set of powers lay on the periphery that would forever change the balance. These were the five key states of northwestern Europe: the kingdoms of Portugal, Spain, and France; the peculiar kingdom of England, which is best described as a crowned republic; and the Dutch Republic.

- Those five European states launched out on the great Age of Discovery. They had with them oceangoing vessels that would transform not only the military and political balance of power but also the economic balance of the entire world.

New Dynamics of Economics and Trade

- Most significant for the nomads of the central steppes was the circumnavigation of Africa by Vasco da Gama in 1498. His voyages opened up India to direct contact by Portugal. In 1503, a Portuguese fleet mounted with artillery off the coast of India dispersed the Ottomans in a great battle.

- Henceforth, the Indian Ocean would be dominated by European powers. In the 16th century, the Portuguese colonized the Malabar Coast and Sri Lanka. They penetrated to the East Indies and even opened up trade with Japan. They were followed in the 17th century by the Dutch, English, and French.

- As a result, these great European imperial powers, which also colonized new lands in the Americas, Australia, and New Zealand, took over control of ocean commerce. This changed the entire dynamic of world trade. A great transoceanic economy was born and, with it, came the globalization of today. Population and economic centers moved to the coasts.

- As a result, the caravan cities and trade routes across Eurasia that had been so crucial to the nomadic peoples simply faded away. They declined to the point of becoming provincial frontiers of great empires—most notably, of Russia, later the Soviet Union, and China.

Legacy of the Steppe Empires

- The first Indo-European pastoralists, or nomads, mastered the use of wheeled vehicles and domesticated the horse. Those innovations were as significant as the invention of farming; they opened up the Eurasian steppes to colonization by humans.

- The steppes then became the highway that linked the civilizations that emerged in the great river valleys of the Tigris-Euphrates, the Nile, the Indus, and the Huang He.

- The invention of light chariots and the improvement of wheeled vehicles led to the dispersion of Indo-European speakers across Europe, across much of western Eurasia, into India. In turn, this led to the evolution of many significant language families.

Contact with China

- The steppe nomads were able to create political orders—great confederations—that could challenge the powerful urban, literate civilizations.

- Modu Chanyu's confederation dramatically altered the balance of power. It led to migrations from east to west. It brought the steppe peoples directly and indirectly into contact with Chinese civilization.

- Chinese civilization was arguably one of the great forces that transformed the steppe peoples. Many of the achievements of

Chinese civilization through the Mongol period were disseminated to the rest of humanity via the trade routes and empires built by these so-called barbarians of the steppes. The achievements in antiquity were astonishing.

Role of the Turks

- The early Middle Ages was characterized by another set of migrations from east and west and the expansion of the Turkish tribes. We saw this in the 6th century with the success of the Gök Turks.

- The Turks represented an explosive and powerful force across the steppes. They transformed the steppes ethnically and linguistically and introduced superior military technology: metal stirrups, improved saddles, and better composite bows.

- The Turks also played another important role: They brought the peoples of the steppes into closer association with Islam. Before that, Buddhism had been the major religious force on the steppes as a result of the achievements of the Kushan emperors and the Hephthalites.

- Starting in the 7th century, Islam came to play an increasingly important role. Islam resulted in a remarkable exchange with the Turks, and the Turks adapted it to create an identity that was both Turkish and Islamic.

- When the Seljuk Turks captured Baghdad in 1055, they were seen differently from all previous steppe conquerors; they were Muslims. They were accepted, however reluctantly, by the Muslim populations, by the Abbasid caliphs, and by the merchant princes of Transoxania and Iran.

- A unique partnership emerged between the Turks and the Persians— those Iranians who came to define Islamic civilization. There was a new expansion of Islam into Asia Minor and, ultimately, into northern India.

Terror and Destruction

- The period starting in the late 12th century and going into the 14th century was dominated by the Mongols. The Mongols were both the exception and the epitome of everything that preceded them. They made a decisive impact in history, but the costs were high.

- Mongol conquests brought misery and destruction on a scale hitherto unknown. Genghis Khan and his grandsons and Tamerlane—who, although not a Mongol in birth and descent, was certainly a Mongol in his military and political conceptions—waged a war of terror on a colossal scale.

- The destruction of the great cities of Iran and Transoxania by repeated Mongol attacks was devastating; many cities never recovered.

- We saw similar destruction in northern China, when Genghis Khan deliberately ravaged irrigated fields. One could argue this was a typical nomadic reaction. They needed the products of civilization, but they feared the urban populations.

The Mongol Century

- Whatever the concentration of good and evil, whatever the intentions, whatever the unintended consequences, the results were undeniable: The Mongols made the 13th century their own.

- They played a pivotal role in the revival of prosperity. To be sure, part of this was for pragmatic reasons; they needed to rehabilitate many of the areas that had been devastated in order to raise revenue to support their steppe armies.

- Because of the Mongols, the Islamic and Chinese worlds were brought into close association. Arabic numbers and astronomy made their way to China, as did sophisticated instruments for measuring the earth and for making maps.

- In turn, the knowledge of the Chinese, in aesthetics and arts, science, and medicinal lore, was then received by the Islamic world. These cultural exchanges ultimately resulted in better civilizations on both ends.

- One of the bitter ironies we encountered was in the transmission of military technology. The people who embraced the changes in military technology were the least important in the cultural exchanges of the 13th century. In fact, they were the least impressive in the eyes of the Mongol khans.
  - To Khan Güyük or Möngke, the embassies sent by Pope Innocent IV or the French Crusader king Louis IX were pitiful envoys of a distant set of pale rulers. A group of Franciscans who showed up barefooted and bringing trivial gifts could not compare with the multitudes of powerful and distinguished envoys from around the world who had come to seek the patronage of the Great Khan.

  - Yet it was those unimpressive Europeans who picked up the technology of black gunpowder and went on to crush the steppe nomad empires and create modern Western civilization.

Making of the Modern World
- In addition, Marco Polo's experiences in the Far East, the seductive images of Xanadu and Cathay, provided the inspiration and motivation for the Age of Discovery.

- Our course has given us a unique glimpse into the development of all these civilizations and the making of the modern world.

- It is still remarkable how much of modern civilization was influenced by the fact that 130,000 Mongol warriors mounted on cavalry horses followed Genghis Khan into battle and glorious conquest. If those conquests had never happened, it's difficult to imagine what the world would look like today.

Suggested Reading

Barefield, *The Perilous Frontier*.

Braudel, *Civilization and Capitalism, 15th–18th Century*, vols. I–III.

Dale, *The Muslim Empires of the Ottomans, Safavids, and Mughals*.

Headrick, *The Tools of Empire*.

Hopkirk, *The Great Game*.

Khodarkovsky, *Russia's Steppe Frontier*.

Lincoln, *The Conquest of a Continent*.

Mote, *Imperial China, 900–1800*.

Questions to Consider

1. What were the principal reasons for the passing of the power of the nomadic peoples of the Eurasian steppes? Why did the empire of Tamerlane represent not only the end of the Mongol legacy but also the end of imperial power for steppe nomads?

2. How did tsarist Russia and the Xing Empire of China partition the Eurasian steppes after 1689? Why did Russia emerge with control over the Eurasian steppes and the cities of Transoxiana? Did the Xing emperors of China buy frontier security at too high a price?

3. What were the decisive roles played by early Indo-European–speaking nomads on the Eurasian steppes in 4800 to 1200 B.C.? How significant were their contributions?

4. What was the role of the Scythians for the Persian Empire and the Greek world? How should the relationship between Scythians and their civilized neighbors be characterized? What were the contributions of Parthians, Sacae, and Kushans?

5. How did Modu *chanyu* of the Xiongnu set the standard for future conquerors from the steppes? What was the importance of the interaction of the Xiongnu and, later, Turkish tribes with the Han and Tang empires of China? How was each side transformed by trade, wars, and cultural exchange?

6. What role was played by the nomads in promoting trade and cultural exchange along the Silk Road? Why was the transmission of Buddhism so important?

7. How did imperial Rome respond to Attila the Hun? How did this experience dictate the future interaction of the Byzantine world with the nomads of the western Eurasian steppes? How did the interaction of the Sassanid shahs with Turks and Hephthalites in the 6th and 7th centuries anticipate the relationship of the caliphate and the Turks between the 9th and 11th centuries?

8. How did the Turkish khaganates of the Gök Turks, Khazars, and Uighurs transform the Eurasian steppes? Why did the Turks play a decisive role in the Islamic world from the 11th century on?

9. In what ways was the 13th century the Mongol century? What accounts for the success of the Mongol khans? What were the results of the Mongol peace?

Legacy of the Steppes
Lecture 36—Transcript

In this final lecture, I wish to deal with two issues. One is, briefly: Why was it that by 1500 the various nomadic peoples of the Eurasian steppes ceased to play the type of decisive role that they had done for nearly 6,000 years, both as a military force but also as a force that led to cultural exchange, to trade, to prosperity, which linked the great sedentary urban civilizations of Eurasia, the Mediterranean world, the Near East, India, and China? Then, once we look at that question and why this happened, really in the 16th and early 17th century, I believe we should then turn and see where we have been, where we have come from, and what does this legacy mean to us today? We have covered some 6,000 miles and 6,000 years in a great exercise to understand how the nomadic peoples of the Eurasian steppes played decisive roles in history over that long period and over those great distances. We have really two issues to address in this final lecture.

As to the first question—and we can handle that fairly briefly—part of it really hinges on the military revolution of the 15th and 16th centuries. This originated in Northwestern Europe with the introduction of handheld firearms, the use of artillery on the battlefield, and the European mastery of oceangoing vessels that could mount artillery. Ironically, this revolution was possible in part—not exclusively, but in part—because of the Mongol peace that had disseminated the knowledge of black gunpowder west during the 14th century; and the Europeans then took this technology and ran with it. As I mentioned, ironically it was about the only thing the Europeans really got out of that vast cultural exchange between the Islamic world and the Mongol Empire during the 13th and 14th centuries. The Europeans were really at the far end of that cultural exchange and very little seemed to have penetrated Europe. Those changes meant that from the 16th century on, increasingly the horse archer, who was clearly the premier warrior since the early Iron Age, since the 10th century, now had to face on the battlefield forces that could annihilate him at a capacity hitherto unknown. Tamerlane was really the last of the great conquerors who could depend essentially on the great cavalry armies. Bābur, who built the Mughal Empire, too used steppe cavalry; but he had to marry it with the infantry carrying matchlocks, the very primitive firearm, as well as field artillery. Already in the 16th century, there was a shift;

and you can actually look at the great victories of Tamerlane and Bābur as representing the passing of an old age in which nomadic cavalry dominated that battlefield. One thinks of the great victories outside of Delhi and Angora in 1402, and then the victory of Bābur at Panipat, the first battle of Panipat in 1526; there were actually three battles fought there, which represented the beginning of a new age.

In addition, there were new political orders that now emerged that would restrict ever more the migration of nomadic peoples and would begin to encroach on those very steppes; the very homeland where the nomads had drawn strength to launch out in raids, to launch out in migrations and invasions, or to dominate the Silk Road and the caravan routes, exact tribute, engage in exchange with the merchants, and religious-inspired ones from the sedentary civilizations. That type of order was passing in the 16th and 17th centuries. Among those states in the Islamic world were the Ottoman Empire and Safavid Iran, both of which had a very, very remote connection to the nomadic traditions. In each case, the dynasties could trace their descent back to Turkish conquerors going back into the 11th or 10th centuries. They both represented great Islamic states. The Ottoman Empire, a combination of the Byzantine Empire and the Abbasid Caliphate; the shahs of Iran drew not only on a distinctly Shi'a tradition of Islam, but also on the great bureaucratic traditions of the Sassanid Shahs; the Achaemenid Kings of Persia; and the great Near Eastern monarchies going back to the first conqueror Sargon of Acad. These were the great states that brought portions of the steppes under their control; and I mentioned how the remnants of the Golden Horde only survived by acting as vassals of the Ottoman port, the sublime port—that is, the government of Constantinople—from conquests by the Russian tsars. On the central steppes, the Uzbeks and other coalitions were very much tied to the shahs of Iran. In their early stages, the first two Mughal emperors also were virtual dependents on the Shah of Iran for military forces. Those two Muslim states emerged in the 15th and 16th centuries, and the relationship definitely changed.

The other two great powers that I discussed in this course were the Russians and the Chinese, the later Chinese emperors of the Ming and the Qing Dynasties. They, in effect, partitioned the steppes. There were a number of reasons for this; and we went into some detail how the threat of the Golden

Horde galvanized the grand princes of Moscow to serve first as literally the collection agents for the Golden Horde and then to become their rivals. Starting in 1480 with the victory of Ivan III over the Taters—in that absurd victory where the Taters essentially refused to face the infantry and artillery of the Tsar—starting from that point and especially with his successor Ivan the Terrible, the Russian tsars gathered not only the Russian principalities together, became the embodiment of the third Rome (the traditions of Orthodox Byzantium), but they started their relentless march across Siberia, the Eurasian land mass, and they brought the tundra, the taiga, and the steppes largely under their control. They had a number of motives for doing this. At the same time, the Xing emperors of China, who were the heirs of the Chinese policies really going back to the emperor Wudi—the man who initiated the first wars against the Xiongnu; that emperor who ruled from 141–87 B.C.—they achieved the traditional Chinese aims. They controlled the key border areas of Inner Mongolia, the Ordos triangle, the Gansu corridor, the Tarim Basin. They made sure that the Mongolian homeland, the Eastern Eurasian steppes, would never again emerge as a threat to China. This was symbolized in the Treaty of Nerchinsk in 1689, concluded by Peter the Great and his younger brother Ivan and the Xin court, which essentially partitioned the great steppes.

That partition then gave the go ahead for later tsars to expand into Transoxiana. This was a natural expansion; the tsars essentially control the steppes, they crossed the Jaxartes. In the 19th century, the great caravan cities of Transoxiana, ruled by various emirs—particularly notable are the emirs of Bukhara, also of Samarkand—they submitted to the Orthodox tsar; and it is a supreme irony to me that these rulers who depended so much on nomadic power, the embodiment of Islam, in effect became *dhimmi* themselves to an Orthodox Christian Russian tsar in Moscow. It almost symbolizes the end of that unique relationship between the cities of Transoxiana, the central and western steppes, which had been the basis of so many of these steppe empires. That situation persisted down to 1920 when Lenin got rid of the emirs and, of course, these states have since become independent republics after 1991.

Besides these four great orders, there was also another set of powers, really on the periphery, certainly outside of the vision of the Mongol emperors of the 13th century, which would forever change the balance. These were the five key states of Northwestern Europe, the Atlantic powers: the kingdoms of Portugal and Spain; the kingdom of France; that peculiar kingdom of England, which best is described as Crown Republic; and, of course, the Dutch Republic. Those five European states launched out on the great Age of Discovery. They had with them oceangoing vessels that would transform not only the military and the political balance, but also the entire economic balance of the globe.

Most significant for the nomads of the central steppes was the circumnavigation of Africa by Vasco De Gama in 1498. Without a doubt, Vasco De Gama, whatever his other faults may have been, was really one of the great navigators of the Age of Discovery, on par with Columbus and Magellan. His circumnavigation opened up India to direct contact by Portugal. The Portuguese quickly arrived. In 1509, off the shores of India, a Portuguese fleet of only 18 of these vessels, ships of the line, mounted with artillery dispersed the Ottoman fleet and its various Hindu supporters and vassals in a great battle that essentially determined that henceforth the Indian Ocean would fall into the hands of those European powers that had those vessels. The Portuguese went on in 16th century to colonize the shores of India, particularly of the Malabar Coast. They were active in Sri Lanka. They penetrated to the East Indies and even opened up trade with Japan.

They were followed in the 17th century by the Dutch, the English, and the French. As a result, these great European imperial powers, which colonized new lands in the Americas, in Australia, and New Zealand, also took over the control of ocean commerce. But it was more than just the control of ocean commerce; they had changed the entire dynamics. I had argued earlier, in the beginning of the Silk Road—which we can trace back into antiquity, certainly from the third century B.C. on, probably going back earlier— that all of those caravan routes that linked the Eurasian land mass were accompanied by a group of complementary ocean and sea routes; especially the Romans, pioneering, the sailing down the Red Sea across the Erythraean Ocean to the Indian ports where they picked up Chinese silks. These silks were brought in, of course, by the caravans of the Silk Road. This continued in the Islamic period. It was also fostered by Kublai Khan and the later Ming emperors. But in the 16th century, the scale and balance of this trade changed.

Oceangoing trade, the great transoceanic economy, was born, and with it the globalization of today. Population centers, economic centers now moved to the coasts.

Overwhelmingly the density of the world's population was lined up on the great port cities. This was symbolized at different points. Perhaps one of the most important ones affecting Central Asia was the opening of the Suez Canal in 1869, which really shortened that trip from Western Europe; in this case, from Britain to Britain's Indian possessions and points farther east. The laying down of the great Transatlantic cable, the whole development of what scholars now speak of the Atlantic World—that is, between the Americas and Northwest Europe, and then sweeping up also the African continent—all of what we think the transoceanic trade and globalization is comes out of these developments of the 16th and 17th century. As a result, the caravan cities of Transoxiana, those trade routes across Eurasia that had been so important to the nomadic peoples, really declined. They faded, they became the memories of romance. It is scholars like Sir Aurel Stein, who went back into these cities in the early 20th century and rediscovered the splendor and the importance of these cities, because the caravan cities, the steppes, had essentially declined to the provincial frontiers of great empires, notably of Tsarist Russia, later the Soviet Union, and, of course, of China. In the 16th century, the situation significantly changed and there would no longer be conquerors from the steppes that would play the kind of role that they had played for so long in Eurasian history.

With that conclusion, what was the importance of this legacy? Why did we take this journey across 6,000 years and across 6,000 miles of steppes? That is what you are looking at when you count all of those steppes as well as their extensions; as I mentioned earlier, it was a great highway with exit ramps into Central Europe, into Transoxiana, into China. There were associated desert zones. One could argue that some two-and-a-half million square miles of real estate of the globe was involved in this course. To review for a moment, think of what was achieved; think what happened in those three distinct periods of antiquity, the early Middle Ages, and above all the final legacy of the Mongol Empire. We opened this course with the first Indo-European pastoralists, nomads, who mastered the use of wheeled vehicles, domesticated the horse; and those innovations were as significant as the invention of farming, in my opinion. It opened up the Eurasian steppes to colonization by humans. It turned those vast grasslands, which up until that point were largely populated by horses, into a harsh landscape indeed, but into a home to people who could move at will on those steppes, who could turn that grass into horseflesh, into milk—particularly the fermented mare's milk that was the staple of Mongol armies—and as a result, the steppes came under human occupation and became that highway; that highway that linked the settled civilizations that emerged in the great river valleys of the Tigris-Euphrates, the Nile, the Indus, and, of course, the Yellow River in China.

The invention of light chariots and the improvement of wheeled vehicles led to the dispersion of Indo-European speakers across Europe, across much of Western Eurasia, into India. It led to a very, very important peopling of many significant language families to this day. The invention of horseback riding, with good saddles and with the first efforts of composite bows—and this was achieved in the early Iron Age by the Scythians—that opened up the steppes to a new wave of migrations. It brought Iranian-speakers east to the borders of China; it brought them into India; and it set off a new set of migrations and relationships. We investigated some of these in antiquity, particularly the relationship of the steppe nomadic peoples with the Greek world and the great empire Persia, the Achaemenids; and that was then inherited by the Romans and their successors, the Sassanids. We have seen how steppe nomads could actually build states within that wider world of the Mediterranean world and the Middle East, particularly the Parthians, the first nomadic people to rule by horseback; the Kushans, so important in the spread of Buddhism and the expansion of the Silk Road. Above all, we looked at China; especially Han China: its relationship with the Xiongnu; the ability of steppe peoples now to create political orders, great confederations that could challenge the great urban literate civilizations. Modu Chanyu was really the model of the great conquerors to follow; and would that we have the kind of information we have on Genghis Khan in the *Secret History* or the biography of Bābur to know this man better. But his confederation dramatically changed the balance. It led henceforth to migrations from east to west. It brought almost all of the steppe peoples directly and indirectly into contact with Chinese civilization. Chinese civilization arguably was one of the great forces that transformed the steppe peoples. So many of the achievements of Chinese civilization through the Mongol period were disseminated to the rest of humanity compliments of the trade routes and the empires built by these so-called barbarians of the steppes. The achievements in antiquity are astonishing.

We then moved to the early Middle Ages. That was a period in itself characterized by another set of migrations, again from east and west, and the expansion of the Turkish tribes. We started in the 6th century with the success of the Gök Turks; the construction of Khagnates on the western branch of the steppes that came into contact with Constantinople; with the khanates on the eastern steppes such as the Uighurs, who came into contact with Tang China. The Turks represented an explosive and powerful force across the steppes. They transformed the steppes ethnically and linguistically. They brought new methods of fighting, especially the metal stirrups, the improved saddles, the better composite bows. Starting in the 6th century, and really almost down to the 16th century, for 1,000 years, the improved version of the steppe way of war dominated so many of the battlefields, so many of the Eurasian battlefields, and only very, very few opponents in the civilized kingdoms, in the civilized states, mastered tactics necessary to counter this. There were a few, and they were remarkably similar, created at different times and different places: I mentioned the Roman tactician and governor Aryan; the Chinese generals, above all Li Jing, the Tang general who defeated the Gök Turks. Those who did not follow those rules, those who sought to fight the Turkish nomads on his own terms, they courted disaster; and there were a number of the cases of those disasters that significantly transformed the worlds of Islam, Byzantium, India, and China.

The Turks also played another important role: They brought the peoples of the steppes into closer association with Islam. Buddhism had been the major religious force on the steppes as a result of the achievements of the Kushan emperors and the later states that followed the Kushans, notably the Hephthalites. But starting in the seventh century A.D., Islam came to play an ever more important force in the lives of more and more people across the steppes. Islam resulted in a remarkable exchange with the Turks; the Turks adapted it on their own terms, they created an identity that was both Turkish and at the same time is Islamic, and they created the third great literary language of the Islamic world. This proves significant, because when the Turks arrived in the Islamic world in force—starting with

Toghrul Bey and the Seljuk Turks when they captured Baghdad in 1055—they differed very much from all previous steppe conquerors. They were Muslims. They received a pass. They were accepted, however reluctantly, by the Muslim populations, by the Abbasid caliphs, by the various emirs and cities, and the merchant princes of Transoxiana and Iran. Because of that, a unique partnership emerged between the Turks and the Persians, the Iranians, who essentially came to define Islamic civilization, and that saw the new expansion of Islam into Asia Minor after the battle of Manzikert in 1071; ultimately into Northern India with the victories that resulted in the emergence of the Delhi sultanate in 1260; and finally, the great Mughal conquest in 1526. Islam received a remarkable rejuvenation and expansion compliments of the Turks, and went onto a second great period in the later Middle Ages.

Finally, for that third period—starting in the late 12th century, 13th and 14th centuries—that third period was dominated by the Mongols. I have argued, I hope persuasively, that the Mongols had a decisive impact. We have argued that they were the exception and the epitome of everything that preceded them in many ways. Again, I have tried to stress that the costs were high. The costs of all of these steppe empires could be very high; they could be extremely disruptive to those who fell to the conquests of the steppe tribes. On the other hand, the Mongol invasions, the Mongol conquests, brought misery and destruction on a scale that had hitherto been unknown. One could argue in part it came out of the harsh way of war, the harsh life on the steppes; that when tribes and clans fought there was no quarter, those who won liquidated the opponents. But Genghis Khan and his grandsons, and above all Tamerlane—while not a Mongol in birth and descent, he was certainly a Mongol in his military and political conceptions—they practiced the war of terror on a colossal scale; and the destruction of the great cities of Iran and Transoxiana by repeated Mongol attacks was extremely devastating. Many cities never recovered; and those cities had to be rebuilt later, ironically by some of the descendants of Genghis Khan, notably the Ilkhans of Tabriz. In Northern China, we saw similar types of destruction where Genghis Khan almost deliberately rode down irrigated fields and tried to turn them back into pastureland. One could argue this was, again, a typical nomadic reaction. They needed the sedentary civilizations, they needed the products of the cities, but they always feared them; they always saw that they were a minority vis-à-vis the urban and sedentary populations, and so they returned areas to pastures as a way of asserting themselves. But that just does not explain it all the way. The conquest of Batu was in the same category; the destruction in Russia and Hungary were on a remarkable scale; and these must be faced in assessing the total legacy. There was a high price, particularly in that final third phase.

On the other hand, whatever the good and the evil, whatever the intentions, whatever the unintended consequences, the results are undeniable. The Mongols made the 13th century their century and they played a pivotal role, especially in the later 13th century, in the revival of prosperity. To be sure, part of this was for pragmatic reasons: They wanted the revenues to support their steppe armies; and after all, they had to rehabilitate many of the areas that had been devastated in the earlier 13th centuries. But the results are undeniable. We have looked at some of the remarkable cultural exchanges in medicine, in the exchange of food and various types of clothing, aesthetics and arts, especially between the court of Kublai Khan and the Ilkhans of Tabriz. The Islamic and Chinese worlds were brought into close association, and that was because of the Mongols. Arabic numbers, Arabic astronomy made its way to China; sophisticated instruments for measuring the earth, for making maps and cartography also arrived in China; and then the knowledge of the Chinese, their mathematics, their medicine, their knowledge in all sorts of herbs and biology was then received by the Islamic world. These are undeniable improvements that gave ultimately birth to better civilizations on both ends.

Above all was the military technology; and I saw a very, very bitter irony in this. First, the people who embraced the changes in military technology were the least important in the cultural exchange of the 13th century. In fact, they were the least important in the eyes of the Mongol khans. The embassies sent by Pope Innocent IV or the French Crusader King St. Louis IX were pitiful envoys of a distant set of pale rulers. The khans Güyük or Möngke really wondered, "Who are you guys?"; a bunch of Franciscans who showed up barefooted bringing really trivial gifts and were the most unimpressive members of great choruses of 3,000, or 4,000, or 5,000 envoys from across the world who had come to seek the patronage of the Great Khan. Yet, it was these Europeans who picked up the black gunpowder and then went on to create artillery, handheld firearms, to create those oceangoing vessels to launch out on the great transoceanic expansion that would forever change the world. The Europeans got that other strange benefit, and those are the tales attributed to Marco Polo. Probably Marco Polo existed, and how much is real and not real in the account is irrelevant. The image of Xanadu and Cathay provided the inspiration and motivation for that Age of Discovery. As a result, it was these Europeans, these Western Europeans, who are heirs to this legacy of the Mongol peace, who in the end did in the great routes across Eurasia and ended a steppe power.

Perhaps it is useful to think upon all these civilizations we have looked at. To take the map of Eurasia and turn it around; to look north, south, to see how the nomads for 6,000 years had seen that world and how they had interacted with those civilizations and what they had contributed; what their fears, what their abilities, and what their successes were. It gives us a unique vision into the development of all of these civilizations and the making of the modern world. Above all, it is still remarkable to me, in doing this course, how much of modern civilization is influenced by the fact that 130,000 Mongol warriors mounted on those horses, followed Genghis Khan. If those conquests had never happened, one thinks of what the world would look like today.

Maps

Silk Road Routes

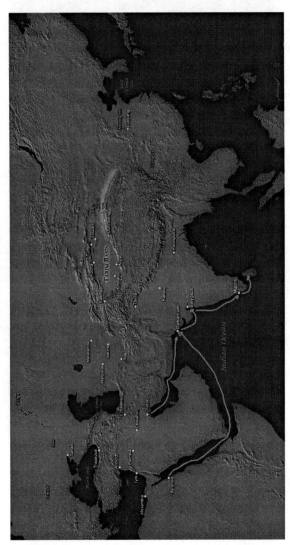

Eurasian Steppes

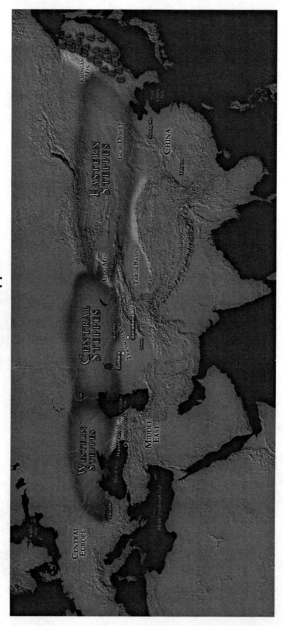

Timeline

6500–5000 B.C. .... Proto-Indo-European speakers
settle the Pontic-Caspian steppes

5000–4000 B.C. .... Domestication of the horse

Beginning of the Chalcolithic Age
(4200–3800 B.C.): metallurgy on
the Pontic-Caspian steppes

Riding of horses and herding on
the Pontic-Caspian steppes

Migration of Proto-Anatolian
speakers into the Balkans

4000 B.C.–3000 B.C. .... Emergence of Yamnaya culture on
the Pontic-Caspian steppes (PIE)

Invention of wheeled vehicles

Migration of Proto-Tocharian speakers
to Altai Mountains (Afanasevo culture)

Emergence of literate, urban
civilization of Sumer (southern Iraq)

Unification of Egypt under Narmer:
birth of Egyptian civilization

3000–2000 B.C. .... Emergence of urban civilization
of Meluhha in India (Indus Valley
civilization, 2600–1700 B.C.)

Anatolian speakers (Hittites, Luvians,
and Palaic speakers) cross the
Bosporus and enter Asia Minor

Division of Indo-European languages
into centrum and satem branches

First known light chariots
in central Asia

2000–1500 B.C. .... Chariots at Nesa (Kültpe)
in central Asia Minor

Erlitou culture in the Yellow River
valley: origins of Chinese civilization

Andronovo culture in Khazkhstan

Proto-Indo-Iranian speakers
migrate to Transoxiana (BMAC)

Domestication of the Bactrian camel

Migrations of Eastern Iranian
speakers across Central and
Eastern Eurasian steppes

Hattusilis I founds the Hittite Empire
in Asia Minor; spread of chariot
warfare across the Near East

Migration of Indo-Aryan speakers
of Mitanni from Transoxiana
into northern Mesopotamia

Shang Dynasty (1600–1046 B.C.):
urban, literate civilization in China

1500–1000 B.C. .... Indo-Aryans migrate into northern
India, completing the end of
urban civilization of Meluhha
(Indus Valley civilization)

Introduction of chariot
and horses to China

Collapse of the great states of the
Bronze Age in the Near East and Greece

Zhou Dynasty in China
(1046–256 B.C.)

1000–500 B.C. .... Beginning of widespread
use of iron technology

Migration of Tocharian-speakers
into the Tarim Basin

Earliest mummies of Tarim Basin
(Ur David and Beauty of Loulan)

Spread of cavalry across
Eurasian steppes

Migration of Medes and
Persians into western Iran

Scythians dominate the
Pontic-Caspian steppes

Sacae dominate the central
Asian steppes

Sacae migrate into the Tarim Basin
and upper valley of Yellow River

Cultural exchange between
Iranian nomads and Chinese

Scythians compel Cimmerians to
migrate across the Caucasus

Cimmerians invade Urartu, Phrygia,
and the Assyrian Empire

Life and teachings of Mahavira
Vardhamana, founder of Jainism

Cyrus I (559–530 B.C.) unites Iran
and Transoxiana and conquers
Asia Minor and Babylonia: birth of
Persian (Achaemenid) Empire

King Cyrus slain by Massagetase north
of the Jaxartes River (Syr Darya)

Life and teachings of Siddhartha
Gautama, the Buddha

Reign of Darius I: consolidation
of the Persian Empire

Scythian expedition of King
Darius I of Persia

Founding of the Roman Republic

500–400 B.C. .... Period of Warring States in
China (down to 221 B.C.)

Herodotus visits Olbia and receives
reports about the Scythians

400–300 B.C. .... Alexander the Great conquers
the Persian Empire

Alexander battles the nomadic
Sacae and Dahae across Jaxartes

Greco-Macedonian colonies
founded in Bactria and Sogdia

Diadochoi: wars of successors and
partition of Alexander's empire

Chandragupta (322–298 B.C.) ends
Macedonian rule in northern India

Foundation of Mauyran
Empire (326–187 B.C.)

Seleucus I (312–281 B.C.) establishes
Seleucid Empire (312–63 B.C.)

Hellenization of the Near East
and expansion of the Silk Road

Genesis of Sarmartian tribes on the
steppes between Volga and Ural rivers

300–200 B.C. .... Accession of Ashoka (268–232
B.C.): height of Mauyran Empire

Rome defeats Carthage in
the First Punic War

Conversion of Ashoka to Buddhism

Diodotus of Upper Satrapies
founds Greco-Bactrian kingdom

Third Buddhist Council: division
of Buddhism into Theravada
and Mayahana vehicles

Arsaces I (246–211 B.C.)
founds Parthian kingdom

Unification of China by Qin Shi
Huangdi (246–210 B.C.)

First Chinese empire under the
Qin Dynasty (221–206 B.C.)

Building of the Great Wall
to check the Xiongnu

Touman forges the Xiongnu
confederacy on the eastern steppes

Rome defeats Carthage in
the Second Punic War

Roman conquest of the Mediterranean
world (201–31 B.C.)

Reign of Modu Chanyu
(down to 174 B.C.): Xiongnu
dominate eastern steppes

Emperor Gaozu (206–195 B.C.) founds
Former (Western) Han Dynasty

200–100 B.C. .... Sarmatians subject Scythians and
rule the Pontic-Caspian steppes

Sarmatians impose tribute on
Greek cities of the Crimea

Battle of Magnesia: Romans defeat
Seleucid King Antiochus III

Decline of Seleucid Empire
and rise of Parthians

Reign of Mithridates I: expansion
of Parthian kingdom

Gunchen Chanyu expands
Xiongnu confederation

Yuezhi (Tocharians) driven by
Xiongnu west into Ferghana

Yuezhi drive Sacae into
Sogdiana and Bactria

Reign of Han Emperor Wudi

Mithridates I defeats and captures
Seleucid king Demetrius II

Parthians conquer Media,
Persia, and Mesopotamia

Sacae devastate Sogdiana and shatter
the Greco-Bactrian kingdom

Sacae settle in Drangiana
(Seistan; 140–120 B.C.)

Mission of Zhang Qian to the
Yuezhi (Kushans) and Wusun

War between Han China
and the Xiongnu

Expedition of Antiochus VII
Sidetes against Parthia

Tocharians subject the Greek cities
of Bactria (140–120 B.C.)

Phraates II of Parthia (138–128 B.C.)
defeats and slays Seleucus VII

Sacae and Tocharians invade Media
and defeat and slay Phraates II

Tocharians defeat and slay Parthian
king Artabanus I (128–124 B.C.)

Reign of Mithridates II (123–88 B.C.):
consolidation of Parthian Empire

Construction of Ctesiphon
on the Tigris River

Han armies secure Gansu and the
Tarim Basin (western regions)

Eudoxus of Cyzicus discovers use
of monsoons for sailing to India

Development of trade in the
Erthyraean Sea (Indian Ocean)

War of the Heavenly Horses:
Li Guangli invades Sogdiana

Sogdians render tribute of horses
to Han Emperor Wudi

100 B.C.–1 A.D. .... Roxolani migrate into eastern
Rumanian steppes (Wallachia; down
to 50 A.D.)

Iazyges migrate into eastern
Hungarian steppes

Alans occupy Kuban and steppes
north of the Caucasus

King Tigranes the Great of Armenia
expels Parthians from Mesopotamia

Outbreak of Third Mithridatic
War (74–63 B.C.)

L. Licinius Lucullus defeats Mithridates
VI and secures Asia Minor

Battle of Tigranocerta: L. Licinius
Lucullus defeats Tigranes the Great

Parthians subject Mesopotamia
and Media Atropatene

Pompey the Great (Cn. Pompeius
Magnus) imposes Roman
suzerainty over Armenia

Pompey secures the Roman
frontier on the upper Euphrates

Civil war on the eastern
steppes: division into northern
and southern Xiongnu

Battle of Carrhae: Parthians
defeat M. Licinius Crassus

Abortive campaign of Mark Antony
in Armenia and Media Atropatene

Octavian, hailed Augustus by the
Senate, establishes the Roman Empire

Augustus imposes settlement
on King Phraates IV

Return of Roman prisoners
and standards of Carrhae

1–100 A.D. .... Wang Mang overthrows
the Han Dynasty

Reforms in China and collapse
of Chinese frontier policy

Reunification of the
Xiongnu confederacy

Guangwu (25–57) founds Later
(Eastern) Han Dynasty (25–220)

Accession of Kujula Kadphises
(30–80): founding of Kushan Empire

Composition of the *Periplus
Maris Erythraei*

War of the Armenian Succession;
Rome opposes King Tiridates

Cn. Domitius Corbulo
campaigns in Armenia

Settlement between Nero and
King Vologeses I over Armenia

Roman governor Tib. Plautius
Silvanus secures the lower Danube
against the Roxolani and Dacians

Alans cross the Caucasus and
ravage the Near East

Han general Bao Chao subjects the
western regions (Tarim Basin)

Dissolution of the northern
Xiongnu confederacy

Reign of Kushan emperor Vima Taktu

Reign of Kushan emperor Vima
Kadphises (down to 127)

Extension of Kushan power
into the Punjab

Introduction of Kushan gold
currency to facilitate trade

Mission of Han envoy Gan Ying
to Kushan Empire and Parthia

Gao Ying receives reports about
Daqin (imperial Rome)

100–200... Emperor Trajan (98–117)
wages the Parthian War

Roman legions capture and sack
Ctesiphon, the Parthian capital

Trajan crowns Parthamasiris
king of Parthia

Hadrian relinquishes Trajan's
conquests east of the Euphrates

Reign of Kushan emperor Kanishka
I: height of Kushan Empire

Patronage of Iranian and
Hindu gods and Buddhism

Arrian, Roman governor of
Cappadocia, checks attack of Alans

Reign of Kushan emperor Huviskha

War of Marcus Aurelius against Parthia

Roman army sacks Seleucia
ad Tigrim and Ctesiphon

Northern war of Marcus Aurelius
against Germanic and Sarmatian tribes

Reign of Vasuveda I (down to
230): decline of Kushan Empire

War of Septimius Severus
against Parthia

Roman army captures and
sacks Ctesiphon

200–300... War of Caracalla against Parthia

Life and teachings of Mani,
founder of Manichaeism

End of the Han Dynasty:
political disunity in China

Era of Three Kingdoms
(220–280): Wei, Shu, and Wu

Battle of Hormozgan: Shah Shapur
defeats Parthian King Artabanus V

Shapur I (227–240) founds
Neo-Persian (Sassanid) Empire

Reign of Sassanid Shah Ardashir I

Reforms of Kartir:
codification of Zoroastrianism

War of Ardashir against Roman
emperor Severus Alexander (222–235)

Reign of Sassanid Shah Shapur I

Shapur I invades Mesopotamia:
first war against Rome (242–244)

Gordian III (238–244) marches
east against Shapur I

Goths and Samartians raid
Dacia and Danubian provinces
of the Roman Empire

Death of Gordian III; accession
of Philip I (244–249)

Philip I pays Shapur I 10,000
pounds of gold for peace

Battle of Abrittus: Goths defeat
and slay Trajan Decius

Shapur I invades and sacks Syria:
second war against Rome (253–254)

Shapur I invades Syria: third
war against Rome (256–258)

Expedition of Valerian I
(253–260) against Shapur I

Valerian I captured by Shapur I

Sassanid army ravages Mesopotamia,
northern Syria, and eastern Asia Minor

Rally of eastern Roman army by Prince
Odenathus of Palmyra (260–262)

Battle of Nassius: Claudius II Gothicus
decisively defeats the Goths

Aurelian reunites the Roman
Empire and secures frontiers

Aurelian withdraws Roman garrisons
and colonists from Dacia

Emperor Wu (265–290) reunites China
under the Jin Dynasty (280–420)

Accession of Diocletian (284–305):
imperial reform and recovery

Foundation of the Dominate

Sassanid-Persian War: Caesar Galerius
decisively defeats Shah Narses

Sassanid Shah Narses relinquishes
strategic Mesopotamian provinces

300–400... Conversion of Constantine I
(306–337) to Christianity

Accession of Shah Shapur II (309–379)

Chandragupta I founds the
Gupta Empire (219–550)

Constantine I campaigns against
the Sarmatians and Goths

Constantine founds
Constantinople (New Rome)

Yujiulu Muglu establishes the Rouran
(Avar) confederacy (330–551)

First migrations of Turkish speakers
into central Eurasian steppes

Shah Shapur II invades
Mesopotamia and sacks Amida

Outbreak of Roman-Persian
War (359–364)

Failure of the expedition of
Julian II against Ctesiphon

Death of Julian II and accession
of Jovian (363–364)

Jovian cedes Mesopotamian
province to Shapur II

Shah Shapur II settles Hephthalites
(White Huns) in Bactria

Hephthalites, as Sassanid allies, secure
northeastern frontier (375–425)

Huns defeat Gothic King
Ermanaric, who commits suicide

Huns subject Goths and Alans on
the Pontic-Caspian steppes

Goths received as federates by
Roman emperor Valens (364–378)

Battle of Adrianople: Goths
defeat and slay Valens

Accession of Theodosius I,
the Great (379–395)

Rome cedes Armenia to
the Sassanid Empire

Uldin, king of the Huns (down to 414)

Theodosius I declares Nicene
Christianity as the empire's official faith

Death of Theodosius I: division of
western and eastern Roman empires

Honorius, western Roman
emperor (395–423)

Arcadius, eastern Roman
emperor (395–408)

Huns cross the Dariel Pass and invade
the Sassanid Empire (395–396)

Daowu (398–409), ruler of the Tuoba,
founds northern Wei Dynasty (398–535)

400–500... Migration of Visigoths
under Alaric into Italy

Germanic tribes migrate into Gaul and
Spain: collapse of the Rhine frontier

Huns migrate into Pannonia: collapse
of the middle Danube frontier

Accession of Theodosius II, eastern
Roman emperor (408–450)

Goths sack Rome

Construction of the Theodosius
Walls of Constantinople

Reigns of Rugila (420–434) and
Octar (420–430) over the Huns

Death of Jin emperor Gong (419–420):
disunity in China (420–581)

Ruglia raids into Thrace and
receives subsidy to withdraw

Reign of Taiwu, emperor of
the northern Wei Dynasty

Construction of colossal
Buddhas at Yungang Caves

Accession of Valentinian III as
western Roman emperor (425–455)

Aetlius, patrician and *magister militum*,
directs western Roman policy

Third Ecumenical Council at Ephesus:
condemnation of Nestorianism

Nestorian Christians establish
churches in Sassanid Babylonia

Accession of Attila (434–453) and
Bleda (434–445) as kings of the Huns

Attila forges a barbarian empire
from the Rhine to the Volga

Attila invades Thrace and
extorts the Treaty of Margus

Annual subsidy (700 pounds of
gold) paid by Theodosius II

Shah Yazdegerd II wages frontier
wars against the Hephthalites

Huns annihilate Burgundians at Worms;
origins of the legend of the Nieblungs

Attila murders Bleda: Attila
sole king of the Huns

Attila devastates the Balkan provinces
of the eastern Roman Empire

Treaty of Anatolus: Attila ends the
Roman frontier on the lower Danube

Accession of Marcian, eastern
Roman emperor (450–457)

Reform of eastern Roman army
and end of subsidies to Attila

Marriage proposal of Honoria to
Attila rejected by the western court

Attila declares war on the
western Roman Empire

Battle of Chalons: Aetius checks Attila

Invasion of northern Italy by Attila

Death of Attila: civil war and
rebellion within the Hun Empire

Battle of Nedao: collapse
of the Hun Empire

Hephthalites defeat, capture, and
ransom Shah Peroz (457–484)

Odoacer deposes last western
Roman emperor, Romulus
Augustulus (475–476)

End of the western Roman Empire

Hephthalites defeat and slay Shah
Peroz and overrun Transoxiana

Wei emperor Xiaowen (471–499)
locates his court at Luoyang

Sinification of the northern Wei Dynasty

Hephthalites subject northern India
and the Tarim Basin (down to 513)

500–550... Construction of the first colossal
Buddha at Bamiyan

Outbreak of Persian–Roman
War (526–532)

Accession of Roman emperor
Justinian (527–565)

Battle of Daras: Belisarius
defeats the Persian army

Timeline

Accession of Shah Khursau I (521–570)

Perpetual peace between
Justinian and Shah Khurau I

Justinian reconquers North Africa,
Italy, and southern Spain

550–600... Bumin overthrows rule of the
Rouran (Avar) khagans

Turks expel Avars and occupy
the Orkhon valley

Establishment of the Gök Turk
khaganate under the Ashina clan

Istami (552–581), brother of
Bumin and *yabgu* of the western
Gök Turks, pursues the Avars and
secures the central and western
Eurasian steppes to the Volga

Accession of Mukan as
khagan of the Gök Turks

Gök Turks subject Tocharian
cities of the Tarim Basin and
control the Silk Road

Construction of the second
colossal Buddha at Bamiyan

Istami, *yabgu* of the western Turks, and
Shah Khosrow attack the Hephthalites

Turks subject Transoxiana

Avars flee into the
Pontic-Caspian steppes

Avar khagan Bayan and Lombard king
Albion (560–572) defeat the Gepidae

Avars occupy the Pannonian grasslands

Khagan Bayan (560–602) rules the
steppes from the Danube to the Don

Avars raid the Byzantine
Balkan provinces

Beginning of migration of Slavs
into the Balkans

Justin II (565–578) receives a
delegation of the western Turks

Lombards migrate into northern Italy

Justin rejects annual
subsidy to Khosrow I

Outbreak of Roman–Persian
War (572–590)

Tiberius II (578–582) allies with
the Avars; collapse of Byzantine-
Turkish alliance; western Turks attack
Byzantine cities in the Crimea

Accession of Tardush as second
yabgu of the western Turks

Emperor Wen (581–604) unites
China and establishes the
Sui Dynasty (581–618)

Death of Taspar Khagan:
civil war between Ishbara
Khagan and Apa Khagan

Tardush asserts de facto
independence of the western
Turks (On Ok, "Ten Arrows")

Division of the Gök Turks into eastern
and western Turkish khaganates

First Persian-Turkish war
over Transoxiana

Vaharam Chobin defeats
the Western Turks

Vaharam Chobin usurps
the Sassanid throne

Khosrow II flees to Constantinople and
receives an army from Maurice Tiberius

Khosrow II (591–626) occupies
Ctesiphon and restores Sassanid rule

Peace between the Byzantine
Empire and Sassanid Persia

Outbreak of civil war in Turk khaganate

600–650..Phocas (602–610) overthrows
and murders Maurice Tiberius

Shapur II invades Roman
Mesopotamia and northern Syria

Outbreak of the Byzantine–
Persian War (602–626)

Accession of Sui emperor
Yang (604–617)

Reign of Harsha-Vardhan:
unification of northern India

Accession of Shibi Khan to
eastern (Gök) Turk khaganate

Accession of Heraclius
(610–641) as Byzantine emperor

Shibi Khan defeats Sui emperor
Yang at Yanmen (Shanxi)

Gök Turks raid the northern
frontiers of China

Accession of Tong *yabgu* khagan
(Ziebel) of western Turks (On Ok)

Khazars emerge as dominant
Ashina tribe of On Ok

Emperor Gaozu imposes unity in China
and founds the Tang Dynasty (618–907)

Second Persian–Turkish war; Tong *yabgu* khagan raids to Isfahan

Muhammad (575–632) flees from Mecca to Medina (Hegira)

Heraclius launches his eastern campaigns against Persia (622–626)

Alliance of Heraclius and Tong *yabgu* khagan against Shah Khosrow II

Illig, khagan of eastern Turks, defeats Tang emperor Taizong at Xuanwu Gate

Turks raid northern China to Wei River

Avars and Persians besiege Constantinople

Accession of Tang emperor Taizong (626–649)

Turks under Böri Shad cross the Derbent Gates and devastate Azerbaijan

Tang emperor Taizong promotes rebellions within the eastern Turkish khaganate

Campaign of Li Jing smashes the power of the eastern Turkish khaganate

Gök Turks submit to Tang emperor Taizong

Pilgrimage of Buddhist monk
Xuanzang to central Asia and India

Khazars assert domination over the
western Turkish tribes (down to 670)

Bulgars expel Avars from the steppes
between the Don and Dnieper rivers

Death of Muhammad: election of
Caliph Abu Bakr (632–634)

Death of Abu Bakr: election of
Caliph Umar I (634–644)

Battle of the Yarmuk: Arabic
conquest of Syria

Battle of Kadisiya: Arabs conquer
Iraq and western Iran (639–642)

Arabs conquer Egypt

Death of Heraclius; accession
of Constans II (641–668)
as Byzantine emperor

Fragmenting of the western
Turkish khaganate

Arabs conquer Cyrenaica
and Tripolitana

Election of Caliph Uthman (644–656)

650–700...Khazars repel first Arabic invasion
north of the Caucasus

Accession of Tang emperor
Gaozong (650–683)

Death of Shah Yazdgerd III
(632–651): end of Sassanid Empire

Arab armies reach Merv and
secure Oxus River as a frontier

Mutiny of Arab army in Egypt:
Murder of Caliph Uthman

Egyptian army proclaims
Ali caliph (656–661)

Outbreak of Muslim civil war
between Ali and Muawiya

Arabs raid Mawarannhar (Transoxiana)

Tang emperor Gaozong imposes
hegemony over western Turks

Turgesh emerge as leading
tribe of western Turks

Assassination of Ali; Muwayia
proclaimed first Umayyad caliph

Muwayia (661–680) establishes
Umayyad caliphate at Damascus

Succession of Constantine IV
(668–685) as Byzantine emperor

Khagan Busir Glavan (c. 670–715)
consolidates the Khazar Empire

Ziyad ibn Abihi (670–673),
governor of Iraq, fortifies Merv

Tribal armies settled in Khurasan

First Arabic siege of Constantinople

First revolt of eastern Turks under
Ashina Nishu Beg against Tang rule

Tang general Pei Xingjian
crushes Turkish rebels

Pei Xingjian crushes second Turkish
revolt under Ashinde Wenfu and Ashina
khagan Funian; public execution
of Turkish nobility at Chang'an

Khan Asparuch (681–702) settles
Bulgars in Moesia south of the Danube

Third Turkish revolt under Ashina
Kutlag against Tang rule

Kutlag declared Ilterish khagan
(682–694); end of Tang hegemony

Reestablishment of eastern
Turkish khaganate

Accession of Justinian II
(685–695) as Byzantine emperor

Accession of Caliph Abd
al-Malik (695–705)

Creation of Arabic-Muslim
administration in Umayyad caliphate

Accession of Kapagan
(694–716) to eastern khaganate

Overthrow and exile of
Justinian II to Cherson

Battle of Bolchu: Kapagan
khagan imposes hegemony
over the western Turks

Turks occupy Transoxiana in alliance
with Sogdian cities against Arabs

Arab capture of Carthage

700–750.. Qutaibah bin Muslim, governor of Merv

Arab conquest of Transoxiana

Marriage alliance between Justinian
II and Khazar khagan Busir Glavan

Restoration of Justinian II
(705–711) at Constantinople

Khan Tervel of the Bulgars (702–705)
concludes a treaty with Justinian II

Dowager Empress Wu directs
Tang policy (705–712)

Qutaybah ibn Muslim (705–715)
appointed Arab governor of Khurasan

Qutaybah initiates Arab
conquest of Transoxiana

Qutaybah captures Bukhara:
forced conversions to Islam

Arab conquest of Spain (711–713)

Arab conquest of the Sind (711–712)

Accession of Tang emperor
Xuanzong (712–756)

Byzantine–Bulgar treaty: annual tribute
to Bulgars and frontiers confirmed

Tokuz Oghuz Turks, backed by Tang
court, defeat and slay Kapaghan khagan

Kul Tigin and Tonyukuk impose
Bilge as khagan of the eastern Turks

Suluk, khan of Turgesh (716–738),
asserts power over western Turks

Accession of Leo III (717–741),
who founds the Isaurian Dynasty

Byzantine-Khazar alliance against
the Umayyad caliphate

Second Arabic siege of Constantinople

Erection of Turkish monumental
inscription of Tonyukuk
in the Orkhon valley

Arab governor al-Karashi massacres
population of Khujand, Ferghana

General rising of Sogdian cities and
Turkish tribes in Transoxiana

Suluk khagan of Turgesh defeats
Arab expedition ("day of thirst")

Suluk khagan defeats second Arab
expedition into Transoxiana

Byzantine-Khazar marriage alliance

Constantine V marries
Chichek, daughter of Bihar
Khagan of the Khazars

Death of Bilge Khagan; civil wars
in eastern Turkish khaganate

Monumental inscriptions in Orkhon
valley to Bilge and brother Kül Tigin

Arab army under Marwan defeats
Khazars and occupies Balanjar

Khazars compelled to convert to Islam

Assassination of Suluk;
collapse of Turkish resistance
to Arabs in Transoxiana

Nasr ibn Sayyar, Arab governor
of Khurasan (738–748),
secures Transoxiana

Khazar Khagan Bulan renounces
Islam in favor of Judaism

Foundation of new Khazar capital
at Atil on the lower Volga

Rebellion of Uighurs and Karluks:
overthrow of eastern Turkish khaganate

Accession of Umayyad caliph
Marwan II (744–750)

Kurluk Bilge proclaimed first
khagan of the Uighurs

Karluks, vassals of Kurluk Bilge,
secure the central Eurasian steppes

Uighur khagan Bayanchur Khan founds
capital of Baghlasun (Ordu Balik)

Outbreak of rebellion of Arab army in
Khurasan against Caliph Marwan II

750–800... Battle of the Greater Zab: as-
Saffrah defeats Caliph Marwan II

End of Umayyad caliphate

As-Saffrah (750–756) establishes
the Abbasid caliphate

Battle of Talas: Arab-Karluk
army defeats Tang army

Chinese garrisons withdrawn
from the Tarim Basin

Outbreak of An Lushan Rebellion

Uighur khagan Bayanchur Khan
supports Tang court against rebels

Abd ar-Rahman (756–788) proclaims
Umayyad emirate of Cordova

Byzantine emperor wars against Bulgars

Caliph al-Mansur founds Baghdad,
capital of Abbasid caliphate

Uighur khagan Bogu converts
to Manichaeism

Karluks defeat Turgesh and
reorganize the On Ok confederacy

Karluks dominate central Eurasian
steppes as vassals of Uighur khagans

Emergence of Oghuz (Ghuzz)
Turks on the steppes between
the Aral and Caspian seas

Accession of Caliph Harun ar-Raschid
(786–809): height of Abbasid caliphate

Charlemagne, king of the Franks,
smashes the Avar khanate

800–850..Coronation of Charlemagne as
Holy Roman Emperor (800–814)

Magyars migrate into the Pontic-
Caspian steppes (c. 800–830)

Accession of Krum, khan of
the Bulgars (802–813)

Outbreak of Abbasid civil war between
al-Amin and al-Mamun (809–813)

Formation of Turkish bodyguard (*haras*)

Bulgar khan Krum defeats
and slays Byzantine emperor
Nicephorus I at Pliska

Tahir ibn al-Husayn captures
Baghdad: end of Abbasid civil war

Accession of Caliph
al-Mamun (813–833)

Khan Krum defeats Emperor
Michael I at Versinicia

Bulgars devastate the hinterland
of Constantinople

Accession of Leo V (813–820):
extension of Theodosian Walls

Peace between Leo V and the
Bulgar khan Omurtag (814–831)

"Great Fence of Bulgaria"

Ahad obm Asad I appointed Abbasid
governor of Ferghana (819–864)

Foundation of the Samanid
Dynasty (819–1005)

Uighur-Tibetan clash for
control of the Tarim Basin

Caliph al-Mamun appoints
Tahir ibn al-Husayn in Khurasan

Tahirid emirs rule Khurasan
and Transoxiana (821–873)

Pechenegs migrate west from
the central Eurasian steppes

Magyars consolidate power in the
steppes west of the Don (930–895)

Caliph al-Mutasim relocates the
Abbasid capital to Samara

Turkish bodyguard dominates
Abbasid court (836–892)

Caliph al-Mutasim invades Byzantine
Asia Minor and sacks Amorium

Emperor Theophilus wins tactical
victory over Turks at Dazimon

Khazars, with Byzantine
assistance, fortify the fortress
Sarkel against Magyars

Karluks and Krygyz sack Baghlasun:
end of Uighur khaganate

Uighurs migrate into the Tarim Basin

Beginning of migrations of Oghuz
Turks westward (840–925)

Karakhanids dominate central
Eurasian steppes (840–1137)

850–900... Migration of Pechenegs to
steppes west of the Don River

Rurik (Erik) founds Holmgard
(Novgorod) as a Rus settlement

First Rus attack on Constantinople

Saint Cyril fails to convert the
Khazars to Orthodox Christianity

Khan Boris of the Bulgars (852–889)
converts to Orthodox Christianity

Formation of the kingdom of Bulgaria

Tulunid emirs rule over
Egypt (down to 905)

Ahmad ibn Asad ibn Saman appointed
emir of Transoxiana (875–886)

Samanid emirs create the high Persian
culture of eastern Islam (875–1005)

Accession of Oleg (Helgi) as
prince of the Rus (c. 880–912)

Oleg transfers capital to Kiev

Magyars settle on Pannonian grasslands

Accession of Tsar Symeon
of Bulgaria (893–927)

Outbreak of Symeon's first war
against Byzantium (894–897)

Magyars migrate into Pannonian
steppes (Hungary)

Magyars raid into western
Europe (896–955)

900–950... Death of Emperor Li Zhu
(904–909): end of the Tang Dynasty

Period of disunity: Five Dynasties
and Ten Kingdoms (907–980)

Second Rus attack on Constantinople

Abaoji unites the Khitans

Ubaydallah al-Mahdi (909–
934) proclaims the Fatimid
caliphate in North Africa

Accession of Byzantine emperor
Constantine VII (913–959)

Symeon wages second war
against Byzantium (913–924)

Abaoji subjects 16 prefectures and
seizes power of northern China

Abaoji takes Chinese throne
name Taizu (916–926),
establishing the Liao Dynasty

Conversion of Volga Bulgars to Islam

Mission of Ibn Fadlan to the
Bulgars and Khazars

Reign of Khitan emperor
Yelü Deguangr (Taizong)

Ikhshidid emirs rule Egypt and Syria

Accession of Satuk Boghra
Khan (940–955)

Satuk Boghra Khan promotes Islam
among the Karakhanid Turks

Third Rus attack on Constantinople

Khitans conquer Kaifeng

Fourth Rus attack on Constantinople

950–1000... Li Xixing (954–967) establishes the Xi
Xia kingdom in the Gansu Corridor

Battle of the Lech: Otto I of
Germany defeats the Hungarians

Zhao Kuangyin seizes power in
Kaifeng as emperor Taizu (960–976)

Taizu establishes Northern
Song Dynasty (960–1127)

Taizu unites southern China
into a Neo-Confucian state

Alp Tigin (961–975) takes over
the town of Ghazna

Establishment of the Samanid emirate

Prince Sviatoslav of Kiev
(965–967) and Pechenegs sack Atil

Collapse of the Khazar khaganate

Pechenegs dominate the
Pontic-Caspian steppes

Prince Sviatoslav of Kiev
invades Bulgaria (967–971)

Reign of Khitan emperor Yelü
Xian (Jingzong; 969–982)

Sinification of Khitan court

Fatimid army occupies Egypt

Prince Sivatoslav overruns
Bulgaria and attacks Byzantium

Battle of Dorostolum:
Byzantine emperor John I
defeats Prince Sviastoslav

Byzantine annexation of
eastern Bulgaria

Pechenegs defeat and slay Prince
Sviatoslav on the Dnieper River

Fatimid al-Mu'izz transfers
the capital to Cairo

Accession of Byzantine emperor
Basil II (976–1025)

Height of Byzantine Empire under
the Macedonian Dynasty

Accession of Song emperor
Taizong (976–997)

Emergence of the Song bureaucratic
state and examination system

Accession of the Samind
emir Nuh II (976–997)

Sebüktigin (977–997) establishes
the Ghaznavid emirate (977–1163)

Reign of Khitan emperor Yelü
Longxu (Shengzong; down
to 1031)

Migration of Seljuk Turks to the
steppes south of Khwarazm

Sebüktigin raids Kabul and
Punjab—domains of the Shahi
Jayapala (964–1001)

Battle of Langhan: Sebüktigin
defeats Shahi Jayapala

Conversion of Prince Vladimir of Kiev
(980–1015) to Orthodox Christianity

Foundation of Orthodox Russia

Jiqian of the Xi Xia ends vassalage
to Song and Liao emperors

Sebüktigin and Tafgach Bughra Khan
of the western Karakhanids agreed
to partition the Samanid emirate

Mahmud Ghaznavi (998–1030)
succeeds to the Ghaznavid emirate

Karakhanids occupy Bukhara; Samanid
court flees to Tabaristan (999–1005)

Collapse of the Samanid emirate;
Karakhanids control Transoxiana

1000–1050.. Conversion of King Stephen of Hungary
(997–1036) to Latin Christianity

Battle of Peshawar: Mahmud Ghaznavi
annihilates army of Shahi Jayapala

Mahmud raids across the Punjab
and Doab (1001–1024)

Treaty of Chauyuan: Song
emperor Zhenzong (997–1022)
recognizes Khitan control of the
16 prefectures of north China

Mahmud Ghaznavi and Karakhanids
clash along the lower Oxus River

Mahmud Ghaznavi occupies Khwarazm

Mahmud Ghaznavi sacks Somnath,
the sanctuary of Shiva

Tughril Bey and Chagri settle near
Bukhara in Karakhanid service

Mahmud Ghaznavi secures
Khurasan and northern Iran

Mahmud Ghaznavi settles Seljuk
Turks under Tughril Bey in Khurasan

Reign of Yuanhao of the Xi Xia under
the Chinese imperial name Jingzong

Promotion of Buddhism
in Xi Xia domains

Tughril Bey declared sultan at Nishapur

Tughril Bey defeats Ghaznavid
sultan Masud I near Merv

Seljuk Turks conquer cities of
northern Iran (1040–1055)

1050–1100...................................... Tughril Bey and Seljuk
Turks enter Baghdad

Tughril Bey restores the Abbasid
caliphate under Seljuk protection

End of the Macedonian
Dynasty at Constantinople

Clash of civil and military aristocracies:
decline of Byzantine power

Accession of Alp Arslan
(1063–1072) as Seljuk sultan

Alp Arslan directs raids
against Byzantine and Fatimid
empires (1063–1071)

Accession of Byzantine emperor
Romanus IV (1068–1072)

Battle of Manzikert: Seljuk sultan Alp-
Arslan defeats Emperor Romanus IV

Seljuk Turks overrun Byzantine
Asia Minor (1071–1081)

Malik Danishmend (1071–1084)
seizes Niksar as Danishmend emir

Cumans migrate west,
attacking the Pechenegs

Accession of Malik Shah
(1072–1092) as Seljuk sultan

Sulayman (1077–1086) seizes Konya
and is proclaimed sultan of Rūm

Accession of King Ladislaus
of Hungary (1077–1095)

Hungarian–Cuman border wars

Accession of Byzantine emperor
Alexius I Comnenus (1081–1118)

Establishment of Comnenian
Dynasty (1081–1185)

Pechenegs migrate into
Byzantine Empire

Battle of Levounion: Emperor Alexius I
and the Cumans destroy the Pechenegs

First Crusade

Battle of Dorylaeum: First
Crusade defeats Sultan Kilij
Arslan I of Konya

First Crusade captures Antioch

First Crusade captures Jerusalem

1100–1150 .... Accession of Vladimir Monomakh
(1113–1125) of Kiev

Russian–Cuman wars

Wanyan Aguda (1115–1123) unites
the Jurchens in Manchuria

Jurchen rebellion against the Liao
(Khitan) emperor Tianzuo (1101–1125)

Wanyan Aguda assumes Chinese
throne name Taizu of the Jin Dynasty

Alliance of the Sea: Wanyan Aguda and
Song emperor Huizong (1100–1125)
agree to partition the Khitan Empire

Wanyan Aguda conquers the 16
prefectures of China (1121–1123)

Accession of Jurchen emperor
Wanyan Sheng (1123–1135)

Wanyan Sheng ends the
Khitan (Liao) Empire

Yelü Dashi (1124–1143) and the Kara-
Khitans flee to central Eurasian steppes

Yelü Dashi establishes
Kara-Khitan khaganate

Wanyan Sheng conquers from Song the
lower Yellow River valley (1125–1127)

Wanyan Aguda captures
Kiafeng, the Song capital

Gaozong (1127–1162) relocates
the Song capital to Lin'an
(modern Hangzhou)

Beginning of the Southern
Song Dynasty (1127–1279)

Yelü Dashi and the Kara-Khitans
conquer cities of the Tarim Basin

Treaty of Shaoxing:
Song emperor Gaozong
acknowledges loss of north China

Jurchen (Jin) Empire supreme in north
China and eastern Eurasian steppes

Battle of Qatwan: Yelü Dashi defeats
Seljuk sultan Ahmed Sanjar

Kara-Khitans conquer Transoxiana

First reports of legendary Prester
John in western Europe

1150–1200 .... Collapse of the great Seljuk sultanate

Abbasid caliph al-Muqtafi
asserts independence in Iraq

Birth of Temujin (future Genghis Khan)

Tatars poison Yesugei, father of Temujin

Temujin; his mother, Hoelun;
and siblings live in exile

Ghiyath-ad-Din seizes Ghaznva and
establishes the Ghurid sultanate

Muhammad Ghori as emir directs
Ghurid attacks into India (1173–1192)

Battle of Myricoephalon: Sultan Kilij
Arslan II defeats Emperor Manuel I

Decline of Byzantine
power in Asia Minor

Enslavement and escape of Temujin

Temujin, as ally of Toghrul Khan of
the Keraits, wars against the Merkits

Jamukha and Temujin swear
brotherhood and battle the Merkits

Prithviraj III (1149–1192) of
the Chauhan kingdom builds
the capital at Delhi

Marriage of Temujin and
Börte, birth of Jochi

Clashes between Jamukha and
Temujin; Jamukha allies with
the Merkits and Naimans

Jin emperor Zhangzong
(1189–1208) promotes tribal
wars among the Mongols

Expedition of Prince Igor of Novgorod-
Seversk against the Cumans

Second Battle of Tarain; Muhammad
Ghuri defeats Prithviraj III

Muhammad Ghuri occupies Delhi

Qutb ud-din Aybak directs
Ghurid conquest

Aybak orders the construction of the
Quwwatt-ul Islam mosque complex

Bakhtiyar Khilji, Ghurid general, sacks
Nalanda: end of the Pala kingdom

Aybak orders the construction
of the Qutb Minar

1200–1250.................................. Temujin defeats Jamukha, Naimans,
and Merkits near Khingan Mountains

Muhammad Ghori declared
sultan (1202–1206)

Toghrul Khan allies with Jamukha

Toghrul Khan and Jamukha defeat
Temujin at the Battle of Baljuna

Temujin rallies Mongols and the
kurultai declare war on Jamukha

Temujin wins decisive victory
near Karakorum over Jamukha
and Toghrul Khan

Temujin imposes his authority over
the eastern Eurasian steppes

Kuchlug, prince of Naimans,
flees to Kara-Khitan Gurkhan
Mozhu (1178–1211)

Fourth Crusade sacks Constantinople
and partitions the Byzantine Empire

Accession of Sultan Kay-Khusraw
I (1204–1210) of Konya (Rūm)

Theodore I founds the Byzantine
splinter empire at Nicaea

Seljuk conquest of Anatolia:
subjection of Sivas and Kayseri

The *kurultai* declares
Temujin Genghis Khan

Genghis Khan refuses homage to the
Jin emperor Zhangzong (1189–1208)

Aybak establishes the slave
sultanate of Delhi (1206–1290)

Genghis Khan campaigns against
Xiangzong of the Xi Xia (1207–1209)

Birth of Jalal-ud-din Rumi,
the Mevlana (1207–1273)

Mongol siege of Ningxia;
submission of Xiangzong

Accession of Iltutmish
(1210–1236) as sultan of Delhi

Genghis Khan campaigns
against the Jin Empire

Mongol army conquers the 16
prefectures of north China (1211–1214)

Muhammad Shah of Khwarazm defeats
Gurkhan Mozhu and takes Transoxiana

Kuchlug overthrows Mozhu
and rules the Kara-Khitans

Genghis Khan besieges
Zhongdu (future Beijing)

Jin emperor Xuanzong (1213–1224)
relocates his capital to Kaifeng

Mongol army captures
and sacks Zhongdu

Family of Rumi migrates
from Balkh to Baghdad

Mongol army under Jebe defeats
Kuchlug and ends Kara-Khitan khanate

Mongol conquest of Tarim Basin
and central Eurasian steppes

Muhammad Shan of Khwarazm
provokes war with Genghis Khan

Genghis Khan wages campaign against
Muhammad Shah (1219–1220)

Mongol conquest of Transoxiana;
flight of Muhammad Shah

Genghis Khan sacks Bukhara
and Samarkand

Death of Muhammad Shah in exile

Sübetei and Jebe command Mongol
western expedition (1220–1223)

Siege of Urgench: quarrel
between Jochi and Chagatai

Genghis Khan invades Khurasan;
Mongols sack Merv and Nishapur

Jalal al-Din rallies Khwarazmian
forces in India

Sübetei and Jebe ravage
Armenia and Georgia

Genghis Khan invades India and
defeats Jalal al-Din near Multan

Meeting of Genghis Khan and
Daoist sage Qiu Chuji

Genghis Khan orders Mongol rule
in Khurasan and Transoxiana

Sübetei and Jebe cross the Derbent Pass
and invade the Pontic-Caspian steppes

Genghis Khan withdraws to Mongolia

Sübetei and Jebe defeat the Russian-
Cuman army at the Battle of Kalka

Family of Rumi settles in
Karaman, Anatolia

Death of Jochi; Batu assigned the
Western *ulus* (future Golden Horde)

Death of Genghis Khan: regency
and succession crisis (1227–1229)

Partition of Mongol Empire among
Ögödei, Chagatai, and Batu

Family of Rumi settles in Konya
and establishes medrese

Ögödei (1229–1241) elected
as Great Khan by *kurultai*

Ögödei initiates the conquest of
the Jin Empire (1229–1235)

Rumi succeeds to family medrese
at Konya

Rumi reorganizes Maulawiyah
order (whirling deverishes)

Rumi hailed Mevlana

Beginning of the Islamization
of Anatolia

Ögödei and Song emperor
Ningzong (1194–1224) agree
to partition the Jin Empire

Mongols invade Sichaun (Szechwan)

Ögödei ends the Jin Empire

The *kurultai* approves the
conquest of the west by Batu

Timeline

Batu subdues the Kipchak
Turks and secures the lower
Volga steppes as his base

Batu subdues the Volga Bulgars

Accession of Sultana Radiyya
Begum (1236–1240) at Delhi

Civil wars in the Delhi sultanate

Accession of Sultan Kaykubad
(1219–1236) of Konya

Height of the sultanate of Konya

Batu invades Russia and sacks
Ryazan and Moscow

Kay-Khusraw II (1237–1246) seizes
the throne of the sultan of Konya

Kay-Khusraw II seeks to subdue the
Turkmen tribes of eastern Anatolia

Batu captures and sacks
Vladimir-Suzdal

Batu defeats and slays
Yuri II of Vladimir-Suzdal
(1212–1238) at the Sit River

Mongol army devastates southern
Russia, sacking Rostov and Yaroslavl

Mongol army subdues the Cumans
and ravages the Crimea (1238–1239)

Turkish tribes rebel under Baba Ishak
(1239–1242) against Kay-Khusraw II

Turkish rebels appeal to Mongol
general Baiju in Iran

Batu captures and sacks Kiev;
Batu declares war against
King Bela IV of Hungary

Mongol army invades Tibet; sack of
Rwa-sgeng and submission of Tibetans

Batu campaigns against
Poland and Hungary

Battle of Chmielik: Mongols
defeat Duke Boleslav V of
Cracow (1243–1279)

Battle of Liegnitz: Mongols annihilate
the army of Duke Henry II of Silesia

Battle of Mohi: Batu defeats
King Bela IV of Hungary

Mongols ravage Hungary and Croatia
and withdraw to lower Volga

Mongols invade northern
India and sack Lahore

Death of Great Khan Ögödei and
regency of Töregene (1241–1246)

Baiju and the Mongol army in
Iran invade eastern Anatolia

Battle of Köse Dağ: Mongol general
Baiju defeats Sultan Kay-Khusraw II

Sultanate of Konya submits to
Mongol rule

Election of Güyük as Great
Khan (1246–1248)

Mission of papal envoy Giovanni
da Plan del Carpini (1246–1247)

Death of Great Khan Güyük:
succession crisis

Regency of Sorghaghtani Beki,
widow of Tolui (1248–1251)

Marco, Niccolo, and Matteo
Polo journey to court of Kublai
Khan (1251–1257)

Kublai Khan, as deputy of Möngke,
conquers the Dali kingdom

King Louis IX of France sends William
of Rubruck as envoy to Khan Möngke

Mongol conquest of Yunnan
and Annan (North Vietnam)

Hulagu and Mongol army invade Iran

Mongol capture and destruction of
Alamut, stronghold of the Assassins

Berke succeeds to the Western
ulus (Golden Horde)

Western Mongols embrace Islam

Möngke and Kublai Khan
invade Song China

Hulagu sacks Baghdad: end
of the Abbasid caliphate

Hulagu conquers the
al-Jazirah and the Levant

Submissions of Prince Bohemond VI of
Antioch and Armenian King Hethoum I

Death of Great Khan Möngke; Arigh
Böke elected Great Khan by *kurultai*

Mongol army in China acclaims
Kublai Khan Great Khan

Outbreak of civil war in the
Mongol Empire (1260–1263)

Kublai Khan appoints Drogön
Chögyal Phagpa "minister of Tibet"

Drogön Chögyal Phagpa commissioned
to create script for Mongolians

Hulagu sacks Aleppo and Damascus

Hulagu retires from Syria to Azerbaijan

Battle of Ain Jalut: Mamluk
sultan Qutuz defeats Mongol
army under Kitbuka

Baybars (1260–1277) murders Qutuz
and is proclaimed Mamluk sultan

Alliance of Khan Berke and
Sultan Baybars against Hulagu

Kublai Khan invests Hulagu with the
ilkhanate in Iran and Transoxiana

Battle of Shimultai: Kublai Khan
decisively defeats Arigh Böke

Surrender of Arigh Böke;
end of Mongol civil war

Kublai Khan reorders the
Mongol Empire (1263–1268)

Death of Hulagu: accession of
Ilkhan Abaqa (1265–1282)

Kublai Khan recognizes Barak
(1266–1271) as Chagataid Khan

War between Barak and Kaidu
over central Asia (1266–1267)

Kaidu, grandson of Ögödei, seizes
power in the Altai Mountains

Kaidu defies Kublai Khan and
Temür Khan (1266–1301)

Barak and Ilkhan Aqaba
(1265–1282) battle for Transoxiana

Kublai Khan invades Song China

Desultory fighting along the
Yangtze River (1268–1273)

Mongols besiege fortresses at
Xianyang and Fengcheng

Kublai Khan claims the
mandate of heaven and takes the
Chinese throne name Shizu

Establishment of the Yuan
Dynasty (1271–1368)

Mongols capture Fengcheng

Fall of Xianyang: collapse of
Song resistance (1273–1275)

First Mongol expedition against Japan

Surrender of Song court at the
capital of Linan (Hangzhou)

Battle of Yamen: defeat
of the Song army

Second Mongol expedition
against Japan

Appointment of Bolad Aqa as
ilkhanate fiscal minister (1285–1313)

Jalal-ad-Din Firuz Shah II (1290–1296)
overthrows the slave sultanate

Establishment of the Khalji
sultans of Delhi

Departure of Marco, Niccole, and
Matteo Polo to ilkhanate court

Mongol invasion of Java (1292–1293)

Death of Kublai Khan; Temür Khan
(1294–1307) succeeds as Great Khan

Temür Khan renounces Yuan
control over the Tarim basin

Ilkhan Mahmud Ghazan
(1205–1304) coverts to Islam

Marco, Niccole, and Matteo
Polo reach Venice

Accession of Ala-ad-Din
Muhammad Shah I (1296–1316)

Height of the Khalji sultanate of Delhi

Marco Polo, in prison, dictates
Livres des merveilles du monde

1300–1350...................................... Malik Kafir commands Khalji
raid into southern India

Accession of Ilkhan Abu
Sa'id (1317–1335)

Transformation of ilkhanate
into a Muslim state

Tughluq seizes power in Delhi;
Ghiyath-ad-Din Tughluq
Shah (1320–1325)

Establishment of the Tughluq
sultanate of Delhi (1320–1414)

Khan Tamashinin (1226–1334)
succeeds to Chagataid khanate

Khan Tamashinin embraces Islam

Death of Ilkhan Abu Sa'id (1317–
1335), last effective ilkhan of Iran

Fragmenting and collapse of the
ilkhanate of Iran (1335–1353)

Birth of Tamerlane (Timur)

Death of Khan Qazan (1343–1346),
last effective Chagataid khan

Division of Chagataid khanate

Tribal warfare on the central Eurasian
steppes and Transoxiana (1347–1370)

1350–1400... Division of the western Mongol *ulus*
into the White and Blue Hordes

Hongwu (1368–1396) captures
Dadu and expels Khan Toghan
Temür from China

End of Mongol rule (Yuan
Dynasty) in China

Emperor Hongwu establishes the
Ming Dynasty (1368–1644)

Tamerlane crowned Great
Emir at Samarkand

Tamerlane subjects Khwarazm

Tamerlane campaigns in Moghulistan
(Chagataid central Asia)

Civil war on the western Eurasian
Steppes (White and Blue Hordes)

Khan Urus expels Tokhtamish

Tokhtamish flees Saray and is
received by Tamerlane

Tokhatmish, with Tamerlane's
assistance, crowned khan
of the White Horde

Tokhatmish unites White and Blue
Hordes into the Golden Horde

Tamerlane sacks the city of
Urganch in Khwarazm

Battle of Kulikovo Field: Grand
Prince Dmitri Ivanovich (1359–1389)
annihilates a Mongol army

Tokhatmish is received as khan of the
western Mongol *ulus* (Golden Horde)

Tamerlane subjects Khurasan
and Afghanistan

Tokhatmish sacks Moscow and Ryazan:
Russian princes submit to Tokhatmish

Tamerlane launches campaign into
Seistan and Kandahar (1383–1386)

Tamerlane sacks Herat

Tokhatmish declares war against
Tamerlane and sacks Tabriz, Iran

Tamerlane initiates campaign to
conquer Iran (1386–1388)

Tokhatmish invades Khurasan, besieges
Herat, and promotes rebellion in Iran

Tamerlane expels Tokhatmish
and sacks Isfahan

Tamerlane crushes revolts in
Khurasan and Moghulistan

Tamerlane leads first campaign
against Tokhatmish

Timeline

Tamerlane defeats Tokhatmish
at the Battle of Kunduzcha

Tamerlane wages his great
western campaign

Tamerlane overruns Iran and
receives the surrender of Baghdad

Mamluk sultan of Egypt Barkuk
provokes war with Tamerlane

Sultan Barkuk and Tokhatmish
conclude an alliance against Tamerlane

Tamerlane conquers
Armenia and Georgia

Tokhatmish raids into northwestern Iran

Battle of Terek: Tamerlane
decisively defeats Tokhatmish

Tamerlane sacks Saray and
ravages the Golden Horde

Tamerlane celebrates his
triumphs at Samarkand

Ottoman sultan Beyezid I defeats
Crusaders at the Battle of Nicopois

Tamerlane invades northern India

Battle of Delhi; Tamerlane
captures and sacks Delhi

Tamerlane returns to Samarkand
and initiates building program

Tamerlane leads second
western campaign

Ottoman sultan Beyezid besieges
Constantinople (1399–1402)

Tamerlane invades eastern Asia
Minor and sacks Sivas

Tamerlane invades northern
Syria and sacks Aleppo

Tamerlane besieges and
sacks Damascus

Meeting of Tamerlane and
Arab historian Ibn Khaldun

Tamerlane invades Asia Minor

Battle of Angora: Tamerlane defeats
and captures Ottoman sultan Beyezid I

Tamerlane initiates new building
projects at Samarkand

Arrival of Ruy Gonzalez de Clavijo,
ambassador from Castile

Tamerlane declares wars on Ming
emperor Yongle (1402–1424) of China

Tamerlane dies at Otrar on
campaign against Ming China

Western expedition of Ma Huan
and the fleet of Ming China

1450–1500...................................... Ottoman sultan Mehmet II
captures Constantinople

Foundation of the Ottoman
Empire (the Porte)

Grand Prince Ivan III of
Moscow defeats Khan Ahmet
of the Golden Horde

Muscovite army occupies Saray,
capital of the Golden Horde

Ivan III ends the "Mongol yoke"

Birth of Zahir ud-din Muhammad
Bābur, future Mughal emperor

Bābur succeeds as khan of the
Turco-Mongol tribes of Ferghana

1500–1550...................................... Shah Ismail I (1501–1524) founds
the Safavid Shi'ite state in Iran

Muhammad Shaybani of the Uzbeks
defeats Bābur at Samarkand

Bābur secures and rules from Kabul
as a vassal of Shah Ismail I

Shah Ismail I defeats and
slays Muhammad Shaybani
at the Battle of Merv

Ottoman sultan Selim I defeats Shah
Ismail I at the Battle of Chaldarin

Ottoman army occupies Tabriz

Bābur declares war on the Lodi sultan
Ibrahim (1517–1526) of Delhi

First Battle of Panipat: Bābur defeats
Lodi army and occupies Delhi

Foundation of Mughal Empire

Battle of Khanwa: Bābur
defeats the Rajput army under
Rana Sanga (1509–1527)

Death of Bābur; accession of
Humayun (1530–1539; 1555–
1556), as Mughal emperor

Sher Khan defeats Humayun
at the Battle of Chausa

Sher Khan occupies Bengal and
is declared shah of Delhi

Humayun flees to Safavid court

1550–1600...................................... Ivan IV, "the Terrible," conquers the
khanate of Kazan on the middle Volga

Humayun returns to India and
establishes the Mughal Empire

Death of Humayun and accession of
Akbar (1556–1605) as Mughal emperor

Timeline

Ivan the Terrible conquers
the khanate of Astrakhan

Akbar imposes his authority over
Bengal and northern India

Akbar secures Kabul, and the Panthan
tribes to submit to Mughal rule

1600–1700...................................... Death of Akbar and accession
of Jahangir (1605–1627)
as Mughal emperor

Accession of Shah Jahan as
Mughal emperor (1628–1658)

Aurangzeb overthrows his father, Shan
Jahan, and is declared Mughal emperor

Reign of Aurangzeb (1658–1707);
height of Mughal Empire

Treaty of Nerchinsk; Tsar Peter the
Great (1682–1725) and the Qing
emperor Kangxi of China (1661–1721)
partition the Eurasian steppes

Glossary

Abbasid caliphate: The hereditary dynasty of caliphs (749–1258) established by as-Saffah (r. 750–754) and, from 762 on, resident at Baghdad. Hulagu ended the dynasty with the sack of Baghdad in 1258.

Achaemenid: The royal family of the great kings of Persia (559–329 B.C.).

Ahura Mazda: The supreme god of creation in Zoroastrianism.

airak: Mongolian fermented mare's milk; nomadic beverage of choice.

Alani: Sarmatians who settled on the steppes north of the Caucasus in the 1st century B.C. In A.D. 375, many Alani submitted to the Huns, while others, along with Goths, migrated west. The Alani entered the Roman Empire as allies of the Vandals in 406–407.

Altaic languages: A family of languages with common agglutinative grammar and syntax, vowel harmony, and vocabulary. The major branches are Turkic, Mongolian, and Tungusic; Korean and Japanese may also be branches of this language family.

Amber Road: Overland routes between the lands of the Baltic and the Mediterranean and Black seas since the Bronze Age (2200–1500 B.C.), over which amber and the products of the northern forests and Arctic lands were exported south. Pliny the Elder (23–79) first described the route in his *Natural History*.

An Lushan Rebellion: A rebellion (755–762) raised by the Tang general An Lushan against the emperor Xuanzong (712–756). The revolt, even though it failed, wrought great destruction throughout China and compelled the emperor to withdraw garrisons from the Tarim Basin.

Anatolian languages: The first language family to diverge from Proto-Indo-European (4000–3800 B.C.). Speakers of these languages who migrated into Asia Minor circa 2500–2300 B.C. were ancestors of those speaking Hittite, Luwian, and Palaic.

anda: Sworn brothers in Turkish and Mongolian society.

Arsacid: The royal family of the kings of Parthia (246 B.C.– 227 A.D.).

Aryavarta: The "Aryan homeland," which comprises the lands of the upper Indus and Ganges rivers that are home to the sacred cities of Hinduism.

Aryan: From Sanskrit *arya*, meaning "noble": (1) designation of related languages that has been replaced by Indo-European languages; (2) speakers of Sanskrit who entered India circa 1500–1000 B.C.

Ashina: The royal clan among the Gök Turks; descended from the brothers Bumin and Istami.

atman: In Hinduism, the imperishable soul, subject to reincarnation by the rule of *dharma* until enlightenment, when it achieves union with the universal soul (*brahman*).

Avars: Peoples who founded the first confederation of Turkish-speaking tribes on the eastern Eurasian steppe (330–551). In 551–552, Bumin of the Gök Turks overthrew the Avars, who then migrated west to establish a new khaganate on the Pannonian plains (580–796).

Avesta: The compilation of the sacred texts of Zoroastrianism. The Persian language of the texts, known as Avestan, shares close similarities to the Sanskrit of the Rigveda.

Bactria: Today, northern Afghanistan, this is a fertile region of the upper Oxus River. Its principal city, Bactra, was the nexus of routes of the Silk Road between central Asia and India.

Balghasun: Capital of the Uighur khaganate (744–840). The city was sacked by the rebel Kyrgyz tribes and abandoned in 840.

Bamiyan Buddhas: Two colossal statues (created in 507 and 554) carved out of rock in the Bamiyan valley, 140 miles northwest of Kabul. They were destroyed by the Taliban in March 2001.

bashlyk: The distinctive nomadic felt cap.

BMAC: Bactria-Margiana Archaeological Complex (2300–1700 B.C.); the culture centered on the lower Oxus valley that was likely the common homeland to the Indo-Iranian speakers.

brahman: The universal soul of Hinduism to which the enlightened *atman* will return upon *moksha*.

Brahmi: The oldest alphabetic script employed in India, based on Aramaic scripts of the Near East. The earliest inscriptions date from the reign of Ashoka (268–232 B.C).

Brahmin: In Hinduism, the first or priestly caste; see *varna*.

caliph: Ruler of the Muslim community. In 661, Muawiya established the first line of hereditary caliphs.

caravansary: Walled quarters, stables, and storage rooms constructed and maintained by the Turkish Muslim rulers for the benefit of caravans. The upkeep of the caravansary was paid by the profits of a foundation.

cataphracti: Heavily armored shock cavalry wearing chain mail or lamellar armor. This heavy cavalry, first attested among the Sarmatians, was adopted by the Romans during the reign of Hadrian (117–138).

Cathay: Medieval European name for China; it was derived from a misunderstanding of Khitan, Mongolian-speaking nomadic rulers of northern China who ruled as the Liao Dynasty (907–1125).

centum languages: Western language families that evolved out of Proto-Indo-European in 3000–2500 B.C. These language families shared common changes in sound and morphology. They include the language families of Celtic, Italic, Germanic, and Balkan Indo-European languages (the putative mother language for later Greek, Macedonian, Phrygian, Illyro-Thracian languages, and possibly, Armenian).

Chagatais: Descendants of Khan Chagatai (1226–1242), second son of Genghis Khan; they were rulers of the central Asian steppes and Transoxania.

chanyu: Meaning "son of endless sky," this was the title of the ruler of the Xiongnu reported by Han and Song Chinese sources. In the early 5th century, the title was abandoned, and steppe nomadic rulers henceforth styled themselves as khan.

Chihilgan: Meaning "The Forty," the Turkish military elite who dominated the Delhi sultanate in 1240–1290.

Chingisids: Descendants of Genghis Khan (1206–1227).

Cumans: Western Turkish-speaking nomads and scions of the Kipchak Turks, who migrated from the central Asian steppes into the Pontic-Caspian steppes in the 11th century.

cuneiform: The first writing system, devised by the Sumerians circa 3500–3100 B.C. The wedge-shaped writing was inscribed by a stylus on wet clay.

devsirme: The Ottoman levy of Christian youths who were converted to Islam and enrolled in the Ottoman sultan's corps of Janissaries.

dharma: In Hinduism, the moral law that dictates the cycle of reincarnation.

dhimmi: In Islam, members of protected religious communities of the book, who practiced their faith by payment of a special tax. They were originally Jews and Christians; later, Sabians (polytheists of Harran) and Zoroastrians were so protected.

digvijaya: The ceremonial royal progress made by an Indian maharaja atop an elephant.

Doab: The fertile lands between the Punjab and the upper Ganges and Yamuna rivers; Delhi and Agra are in the Doab.

Fatimid caliphate: Shi'ite caliphs (909–1171) who claimed descent from Fatimah, daughter of the prophet Muhammad and wife of Caliph Ali. In 969, the Fatimid caliphs ruled from Cairo and protected the holy cities of Medina and Mecca.

Finno-Ugric languages: A family of the Altaic languages, which includes Magyar (Hungarian), Estonian, Finnish, and the Samoyedic languages of Siberia.

Five Dynasties; Ten Kingdoms: Rival kingdoms (907–960) ruling in China between the Tang (618–907) and Song (960–1279) dynasties.

foederati: Barbarian military units commanded by their own leaders who fought as allies of the Roman Empire in the later 4th and 5th centuries.

Gansu Corridor: The narrow zone between the Eurasian steppe and the Tibetan highlands that connects China with the Tarim Basin.

ger: Portable home on wheels made of felt stretched over a lattice frame. See **yurt**.

ghazi: The epitome of the heroic nomadic warrior, prized by Turks.

Ghaznavid: A dynasty of Turkish slave emirs (963–1186), who ruled from Ghazna (Afghanistan) over Transoxania and Iran and raided northern India.

ghulam, ghilman (pl.): Arabic word for slave soldiers, usually of Turkish origin. See **Mamluk**.

Ghurid sultans: Leaders (1148–1210) of Iranian origin, who used Turkish Mamluks and tribal regiments to establish the first Muslim sultanate in northern India. They clashed with the rival Khwarezm shahs for control of Transoxania and Iran.

Ghuzz Turks: Speakers of western Turkish or Oghuz languages who emerged on the central Asian steppes between the 9th and 11th centuries. They included Seljuk Turks, Cumans, and Kipchak Turks.

Gog and Magog: Figures (or nations) in the Bible and the Qur'an, whose arrival marked the great wars leading to the final days of the Apocalypse. Since the 5th century, Christian and, later, Muslim writers identified them with the nomadic invaders of the Eurasian steppes.

Gök Turks: The "Celestial Turks" who overthrew the Avar khanate in 551–552. Khan Bumin established the senior Gök Turk khaganate (551–744). His brother Istami (551–575) established the western Turkish khaganate (553–659) on the central and western Eurasian steppe. In 681, after ending Tang Chinese overlordship, the western khaganate was reconstituted as the Confederation of the Ten Arrows.

Golden Horde: The western part of the Mongol Empire (1240–1502), established by Khan Batu; see also **Jochids**.

Gupta Empire: The second great empire of India (320–550), founded by Chandra Gupta I (319–335). The Gupta emperors patronized Sanskrit letters and Hinduism and ended Kushan rule in northern India.

Han Dynasty: Rulers of imperial China as the Former or Western Han (206 B.C.–9 A.D.) and then as the restored Later or Eastern Han (25–220). The usurper Wang Mang, who overthrew the Former Han Dynasty, failed to establish his own Xin Dynasty (9–25).

Hephthalites: The "White Huns" were Tocharian-speaking nomads, driven from the eastern Eurasian steppe by the northern Wei emperors of China and Avar khagans. They founded an empire (408–670) encompassing the western Tarim Basin, Transoxania, and northern India.

Hexi Corridor: See **Gansu Corridor**.

Hinayana Buddhism: The "Lesser Wheel," which includes Buddhist ascetics who rejected the doctrines of Mahayana Buddhism and adhered more closely to the teachings of Siddhartha Gautama (563–483 B.C.).

Huns: Altaic-speaking nomads who conquered the Pontic-Caspian steppes circa 375 and, under Attila, forged a barbarian empire from the Rhine to the Volga that challenged the Roman Empire. The Huns were probably descendants of subject or allied tribes of the northern Xiongnu.

ilkhan: Meaning "loyal khan," the title granted by Kublai Khan to his brother Hulagu in 1260. It was carried by his descendants, the Ilkhanids (1265–1353), who ruled over Iran, Iraq, and Transoxania.

Indo-Scythians: See **Sacae**.

iqta: A military tenure granted to Muslim soldiers by the sultans of Delhi.

Jade Gate: The name for the strategic Yumen Pass on the Silk Road that connected the Tarim Basin to China.

Jazyges: Sarmatians who settled as allies of Rome on the eastern Pannonian grasslands west of Dacia in the mid-1st century.

jihad: In Islam, "holy war."

Jin Dynasty: See **Jurchens**.

jinshi: The highest level of mandarin officials in the Song examination system (960–1279).

Jochids: Descendants of Jochi (1181–1227), the first son of Genghis Khan. Jochi's son Batu founded the western part of the Mongol Empire, or Golden Horde.

Jurchens: Tungusic-speaking peoples of Manchuria who overthrew their overlords and ruled northern China under the Chinese dynastic name Jin, or

"Golden" (1115–1234). The Jurchen emperors exercised a loose hegemony over the Mongol tribes.

Karakhanid: A Turkish confederation on the central Asian steppes that ruled Transoxania from Kashgar and Samarkand (840–1212). They converted to Islam in 934.

Kara-Khitans: Sinicized Khitans (1123–1218) who migrated to the central Asian steppes and, thus, escaped the rule of the Jurchens. In 1141, the Kara-Khitans defeated the Karakhanids near Samarkand—a victory that gave rise to the legend of Prester John. Also called the western Liao; see also **Khitans**.

Karakorum: Located on the Orkhon River, the political capital of the Mongol Empire in 1225–1260.

karma: In Hinduism and Buddhism, the individual merit acquired by an individual through meritorious deeds.

kashuik: The bodyguard of 10,000 of the Great Khan of the Mongols.

khagan: Meaning "khan of khans," a Turkish term denoting a great royal figure ruling over many subordinate khans.

Khalji sultanate: The second Persian-speaking dynasty of Turkish sultans in northern India (1290–1320).

khan: Turko-Mongolian royal title, meaning "king."

Kharoshti: Northern Indian alphabet, based on the Aramaic alphabet of the Near East, used to write Sanskrit and vernaculars of Sanskrit.

khatun: Mongolian queen, meaning "lady."

Khazars: Members of the Ashina clan and western Turkish khaganate, who established their own khaganate (c. 670–967) over the Pontic-Caspian steppes. The Khazar court converted to Judaism in the late 8th century. Circa

965–967, the Khazar capital was sacked by Prince Svyatoslav of Kiev and the Pechenegs.

Khitans: Mongol-speaking conquerors who ruled northern China under the Chinese dynastic name of Liao (907–1125). They were overthrown by their vassals, the Jurchens.

Khwarezm: Fertile delta lands of the lower Oxus River, flowing into the Aral Sea; the land has been home to important caravan cities since the 5th century B.C.

Khwarezmian shahs: Persian-speaking Sunni Muslim rulers appointed as governors of Khwarezm by the Seljuk sultans (1077–1231). After 1156, the Khwarezmian shahs clashed with the Ghurids over domination of former Ghaznavid lands in Iran and Transoxania.

Kipchak Turks: Ghuzz or western Turkish-speaking nomads who dominated the central Asian steppes in the 11th through 13th centuries. They submitted to Mongol Khan Batu in 1238–1241 and constituted the majority of tribes of the Golden Horde.

Kshatriya: In Hinduism, the caste of warriors.

kurgan: A stone-and-earth tumulus raised as monumental grave on the Pontic-Caspian steppes and central Asian steppes from the Bronze Age to the 13th century A.D. The kurgans of Scythians, between the 6th and 4th centuries B.C., have yielded the richest burial goods.

kurultai: The national council of Mongols summoned to elect the khan or to declare war or conclude a peace.

Kushans: Tocharian speakers who forged an empire embracing the central Asian steppes, Transoxania, and northern India (30–230). They promoted Buddhism and trade along the Silk Road. See also **Yuezhi**.

lamellar armor: Armor of overlapping plates sewed together and often worn as a second layer of protection over chain mail armor.

Liao Dynasty: See **Khitans**.

limes: Meaning "path," the word originally designated a Roman military highway. The term came to designate the political and cultural boundary between imperial Rome and the foreign peoples.

magister militum: "Master of the soldiers," the supreme commander of field armies in the Roman Empire. From the reign of Constantine I (306–337), commanders of the cavalry and infantry commanded regional field armies. After 395, their supreme commander was designated *magister militum*, one for the western and one for the eastern Roman Empire.

Magyars: Finno-Ugric nomads who migrated from the Siberian forests east of the Urals to the Pontic-Caspian steppes in the 9th century. In 896, they settled on the Pannonian grasslands in 896; they are the ancestors of the Hungarians.

Mahayana Buddhism: The "Greater Wheel" was the school of Buddhism that emerged in India in the 1st century B.C., stressing the divine status of the Buddha. The schools of Mahayana Buddhism today are in East Asia (Tibet, Mongolia, China, Korea, and Japan).

Mamluk: From the Arabic for "servant": (1) Turkish slave soldier in the Islamic world; (2) dynasty of Turkish slave soldiers that ruled Egypt (1250–1517); (3) dynasty of Turkish slave soldiers that ruled the Delhi sultanate (1206–1290).

Manichaeism: The dualist, monotheistic faith proclaimed by the prophet Mani in Sassanid Mesopotamia. The faith was popular among Sogdian merchants of the Silk Road; the khagan of the Uighurs converted to Manichaeism in 763.

Mauryan Empire: The first empire of India (322–185 B.C.), established by Chandra Gupta (320–298 B.C.). The emperor Ashoka (268–232 B.C.) converted to Buddhism.

Mawarannahr: "Land beyond the river," the Arabic name for Transoxania.

maya: In Hinduism, the illusion of the physical world.

Mcluhha: The Sumerian name for the earliest urban civilization of India, known as the Indus Valley civilization (2600–1700 B.C.).

Ming Dynasty: Founded by Emperor Hongwu (1368–1398), who expelled the Mongols, the Ming Dynasty (1368–1644) was the last native dynasty of imperial China.

Mitanni: Indo-Aryan speakers who migrated from Transoxania into northern Mesopotamia in the 16th century B.C., where they established a kingdom over Hurrian- and Amorite-speaking populations. Their language is closely related to Sanskrit and Avestan Iranian.

moksha: The liberation of an enlightened Hindu who is freed from the cycle of rebirths, according to *dharma*.

Mughal Empire: The last Muslim empire (1526–1857) in India; established by Bābur (1526–1530), a descendant of both Genghis Khan and Tamerlane.

muqti: A military governor of the Delhi sultanate who held a military tenure in lieu of a salary.

Nestorian Christianity: The Christian church that followed the teachings of Patriarch Nestorius of Constantinople (429–431), who taught that Mary gave birth only to the man Jesus rather than man and God. The Nestorians, condemned at the Third Ecumenical Council (431), spread their faith across the Silk Road, converting Turkish and Mongol tribes.

northern Wei Dynasty: Sinicized nomadic rulers (386–535) of northern China and the Gansu Corridor. They promoted Buddhism along the Silk Road. They were Turkish-speaking Tuoba, the royal clan of the Xianbei tribes.

oracle bones: Inscribed divination bones of the Shang Dynasty (1600–1046); they are the first examples of Chinese writing.

ordu: Turko-Mongolian army or military encampment.

Orkhon inscriptions: The earliest memorial inscriptions in Turkish (722); written in a distinct runic alphabet.

Parthians: An Iranian-speaking tribe melded into a kingdom, and then a Near East empire of the Arsacid kings (246 B.C.–227 A.D.).

Pechenegs: Turkish-speaking tribes whose confederation dominated the Pontic-Caspian steppes west of the Don River from circa 860 to 1091.

Prakrit: The vernacular language of India that evolved out of Sanskrit after 600 B.C. Buddhist texts were written or translated into Prakrit.

Proto-Indo-European (PIE): The reconstructed mother language of the Indo-European languages, circa 6000–5000 B.C.

Qin Dynasty: The dynasty (221–206 B.C.) founded by Shihuangdi (257–210 B.C.), when he unified China in 221 B.C.

Qing Dynasty: The last imperial dynasty of China, founded by the Manchu conquerors (1644–1911).

Qutb Minar: Built by Sultan Aybak of Delhi in 1198, it is the largest minaret in India.

Quwat ul Islam: Meaning "Might of Islam," the mosque outside of Delhi built from plundered architectural elements of Hindu and Jain temples. It was ordered by Sultan Aybak in 1193.

Rabatak: The site in Afghanistan where a Kushan royal inscription in the Bactrian language was discovered in 1993. The Kushan emperor Kanishka I (127–147) gives his genealogy and names the tutelary gods of the empire.

Rajputs: "Sons of the king"; the Kshatriya or warrior caste who dominated western India between the 9th and 12th centuries. They were later accommodated by the Mughal emperors.

rammed earth: A construction technique using earth, gravel, lime, and clay. The Qin and Han emperors employed this method to build the Great Wall. The construction is simple but labor intensive.

Rashidun caliphs: The first four elected caliphs from among the immediate associates of Muhammad: Abu Bakr (632–634), Umar (634–644), Uthman (644–656), and Ali (656–661).

Rashtrakuta: Prakrit-speaking kings who united most of southern and central India (753–982); they favored Hinduism.

Rigveda: The earliest religious texts of Hinduism. The hymns, written in Sanskrit, have been dated as early as 1500 B.C. and as late as 600 B.C.

Roxolani: Sarmatians who settled on the grasslands between the Carpathian Mountains and the Black Sea in the 1st century.

Sacae: An eastern branch of the Scythians dwelling on the central Asian steppes. In 145–135 B.C., they migrated across Sogdiana and Bactria into the Helmand Valley, then via the Bolan Pass into India in the early 1st century B.C., where they were known as the Indo-Scythians.

Safavids: The dynasty of the Shi'ite shahs of Iran (1501–1732), rivals to the Ottoman sultans.

Samanid: The family of Iranian emirs (819–1005) who ruled from Bukhara, eastern Iran, and Transoxania as the representatives of the Abbasid caliphate. They defined the visual arts and letters of eastern Islam.

sangha: The community of Buddhist believers (laity and ascetics) established by Siddhartha Gautama (563–483 B.C.).

Sanskrit: The sacred literary language of Hinduism.

Sarmatians: Iranian-speaking nomads who succeeded the Scythians on the Pontic-Caspian steppes between the 3rd century B.C. and the 3rd century A.D. The tribes included the Alani, Roxolani, and Jazyges.

Sassanid: The dynasty of Zoroastrian shahs of the neo-Persian Empire (227–651).

satem languages: The eastern branch of language families that evolved out of Proto-Indo-European circa 3000–2500 B.C. The language families share sound changes and morphology. These include the Balto-Slavic and Indo-Iranian language families.

satrapy: A province of the Persian Empire (550–329 B.C.) ruled by a satrap; Darius I (521–486 B.C.) organized the empire into 20 satrapies.

Scythians: The general name applied by classical Greeks to the Iranian-speaking nomads on the Eurasian steppe.

Seljuk Turks: Ghuzz or western Turks who founded the Seljuk sultanate (1055–1194) that revived the power of Abbasid caliphate. Seljuk Turks settled in Asia Minor after the Battle of Manzikert (1071).

Shah-nameh: "*Book of Kings*"; the Middle Persian national epic composed by Abu al-Qasem Mansur (c. 940–1020).

shaman: A mystic prized for insights gained by contact with the spiritual world through trances often induced by hallucinogens, notably hashish.

Shang Dynasty: The first historical dynasty of China (c. 1600–1046 B.C.), centered in the lower and middle Huang He (Yellow River).

Sharia: Muslim religious law based on the Koran.

Shi'ite: The sectarian school of Islam that desired a descendant of Ali (656–661) as the rightful caliph and, thus, upheld the authority of Ali.

Shudra: In Hinduism, the caste of laborers or peasants; see ***varna***.

Silk Road: The network of caravan routes across central Asia that linked China with Europe and the Mediterranean world. The German explorer Ferdinand von Richthofen coined the term in 1877.

Sogdiana: Lands of northern Transoxania and the Fergana Valley; the Sogdians spoke an eastern Iranian language that was long the commercial language of the Silk Road.

Song Dynasty: The Song Dynasty (960–1279) reunited most of China as the successors of the Tang emperors, promoted Confucian traditions, and perfected the bureaucratic state. The Khitans and, later, the Jurchens denied the Song the recovery of northern China.

spolia: Architectural elements or sculpture of older buildings recycled into new buildings.

Strategikon: Byzantine military manual, attributed to the emperor Maurice, with sound recommendations for countering nomadic cavalry.

Sufi: Muslim mystic who follows the Sunni tradition.

Sui Dynasty: The dynasty (581–618) that reunited China and founded the third great imperial order; immediately succeeded by the Tang Dynasty.

Sunni: "The orthodox"; Muslims who accepted the Umayyad caliphate of Muawiya (661–680). The majority of Muslims follow Sunni Islam and the authority of the Qur'an.

suren: The hereditary commander of the Drangiana and Arachosia (today, western Afghanistan and Pakistan). The suren had the right to crown the Arsacid king of Parthia.

sutra: A Buddhist sacred text of aphorisms.

taiga: Forest zones of Siberia.

Tang Dynasty: Founded by Emperor Gaozu, the Tang Dynasty (618–907) represented the greatest imperial family of classical China.

tantric: The higher moral and mystical interpretation of traditional village rites in either Hinduism or Buddhism.

Tarim Basin: An area that encompasses the valleys of the tributaries of the Tarim River between the Tien Shan and the Tibetan highlands. The central zone comprises the Taklamakan Desert, and the eastern end is dominated by the salt depression of the Lop Nur. Today known as Xinjiang or eastern Turkestan, the region was been home to caravan cities on the Silk Road.

Ten Arrows: See **Gök Turks**.

Tengri: The sky god and progenitor of humankind in Turkish and Mongol polytheism.

Three Kingdoms: The period of political division (220–280) in China after the fall of the eastern Han Dynasty.

Tien Shan: "Celestial Mountains" that define the northern boundary of the Tarim Basin (today Xinjiang).

Timurids: Descendants of Tamerlane (1370–1405), who ruled Iran and Transoxania (1405–1506).

Tocharian: The name given to two, possibly three, related Indo-European languages spoken in the Tarim Basin and used to translate Buddhist texts between the 6th and 9th centuries. The ancestors of the Tocharians migrated from the original Indo-European homeland on the Pontic-Caspian steppes to the Altai Mountains and then the Tarim Basin in circa 3700–3500 B.C.

Toluids: Descendants of Tolui (1227–1229), the fourth son of Genghis Khan.

Transoxania: Lands between the Oxus and Jaxartes rivers; in antiquity, known as Bactria and Sogdiana.

Tughluq sultans: Members of the third dynasty of Turkish Muslim rulers in India (1320–1414).

tumen: Mongol military unit of 10,000 soldiers.

tundra: Arctic zones of Siberia.

Tungusic languages: A branch of the Altaic language family, today spoken in Manchuria and eastern Siberia.

türbe: Memorial tomb to a Muslim ruler or mentor.

Uighurs: Turkish-speaking nomads who founded the third Turkish confederation on the eastern Eurasian steppe (744–840). They converted to Manichaeism in 763.

ulema: The religious community of Muslim scholars who interpret Sharia.

ulus: The Turko-Mongolian nation, designating related tribes.

Umayyad caliphate: The first hereditary line of caliphs (661–750), established by Muawiya (661–680) and ruling from Damascus.

ummah: In Islam, the community of believers as proclaimed by the prophet Muhammad (575–634).

Upper Satrapies: The Greek designation of the satrapies of Bactria and Sogdiana (Transoxania) in the Achaemenid Empire of Persia (550–329 B.C.).

Vaishya: In Hinduism, the caste of merchants.

varna: From the Sanskrit for "outward appearance," any one of the original four castes of Indo-Aryan society described in the Rigveda: Brahmins (priests), Kshatriyas (warriors), Vaishyas (merchants), and Shudras (laborers). Only the first three castes were considered twice born; the Shudras represented the subjected populations.

vihara: Meaning "secluded place," the community of Buddhist ascetics.

Vikrama era: The era of reckoning from the year 57 B.C.; widely used by Buddhists in India and Nepal. The year 1 of the era was the accession date of Azes I (57–35 B.C.), king of the Sacae.

Warring States: Kingdoms in the period of political disunity in China following the collapse of effective rule by the Zhou Dynasty (481–221 B.C.).

western regions: Also called Xiyu, the designation by the Han and Tang emperors of their provinces in the Tarim Basin.

White Huns: See **Hephthalites**.

Xi Xia: Sinicized Tanguts who had settled in Gansu and western China in the 10th century as nominal vassals of the Song emperors. With Jingzong (1038–1048), Xi Xia monarchs ruled as Chinese-style emperors who favored Buddhism (1038–1227).

Xia Dynasty: The legendary first dynasty of China (c. 2100–1600 B.C.).

Xinjiang: Eastern Turkestan; see **Tarim Basin**.

Xiongnu: Altaic-speaking nomads who forged the first nomadic confederacy on the eastern Eurasian steppe. In 56–53 B.C., the Xiongnu divided into the southern and northern Xiongnu.

yabgu: The subordinate of a khan or khagan; among the Khazars, the leading commander of the army.

Yassa: Customary Mongol law codified by Genghis Khan; it exalted the authority of the khan over all other legal and religious authorities.

Yuan Dynasty: The Chinese dynasty adopted by Kublai Khan (1260–1294) and his successors who ruled China and Mongolia (1279–1368).

Yuezhi: The Chinese name for Tocharian-speaking nomads who dwelled on the central Asian steppes north of the Tarim Basin. In 155 B.C., the Xiongnu drove the Yuezhi west into Ferghana, where Zhang Qian visited them in 128 B.C. These Tocharian speakers, called Da Yuezhi ("Great Yuezhi") were the ancestors of the Kushans.

yurt: The residence and social bonds of the kinship group of a *ger*. See *ger*.

Zhou Dynasty: The second imperial dynasty of China (1045–256 B.C.), ruling in the early Iron Age. After 481 B.C., Zhou emperors lost control over their vassals, and China lapsed into the period of Warring States.

Zoroastrianism: The monotheistic religion of the Iranians, based on the teachings of Zoroaster, born circa 628 B.C. The Sassanid shahs favored Zoroastrianism as reformed in the 3rd century.

Biographical Notes

Abaoji (b. 872; r. 907–926): Emperor of Liao Dynasty; assumed the Chinese throne name Taizu. He was of the Yila tribe within the confederation of Khitans. In 904, he seized supreme power over the Khitans. In 907, he assumed the name and role of a Chinese emperor, conquering the 16 prefectures in northeastern China and the eastern Eurasian steppe. He established his Sinicized court at Shangjing.

Abd al-Malik (b. 646; r. 685–705): Umayyad caliph who imposed Arabic as the language of administration and forged the first Muslim administrative institutions. He appointed able governors who conquered Carthage in 698 and raided into Transoxania.

Abu Bakr (b. c. 573; r. 632–634): Caliph and friend and associate of Muhammad who succeeded as the first of the Rashidun caliphs after the prophet's death. His reign saw the unification of Arabia under the banner of Islam.

Aetius (d. 454): A *magister militum* (425–454) from a military family in Moesia. By his influence with King Rugila and, later, Attila, Aetius secured Hun *foederati* so that he dominated policy at the court of the western emperor Valentinian III. His policy of alliance with the Huns was ruined by the invasions of Attila in 451–452. In 454, Aetius was executed on grounds of treason.

Ahmad ibn Arabshah (1389–1450): Arabic historian; a native of Damascus who wrote a critical biography of Tamerlane in 1435. He visited the Timurid court at Samarkand, and he consulted Turkish and Persian sources and spoke to eyewitnesses. In his account, Tamerlane is depicted as a savage prince, deformed and spiteful, whose base birth was the reason he committed atrocities.

Akbar (b. 1542; r. 1556–1605): Third Mughal emperor; the son of Humayun. He fiscally and administratively organized the Mughal Empire, laying the foundations of the future British raj. A mystic, he sponsored his own syncretist solar cult of the ruler, Din-i Ilahi ("divine faith"). His personal beliefs and toleration of subjects of all faiths alienated the Sunni *ulema*, and his son and successor, Jahangir (1605–1627), returned to Sunni Islam.

Ala-ad-Din Muhammad Shah I (1296–1316): Khalji sultan of Delhi; greatly extended his sway over the Deccan. Malik Kafur, a Hindu convert to Islam and general, conducted audacious and destructive campaigns into the southern Deccan and Tamil Nadu in 1310–1311. Khalji raids ultimately led to the consolidation of the powerful Hindu kingdom of Vijayanagara (1336–1565) at Hampi.

Ala al-Din Muhammad (r. 1200–1220): Shah of Khwarezm; conquered Iran from the Seljuk Turks in 1205. By 1217, he had secured Transoxania, assumed the title shah, and extended his unwanted protection over the Abbasid caliph al-Nasir. In 1218, he provoked a war with Genghis Khan, who overran the Khwarezmian Empire in 1219–1220. Muhammad Shah died a fugitive on an island in the Caspian Sea near Abaskun.

al-Amin (b. 787; r. 809–813): Abbasid caliph; the unpopular son of Harun al-Rashid. He faced rebellions in Syria and Iraq. In 812–813, the Persian general Tahir ibn al-Husayn besieged Baghdad in the name of al-Mamun (813–833), half-brother of al-Amin. In 813, al-Amin was captured while escaping Baghdad and executed.

Alaric (395–410): King of the Visigoths; served under Theodosius I. Alaric, denied high command by the imperial government, led the Visigoths into Greece in 395–397 and then to Italy in 400–402. Flavius Stilicho checked Alaric until 408. In 410, Alaric sacked Rome in a bid to pressure the emperor Honorius for a command, but he died soon after.

Alexander III, the Great (b. 356 B.C., r. 336–323 B.C.): King of Macedon; son of Philip II (359–336 B.C.) and the Epirote princess Olympias (375–316 B.C.); arguably the greatest commander in history. In 334–329 B.C., he conquered the Achaemenid Empire and defeated the Great King Darius III of Persia (336–329 B.C.). He subdued Bactria and Sogdiana (Transoxania) in 329–327 B.C. and the Indus Valley in 327–325 B.C. Alexander defeated the nomadic Sacae, secured the Upper Satrapies (Bactria and Sogdiana), and established a frontier on the upper Jaxartes. His Greco-Macedonian military colonies in the Upper Satrapies were the basis for the Greco-Bactrian kingdom (c. 250–125 B.C.).

Alexius I Comnenus (b. 1056; r. 1081–1118): Byzantine emperor; seized power in the civil war of 1081 and founded the Comnenian Dynasty (1081–1185). He restored imperial power in western Asia Minor by summoning the First Crusade (1095–1099). He allied with the Cumans to destroy the Pechenegs, who had invaded Thrace, at the Battle of Levounion in 1091.

Al-Hajjaj (b. 661; r. 694–715): Umayyad governor of Khurasan; directed the Muslim conquests of Seistan, Baluchistan, and the Sind.

Ali ibn Abi Talib (b. c. 600; r. 656–661): Fourth of the Rashidun caliphs. Cousin of the prophet Muhammad, Ali married the prophet's only daughter, Fatimah (606–632). Ali was twice passed over for the caliphate. As caliph in 656, he faced opposition from Muawiya in the first Muslim civil war. Ali was slain by sectarian extremists, and in later Shi'ite theology, he was elevated to prophetic status almost on par with Muhammad.

al-Mamun (b. 786; 813–833): Abbasid caliph; son of Harun al-Rashid. In 813, he defeated his half-brother al-Amin and gained the throne. But he surrendered control over Khurasan and the northeastern frontier to Tahir ibn al-Husayn.

al-Mansur (754–775): Second Abbasid caliph; dedicated Baghdad as the new capital in 762 and shifted the locus of Islamic civilization to Iran and Transoxania.

Almish Yiltawar (c. 900–940): Khagan of the Volga Bulgars. Converted to Islam to obtain Abbasid support so that he could renounce his allegiance to the Khazars. In 921–922, he was visited by Ahmad ibn Fadlan, envoy of the Abbasid caliph al-Muqtadir (908–932).

al-Mutasim (833–842): Abbasid caliph. Waged prestige campaigns against the Byzantine Empire. He reformed the army, recruiting a bodyguard of 10,000 Turkish slave soldiers, as well as allied and mercenary Turkish tribal regiments of horse archers.

al-Mustasim Billah (b. 1213; r. 1242–1258): Last Abbasid caliph. Sought to restore the power and authority of the Abbasid state. He blundered into a war against the Mongols. He was slain and his capital, Baghdad, was sacked by the khan Hulagu in February 1258.

Alp-Arslan (b. 1029; r. 1063–1072): Seljuk sultan and nephew of Tughril Beg. Defeated and captured the Byzantine emperor Romanus IV at the Battle of Manzikert. Alp-Arslan opened Asia Minor to settlement by Turkish tribes.

Alp Tigin (961–975): Turkish Mamluk; ruled Ghazna (today Afghanistan) as a vassal of the Samanid emir Mansur I (961–976). He promoted Sunni Islam and raided the Punjab, sacking Hindu temples and Buddhist monasteries. He was succeeded by Ishaq (975–977), and then his son-in-law Sebüktigin (977–997).

al-Tabari (839–923): Persian historian and Qur'anic scholar; was a native of Tabaristan. Tabari wrote in Arabic a universal Muslim history that is the principal source for the Umayyad and early Abbasid caliphates.

Ammianus Marcellinus (c. 325–391): A historian of imperial Rome, a native of Antioch, and a staff officer. He wrote a history of the Roman world from the reign of Trajan (98–117) to Valens (364–378). He provides invaluable information on the Goths, Alani, and Huns, as well as Roman relations with the Sassanid Empire.

An Lushan (c. 703–757): Chinese general of Sogdian-Turkish ancestry. Raised a rebellion against the Tang emperor Xuanzong (712–756). Upon occupying Luoyang, he declared himself the first emperor of the Yan Dynasty. He was murdered by his ministers in January 757, and the rebellion collapsed in 763.

An Shigao (d. 168): Styled a Parthian prince; arrived at the Han court in 148 and translated into Chinese a number of works of the Sarvastivada school of Buddhism. He set the traditions of Chinese Buddhist monasteries.

Antiochus III, the Great (b. c. 241 B.C.; r. 223–187 B.C.): Seleucid king. Restored the power of his empire. In 309–203 B.C., he conducted an eastern expedition and received the homage of the Parthian prince Arsaces II and the Greco-Bactrian king Euthydemus. At the Battle of Panium in 200 B.C., he defeated the Ptolemaic army, conquering Phoenicia, Coele-Syria, and Judaea. He was decisively defeated by the Roman consul Lucius Cornelius Scipio Asiaticus at Magnesia in 190 B.C. Thereafter, the Seleucid Empire fragmented.

Antiochus VII Sidetes (b. c. 158 B.C.; r. 138–129 B.C.): Seleucid king; was crowned after the capture of his brother Demetrius II (146–139 B.C.) by the Parthian king Mithradates I. In 130 B.C., Antiochus recovered Mesopotamia, Babylonia, and Media from the Parthians, but Phraates II decisively defeated and slew Antiochus VII in 129 B.C. and ended the revival of Seleucid power in the Near East.

Antony, Mark (Marcus Antonius) (83–30 B.C.): Roman senator and commander; a member of the Second Triumvirate, along with Octavian and M. Aemilius Lepidus in 43–30 B.C. He was awarded the eastern half of the Roman Empire in 42 B.C., but he steadily broke with his colleague Octavian and allied with Ptolemaic queen Cleopatra VII (51–30 B.C.). In 39 and 37–36 B.C., he waged two unsuccessful Parthian wars. In 31 B.C., he was defeated at the Battle of Actium and subsequently committed suicide.

Arcadius (b. 377; r. 395–408): Elder son of Theodosius I. He was proclaimed Augustus in 383 and, in 395, succeeded to the eastern half of the Roman Empire. He proved a weak-willed emperor, dominated by his ministers, who averted the crisis posed by Alaric and the Visigoths.

Ardashir I (227–240): Shah of Persia; overthrew Parthian rule and founded the Sassanid Neo-Persian Empire. He initiated the first of a series of wars by the Sassanid shahs to conquer the eastern provinces of the Roman Empire.

Arigh Böke (b. 1219; r. 1259–1264): Mongol khan; the fourth and youngest son of Tolui. He was entrusted with the Mongolian homeland by Great Khan Möngke. In 1259, upon the death of Möngke, Arigh Böke was declared Great Khan, but the Mongol army in China acclaimed Kublai Khan. Arigh Böke was defeated in the ensuing civil war in 1260–1254 and forced to abdicate.

Arrian (Lucius Flavius Arrianus) (86–160): Native of Nicomedia (Izmit); a Roman senator and historian who composed a history of Alexander the Great. He also wrote a treatise of his battle line against the Alani in 135, when he was governor of Galatia-Cappadocia.

Arsaces I (246–211 B.C.): Prince of the Iranian-speaking tribe Parni and founder of the Arsacid Dynasty in northeastern Iran. His descendants ruled as the kings of Parthia.

Arsaces II (211–191 B.C.): King of Parthia and a vassal of the Seleucid kings. In 190 B.C., he asserted his independence after the Romans decisively defeated the Seleucid king Antiochus III (223–187 B.C.) at the Battle of Magnesia.

Artabanus II (128–124 B.C.): King of Parthia; the uncle and successor of Phraates II. He was defeated and slain by the Tocharians, ancestors of the Kushans, when they invaded Margiana.

Artabanus V (216–227): King of Parthia; faced an invasion by the Roman emperors Caracalla and Macrinus in 214–218. He was defeated and slain by the Sassanid shah Ardashir I at the Battle of Hormozgan.

Ashoka (b. 304 B.C.; r. 268–232 B.C.): The greatest Mauryan emperor. He ruled most of the Indian subcontinent and published the earliest surviving royal edicts in India that were erected as monumental inscriptions. By 263 B.C., he converted to Buddhism; he promoted the faith throughout India and encouraged Buddhist missionaries on the Silk Road.

as-Saffah (b. 721; r. 749–754): Abbasid caliph; governor of Khurasan who overthrew the Umayyad caliphate in 749–750. He founded the Abbasid caliphate, a Muslim, as opposed to Arabic, state based on the lands of eastern Islam.

Attila (b. c. 410; r. 434–452): Regarded as the second greatest conqueror of the steppes. He and his brother Bleda succeeded their uncle Rugila as joint kings of the Huns. Circa 445, Bleda was murdered by Attila. In 442–443 and 447, Attila launched devastating raids into the Balkans, earning the sobriquet "Scourge of God." In 451, he invaded Gaul and suffered at Châlons a strategic defeat from a Roman-Gothic army under Aetius. In 452, he invaded northern Italy but withdrew due to the intercession of Pope Leo I. Attila died in 452 from overindulgence at his wedding celebrations. The Hun Empire collapsed within two years after his death.

Augustus (Gaius Julius Caesar Octavianus) (b. 63 B.C., r. 27 B.C.– 14 A.D.): Roman emperor; the nephew and adopted son of Julius Caesar (101–44 B.C.). Augustus ended nearly 60 years of civil war and, in 27 B.C., founded the principate.

Aurangzeb (b. 1618; r. 1658–1707): Son of Shah Jahan (1628–1658) and grandson of Akbar. Hailed Alamgir ("world conqueror"), he united nearly all of India under Mughal rule. A zealous Muslim, he alienated his Muslim subjects, and his campaigns in the Deccan exhausted the imperial treasury.

Azes I (c. 58–38 B.C.): Indo-Scythian king, conquered the Indus valley, and was remembered by Buddhists, who took his year of accession as the first year for reckoning by the Vikrama era.

Bābur (Zahir al-Din Muhammad) (b. 1483; r. 1526–1530): First Mughal emperor of India; a descendant of Genghis Khan and Tamerlane. A Timurid prince of Ferghana, he lost his realm in the wars between the Uzbeks and Safavid Iran. In 1504, he seized Kabul and acknowledged the Safavid shah Ismail I as his overlord. In 1526, he invaded India and defeated Ibrahim Lodi, sultan of Delhi, at the Battles of Panipat on April 26, 1526; he then occupied Delhi and founded the Mughal Empire. He composed an engaging autobiography, *Baburnama*, in literary Turkish.

Baiju (d. 1260): Mongol general; appointed by Töregene to the command of Mongol forces in Iran in 1242. He decisively defeated the Seljuk sultan Kay-Khusraw at the Battle of Köse Dag on June 26, 1243. In 1246, Khan Güyük recalled the popular Baiju, but he was restored to his command by Khan Möngke in 1251–1255.

Ban Chao (30–102): Han general who completed the subjection and organization of the western regions in 75–91 and ended the power of the northern Xiongnu.

Baraq, Ghiyas-ud-Din (1266–1271): Mongol khan recognized by Kublai Khan as ruler of the Chagatai khanate in central Asia. He converted to Islam and assumed the Muslim name Ghiyas-ud-Din. He was opposed by rival Khan Kaidu, grandson of Ögödei. In 1267, they concluded a truce so that Kaidu could move against Kublai Khan. In turn, Baraq warred with little success against Ilkhan Abaka (1265–1282) for control of Transoxania.

Batu (b. 1207; r. 1227–1255): Mongol khan; the son of Jochi (the eldest son of Genghis Khan). In 1227, he succeeded to the western *ulus* (the future Golden Horde). He conquered the Cumans in 1235–1236. In 1237–1240, he subdued the Russian principalities. He won a brilliant victory over King Bela IV of Hungary at the Battle of the Mohi on April 11, 1241. The news of the Mongol victory panicked Western Christendom, but in 1242, Batu withdrew to the grasslands of the Volga when he received news of the death of Khan Ögödei. Thereafter, Batu ruled in splendid isolation, professing loyalty to Güyük and Möngke.

Bayan (c. 560–602): Khagan of the Avars; settled his nation on the Pannonian grasslands (eastern Hungary) after defeating the Gepidae in 562. His allies, the Lombards, thereupon invaded Italy, while Bayan raided the Byzantine provinces of Thrace and Moesia in the Balkans.

Bayan (1236–1295): Mongol general; the leading field commander of Kublai Khan in the conquest of Song China. He received the final surrender of the dowager empress Xie Daoqing and the boy emperor Gong (1275–1276) at the Song capital of Linan (Hangzhou).

Bayanchur Khan (747–759): Second Uighur khagan; extended the power of the Uighur khaganate, exploiting Chinese weakness due to the An Lushan

Rebellion (755–763), and welcomed Sogdian merchants from the Tarim Basin to the Uighur capital.

Baybars (1260–1277): Mamluk sultan of Egypt; architect of the victory over the Mongols at Ain Jalut in 1260. Soon afterwards, he seized power in Cairo and reoccupied the Levant. He also claimed to have removed the Abbasid heir from the ruined city of Baghdad to Cairo; thus, he was hailed as the champion of Islam against the Mongols and Crusaders.

Bela IV (b. 1206; r. 1235–1270): King of Hungary; a conscientious ruler who extended royal justice and restored his kingdom after the Mongol invasion. He was, however, decisively defeated by Khan Batu at the Battle of the Mohi on April 11, 1241.

Berke (b. c. 1208; r. 1257–1266): Mongol khan; the son of Jochi and brother of Batu. He succeeded to the western *ulus* of the Mongol Empire (then known as the White and Blue Hordes). He had converted to Islam; thus, he aligned with Mamluk Egypt against his cousin, the ilkhan Hulagu (1256–1265).

Bilge (b. c. 683; r. 717–734): The fourth Ashina khagan of the Gök Turks (or eastern Turks) since the end of the Tang overlordship in 681. The protégé of his *yabgu* and father-in-law Tonyukuk, Bilge restored the power of the Gök Turks on the eastern Eurasian steppe. His deeds are celebrated on the memorial inscriptions in the Old Turkic language in the Orkhon Valley (today Mongolia).

Bleda (434–445): King of the Huns and elder son of Octar. He ruled jointly and clashed repeatedly with his brother Attila, who ordered Bleda's murder.

Bögü Khan (759–780): Uighur khagan; promoted trade and settlements within the Uighur khanate. In 762, he converted to Manichaeism.

Bolad (d. 1313): Mongol chancellor and cultural advisor; served Kublai Khan in 1260–1285. He established a directorate to gather and analyze geographic information and maps. In 1285, he arrived as the Great Khan's envoy and entered into the service of the ilkhans Arghun (1282–1291),

Gaykhatu (1291–1295), and Mahmud Ghazan (1295–1304) as a fiscal expert. He introduced Chinese-style paper money.

Boris I (r. 858–899): Tsar of Bulgaria; converted to Orthodox Christianity in the 860s and, thus, assured the conversion of the southern Slavs. He presided over the conversion of the Bulgar khanate into a Christian Slavic kingdom.

Börte (1161–1230): Principal wife of Genghis Khan. She was affianced to marry him to link their clans, but around 1180, she was abducted by the Merkits; eight months later, she was rescued by Genghis Khan and married. It was widely believed that her first son, Jochi, was the son of Börte's captor, Chilger Bökh. She bore Genghis Khan three sons: Chagatai, Ögödei, and Tolui. Both Genghis Khan and Ögödei valued her for her shrewd judgment.

Buddha: see **Siddhartha Gautama**.

Bumin (546–553): Khagan of the Gök Turks and a member of the Ashina clan. He ruled as vassal king to the Avars over the Turks dwelling in the Altai Mountains. In 552–553, he overthrew his Avar overlord Anagui and established the Gök Turk khaganate on the eastern Eurasian steppe.

Caracalla (b. 188; r. 198–217): Roman emperor; son of the emperor Septimius Severus (193–211). He ruled as co-emperor with his father and, later, his brother Geta (209–212). In 212, he murdered Geta and was remembered as a savage emperor. He waged successful campaigns in Germania, but he was murdered while on campaign against the Parthians (214–217).

Carpini, Giovanni Da Pian Del (1182–1252): Franciscan friar; the envoy of Pope Innocent IV (1243–1254) to the Mongol court in 1246–1247. His party traversed the steppes from Kiev to Karakorum in 106 days. Carpini witnessed the *kurultai* that elected Güyük (1246–1248), and he records important details about the court a generation after the death of Genghis Khan.

Chagatai (b. 1183; r. 1227–1242): Mongol khan; the second son of Genghis Khan and Börte and founder of the Chagatai khanate. In 1227, he was assigned the ulus in central Asia, originally comprising the central Eurasian steppes, Tarim Basin, and Transoxania. He was notorious for his violent temper, but he ruled justly and was praised for his adherence to Mongol traditions. He resented his brother Ögödei, but he supported Töregene as regent in 1241–1242.

Chao Cuo (c. 200–154 B.C.): Han minister and legalist writer; composed a memorandum to Emperor Wen (180–157 B.C.) in which he presented the strategy for battling the Xiongnu. The emperor Wudi (141–87 B.C.) based his strategy on the recommendations of Chao Cuo.

Charlemagne (Charles the Great) (b. c. 747; r. 768–814): King of the Franks; forged the Carolingian Empire. He was crowned Roman emperor in 800, thereby founding the Holy Roman Empire. He built the first effective state in western Europe since the collapse of Roman power. In 791–796, he destroyed the Avar khaganate.

Comnena, Anna (1083–1153): Byzantine historian and daughter of Alexius I; wrote the *Alexiad*, a primary source on the Pechenegs and Cumans of the Pontic-Caspian steppes.

Constantine I, the Great (b. 272; r. 306–337): First Christian Roman emperor; founded New Rome, or Constantinople, in 330 and reorganized the Roman state as an autocracy known as the Dominate. In 323–324, he imposed treaty obligations on the Goths and Sarmatians on the Pontic-Caspian steppes that lasted down to the arrival of the Huns in 375.

Corbulo, Gnaeus Domitius (6–67): Roman senator and consul; a distinguished general under the emperors Claudius (41–54) and Nero (54–68). He commanded the eastern legions in the War of Armenian Succession (54–66), but his success and fame gained him the enmity of Nero, who ordered his loyal commander to commit suicide in 67.

Crassus, Marcus Licinius (115–53 B.C.): Roman senator and consul in 70 and 55 B.C.; a leading commander of the republic and a member of the First Triumvirate. He was defeated and slain by the Parthians at the Battle of Carrhae in 53 B.C.

Cyril (827–869) and **Methodius** (826–885): Fraternal monks, born at Thessalonica. They are hailed "Apostles to the Slavs," converting Moravians, Serbians, and Bulgarians. Cyril devised the Cyrillic alphabet and translated the Bible into Slavic.

Cyrus the Great (b. c. 590 B.C., r. 559–530 B.C.): Achaemenid king; founded the Persian Empire, conquering Lydia in 546 B.C. and Babylonia in 539 B.C. He was hailed in classical sources as the greatest conqueror before Alexander the Great. He was killed in a frontier war against the Massagetai, a Scythian tribe, north of the Jaxartes River.

Darius I (b. c. 550 B.C.; r. 521–486 B.C.): Achaemenid king of Persia; succeeded to the throne during the Great Revolt of 522–521 B.C. He organized the satrapies of the Persian Empire and built the capital of Persepolis. In 515 or 512 B.C., he waged unsuccessful war against the Scythians on the Pontic-Caspian steppes.

Demetrius II Nicator (b. c. 160 B.C.; r. 147–141 B.C., 129–125 B.C.): Seleucid king and son of Demetrius I Soter (161–150 B.C.). This dashing monarch was defeated and captured by the Parthian king Mithradates I in 141 B.C. Demetrius lived in gilded captivity at the Arsacid court and married the sister of Phraates II. In 129 B.C., King Phraates II, at war with Demetrius's brother Antiochus VII, released Demetrius to raise a rebellion in Syria. Demetrius regained his throne but failed to restore Seleucid power.

Diodotus I (250–230 B.C.): Greco-Bactrian king who declared his independence from his Seleucid overlord Antiochus II (261–246 B.C.).

Drogön Chögyal Phags-pa (1235–1280): Fifth leader of the Sakya school of Buddhism in Tibet and the spiritual mentor to Kublai Khan. In 1268, at the behest of Kublai Khan, he devised the Phags-pa script, an adaptation of the Tibetan script, so that all official documents could be published in Mongolian.

Duzong (b. 1240; r. 1264–1274): Song emperor; faced rebellions and a fiscal crisis and, thus, was ill prepared to face the renewed Mongol conquest by Kublai Khan in 1268. In March 1273, the fall of Xianyang, the last strategic fortress on the Yangtze River, signaled the doom of the Song Dynasty, and Duzong died as the Mongol army advanced against his capital in August 1274.

Ermanaric (d. 376): King of the Goths; committed suicide upon the defeat of his people by the Huns. He was remembered in the Norse legend of the Volsungs as the tyrant Jörmunrek.

Eucratides (c. 175–145 B.C.): Greco-Bactrian king; overthrew the royal family of Euthydemus and issued an extensive coinage used along the Silk Road. He lost Herat and other western provinces to the Parthian king Mithradates I.

Eudoxus of Cyzicus (fl. c. 130–90 B.C.): Greek navigator for King Ptolemy VIII (126–116 B.C.); credited with the discovery of the use of the monsoon season to sail the Indian Ocean.

Euthydemus (230–185 B.C.): Greco-Bactrian king who submitted to Seleucid king Antiochus III (223–187 B.C.). His reign witnessed the height of prosperity of the Greek cities of Bactria.

Fadlan, Ahmad ibn (fl. 10th c.): Persian geographer and envoy to the Bulgars in 921–922 who wrote a detailed account of his encounters with the Khazars, Bulgars, and Rus on the Volga River.

Faxian (337–422): Chinese Buddhist monk who visited India in 399–412 and penned an account of his travels.

Ferdowsi (Abu al-Qasem Mansur) (940–1020): Persian poet; wrote the epic *Shah-nameh* ("*Books of Kings*") in 977–1010. This national epic celebrated Persian historical traditions before the advent of Islam and set the standard of expression in literary Middle Persian.

Galla Placidia (c. 388–450): The daughter of Theodosius I; married to King Ataulphus of the Visigoths in 410–414. In 417, she married the Roman general Constantius III, who was briefly emperor in 421. She acted as the regent for her son, the western emperor Valentinian III.

Gan Ying (fl. 1st c. A.D.): Han envoy; sent by Ban Chao on a mission to contact imperial Rome in 97. He visited Sogdiana, Bactria, Gandhara, and Parthi, and likely reached the shores of the Persian Gulf. He wrote the only Chinese account about the Roman world and gained important new information on the lands of the Near East and Transoxania.

Gao Xianzhi (d. 756): Tang commander of the Four Garrisons (Tarim Basin) and an experienced general of Korean ancestry. He commanded the Tang army that was defeated by the Arabs and Karluks at the Battle of Talas in 751.

Gaozong (b. 628; r. 649–683): Tang emperor of China; ruled in the Confucian tradition. He faced serious rebellions, and in 679–681, the Gök Turks regained their independence. After he suffered a series of strokes, his principal wife and empress took charge of policy and, later, succeeded as regent empress (690–705).

Gaozu (b. 247 B.C.; r. 206–195 B.C.): First Han emperor of China. Overthrew the Qin Dynasty. Born Liu Bang and of humble origin, he preferred negotiation to war with Modu Chanyu after he suffered an embarrassing defeat at Mount Baideng in 200 B.C. Gaozu instituted the tribute system whereby nomadic tribes could be turned into allies dependent on Chinese silk and goods.

Gaozu (b. 566; r. 618–626): Tang emperor of China. One of the greatest soldier-emperors of Chinese history. Under the Sui emperors, Gaozu, or Li Yuan, ruled strategic borderlands in Shanxi. In 618, he seized power. He waged war against the Gök Turks of the eastern khaganate.

Gautama, Siddhartha (563–483 B.C.): The Buddha, a prince of the Kshatriya Shakya clan, was the sage who founded Buddhism. Around 534 B.C., he assumed an ascetic life to achieve understanding of human suffering. In the deer park at Sarnath, he achieved enlightenment and went on to teach the noble truths of the Middle Way, the fundamental tenets of Buddhism.

Genghis Khan (b. 1162 or 1167; r. 1206–1227): Born Temujin, he was the son of Yesugei (d. c. 1171). He was the greatest conqueror of the steppes and founder of the Mongol Empire. In 1180–1204, he defeated his rival,

Jamukha, and united the Mongol tribes. In 1206, the *kurultai* acclaimed Genghis Khan "Universal Lord." In 1209–1210, he compelled the Emperor Xiangzong (1206–1211) of Xi Xia to submit. In 1211–1216, he wrested northern China from the Jin (Jurchen) Empire. In lightning campaigns, he overthrew the empire of Khwarezm in 1218–1223 and, thus, opened the lands of eastern Islam to Mongol conquest. He died while planning his final campaign against the Jin Empire. His generalship and organizational genius place him among the great captains of warfare. By his principal wife, Börte, he had four sons: Jochi, Chagatai, Ögödei, and Tolui.

Ghazan (b. 1271; r. 1295–1304): Ilkhan of Iran; assumed the name Mahmud upon his conversion to Islam. Although he tolerated Buddhism and shamanism, he promoted the high Persian culture of Islam and initiated the first major building program of Muslim monuments at Tabriz.

Guangwu (b. 5 B.C.; r. 25–57 A.D.): Han emperor; restored the Han Dynasty and moved the capital to Luoyang. He pursued a defensive policy against the nomadic tribes, but he reimposed Chinese rule over what is now Korea and Vietnam.

Gunchen (161–126 B.C.): *Chanyu* of the Xiongnu; long abided by treaty arrangements with Han China. Raiding by the Xiongnu and Han retaliatory measures led to the outbreak of war in 133 B.C.

Güyük (b. 1206; r. 1246–1248): Mongol khan; the son of Ögödei and Töregene. The strong-willed Töregene assumed a regency in 1241–1246, until she could arrange for the acclamation of Güyük as Great Khan by the *kurultai*. Güyük, a suspicious ruler and an alcoholic, discredited the house of Ögödei in the eyes of many Mongols. He died while en route to settle scores with his cousin Batu.

Harshavardhana (b. c. 590; r. 606–647): Ruled the Indo-Gangetic Plain from Kannauj. A convert to Buddhism, Harshavardhana maintained the aesthetics and arts of the Gupta Empire. The Chinese pilgrim Xuanzang wrote a description of his court.

Harun al-Rashid (b. 763; r. 786–809): Abbasid caliph; celebrated for his patronage of letters and arts. He proved a foe of Byzantium, and he concluded a treaty with Charlemagne guaranteeing the safety of Christian pilgrims to the Holy Land. With his death, the caliphate experienced civil war and fragmentation.

Heraclius (b. c. 576; r. 610–641): Byzantine emperor and exarch of Carthage; overthrew the usurper Phocas (r. 602–610). Heraclius rescued the eastern Roman Empire from near collapse and transformed it into the Byzantine state. He defeated Shah Khosrow II in 626–628 and recovered the eastern provinces. He nearly succeeded in reconciling the monophysites and Chalcedonians. Incapacitated by illness, the aging Heraclius failed to prevent the loss of Syria and Egypt to the Arab armies in 636–641.

Heraios (c. 1–30): Ruler of the Tocharians and ancestor to the Kushan kings; he is known from his coins, on which he is styled "tyrant."

Herodotus (c. 490–425 B.C.): Known as the father of history. A native of Halicarnassus, he traveled the Persian Empire and the lands around the Black Sea. He wrote his *History* to explain the wars between the Greeks and Persians. He gives a detailed account of the nomadic Scythians on the Pontic-Caspian steppes in the fourth book of the *History*.

Hongwu (b. 1328; r. 1368–1398): Ming emperor of China and the peasant rebel leader and Buddhist monk Zhu Yuanzhang. In 1353–1367, he secured the Yangtze valley and, in 1328, occupied Dadu. He expelled the Mongol emperor Togon-temür (1333–1368) and was hailed emperor of the Ming Dynasty (1368–1644). He razed the Mongol palace and replaced Dadu with the new Chinese city of Beijing.

Honoria (417–454): Daughter of Galla Placidia and Constantius III; created Augusta in 425. Honoria, who despised her brother, the western emperor Valentinian III, precipitated the invasion of Attila in 451.

Honorius, Flavius (b. 384; r. 395–421): Second son of Theodosius I; was created Augustus in 393 and succeeded as western emperor in 395. Real power was in the hands of Stilicho down to 408. Honorius, at his capital at Ravenna from 402 on, witnessed the loss of northwestern and Spanish provinces.

Hulagu (b. 1218; r. 1256–1265): Mongol ilkhan; the son of Tolui and founder of the ilkhanate. In 1256–1260, he waged a war of conquest of the Islamic world, destroying Alamut, the seat of the Assassins, and sacking Baghdad in 1258. He halted his campaign against Mamluk Egypt and withdrew to support his brother Kublai Khan in his civil war against Arigh Böke. Kublai Khan bestowed on Hulagu the rank of *ilkhan*, "loyal khan"—the title held by his successors.

Humayun (b. 1508; r. 1530–1539, 1555–1556): Mughal emperor of India; succeeded his father, Bābur. In 1539, he was expelled from India by Sher Khan, who had rallied the former Lodi mercenary bands of Afghans that had retired to the Bengal after 1527. With Safavid assistance, Humayun reconquered northern India in 1555–1556.

Huo Qubing (c. 140–117 B.C.): Han general; nephew of the general Wei Qing. He distinguished himself as a tactician against the Xiongnu. In 119 B.C., he and his uncle Wei Qing captured Mobei, the encampment of Ichise Chanyu. A favorite of Emperor Wudi, Huo Qubing died prematurely from plague and was honored with a spectacular burial.

Huvishka (147–180): Kushan emperor, succeeded Kanishka I. He consolidated Kushan rule in India and patronized Buddhism and the leading Hindu cults. His coinage reveals that he venerated all the gods of his empire.

Ibn Khaldun (1332–1406): Arab historian; born in Tunis of an Arab family from Andalusia. He wrote the influential *Muqaddimah*, a treatise on the rise and fall of Islamic governments. At the siege of Damascus in 1401, he reportedly met with Tamerlane and conversed on statecraft and proper government.

Ichise (126–114 B.C.): *Chanyu* of the Xiongnu; suffered successive defeats at the hands of Han armies. In 121 B.C., he was driven out of the Gansu Corridor, and he suffered a humiliating defeat and the loss of his capital Modei in 119 B.C. Repeated defeats undermined his authority, and he was assassinated by a disaffected general.

Igor Svyatoslavich, "the Brave" (b. 1151; r. 1180–1202): Prince of Novgorod-Seversky. Led an abortive expedition against the Cumans. He is celebrated in the earliest Russian epic poem.

Illig Khagan (r. 620–630): Ruled over the eastern Turkish khaganate. His raids into northern China precipitated war with the Tang emperor Taizong. In 626–630, the Tang general Li Jing defeated and captured Illig, thereby ending the eastern Turkish khaganate and imposing Chinese overlordship in 630–681.

Ilterish Khagan (682–694): Khagan of the eastern Turks. Ended Chinese rule in 681 and in 682 reestablished the eastern Turkish khaganate.

Iltutmish (r. 1210–1236): Sultan of Delhi; succeeded his father-in-law, Aybak, and reestablished the capital at Delhi. He organized a system of land grants to his emirs and soldiers, but he also co-opted loyal Hindu princes into the military hierarchy.

Ishbara Khagan (650–658): Khagan of the western Turks. Was defeated by a Tang army under Su Dingfang in 657. Henceforth, the western Turks acknowledged as their overlord the Tang emperor Gaozong (649–683).

Isidore of Charax (fl. 1ˢᵗ c. B.C.): Wrote *Parthian Stations*, an itinerary of the Silk Road across the Parthian Empire.

Ismail I (b. 1487; 1501–1524): First Safavid shah of Iran. Founded the Shi'ite state in Iran and revived Iran as one of the great Islamic powers. He fought for Transoxania against Muhammad Shaybani (1500–1510), who had united the Turkish tribes of the central Eurasian steppe as the Uzbek confederation. On December 2, 1510, Shah Ismail decisively defeated and slew Muhammad Shaybani at the Battle of Merv. But Shah Ismail had to confront the Ottoman threat from the west. He was defeated by the Ottoman sultan Selim I (1512–1520) on August 23, 1514.

Istami (553–575): *Yabgu* of the western Gök Turks; brother of Khagan Bumin, who commissioned Istami to pursue the Avars, who had fled west. Istami established western Turks on the central Eurasian steppe. In 557–561, in alliance with Shah Khosrow I, he occupied Transoxania and ended the Hephthalite Empire.

Ivan I Danilovich (b. 1288; r. 1325–1340): Grand prince of Moscow; a loyal vassal of the khan of the Golden Horde (1312–1341). In 1328, the khan rewarded Ivan I with Vladimir and the right to collect from the other Russian princes the tribute due to the Mongols. Ivan, nicknamed Kalita ("Moneybags"), exploited his position to turn Moscow into the premier Russian principality.

Ivan III Vasilyevich (b. 1440; r. 1462–1505): Grand prince of Moscow; renounced his allegiance to the Golden Horde. In 1480, he won a strategic victory over Khan Ahmed (1465–1481) on the Ural River. Vasilyevich secured Saray, capital of the Golden Horde.

Ivan IV (b. 1530; r. 1547–1584): Ivan the Terrible, tsar of Russia. Reformed the Russian army and conquered the khanates of Kazan (1152) and Astrakhan (1556). He ended the Mongol threat, securing the lower Volga valley and, thus, enabling Russian expansion across Siberia.

Jalal al-Din Mingburnu (1220–1231): Khwarezm shah; the son and successor of Muhammad Shah. In 1221, he was forced to retreat across the Hindu Kush into India. In 1224, he returned from exile, but he failed to regain his kingdom.

Jalal al-Din Rumi (1206–1273): Persian mystic and poet; known as Rumi. He was born in Balkh, the son of the Baha al-Din Walad, a celebrated jurist and theologian. His family relocated to Konya in 1228, where Rumi succeeded his father as head of the madrasah in 1232. In 1244, he adopted an ascetic life and founded the Mevlevi mystical order of Sufism. The members of this order, the dervishes, converted the Christians of Anatolia in the 13th and 14th centuries.

Jalal-ud-Din Firuz (1290–1296): Khalji sultan of Delhi; ended the rule of the slave sultans and founded the second Muslim dynasty in India, the Khilji. His talented nephew and successor, Ala-ud-Din Khilji, repelled Mongol attacks and campaigned in the Deccan.

Jamal al-Din (fl. c. 1250–1300): Persian astronomer and native of Bukhara. Entered the service of Kublai Khan circa 1255. In 1285, he presented to Kublai Khan a massive geographical compendium and introduced sophisticated instruments for measuring the earth. He played a pivotal role in the transfer to China of the science of the Islamic world.

Jamukha (c. 1165–1206): Mongol prince; the sworn brother and then rival of Temujin, Genghis Khan. In 1197–1202, he fought against Temujin and Wang Khan and, in 1203, in alliance with Wang Khan, defeated Temujin at the Battle of Baljuna. Temujin, however, later rallied and defeated Jamukha.

Jayapala Shahi (964–1001): Rajput ruler over the Punjab and Kabul Valley. Devoted to Shiva. He was decisively defeated by Sebüktigin at the Battle of the Neelum River in Kashmir in 986. The victory gained Kabul and Peshawar, the future bases for Muslim expansion into India.

Jebe (d. 1225): Mongol general; born as Zurgadai but received his nickname Jebe ("Arrow") when he boldly confessed that he had accidentally wounded Genghis Khan in battle in 1201. He was a trusted field commander and, thus, he shared with Subutai command of the western expedition in 1221–1223.

Jiu Zhuji (1148–1227): Daoist Chinese monk. Was invited to converse with Genghis Khan on matters of immortality and just rule. Jiu Zhuji departed his home in Shandong in 1220 and journeyed west, meeting Genghis Khan at the Mongol camp at the base of the Hindu Kush in May 1222. Even if embroidered, the exchange captures the religious outlook of Genghis Khan.

Jizhu Chanyu (178–154 B.C.): Ruler of the Xiongnu, whose attacks drove the Yuezhi (Tocharian speakers) westward to Ferghana.

Jochi (1181–1227): Mongol prince; the first son of Genghis Khan and Börte, but he was suspected to be the son of the Merkit warrior Chilger Bökh, who had held Börte captive for eight months. Genghis Khan accepted Jochi as his son. Jochi, while personally brave, was perceived as lacking the qualities of a khan. He also had quarreled with his brother Chagatai during the Khwarezmian campaign in 1220. Hence, Genghis Khan decided to assign to

Jochi the western *ulus*. Because Jochi predeceased his father, Jochi's domain (the future Golden Horde) was assigned to his son Batu.

Julian the Apostate (b. 331; r. 360–363): Roman emperor and Neo-Platonic philosopher; nephew of Constantine I. Julian restored the worship of the pagan gods. He waged an unsuccessful campaign against Persia in 363. He failed to capture the Persian capital Ctesiphon, and he was slain in a skirmish in upper Mesopotamia during the retreat of his army.

Justin II (b. c. 520; r. 565–578): Byzantine emperor; nephew and heir of Justinian I. He precipitated a Persian war in 572 and, from 574, because of mental illness, was under the regency of his wife, Sophia (niece of Theodora), and Tiberius II.

Justinian I (b. 482; r. 527–565): Known as Justinian the Great; the greatest emperor since Constantine. He promoted the most talented at his court without regard to birth. He restored imperial rule in Italy and Africa, sought religious reconciliation, and sponsored arts and letters. His most enduring achievements are the Hagia Sophia and the *Corpus Juris Civilis.*

Justinian II (b. c. 669; r. 705–711): The last Heraclian emperor and an unbalanced tyrant. He was overthrown, mutilated (by slitting his nose), and exiled to Cherson. He escaped to the Khazar court and returned with a Khazar army to regain his throne. He was deposed in 711. His foreign policy led to defeats at the hands of the Arabs and exposed Constantinople to a second Arabic siege.

Juvayni (1226–1283): Persian historian and native of Khurasan, served both Khwarezmian shah Jalal al-Din (1220–1231) and the Mongol khans Ögödei (1229–1241) and Hulagu (1256–1625). He wrote his *History of the World Conqueror* based on contemporary sources. He witnessed the sack of Baghdad, and he twice visited the court at Karakorum.

Kaidu (b. 1230; r. 1260–1301): Mongol khan; a grandson of Ögödei with aspirations to the throne of the Great Khan. In the civil war of 1259–1264, he dominated the central Eurasian steppe and clashed with the Chagatai khan Baraq for control of Transoxania. In 1267, he concluded a truce with Baraq and turned against Kublai Khan and his successor, Temür Khan (1294–1307). Based in the Altai Mountains, he waged local rebellion down to his death in 1301.

Kanishka (127–140): Fourth Kushan emperor; revered as convert to Buddhism, although he was more likely a patron who promoted favorable conditions for the spread of Buddhism into central Asia and Han China. He is credited, anachronistically, by a later Buddhist tradition with summoning a Fourth Buddhist Council in 78.

Kartir (fl. 3rd c.): Zoroastrian priest who reformed the monotheistic faith; he was patronized by shahs Ardashir I (227–240) and Shapur I (240–272).

Kay-Khusraw I (1204–1210): Seljuk sultan of Konya (Rūm). United the Turkish tribes in central and eastern Anatolia. He turned Konya into a Muslim capital. He promoted the caravan trade and minted the first Muslim silver coinage in Asia Minor.

Kay-Khusraw II (1237–1246): Seljuk sultan of Konya (Rūm). He failed to maintain control over the Turkish tribes and, thus, faced repeated rebellions. He refused to render homage to the Mongol khan Ögödei (1228–1241). Bayju, the Mongol commander in Iran, invaded Asia Minor and decisively defeated Kay-Khusraw at the Battle of Köse Dag on June 26, 1243. Thereafter, the sultans of Konya, as Mongol vassals, lost control over the emirs and Turkish tribes of Asia Minor.

Khalid ibn Barmak (705–782): Abbasid vizier; first appointed by as-Saffah (750–754). He was descended from the Barmakid family of Balkh, which had converted from Buddhism to Islam circa 670. He patronized scientists, mathematicians, and physicians and promoted the study of Buddhism among Muslim scholars.

Khosrow I (531–579): Sassanid shah; waged two wars against Justinian, emperor of the eastern Roman (Byzantine) Empire, in 530–532 and 550–545. He sought prestige, plunder, or subsidies of gold under treaty from Justinian rather than conquest. In 557–561, he allied with Istami, *yabgu* khagan of the western Turks, to defeat the Hephthalites.

Khosrow II (591–628): Last great Sassanid shah. He gained his throne with the support of the Byzantine emperor Maurice. In 602–628, he waged a war of conquest of the eastern provinces of the Byzantine Empire. In alliance with the Avars, he besieged Constantinople in 626. In 622–628, the emperor Heraclius, along with Turkish nomadic allies, launched offensives in Armenia, Iran, and Mesopotamia that led to the defeat and overthrow of Khosrow II. Heraclius recovered his lost eastern provinces, so weakening the Sassanid state that it fell to Arab armies in 636–651.

Kitbuqa (d. 1260): Mongol general; the leading field commander of Hulagu in 1256–1259. He was defeated and slain by the Mamluk army at the Battle of Ain Jalut on September 3, 1260.

Kokchu (d. 1206): Shaman and advisor to Genghis Khan; credited with great influence over the khan. He was executed on grounds of treachery based on information supplied by Börte, principal wife of Genghis Khan.

Krum (r. c. 803–814): Khan of the Bulgars; defeated the Byzantine emperors Nicephorus I and Michael I. He negotiated the first treaty with Byzantium that delineated the Bulgar state.

Kublai Khan (b. 1215; r. 1260–1294): Mongol khan; the second son of Tolui. Kublai Khan distinguished himself in campaigns against the Jin Empire in 1234–1235 and against Song China in 1257–1259. He was proclaimed khan by the Mongol army in 1260 and defeated his rival brother, Arigh Böke, in the civil war of 1260–1264. In 1268–1279, he completed the conquest of Song China. In 1274 and 1281, he launched two costly, abortive expeditions against Japan. In 1271, he assumed the Chinese temple name Shizu, the first of a new Yuan Dynasty (1271–1368). He founded a new capital, Dadu (Beijing), which Marco Polo called Kanbalu (Xanadu). Kublai Khan ruled through imperial servants of various nationalities rather than the Confucian bureaucratic classes. A convert to Buddhism, he assured the eventual triumph of Buddhism among the Mongol tribes.

Kuchlug (d. 1218; r. 1211–1218): Prince of the Naimans. Refused to submit to Genghis Khan in 1204 and took service with the Kara-Khitan *gurkhan* Mozhu (1178–1211). In 1211, he seized power at Balasagun, deposed the king, and intrigued with Muhammad Shah of Khwarezm against Genghis Khan. A zealous convert to Buddhism, Kuchlug persecuted his Muslim subjects. In 1218, he was overthrown and died an exile when the Mongol army under Jebe invaded the Kara-Khitan Empire.

Kujula Kadphises (30–80): Kushan emperor; crossed the Hindu Kush and conquered Taxila and Punjab. He forged a confederation of the Tocharian tribes in Bactria into a bureaucratic state. He is hailed in the Rabatak inscription as the founder of the Kushan royal family.

Leo I, the Great (b. c. 390; r. 440–461): The first pope of a noble Roman family. Leo upheld papal primacy against the patriarch of Constantinople. He defined the creed of the western church in his *Tome* (449), accepted at the Fourth Ecumenical Council in 451. He won a moral victory by convincing Attila to withdraw from Italy in 452.

Li Guangli (fl. 1st c. B.C.): Courtier and general of Emperor Wudi (141–87 B.C.). Commanded two expeditions to subdue Sogdiana in the so-called War of the Heavenly Horses (104–102 B.C.). In 102 B.C., Li Guangli forced the Sogdians to capitulate and pay a tribute of horses, but he lost most of his army and the horses on his return.

Li Jing (571–649): Tang general and chancellor; proved the ablest commander under emperors Gaozu and Taizong. In 629–630, he defeated and captured Khagan Illig, thereby ending the eastern Turkish khaganate.

Li Shiji (594–669): Tang general; distinguished himself in the campaign against the Gök Turks in 629–630. He pacified the caravan cities of the Tarim Basin and defeated the nomadic Xueyantuo, who occupied the grasslands of eastern Mongolia.

Lizong (b. 1205; r. 1224–1264): Song emperor. He was a noted patron of letters and architecture, but he proved unequal to the task of facing renewed Mongol attacks in 1257. He was saved by the outbreak of the Mongol civil war in 1269–1264.

Lokaksema (b. c. 147): A Kushan from Gandhara and a Buddhist monk at the Han capital of Luoyang. In 178–189, he translated a number of Sanskrit sutras into Chinese. His student Zhi Yao, also styled a Kushan monk, translated a number of Mahayana Buddhist texts in the late 2nd century.

Longjumeau, Andrew of (d. after 1253): Dominican friar. Sent as the envoy of Pope Innocent the IV (1243–1254) to the ilkhanate court in 1245–1247. In 1248–1251, he traveled to Karakorum as the envoy of King Louis IX of France (1226–1270). In 1249, he reached the Mongol Empire after the death of Güyük. The regent Sorghaghtani Beki, although a Nestorian Christian, received the letters and gifts as token of submission by both Pope Innocent IV and King Louis IX.

Lucullus, Lucius Licinius (118–56 B.C.): Consul in 74 B.C.; assumed the command as proconsul against Mithradates VI, king of Pontus, in 73–66 B.C. In 69 B.C., his victory at Tigranocerta over King Tigranes II of Armenia and Mithradates VI made Rome the premier power in the Near East.

Ma Huan (1380–1460): Admiral of Ming China; a Muslim and Arabic speaker. At the command of the Ming emperor Yongle (1402–1424), he set sail with 57 ships in a great expedition to the western lands in 1413. He visited Champa, Java, Sumatra, Malaya, the southern Indian port of Cochin, Hormuz, and ultimately, Mecca.

Mahavira (599–527 B.C.): Sage and teacher; the founder of Jainism. He is hailed as the 24th and last Tirthankara, or teacher, of the Jain faith. Born into a royal family of Bihar, of the Kshatriya caste, he assumed an ascetic life, attained enlightenment, and taught the cardinal principles of a life based on *ahimsa*, or nonviolence, and respect for all living creatures.

Mahmud al-Kashgari (1005–1102): Turkish poet and scholar under the Karakhanids; wrote the first compendium on the Turkish language, *Diwan lughat at-Turk*, and adapted the Arabic-Persian script for writing Turkish. His work contains a wealth of information about early Turkish history and religious traditions. He also drew the first world map showing the location of Turkish tribes.

Mahmud of Ghazni (b. 971; r. 997–1030): Ghaznavid sultan; the son and successor of Sebüktigin. He waged 17 campaigns in northern India, whereby he gained the loot and slaves to sustain his professional army. He clashed with the Karakhanids over Transoxania, and in 1015–1071, he secured Khwarezm. In 1027–1028, he extended his sway over the caravan cities of northern Iran.

Malik-Shah (b. 1055; r. 1072–1092): Seljuk sultan; son of Alp-Arslan. He concentrated on war against the Fatimid caliphate at Cairo, and he faced threats in Transoxania. Independent *ghazi* warriors, who only nominally recognized Malik-Shah, migrated into Asia Minor and established their own states at Konya and Sivas.

Marcus Aurelius (161–180): Roman emperor; considered the last and noblest of the so-called Five Good Emperors of Rome. A Stoic in outlook, he ruled judiciously and waged successful Parthian (161–166) and German (167–180) wars. Merchants, claiming to represent the emperor, are reported to have arrived by sea and were received at the Han court in 166.

Marwan II (b. 688; r. 744–750): Umayyad caliph; moved the capital from Damascus to Harran. In 737, as governor in Armenia, he waged a campaign north of the Caucasus and compelled the Khazars to accept Islam. In 750, he was defeated by as-Saffah at the Battle of the Zab and, later, captured and executed.

Maurice (582–602): Byzantine emperor; waged campaigns against the Avars in the Balkans and ended the Persian war (572–590) by supporting Shah Khosrow II to the Sassanid throne. He is credited with writing the *Strategikon*, a manual of tactics against nomadic horse archers.

Mawlana: see **Jalal al-Din Rumi**.

Meng Tian (d. 210 B.C.): The leading general of the Qin emperor Shihuangdi. In 221 B.C., he led a major expedition against the Xiongnu and established the empire's northern frontier. He directed the construction of the continuous Great Wall of China.

Midas (c. 725–696 B.C.): King of Phrygia. Constructed a great royal tumulus near his capital, Gordion. He was remembered by Greeks for his patronage of the oracle of Delphi. He committed suicide after the Cimmerians, Iranian-speaking nomadic invaders, destroyed his kingdom.

Mithradates I (171–138 B.C.): King of Parthia, defeated and captured the Seleucid king Demetrius II in 140 B.C. and then the Greco-Bactrian king Eucratides. He conquered Media, Persia, Mesopotamia, Margiana, and Aria.

Mithradates II (137–88 B.C.): King of Parthia. Turned the Arsacid state into a Near East monarchy. He founded the capital Ctesiphon.

Mithradates VI Eupator (121–63 B.C.): King of Pontus. Fought three wars with Rome (89–85 B.C., 83–81 B.C., and 74–63 B.C.) for mastery of Asia Minor. He was finally defeated by Pompey the Great, fled to the Tauric Chersonese, and committed suicide.

Modu Chanyu (b. c. 234 B.C.; r. 209–174 B.C.): Succeeded his father, Touman, as *chanyu* of the Xiongnu. He gave the tribal confederation administrative organization and effective leadership in raiding China, and he defeated the army of Han emperor Gaozu at the Battle of Mount Baideng in 200 B.C. Thereafter, he received gifts and silk from the Han court in return for an alliance and sale of horses to the Han armies.

Möngke (b. 1209; r. 1251–1259): Mongol khan and eldest son of Tolui and Sorghaghtani Beki. He proved an intelligent ruler, who commissioned his brother Hulagu to conquer the Islamic world in 1256. In 1257–1259, he along with his brother Kublai Khan, invaded Song China. He died of dysentery while besieging the fortress Diaoyu on the Yangtze River. His death precipitated a civil war.

Montecorvino, Giovanni da (1247–1328): Franciscan missionary; ordained in Cathay in 1307. He had Christian works translated into Uighur. He was credited with converting 6,000 Mongols, including Temür Khan, after 35 years of proselytizing.

Muawiya (b. 602; r. 661–689): Umayyad caliph; general of the Syrian army and father of the Arabic navy. In 656, he refused to accept Ali, the cousin of Muhammad, as the fourth Rashidun caliph because of Ali's implication in the murder of Caliph Uthman (644–656). Muawiya triumphed over the forces of Ali and, thus, founded the first hereditary Umayyad caliphate at Damascus.

Muhammad (570–632): The prophet of God (Allah), he was called to cleanse the religion of Abraham and, thus, founded Islam. His revelations were collected into the Qur'an. Driven from his native Mecca in 622, Muhammad created an *ummah* (community of believers) at Medina that defeated the Meccans. At his death, Muhammad had united all of Arabia under Islam.

Muhammad Ghuri (b. 1150, r. 1202–1206): Ghurid emir; extended the Ghurids into northern India. He conquered the Punjab and Doab in the name of his older brother Ghiyas al-Din (1163–1203). His decisive victory over the Rajput King Prithviraja III (1149–1192) in 1192 gained him control of Delhi. As emir, he entrusted the administration of the Indian conquests to his Turkish general Qutb al-Din Aybak.

Muhammad Shaybani (b. 1451; r. 1500–1510): Khan of the Uzbek confederation, who occupied Bukhara and Samarkand. He clashed with Ismail I, Safavid shah of Iran, and Bābur, who quit his homeland in Ferghana to invade India. On December 2, 1510, Shah Ismail decisively defeated and slew Muhammad Shaybani at the Battle of Merv.

Nasr ibn Ahmad (864–892): Samanid emir; ruled as the Abbasid deputy over Khurasan and Transoxania. Nasr secured the frontier on the Jaxartes and gained wealth from the slave trade with the Turkish tribes. He turned Bukhara into the model of a Muslim city, with its architecture and arts, and sponsored the Persian literary culture of eastern Islam.

Nasr ibn Sayyar (b. 663; r. 738–748): Umayyad governor of Khurasan; completed the conquest of Transoxania. He pursued conciliatory policies toward all religions and reformed taxation and administration.

Nicephorus I (802–811): Byzantine emperor; served as treasurer of the empress Irene (797–802). He was an Arabian by birth and seized power as Irene lost popularity. He suffered humiliating defeats at the hands of the Abbasid caliph Harun al-Rashid. He was defeated and slain by Khan Krum of the Bulgars.

Ningzong (b. 1168; r. 1194–1224): Song emperor of China. Allied with Khan Ögödei to partition the remaining domains of the Jin Empire in 122. But the Song army sought to retake Kaifeng and, thus, precipitated an inconclusive war in 1234–1241.

Octar (c. 420–430): Ruled over the western Huns on the Pannonian grasslands; he was the father of Attila (434–453) and Bleda (434–445). See also **Rugila**.

Octavian: See **Augustus**.

Ögödei (b. 1186; r. 1229–1241): Mongol khan; the third son of Genghis Khan and Börte. Ögödei, popular and affable, was elected by the *kurultai* as successor to Genghis Khan. He ruled directly over the Mongolian homeland, but he was recognized as Great Khan by his brothers Chagatai and Tolui and his nephew Batu. He transformed Karakorum into a capital city and authorized Batu's conquest of the west. His death precipitated the first succession crisis of the Mongol Empire.

Otto I (b. 912; r. 936–973): Holy Roman Emperor; duke of Saxony and son of Henry the Fowler. Otto was elected king of Germany. In 955, he decisively defeated the Hungarians on the Lech, and his campaigns against the Danes and Slavs secured imperial frontiers. In 962, he was crowned Holy Roman Emperor.

Ouyang Xiu (1007–1072): Song official and polymath; rose from obscure origins to high rank through the examination system. He sponsored the literary movement stressing clear expository prose within the tradition of Confucian classics. He epitomized the neo-Confucian scholar-official.

Peroz I (457–484): Sassanid shah; was deposed by his brother Hormizd II. He regained his throne with a Hephthalite army provided by King Khush-Nevaz. Peroz twice waged campaigns against his former ally Khush-Nevaz. In either 469 or 472, Peroz suffered a defeat and had to pay a ransom for his release. In 484, he was slain near Herat, enabling the Hephthalites to raid deep into Iran.

Phraates II (138–128 B.C.): King of Parthia; defeated Antiochus VII Sidetes and ended Seleucid power in the Near East. Phraates, however, was defeated and slain by the Sacae, who had migrated into Aria and Drangiana.

Phraates IV (38–2 B.C.): King of Parthia; negotiated with Augustus the return of the Roman standards and prisoners taken at the Battle of Carrhae in 20 B.C. He recognized Roman hegemony in Armenia—an agreement that lasted down to 54. In turn, Augustus sent the Greek courtesan Musa Urania, who became Phraates's principal wife and mother to his heir, Phraates V (2 B.C.–A.D. 4).

Plautius Silvanus Aelianus, Tiberius (c. 15–85): Roman senator and consul (45 and 74) of patrician lineage. As legate of Moesia in 66–67, he repelled Sarmatian attacks against the Greek cities and secured the lower Danube against nomadic invaders.

Pliny the Elder (23–79): Roman senator, naturalist, and philosopher. He wrote the encyclopedic *Naturalis Historia*, which has a wealth of information on the Amber Road, Silk Road, and trade routes of the Indian Ocean. He died on August 25, 79, while attempting to effect rescues of friends trapped by the eruption of Mount Vesuvius.

Polo, Marco (1254–1324): Venetian adventurer; took service with Kublai Khan as the administrator of the salt monopoly at Yangzhou and as an emissary to the Burmese court. In 1251–1257, Marco Polo, along with his father Niccolò, and uncle Maffeo (who had previously visited the ilkhanate court), journeyed to Dadu. In 1292–1294, the three returned to Venice. In 1298, Marco was captured by the Genoese at the Battle of Curzola. While in prison in 1298–1299, he dictated his adventures of 23 years (1271–1294) to fellow prisoner Rustichello da Pisa, who composed the *Livres des merveilles* *du monde.* Marco's book was an instant success and fired the European imagination and desire to reach Cathay.

Pompey the Great (Gnaeus Pompeius Magnus) (106–48 B.C.): Roman senator and consul (70, 56 and 52 B.C.); a member of the First Triumvirate, along with Gaius Julius Caesar and Marcus Licinius Crassus (59–51 B.C.). He commanded the republican forces against Julius Caesar in the civil war and was decisively defeated at the Battle of Pharsalus (48 B.C.), fled to Egypt, and was murdered on orders of King Ptolemy XIII. In 66–63, Pompey had ended the war against King Mithradates VI of Pontus, reorganized the eastern province, and secured Rome's frontier on the upper Euphrates with an overlordship over Armenia.

Prester John: "Priest John"; a legendary Christian king in inner Asia who would deliver Jerusalem from the Muslims. He was probably inspired by garbled reports about Yelü Dashi (1124–1143), khan of the Kara-Khitans, who had defeated Seljuk sultan Ahmad Sanjar (1118–1153) at the Battle of Qatwan on September 9, 1141. Genghis Khan was later hailed by western European Christians as Prester John or his descendant, David.

Priscus of Panium (c. 410–472): Roman diplomat. Accompanied the mission of the emperor Theodosius II to the court of Attila, king of the Huns, in 441–442. He wrote a perceptive account about the customs of the Huns and the character of Attila.

Procopius (500–565): Byzantine historian and native of Caesarea. He wrote a narrative history of the wars of the emperor Justinian (527–565) and *Buildings* (a monograph of the emperor's building programs). In his *Secret History*, or *Anecdota*, he vents his outrage over Justinian and the empress Theodora. He provides invaluable information on the nomadic peoples of the western and central Eurasian steppes and the Sassanid Empire.

Ptolemy (Claudius Ptolaemeus) (90–168): Mathematician, scientist, and geographer of Alexandria. He composed the *Geographica*, which included a map of the known world to Romans, in the mid-2nd century. He also measured the circumference of the earth and wrote treatises on optics, astronomy, and music.

Qapaghan (694–716): Khagan of the eastern Turks. Restored Turkish power on the eastern Eurasian steppes. He was acknowledged overlord by the western Turks of the Onoq confederacy. He battled both Tang armies and Tibetans for control of the Tarim Basin, and he clashed with Qutaybah ibn Muslim, Umayyad governor of Khurasan, for control of Transoxania.

Qilij Arslan I (1092–1107): Seljuk sultan of Konya (Rūm). Suffered serious defeats at the hands of the First Crusade in 1097. In 1097–1098, the Byzantine emperor Alexius I thus recovered the western third of Asia Minor.

Qilij Arslan II (1156–1192): Seljuk sultan of Konya (Rūm). Defeated the Byzantine emperor Manuel I (1143–1180) at the Battle of Myriocephalon on September 17, 1176. The victory checked the revival of Byzantine power in Asia Minor.

Qutaybah ibn Muslim (b. 699; r. 705–715): Umayyad governor of Khurasan; waged a destructive war against the cities of Transoxania, looting Manichaean, Zoroastrian, and Buddhist sanctuaries. He took Bukhara in 709 and Samarkand in 712. His ruthless efforts to impose Islam galvanized the Sogdian populations to invite Suluk, *yabgu* of the western Turks, to intervene. Qutaybah was executed on grounds of treason on the orders of Caliph Sulayman.

Qutb ud-Din Aybak (1206–1210): Sultan of Delhi; was the leading general of Muhammad Ghuri (1202–1206), who entrusted Aybak with the conquest of the Ganges. In 1206, he made himself sultan of the Turkish slave soldiers and, thus, founded the slave sultanate of Delhi.

Qutlugh Bilge Köl Khagan (744–747): Khagan of the Uighurs; ended the Gök Turk khaganate. He was acclaimed khagan by the *kurultai* of the Uighurs and entered into alliance with Tang China.

Qutuz, al-Muaaffar Sayf al-Din (1259–1260): Mamluk sultan. He refused to submit to Hulagu and planned the campaign of Ain Jalut. He was overthrown and murdered by his leading general, Baybars.

Rashid al-Din (1247–1318): Persian polymath and scholar; was a Jewish convert to Islam and native of Hamadan. At the ilkhanate court, he wrote an encyclopedic history of the Islamic world, *Jami' al-tawarikh*, in which he made extensive use of Chinese sources and the *Secret History of the Mongols*. He also translated Buddhist texts and Chinese works on statecraft into Persian.

Radiyya Begum (b. 1205; r. 1236–1240): Daughter of Iltutmish; was the first Muslim woman to rule in her own right as sultana of Delhi. She failed to win over the Turkish military elite, who were scandalized by her manners and liaisons. Her murder in 1240 marked the end of effective rule by the slave sultans of Delhi.

Romanus IV Diogenes (b. c. 1030; r. 1068–1072): Byzantine emperor; candidate of the officers of the eastern army. He married the empress Eudocia, widow of Constantine X Ducas (1059–1067). Romanus was decisively defeated and captured by the Seljuk sultan Alp-Arslan at the Battle of Manzikert in 1071. In 1072, Romanus was released by Alp-Arslan, but Michael VII ordered him deposed and blinded. Romanus died in exile.

Rubrouck, William of (1220–1293): Flemish Franciscan friar; sent as envoy of French king Saint Louis IX (1226–1270) to the Mongol court in 1253–1255. William of Rubrouck failed in his mission to convert the Mongols, but he wrote a perceptive account on the court of Great Khan Möngke (1251–1259).

Rugila (r. c. 420–434): King of the Huns; ruled over the eastern tribes of the Huns between the lower Danube and the lower Volga. His brother Octar (r. c. 420–430) ruled over the western Huns on the Pannonian grasslands. He was succeeded by his nephews Attila and Bleda.

Salam ibn Ziyad (681–683): First Umayyad governor of Khurasan; conducted raids into Transoxania and settled Arab military colonists on the Oxus River.

Sargon II (722–705 B.C.): Assyrian king; seized the throne in a brief civil war and claimed to be the son of Tiglath-Pileser III (745–727 B.C.). He campaigned against the neo-Hittite and Aramaic kingdoms of the Levant and Babylon. He fell fighting an invasion by the Cimmerians, Iran-speaking nomads from the Pontic-Caspian steppes who had crossed the Caucasus Mountains.

Satuk Bughra Khan (b. 922; r. 934–955): Karakhanid Black Camel khan; ruled the Yaghma Turks in the valley of the Talas River. He had converted to Islam in 934. In 940, he seized power over the Karakhanid khaganate and promoted Islam among the Turkish tribes of the central Eurasian steppes.

Sebüktigin (b. 942; r. 977–997): Ghaznavid emir and sultan; known as the Lion of Ghazni. He was the Turkish commander and son-in-law of Alp Tigin. In 977, he was declared emir by his Turkish soldiers. He forged the Ghaznavid emirate into a Muslim state and conquered the Kabul valley. In 994–999, he secured the Samanid lands south of the Oxus River, while the Karakhanids occupied Transoxania.

Seleucus I Nicator (b. 358 B.C.; r. 312–281 B.C.): Macedonian noble and general. A minor figure in the initial succession wars after the death of Alexander the Great in 323–321 B.C. In 320 B.C., he obtained the satrapy of Babylonia, and between 312 and 281 B.C., he fell heir to the Asia domains of Alexander's empire.

Septimius Severus (b. 145; 193–211): Roman emperor; member of a senatorial family from Leptis Magna in North Africa. He seized the throne in the civil war of 193–195 and founded the Severan Dynasty (193–235). He waged two successful Parthian wars (195–196; 198–201) and organized the Roman province of Mesopotamia in northern Iraq.

Shapur I (240–270): Sassanid shah; waged three major wars against the Roman Empire, in 242–244, 253, and 254–260. In the third war, he took the Roman Valerian captive. His victories are celebrated on the rock reliefs at Naqsh-e Rostam. Shapur failed to conquer Roman territory, and in 262, he faced a counterinvasion by Odenathus, merchant prince of Palmyra and ally of Rome.

Shapur II (309–379): Sassanid shah; waged two wars against the Roman Empire, in 335–350 and 358–363. He repelled the Roman invasion of lower

Mesopotamia led by the emperor Julian II. The retreat and death of Julian enabled Shapur II to conclude a favorable treaty from the new emperor, Jovian, who relinquished the strategic fortresses of upper Mesopotamia.

Sharaf ad-Din Ali Yazdi (fl. c. 1425–1450): Persian historian who served at the Timurid court of Shah Rukh (1405–1447). He wrote a favorable biography of Tamerlane, *Zafernameh.*

Shihuangdi (b. 259 B.C.; r. 246–210 B.C.): Founded the Qin Dynasty and united the warring states of China. He took strong measures against the Xiongnu and ordered the construction of the Great Wall.

Shulu Ping (879–953): Khitan empress of the Liao Dynasty; wife of Abaoji (907–926). She manipulated the court to place on the throne her younger son, Yelü Deguang, who assumed the Chinese throne name Taizong (927–947). She again intrigued in the succession war following the death of Yelü Deguang in 947–950.

Sima Qian (c. 140–86 B.C.): Historian of Han China; wrote a dynastic history in *Shiji* (*Historical Records*). A meticulous scholar, Sima Qian incorporated a number of earlier sources, notably, the account of Zhang Qian about his travels among the Xiongnu and Yuezhi (Tocharians).

Simeon (893–927): Tsar of Bulgaria; second son of Tsar Boris. He had been destined for a religious career, studying at Constantinople. In two wars (894–899; 912–924), he challenged the Macedonian emperors for domination of the Balkans. In 895–896, he courted the Pechenegs as allies against the Magyars, who were allied to the Byzantine emperor Leo VI (886–912). The Pechenegs drove the Magyars, ancestors of the Hungarians, into the Pannonian grasslands.

Sorghaghtani Beki (1204–1252): Kereyid princess and wife of Tolui, son of Genghis Khan, and the niece of Wang Khan. She was the mother of Möngke, Kublai Khan, Hulagu, and Arigh Böke. A Nestorian Christian, she favored her co-religionists at court. In 1248–1251, after the death of Khan Güyük (1246–1248), she secured the support of Batu and the majority in the *kurultai* to elect her son Möngke as Great Khan.

Stein, Sir Aurel (1862–1943): An explorer, archaeologist, and officer of the British army. Stein, born of a prominent Jewish family in Budapest, took British citizenship. He led four archaeological expeditions into the Tarim Basin (1900–1901, 1906–1908, 1913–1916, and 1930). He visited the caravan cities of the Tarim Basin and found the Buddhist cave monasteries at Mogao near Dunhuang.

Stilicho, Flavius (d. 408): *Magister militum* of the western army (395–408); directed the policy of the western court. In 395–397 and in 402–408, Stilicho used the threat posed by Arcadius to secure control over Honorius. Stilicho's policies led to the loss of the northwestern provinces in 406. In 408, he was arrested and executed on grounds of treason.

Strabo of Amaseia (63 B.C.–A.D. 24): Geographer; wrote the definitive account of the geography of the Roman Empire and the surrounding lands. His account includes invaluable information on the trade in the Erythaean Sea and the western routes of the Silk Road.

Stroganov, Anika (1488–1570): Russian merchant prince. A native of Novgorod, who received the right from Ivan the Terrible to develop the fur trade from Solvychegodsk (on the Vychegda River). These rights were confirmed in 1552, 1555, and 1560. The Stroganov family undertook the colonization of Siberia—tundra, taiga, and steppe—establishing trading posts and exacting tribute in furs.

Subutai (1175–1248): Mongol general and early companion of Temujin (the future Genghis Khan); commanded 20 campaigns. He was an expert in strategy and siege warfare. In 1221–1223, he and Jebe conducted a brilliant western campaign that climaxed at the Battle of the Kalka River on May 31, 1223. He distinguished himself in the western campaigns of Batu in 1237–1241 and in the campaign against Song China in 1246–1247.

Suluk (717–738): *Yabgu* of the Turgesh, a leading tribe of the western Turkish khaganate. He waged a brilliant war of attrition against the Umayyad governor in Transoxania.

Sviatoslav (b. c. 942; r. 964–972): Rus prince; son of Prince Igor (914–945) and Queen Olga (Helga), who had embraced Orthodox Christianity in 957. He defeated the Khazars circa 965, but he suffered defeat at the hands of Byzantine armies in Bulgaria (967–971). On his retreat to Kiev, he was defeated and slain by the Pechenegs.

Tacitus, Publius Cornelius (56–117): Roman historian and senator. He wrote two narrative histories, *Annals* and *Historiae*, covering the reigns of Tiberius (14–37) through Domitian (81–96), and the treatises *Germania*, *Agricola*, and *Dialogus*.

Tahir ibn al-Husayn (d. 821): Persian general and emir. Won the civil war of 812–813 for al-Mamun (813–833). He was rewarded with the governorship of Khurasan, which his heirs, the Tahirids, turned into a hereditary emirate.

Taiwudi (b. 408; r. 424–452): Emperor of the northern Wei Dynasty; secured northern China from Avar attacks. A devoted Buddhist, he constructed the five colossal statues of Buddha at Yungang.

Taizong (b. 598; r. 626–649): Tang emperor of China. Defeated the Gök Turks in 629–630 and brought the eastern Eurasian steppe under Chinese rule. His generals Li Jing and Li Shiji subjected the Tarim Basin, defeated the Tibetans, and advanced Chinese influence to the Jaxartes River.

Taizong (b. 939; r. 976–997): Song emperor of China; succeeded his brother Taizu. He is credited with the foundation of the Neo-Confucian bureaucratic state based on the examination system.

Taizu (b. 927; r. 960–976): Song emperor of China; the accomplished general Zhao Kuangyin, who founded the Song Dynasty. In 960, he ended the regional Zhou Dynasty at Kaifeng and then imposed order over the southern Chinese kingdoms. He ruled as the political heir of the earlier Han and Tang dynasties.

Tamerlane (b. 1336; r. 1370–1405): "Prince of Destruction"; regarded as the third greatest conqueror of the steppes (after Genghis Khan and Attila). He was the heir to the Mongol military tradition, recruiting professional regiments of cavalry based on loyalty and rewards. Tamerlane, emir of the Turko-Mongol Barlas tribe, emerged as the leading emir in the tribal wars in Transoxania in 1360–1370. In 1370, Chagatai khan Suurgatmish (1370–1384) named Tamerlane grand emir. Tamerlane also married Saray Mulk Khanum, a descendent of Genghis Khan. From his capital, he waged six campaigns of conquest between 1381 and 1401, in which he conquered most of the western half of the Mongol Empire. In 1391–1392 and 1393–1396, he defeated Tokhtamysh and broke the power of the Golden Horde. He won his greatest victories near Delhi over the Tughluq army in 1398 and at Angora over the Ottoman army of Bayezid Yildirim in 1402. Yet neither campaign resulted in territorial expansion. In February 1405, he died en route to his seventh campaign against Ming China. His exploits inspired legends; he is credited he with writing the flattering *Memoirs of Temur*.

Tardu (581–602): Succeeded Istami as *yabgu* of the western Turks (575–581). In 581, he assumed the title khagan and established the western Turkish khaganate.

Temujin: See **Genghis Khan**.

Theodosius I, the Great (b. c. 346; r. 379–395): The son of Count Theodosius, a leading general of Valentinian I, Flavius Theodosius rose to high command under Gratian. In 379, as Augustus of the east, Theodosius restored order, granting a treaty to the rebellious Goths, who henceforth served as *foederati*. In 395, he was succeeded by Arcadius and Honorius, his sons by his first wife, Aelia Flacilla.

Theodosius II (b. 401; r. 408–450): Flavius Theodosius, the son of Arcadius and Eudocia (daughter of the Frankish general Bauto); succeeded as a minor. The emperor was directed by his ministers and his older sister, Aelia Pulcheria. Theodosius agreed to humiliating treaties dictated by Attila the Hun in 443 and 447.

Tiridates (r. 53–c. 75): Arsacid king of Armenia and brother of King Vologeses I of Parthia. He was received by the Armenian nobility and refused to acknowledge the suzerainty of Rome. In 38–59, the Roman commander Gnaeus Domitius Corbulo expelled Tiridates from Armenia and crowned Tigranes V (60–62). Vologeses I intervened on behalf of Tiridates, but he was checked by Corbulo. In 64, a diplomatic settlement was reached whereby Tiridates regained the Armenian throne, but he was required to journey to Rome and receive his crown from Nero in 66.

Todar Mal (d. 1589): The Hindu finance minister of Akbar (1556–1605); of the Kshatriya caste. He entered the service of Akbar in 1560 and managed the mint, introduced a census, and reformed the system of taxation.

Togon-temür (b.1320; r. 1333–1368): Last Mongol khan and Yuan emperor; ruled China under the throne name of Huizong. He ruled as a figurehead, and in 1358, he fled from Dadu to Mongolia, where he died in exile in 1370.

Tokhtamysh (d. 1406; r. 1376–1395): Khan of the Golden Horde. Fled to Tamerlane in 1376 after he failed to unseat his uncle Urus Khan (1361–1375). With the support of Tamerlane, he was received as khan of the Golden Horde. In 1382, he avenged the Mongol defeat at Kulikovo Field by sacking Moscow and forcing Grand Prince Vasily to return to his Mongol allegiance. In 1395, Khan Tokhtamysh blundered into a war with his overlord Tamerlane (1370–1405), who ruthlessly sacked Saray and appointed as his vassal a new khan, Temür Kutlugh (1395–1401). Tokhtamysh died in exile in 1406.

Tong Yabgu (618–630): Khagan of the western Turkish khaganate. Ended civil war and reorganized the tribes into the Confederacy of the Ten Arrows. In 626, he allied with the Byzantine emperor Heraclius against the Sassanid shah Khosrow II and, thus, regained the cities of Transoxania.

Tonyukuk (646–726): A *yabgu* of the eastern Turkish khaganate and advisor to Bilge Khan (717–734). He restored the power of the khaganate after the end of the Tang overlordship in 681. In 716, he erected a memorial inscription of his deeds and his advice in the Old Turkic language at Bayn Tsokto in the Orkhon Valley (today Mongolia).

Töregene (c. 1185–1248): Naiman princess; married Ögödei in 1204. In 1241, upon the death of her husband, she assumed the role of Great Khatun (regent) and arranged for the election of her son Güyük as Great Khan in 1246. She directed imperial affairs and appointed ministers at court and generals. She retired from the regency in 1246 and died out of favor with her son.

Touman (c. 220–209 B.C.): First known *chanyu* of the Xiongnu; organized the first nomadic confederation on the eastern Eurasian steppe. He warred with the Qin emperor Shihuangdi and with the rival Yuezhi (Tocharians) for control of the Gansu Corridor.

Trajan (b. 53; r. 98–117): Roman emperor; hailed the best of emperors (*optimus princeps*). He conquered Dacia (101–106) and waged a successful Parthian war (114–117). Trajan briefly occupied Mesopotamia and appointed his own Arsacid king, Parthamaspates (116–118). His successor, Hadrian (117–138), withdrew from Trajan's conquests.

Trajan Decius (b. 201; r. 249–251): Roman emperor; seized the imperial throne with support of the legions of the Danube frontier. He and his son Herennius Etruscus were defeated and slain by the Goths at the Battle of Abrittus. He also initiated the first empire-wide persecution of Christians in 250–251.

Tughluq, Ghiyas-ud-Din (1320–1325): Sultan of Delhi; a leading Khalji general of mixed Turkish and Jat descent. He seized power and established the third line of Muslim sultans at Delhi, the Tughluqs (1320–1412).

Tughril Bey (b. 999; r. 1037–1063): Seljuk sultan; restored the power of the Sunni Abbasid caliphate at Baghdad. In 1025, Tughril Beg and his brother Chaghri had settled their Ghuzz Turks in Khurasan as vassals of Sultan Mahmud of Ghazna. In 1030–1037, Tughril Beg conquered Transoxania and took the title sultan. In 1040, he defeated the Ghaznavid sultan Masud (1031–1041) and conquered the former Ghaznavid domains in northern Iran. In 1055, he entered Baghdad and was received as great sultan by Caliph al-Kasim (1031–1075).

Uldin (r. c. 395–412): King of the Huns. Directed attacks of the Huns into the Balkans to extort subsidies and trading privileges from the eastern Roman emperor Arcadius. He commanded Hun contingents sent on request of the western Roman emperor Honorius in 406.

Umar I (b. 584; r. 634–644): Second of the Rashidun caliphs; was elected in preference to Ali. He directed the conquests of Byzantine Syria, Egypt, and Libya and the Sassanid Empire of Persia.

Uthman (b. 577; r. 644–656): Third of the Rashidun caliphs; was elected in preference to Ali. He headed the powerful Umayyad clan but personally lacked the will to govern effectively from Medina. He was slain by mutinous soldiers of the Egyptian army, who then offered the caliphate to Ali.

Valentinian III (Flavius Placidius Valentinianus) (b. 419; r. 425–455): Son of Galla Placidia and Constantius III. As western Roman emperor, Valentinian lost the remaining provinces in Spain and North Africa. His mother, who directed affairs of state, clashed with the powerful *magister militum* Aetius. Valentinian III, murdered by a clique of senators, left no heirs; thus, the western Roman Empire disappeared within 20 years of his death.

Valerian (b. c. 193; r. 253–260): Roman emperor; waged two Persian wars. He was captured by Shah Shapur I and died ignominiously in captivity. As a result of Valerian's defeat and capture, Shah Shapur ravaged Roman provinces in eastern Asia Minor and northern Syria in 260. He ordered the second empire-wide persecution of Christians in 258–260.

Vasily I Dmitriyevich (b. 1371; r. 1389–1425): Grand prince of Moscow; the grandson of Ivan I. He defeated a Mongol army of 35,000 on Kulikovo Field on September 8, 1380. In 1382, Khan Tokhtamysh invaded and stormed Moscow and sacked the city, forcing Grand Prince Vasily to return to his Mongol allegiance.

Vasudeva I (190–225): The last effective Kushan emperor; witnessed the fragmenting of the Kushan state. His heirs ruled as vassals of the Sassanid shahs of Iran.

Vespasian (b. 23; r. 69–79): Roman emperor; established the Flavian Dynasty of Rome. He proved a practical emperor who corrected a fiscal crisis and secured imperial frontiers. Vespasian commenced the construction of the *limes* (highways and fortifications) on the upper Euphrates.

Vima Kadphises (105–127): Kushan emperor; received envoys from the Roman emperor Trajan. He extended Kushan domains in India and introduced gold coinage.

Vima Taktu (80–105): Kushan emperor; the son and successor of Kujula Kadphises. He is known from the Rabatak inscription and minted an extensive coinage but without the royal name.

Vladimir (b. c. 958; r. 980–1015): Rus prince of Kiev; he embraced Orthodox Christianity around 989 as part of a marriage alliance with the Byzantine emperor Basil II (976–1025). He founded the royal institutions of the Christian Russian state.

Vologeses I (51–78): Arsacid king of Parthia. Supported his brother Tiridates to the throne of Armenia in a war against Rome. In 66, he concluded a peace with the emperor Nero, whereby Tiridates retained the Armenian throne but recognized the hegemony of Rome.

Wang Khan (d. 1203; r. c. 1175–1203): Khan of the Keraits. His personal name was Toghrul; in 1197, he received the Chinese title Wang ("King") from the Jin (Jurchen) emperor Zhangzong (1189–1208). The sworn brother of Yesugei, the father of Temujin, he received Temujin into his service in 1180. He supported Temujin against Jamukha, but in 1203, he switched his loyalty to Jamukha. Temujin captured the Kerait encampment, and Wang Khan fled and was slain by the Naimans.

Wang Mang (b. 45 B.C.; r. 9–23 A.D.): Usurper who overthrew the Former Han Dynasty and issued sweeping reforms. He failed to maintain the northern frontier against the Xiongnu.

Wanyan Min (b. 1068; 1115–1123): Jurchen emperor of the Jin Dynasty; assumed the Chinese throne name Taizu. He united the Jurchens and overthrew the Khitan Empire. In 1121, he concluded with Song emperor Huizong (1100–1125) the so-called Alliance of the Sea that called for the partition of the Khitan Empire.

Wanyan Sheng (b. 1075; r. 1123–1135): Jurchen emperor of the Jin Dynasty; assumed the Chinese throne name Taizong. He succeeded his brother Wanyan Min and completed the conquest of the Khitan state. In 1127, he captured Kaifeng and the Song court, including the retired emperor Huizong. The new Song emperor Gaozong (1127–1162) agreed to cede northern China to Wanyan Sheng.

Wei Qing (d. 106 B.C.): Han general of imperial descent; the strategic genius behind the victories over the Xiongnu. He and his nephew Huo Qubing captured the Mobei, the tent capital of Ichise Chanyu. Thereafter, he retired from active service and served as strategic advisor to Emperor Wudi.

Wen (b. 541; r. 581–604): Sui emperor; reunited China under the Sui Dynasty (581–618). He promoted Buddhism, secured the northern frontiers by reconstructing the Great Wall, and initiated the Grand Canal.

Wudi (b. 157 B.C., r. 141–87 B.C.): Han emperor; presided over the territorial expansion of China. In 133 B.C., Wudi initiated war against Gunchen, *chanyu* of the Xiongnu. By campaigning across the Gobi in 127–119 B.C., his general broke the power of the Xiongnu. In 121–115 B.C., Wudi's armies imposed Han suzerainty over the western regions (Tarim Basin). His wars, however, proved costly and nearly bankrupt the imperial treasury.

Xuanzang (596–664): Buddhist monk and Chinese pilgrim; wrote an account of his travels in the western regions and India in 629–645. He visited the court of Harsha Vardhana (606–647) at Kannauj on the Ganges. He revealed the international network of Buddhist monasteries in central Asia and India on the eve of the Islamic conquests.

Xuanzong (712–756): Tang emperor of China, who had to evacuate the western regions (Tarim Basin) soon after the defeat at the Battle of Talas (751) to face the An Lushan Rebellion (754–763). He was noted for his taste in exotic luxury items and musicians arriving on the Silk Road.

Yangdi (b. 569; r. 604–618): Sui emperor; reorganized the imperial army, recruiting Turkish cavalry. He initiated the conquest of what is now Vietnam, but expeditions against Korea proved costly failures. His assassination precipitated a brief civil war, whereby the general Li Yuan seized the throne as Gaozu, first emperor of the Tang Dynasty.

Yazdegerd III (632–651): Last Sassanid shah and grandson of Khosrow II; lost his empire to the Arab armies. In 636 (or 639), the Arabs occupied his capital Ctesiphon after their victory at the Battle of al-Qadisiyyah. In 642–651, Yazdegerd failed to check the Arab advance into Iran and was murdered near Merv. His son and heir, Peroz, died an exile at the Tang court.

Yelü Chucai (1190–1244): Khitan minister; a noted scholar of Buddhist and Confucian classics. He served under the Jin (Jurchen) court, but in 1218, he entered the service of Genghis Khan and, later, of Ögödei. He was credited with admonishing Ögödei that China was won on horseback, but it could not be ruled from horseback.

Yelü Dashi (b. 1087; r. 1124–1143): Kara-Khitan khan; a descendant of Abaoji who refused to accept Jurchen rule. In 1130–1131, he led a migration of Khitans into the Tarim Basin; in 1137, he overthrew the Karakhanid khaganate and founded a new Kara-Khitan Empire in central Asia. On September 9, 1141, Yelü Dashi decisively defeated the Seljuk sultan Ahmet Sanjar (1118–1153) at the Battle of Qatwan—the event that gave rise to the legend of Prester John. The victory delivered Transoxania to the Kara-Khitans.

Yelü Deguang (b. 902; r. 927–947): Khitan emperor of the Liao Dynasty; assumed the Chinese throne name Taizong. He proved a valiant warrior-emperor who conquered the lower Huang He valley and occupied Kaifeng. His premature death plunged the Khitan Empire into a succession crisis in 947–950.

Yelü Longxu (b. 972; r. 982–1031): Khitan emperor of the Liao Dynasty; assumed the Chinese throne name Shengzong. He presided over the transformation of the Khitan Empire into a Chinese bureaucratic state. In 1005, he concluded the Treaty of Chanyuan with the Song emperor Zhenzong (997–1022), who recognized the Khitan Empire and agreed to pay an annual subsidy.

Yuri II (b. 1189; r. 1212–1238): Prince of Vladimir-Suzdal; campaigned against the Volga Bulgars and Russian rival princes. In 1238, Batu captured Vladimir. Yuri II escaped, but his capital was sacked and the population slaughtered. On March 8, 1238, he and his army were annihilated by the Mongols at the Battle of Sit River.

Yusuf Khass Hajib (1019–1085): Turkish poet and native of Balasagun; composed *Kutadgu Bilig* for the Karakhanid prince of Kashgar. The work is a guide to proper rule, combining Turkish martial traditions with Islamic political and religious ideals.

Zhang Qian (200–114 B.C.): Official of the Han court. Sent by emperor Wudi as envoy to the Yuezhi (Tocharians) to form an alliance against the Xiongnu in 137–125 B.C. Zhang Qian failed in this mission; twice he was captured by the Xiongnu. His account of the western regions is an invaluable source on the customs of the Xiongnu and the reigns of the *chanyus* Gunchen (161–126 B.C.) and Ichise (126–114 B.C.). His account was incorporated into the *Shiji* ("*Historical Records*") by the historian Sima Qian in the 1st century.

Zhu Xi (1130–1200): Neo-Confucian philosopher and philologist of the Song Dynasty who edited the Confucian classics and wrote commentaries. He also wrote the *Daxue* (*Great Learning*), a moral guide for the Mandarin scholar class.

Ziyad ibn Salih (748–751): Arabic governor of Khurasan who commanded the Arabic-Turkish Karluk army that defeated the Tang army at the Battle of Talas in 751.

Ziyad ibn Abi Sufyan (d. 673): Umayyad governor of Basra (664–673) who commanded Arab expeditionary forces in Iran. In 670–673, he ordered the fortification of Merv as a military base on the northeastern frontier.

Bibliography

Agusti, Alemany. *Sources on the Alans: A Critical Compilation*. Leiden: Brill Academic Publishers, 2000.

Alam, Muzaffar, and Sanjay Subramanyam, eds. *Mughal State, 1526–1750*. Oxford: Oxford University Press, 2011.

Allsen, Thomas T. *Culture and Conquest in Mongol Eurasia*. Cambridge: Cambridge University Press, 2001.

———. "Mongols as Vectors of Cultural Change." In *Cambridge History of Inner Asia: The Chinggisid Age*. Edited by Nicola di Cosmo, Allen J. Frank, and Peter B. Golden, pp. 135–156. Cambridge: Cambridge University Press, 2009.

Ammianus Marcellinus. *The Later Roman Empire (A.D. 354–378)*. Translated by Walter Hamilton. New York: Penguin Classics, 1986.

Angold, Michael. *The Byzantine Empire, 1025–1204: A Political History*. London: Longman, 1984.

Anthony, David W. *The Horse, the Wheel, and Language: How Bronze Age Riders from the Eurasian Steppes Shaped the Modern World*. Princeton: Princeton University Press, 2007.

Bachrach, Bernard S. *A History of the Alans in the West from Their First Appearance in the Sources of Classical Antiquity through the Early Middle Ages*. Minneapolis: University of Minnesota Press, 1973.

Barfield, Thomas J. *The Perilous Frontier: Nomadic Empires and China, 221 B.C. to A.D. 1757*. Oxford: Blackwell, 1989.

Bosworth, C. E. *The Ghaznavids, 994–1040*. Edinburgh: Edinburgh University Press, 1998.

Brian, Michael. "The Mongols of Central Asia from Chinggis Khan's Invasion to the Rise of Temür: The Ögedeid and Chaghandaid Realms." In *The Cambridge History of Inner Asia: The Chinggisid Age*. Edited by Nicolas di Cosmo, Allen J. Frank, and Peter B. Golden, pp. 46–66. Cambridge: Cambridge University Press, 2009.

Braudel, Ferdinand. *Civilization and Capitalism, 15ᵗʰ–18ᵗʰ Century*. Vol. I: *The Structure of Everyday Life*. Berkeley: University of California Press, 1992.

———. *Civilization and Capitalism, 15ᵗʰ–18ᵗʰ Century*. Vol. II: *The Wheels of Commerce*. Berkeley: University of California Press, 1992.

———. *Civilization and Capitalism, 15ᵗʰ–18ᵗʰ Century*. Vol. III: *The Perspective of the World*. Berkeley: University of California Press, 1992.

Brook, Levin Alan. *The Jews of Khazaria*. 2ⁿᵈ ed. New York: Rowman and Littlefield, 2009.

Bulliet, Richard W. *The Camel and the Wheel*. New York: Columbia University Press, 1990.

———. *Cotton, Climate and Camels in Early Islamic Iran: A Moment in World History*. New York: Columbia University Press, 2009.

Burns, T. R. *A History of the Ostrogoths*. Bloomington: Indiana University Press. 1984.

Cahen, Claude. "The Mongols and the Near East." In *A History of the Crusades*. Edited by Kenneth W. Setton, vol. II, pp. 715–734. Madison, WI: University of Wisconsin Press, 1969.

———. *Pre-Ottoman Turkey: A General Survey of the Material and Spiritual Culture and History, c. 1071–1330*. Translated by J. Jones-Williams. London: Sidgick and Jackson, 1968.

————. "The Turkish Invasion: The Selchukids." In *A History of the Crusades*. Edited by Kenneth W. Setton, vol. I, pp. 135–176. Madison, WI: University of Wisconsin Press, 1969.

Canepa, Matthew P. *The Two Eyes of the Earth: Art and Ritual Kingship between Rome and Sasanian Iran*. Berkeley: University of California Press, 2009.

Chang, Kwang-Chih. *Shang Civilization*. New Haven: Yale University Press, 1980.

Comnena, Anna. *The Alexiad*. Translated by E. R. A. Sweter. New York: Penguin Books, 1960.

Cribb, Joe, and Georgina Herrmann, eds. *After Alexander: Central Asia before Islam*. Oxford University Press, 2007.

Crone, P., and G. M. Hinds. *God's Caliph: Religious Authority in the First Centuries of Islam*. Cambridge: Cambridge University Press, 1980.

Curta, Florin, and Roman Kovaley, eds. *The Other Europe in the Middle Ages: Avars, Bulgars and Cumans: East Central and Eastern Europe in the Middle Ages, 450–1450*. Leiden: Brill, 2007.

Curta, Florin, *Southeastern Europe in the Middle Ages, 500–1250*. Cambridge: Cambridge University Press, 2006.

Curtis V. S. S., and Sarah Stewart, eds. *The Age of the Parthians*. London: I. B. Tauris, 2007.

Dale, Stephen F. *The Muslim Empires of the Ottomans, Safavids, and Mughals*. Cambridge: Cambridge University Press, 2010.

————. "The Later Timurids, c. 1450–1526." In *Cambridge History of Inner Asia: The Chinggisid Age*. Edited by Nicola di Cosmo, Allen J. Frank, and Peter B. Golden, pp. 199–220. Cambridge: Cambridge University Press, 2009.

Daryaee, Touraj. *Sasanian Persia: The Rise and Fall of an Empire.* New York: J. B. Taurus & Co., Ltd., 2009.

Debevoise, N. C. *A Political History of Parthia.* Chicago: Chicago University Press, 1938.

Donner, Fred M. *The Early Islamic Conquests.* Princeton: Princeton University Press, 1981.

Dunlop, D. N. *The History of the Jewish Khazars.* Princeton: Princeton University Press, 1954.

Elverskog, Johan. *Buddhism and Islam on the Silk Road.* Philadelphia: University of Pennsylvania Press, 2010.

Ferrill, Arther. *The Fall of the Roman Empire: The Military Explanation.* London: Thames and Hudson, 1986.

Foltz, Richard. *Religion of the Silk Road: Premodern Patterns of Globilization.* 2nd ed. New York: Palgrave Macmillan, 2010.

Fowden, Garth. *From Empire to Commonwealth: Consequences of Monotheism in Late Antiquity.* Princeton: Princeton University Press, 1993.

Franke, Herbert. "The Forest Peoples of Manchuria." In *The Cambridge History of Early Inner Asia.* Edited by Denis Sinor, pp. 400–423. Cambridge: Cambridge University Press, 1990.

Franklin, Simon, and Jonathan Sheppard. *The Emergence of the Rus, 750–1200.* New York: Addison Wesley Longman, 1996.

Frye, Richard N. *The Heritage of Central Asia: From Antiquity to the Turkish Expansion.* Princeton: Markus Wiener Publishers, 1998.

———. *The Heritage of Persia.* New York/London: Mentor Books, 1966.

Fuller, J. F. C. *The Generalship of Alexander the Great*. New York: Minerva Books, 1960.

Golden, Peter B. *Central Asia in World History*. Oxford: Oxford University Press, 2011.

———. "Inner Asia, c. 1200." In *The Cambridge History of Inner Asia: The Chinggisid Age*. Edited by Nicolas di Cosmo, Allen J. Frank and Peter B. Golden, pp. 9–25. Cambridge: Cambridge University Press, 2009.

———. "The Karakhanids and Early Islam." In *The Cambridge History of Early Inner Asia*. Edited by Denis Sinor, pp. 343–370. Cambridge: Cambridge University Press, 1990.

———. "The Peoples of the Russian Forest Belt." In *The Cambridge History of Early Inner Asia*. Edited by Denis Sinor, pp. 230–255. Cambridge: Cambridge University Press, 1990.

———. "The Peoples of the South Russian Steppes." In *The Cambridge History of Early Inner Asia*. Edited by Denis Sinor, pp. 246–284. Cambridge: Cambridge University Press, 1990.

———, et al., eds. *The World of the Khazars*. Leiden: Brill, 2007.

Goldsworthy, A. K. *The Roman Army at War, 100 B.C.–A.D. 200*. Oxford: Oxford University Press, 1996.

Gonzalez de Clavijo, Ruy. *Embassy to Tamerlane, 1403–1406*. Translated by Guy Le Strange with revised introduction by C. Sonte. The Roan, Scotland: Hardinge Simpole Ltd., 2009.

Gordon, C. D. *The Age of Attila: Fifth-Century Byzantium and the Barbarians*. Ann Arbor, MI: University of Michigan Press, 1972.

Graff, David A. *Medieval Chinese Warfare, 300–900*. London/New York: Routledge, 2002.

Gupta, Parmeshwari Lal, and Sarojini Kulashreshtha. *Kuṣāna Coins and History*. Delhi: D. K. Printworld, Ltd., 1994.

Hansen, Valerie. *The Silk Road: A New History*. Oxford: Oxford University Press, 2012.

Harl, Kenneth W. *Coinage in the Roman Economy, 300 B.C.–700 A.D.* Baltimore: Johns Hopkins University Press, 1996.

Headrick, Daniel R. *The Tools of Empire: Technology and European Imperialism in the Nineteenth Century*. Oxford: Oxford University Press, 1981.

Herodotus. *The Histories*. Translated by A. de Selincourt. Rev. ed. New York: Penguin, 1972.

———. *The Histories*. Rev. ed. Translated by J. M. Marcincola and Aubery de Selincourt. New York: Penguin, 2003.

Hildinger, Erik. *Warriors of the Steppe: A Military History of Central Asia, 500 B.C. to 1700 A.D.* Cambridge, MA: Da Capo Press, 1997.

Hill, John E. *Through the Jade Gate to Rome: A Study of the Silk Routes during the Later Han Dynasty, 1st to 2nd Centuries C.E.* Charleston, SC: Book Surge Publishing, 2009.

Hirth, F. *China and the Roman Orient: Researches into Their Ancient and Medieval Relations as Represented in the Old Chinese Records*, Chicago: Ares Press, 1975; reprint of Shangai–Hong Kong, 1885.

Holt, Frank L. *Alexander the Great and Bactria: Formation of a Greek Frontier in Central Asia*. Leiden: E. J. Brill, Mnemosyne Supplement, 1988.

Hopkirk, Peter. *The Great Game: The Struggle for Empire in Central Asia*. New York: Kodansha America, 1990.

Hucker, Charles. *China's Imperial Past: An Introduction to Chinese History and Culture.* Stanford: Stanford University Press, 1995.

Isaac, Benjamin. *The Limits of Empire: The Roman Army in the East.* 2nd ed. Oxford: Clarendon Press, 1993.

Istvan, Vasary. *Cumans and Tatars: Oriental Military in the Pre-Ottoman Balkans, 1185–1365.* Cambridge: Cambridge University Press, 2005.

———. "The Jochid Realm: The Western Steppes." In *The Cambridge History of Inner Asia: The Chinggisid Age.* Edited by Nicolas di Cosmo, Allen J. Frank, and Peter B. Golden, pp. 67–88. Cambridge: Cambridge University Press, 2009.

Jackson, Peter. *The Delhi Sultanate: A Political and Military History.* Cambridge: Cambridge University Press, 1999.

———. "The Mongol Age in Eastern Inner Asia." In *The Cambridge History of Inner Asia: The Chinggisid Age.* Edited by Nicolas di Cosmo, Allen J. Frank, and Peter B. Golden, pp. 26–45. Cambridge: Cambridge University Press, 2009.

———. *The Mongols and the West, 1221–1410.* New York: Pearson Longman, 2005.

Keay, John. *India: A History.* New York: Grove Press, 2000.

Kelenkna, Pita. *The Horse in Human History.* Cambridge: Cambridge University Press, 2009.

Kennedy, Hugh. *The Armies of the Caliphate: Military and Society in the Early Islamic State.* New York/London: Routledge, 2001.

———. *The Great Arab Conquests: How the Spread of Islam Changed the World We Live In.* Philadelphia: Da Capo Press, 2007.

————. *The Prophet and the Age of the Caliphates: The Islamic Near East from the Sixth to the Eleventh Century.* 2nd ed. London: Pearson Longman, 2006.

Khodarkovsky, Michael. *Russia's Steppe Frontier: The Making of a Colonial Empire, 1500–1800.* Bloomington, IN: Indiana University Press, 2002.

Kinoshita, Hiromi, and Jane Portal. eds. *The First Emperor: China's Terracotta Army.* London: British Museum, 2007.

Kuhn, Dieter. *The Age of Confucian Rule: The Song Transformation of China.* Cambridge, MA: Harvard University Press, 2009.

Lange, Christian. The *Seljuqs: Politics, Society, and Culture.* Edinburgh: Edinburgh University Press, 2012.

Lewis, Mark E. *China between Dynasties: The Northern and Southern Dynasties.* Cambridge, MA: Harvard University Press, 2009.

Li, Rongxi, trans. *The Great Tang Dynasty Record of the Western Regions.* Berkeley: Numata Center for Buddhist Translation and Research, 1995.

Lieu, Samuel N. C. *Manichaeism in the Roman Empire and Medieval China.* Tubingen: J. C. R. Mohr, 1992.

Lincoln, W. Bruce. *The Conquest of a Continent: Siberia and the Russians.* Ithaca, NY: Cornell University Press, 1994.

Liu, Xinbu. *The Silk Road in World History.* Oxford: Oxford University Press, 2010.

Macartney, C. A. *The Magyars in the Ninth Century.* Cambridge: Cambridge University Press, 2008; reprint of 1930 edition.

MacKerras, Colin. "The Uighurs." In *The Cambridge History of Early Inner Asia.* Edited by Denis Sinor, pp. 317–342. Cambridge: Cambridge University Press, 1990.

Magdalino, P. *The Empire of Manuel I Komnenos, 1143–1180*. Cambridge: Cambridge University Press, 1993.

Mallory, J. P. *In Search of the Indo-Europeans: Language, Archaeology, and Myth*. London: Thames and Hudson, 1989.

Mallory, J. P., and Victor H. Mair. *The Tarim Mummies: Ancient China and the Mystery of the Earliest Peoples from the West*. London: Thames and Hudson, 2000.

Manz, Beatrice F. *The Rise and Rule of Tamerlane*. Cambridge: Cambridge University Press, 1989.

————. "Temür and the Early Timurids to c. 1450." In *Cambridge History of Inner Asia: The Chinggisid Age*. Edited by Nicola di Cosmo, Allen J. Frank, and Peter B. Golden, pp. 182–198. Cambridge: Cambridge University Press, 2009.

Marozzi, Justin. *Tamerlane: Sword of Islam, Conqueror of the World*. Cambridge, MA: Da Capo Press, 2004.

Meaenchen-Helfen, Otto J. *The World of the Huns: Studies in Their History and Culture*. Edited by Max Knight. Berkeley: University of California Press, 1973.

Melyukova, A. I. "The Scythians and Samartians." In *The Cambridge History of Central Asia*, edited by D. Sinor, pp. 97–117. Cambridge, 1990.

Millar, Fergus. *The Roman Near East, 31 B.C.–A.D. 337*. Cambridge, MA: Harvard University Press, 1993.

Mote, F. W. *Imperial China, 900–1800*. Cambridge, MA: Harvard University Press, 1999.

Narain, A. K. "Indo-Europeans in Inner Asia." In the *New Cambridge History of Inner Asia*. Edited by Denis Sinor, pp. 151–176. Cambridge: Cambridge University Press.

Oblensky, Dimitri. *The Byzantine Commonwealth: Eastern Europe, 500–1453.* Crestwood, NY: St. Vladimir's Seminary Press, 1982.

O'Flynn, John Michael. *Generalissmos of the Western Roman Empire.* Edmonton: University of Alberta Press, 1983.

Okladnikov, A. P. "Inner Asia at the Dawn of History." In *The Cambridge History of Inner Asia.* Edited by Denis Sinor, pp. 41–96. Cambridge: Cambridge University Press, 1990.

Ostrer, Harry. *Legacy: A Genetic History of the Jewish People.* Oxford: Oxford University Press, 2012.

Peacock, Andrew, and Sara Nur Yildez, eds. *The Seljuks of Anatolia: Court and Society in the Medieval Middle East.* London: I. B. Tauris, 2012.

Piggott, Stuart. *The Earliest Wheeled Vehicles from the Atlantic Coast to the Caspian Sea.* Ithaca, NY: Cornell University Press, 1983.

Polo, Marco. *The Travels of Marco Polo, the Venetian.* Translated and edited by Thomas Wright. London: George Bell and Sons, 1907.

Pourshariati, Parvaneh. *Decline and Fall of the Sasanian Empire: The Sasanian-Parthian Confederacy and the Arab Conquest of Iran.* New York: J. B. Taurus, 2008.

Ratchnevsky, Paul. *Genghis Khan: His Life and Legacy.* Oxford: Blackwell Publishing, 1999.

Reder, Ellen, and Michael Treiser. *Scythian Gold.* New York: Harry N. Abrams, 1999.

Rice, Tamara Talbot. "The Scytho-Sarmatian Tribes of South-Eastern Europe." In *The Roman Empire and Its Neighbors*, by Fergus Millar, 2nd ed., pp. 281–294. New York: Holmes & Meier, 1981.

———. *The Seljuk Turks.* London: Thames and Hudson, 1961.

Richards, John F. *The Mughal Empire*. Cambridge: Cambridge University Press, 1996.

Rossabi, Morris. *Kublai Khan, His Life and Times*. Berkeley: University of California Press, 2006.

―――. *The Mongols and Global History*. New York: W. W. Norton and Company, 2011.

Runciman, Stephen. *A History of the First Bulgarian Empire*. London: G. Bell and Sons, 1930.

Saunders, J. J. *A History of Medieval Islam*. London: Routledge and Kegan Paul, 1965.

―――. *The History of the Mongol Conquests*. Philadelphia: University of Pennsylvania Press, 1971.

Shaban, M. A. *The Abbasid Revolution*. Cambridge: Cambridge University Press, 1970.

Shavegan, M. R. *Arsacids and Sasanians: Political Ideology in Post-Hellenistic and Late Antique Persia*. Cambridge: Cambridge University Press, 2011.

Sinor, Denis, ed. *The Cambridge History of Early Inner Asia*. Cambridge: Cambridge University Press, 1990.

―――. "The Establishment and Dissolution of the Türk Empire." In *The Cambridge History of Early Inner Asia*. Edited by Denis Sinor, pp. 285–316. Cambridge: Cambridge University Press, 1990.

―――. "The Hun Period." In *The New Cambridge History of Inner Asia*. Edited by Denis Sinor, pp. 177–205. Cambridge: Cambridge University Press, 1990.

Skaff, Jonathan K. *Sui-Tan China and Its Turko-Mongol Neighbors: Culture, Power, and Connections, 580–800*. Oxford: Oxford University Press, 2012.

Sulimirski, T., and T. Taylor. "The Scythians." In *The Cambridge Ancient History*. Vol. III, part 2. Edited by John Barodman et al.. pp. 547–590. Cambridge: Cambridge University Press, 1991.

Szádeczky-Kardoss, Samuel. "The Avars." In *The Cambridge History of Early Inner Asia*. Edited by Denis Sinor, pp. 206–228. Cambridge: Cambridge University Press, 1990.

Tacitus. *Annals of Imperial Rome*. Translated by Michael Grant. New York/London: Penguin Books, 1975.

Tarn, William Woodthorpe. *The Greeks in Bactria and India*. 3rd ed., rev. by Frank L. Holt. Chicago: Ares Publishers, 1984.

Thapar, Romila. *A History of India*. Vol. I. New York/London: Penguin Books, 1966.

Thompson, E. A. *The Huns*. Oxford: Blackwell Publishers, Ltd., 1996.

Vásáry, István. *Cumans and Tatars: Oriental Military in the Pre-Ottoman Balkans, 1185–1365*. Cambridge: Cambridge University Press, 2009.

Veith, Veronika. "The Eastern Steppe: Mongol Regimes after the Yuan (1368–1636)." In *Cambridge History of Inner Asia: The Chinggisid Age*. Edited by Nicola di Cosmo, Allen J. Frank, and Peter B. Golden, pp. 157–181. Cambridge: Cambridge University Press, 2009.

Vyrnos, Speros. *The Decline of Medieval Hellenism in Asia Minor and the Process of Islamization from the Eleventh through the Fifteenth Century*. Berkeley: University of California Press, 1964.

Waldron, Arthur. *The Great Wall of China: From History to Myth*. Cambridge: Cambridge University Press, 1990.

Watt, W. Montgomery. *Muhammad, Prophet and Statesman*. Oxford: Oxford University Press, 1975.

Weatherford, Jack. *Genghis Khan and the Making of the Modern World*. New York: Three Rivers Press, 2004.

Whitby, Michael. *The Emperor Maurice and His Historian Theophylact Simocattta on Persian and Balkan Warfare*. Oxford: Clarendon Press, 1988.

Whittlow, Mark. *The Making of Byzantium, 600–1025*. Berkeley: University of California Press, 1996.

Yarshater, E., ed. *The Cambridge History of Iran*. Vol. III: *Seleucid, Parthian, and Sasanian Periods*. Cambridge: Cambridge University Press 1983.

Ying-shi Yu. "The Hsiung-nu." In *The Cambridge History of Inner Asia*. Edited by Denis Sinor, pp. 118–150. Cambridge: Cambridge University Press, 1990.

———. *Trade and Expansion in Han China: A Study in the Structure of Sino-Barbarian Economic Relations*. Berkeley: University of California Press, 1967.

Zakaria, Rafiq. *Razia, Queen of India*. Oxford: Oxford University Press, 1966.

Notes

Notes